Friedrich Ueberweg

System of logic and history of logical doctrines

Friedrich Ueberweg

System of logic and history of logical doctrines

ISBN/EAN: 9783742817501

Manufactured in Europe, USA, Canada, Australia, Japa

Cover: Foto ©Thomas Meinert / pixelio.de

Manufactured and distributed by brebook publishing software
(www.brebook.com)

Friedrich Ueberweg

System of logic and history of logical doctrines

SYSTEM OF LOGIC

AND

HISTORY OF LOGICAL DOCTRINES.

BY

DR FRIEDRICH UEBERWEG,

PROFESSOR OF PHILOSOPHY IN THE UNIVERSITY OF KÖNIGSBERG.

TRANSLATED FROM THE GERMAN, WITH NOTES AND APPENDICES,

BY

THOMAS M. LINDSAY, M.A., F.R.S.E.,

EXAMINER IN PHILOSOPHY TO THE
UNIVERSITY OF EDINBURGH.

LONDON:

LONGMANS, GREEN, AND CO.

1871.

TO

ALEXANDER CAMPBELL FRASER,

M.A., LL.D., F.R.S.E.,

PROFESSOR OF LOGIC AND METAPHYSICS IN THE
UNIVERSITY OF EDINBURGH,

THIS ATTEMPT

TO FOSTER THE HIGHER STUDY OF LOGIC

BY THE TRANSLATION OF

ONE OF THE BEST GERMAN MANUALS,

IS DEDICATED

BY

AN OLD PUPIL.

TRANSLATOR'S PREFACE.

PROFESSOR UEBERWEG'S 'System of Logic' enjoys a popularity among German students which is shared by no other manual. It has already reached three editions, and will soon appear in a fourth. Acquaintance with these facts, personal experience of the value of the book, and the knowledge that there is no really good logical text-book for advanced students in our language, led me to undertake this Translation. While it is not especially intended for beginners, and while the student is recommended to make himself previously familiar with the outlines of Logic as given in such excellent little books as those of Fowler or Jevons, some judicious 'skipping,' in the more difficult parts, will bring this manual down to the level required by those who begin it entirely ignorant of the science.

This Translation is from the text of the third edition, published in 1868, and contains *all the additions and alterations which are to be inserted in the next German edition.* Although I am responsible for the translation, and liable to censure for its many faults and defects, it is but right to mention that anyone who compares it with the original will find numerous small omissions, additions, and alterations—indeed, there are few pages which do not differ in some particular from the text of the third edition,—*all* of which have been made by the author. Dr. Ueberweg has himself revised the sheets; and, as he knows English well, this Translation may be held to give his opinions as he wishes them expressed in our language.

In order to make the book more useful to students, the opinions of the more prominent English logicians on the points discussed have been from time to time inserted. Such passages are distinguished by the brackets [ ]. For these and for the first three Appendices I am alone responsible; but my friend Professor W. R. Smith has furnished the account of the late Professor Boole's logical opinions in Appendix A. Appendix D will appear in the fourth German edition, and has been added in deference to the author's wishes.

It need only be added, that while agreeing in the main with the logical opinions of Professor Ueberweg, I must not be held responsible for every theory advanced in the text-book, and must dissent from some of the statements regarding the Logic of Mathematics. The remarks made at page 577 in Appendix A seem almost as applicable to Dr. Ueberweg's views as to Mr. Mill's.

THOMAS M. LINDSAY.

7 GREAT STUART STREET, EDINBURGH:
June 1st, 1871.

NOTE.—Since writing these lines the sad and unexpected news of Dr. Ueberweg's death has reached me. These pages will have a mournful interest to his many friends, for their revisal was the last bit of work he was able to do. He had just finished them when death ended his labours.

T. M. L.

June 15th.

AUTHOR'S PREFACE

TO

THE FIRST EDITION.

SCHLEIERMACHER, whose philosophical significance has but too often been overlooked for his theological, in his Lectures upon ' *Dialektik* ' (ed. by Jonas, Berlin, 1839), sought to explain the forms of thinking from science, which is the end and aim of thinking, and to make good his opinion by proving their parallelism with the forms of real existence. This apprehension of the forms of thought holds a middle place between the subjectively-formal and the metaphysical Logics, and is at one with the fundamental view of Logic which Aristotle had. The subjectively-formal Logic—that promulgated by the schools of *Kant* and *Herbart*—puts the forms of thought out of all relation to the forms of existence. Metaphysical Logic, on the other hand, as *Hegel* constructed it, identifies the two kinds of forms, and thinks that it can recognise in the self-development of pure thought the self-production of existence. *Aristotle*, equally far from both extremes, sees thinking to be the picture of existence, a picture which is different from its real correlate and yet related to it, which corresponds to it and yet is not identical with it.

Ritter and *Vorländer*[1] have worked at Logic from the standpoint of Schleiermacher: the investigations into the theory of knowledge of most of our modern logicians, who do not belong to any definite school, lie more or less in the same direction. *Trendelenburg*, who has revived the true Aristotelian Logic, comes in contact in many ways with Schleiermacher's Platonising theory of knowledge, without being dependent[2] upon him, and has a basis of metaphysical categories acquired independently in a polemic against Hegel and Herbart. The view of *Lotze* is more distantly related. It approaches nearer to Kant's, and represents that in the laws and forms of thought only the necessary metaphysical presuppositions of the human mind upon nature and the universe mirror themselves. Essentially accepting Schleiermacher's fundamental axioms concerning the relation of thought to perception

---

[1] Now (1868) also George. (Added to the third edition.)

[2] At least without any direct dependence. Schleiermacher's *lectures on Dialectic*, published in 1839, are only quoted here and there. But the influence of Ritter's *Logic* apparently shows itself in his doctrine of the notion and of the judgment. (Added to the second edition.)

and of perception to existence, *Beneke* has proceeded to blend these with his psychological theory, partly constructed after Herbart's, into a now whole.

This present work on Logic proceeds in the direction denoted by the labours of these men, while conscious of the right of complete independence in the mode of procedure. It sets before it both the *scientific* problem of aiding in developing Logic, and the *didactic* one of assisting to its study.

In the *first* reference, the Author hopes that he may succeed in the present work in answering the principal questions relating to the problem, sphere, and arrangement of Logic, and to the standpoint from which Logic is treated as a theory of knowledge, and in furnishing a not worthless contribution to the solution of many single problems. Polemic is used sharply enough where occasion demands, but only against those of whom I can say with truth—' verecunde ab illis dissentio.' That truth was the single interest, determining me in each case to agree with or contradict, need not require previous assurance, but will appear from the work itself. On my side, I will welcome every thoroughgoing criticism as heartily as agreement. One thing I do not wish, and that is, that this independently thought-out work be laid aside by classing it under this or that general formula—Empiricism, Rationalism, Eclecticism. For this would falsely represent my work to be the mere exposition of a one-sided antiquated party standpoint, or, since it is essentially related to the whole of the philosophical tendencies, would accuse it, mistaking its leading fundamental thought, of want of principle. The Author would least of all object to have his system entitled an Ideal-Realism.

In the *didactic* reference, I have striven to exhibit general Logic clearly, exactly, comprehensively, and so far completely, as a theory of knowledge, and to describe the chief moments in its historical development. What is universally recognised has been rendered in a precise and strictly systematic form. What is doubtful and debatable will be explained, not with the prolixity of the monograph, but with a sufficient consideration of the points which decide the question. A systematic representation of scientific Logic must, in so far as it is meant to serve as a text-book to those entering upon the study, presuppose genuine students of science, who do not mean to shirk difficulties, but to overcome them. Particular parts may always be passed over in a first study. These will meet the want of those who, already familiar with the elements, may wish to extend their studies. The examples will show the importance of the logical laws in their application to all the sciences. Finally, by means of historico-literary examples and investigations, in which the Aristotelian point of view of thankful reference to all essential moments of development of scientific truth is preserved, this work strives to encourage the most many-sided study of Logic possible.

BONN :

August, 1857.

THE SECOND EDITION.

. . . . . I might recommend this work more especially to the attention of those engaged in the investigation of Nature as a thorough-going attempt at a comparatively objective theory of knowledge in opposition to Kant's subjective criticism. It may serve to give a philosophic basis to their more special methodic. The kernel of my opposition to *Kant* lies in the thoroughgoing proof of the way by which scientific insight is attained, an insight which mere experience in its immediateness does not warrant, which is not brought about by à priori forms of purely subjective origin, finding application only to phenomenal objects present in the consciousness of the subject (and has not, as Hegel and others desire, an à priori, and yet objective validity), but is reached by the combination of the facts of experience according to the logical rules, which are conditioned by the objective order of things and whose observance ensures an objective validity for our knowledge. I seek more especially to show how arrangement, according to time, space, and cause, on whose knowledge apodicticity rests, is not first of all imposed upon a chaotically given matter by the perceiving thinking subject, but is formed in the subjective consciousness in accordance with the (natural and spiritual) reality, in which it originally is, successively by experience and thinking. . . . .

то

THE THIRD EDITION.

. . . . . University education and its lectures, to bring forth good fruit, must presuppose a knowledge of the elements of Logic, and a familiarity with them such as is only to be got by school training. Philosophical propaedeutic is of value in the studies of the gymnasia, both as a very suitable conclusion to intellectual education, and more especially as a means in the teaching of one's own language and literature. . . . I have exerted myself in the present third edition of this book not only to increase its scientific value by a more acute treatment of many problems, and by a thoroughgoing reconsideration of newly-risen difficulties, but, more than hitherto, by the kind of explanations and the choice of examples, to supply the needs of the teacher who gives preparatory instruction, and to meet the wants of the student for whom it is to serve as a solid foundation for philosophical instruction. . . . .

Königsberg:
September, 1868.

F. Ueberweg.

CONTENTS.

INTRODUCTION.

Notion, Division, and General History of Logic.

Contents.

PART I.

Perception in its relation to Objective Existence in Space and Time.

A.—EXTERNAL OR SENSE-PERCEPTION.

B.—INTERNAL OR PSYCHOLOGICAL PERCEPTION.

C.—THE COMBINATION OF OUTER AND INNER PERCEPTION.

PART II.

The Individual Conception or Intuition in its relation to the Objective Individual Existence.

PART III.

*The Notion according to Content and Extent in its relation
to the Objective Essence and the Genus.*

PART IV.

*The Judgment in its reference to the Objective Fundamental
Combinations or Relations.*

SYSTEM OF LOGIC.

INTRODUCTION.

§ 1. *Logic is the science of the regulative laws of human
knowledge.* The act of knowing is that activity of the
mind by means of which it consciously reproduces in
itself what actually exists. The act of knowing is
partly immediate or outer and inner perception, partly
mediate or thinking. The regulative laws (injunctions,
prescriptions) are those universal conditions to which
the activity of knowledge must conform in order to attain
to the end and aim of knowledge.

Logic, as the doctrine of knowledge, occupies the mean
between what is commonly called *formal,* or, more definitely,
subjectively-formal Logic, which treats of the act of thinking
apart from any relation to objective existence, and *Logic
identified with Metaphysics,* which would represent along with
the laws of the act of knowing, the most universal (metaphysical
or ontological) contents of all knowledge. This middle position
is described and justified in §§ 3 and 6, and in the sketch of
the general history of Logic, especially in §§ 28–35.

D

2   § 1. *Definition of Logic.*

___

Knowledge, in the wider sense in which we here use the word, comprehends both *cognition*, which rests on perception (and on the evidence transmitting perceptions of which we are ignorant), and also *knowledge in the stricter sense*, which is attained by thinking.

The act of knowing, in so far as it is the copying in the human consciousness of the essence of the thing, is an *after-thinking* of *the* thoughts which the divine creative thinking has built into things. In *action* the preceding thought determines what actually exists, but in *knowing* the actual existence, in itself conformable to reason, determines the human thought.

Plato declares that knowing is conditioned by being.[1]

Aristotle says almost the same in reference to the judgment:[2] ἔστι δὲ ὁ μὲν ἀληθὴς λόγος οὐδαμῶς αἴτιος τοῦ εἶναι τὸ πρᾶγμα, τὸ μέντοι πρᾶγμα φαίνεταί πως αἴτιον τοῦ εἶναι ἀληθῆ τὸν λόγον· τῷ γὰρ εἶναι τὸ πρᾶγμα ἢ μὴ ἀληθὴς ὁ λόγος ἢ ψευδὴς λέγεται.[3] ἀληθεύει μὲν ὁ τὸ διῃρημένον οἰόμενος διαιρεῖσθαι καὶ τὸ συγκείμενον συγκεῖσθαι, ἔψευσται δὲ ὁ ἐναντίως ἔχων ἢ τὰ πράγματα· . . . οὐ γὰρ διὰ τὸ ἡμᾶς οἴεσθαι ἀληθῶς σε λευκὸν εἶναι εἶ σὺ λευκός, ἀλλὰ διὰ τὸ σὲ εἶναι λευκὸν ἡμεῖς οἱ φάντες τοῦτο ἀληθεύομεν.[4] τρόπον τινὰ ἡ ἐπιστήμη μετρεῖται τῷ ἐπιστητῷ.

Schleiermacher[5] says: 'To the proposition that thinking must conform to being, must be added another, that being must conform to thinking. The latter proposition is the principle and measure for every activity of the will, the former for every activity of thought.'[6]

Lotze's remark that mind is better than things, and does not need to be their mirror in knowledge, does not invalidate our logical principle, because—1. The objective existence to be

[1] *Rep.* v. 477, ed. Steph.   [2] Arist. *Cat.* xii. 14 a, 18.
[3] Arist. *Metaph.* ix. 10, § 2 ed. Schwegler., p. 1051 b, 3 ed. Bekker.
[4] Arist. *Metaph.* x. 6, 18, p. 1057 a, 11.
[5] *Dialektik*, ed. by Jonas, p. 487.
[6] Cf. Schelling, *System des transscendentalen Idealismus*, 1800, p. 13 ff.; Hegel, *Encycl.* § 225.

known consists not merely of natural objects, but also (as in history, &c.) of mental contents. 2. The mirroring in consciousness, although reproduction, cannot be accomplished without a peculiar activity of the mind. 3. The whole activity of the mind is not exhausted in knowledge. There is besides the creative power of the phantasy, reforming and refining what is given in the conception, and ethical action. Cf. § 6. The definitions in the introduction are to be considered only as nominal definitions, and their enunciations as theses to be proved afterwards in an independent investigation (e.g. in § 37).

§ 2. Since the human mind must consciously reproduce what actually exists (§ 1), the act of knowing is *conditioned in two ways* : a. *Subjectively*, by the essence and natural laws of the human mind, especially by those of the human powers of knowledge ; b. *Objectively*, by the nature of what is to be known. The constitutions and relations of what is to be known, so far as these require different ways of representation in the act of knowing, we call *forms of existence* (e.g. subsistence and inherence). The notions of these forms of existence are the *metaphysical categories.* The different ways, corresponding to these forms of existence, in which what actually exists is taken hold of and copied in the act of knowledge, are the *forms of knowledge* (e.g. the categorical judgment). The actual copy, the result of the activity of knowledge, is the *content of knowledge.* The notions of the forms of knowledge are the *logical categories.* Since the laws of knowing, as such, determine only the ways of representation (copying), or the forms of knowledge, not its contents, Logic can be explained to be the *doctrine of the laws of the forms of knowledge.* In this way Logic is a *formal* science ; but since the forms which it treats of correspond to the forms of existence, they are conditioned by the objective reality. They stand in essential relation not only to the content of knowledge in general, but also to the particular nature of the content in the modifications they take for the time being.

Logic has both a metaphysical and an anthropological side, inasmuch as it is founded upon the universal laws of existence, and also upon the laws of the life of the mind. These two elements, however, do not make independent parts of logic, but only serve for the foundation of the regulative laws. They are consequently, in the treatment of individual portions of the part concerned, to be borrowed from Psychology and Metaphysics as auxiliary axioms, or to be explained only in so far as this is necessary for the purpose of Logic. Logic does not *directly* treat of Being, Essence, Causality, the moving cause, the final cause, &c., nor yet of the principles of Psychology, any more than does Dietetic the chemical and physiological processes; but it can refer to such investigations as preparatory or following. At the same time, such investigations as those regarding the possibility of knowing things, regarding the validity of our notions of Space, Time, Causality, &c., are not to be excluded from Logic,[1] for these investigations have to do with our knowledge, not with the forms of existence *as such.*

The relation of subject and predicate in the categorical judgment to the forms of existence, subsistence and inherence, or the relation of superordinate and subordinate notions to the way in which things exist in genera and species—may provisionally serve to give a clearer idea of the connection between logical and metaphysical or ontological forms. Cf. § 8.

Many writers[2] wrongly interpret the expression ' *Formal Logic,*' as if it necessarily involved the abstraction of every

[1] As Drobisch thinks, *Log.* 3rd ed. prof. p. xvii.
[2] E.g. Steinthal, *Gram. Log. and Psych.* (Berlin, 1855), p. 146.

relation to the actual. Logic is *formal* because it is the doctrine of the correct *form* or way of thinking, even if this form
is conditioned by the endeavour after an agreement of the contents of thought with actual existence. It is *Subjectively-formal*
Logic which directs its attention *exclusively* to the subjective
agreement of thinking with itself.

Kant and his school have connected the distinction of *formal
Logic*, in the sense that it exhibits only the laws of *analytical*
knowledge, and the *criticism of the pure reason*, which inquires
into the possibility of a universally valid *synthetic* knowledge,
with the distinction of the analytic and synthetic formation of
judgments (§ 83). The Aristotelian Logic is an *analytical
theory of thinking*, but the formal Logic, in the Kantian sense,
a *theory of analytical thinking*.

Beneke's distinction of analytical or ' logical ' thinking from
the synthetic elements of thinking, and *Ulrici's* division of
thinking into productive (synthetic) and separative (analytic),
are related to Kant's.

It does not seem proper that a distinction, which of course
is valuable and true in connection with the formation of judgments, should be raised to be the principle of a division of the
whole of Logic into two separate parts. This procedure would
be like a geometer's, who divides his science into two separate
divisions, as its propositions could be proved with or without
the eleventh axiom of Euklid. Such methods of treatment
have their full scientific value as *monographs* on single axioms,
but cannot determine the whole articulation of a system, which
must rest on a more comprehensive point of view.

§ 3. The *aim* of knowledge is *TRUTH*. Knowledge
arrived at the certainty of truth is *SCIENCE*. Material
(or real) truth must be distinguished from (formal)
correctness. Material truth in the absolute sense,
or simply truth, is the agreement of the content of
knowledge with what actually exists. Material truth
in the relative sense, or phenomenal truth, is the

agreement of the mediately acquired content of thought
with the immediate outer or inner perceptions which
exist when the soundness of the mind and of the
bodily organs is undisturbed, or would exist under
the corresponding outer conditions. According to
some logicians formal truth is the absence of contradiction, or the agreement of thoughts with one
another. Material truth includes formal, in the sense
of absence of contradiction; but there may be the absence of contradiction without material truth. In the
fuller sense of the term, formal truth or correctness is
the consistency of the activity of knowledge with its
logical laws. When the form of perception, as well as
of thinking, meets all the logical demands, then (at least
the relative) material truth must exist; and formal correctness in the fuller sense guarantees this. But correctness of thought only warrants that the connection
between the antecedents and consequents is known, as
it really is, with truth, and that therefore where the
antecedents have material truth the consequents have it
also. With respect therefore to the aim and end of knowledge, *Logic is the scientific solution of the question relating
to the criteria of truth; or, the doctrine of the regulative
laws, on whose observance rests the realisation of the idea
of truth in the theoretical activity of man.*

In opposition to truth in the logical sense—the agreement of
the thought with its object, and supplementary to it, is the
ethical meaning of the word—the correspondence of the object
with its idea or inner determination. The explanation of the
so-called 'formal truth,' as 'the harmony of knowledge with
itself in complete abstraction from all objects whatever and

from all their differences, is insufficient."¹ The explanation of the so-called transcendental truth, as the orderly arrangement of real objects, goes as far on the other side : ' Veritas, quae transscendentalis appellatur et rebus ipsis inesse intelligitur, est ordo eorum, quae cuti conveniunt.'¹

In so far as Logic seeks to determine whether and how far agreement between the content of knowledge and objective reality is attainable, it is a *critique of knowledge*. In so far as it teaches the procedure by which the measure of agreement attainable is actually attained, it is *Logic in the stricter sense*. In the doctrine of perception the one side, and in the doctrine of thought the other side of Logic is the prevalent. Without any inner contradiction, general criteria can be found according to which the agreement of a plan, a picture, a notion, a proposition, &c. with its object can be decided. The reference, what the particular objects are in each case, first comes in the *application*.

Scepticism and the *Critical Philosophy* raise weighty objections against - the *possibility* of arriving at and being certain of material truth. In order to be assured of truth in the absolute sense, we must be able to compare our conception with its object. But we never have (says the Critical Philosophy) the object otherwise than in our conception ; we never have it pure in itself. We only compare our conceptions with our conceptions, never with the things in themselves. Material truth in the relative sense succumbs to the difficulty which the old Skeptics expressed in the question: Τίς κρινεῖ τὸν ὑγιεινόν; or τίς ὁ κρινῶν τὸν ὑγιαίνοντα καὶ ὅλως τὸν περὶ ἕκαστα κρινοῦντα ὀρθῶς?² Formal validity, lastly, in the sense of absence of contradiction, does not carry us beyond what we, at least implicitly, possess already. How then do we get at the first knowledge, and how can we advance in knowledge ? To these general difficulties are to be added particular ones belonging to single forms of knowledge, which will be men-

¹ Kant, *Log.* ed. by Jäsche, p. 66.
² Christian Wolff, *Ontolog.* § 495.
³ Arist. *Metaph.* iv. 6, p. 1011, A, 5.

tioned afterwards. Their solution is the problem of the whole system of Logic, and cannot therefore be given in this place.[1]

It has been urged against the identification of Logic with the doctrine of the regulative laws of human knowledge, that the principles of Logic would remain were there no things and no knowledge, and that thinking, e.g. a logical inference, can be (formally) correct when it is materially false (because false in the premisses).[2] But this exception in its first part amounts to a petitio principii. Of course there are certain logical principles in which the relation of thought to things can be got rid of by abstraction. This is true of the law of Identity and Contradiction, which requires the harmony of thoughts with one another (the condition of their agreement with actual existence), as well as of all other laws derived from it. Whoever limits Logic to these portions must maintain that logical principles are valid without reference to objective reality; but he who assigns to Logic a more comprehensive sphere will not admit the correctness of that assertion in its universality. Whoever maintains that Logic does not fulfil its task unless it provides laws for the rigid construction of the scientific notion in its distinction from the mere general conception, for natural division, for the scientific form of Deduction, Induction, and Analogy—whoever does not consider the principle of Logic to be the mere consistency of the thinking subject with itself, but recognises truth to be the agreement with existence, and therefore no mere necessity of thought immanent in the subjective spirit, but rather a correspondence of the logical with the ontological categories, cannot assert that the logical laws, having reference to truth, would be quite as valid if there were neither things nor knowledge. What is brought forward in the second part of the above objection is so

---

[1] Cf. especially § 31, and the tract quoted there on Idealism, &c.; also §§ 37, 40–44.

[2] Ulrici; cf. Drobisch, *Log.* 2nd ed. § 7, 3rd ed. § 5, and Pref. p. xviii. According to Drobisch, in his introduction to Logic, only so much is to be taken from the doctrine of knowledge as is needful to get at the data for the peculiar problems.

far true that thinking may be conformable to *single* logical
laws—to single laws of Logic even as the science of knowledge
—without having material truth : but the agreement of the
whole activity of knowledge with *all* these laws ensures
material truth. He who has observed all the laws of perception and of thinking cognition in a conclusion and in the
structure of the premisses and in the foregoing operations, has
arrived in the conclusion (be it immediately, or, as in indirect
proof, mediately) at material truth. The Novel does not proceed upon (historical) knowledge, and yet must follow logical
laws : but it must follow them only in the combination of
antecedents with consequences. If the poet constructed his
antecedents from the contents of perception according to logical
laws, as the historian and the judge do, he too would arrive
throughout at material truth : if he follows logical laws in the
combination of antecedents and consequences, he thus gains for
this combination more than mere agreement with itself; he
gains for it agreement with the *laws* of objective reality. The
formal correctness of the mere conclusion, or generally of any
definite *part* of the whole activity of knowledge, ensures
material truth so far as it goes, i.e. it warrants that we, so far
as we proceed from materially true antecedents (e.g. in concluding the return of a comet or the approach of an eclipse),
will continue in material truth, and arrive at materially true
results. And this is just what must be expected from the view
that logical rules rest on the principle of material truth ; while
it does not at all agree with the opposite view, which would
understand logical rules in abstraction from material truth.
According to this view material truth could be ensured neither
absolutely nor partially (e.g. from premisses to conclusion)
through the observance of logical rules. It must explain con-
tinuance in truth from this stand-point—that no logical operations carry us beyond the previously actually existing content
of knowledge, but only raise it to fuller clearness and completeness. The *fact* of the enlargement of knowledge by logical
combination, especially by inference (both deductive and inductive), contradicts this. The rules which thinking follows in

practical life and in scientific investigation can only be
comprehended and established, when we advance from the
consideration of the relation of thought to itself to the consideration of its relation to the objective reality.

§ 4. The *possibility* of the conscious apprehension
and systematic representation of logical laws rests on
their previous unconscious activity; and so *Logic* as
science rests on the previous *exercise of the activity of
knowledge.* On the other hand, the science of Logic
makes possible a conscious application of the laws of
Logic and a conscious logical activity of thought.

On these relations rests the scholastic distinction of *Logica
naturalis* (connata et acquisita), *Logica scholastica docens,*
and *Logica scholastica utens.* Still, the name Logic, strictly
taken, belongs to the Logica scholastica docens, and is therefore rightly used in this sense chiefly by modern logicians.
The use of logical forms and the application of logical laws
can and must precede their theory, since the theory itself is
only possible through such use; but by the theory the use
becomes more regulated and stricter. Historically, single
axioms upon thinking have first of all become connected with
thinking, and a logically regulated representation of the sciences,
and Logic itself in gradual development, does not follow without application of these axioms.

§ 5. Logic has partly an *absolute,* as scientifically an
end in itself, partly a *relative value,* in virtue of the
relation in which it, as the theory of the art of thinking
and of knowing, stands to the exercise of the activity of
knowledge, aiding and furthering it. The theory of
thinking exerts an influence upon thinking: (a) Essentially by the enunciation of the regulative laws themselves, since the scientific consciousness of these laws

furthers their practical application; it can besides (b),
by pointing out the most appropriate procedure, enable
the requirements of the logical laws to be fulfilled
under subjective limitations and hindrances. In technical relation Logic is a mere *canon* and *purifier* of
thought, if it be looked at only as the doctrine of the
agreement of thought with itself; but it is also a *canon*
and *organon of knowledge*, although only mediately in
the application of its laws to a given material of knowledge, if it be represented as a criterion of material
truth.

It is equally false to consider Logic valid only as an organon
or canon, or mean, and only as something to be studied for
its own sake. *Hegel* rightly remarks, so decidedly does he
declare both against the first one-sided view,[1] and also against
the second,[2] that whatever is in itself of the most worth,
importance, freedom, and independence, is also the most useful,
and that Logic forms no exception to the rule.

§ 6. Logic is *an integral part of the system of philosophy.* Philosophy may be defined as the science of
the universe, not according to its individual existences,
but according to the principles which condition every
individual, or the science of the principles of what is to
be known in the special sciences. The principles are in
the absolute or relative sense the first elements on
which the series of other elements depend. In the
system of Philosophy, metaphysics, including general
rational theology (πρώτη φιλοσοφία, Arist.), makes the
first great division, because it is the science of principles in general, in so far as they are common to all

[1] *Wiss. der Logik*, ed. 1833–31, I. 13–17.   [2] *Encycl.* § 19.

existence. The philosophy of Nature and the philosophy of Spirit make the second and third divisions,
because they are sciences of the special principles of the
two great spheres of existence, which are distinguished
by the opposition of impersonality or of the absence
of self-consciousness, and of personality or the capacity for the thinking cognition of what actually exists,
for perfection, and for ethical self-determination. In
the philosophy of Spirit three regulative sciences—
Logic, Ethics, and Aesthetics, the sciences of the laws
on ·the observation of which depends the realisation
of the ideas of the true, the good, and the beautiful—connect themselves with Psychology, the science
of the essential nature and natural laws of the human
soul. The true is knowledge which agrees with what
actually exists. The good is what corresponds to its
inner determination or idea, as the object of will and
desire. The beautiful is what corresponds to its inner
determination or idea, as the object of representation
and feeling.

To these sciences is further to be added, as both con-
templative and regulative, Paedagogic, or the doctrine
of training the capacities, determined by the genetic
laws of the mental life, to develope themselves to their
ideal ends, i.e. to the knowledge of the true, to will the
Good, and to the sense of the Beautiful; and the Philosophy of History, or the science of the actual development of the human race, in so far as it proceeds in
agreement or disagreement with the ideal rules of development. It includes the philosophical consideration
of the development of culture, religion, art, and science.

The complete justification of this description of the notion and of the division of philosophy would lead us beyond the bounds of this Introduction. We therefore limit ourselves here to the following remarks. If we were to understand by *principle* what is thought to be absolutely without antecedent, our discourse must needs be of one principle only; but, according to the definition of the notion given above, a plurality of principles can be accepted, each of which in its own series is the ruling one, but when admitted into other series depending upon other principles, can also subordinate itself to a higher principle from which it now derives its authority. In this sense the common principles of all existence are to be distinguished from the particular principles of individual spheres. The science which treats of the earlier evidently makes the first great division in any systematic arrangement. It bears the name of first philosophy [1] ever since Aristotle won for it an independent place, and is also called metaphysics from its position, *after* the physics in the system of the Aristotelian works. (This arrangement is not Aristotle's. It dates from a later time, and is due probably to Andronicus of Rhodes; but it corresponds to Aristotle's didactic maxim, that what lies nearer the senses is the earlier for us in inductive cognition, but the later in deductive cognition.) The divisions of philosophy which treat of the special principles of the individual spheres of being stand opposed to metaphysics. The division of these spheres into the two great groups of nature and of mind (Geist), of impersonal and personal existence, does not here require vindication, as it is commonly recognised by science. It follows from this presupposition that the philosophy of nature and the philosophy of mind must come after metaphysics, and make the second and third great divisions of the system of philosophy. The division of the philosophy of mind rests upon the law recognised by Aristotle, that in the gradation of earthly existence every higher carries in itself the modified character of the lower, while raised above it by its higher characteristics. Thus, mind

[1] Arist. *Phys.* i. 4; *Metaph.* iv. 3; ibid. iv. 1.

(Geist) has in itself the elements of nature and conformity to natural law; and the series of the branch sciences of the philosophy of mind begins with the science of mental life from the side of nature and natural law—viz. with Psychology. The personal power of self-determination, by which mind is raised above nature, is conditioned by the consciousness of regulative laws or laws of what should be. Since these laws follow from the universal demand to realise ideas in life, each of the three chief tendencies of the life of the spirit—knowledge, will, and feeling—is governed by its special idea. Thus arise three sciences of ruling or ideal laws, co-ordinate to each other—viz. the sciences of the laws of truth, goodness, and beauty. Lastly, since the opposition of the laws of nature and of the regulative laws points towards an adjustment in which the opposites become one (for, under the government of the divine spirit, what should be and what is are one and the same), the theory of Paedagogic and the philosophy of history must follow psychology and the regulative sciences, and close the series of the branch sciences of the philosophy of mind.

The ideas of truth and beauty stand in essentially like relation to the idea of moral goodness. They can and should all be placed in relation to the divine spirit, for all earlier categories are destined to return as moments in the last and higher sphere; but truth and beauty, as well as moral goodness, must find their nearest scientific explanation from the essence of the finite spirit. We cannot, therefore, find (with *Hegel*) the opposition to the 'subjective spirit' yet linked with nature, and running through the first course of its self-liberation, in the ethical relations exclusively, but must assign aesthetic and logic, as well as ethics, to the second sphere.

The doctrine of the regulative laws of *thought* forms part of the doctrine of the regulative laws of *knowledge*. It has no claim to the rank of an independent philosophical doctrine.

The attempt to unite the doctrine of knowledge with metaphysics in one and the same science—*metaphysical* or *onto-*

logical logic—is untenable; because it contradicts the fundamental principles of any rational attempt at systematisation, by placing under the same notion with one of the branch sciences of the philosophy of spirit that philosophical science which has to do with the most general principles. This difficulty would vanish, if we could (as Hegel does) explain the laws of knowledge to be the universal forms of all existence—of things in nature as well as of spiritual existences. But this is a violent proceeding. Hegel's metaphysical logic treats not only of notion, judgment, and inference, but also of the analytic and synthetic methods, of definition, of division, of theorem, of construction, of proof, &c. All these forms must be explained as metaphysical, and, consequently, as forms of nature and of spirit; but this is evidently incorrect. And even if this presupposition could be granted, the essential distinction would still exist, that those forms attain in the outer world only to an unconscious and limited, but in the knowing spirit to a free conscious existence. This distinction is significant enough to require a special consideration of these forms as forms of spirit; and, in fact, with Hegel, the doctrine of the notion has three different positions in the system. It is ever coming forward in Logic, in the phenomenology of reason and in the psychology of the intelligence. Even if Hegel's presupposition, therefore, were true (which it is not), we would need a special theory of human knowledge besides metaphysics; and of the two disciplines, the doctrine of knowledge, both on verbal and historical grounds, has the better right to the name of Logic.

§ 7. In a system of philosophy divided according to purely scientific principles, Logic would not have the first place; yet it is both lawful and suitable that the *study* of Logic should precede that of the other philosophical disciplines as a propaedeutic—*lawful*, for its purposes are served when a few universal definitions, which are comprehensible and capable of a certain justi-

16   § 8. *Division of Logic.*

fication outside of their own peculiar science, are taken out of the preceding disciplines, Metaphysics and Psychology; *suitable* for these reasons: (a) The study of Logic offers less difficulty than that of those philosophical disciplines which go before it in scientific arrangement. (b) Logic makes us conscious of the methods which find application in itself and in the other branches of philosophy, and the study of Logic is a valuable exercise of thinking. In formal reference, therefore, it is convenient that Logic should be placed at the beginning of the whole study of philosophy. (c) The scientific representation of the system of Philosophy requires an introduction, in order to lead the consciousness to the stand-point of the philosophical treatment by means of the theory of the relations which exist between phenomena and Being ; and the task of this introduction is most completely and most scientifically accomplished by Logic as the critical theory of knowledge.

Hegel says, in his Letters to v. Raumer[1] on philosophical propaedeutic, that it has to see to the education and exercise of thinking. It is able to do this by removing thinking entirely from the region of the phantastic, by means of the determinateness of its notions and its consistent methodical procedure. It is able to do this in a higher measure than mathematics, because it has not the sensible content which mathematics has.[2]

§ 8. The forms and laws of knowledge can be treated partly in their general character and partly in the particular modifications which they take according to the

[1] Worke, xvii. 355.
[2] It is this thought which is the grain of truth in Sir W. Hamilton's ill-judged attack on mathematics. Cf. *Discussions*, p. 282 ff.

different nature of the object-matter known (§ 2).
The first is the problem of *pure* or *general*, the second
that of *applied* or *particular* Logic. Pure Logic teaches
both the laws of immediate knowledge or perception,
and those of mediate knowledge or thought. And
since, speaking generally, knowledge mirrors the actual
in its forms of existence, so more particularly—

Perception mirrors the outer order of things or their
existence in space and time, and represents or copies
their real motion in an ideal way; and—

Thought mirrors their inner order, which is the foundation of the outer.

The forms of thought separate into as many divisions
as there are forms of existence in which the inner order
of things exists, and correspond to them in the following way:—

Intuition or individual conception, to the objective
individual existence;

Notion, with content and extent to the essence and
genus or species;

Judgment, to the fundamental relations among things;

Inference, to the objective reign of law; and

System, to the objective totality of things.

The division of *Applied* or *Particular* Logic depends
upon the sciences to which the logical doctrines find
application. It treats of, for instance, the methods of
mathematics or of the science of quantity and form,
of the explanatory and descriptive sciences of nature,
of the explanatory and descriptive sciences of spirit,
and of philosophy or the science of principles.

c

18 § 8. *Division of Logic.*

The justification of this division in its particulars, so far as it rests on logical principles, remains to be considered below, cf. §§ 36, 45, 56, 67, 74, 138; but in so far as it depends on metaphysical principles, cf. the first remark to § 2. The most common division of Logic since Kant's time has been—A. General Logic: 1. Pure General Logic: *a.* The doctrine of elements; *b.* The doctrine of method. 2. Applied General Logic. B. Special Logic. Comparing this with our division, we remark: In so far as Applied Logic is understood to mean the doctrine of perception and of the relation of thought to perception, it belongs to our Pure Logic; but in so far as it means the practical hints for the most suitable behaviour under the many subjective hindrances to thinking[1] —[or as it is said to exhibit the laws of thought modified in their actual applications by certain general circumstances, external or internal, contingent in themselves, but by which human thought is always more or less influenced in its manifestations[2]]—it cannot be allowed to form a special division of Logic, because it has more a didactic than a logical character (cf. § 5); and Applied Logic can only be understood in the same sense as we speak of applied mathematics, &c., viz. the application of its general rules to particular wider spheres in which they hold good, and the consideration of the modifications under which they find application to each one of them. In this sense the notion of applied Logic does not differ from that of special Logic, while, on the other hand, Pure Logic is identical with General Logic.

The division of Pure Logic into the doctrine of Elements and doctrine of Method[3] confuses its scientific interest with its didactic. Scientifically, notion, judgment, and inference are not merely elements of method. The notion is also an element in the judgment, and both are elements in inference. Besides, the notion, the doctrine of elements, is too relative to denote the opposite of Methodology.

[1] Cf. Kant, *Kritik der r. Vern.* Werke, ed. Hartenstein, iii. 84 ; *Logik*, viii. 18.
[2] [Hamilton, *Lect. on Logic*, i. 60.]   [3] [Cf. Hamilton, ibid. i. 61.]

§ 9. The *History of Logic* has worth and meaning in a double relation : (a) *for its own sake,* inasmuch as it brings clearly before us the ever-ongoing struggle of the human mind to obtain an understanding of the laws of its thinking and knowing; (b.) *as a mean* to understand the present position of Logic, since it informs us of the genesis both of the parts scientifically certain, and of the diverse opinions prevailing at present.

Of the works which treat of the general history of Logic, the most complete and thoroughgoing is the Geschichte der Logik im Abendlande, by *C. Prantl,* 1st vol. (containing the development of Logic among the ancients), Leipzig, 1855, 2nd vol. (referring to the first half of the Middle Ages), do., 1861, 3rd vol.. do., 1867, and 4th vol., do., 1870 (referring to the latter half of the Middle Ages).

§ 10. The *foundation* of Logic as a science is a work of the *Greek* mind, which, equally removed from the hardness of the Northern and the softness of the Oriental, harmoniously united power and impressibility.

For its general characteristic, cf. *Plato,* De Republ. iv. 435 ε (ed. Steph.), and *Arist.* Polit. vii. 7. The impressible fancy of the Oriental has not the measure nor grip of strong thinking : it wants the mental power of the genuinely scientific mind. In its attempts to philosophise it is not ruled by the tendency to strict demonstration and to representation in a scientific form ; and where the *art* of strictly scientific thinking is absent, the *theory* can still less develope itself. Yet some true, deep fundamental thoughts appeared which, if they had been consistently followed out, would have served very well to be a foundation of a system of Logic. Thus the *Chinese* Meng-tse, a disciple of Kon-fu-tse, says, 'The human mind has in itself the possibility of knowing all things; it must therefore look to its own nature and essence, otherwise it errs.

Only the virtuous can fathom his own essence: he who has fathomed his own nature can also know that of other men, he can fathom the essence of things.' According to this writer the general original power of reason shows itself in man as the law of duty.[1]

Among the Hindoos we find, in the philosophies of the Sankhya and the Nyaya, an enumeration of the kinds and objects of knowledge. The three ways of obtaining knowledge, according to the Sankhya doctrine, are, (1) Perception; (2) Conclusion (from the cause to the effect and from the effect to the cause, and also by analogy); and (3) Tradition (by human testimony and Divine revelation): the Nyaya adds Comparison. The Nyaya, which perhaps first arose under Greek influence, recognises the syllogism Nyaya (from which the system takes its name) in the form of five propositions, which arise out of the three propositions by the repetition of the minor premise and conclusion, according to the following scheme:—

Thesis—The hill is fiery. | Proof—What smokes is fiery.
Reason—For it smokes. | Application—The hill smokes.

Conclusion—It is fiery.[2]

It is very doubtful whether the *Egyptians* constructed a logical theory. Plato praises the antiquity of their knowledge, but by no means the elevation of their philosophy. The Greek thinkers, even if acquainted with Egyptian wisdom, had to find out for themselves both the fundamental doctrines of Logic and the proofs of the elementary propositions in Geometry.

The *Greeks* have undoubtedly learned much of the material of their knowledge from the Egyptians, and from the Orientals generally. The Greek mind may have needed an impulse from without for its development, but it owes to its own inborn independent power, not to foreigners, what is the more essential, its scientific and artistic form, however actively impressible it may have made their treasures its own. Cf. *Hegel*,[3] ' From

[1] Cf. Wuttke, *Das Heidenthum* (Breslau, 1853), ii. 102.
[2] [Cf. Colebrooke's *Misc. Essays*, i. 8, and the *Aphorisms of the Nyaya Philos.*, by Gautama, Allahabad, 1850.]
[3] *Philos. der Geschichte*, 1837, p. 216.

what they have naturally received the Greeks have created the spiritual.' The assertion of *Lepsius* agrees also with this:[1] 'The Greeks of this great period (Thales, Pythagoras, &c.) collected the learning of the barbarians of all regions as ripe corn to the threshing-floor, to be new seed for their own fertile soil.'

§ 11. The speculation of the *older Ionic natural philosophers* (in the sixth century B.C.)—of Thales, Anaximander, Anaximenes—was immediately directed to things only, not to the human knowledge of things. The *later natural philosophers* (in the fifth century B.C.) —Heraklitus, Anaxagoras, Leukippus, and Demokritus— showed that sense-perception as such was not trustworthy. It is the reason mingled with it, and going all through it, which decides what truth is. Empedocles taught that things and man came from the same material and ideal elements, and that like is known by like. The *Pythagoreans* held that the elements of number, limit and the limitless, are the elements of all objects. They seek therefore, by means of mathematical investigation and speculation on numbers, to get at all knowledge. Xenophanes of Colophon, the founder of the *Eleatic* philosophy, led on by his theological speculation, distinguished certain knowledge from accidentally correct opinion. His immediate follower, Parmenides, the most developed of the Eleatic philosophers, in his polemic against the Heraklitic doctrine of the universal flow of all things, and of the identity of contradictories, first reaches the theoretic consciousness of the axioms of identity and contradiction, although as yet in an incomplete form. Similarly, Parmenides taught the identity of thought with the exist-

[1] *Chronologie der Aegypter*, i. 55.

ence which is thought. He set in strict opposition to *opinion* about the multiplicity and change of what exists, resting on the deception of the senses, the *knowledge* of the One, which is truth, able to produce conviction, and attained by means of thinking. His young contemporary, Zeno the Eleatic, was the first to use in its strict form the art of managing philosophical dialogue, especially the art of indirect proof. Hence Aristotle calls him the founder of Dialectic.

Heraklitus in Sext. Empir. adv. Math. vii. 126: Κακοὶ μάρτυρες ἀνθρώποισιν ὀφθαλμοὶ καὶ ὦτα, βορβόρου ψυχὰς ἔχοντος (according to the conjecture of Jac. Bernays; commonly: βαρβάρους ψυχὰς ἐχόντων). In Diog. Laert. ix. 1: Πολυμαθίη νόον οὐ διδάσκει · . . . . ἓν τὸ σοφόν · ἐπίστασθαι γνώμην, ἥτε οἰακίζει (according to the conjecture of Bernays; commonly: ἥτε οἱ ἐκυβερνήσει, Schleiem. ἥτε οἴη κυβερνήσει) πάντα διὰ πάντων. Yet the thinking through which wisdom is attained is, according to the view of Heraklitus, not so much an activity of the mind separable from sense-perception, and opposed to it, but rather the sense lying open and submitting itself to the universal all-ruling reason, while its isolation produces error.[1]

Anaxagoras in Sext. Emp. adv. Math. vii. 90: ὑπὸ ἀφαυρότητος αὐτῶν (τῶν αἰσθήσεων) οὐ δυνατοί ἐσμεν κρίνειν τἀληθές. According to Anaxagoras,[2] the divine reason knows all things, and the human is homogeneous with it: πάντα ἔγνω νόος ·—νόος δὲ πᾶς ὁμοῖός ἐστι καὶ ὁ μείζων καὶ ὁ ἐλάσσων.

Demokritus, Sext. Emp. adv. Math. p. 138, informs us, divided knowledge into what is attained through sense-perception, and what through the understanding. The former he calls the dark (σκοτίη), the latter the genuine (γνησίη). Demokritus says (p. 140) that the work of the ἔννοια is Ζήτησις, the investigation of the unknown upon the ground of the sense-phe-

[1] Cf. Sext. Emp. adv. Math. vii. 129.
[2] In Simplic. in Arist. Phys. fol. 39 sqq.

nomena. Yet this thinking warrants only relatively a higher
certainty. Man has no science in the strict sense of the
word. *Demokritus* in Diog. Laërt. ix. 72: ἐτεῇ δὲ οὐδὲν ἴδμεν·
ἐν βυθῷ γὰρ ἡ ἀλήθεια.—*Empedokles* in Aristot. de Anima, i. 2:

γαίῃ μὲν γὰρ γαῖαν ὀπώπαμεν, ὕδατι δ᾽ ὕδωρ,
αἰθέρι δ᾽ αἰθέρα δῖον, ἀτὰρ πυρὶ πῦρ ἀΐδηλον,
στοργῇ δὲ στοργὴν, νεῖκος δέ τε νείκεϊ λυγρῷ.

The doctrines of the early *Pythagoreans* are not accessible to us
as they themselves represented them, since the writing ascribed
to Philolaus,[1] which gave us access to many fragments, cannot
be held to be genuine according to the investigations of
Schaarschmidt.[2] We can only trust to a sketch given by
Aristotle.[3] Quotations such as the following are valuable
only as bearing witness to the tendency of the *later Pytha-*
gorean philosophy:—*Pseudo-Philolaus* in Stob. Eclog. i. 2, 3:[4]
οὐ γὰρ ἦς' δῆλον οὐθενὶ οὐθὲν τῶν πραγμάτων, οὔτε αὐτῶν ποθ'
(πρὸς) αὐτὰ οὔτε ἄλλω ποτ᾽ ἄλλο, εἰ μὴ ἦς ἀριθμὸς καὶ ἁ τούτω
ἐσσία. Νῦν δὲ οὗτος κατὰ τὰν ψυχὰν ἁρμόζων αἰσθήσει πάντα
γνωστὰ καὶ ποτάγορα (i.e. προσήγορα, corresponding to and
connected by friendship) ἀλλάλοις ἀπεργάζεται. In Sext.
Emp. adv. Math. vii. 92:[5] ὑπὸ τοῦ ὁμοίου τὸ ὅμοιον κατα-
λαμβάνεσθαι πέφυκεν.

Xenophanes in Sext. Emp. adv. Math. vii. 49; 110; viii. 326:

καὶ τὸ μὲν οὖν σαφὲς οὔτις ἀνὴρ ἴδεν οὐδέ τις ἔσται
εἰδὼς, ἀμφὶ θεῶν τε καὶ ὅσσα λέγω περὶ πάντων·
εἰ γὰρ καὶ τὰ μάλιστα τύχοι τετελεσμένον εἰπών,
αὐτὸς ὅμως οὐκ οἶδε, δόκος δ᾽ ἐπὶ πᾶσι τέτυκται.

Parmenides enunciates the axiom of Identity, in the metaphysical sense, in the words : ἔστιν or ἔστι γὰρ εἶναι, and the
axiom of Contradiction in the words: οὐκ ἔστι μὴ εἶναι or
μηδὲν δ᾽ (ἐστὶν) οὐκ εἶναι. He explains to be false the opinion
of erring two-headed (δίκρανοι) mortals, of the uncritical tribes

[1] Edited and commented on by Boeckh, Berlin, 1819.
[2] *Die angebliche Schriftstellerei des Philolaus und die Bruchstücke
der ihm zugeschriebenen Bücher*, Bonn, 1864.
[3] *Metaph.* i. 5. [4] See Boeckh, *Philol.* 141. [5] Ibid. 191, 192.

(ἄκριτα φῦλα) who hold Being and Not-Being to be identical, and at the same time not identical, and change every thing into its opposite :

οἷς τὸ πέλειν τε καὶ οὐκ εἶναι ταὐτὸν νενόμισται
κοὐ ταὐτόν, πάντων τε παλίντροπός ἐστι κέλευθος.[1]

Parmenides in these verses[2] refers most probably to Heraklitus, for it is Heraklitus who has enunciated this doctrine: ταὐτό τ' ἔνι (leg. ταὐτόν ἐστι) ζῶν καὶ τεθνηκός, κ.τ.λ., πάντα εἶναι καὶ μὴ εἶναι,[3]—παλίντονος (παλίντροπος) ἁρμονία κόσμου, ὅκωσπερ λύρης καὶ τόξου.[4] He does not, however, refer to Heraklitus as a solitary thinker, but as a representative of the ' uncritical many,' who, trusting to the senses, get involved in that mode of viewing things, full of contradictions, to which Heraklitus has given a philosophical form.[5] Since Heraklitus called the synthetic unity of opposites, their identity, and their existence in combination, a oneness of existence, he provoked that strong thinker, Parmenides, to the counter-assertion, and to seize on the opposite extreme. Parmenides denied that true existence could have any multiplicity or any change. (This is the very opposition of fundamental philosophical conception which appears in the Hegelian and Herbartian systems. The difference is that the perception of Heraklitus has been absorbed in the dialectic method of Hegel, and that Herbart believes that the multiplicity and change of the qualities

[1] Parm. Fragm. ed. *Mullach*, vv. 35, 43–51.

[2] To which Steinhart in the *Hall. Allg. Litteraturz*, 1845, p. 892 f, and Bernays in the *Rhein. Museum*, vii. 114 f., have paid careful attention.

[3] Plut. *Consol.* c. 10 ; Arist. *Metaph.* iv. 7, cf. iv. 3.[*]

[4] Plutarch, *De Is. et Os.* c. 45 ; *De An. Procr.* 27, 2.

[5] So also Aristotle, *De An.* i. 2 : ἐν κινήσει δ' εἶναι τὰ ὄντα κἀκεῖνος ᾤετο καὶ οἱ πολλοί, cf. Plut. *Theaet.* p. 179. In a wholly analogous way Herbart accuses Hegel of empiricism.

[*] *Metaph.* iv. 3, § 14, perhaps καθάπερ τινές οἴονται 'Ηράκλειτον should be read, and ἀπολαμβάνειν, not λέγειν, understood ; for Heraklitus actually said that the same was and also was not (cf. εἶμεν καὶ οὐκ εἶμεν, Her. *Alleg. Hom.* c. 24), but could not accept it or *think* it because it was not at all possible.

of ono thing are contradictory, but grants the multiplicity of individual real essences. Herbart also attempts the problem, not considered by Parmenides, to derive philosophically the illusion of the changeable from the being of the changeless.) Parmenides further teaches that thought belongs to the One, to the truly existing, which is thought of and is identical with it. What exists, is itself thinking, the νοῦς. *Parm.* Frag. vv. 94–97:

ταὐτὸν δ' ἐστί νοεῖν τε καὶ οὔνεκέν ἐστι νόημα·
οὐ γὰρ ἄνευ τοῦ ἐόντος, ἐν ᾧ πεφατισμένον ἐστίν,
εὑρήσεις τὸ νοεῖν· οὐδ' ἦν γὰρ ἢ ἔστιν ἢ ἔσται
ἄλλο παρὲκ τοῦ ἐόντος.

The deceiving senses do not judge of truth, the reason does. *Parm.* Frag. vv. 54–57:

μηδέ σ' ἔθος πολύπειρον ὁδὸν κατὰ τήνδε βιάσθω,
νωμᾶν ἄσκοπον ὄμμα καὶ ἠχήεσσαν ἀκουὴν
καὶ γλῶσσαν· κρῖναι δὲ λόγῳ πολύδηριν ἔλεγχον
ἐξ ἐμέθεν ῥηθέντα.

Of *Zeno* the Eleatic, Diogenes Laertius informs us (ix. 25): φησὶ δὲ Ἀριστοτέλης ἐν τῷ Σοφιστῇ, εὑρετὴν αὐτὸν γενέσθαι διαλεκτικῆς. Zeno's dialectic art consisted essentially in this, that by reasoning against the existence of the many [1] and of motion [2] he undertook to bring forward indirect proof for the truth of Parmenides' doctrine of the One, which was genuine.[3] His dialogues appear, according to (Plato's?) *Parmenides*, p. 127, to have contained regular courses of reasoning (λόγους).

§ 12. The *Sophists* elaborated the dialectic art, but often misapplied it to the purposes of subjective caprice.

Sokrates (470–399 B.C.), who was animated by the idea of science, made it serve to aid the striving after that objectively valid knowledge, which may be recognised by every thinking subject to be true in the same way, and

[1] *Simplic. in Phys.* fol. 30 a.   [2] *Arist. Phys.* vi. 9.
[3] Cf. (Plato's?) *Parmen.* p. 128.

necessarily. He sought by collecting and testing instances to recognise the general from the basis of individuals. When he had discovered the universal, he endeavoured to describe it by means of the definition of the notion. He is therefore the founder of Induction and Definition, but only in their application to ethical problems, and apart from any logical theory.

Protagoras ap. Diog. l. 9. 51: πάντων χρημάτων μέτρον ἄνθρωπος, τῶν μὲν ὄντων ὡς ἔστι, τῶν δὲ οὐκ ὄντων ὡς οὐκ ἔστιν. Ibidem: πρῶτος ἔφη δύο λόγους εἶναι περὶ παντὸς πράγματος ἀντικειμένους ἀλλήλοις. (*Arist.*?) do Melisso, Xenophane, Gorgia, c. 5: (ὁ Γοργίας) οὐκ εἶναί φησιν οὐδέν· εἰ δὲ ἔστιν, ἄγνωστον εἶναι· εἰ δὲ καὶ ἔστι καὶ γνωστόν, ἀλλ' οὐ δηλωτὸν ἄλλοις. *Arist.* Metaph. xiii. 4: δύο γάρ ἐστιν ἅ τις ἂν ἀποδοίη Σωκράτει δικαίως, τούς τ' ἐπακτικοὺς λόγους καὶ τὸ ὁρίζεσθαι καθόλου· ταῦτα γάρ ἐστιν ἄμφω περὶ ἀρχὴν ἐπιστήμης. *Arist.* Metaph. i. 6: Σωκράτους δὲ περὶ μὲν τὰ ἠθικὰ πραγματευομένου, περὶ δὲ τῆς ὅλης φύσεως οὐθέν, ἐν μέντοι τούτοις τὸ καθόλου ζητοῦντος καὶ περὶ ὁρισμῶν ἐπιστήσαντος πρώτου τὴν διάνοιαν.[1]

§ 13.

Of the *one-sided Sokratic Schools*, the *Cynic* of Antisthenes, and the *Cyrenaic* or Hedonist of Aristippus, treat of ethical problems chiefly. Their contributions to Logic rest on their negative polemic against contemporary systems. The *Megaric* School of Euklid, and *Eretric* School of Phaedo and Menedemus allied to it, mix together the principles of Sokrates and the doctrines of Parmenides. Since the Megarics, in order to defend the unity of existence, deny the truth of sense-phenomena, their dialectic became gradually more and more a mere Eristic, which takes special delight to find out numerous captious and sophistical arguments.

[1] Cf. Xenoph. Memorab. iv. 5, 12; iv. 6, 1.

Antisthenes objected to the Platonic doctrine of ideas :—It could easily be said to what things were similar, but not *what* things were. Definitions of simple notions were a useless waste of words (μακρὸς λόγος).[1]

The *Cyrenaics* restricted science to the consciousness of the sense-affections as such; what the real object was which excited these, and whether it was in itself white or sweet, &c. could not be known.[2]

Euklid of Megara identified the *One*, the true existence of the Eleatics, with the *Good* of Sokrates.[3] He vindicated his doctrine, as Zeno did, by indirect argument, and sought to show the absurd consequences which flow from the opposite view, which ascribes plurality and change to reality.[4] For this purpose his followers, Eubulides, Diodorus Kronus, and Alexinus, invented a number of captious arguments ; e.g. 'The Liar,' 'The Veiled,' 'The Horned,' 'The Heap,' and 'The Baldhead.'

The doctrine that no subject can be joined to a predicate which can be separated from it (e.g. man is wise), but that each must be predicated of itself only (e.g. man is man), is to be ascribed partly to the Megarics in general, but more especially to *Stilpo*, who mixed up their doctrines with those of the Cynics,[5] and also to *Menedemus* the Eretrian.[6] It is an immediate consequence from the doctrine of the oneness and unchangeableness of true existence.

§ 14. Proceeding from the Sokratic method of Induction and Definition, *Plato* (427–347 D.C.) developed the *art* of Logic in many ways—

(a) He enriched it with the methods of Division and Deduction.

---

[1] *Simplic. in Arist. Categ.* fol. 51 B.; Arist. *Metaph.* viii. 3, cf. Plat. *Theaet.* 201, Soph. 251.

[2] Sext. *Emp. adv. Math.* vii. 191.

[3] Diog. *Laert.* ii. 106 ; Cic. *Acad. pr.* ii. 42.

[4] Diog. *Laert.* ii. 107.   [5] Plut. *adv. Col.* 23.

[6] *Simplic. in Phys.* 20 A.

(b) He removed its limitation to ethical inquiry, and extended it to the whole sphere of philosophical thought.

(c) He used it with ingenious sagacity, scientific exactness, care, and depth; and still more increased the value of these advantages by his masterly artistic representation.

Plato also developed the *theory* of thinking in many relations—

(a) He surveyed the art of philosophical thinking in the general, and comprehended it under a general notion (the notion of *Dialectic*).

(b) He strictly distinguished philosophical thinking, not only from sense-perception, as his predecessors had done, but from mathematical thinking.

(c) He brought under observation also, and undertook to give an account of, the main operations of thought, more especially the formation of notions, Definition, Division, and partly also Deduction.

But Plato's logical theorems, showing throughout the traces of their origin from reflection upon ideological thinking, want both a strict separation of the logical from the metaphysical elements, a scientific completeness, and representation in a systematic form.

If Plato's lofty art of thinking and of representation rightly excites our admiration, his developments of logical theory have no less significance for the history of our science. Plato finds in existence the measure of thinking: Rep. v. 477 (cf. Cratyl. p. 385 B): λόγος,—ὃς ἂν τὰ ὄντα λέγῃ ὡς ἔστιν, ἀληθής, ὃς δ' ἄν, ὡς οὐκ ἔστι, ψευδής, Soph. p. 263 B; λέγει δὲ ὁ μὲν ἀληθὴς λόγος τὰ ὄντα ὡς ἔστιν, ὁ δὲ ψευδὴς ἕτερα τῶν ὄντων, τὰ μὴ ὄντα ἄρα ὡς ὄντα λέγει). Plato theoretically assigns this double problem to the art of Dialectic, which he also seeks to explain in actual thinking—(1) to collect together into one form what appears scattered everywhere, in order to determine strictly each single one (Phaedr. p. 266, the mode of forming the notion by *Abstraction* and *Definition*), and in this way by the same manner to ascend further to higher notions, until the very highest is reached;[1] (2) then to descend again from the higher notions to the lower, which are subordinate to it, ' to be able to distinguish how each individual has grown by means of the notions of the kinds' (Phaedrus, l. i.—*Division*), and to examine what proceeds from the presuppositions laid down as a basis (Phaedon, 101—*Deduction*), in order to follow it out to the last consequences. Real essences correspond to the notions, rightly constructed, by which they are known, the *ideas*, and these separate into the graduated series which the notions have, from the lower up to the absolutely highest, the idea of the Good.[2] Mathematics proceeds from postulates which are not the highest. Dialectic uses these said postulates as the basis on which to rear its ideal principles. Mathematics takes the opposite course, and derives from its postulates individuals and particulars. For this reason, mathematical knowledge takes a position between pure thought and sense-perception, and the objects of Mathematics are intermediate existences between ideas and sensible things. Since Plato distinguished in sense-knowledge between the trust in sense-perception and mere conjecture, and, in a corresponding way, in sensible objects between things perceived in sense and pictures or shadows, he arrives at the following division of ways of knowing :—

Νόησις		Δόξα	
ἐπιστήμη	διάνοια	πίστις	εἰκασία,

and at the following analogous division of the whole of existing objects :—

Νοητὸν γένος		Ὁρατὸν γένος	
ἰδέαι	μαθηματικά	σώματα	εἰκόνες

[1] *De Rep.* vi. 511 ; cf. vii. 532 *sqq.*   [2] Ibid. p. 509.

It is not only characteristic of Plato's method that he carries on together investigations into thinking and into what is thought about; it is also the peculiarity of the content of his doctrine that he transfers the whole relation of his forms of thought to the objects thought about. With him the logical and the metaphysical stand in a very close relation, and almost in immediate unity. (Yet he does not proceed to identify them.)

§ 15. Plato's followers in the *Academy* felt the need of a stricter systematic form for the purpose of a connected exposition of doctrines. Hence Speusippus was induced to divide the sciences in general, and Xenokrates the philosophical disciplines in particular. Xenokrates was the first to enunciate expressly the division of Philosophy into Physics, Ethics, and Dialectic. The second and third Academic Schools in the so-called *Intermediate Academy*, founded by Arkesilaus and Karneades, inclined to scepticism; the fourth and fifth, founded by Philo and Antiochus of Askalon, inclined to dogmatism and syncretism.

For *Speusippus* s. Diog. Laërt. iv. 2 : οὗτος πρῶτος ἐν τοῖς μαθήμασιν ἐθεάσατο τὸ κοινὸν καὶ συνῳκείωσε καθόσον ἦν δυνατὸν ἀλλήλοις. For *Xenokrates* s. Sext. Empir. adv. Math. vii. 16 : ὧν δυνάμει μὲν Πλάτων ἐστὶν ἀρχηγός, περὶ πολλῶν μὲν φυσικῶν, περὶ πολλῶν δὲ ἠθικῶν, οὐκ ὀλίγων δὲ λογικῶν διαλεχθείς· ῥητότατα δὲ οἱ περὶ τὸν Ξενοκράτη καὶ οἱ ἀπὸ τοῦ Περιπάτου, ἔτι δὲ οἱ ἀπὸ τῆς Στοᾶς ἔχονται τῆσδε τῆς διαιρέσεως. For *Karneades*, who allowed no criterion of truth, but enunciated the doctrine of probability, s. Sext. Empir. adv. Math. vii. 159 sqq.; 166 sqq. For *Philo* Cic. Acad. pr. ii. 0 : and for *Antiochus*, Cic. ib. ii. 6-18, 43.

§ 16. *Aristotle* (384-322 B.C.) established his theory of Logic, as he did every branch of his system, on the foundation laid by Plato. But his peculiar service is: (a) his critical remodelling of Plato's logical doctrines ; (b) their development ; and (c) their systematic representation. The critical remodelling consists, in general, in this, that Aristotle sought to define more strictly the relation of the logical and metaphysical elements. The development belonged to every part of Logic; but, more especially, Aristotle created the theory of syllogism, which before him had scarcely been worked at. The systematic division extended equally to the representation of the whole, and of individual parts. Aristotle dedicated special treatises to the whole of the chief parts of Logic as the doctrine of thinking, and has given a strict scientific form to each one of them. For this service he has been rightly called the Father of Logic as a science. Aristotle collects together the most important part of his logical investigations— the doctrine of inference and proof—under the title *Analytic*, because the logical structure of thought is here as it were analysed, i.e. separated and reduced to its elements. He does not give one common name to all the parts. His successors and commentators called his collected logical writings the *Organon*. *Dialectic* with Aristotle is the art of the critical ἐξέτασις of a thesis, or proceeding from propositions which are held to be true, but are doubtful, to derive conclusions, in order to get at some decision upon their truth or falsehood. The propositions it deals with are mainly probable (ἔνδοξα). *Logical* means with Aristotle the explanation of mere general notions (λόγοις), after the manner of Sokrates and Plato, in opposition to physical treatment, which

has to do with the specific and individual qualities.
The science which is represented in the Organon was
called *Logic* by the Stoics and by some of the commentators of Aristotle.

The Aristotelian remodelling of the Platonic doctrines cannot be understood, although modern writers have often so misunderstood it, in the sense that Aristotle considered the form of
thought without any reference to objective reality. The stand-
point of the Aristotelian is by no means identical with that of
the modern Subjective-formal Logic. This has been proved by
Ritter,[1] Trendelenburg,[2] Zeller,[3] Bonitz,[4] Brandis[5] (although
he accepts an essential relationship between the Aristotelian and
the modern Formal Logic), and by Prantl.[6] Aristotle finds
the standard of truth, as Plato had, in the agreement of thought
with what actually exists, which is the limit of science.[7] The
notion, rightly formed, corresponds, according to Aristotle, to
the essence of the thing (οὐσία or τὸ τί ἦν εἶναι, cf. § 56); the
judgment is an assertion about an existence or a non-existence; affirmation and negation correspond to union and separation in things; the different forms which the notions take in
the judgment (or the kinds of denotation of existences, σχήματα τῆς κατηγορίας τῶν ὄντων) determine themselves according
to the forms of existence; the middle term in a syllogism
correctly constructed corresponds to the cause in the connected
series of real events; the principles of scientific knowledge
correspond to what is actually the first in the nature of things.

Aristotle gives to the whole of his logical investigations the

[1] In his *Geschichte der Philos.* iii. 117 ff. 1631.
[2] In his *Logischen Untersuchungen*, 1st ed. 18-21, 1810; 2nd and 3rd
ed. 30-33, 1862, 1870; cf. *Elem. log. Arist.* 6th ed. 1868, ad § 63.
[3] *Philos. der Griechen*, ii. 373 ff., 1816; 2nd ed. ii. 2, 131 ff., 1860.
[4] *Commentar zur Arist. Metaph.* 187, 1849.
[5] *Gesch. der Gr.-R. Phil.* ii. 2nd ed. 371 ff.; 432 ff., 1853.
[6] *Gesch. der Logik*, i. 87 ff.; 104 ff.; 135, 1855.
[7] *Metaph.* iv. 7; ix. 10; x. 6; cf. *Categ.* 12, 14 a. 21: τῷ γὰρ
εἶναι τὸ πρᾶγμα ἢ μὴ ἀληθὴς ὁ λόγος ἢ ψευδὴς λέγεται.

§ 16. *Aristotle.* 33

name *Analytic* (τὰ ἀναλυτικά), i.e. the analysis of thought (not the doctrine of merely analytic thinking), and desires that every one will first make himself familiar with it before he proceeds to study the First Philosophy or Metaphysic.[1] With regard to the single logical writings, the book De Categoriis, περὶ κατηγοριῶν (whose authenticity is not quite undoubted; perhaps caps. x.–xv. have been inserted by a stranger), treats of the forms of notions and of the corresponding forms of existence. The book De Interpretatione, περὶ ἑρμηνείας (whose authenticity was doubted by Andronikus of Rhodes), treats of the proposition and judgment. The two books Analytica Priora, ἀναλυτικὰ πρότερα, treat of inference. The two books Analytica Posteriora, ἀναλυτικὰ ὕστερα, treat of proof, definition and division, and the knowledge of principles. The eight books of the Topica, τοπικά, treat of dialectical or probable inferences. Lastly, the book De Elenchis Sophisticis, περὶ σοφιστικῶν ἐλέγχων, treats of the deceptive inferences of the Sophists and of their solution. The best new collected edition of these writings is Aristotelis Organon, ed. Theod. *Waitz.*[2] *Trendelenburg's* Elementa Logices Aristoteleae is a very good help to the study of the chief doctrines of *Aristotle's* Organon.[3] For a wider and more thorough-going acquaintance, the student may be referred to the well-known historical work of *Prantl*, Geschichte der Logik, and more especially to the representation of the Aristotelian philosophy given by *Brandis* in his Handbuch der Geschichte der Griech.-Röm. Philos. ii., 2nd pt., 1853. *Biese* (Die Philosophie des Arist. Logik und Metaphysik, 1835) may also be consulted. For the meaning of the expressions *Analytic* and *Dialectic* in Aristotle, see *Trendelenburg*, Elem. Arist., Int. and § 33; and *Charles Thurot*, Études sur Aristote, Paris, 1860, p. 118 ff. For the meaning of Λογικόν, see *Waitz* ad Organon Arist. 82 n, 35; *Schwegler* ad Arist. Metaph. vii. 4; xi. 10; *Prantl*, Geschichte der Logik, i. 535 f. Aristotle refers the Λογικῶν

[1] *Metaph.* iv. 3; vii. 12.   [2] Lips. 1844–46.
[3] Berol. 1836, 5th ed. 1862.

D

34 § 17. *The Peripatetics.*

Ζητεῖν (in opposition to the φυσικὴ σκέψις) more particularly to
Plato and the Platonists,[1] partly with recognition of the
superiority of their investigation into notions,[2] partly and
chiefly blaming them, because the merely logical treatment,
the more it proceeds upon the general notion, the further it
is from the particular qualities. He says:[2] λέγω δὲ λογικὴν
(τὴν ἀπόδειξιν) διὰ τοῦτο, ὅτι ὅσῳ καθόλου μᾶλλον, πορρωτέρω
τῶν οἰκείων ἐστὶν ἀρχῶν. In the time of Cicero Λογική
was in common use to denote the doctrine of knowledge
and representation (especially whilst the influence of the
Stoics lasted). He says, e.g. De Fin. i. 7: in altera philosophiae parte, quae est quaerendi ac disserendi, quae Λογική
dicitur. The expression ἡ λογικὴ πραγματεία is common
with Alexander of Aphrodisia, the Interpreter of Aristotle. Boethius says: logicen Peripatetici veteres appella-
verunt. Seneca and Quintiliau use the expression, rationalis
philosophia, rationalis pars philosophiae. Thomas of Aquino
rightly explains the sense of this in his Commentary on
Arist. Anal. Post.: Ratio de suo actu ratiocinari potest—
et haec est ars logica, i.e. rationalis scientia, quae non solum
rationalis ex hoc, quod est secundum rationem, quod est omnibus artibus commune, sed etiam in hoc, quod est circa ipsam
artem rationis sicut circa propriam materiam. Cf. Kant,[1]
who says, 'that it (Logic) is a science of the reason, not of
its forms merely, but also of its matter, since its rules cannot
be derived apart from experience, and since it has at the same
time reason for its object.'

§ 17. The earlier *Peripatetics*, giving their attention to empirical investigation, developed the Logic of
Aristotle in a few particulars only. The later Peripatetics restricted themselves to the task of advancing
the study of Aristotle's labours by commentaries.

1 *Metaph.* xii. 1, and elsewhere.   2 Ibid. xiii. 5.
2 *De General. Animal.* ii. 8, p. 717 b, 28.
1 *Logik*, Werke, viii. 14, Harten. ed. Leip. 1868.

Theophrastus and Eudemus established the theory of Hypothetical and Disjunctive Inference. They developed the theory
of the Categorical Syllogism by adding five new ones, moods
of the first figure, to the fourteen Aristotelian moods. The
so-called Fourth Figure was afterwards constructed out of
these. For the particulars, see § 103. Of the Later Peripatetics, the most prominent were *Andronikus* of Rhodes, who
classified the works of Aristotle, and *Alexander* of Aphrodisias,
the Interpreter. The labours of *Galen* and of the Neo-
Platonists are to be added to theirs. See Brandis upon the
Greek expounders of the Organon of Aristotle in the Proceed-
ings of the Berlin Academy of Sciences, 1833.

§ 18. *Epikurus* (341–270 B.C.) lowers the value of
Logic, which he calls Canonic. He places it exclusively
at the service of his Hedonist Ethics, passes over the
harder doctrines, and makes sense-perception and the
conception proceeding from it the final judge of truth.

The *Stoics*, whose mode of thought owed its origin
to Zeno of Cittium (circa 300 B.C.), and was built up
into a system by Chrysippus (282–209 B.C.) chiefly,
developed the Aristotelian doctrine of thought in particular parts, by their elaboration of the doctrine of the
hypothetical and disjunctive syllogism, and added to it
the beginnings of a theory of perception and of its
value for knowledge. From their investigations into
the criterion of truth, their Logic, more distinctly than
Aristotle's, acquired the character of a theory of knowledge. They attribute to sense-perception, and in a
higher degree to thinking, the capacity to become a
true picture of actual existence. Some of the Stoics
comprehended, under the name Logic, dialectical doctrines (i.e. those of the theory of thinking and knowing) and those of grammar and rhetoric.

D 2

36 § 18. *The Epikureans, Stoics, and Skeptics.*

The *Skeptics* combated dogmatism in general, and especially that of the Stoics. The chief representatives of Skepticism are the followers of Pyrrho of Elis (circa 320 B.C.), and the Philosophers of the Intermediate Academy.

For *Epikurus* see *Diog. Laert.* x. 31 : ἐν τοίνυν τῷ Κανόνι λέγει ὁ Ἐπίκουρος, κριτήρια τῆς ἀληθείας εἶναι τὰς αἰσθήσεις καὶ προλήψεις καὶ τὰ πάθη. Cicero[1]: tollit definitiones, nihil de dividendo ac partiendo docet; non quo modo efficiatur con-cludaturque ratio tradit; non qua via captiosa solvantur, ambigua distinguantur ostendit; iudicia rerum in sensibus ponit.[2] Some later Epikureans, Zeno (circa 100 B.C.) and his scholar Philodemus, following in the steps of Epikurus, have treated of the mode of concluding from signs (σημεία, σημει-οῦσθαι).

For the *Stoical* division of Logic see *Diog. Laert.* vii. 41: τὸ δὲ λογικὸν μέρος φασὶν ἔνιοι εἰς δύο διαιρεῖσθαι ἐπιστήμας, εἰς ῥητορ-ικὴν καὶ εἰς διαλεκτικήν, cf. *Senec.* Ep. 89; upon the φαντασία καταληπτική and the πρόληψις issuing from it, *Diog. L.* vii. 46 ; *Cic.* Acad. Post. i. 11 : visis non omnibus adiungebant fidem, sed iis solum, quae propriam quandam haberent declarationem earum rerum, quae viderentur—unde postea notiones rerum in animis imprimerentur.—*Stob.* Eclog. Eth. ii. 128 : εἶναι δὲ τὴν ἐπιστήμην κατάληψιν ἀσφαλῆ καὶ ἀμετάπτωτον ὑπὸ λόγου.

The *Skeptics* find no sure ground for distinguishing between two opposite opinions either in perception or in the notion, and therefore limit themselves to the acceptance of the phe-nomena as such, abstaining (ἐποχή) from any judgment upon their objective truth.[3] The grounds of doubt which, accord-ing to Aristokles,[4] seem to have been collected by Aenesidemus are quoted by Sext. Emp.[5] They rest chiefly upon subject-ive differences conditioned by the relativity of conceptions. Sextus, a physician of the Empirical School, gives a very

[1] *De Fin.* i. 7.   [2] Cf. ib. ii. 6.   [3] Diog. Laert. ix. 103 sqq.
[4] Ap. Euseb. praepar. Evang. xiv. 18.
[5] *Hypotyp. Pyrrhon.* i. 36 sqq.; Diog. Laert. ix. 79 sqq.

copious collection of the whole of the Skeptical arguments of
antiquity in his two works which are extant: Πυῤῥωνίων
ὑποτυπώσεων βιβλία τρία and Πρὸς μαθηματικοὺς βιβλία ἕνδεκα.

§ 19. The *Neo-Platonists* (whose mode of thought
appeared in the third century A.D.), inclining to meta-
physical-theosophic speculations, placed the ecstatic intuition of the divine high above scientifically elaborated
knowledge. They diligently studied the logical investigations of Plato and Aristotle, without essentially
advancing them in an independent way.

Plotinus (204–269 A.D.) tried to remodel the Aristotelian
doctrine of the Categories; the later Neo-Platonists went
back to it. *Porphyry* (232–304 A.D.), scholar of Plotinus,
was the author of the introduction to the Organon of
Aristotle, so much read in the Middle Ages. It treats of the
logical notions of Genus, Species, Difference, Property, and
Accident. Their numerous commentaries upon the writings
of Plato and Aristotle, in part still extant, evidence the
studies of the Neo-Platonists.

§ 20. The Philosophy of the *Church Fathers* is essentially a philosophy of religion, and, grappling with the
difficulty of the problems nearest it, takes only a secondary interest in the problems of Logic. The Platonic
doctrine of ideas attracted their attention, but in a sense
which departs essentially from the original one. Augustine, following Plotinus, makes the idea immanent
in the divine mind. The chief doctrines of the Aristotelian organon were incorporated in the text-books of
the so-called seven liberal arts, and thus became an
object of instruction in the Christian Schools from the
sixth century. The Organon, as well as the Aristotelian

works generally, was also diligently studied by the Arabian and Jewish literati.

The relation of the Church Fathers to Greek Philosophy is a various one. *Justin Martyr* (circ. 150 A.D.) thus asserts his conviction : οἱ μετὰ Λόγου βιώσαντες Χριστιανοί εἰσι, κἂν ἄθεοι ἐνομίσθησαν, οἷον ἐν ῞Ελλησι μὲν Σωκράτης καὶ ῾Ηράκλειτος καὶ οἱ ὅμοιοι αὐτοῖς.[1] *Clement* of Alexandria, *Origen*, and others are friends of the Greek Philosophy, and place it at the service of Christian Theology. Others, as *Irenaeus*, his disciple *Hippolytus*, and *Tertullian*, frightened by the Gnostic Syncretism, were afraid of danger from it to Christian doctrine. Others, again, such as *Augustine* (354–430), keep a middle course. The contact with Neo-Platonism was partly friendly, partly antagonistic. Augustine grounded the truth of knowledge in general on the truth of the knowledge of our inner life (cf. § 40). Ideas are for him : principales formae quaedam vel rationes rerum stabiles atque incommutabiles, quae in divina intelligentia continentur.[2] *Boëthius* (470–525) translated and commented on several treatises of Aristotle's Organon, and explained the Introduction of Porphyry.

Marcianus Capella (circ. 430) and *Cassiodorus* (circ. 500), in their text-books of the seven liberal Arts (Grammar, Rhetoric, *Dialectic*, Arithmetic, Geometry, Astronomy, and Music), treat, among others, of Dialectic or Logic, following the course of Aristotle. *Isidorus Hispalensis* (circ. 600), *Bede* (circ. 700), *Alcuin* (736–804), follow in their footsteps.

Among the Arabian Aristotelians, *Avicenna* (Ibn Sina, circ. 1000 A.D.) and *Averroës* (Ibn Roschd, circ. 1175) were specially famed. The most noted of the Jewish Aristotelians was the contemporary of Averroës, *Moses Maionides* (Moses Ben Maimun, 1135–1204), ‘the light of the Jews of the Middle Ages.’

§ 21. In the Middle Ages the *Scholastic* Philosophy developed itself partly under the influence of the Church Fathers, partly under that of the logical writ-

---

[1] Iustin. *Apolog.* i. 46, 83 c.   [2] *De Div.* qu. 46.

ings of Aristotle, and later (about the beginning of the thirteenth century) under that of his other works. The essential characteristic of the Scholasticism of the Middle Ages is the application of the understanding, arranging and inferring, to the formal outside of dogmatic, and of sciences whose contents have been traditionally given. It has significance for Logic in a double reference: (a) by its subtle extensions of the Aristotelian Syllogistic; and (b) by the struggle of Realism with Nominalism in the question about the real existence of universals. Realism acquired an almost unlimited sovereignty in the bloom-time of Scholasticism; Nominalism, asserting that the universal was not something real, but only existed in the word, or at least in the conception (conceptualism), and thereby threatening to lower the value of Scholastic Art, appeared in the beginning of Scholasticism only in an isolated and transitory way, and in its last period more generally and victoriously.

The universal tendency of Scholasticism is summed up in the maxim of *Anselm* of Canterbury (1033-1109), 'credo ut intelligam.' As was natural, this striving after a scientific rational insight, when it first came into power, busied itself with a formal systematising of the given contents of the doctrines of faith and of the sciences. The knowledge of the logical works of Aristotle was, until the time of Abelard (1079-1142 A.D.), limited to the Categories and the De Interpretatione, along with the Isagoge of Porphyry. The contents of the other parts of the *Organon* were known through the text-books of Boëthius, the *Principia Dialect.* of Augustine, and the pseudo-Augustinian treatise on the ten Categories.[1] Soon after, about the middle, and even

[1] According to the testimony of Abelard in *Cousin, Oeuvres inéd.*

before the middle, of the twelfth century, the knowledge
of both Analytics, of the Topics, and of the Soph. Elench.
had gradually diffused itself, partly in the translations of
Boëthius, partly in other new and more literal translations.
John of Salisbury (d. 1180, Bishop of Chartres) knew the
whole Organon. Partly perhaps in the course of the twelfth
century, partly in the beginning of the thirteenth, Logic
received an addition, which consisted essentially in the re-
ception of grammatico-logical notions and doctrines. These
new forms were made popular by the Compendium of Petrus
Hispanus (d. 1277, Pope John XXI.), the Summulae
Logicales, in which, among other things, the mnemonic words
for the forms of the Syllogism are found. The logical
doctrines were here expounded in six parts (tractatus); the
first of which gives a summary of the contents of the book De
Interpretatione. The second treats of the 'quinque voces'
of Porphyry—Genus, Species, Difference, Property, and
Accident; the third, of the Categories; the fourth of the
Syllogism; the fifth, of the Topics; the sixth, of the Soph.
Elench. A seventh part treats of De Terminorum Proprieta-
tibus. It speaks of the use of substantives, and especially of
their 'suppositio,' i.e. the representation of the more special
by the more general, of proper nouns by common nouns, also
of adjectives and verbs, and of the 'syncategoremata,' i.e.
the other several parts of speech. This seventh part is also
called the Parva Logicalia, and is often published separately under this title. The part of the Aristotelian Logic
which was the earlier known was called the Vetus Logica,
and the part which became known about 1140, the Nova
Logica. The representatives of Logic extended by the doctrine 'de term. prop.' were called 'Moderni,' and the corresponding parts of the whole of Logic, 'Tractatus Modern-
orum.' *Occam,* the reviver of Nominalism (circ. 1320), has
'woven into the whole doctrine of Universals' the pro-

p. 228, cf. Prantl, *Gesch. der Logik*, ii. 100. Besides this, Abelard
perhaps knew indirectly single sentences which Aristotle had enunciated
in other logical treatises.

positions and terms of this part of Logic.[1] It is better not to
assume (as Prantl does) that this 'Modern Logic' rests on a
Byzantian influence. A Greek compend, which contains
these additions, and quite in the same way as the Summulae
of Hispanus, has been ascribed by some to Michael Psellus,
who lived in the eleventh century. If this be true, it must
have been copied by Hispanus and other later Logicians, but
it is more correctly believed to be a translation of the text-
book of Petrus Hispanus. The metaphysical and physical
writings of Aristotle[2] were known in the West since the end
of the twelfth and beginning of the thirteenth centuries ; for
the Arabian and Hebrew translations were then translated into
Latin. Soon after, also, the Greek texts were obtained from
Constantinople, when once the taking of that city by the
Crusaders (1204) had opened up this way.

Realism had among its followers *Anselm, Albertus Magnus,
Thomas* of *Aquino, Duns Scotus*; to Nominalism belonged
Roscellinus, and also *Abelard* (with an approach to Conceptualism); and later, after the fourteenth century, *William* of
Occam, Buridan, Peter of *Ailly, Biel*, and others. *Melanchthon* was also a Nominalist. The chiefs of Scholasticism
themselves, *Albertus Magnus* (1193–1280), *Thomas* of *Aquino*
(1225–1274), and *Duns Scotus* (d. 1308), did not disdain to
write commentaries on the logical writings of Aristotle.

Of the fantastic ' ars magna et ultima' of *Raymond Lully*
(1234–1315), a kind of combining topic, Des Cartes rightly
judged when he said,[3] that it served only ' ad copiose et sine
iudicio de iis, quae nescimus garriendum.'

§ 23. The revival of the study of the *old classical
literature*, and the great struggle for the reformation of
the Church, made the questions disputed by Scholastics

---

[1] According to Prantl, *Sitzungsber. der Münchener Akad.* 1861,
ii. 1, p. 65. Cf. *Geschichte der Log.* iii. 334 ff.

[2] Cf. A. Jourdain, *Recherches crit. sur l'âge et l'origine des Trad.
lat. d'Aristote*, Paris, 1819, 2nd ed. 1843.

[3] *Disc. de Methodo*, ii.

lose all their interest. Yet in the universal break with traditionalism lay the germ of a new independent development of Logic, as well as of Philosophy in general. The study of Logic was retained and advanced by the reformers. Text-books written by *Melanchthon,* and based upon the works of Aristotle, long served in Protestant schools to give the elements of logical instruction. *Ramus* stood forth as the opponent not only of Scholastic but of Aristotelian Logic.

Among the classically trained men of the time, *Laurentius Valla* (1415–1465), *Agricola* (1442–1485), and *Ludovicus Vives* (1492–1540) helped to purify Logic from Scholastic subtlety. *Melanchthon* (1497–1560) in his treatises—Dialectica, 1520; Erotemata Dialectices, 1547—placed the didactic side of Logic in the foreground, for he explained Dialectic to be the ' ars et via docendi.' His example and precept, ' carere monumentis Aristotelis non possumus,' restored again amongst Protestants the authority of Aristotle, which the assaults of Luther had at first threatened to overthrow.

Peter Ramus (*Pierre de la Ramée,* 1515–1572)—in his Dialecticae Partitiones, 1543; Institutiones Dialect., 1547; Scholae Dialect., 1548—has done more to agitate than to positively advance the science. The like may be said of the tumultuous endeavours of the contemporary Natural Philosophers of Italy —Telesius, Campanella, Bruno, and Vanini, and also of the Natural Philosopher and physician Paracelsus, and others— who have, with all their fancifulness, done a lasting service, inasmuch as they founded their doctrine of nature, and their view of the universe, upon observation and mathematics. By his maxim ' to begin from experience, and by means of it to direct the reason,' *Leonardo da Vinci* (1452–1519) became a predecessor of Bacon.

§ 23. *Bacon of Verulam* (1561–1626), a champion of the anti-scholastic tendency of his time spending it-

self on the investigation of Nature, brings into Logic
an essentially new element by his theory of *inductive*
knowledge. He wished Induction to ascend from the
individuals which are the objects of experience, first to
notions and propositions of intermediate universality,
then by degrees to knowledge of higher universality.
Bacon holds that the syllogism is not valid as a means
of scientific investigation, because it does not lead to
principles, and in the descents from principles cannot
increase the subtlety of Nature, and that it is only
suitable for disputations. Bacon undervalued the
worth of the deduction of the particular from the
general, and the significance which the syllogism has
for deductive and mediate, and also for inductive knowledge.

Bacon has stated his opinions in his treatise De Dignitate
et Augmentis Scientiarum, and in the Novum Organum. He
says:[1] Scientia nihil aliud est, quam veritatis imago; nam
veritas essendi et veritas cognoscendi idem sunt, nec plus a se
invicem differunt, quam radius directus et radius reflexus.[2]—
Syllogismus ad principia scientiarum non adhibetur, ad media
axiomata frustra adhibetur, quum sit subtilitati naturae longe
impar. Assensum igitur constringit, non res.[3]—Syllogismus ex
propositionibus constat, propositiones e verbis, verba notionum
tesserae sunt. Itaque si notiones ipsae, id quod basis rei est,
confusae sint et temere a rebus abstractae, nihil in iis quae su-
perstruuntur est firmitudinis. Itaque spes una est in inductione vera. According to the Nov. Org.,[4] Inductive Logic
is not, like the common Logic, to be a standard for an intellectual activity only abiding in itself, but is to be a standard
for the knowledge of things: ita mentem regimus, ut ad rerum

[1] De Augm. i. 18.   [2] Novum Org. i. aphor. xiii.
[3] Ibid. xiv.   [4] Ibid. i. 127.

naturam se applicare possit. This Logic boasts itself to be a
key to every science, since it directs and strengthens the
thinking mind in its striving after knowledge:[1] Rationales
scientiae reliquarum omnino claves sunt; atque quemad-
modum manus instrumentum instrumentorum, anima forma
formarum, ita et illae artes artium ponendae sunt. Neque
solum dirigunt, sed et roborant, sicut sagittandi usus non
tantum facit, ut melius quis collineet, sed ut arcum tendat
fortiorem. In the Nov. Org.[2] Bacon asserts that his inductive method is applicable to the intellectual and moral sciences,
but does not proceed to apply it. This application was only 'a
dark presentiment from afar '(Beneke). Bacon has seldom
given the correct methods of investigation in particular cases,
still seldomer reached good scientific results in his investigations, and has not even recognised as valuable nor appropriated
the best of the discoveries already made in his day by others
(all which *Lasson* and *Liebig* have made manifest, while they
were opposing the previously very widely-extended over-
estimation of Bacon); but he did this service, he more
strongly opposed than any of his predecessors the trivialities
of Scholasticism, he firmly established universal laws of inductive investigation, and he gave a place in Logic to the
new tendency, with its methods and principles. Cf. § 134, on
Hypothesis and the ' Experimentum crucis.'

§ 24. If Bacon paid almost exclusive attention to
sense-perception and outer nature, *Des Cartes* (1596–
1650), on the other hand, found in the inherent certainty
of the thought of his own existence the one starting-
point of philosophical knowledge which could with-
stand every doubt. He made the subjective clearness
and distinctness the criterion of objective truth, and
found security for the validity of this criterion in the
divine truthfulness, which could not allow a clear and

[1] *De Augm.* v. 1.   [2] Ibid. i. 127.

distinct conception to be a deceptive one. Des Cartes accordingly believes that by means of this criterion the human mind can truly know both its own thinking in the widest sense of the word, or its whole inner conscious activity, the divine nature, and, as the properties of extended things, extension in space and its modes. He calls immediate knowledge *Intuition*; every mediate way of knowledge he comprehends under the general notion of *Deduction*. In mediate knowledge Des Cartes occasionally distinguishes a double *method* of exhibiting his fundamental doctrines—the *analytic* and the *synthetic*: the former, which proceeds from what is immediately given to principles, serves for discovery; the latter, which proceeding from principles deduces single theorems, serves for strict demonstration.

Des Cartes believes that in four general directions he exhausts all that can be said about method. The first rule demands evidence which is founded on perfect · clearness; the second, a division of the difficulties; the third, an orderly; and the fourth, a continuous advance in investigation. Every error is due to an abuse of the freedom of the will, leading to hasty judgment.

Des Cartes enunciates [1] the following definition of Clearness and Distinctness:—Claram voco illam perceptionem, quae menti attendenti praesens et aperta est, distinctam autem illam, quae quum clara sit, ab omnibus aliis ita sciuncta est et praecisa, ut nihil plane aliud, quam quod clarum est, in se contineat. The four rules of method (which are not so much logical laws as rules, which we must receive subjectively in order to be able to comply with the logical standard, and so escape errors) are to be found in

[1] *Princip. Phil.* i. § 15.

Discours de la Méthode pour bien conduire sa raison et chercher la vérité dans les Sciences, 1637,[1] sec. part. Des Cartes says : ' Thus, instead of the great number of precepts of which Logic is made up, I thought that the four following would be sufficient, provided I firmly and constantly resolved not to fail even once in observing them. The first was, never to accept anything as true, unless I recognised it to be so evidently, i.e. to avoid carefully haste and anticipation, and to include nothing in my judgments but what should present itself so clearly and distinctly to my mind that I should have no occasion to doubt it. The second was, to divide each of the difficulties I had to examine into as many parts as would be requisite for better resolving them. The third was to arrange my thoughts in an orderly fashion, beginning with the most simple objects, and those most easily understood, to ascend little by little, by degrees as it were, up to the knowledge of the most compound, and to imagine an order even between those which do not precede each other naturally. And the last was, to make everywhere such complete enunciations and such general reviews, that I should be certain I had omitted nothing.' In the same place, Des Cartes says of the Syllogism, and of most of the other doctrines of Logic, that they have more a didactic than a scientific value : ' As for Logic, its syllogisms and the majority of its other precepts are of avail rather in the communication of what we already know than in the investigation of the unknown.' Des Cartes touches upon the distinction between Analytic and Synthetic methods in his replies to objections against his Meditationes de Prima Philosophia, Respons. ad secund. obiect. In the treatise, Regulae ad Directionem Ingenii (first published in his Opuscula Posthuma, Amstelod. 1701), Des Cartes distinguishes Intuition, or Knowledge immediately certain, by which we become conscious of principles, and Deduction, or the operation by which we deduce a knowledge, which is the necessary consequent of an other, and recognise it because of the other. The demands contained in the

---

[1] *Discursus de Methodo recte utendi Ratione*, 1644. · [Translated into English by Prof. Veitch, p. 61, Edin. 1863.]

four directions for method in the Discours are further developed by Des Cartes into rules when he applies them to single
philosophical, and especially mathematical, problems. The
most celebrated logical work which has proceeded from the
School of Des Cartes is La Logique, ou l'art de penser, Paris,
1662,[1] in which the doctrines of Aristotle are combined with
the principles of Des Cartes. It defines Logic to be the art
of the right use of reason in the knowledge of things (l'art
de bien conduire sa raison dans la connaissance des choses, tant
pour s'instruire soi-même que pour en instruire les autres).
This work is probably due to Antony Arnauld, assisted by
Nicole and other Jansenists of the Port-Royal.

Nicole Malebranche (1638–1715), the representative of the
doctrine that we see all things in God, in his work, De la
Recherche de la Vérité, Paris, 1673, proceeds upon the fundamental principles of Des Cartes.

Among the opponents of Des Cartes, *Gassendi* (1592–1655)
deserves special mention for his clear and well-arranged representation of Logic.

§ 25. *Spinoza* (1632–1677) traced false or inadequate
knowledge to the influence of the imagination, true or
adequate knowledge to thought. Truth is the agreement of the idea with its object. Truth makes clear
both itself and error. The intuitive understanding
recognises each individual from its causes, and the finite
generally from the infinite. It attends, in the first
place, to the idea of one substance whose essence
includes in it existence, in order to know thought
and existence as its attributes, and individual beings as
their modes. The arrangement and connection of
thoughts correspond to the arrangement and connection of things. The philosophical method is identical
with the mathematical.

[1 Translated into English by Prof. Baynes, 2nd ed. 1851, Edin.]

Of the works of Spinoza, the Tractatus de Intellectus Emendatione, in the Opera Posthuma, Amstelod. 1677, belongs more especially to our subject. Several passages in the Ethics are to be compared with it. The fundamental postulate of Spinoza is: ' Ut mens nostra omnino referat naturae exemplar, debet omnes suas ideas producere ab ea, quae refert originem et fontem totius naturae, ut ipsa etiam sit fons ceterarum idearum.' He defines truth to be ' convenientiam ideae cum suo ideato.' He distinguishes three kinds or grades of knowledge: imaginatio (φαντασία), ratio (the ἐπιστήμη of Aristotle), and intellectus (the intuitive knowledge of principles, almost equivalent to the Aristotelian νοῦς). The philosopher considers all things as moments of one substance, sub specie aeternitatis. The ' concatenatio intellectus ' should ' concatenationem naturae referre.'

Kaffeler treats of the method of philosophical investigation from the stand-point of Spinoza, in his Specimen Artis Ratiocinandi naturalis et artificialis, ad pantosophiae principia manducens, Hamb., 1684.

§ 26. *Locke* (1632–1704), applying the method of Bacon to the objects of inner experience, investigated the psychological problem of the origin of human knowledge, with the view of reaching a sure fundamental position for the decision of the logical question (of the question belonging to the theory of knowledge) of the objective truth of our notions. Locke distinguished sensation or sense-perception from reflection or perception of the inner activities to which the soul is aroused on occasion of the outer affections. From these two sources all conceptions arise. There are no 'innate ideas.' Nihil est intellectu, quod non fuerit in sensu. Locke, like Des Cartes, attributes full truth to the internal perceptions, partial truth only to the external. Locke, by his *results*, was the forerunner of the sensationalism of

Condillac, who sought to reduce all reflection to sensation, and by his *method* the forerunner of the Idealism of Berkeley, of the Skepticism of Hume, of the Empiricism of the Scottish School, and of the Critical Philosophy of Kant.

Locke's chief work, An Essay concerning the Human Understanding, was first published in London, 1690. Since he would not admit that the conceptions arrived at by sense-perception are true pictures of the objects (figure in space may be objective; colours, sounds, &c. are not), he limited the truth of our thoughts to the objectively correct union and separation of the signs of things.[1] Connected with Locke are J. P. de Crousaz,[2] Is. Watt,[3] Condillac,[4] and Hume.[5] The Idealism of Berkeley[6] (1685–1753), according to which only spirits and their ideas exist, since all unthinking objects are ideas of a percipient and thinking existence, and the Scottish School (Reid, Stewart, &c.), which returned to the assertion of innate activities as facts of inner experience, are, in spite of their polemic against it, essentially connected with the Lockian tendency.

§ 27. *Leibniz* (1646–1716) maintained against Locke the doctrine of innate ideas; but he explained every part of the contents of consciousness to be the production of the inner self-development of the mind (Seele). Leibniz found warrant for the objective truth of clear and distinct conceptions in a *harmony* between the soul

---

[1] *Essay*, bk. iv. ch. v. § 2.
[2] *La Logique*, Amst. 1712.   [3] *Logic*, 1736.
[4] *Essai sur l'Origine des Connaissances humaines*, 1745; *Traité des Sensations*, 1751; *Logique*, 1781.
[5] *Enquiry concerning the Human Understanding*, 1748 [best edition by T. H. Green and T. H. Grose, London, 1870].
[6] [Best edition is the *Collected Works of George Berkeley, D.D.*, Bishop of Cloyne*, ed. by Prof. Fraser, Clarendon Press, 1871.]

and outer things *pre-established* by God. Error arises from a want of clearness and distinctness. Dark and confused knowledge may be raised by demonstration to clearness and distinctness. Leibniz (in opposition to Des Cartes) declared the logical rules to be criteria of truth not to be despised, because correctness of demonstration depended on their being followed. He held the principles of Contradiction and of Sufficient Reason to be the most general principles of all demonstration.

Taking his stand upon the Leibnizian theory, *Wolff* presented Logic (as he did all the philosophical disciplines) in systematic connection, according to mathematical method. He treated Logic as the doctrine of knowledge, and placed the logical forms in essential relation both to ontological forms and psychological laws.

The opinions of *Leibniz* upon the doctrine of knowledge are contained partly in small tracts, partly in his Nouveaux Essais sur l'Entendement humain, directed against Locke, and first published posthumously by Raspe, in 1765. Leibniz approved generally of the Cartesian principle, ' quicquid clare et distincte de re aliqua percipio, id est verum seu de ea enunciabile ;' but he held it necessary to prevent the frequent abuse of the principle by laying down criteria of clearness and distinctness. He, accordingly, defines the clear conception (notio clara) to be that which can recognise the object conceived, and distinguish it from others. The clear conception is either confused (confusa) or definite and distinct (distincta). Confusion is want of clearness in the particular attributes (notae). Distinctness or definiteness, on the other hand, is the clearness of the particular individual attributes which together make up the conception. In absolutely simple conceptions there is no distinction between clearness and distinctness. The distinct conception, finally, is adequate when the attributes of the attributes, on to the last simple elements,

are clearly conceived.[1] These definitions are not in themselves free from fault. Distinctness and Confusion are specifically, not gradually, to be distinguished from Clearness and
Unclearness, just as the accuracy and inaccuracy of a drawing
are from the clearer and fainter outline. But the system of
Pre-established Harmony cannot admit that error has a source
specifically distinct from that of want of clearness. The possibility, which consists in freedom from inner contradiction, and
becomes known by the complete resolution of conceptions into
their component parts, is, according to Leibniz, the warrant of
objective validity or truth. He says, in the above quoted tract:
' Patet etiam, quae tandem sit idea vera, quae falsa ; vera scilicet
quum notio est possibilis, falsa quum contradictionem involvit.'
By the separation of a conception into its non-contradictory attributes, we recognise à priori its validity, but we recognise
à posteriori its validity by experience. The truth of a
proposition consists in its correspondence with the objects to
which it refers. It is reached by accurate experience and
correct logical proof. Meditationes (as above): De caetero
non contemnenda veritatis enunciationum criteria sunt regulae
communis Logicae, quibus etiam Geometrae utuntur, ut
scilicet nihil admittatur pro certo, nisi accurata experientia
vel firma demonstratione probatum ; firma autem demonstratio
est, quae praescriptam a Logica formam servat. For the
principles of contradiction and sufficient reason as the grounds
of all demonstration, see the Monadology (Principia Philosophiae), §§ 30–31. Leibniz wished to see a doctrine of probability added to Logic, as a second part.

Christian Wolff gave a systematic representation of Logic
in his shorter German treatise—Vernünftige Gedanken von
den Kräften des menschlichen Verstandes, 1710; and in his
extensive work—Philosophia Rationalis sive Logica, 1728.
He defined Logic to be scientiam dirigendi facultatem cogno-
scitivam in cognoscenda veritate.[2] The rules, according to

---

[1] See *Leibnitii Meditationes de Cognitione, Veritate et Ideis* [appended
to Prof. Baynes' ed. of the *Port-Royal Logic*, 2nd ed. pp. 424–30].

[2] *Log. Discursus Praeliminaris*, § 61 ; *Prolegomena*, § 10.

which the human mind learns the essences of things, must on
the one hand be psychological, and on the other ontological
principles.[1] It is advisable, because of its suitableness for
Didactic, that Logic should precede Ontology and Psychology,
and so Wolff makes it.[2] The proof, however, of the logical
axioms is not, therefore, to be omitted, but the more important doctrines of Ontology and Psychology must be presupposed in Logic, where they from the first vindicate their
position, both by immediate evidence, and by their agreement
with experience.[3] Accordingly, Wolff places some psychological considerations,[4] and a section ' de notitiis quibusdam
generalibus entis,'[5] at the head of his logical system. He
divides Logic into theoretical and practical. The former
treats of Notion, Judgment, and Inference; the latter, of
the use of Logic in judging, and in the investigation of truth,
in the study and composition of books, in the division of
knowledge, in the comparative valuing of the individual
powers of knowledge, and, lastly, in the practice of life, and in
the study of Logic itself. Wolff gives as the nominal definition
of truth—' Est veritas consensus iudicii nostri cum obiecto
seu re repraesentata;'[6] and as its real definition—' Veritas
est determinabilitas praedicati per notionem subiecti.'[7] The
possible notion corresponds to the true affirmative judgment.[8]
Possibility consists in absence of contradiction.[9] To this
(Leibnizian) criterion Wolff refers the Cartesian, and also the
criterion of conceivability given by *Tschirnhausen* (1651–1708),
the contemporary of Leibniz, in his Medicina Mentis, 1687—
' verum est quicquid concipi potest, falsum vero quod non
concipi potest.'[10]

Among the contemporaries of Leibniz, besides Tschirnhausen, *Christian Thomasius* (1655–1728) is to be mentioned,

---

[1] *Discursus Prael.* § 89 ; *Prolegom.* § 28.

[2] *Discurs. Praelim.* § 91 : ' Methodum studendi praeferro maluimus
methodo demonstrandi.'

[3] *Log.* §§ 2, 28.   [4] Ibid. § 30 ff.   [5] Ibid. § 59 ff.

[6] Ibid. § 505.   [7] Ibid. § 513.   [8] Ibid. § 520.

[9] Ibid. § 518.   [10] Ibid. §§ 522, 528.

who sought to make Logic more practical, and believed that he had pointed out a middle way between the Aristotelian and Cartesian Logics. His special service (as Wolff's was later) consisted in teaching men by his example to express scientific thought in the German language. Among the opponents of Wolff are to be mentioned *Lange, Crusius, Daries,* and *Euler.* More or less nearly related to Wolff are *Baumeister, Baumgarten, Meier, Reimarus,*[1] and *Ploucquet.*[2] *Lambert,* with much which lacks substance and logical form, gives much that has meaning and originality. His Neues Organon[3] is divided into four parts, which Lambert calls— Dianoiologie, Alethiologie, Semiotik, and Phänomenologie. According to his explanation, they comprehend more completely what Aristotle and, after him, Bacon have called an organon. These sciences are 'instrumental,' or are instruments of the human understanding in the examination of truth. Dianoiologic is, according to Lambert, the doctrine of the laws of thought which the understanding must follow if it would advance from truth to truth. Alethiologie is the doctrine of truth, in so far as it is opposed to error, of the possibility of knowing truth. Semiotik is the doctrine of the expression of thought (especially of its expression in language). Phänomenologie is the doctrine of error, and of the means of avoiding it. *Bilfinger* (who wished also a logical theory for the 'subordinate cognitive faculties '), *Feder,*[4] *Eberhard,*[5] and *Ernst Platner*[6] proceeded more or less on Leibnizian principles.

---

[1] *Vernunftlehre,* 1756; 5th ed. 1790.

[2] *Methodus calculandi in Logicis,* 1753; *Methodus tam demonstrandi Omnes Syllogismorum Species, quam Vitia Formae detegendi ope unius Regulae,* 1763.

[3] Leipzig, 1764.

[4] *Grundsätze der Logik und Metaphysik,* 1769, and *Institutiones Logicae et Metaphysicae,* 1777.

[5] *Allgemeine Theorie des Denkens und des Empfindens,* 1776.

[6] *Philo. Aphorismen,* 1776, and *Lehrbuch der Log. und Metaph.* 1795.

§ 28. *Kant* (1724–1804) denied the identity of clearness, distinctness, and absence of contradiction, with the material truth of knowledge, which had been asserted by Des Cartes and Leibniz. He returned to Locke's view, that the origin of knowledge can alone decide upon its truth, without adopting Locke's theory of the empirical origin of all human knowledge. Accordingly, Kant investigated anew, in his Kritik der reinen Vernunft, the origin, extent, and limits of human knowledge. He distinguished analytical or explanatory judgments, which alone rest upon the axiom of contradiction, from synthetic or amplifying judgments, and, among the latter, judgments which have an accidental limited validity from those by which the universal and the necessary is known. Kant believed that all strict generality and necessity must be traced back to an origin à priori, i.e. a purely subjective origin independent of all experience. His presupposition ruled his whole course of thought, and involved a leap from apodicticity to the merely subjective, accomplished by means of the ambiguous middle term à priori. Under its influence he proceeded from the fundamental question, 'How are synthetic judgments à priori possible?' to the result, that the material of knowledge comes to us from without by means of the sense-affections, but that its forms are added à priori by the human mind. These à priori forms of knowledge are, according to Kant: (a) the forms of Intuition of outer and inner sense;—(b) the Twelve Categories, or the pure original notions of the understanding: (1) Three Categories of Quantity—Unity, Plurality, Totality; (2) Three Categories of Quality—Reality, Negation, Limitation ; (3) Three Categories of Relation—Substantiality, Causality, Reciprocity; (4) Three Categories of Modality —Possibility, Existence, Necessity ;—(c) the ideas of reason—of the Soul, the World, and God. These à priori elements of knowledge, because of their subjective origin, are, according to Kant, unable to reveal to us the peculiar essence of things. Human knowledge extends only to the world of phenomena, into which we unconsciously bring these forms, and which must shape itself according to them. It cannot extend to things as they exist in themselves, or as they exist beyond our capacities of knowledge. Consequently, no theoretical insight into the essence of the human soul, of the intelligible world, and of God, can be reached. We can however attain a securer practical faith from the ground of the moral conscience. All these considerations, belonging to the theory of knowledge, Kant separates completely from general formal Logic. He defines this to be the rational science of the necessary laws of thought, as they have to do with, not their particular objects, but all objects generally ;—or the science of the pure form of thought in general ;—or the science of the right use of the understanding and reason, according to à priori principles, as the understanding thinks. Kant divides general Logic into pure and applied. The former treats of the understanding considered in itself; the latter, which belongs to psychology, treats of the understanding in its conjunction with the other psychological faculties. Pure general Logic is divided into the doctrine of the elements and the doctrine of method. Special Logic treats of the special methods of the par-

ticular sciences. Transcendental Logic belongs to the
Kritik of Pure Reason, and forms that part of it which
treats of the categories of the understanding and their
worth in knowledge. Pure general Logic endeavours
to comprehend thoroughly the forms of thought, ab-
stracting them from every metaphysical and psychological relation, and only allowing reference to the laws
of Identity and Contradiction. This tendency produces
the subjectively formal character of the Kantian Logic.

Kant's chief theoretical work, the Kritik der reinen Vernunft, first appeared in 1781, was formally remodelled in the
second edition[1] of 1787, and since then has appeared unchanged

[1] Kant expressly says, in his preface to the second edition, that the
remodelling has to do with the form of representation only, not with
the contents. For the realist moment, which is not wanting in the first
edition, but is kept in the background because self-evident, is expressed
more distinctly and forcibly in the second edition, in order to oppose a
misunderstanding introduced in a review, which has overlooked it, and
made Kant's doctrine approach to near to that of Berkeley. Yet Michelet
Schopenhauer and others have believed that they can see a reconstruction of the Kantian stand-point itself. But I have endeavoured to show in
my tractate (*De priore et posteriore Forma Kantianae Critices Rationis
Purae*, Berol. 1862) that Kant's assertion is confirmed by a thorough
comparison of the two editions, and retain my opinion after Michelet's
answer,* who, with his Hegelian tendencies, makes the 'things-in-themselves,' which give the matter to the empirical intuitions, mean 'the
unity of Essence in the manifold of phenomena.' Michelet and
Schwegler assert that Kant in the first edition of his *Kritik of Pure
Reason* expresses the opinion that the Ego and the thing-in-itself may
be one and the same thinking substance, and that he may therefore
here enunciate hypothetically what Fichte afterwards taught, that the
Ego is not affected by a strange thing-in-itself, but purely by itself.
But these assertions of Michelet and Schwegler rest on a misinterpretation of the passages quoted.† Kant does not believe that the Ego

* *Gedanke*, iii. pp. 2: 7–13, 1862.
† *Krit. d. r. Vern.* 1st ed. 357–359, 379 f.

in the later editions. The Logic was published by Jäsche in 1800, with Kant's manuscript notes and explanations on his copy of Meyer's Handbook of Logic (which Kant purposely added to his Lectures). In Logic Kant was connected with Reimarus in several ways, partly agreeing with him, partly combating him. Kant seeks to establish his isolation of Formal Logic by the axiom that sciences are not increased, but disfigured, when their boundaries are allowed to run into each other. The limits of Logic, he says, are enough defined by this, that it is a science which fully represents and strictly proves nothing save the formal laws of all thinking. Logic, since Aristotle's time, has followed the sure course of a science. It has taken no step backwards, i.e. it has not needed to give up any of Aristotle's acquisitions as useless and illusory ; but it has made no advance, and has not been able to attain any essential development. It must thank its narrowness only for its scientific certainty and completeness, which entitles and compels it to withdraw its attention from every object of knowledge and from the differences of objects, and limit its enquiries to the understanding only in itself and in its forms.[1]

Of course we must recognise with Kant that the object of Logic is the correct *form* of thought. We must also allow that Logic cannot have the same problem as Metaphysics and Psychology, and that it does not teach single parts of these sciences. But it is by no means to be granted that Logic as a science does not need to refer to psychological and metaphysical principles, in order to establish its laws concerning the correct form of thought. Therapeutic, as the science of the restoration of health, or of the correct *form* of corporeal life, does not teach physiology or general natural science either wholly or

affects itself merely, but holds that a substance different from us, which, if it affects us, is perceived by us to be in space, can itself appear to be a thinking essence.*

[1] *Kritik d. reinen Vernunft*, 2nd ed. pref. viii. ix.; cf. p. 71 ff.; and *Logik*, p. 3 ff. Werke, Hart. ed. viii. 12 ff.

* Cf. my remarks in my *Grundr. der Gesch. der Phil.* iii. § 16, 2nd ed., Berlin, 1868, pp. 157, 181-83.

in part, but it must refer to the principles of these two sciences in order to give its prescriptions a scientific basis. That form of thought is the correct one which capacitates the human spirit for the knowledge of things, and therefore the double reference is indispensable in Logic (cf. § 2). The abstraction of the relations of the forms of thought to the forms of existence, to the psychological laws, and to the contents of thought in general (which is to be carefully distinguished from the several contents of thinking), and their separation from the forms of perception—in short, the removal of the harder problems—has undoubtedly its advantages in didactic reference. Such a representation of Logic may be suitable as a preliminary propaedeutic, and perhaps now and then indispensable; but if it be taken, and if it be reckoned, as the last and highest representation, it robs Logic of an essential part of its scientific character. If the fundamental doctrine of Kant were true, that the things-in-themselves are unknowable, then the logical forms, to be scientifically understood, must be taken with reference to the metaphysical forms of the world of phenomena (Substantiality, Causality, &c.). Kant himself recognises this in his Kritik der reinen Vernunft, at least in reference to the *judgment*, where he (p. 140, 2nd ed.) blames as insufficient its explanation as the conception of a relation between two notions, and prefers the definition—it is an *objectively* valid relation (p. 142)—it is the way to bring given knowledge to the *objective* unity of apperception (p. 141); and where, in accordance with this, he refers the functions of the judgment to the categories, because the metaphysical categories express the different objective relations. For example, the logical relation of subject and predicate, in the categorical judgment, is related, according to Kant, to the metaphysical relation of Subsistence and Inherence, the logical relation of the conditioning and conditioned judgment to the metaphysical relation of Causality and Dependence, and so on. Had Kant kept to this stand-point in his Logic, and consistently followed it out, the science would have got from him, in all essential points, *the* place afterwards given it by *Lotze*. But

Kant has not let that knowledge bring forth fruit for his Logic. He abstracts the science from all objective relations. When it is seen that Kant's fundamental doctrine, that real objects are unknowable, is untenable, and that metaphysical forms have a real meaning, as will be shown in our systematic development of Logic, this abstraction will be found to be still less scientifically justifiable. The limits of knowledge set up by Kant are not, however, to be violently broken through, either by an axiom postulating the identity of thought and existence, or by an unconscious transference of the laws of thought to things in themselves. They are to be gradually, as it were, and methodically levelled and removed, and to accomplish this task is the aim of this work.[1]

Kant's fallacy may be put shortly,—What is apodictic is à priori; what is à priori is merely subjective (without relation to ' things-in-themselves '); therefore, what is apodictic is merely subjective (without relation to ' things-in-themselves '). The first premise (the minor), however, is wrong if à priori is understood in the Kantian sense to mean being independent of all experience. Kant wrongly believes that certainty to be à priori (independent of all experience) which we really attain by a combination of many experiences with one another according to logical laws; and these laws are conditioned by the reference of the subject to the objective reality, and are not à priori forms. He erroneously maintains that all orderly arrangement (both that in time and space and that which is causal) is merely subjective.

Upon the relation of the Kantian Logic to the Aristotelian, cf. §§ 2, 16.

§ 29. The Logic of *Kant's School*—viz. of *Jacob, Kiesewetter, Hoffbauer, Maass, Krug,* &c.—is to be treated in the same way as Kant's. The logical works of *A. D. Chr.*

---

[1] Cf. specially §§ 38, 40–44, and the remarks to §§ 129, 131, 137 ; cf. also my tractate upon *Idealismus, Realismus* und *Idealrealismus* in Fichte's *Zeitschr. für Philos.* xxxiv. 63–80, 1859.

Tweston, Ernst Reinhold, Bachmann, Friedrich Fischer, &c. are more or less related to this formal stand-point. *Fries* gives Logic a psychological foundation. He understands Logic to be the science of the laws of thought, and divides it into: Pure Logic, which treats of the forms of thought; and Applied Logic, which treats of the relation of these forms of thought to the whole of human science. Pure Logic, again, is divided into Anthropological Logic, which considers thought as an activity of the human spirit; and Philosophical or Demonstrative Logic, which enunciates the laws of the thinkable. He divides Applied Logic into the doctrine of the relation of thought to knowledge in general, the doctrine of the laws of knowledge which has been thought, or of the illumination of our knowledge, and the doctrine of method. Friedrich van Calker is allied to Fries. He explains the doctrine of thought, or Logic and Dialectic, to be the science of the form of the higher consciousness; and divides it into the doctrines of experience, laws, and art of thinking.

Herbart defines Logic to be the science which treats generally of distinctness in notions and the connection (arising out of this) of these notions to judgments and inferences. He entirely separates from Logic, and refers to Metaphysics, the question of the significance of the forms of thought in knowledge. He believes that the logical laws neither can nor should be established on a scientific basis by means of metaphysical and psychological considerations.

Allied to Herbart are *Drobisch,* Hartenstein, Waitz, Allihn, and others.

The logical works which proceed from the Kantian School, or which essentially share its tendency, refrain from entering upon the deeper problems, and do not make up for this want by perfect accuracy, sufficiency, and clearness in the problems to which they have limited themselves. *Jacob's* Grundriss der allgemeinen Logik appeared first in 1788; *Kiesewetter's* Grundriss der Logik in 1791; *Hoffbauer's* Analytik der Urtheile und Schlüsse in 1792, and his Anfangsgründe der Logik in 1794; *Maass's* Grundriss der Logik in 1793; *Krug's* Logik oder Denklehre in 1806; *Ernst Reinhold's* Versuch einer Begründung und neuen Darstellung der logischen Formen in 1819; Logik oder allgemeine Denkformenlehre in 1827; Theorie des menschlichen Erkenntnissvermögens in 1832; *Twesten's* Logik, especially the Analytic, 1825; *Bachmann's* System der Logik in 1828 (a very instructive work); *Friedr. Fischer's* Lehrbuch der Logik in 1838; *Fries'* Grundriss und System der Logik, 1811; *Herbart's* Lehrbuch zur Einleitung in die Philosophie, 1813 (5th ed. 1850), in which §§ 33–71 contain an epitome of Logic; Drobisch, Neue Darstellung der Logik nach ihren einfachsten Verhältnissen, nebst einem logisch-mathematischen Anhange, 1836 (2nd completely remodelled edition, 1851; 3rd edition written afresh, 1863; worth looking at as the best representation of Logic from that stand-point, very valuable for its clearness, acuteness, and relative completeness).

§ 30. *Fichte* (1762–1814), in his Wissenschaftslehre, in order to overcome the inner contradiction of the Kantian doctrine of knowledge, traced not only the form, but also the material of knowledge to the thinking-subject, or the Ego exclusively, and thereby established a subjective idealism in the strictest sense. He considered Formal Logic no philosophical science, because it broke up the connection in which the form and content of knowledge stand to each other and to the highest principles of knowledge.

Schelling (1775–1854) passed a like judgment upon Formal Logic. He also traced form and content, and therefore the subjective and objective reason, back to one single principle—the Absolute, whose existence he believed to be known by an intellectual intuition.

Neither has developed Logic itself.

Johann Gottlieb Fichte, in his work upon the Begriff der Wissenschaftslehre (1794), laid down the postulate, that all science should be derived from one simple principle, and sought in his Grundlage der gesammten Wissenschaftslehre to satisfy this postulate by deducing all knowledge, both in content and form, from the principle of the Ego. He considers the logical axioms to be the *cognitive* basis of the higher axioms of the Wissenschaftslehre, and these again the *real* basis of the former.   Fichte at first wished to make Formal Logic co-ordinate with the Transcendental, as Kant had done, but later [1] he sought to abolish it altogether, and supplant it by the Transcendental Logic.   He accuses it of assuming as granted that which is itself the product of the thought to be explained, and therefore of reasoning in a circle when it attempts to explain thinking.

Schelling teaches that the original content and the original form of science are conditioned the one by the other.   The principle of all science is the point whence by an indivisible act of intelligence the form and content of science spring up together.   If Logic arises in a scientific way, its fundamental principles must proceed by abstraction from the highest axioms of knowledge.   Logic, in its usual pure formal state, belongs wholly to empirical attempts in philosophy.   *Dialectic* is, according to Schelling, Logic, in so far as it is the science of the form and the pure art of Philosophy.[2]

[1] Particularly in his lecture on the relation of Logic to Philosophy in his *Posthumous Works*, ed. by I. H. Fichte (Bonn, 1834–35), i. 111 f.
[2] *System des transcendentalen Idealismus*, pp. 35–37, 1800; *Lectures on the Methode des Akademischen Studiums*, pp. 17 ff., 122–29, 1803.

Franz von Baader's view (1765–1841) is also related to Schelling's. The School of Baader distinguish theosophic from anthroposophic Logic, which are related as original and copy. The former considers the totality of the absolute forms of thought and knowledge of the infinite spirit; the latter, the totality of the laws and forms which the copying knowledge of the finite spirit obeys. Franz Hoffman,[1] conformably to Baader's principles, represents the divine knowledge a moment of the divine immanent process of life. *Krause's* Logic and *Schleiermacher's* Dialectic (cf. § 33) are also essentially related to Schelling's principles.

§ 31. *Hegel* (1770–1831), following the principles of Fichte and Schelling, founded the Metaphysical Logic. Kant held that the form and content of thought were mutually independent, and referred the form exclusively to the thinking spirit, and the content exclusively to the things affecting. Hegel's Logic, on the contrary, rests on the double identification of: (1) Form and Content; (2) Thought and Being. Hegel judged (1), with Fichte and Schelling, that a separation of form and content is inadmissible, and that the most general content of knowledge must be conceived along with the form. (2) With Schelling, he believed that the necessary thoughts of the human spirit, according to content and form, stand in absolute correspondence to the essence and forms of the development of things. Hegel adds (3) the postulate of method, that pure thought in its dialectical self-development advances creatively from

[1] In the work *Speculative Entwicklung der ewigen Selbsterzeugung Gottes*, Amberg, 1835, and in the *Vorhalle zur speculativen Lehre Franz Baader's*, Aschaffenburg, 1836. Cf. also Hoffmann, *Grundzüge einer Geschichte des Begriffs der Logik in Deutschland von Kant bis Baader*, Leip. 1851.

the widest and most abstract notions to the ever fuller
and more concrete up to the absolutely highest, by means
of negation and identity dwelling in the notions, and
also in absolute unity with the self-production of
existence, so that the subjective necessity of thought
must be also the criterion of objective truth. Hegel's
Logic traces this self-development of the notion from
pure being up to the absolute idea; his natural philosophy
from space and time up to the animal organism; and
his philosophy of the spirit from the subjective up to
the absolute divine spirit. Logic is, according to Hegel,
the system of pure reason,—thought as it is in itself
without its wrappings,—the science of the pure idea,
i.e. of the idea in its being in-and-for-itself,—or the idea
in the abstract element of its being. It divides into
three parts: the doctrine of being, of essence, and of
the notion. The first part treats of the categories of
Quantity, Quality, and Proportion ; the second, of the
essence as the ground of Existence, of the Phenomenon,
and of the Actual ; the third, of the Subjective Notion
(i.e. of the Notion, Judgment, and Inference), of Objectivity (i.e. of Mechanism, Chemism, Teleology), and
of the Idea. The moments of the idea are life, knowledge, and the abstract idea. The abstract idea is the
abstract truth,—the idea thinking itself,—the pure
form of the notion which perceives its content to be
itself. In the doctrine of the Subjective Notion Hegel
brings in the chief definitions of Formal Logic, but he
submits them to an essential transformation, according
to the demands of the Dialectic method, and at the same
time gives them an objective significance.

Hegel's logical works are—Wissenschaft der Logik, 1812–16, 2nd ed. 1833–34 (I. Objective Logic: A. The doctrine of Being: B. The doctrine of Essence.—II. Subjective Logic), and Encyclopädie der philosophischen Wissenschaften im Grundrisse, 1817; the first part, the Science of Logic, §§ 19–244. The more Hegel's polemic is justifiable the less are his own definitions tenable. He justly blames Kant's attempt to abstract Logic from all relation to existence; but he himself has gone to the opposite extreme of exaggerated identification. 'The critical method separates what God has joined, the method of identification would unite what God has separated ' (Troxler).

1. As to the identification of the sciences of the form and of the most general content of Thought, i.e. of Logic and Metaphysics. It is true that form and content are not independent of each other and demand a scientific explanation of their opposite relations, but nevertheless they make two essentially different objects of knowledge, whose consideration accordingly engages two distinct branches of the one whole philosophical science. A separate representation of Logic, if the metaphysical relations are not disowned, is not only admissible, but also a necessary condition of scientific completeness. Schelling, among others, recognises it to be legitimate when he believes Dialectic, the science of the form of philosophical thought, to be a science philosophically correct, and considers admissible, as a special power in the universal science of reason, a Logic which derives the laws of 'reflexive knowledge' from speculative grounds. The union of the sciences by Plato (which, besides, was only relative) was natural in that stage of origination, when both sciences began to develope themselves from the common germ of philosophical thinking. The complete isolation of Logic from metaphysics, on the other hand, was an error, which had for its basis the right feeling that a strict distinction of the two sciences was necessary. A return for a time to the old state of union might be good as a reaction against this isolation with its empty, barren abstractions; but, in the long run, it is difficult to deny that the true connection lies in relative independence. Hence those categories of which

66   § 31. *Hegel.*

Hegel treats in the two chief divisions, of Being and of
Essence, should be taken out of Logic and relegated to
Metaphysics. Further, what Hegel introduced in the section
on Objectivity (Mechanism, Chemism, and Teleology) belongs
to natural philosophy. Only the problems which Hegel treats
of in the section upon the Subjective Notion, and partly those
in the section on the Idea, belong to Logic. The proper place
of Logic, which is the doctrine of knowledge, is not within
Metaphysics (although it may precede it as a propaedeutic; cf.
§ 7), but among the subordinate sciences of the philosophy of
Spirit. Cf. § 6.

2. As to the identity of the forms of thought with the
forms of existence, and especially the objective meaning as-
signed to the Notion, Judgment, and Inference. Hegel has
thought that he has here also discovered a relation of sameness,
while there is really only that of reciprocal reference and of
parallelism. Notion, judgment, and inference are forms of the
thinking and knowing spirit. They find their correlates in the
objects of knowledge—the notion in the essence of things, the
judgment in the relation of subsistence and inherence, inference
in the regular connectedness of what actually happens. In
opposition to the Subjectively-formal Logic, which disowns
these relations, one might be reminded of them in the para-
doxical form—'The notion is immanent in things, things
judge and infer, the planetary system, the state, everything in
accordance with reason, is an inference.' Expressions of this
kind are true as poetical metaphors, and very appropriate to
awaken deeper reflection; but they cannot be considered to
be strictly scientific, for they include under the same notion
forms of thought and existence which are related only in
certain essential determinations, but do not agree in all.[1]
Hegel has hardly touched upon the problem of how far the

[1] This figurative character is recognised by Zeller in his introductory
lecture at Heidelberg, *Ueber die Bedeutung und Aufgabe der Er-
kenntniss-Theorie*, p. 6, Heidelb. 1862. Michelet endeavours to justify
the Hegelian stand-point, in opposition to this, in his journal, *Der
Gedanke*, iii. pt 4, p. 288 ff., 1862.

forms of *perception* are related to the outer reality; yet if, whenever we speculate upon the manner and possibility of the affection, it is hardly to be denied that perception is brought about by a co-operation of the perceiving individual with the outer world, then Kant's deliberate separation of a subjective and objective element in perception cannot be wholly rejected. The admission of a *thorough-going* agreement of the element added by subject with the peculiar existence of the outer world is at most only an uncertain hypothesis, and cannot once be maintained with reference to colours, sounds, &c. even as a mere hypothesis, in opposition to the results of modern physics and physiology. Cf. § 38.

When Hegel generally rejects the whole Kantian attempt to test our capabilities for knowledge, because the knowledge of what knows cannot precede the knowledge of reality, we reply that the knowledge of what knows, although the second stage of knowledge in general, may quite well be the first stage in philosophical knowledge. Man's activity of knowledge is first directed to the outward world, and gradually to many psychological relations; then turned to critical reflection on itself and its own capacities for knowing; and lastly, if the result of this testing process be a positive one, directs itself to reality in general, in nature and spirit. We must set out from faith, not from mistrust, in our own power of knowledge, if we are to reach any good result; but this faith, originally blind, must not remain a blind one. In so far as distinct grounds present themselves for denying material truth or agreement with existence to perception or to thought in particulars or in general, these may not be set aside for the sake of this faith. This testing can only be carried out by thinking. We must trust to the power of the thinking which tests, to ascertain the right relations so long as definite reasons do not present themselves for denying this power: the same holds good in again testing these grounds. This procedure does not lose itself in an ad infinitum, because no necessity compels the constant recurrence of new grounds for mistrusting the thinking which tests. At any one point a conclusion can be rightly attained, as satisfactory as that in mathematical demonstration. Hegel's axiom of an identity of thought and existence is rather an escape from the Kantian criticism than a victory over it.[1]

3. The dialectic method sets before itself a false problem, and solves it only apparently. The problem is wrongly stated. For, just as from the Hegelian stand-point a morality is rightly demanded that may be above the compulsion of nature and yet not unnatural, so, in the province of the intellectual, the analogous proposition holds good, that thought should be free from the compulsion of experience but not void of experience. It is not thinking, resting and remaining in itself, but thinking which works up the material originally obtained in outer and inner sense-perception according to laws founded on the idea of truth, that actually produces human knowledge and forms the object of consideration in Logic. The dialectic problem is insoluble. For: *a.* The more abstract notion cannot produce from itself alone the more concrete notion in the mind of the thinking subject, for 'the product cannot contain more than what the factors have given' (Beneke); and then Hegel's single dialectic transitions really contain logical fallacies, as has been abundantly proved by acute opponents.[2] *b.* When the dialectic process is transferred to reality, the 'logical categories' are hypostatised and treated as independent essences, which are capable of a peculiar development and of passing over the one into the other. This is analogous to the Platonic hypostasis of ideas combated by Aristotle. How the outgoing in the objective reality from Being to Nothing, and then to Becoming, and so on to the Absolute Idea, can find place as a timeless prius in the development of nature and spirit (treated of in the philosophy of nature and spirit), is neither conceivable nor thinkable; and it would contradict Hegel's principles to hold that the priority of the logical categories and their dialectical succession is a merely subjective abstraction.

[1] Cf. the Author's tract, *Ueber Idealismus, Realismus und Idealrealismus,* in Fichte's *Z. f. Philos.* xxxiv. pp. 63–80, 1859.

[2] Especially by I. H. Fichte, Schelling, Trendelenburg, Kym, Lotze, Chalybäus, George, Ulrici, v. Hartmann, and the Herbartian School.

The truth which lies at the basis of the dialectical method is the teleological consideration of nature and mind (Geist), according to which both, advancing by means of the strife and change of opposites, are developed from the lower to the higher stages, by a necessity conformable to reason dwelling consciously or unconsciously in them. Human thought can know the gradual series of the developments, because this series rests on outer and inner experience. The dialectic method proceeds from notion to notion *apparently* by the purely logical mean of negative and identity, but *really* by this, that the thinker, whose consciousness is developed by other means, already perceives or anticipates each higher stage, and finds the lower, when compared with it, unsatisfactory.

§ 32. *Erdmann, Rosenkranz, Kuno Fischer*, and others belonging to the *Hegelian School*, have partly represented the system of Logic scientifically, partly treated the principle, method, and single problems of Logic in works of explanation or defence.

The chief works of the Hegelian school are—*J. E. Erdmann*, Grundriss der Logik und Metaphysik, Halle, 1841, 4th ed. 1864; *Rosenkranz*, Die Modificationen der Logik abgeleitet aus dem Begriffe des Denkens, Leipzig, 1846; System der Wissenschaft, ein philosophisches Enchiridion, Königsberg, 1850; Wissenschaft der logischen Idee, Part I.: Metaphysik, Königsberg, 1858; Part II.: Logik und Ideenlehre, Königsberg, 1859; *Kuno Fischer*, Logik und Metaphysik oder Wissenschaftslehre, Heidelberg, 1852; 2nd ed. (wholly remodelled), 1865.

§ 33. *Schleiermacher* (1768–1834) means by Dialectic the art of scientific thinking, or the system of axioms for technical expression in the department of pure thinking. Pure thinking (in distinction from the artistic and from that of ordinary life) is

thinking with a view to science. Science is what is
identical in all the thinking minds producing it, and
agrees with the existence which is thought about.
The transcendental part of Dialectic considers the
essence of science or the idea of science in itself; the
formal or technical part considers the becoming of
science or the idea of science in motion. Schleiermacher attacks the (Hegelian) position, that pure
thought can have a peculiar beginning distinct from all
other thinking, and arise originally as something
specially for itself. He teaches that in every kind of
thinking the activity of the reason can be exercised
only on the basis of outer and inner perception, or that
there can be no act without the 'intellectual' and none
without the ' organic function,' and that only a relative
preponderance of the one or other function exists in
the different ways of thinking. Agreement with existence is immediately given in inner perception, and is
attainable mediately also on the basis of outer perception. The forms of thought, notion and judgment, are
made parallel, by Schleiermacher, to analogous forms
of real existence—the notion to the substantial forms,
and the judgment to actions.

Schleiermacher's ' Dialektik ' has been published by Jonas,
in 1839, from his manuscripts and written lectures, as the
second subdivision of the second volume of his literary
remains, or as the second part of the fourth volume of the
third division of his collected works. Schleiermacher has taken
the idea and the name of Dialectic partly from Plato, partly
from Schelling. He seeks to realise by actual representation Schelling's postulate of Dialectic as ' a science of the
form and as it were the pure art of philosophy.' Schleier-

macher held that the technical form of scientific thought is separable by abstraction from its content, and forms the object of a relatively independent philosophical discipline. He recognised a parallelism but not an identity between the forms of thinking and knowing, and the forms of real existence. He believes that thinking rests upon perception, and perception arises from the influence, affection, or impression which comes from the objects or being without us. His views, in all these relations, agree with the results of unprejudiced scientific investigation, and correspond more truly than Hegel's do to the idea of the universe as one whole organism, in which the unity of the whole does not interfere with the manifold and relative independence of single sides and members; sameness in common fundamental characters does not remove or render meaningless difference in specific and individual properties, and no one member can be freed, with respect to his actions, or even his existence, from being conditioned by any other. On the other hand, we cannot agree with Schleiermacher when he puts the art of thinking in the place of Metaphysics, for the system of philosophy has room for both sciences, and assigns to each a special meaning and problem (§ 6). Again, Schleiermacher's mode of defining the relation of thinking to perception, and the parallelism of forms of thought and forms of knowledge, appears to require correction in some particulars. This will afterwards be shown in our systematic representation of Logic. Finally, we cannot approve of Schleiermacher's division of Dialectic, according to which he distinguishes a transcendental from a technical or formal part; and, in the former, considers the notion and judgment, in their relation to the corresponding forms of existence, to be forms of science in itself; while in the latter, the syllogism, induction, deduction, and the complex forms of thought, are considered to be forms of the genesis of science, or of the idea of science in motion. For the forms which Schleiermacher relegates to the second class, correspond to certain forms of existence, with this distinction only—that the notion and the judgment, the most elementary forms of thought, mirror the simplest forms, while inference and the other ways of construction and combination mirror the wider and more general interdependence of existence. Schleiermacher is wrong when he says that these latter forms belong to the genesis of science, and become unmeaning and superfluous after that thought has reached its completion in science; for complete science can only exist in them. Again, these forms have a relation to existence as 'transcendental,' and belong to 'science as such' as essentially as do the notion and judgment. They must therefore all be relegated to the 'transcendental part.' There remains for the 'formal or technical part' only certain psychological considerations and rules of procedure; and they, so far as their treatment is of any use, may be more conveniently dispersed over the single sections than gathered together into a special part. Cf. § 5.

These criticisms of details by no means prevent us from recognising that Schleiermacher's fundamental dialectical principles in general point to the direction in which the true mean is to be sought, between the opposites of the subjectively formal and the metaphysical Logics.

§ 34. *Ritter* and *Vorländer* follow Schleiermacher generally in his treatment of Logic. *Beneke, Trendelenburg,* and *Lotze,* in single essential relations proceed upon his fundamental opinions about Logic. Then the whole post-Hegelian labours in the province of the doctrine of thought and knowledge, so far as they do not belong to any one of the Schools already mentioned, occupy a common middle place between the opposites of the Subjectively-formal and the Metaphysical Logics.

Schleiermacher neither founded nor wished to found a philosophical school in the strict sense of the word. He wished to rouse on all sides and waken individuality. His treatises and writings are as fitted, by their wealth of ingenious and acute thoughts, to quicken and bear fruit on all sides, as they

are unfitted, by the absence of a complete systematic form and
a strict terminology (which Schleiermacher designedly avoided,
partly from a horror of the danger of dogmatic stiffness),
to form the uniting symbol of a school. Those of Schleiermacher's philosophical works in which he strove after a stricter
systematic form were not published until after his death.
Hence, those Logicians who follow Schleiermacher most
closely can only be called his scholars in the wider sense that
they chiefly move within the circle of thoughts awakened
by him.

The logical writings of the above-named philosophers are
the following: *Heinr. Ritter*, Vorlesungen zur Einleitung in
die Logik, 1823; Abriss der philosophischen Logik, 1824, 2nd
ed., 1829; System der Logik und Metaphysik, 1856; Encyclopädie der philos. Wissenschaften, 1862 ff.—*Franz Vorländer*,
Wissenschaft der Erkenntniss, Marburg u. Leipzig, 1847.—
Ed. Beneke (1798–1854), Erkenntnisslehre in ihren Grund-
zügen dargelegt, Jena, 1820; Lehrbuch der Logik als Kunstlehre des Denkens, Berlin, 1832; System der Logik als
Kunstlehre des Denkens, Berlin, 1842.—*J. G. Dressler* follows
Beneke, Praktische Denklehre, Bautzen, 1852; Die Grund-
lehren der Psychologie und Logik, ein Leitfaden zum
Unterricht in diesen Wissenschaften für höhere Lehranstalten,
sowie zur Selbstbelehrung, Leipzig, 1867.—*Trendelenburg*,
Logische Untersuchungen, Berlin, 1840; 3rd enlarged ed.
Leipzig, 1870; cf. *Karl. Aug. Jul. Hoffmann*, Abriss der
Logik für den Gymnasialunterricht, Clausthal, 1859; 2nd ed.,
1868.—*Rud. Herm. Lotze*, Logik, Leipzig, 1843.

We may further mention in this place some logical writings
which, when the one is compared with the other, have very
various characters, but have this at least in common, that
they belong neither to the pure subjectivism of the Kantian
Logic, nor yet to the Hegelian identification of thinking and
being, but seek an intermediate direction:—*Jul. Branis*
(inspired by Schleiermacher and by Steffens, the friend of
Schelling), Die Logik in ihrem Verhältnisse zur Philosophie
geschichtlich betrachtet, 1823; Grundriss der Logik, 1830.—

Imm. Herm. Fichte (b. 1797), Grundzüge zum System der Philosophie, Part I., Das Erkennen als Selbsterkennen, Heidelberg, 1833.—*Bernh. Bolzano*, Wissenschaftslehre, Sulzbach, 1837.—*H. M. Chalybäus* (1792-1862), Wissenschaftslehre, Kiel, 1846; Fundamentalphilosophie, Kiel, 1861.—*Hermann Ulrici* (b. 1806), System der Logik, Leipzig, 1852; Compendium der Logik, Leipzig, 1860 (Ulrici treats of *separative* thought only in this work).—*Martin Katzenberger*, Grundfragen der Logik, Leipzig, 1858.—*J. Sengler*, Erkenntnisslehre. Heidelberg, 1858.—*Ernst Ferd. Friedrich*, Beiträge zur Förderung der Logik, Noëtik und Wissenschaftslehre (i.e. upon the 'science the rational existence of things, the theory of thinking, and the doctrine of evidence;' or the 'Metaphysic, Formal, and Inductive Logic'), vol. i., Leipzig, 1864.—*J. H. v. Kirchmann*, Die Philosophie des Wissens, vol. i., Berlin, 1864.—*Rud. Seydel*, Logik oder Wissenschaft vom Wissen, Leipzig, 1866.—*Wilh. Rosenkrantz*, Die Wissenschaft des Wissens, München, 1866-69.—In the Aristotelian-Scholastic sense. yet with reference to modern enquiries, *Georg Hagemann*, Logik und Noëtik, Münster, 1868.—*L. Rabus*, Logik und Metaphysik, I. Erkenntnisstheorie, Geschichte der Logik, Syst. der Logik, Erlangen, 1868 (1867).—*J. Hoppe*, Die gesammte Logik, Paderborn, 1868 (1867).—Many articles in the philosophical journals edited by J. H. Fichte, Ulrici, and Wirth, by Allihn and Ziller, and by Michelet and Bergmann, refer to the debated questions about the general character, and about single problems of Logic. *Karl Alexander von Reichlin-Meldegg*, System der Logik, nebst Einleitung in die Philosophie, Wien, 1870, appeared quite recently.

The general reference to their works will suffice for the logical labours of the philosophers named here, as they belong not so much to history as to the present.

§ 35. Recent German speculation has had in general little influence upon *logical studies beyond Germany.* The theory of Induction, especially in its application to natural science, has been advanced by *Comte, J. Her-schel, Whewell,* and *Mill.*

Among logicians who have kept to the old ways of regard-ing the science may be named :—(Archbishop) *Whately,* Ele-ments of Logic, 9th ed. 1860, London ;—*Karslake,* Aid to the Study of Logic, Oxford, 1851 ;—*J. L. Balmes* (pres-bytero), El Criterio, Barcelona, 1845 ; Curso de Filosofia elemental (Logica, Metafisica, Etica, Historia de la Filosofia), Madrid, 1837, Barcelona, 1847, Paris, 1851, translated into German by F. Lorinser, Regensburg, 1852.

Garelli, Della Logica, o Teoria della Scienza, 2nd ed. Torino, 1859. *J. G. Ulber,* Logica, ossia Teoria del Pensiero, Napoli, 1863.

The following have been influenced by the Kantian doctrine of knowledge :—*A. Tandel,* Cours de Logique, Liége, 1844 ;—*W. Whewell,* The Philosophy of the Inductive Sciences, founded upon the History of the Physical Sciences, London, 1840, 2nd ed. 1847, 3rd ed. 1857; cf. his History of the Inductive Sciences, 1837, translated into German by Littrow, 1839–42 ;—*Henry Longueville Mansel,* Prolegomena Logica, an Inquiry into the Psychological Character of Logical Pro-cesses, Oxford, 1851, London, 1861 ; Artis Log. Rudimenta, 2nd ed., Oxford, 1852 ;—*W. Thomson,* An Outline of the Necessary Laws of Thought, 3rd ed., London, 1852 ;—*Sir W. Hamilton,* Discussions on Philosophy and Literature, 1852, 2nd ed. 1869; Lectures on Logic, edited by H. L. Mansel and J. Veitch, Edinburgh, 1859, 2nd ed. 1869 ;—*A. C. Fraser,* Rational Philosophy in History and System, Edin-burgh, 1857.

The Logic of Chance—an Essay on the Foundations and Province of the Theory of Probability, with especial reference to its Applications to Moral and Social Science, London and Cambridge, 1866.

The following profess a strict Empiricism :—*Sir John Herschel,* A Preliminary Discourse on the Study of Natural Philosophy, London, 1831 ; cf. his review of the works of Dr.

Whewell in the Quarterly Review, June, 1841;—*John Stuart Mill*, A System of Logic, Rationative and Inductive, 7th ed. 1868, London, translated into German by *J. Schiel*, 2nd ed. from the 5th ed. of the original, Braunschweig, 1862–63; cf. Die Methode der inductiven Forschung als die Methode der Naturforschung, in gedrängter Darstellung, hauptsächlich nach John Stuart Mill, by J. Schiel, Braunschweig, 1865.[1]

C. W. Opzoomer inclines to Empiricism in another sense, De Waarheid en hare Kenbronnen, 2nd ed., Leyden, 1863; Het Wezen der Kennis, een Leesbock der Logika, Amsterdam, 1863; cf. his Die Methode der Wissenschaft, ein Handbuch der Logik, from the Dutch by G. Schwindt, Utrecht, 1852.

In France, 'Positivism,' based on the investigation of nature and on Mathematics, is represented by *A. Comte*, Cours de Philosophie positive, Paris, 1830–42.

The principal part of the contents of the work of *E. Vacherot*, La Métaphysique et la Science, Paris, 1858, 2nd ed. 1863, belongs to the theory of knowledge; also *J. Tissot's* Essai de Logique objective, ou Théorie de la connaissance de la vérité et de la certitude, Dijon, 1867. *J. M. C. Duhamel* treats of the doctrine of Method in his Des Méthodes dans les sciences du raisonnement, Paris, 1865.

Ch. Waddington, Essai de Logique; Leçons faites à la Sorbonne de 1848 à 1856, Paris, 1858; and *Pellissier*, Précis d'un cours élémentaire de Logique d'après les programmes officiels de 1857, 2nd ed., Paris, 1860.

Logicians who, seeking a mean between Kant and Hegel, apprehend Logic to be the science of rules, which when followed enable one to attain to science, i.e. to knowledge conformable to things, are represented by *Joseph Delbœuf*, Prolégomènes philosophique de la Géométrie, Liége, 1860; and Essai de Logique scientifique, Prolégomènes, Liége, 1865. His doctrines in many considerations approach the method pursued in this work.

[1] A fuller account of the recent history of Logic in England will be given in Appendix A.

PART FIRST.

PERCEPTION IN ITS RELATION TO OBJECTIVE EXISTENCE IN SPACE AND TIME.

§ 36. PERCEPTION is the immediate knowledge of things existing together and in succession. Outer or sense-perception has to do with the outer world, inner or psychological perception with the mental (psychic) life.

Perception is the first and most immediate form of knowledge, because in it the relation of subject to object rests on given natural relations. It thus presupposes no other forms of knowledge, but is the foundation of all others, and is conditioned only by the presence of its object. The mental (geistige) element in it is connected in the closest way with the definite constitution of nature, and this connection is the earlier form according to the universal law of the development of spirit. Yet the immediateness of knowledge in perception is relative, since many influencing mental (geistige) operations are blended in it with the sense-activity, although only their collective product appears in consciousness, and not they themselves individually. [If this distinction had been as clearly stated by Hamilton, he might have escaped the charge of inconsistency which J. S. Mill and J. H. Stirling advanced against his doctrine of perception.[1]]

Perception is distinguished from mere *Sensation*, which can

[1 Cf. Mill's *Examination of Sir W. Hamilton's Philos.* 3rd ed. Lond. 1867, p. 17 ff.; Stirling's *Philosophy of Perception*, p. 2 ff.]

be more particularly treated in Psychology, by this, that in sensation consciousness clings to the subjective occasion merely, while in perception it goes out upon something which has been perceived, and which therefore, whether it belongs to the outer world or to the subject itself, opposes itself to the act of perception as something objective.[1] Its (relative) immediateness distinguishes *perception* from *thinking* which produces mediate knowledge, separates perceptions into their elements, and re-combines them with each other. *Thinking*, however, may be taken in a wider sense, and understood to mean the totality of the (theoretic) functions, which aim at the representation of any object in our consciousness. In this case perception itself may be called a kind of thinking.

Perception is the object of Psychology in reference to the way it happens, but with regard to the agreement or want of agreement of its contents with nature, it is the object of Logic. The *logical* theory of perception is an integral part of Logic, the doctrine of knowledge, and not a ' mere psychological introduction ' to the representation of the normative laws of the operations of thought.

There is no contradiction in believing that the laws of perception and thought are conditioned by things-in-themselves, and that our understanding of the laws of perception and thought is conditioned by our scientific knowledge of those things in themselves. The opinions of some writers [e.g. Prof. Bain] that there is such a contradiction arises from the erroneous supposition that in order to know the thing-in-itself, *it* must be in our consciousness. The external thing-in-itself cannot be in us, but a knowledge of it on which we may depend can be in us. We get this knowledge by reflecting upon perception and upon thought itself, and in this way can reason back from the results to the cause. There is no contradiction in the assertion that a true knowledge of what is outside my consciousness may be in my consciousness.

[1 Cf. Hamilton, *Lect. on Metaph.* ii. 93; his edition of Reid's *Works*, p. 876 ff.]

A.—EXTERNAL OR SENSE-PERCEPTION.

§ 37. The special question of Logic as the doctrine of knowledge, is, *Whether in sense-perception things appear to us as they actually exist, or as they are in themselves?* Skeptics assert the negative. Their arguments are: The agreement of thought with existence, even if there were such a thing, could never be known, for the sense-perception can only be compared with other perceptions, never with its object. The doubt is strengthened when we reflect upon the essential nature of sense-perception. The perception as an act of the mind (Seele) must either be of a purely subjective origin, or at least include a subjective element. In either case the assertion that the mind reflects undistortedly and exhaustively the peculiar real being of what is perceived, can only be supported by artificial hypotheses which are difficult to be confirmed. The constitution of the world of phenomena is at least partly conditioned by the subjective nature of our sense. Sense may be different in other beings, and so may produce other kinds of worlds of sense-phenomena. What actually exists as such, as it is in itself independent of any way of apprehending it, or the thing-in-itself, is different from all of these.

The uncertainty of sense-perception was maintained by the *Eleatics*, in a certain degree by *Demokritus* and other natural philosophers, then by *Plato*, and with new arguments by the earlier *Skeptics*. The *Stoical* criterion, the φαντασία καταληπτική, was a superfluous assertion, which could not overcome Skepticism. Among modern philosophers who take up the position that sense-perception cannot impart, at least, full material

truth, we may mention specially, *Des Cartes*,[1] *Locke* (with
regard to the secondary qualities), *Kant*,[2] *Herbart*,[3] and
Beneke.[4] *Jos. Delbœuf* has discussed afresh the questions
which belong to the inability to compare the conception with
its object.[5] He uses the formula : $A = f (a, x)$—that is,
the real result, A, is not known as such, but must be brought
about by a, that is, the object-phenomenon, and x, that is, the
nature of our mind (Geist).

[*Sir W. Hamilton's* explanation is not unlike Delbœuf's—
' Suppose that the total object of consciousness in perception is
$= 12$, and that the external reality contributes 6, the material
sense 3, and the mind 3 : this may enable you to form some
rude conjecture of the nature of the object of perception.'[6]]

§ 38. The *Subjective* element in sense-perception cannot be separated from the *Objective* in *this* way, that
space and time can be referred to the subject only,
and what *fills space and time*, or its *material* (colour,
sound, &c.), to external things affecting our senses.
For on this presupposition, although it would be necessary to apprehend the matter of sense-perception in any
form of space and time, each particular matter would
not be referred back to each particular form, and,
consequently, might be perceived in another form from
that in which it actually appears, without having un-
dergone any real change. But in perception we feel
ourselves actually confined to the union of definite
forms with definite matters. Again, modern physics

1 *Méditat. init.*
2 *Kritik der r. Vern.*; *Elementarlehre*, Pt. I. ; *Transcendentalen Aesthetik*; and *Logik*, ed. by Jäsche, p. 69 f.
3 *Einl. in die Philosophie*, § 19 ff.
4 *Metaphysik*, pp. 91–119.
5 *Log.* pp. 35 ff., 71 ff., 99 ff.; 105.
6 [*Lect. on Metaphysics*, ii. lect. xxv. p. 129.]

and physiology, because they trace sound, warmth, and colour back to the perception of vibrations of air and of aether, smell and taste to the perception of certain motions connected with chemical occurrences, prove the dependence of the content of perception on motions, i.e. on changes belonging to the forms of space and time. It involves a contradiction therefore to admit that content rests on affections which come from without, and to believe that these forms nevertheless are derived from the perceiving subject only, and are not conditioned by the external world affecting us.

The view here combated is that which *Kant* enunciated (Kritik d. r. Vernunft, Part I., Transcendentale Aesthetik). The truth that a *subjective* and an *objective* element is to be distinguished in perception was applied in a very unfortunate and misleading way, when Kant called the former element the *form* and the latter the *content* or matter of perception, and still further defined the *form* to be *intuition of space and time.* According to *Kant*, the qualities of sensation, such as blue, green, sweet, &c., as such, are only subjective, but rest on determinate outward affections, which determine the peculiar nature and character of each. This doctrine (which was afterwards developed by Joh. Müller into that of special sense-energies) is correct enough. The form of intuition-in-space-and-time, on the other hand, is something *purely* subjective, because à priori : but it is quite inadmissible not to attribute to intuition-in-space *at least* a measure of the objective conditionality, which is attributed to the sense-qualities, which, as Physics show, depend upon distinct motions. Kant's doctrine of the forms of intuition-in-space-and-time wavers. For, on the one side (on the side on which our statement given above rests), these forms even in their particular determinations *must originate in the subject only,* which can

G

only impose on a chaotic matter its à priori forms and laws; and, on the other side, the *particular* determinate forms and the *special* natural laws must be given *empirically*, and *their determinate nature and character cannot in each case grow out of the subject alone.* They must depend upon the way in which the subject is each time affected from the side of 'things-in-themselves,' according to their own peculiar construction.[1]

Fichte, seeing the separation to be untenable, explained both the matter and the form of perception to be merely subjective; *Schelling* and *Hegel* made it at the same time subjective and objective. *Herbart* subjects the Kantian opinion to a very thorough criticism.[2]

[*Sir W. Hamilton* and his *School* have devoted much labour to distinguish the formal from the empirical elements in sense-perception. The formal element is called the primary qualities of matter, the empirical the secondary. The primary qualities are attributes of *body as body*, are thought of as essential to body, and are conceived as modes of a not-self. The secondary are attributes of *body as this or that kind of body*. They are thought of as accidental, and are conceived as modes of self in relation to bodies. Hamilton has also

[1] For a criticism of the Kantian doctrine, cf. my *Grund. der Gesch. d. Phil.* iii. § 16, 2nd. ed.

[2] *Einl. in die Philosophie*, § 127; *Psychol. als Wissenschaft*, in Herb. *Sämmtlichen Werken*, v. 504 ff. Upon the stimuli of sense as vibrations in matter, see especially Joh. Müller, *Physiologie*, 4th ed. i. 667 ff., ii. 249 ff. [English translation by Daly, i. 613 ff., ii. 903 ff., 1842; Carpenter, *Principles of Human Physiology*, 7th ed. 663–722]; cf. George, *Die Fünf Sinne*, pp. 27–42; Maximilian Jacobi, *Natur- und Geistesleben*, pp. 1–31; Lotze, *Medicinische Psychologie*, p. 174 ff., 1852; *Mikrokosmus*, i. 376, 1869; Helmholtz, *Ueber die Natur der menschlichen Sinnesempfindungen*, p. 20 ff., 1852 (where the distinction between the sensations and the relations of vibrations is emphasised, and the senses are 'thanked' very rightly for 'conjuring' out of these vibrations, colours, sounds, &c., and for bringing us intelligence of the outer world by these sensations, as if by 'symbols'); *Ueber das Sehen des Menschen*, Leipzig, 1855.

secundo-primary qualities, which are intermediate between the other two.[1]

Mr. Mill and his *School* 'do not think it necessary to ascribe to the mind (either in perception or in any other cognitive faculty) certain innate forms, in which objects are, as it were, moulded into these appearances, but hold that Place, Extension, Substance, Cause, and the rest, are conceptions put together out of ideas of sensation by the known laws of association.'[2]]

§ 39. Neither the proportion which the external reality contributes to the generation of perceptions, nor even the *existence of the object affecting us*, can be known from the ground of sense-perception alone. Perceptions are acts of our mind, and as such do not carry us beyond ourselves. The conviction of the existence of external objects which affect us depends upon the presupposition of causal relations which do not belong to sense-perception only.

The doctrine of Common Sense of the *Scottish School* (Reid, Stewart, Beattie, &c.), as well as the allied doctrine of *F. H. Jacobi*, which asserts that a faith which cannot be scientifically explained reveals to us the existence of an external world, is a fiction which has no foundation.

The problem stated in this section can only be settled below (in §§ 41–44).

[1 Cf. Hamilton's ed. of *Reid's Works*, Appendix, Note D, pp. 825–75; cf. Mansel's *Metaphysics*, p. 105 ff., 1860; cf. also, for remarks upon the same distinction in Bacon's philosophy, the general Preface to his philosophical works, by James Spedding and R. L. Ellis, i. 29. Cf also Berkeley's *Works*, Fraser's Ed. i. pp. 122 ff., 160 ff., 249 ff., and passim.

2 Cf. Mill's *Exam. of Sir W. Hamilton's Philos.* pp. 219 ff., 258 ff., 3rd ed. 1867; Bain's *Senses and Intellect* passim; *Deductive Logic*, p. 10.]

B.—INTERNAL OR PSYCHOLOGICAL PERCEPTION.

§ 40. *Internal Perception, or the immediate knowledge of mental (psychic) acts and constructions, can apprehend its objects as they are in themselves with material truth.* For internal perception results when the individual production is apprehended by means of the process of Association as an integral part of our whole mental production. It reaches its most developed form, blended with thought, when the mental production under consideration is placed under the notion to which it refers, and when at the same time the consciousness, which he who performs the internal perception has of himself, has reached the form expressed by 'Ego.' But: (a) The association of a single act with others cannot change its content and form. It remains what it is. We are conscious of our present conceptions, thoughts, feelings, desires, and in general of the elements of our mental (psychic) life, and of their mutual relations as they actually exist ; and they actually exist as we are conscious of them. In mental acts, consciousness and existence are one and the same. (b) In the recollection of earlier mental acts, their thought-pictures, remaining in unconsciousness, are again aroused. Earlier acts may be reproduced, with less intensity it is true, but in actual agreement with their original existence. (c) By the subsumption of individual acts and productions under the corresponding general notion, the strength of consciousness is directed to their common character, without the admixture of any foreign element. The consciousness attained by this of our mental acts and productions

naturally harmonises with the real existence of these
elements. But the possibility of error increases as we,
in order to determine its notion, go beyond the act itself,
and consider its genesis and relations (e.g. as in the question whether a certain conception be a perception or an
illusion). (d) Self-consciousness in the strict sense, or
consciousness of the Ego, developes itself in three moments. The first moment is the unity of an individual
capable of consciousness, by means of which every particular in it must be viewed not as an independent
existence, which together with others is found in an
accidental aggregate, but as a member of a single
whole organism. The second moment is the consciousness which the individual has of itself as one individual, or the coherent perception of single mental acts and
productions in their mutual combinations, according to
which they belong collectively to the same being. The
third moment is the further perception, that that consciousness which the individual has of itself as an individual belongs again to the same being as the acts and
productions to which it is directed,—in other words, the
perception that the being conceived and conceiving, or
the object and the subject of the conception, is one and
the same. The first and second moments constitute the
presuppositions or foundations; the third constitutes
the essence of the self-consciousness as consciousness of
the Ego. This moment is only an inner perception
become potential, and so does not introduce anything
different from the actual existence. Accordingly, in
every form of internal perception directed to *one's own*
mental life, and in every form of thought combining

with it and working it up in *internal experience*, the phenomenon is in essential agreement with the mental actual existence.

That my pain appears to me as my pain, my sensation of colour as my sensation of colour, &c. is self-evident, and to wish to prove this were quite superfluous. But the psychological transcendentalist would distinguish from the pain, from the sensation of sound or of colour, (not only the essence and substance of the soul, and the inner conditions of individual mental occurrence, and not only the outer affections inducing them, with all of which the present investigation has nothing to do—but also) an existence *in-itself* even of those psychological modifications in me, which appear to me as pain, sensation of colour, sound, &c. The present argument aims at proving the incorrectness of this distinction. I perceive by sense-perception a sound, a colour, &c. correctly, in the empirical sense, if I perceive it as it must be perceived by the normal sense-perception. I remember rightly when my memory-conception corresponds with this normal perception. Yet the question ever arises, whether this normal perception agrees with the fact as it took place in itself outside my consciousness, and, by working on my sense, gave rise to my perception. This question is, however, meaningless when it refers to the psychological apprehension of one of my sensations or of any of my mental productions. The distinction of truth in the ' empirical ' and in the ' transcendental ' sense which is valid of sense-perception can only be applied by a false analogy to internal perception. There is meaning not only in seeking to know what are the external, but also what are the internal conditions of the origin of a mental act; but when the mental image as such is the object of my apprehension, there is no meaning in seeking to distinguish its existence in my consciousness (in me) from its existence out of my consciousness (in itself)—for the object apprehended is, in this case, one which does not even exist, as the objects of external perception do, in itself outside my consciousness. It exists only within me. In the external perception the sensation of the subject contains not only elements which correspond with objective existence, but also elements which differ from it; and these last, the subjective elements, make a discrepancy between the image and the objective reality. In internal perception, on the other hand, so far as this has to do with my own acts immediately present in my consciousness (unless memory requires to come forward to introduce them), the subjective action, because it is itself the object of the apprehension, cannot, as purely subjective, contain elements which establish an inconsistency with the object to be apprehended. Every subject in *this* self-apprehension is also object. We have not to distinguish between two things which might or might not correspond with each other. There is only one thing identical with itself. The question of agreement, of course, enters into the conceptions of memory, and the subsumption of mental productions under psychological notions. The relation is no longer that of identity; but what apprehends can be homogeneous with what is to be apprehended, for both belong to the same animate existence. It cannot be presumed to be so in sense-perception; for there, what apprehends is mind, and what is apprehended belongs to the external world.

To understand the nature of *self-consciousness* one must not confound the identity of the conceiving with the conceived essence, or the identity of the person with a supposed identity of the act of self-conception with the acts and productions to which the self-conception is directed. Nor must one, with Hegel, confound the identity of the person, as the *concrete* unity embracing in itself all acts, with the pretended identity of a supposed monad reduced to a simple quality which remains over after the *abstraction* of all actual acts. If we call the totality of these mental elements (conceptions, feelings, desires, &c.), to which the internal perception is directed, A, and the inner perception itself B, then B is not identical with A (however much correspondent), it is only very closely associated. But the essence to which both belong, as integral parts, is identical, or one and the same essence. *That* B is only the consciousness of the singularity of itself as a person, which consciousness is expressed in language by naming one's proper name. Self-consciousness, however, as consciousness of the Ego, c, is the consciousness of the co-existence of A and B in one and the same essence, the Ego, which includes in itself the totality of all my mental acts.

The objection quoted in § 3, and § 37, against the possibility of truth and of the certainty of truth in the material sense, because a comparison of our conceptions with existence is never possible, but only their comparison with other conceptions, does not find application to what has been said about the internal perception of our mental acts and productions. We take to ourselves only an *uncertain picture* of *material external things.* We picture within ourselves in a more *adequate* form the *thoughts, feelings,* and *volitions* of *others.* Still more, memory may be *true* to my own earlier received thoughts, to my own feelings and volitions. The immediate apprehension of the *mental images immediately presented to me is necessarily true. Error* is *possible* only when they are *subsumed* under a general notion. In this sense, internal perception, more trustworthy than external, is the foundation of all philosophical knowledge. That we have a perception of our own inner mental (psychic) life, into which existence immediately enters, without the admixture of a foreign form, is the first stronghold of the theory of knowledge.

Melissus the Eleatic asked: ' If nothing existed, how could men speak as of something?' The certainty of the existence of speech (and therefore also of thought) was to him the prius. The certainty of the thought of his own existence lies at the bottom of all the utterances of *Parmenides* about thought. After the subjective individualism of *Protagoras* had identified appearance and existence, *Aristippus* insisted upon the subjective truth of sensations. We only know that outer things which work upon us by the affections, exist, not how they exist; but sensation itself is in our consciousness.'

---

[1] τὸ πάθος ἡμῖν ἐστι φαινόμενον, *Aristippus in Sext. Emp. adv. Math.* vii. 91.

The Socratic study of Ethics and the church doctrine of Salvation made men look to the inner life. *Augustine* recognised that the conception which we have of external things may deceive us, but that the consciousness by the spirit of its own life, memory, thought, and volition, is free from deception. In this sense he puts forward the claim (De Vera Religione, pp. 39,72): ‘Noli foras ire, in te redi, in interiore homine habitat veritas (et si animum mutabilem inveneris, transcende te ipsum).’ Cf. contra Academicos, iii. 26: noli plus assentiri, quam ut ita tibi apparere persuadeas, et nulla deceptio est. Soliloqu. ii. 1: tu qui vis te nosse, scis esse te? scio; unde scis? nescio; simplicem te scis an multiplicem? nescio; moveri te scis? nescio; cogitare te scis? scio. De Trinitate, x. 14: si dubitat, vivit; si dubitat, unde dubitet, meminit; si dubitat, dubitare se intelligit; si dubitat, certus esse vult; si dubitat, cogitat; si dubitat, scit se nescire; si dubitat, iudicat non se temere consentire oportere. Cf. de Civ. Dei, xi. 26.

So also, in the Middle Ages, *Occam* the Nominalist taught that the propositions, such as, I know that I live, think, &c. are surer than sense-perceptions.

Des Cartes, however, was the first to found a system of philosophy on this principle. Thought (cogitare) is to him the most certain of all things; but ‘under thought,’ he explains, ‘I include all that enters into our consciousness, so far as we are conscious of it, and so volitions, conceptions, and sensations.’[1]

Kant, on the other hand, disputes the truth of self-knowledge also. Development in time belongs to our existence, not actually as it is in itself, but only as it is phenomenal; and this development in time depends upon this, that the ‘internal sense’ is accompanied by the intuitional form of time. Our true being remains completely unknown to us. But if there were an inner sense of such a kind as Kant imagined, so that, when our being, in itself timeless, affected it, then the phenomenon of our conscious life in time resulted, this would yet be a result

[1] *Médit.* ii.; *Princ. phil.* i. 9.

which has actually happened. Consciousness and existence would still be identical in relation to our development in time, and the proposition would remain valid,—our mental (psychic) life in time exists in itself as we are conscious of it, and we are conscious of it as it exists. A stricter psychological treatment of the nature of internal perception makes it evident that the Kantian hypothesis about our internal sense is untenable. We apprehend also our self-apprehension, which, according to Kant, exists in time. By what ' internal sense ' and by what form does this happen? Internal perception cannot bring time into what is in itself timeless, but can only recognise that what has already the attribute of time in itself, is in time. (It is a wholly different question, and one belonging not to the doctrine of knowledge but to metaphysics, to ask — Has time any independent power or subsistence, or is it only an outflow of the essence of things, and in this sense merely phenomenal? and if so, how far does each thing bear about in itself its own measure of time? *The confusion of the metaphysical opposition between essential existence and what is outside of essential existence, where the two sides belong to the peculiar nature of things, with the opposition in Logic or in the doctrine of knowledge between the peculiar existence of things or their existence in themselves, and the phenomenon which is only considered to be a true or untrue mirroring of things, has caused unspeakable confusion in these investigations.*)

Hegel makes internal perception, as he makes external, the propaedeutical starting-point, not the scientific foundation, of philosophy, and allows truth to mental (psychic) processes in so far as they make moments in the dialectical self-development of the Absolute.[1]

Schleiermacher rightly finds in self-consciousness the point where thought and being are originally identical : ' We exist thinking, and we think existing.'[2]

Beneke, in agreement with Schleiermacher, teaches, ' All

---

[1] *Phän. des Geistes*, and *Encyclopädie*, § 413 ff.
[2] *Dial.* § 101 ff. p. 53, and *Erläut.* p. 51 ff.; cf. Beil. *D.* xviii. xix. p. 452 ff., and Beil *E.* xx.–xxiii. 488 ff.

knowledge of our mental (psychic) activities is a knowledge of
an existence in itself, i.e. the knowledge of an existence
appears as it is in and for itself, or is independent of its being
conceived,'[1] and makes this proposition the basis of his doctrine
of Metaphysics (with him comprehending in itself the doctrine
of knowledge).[2]

[*Hamilton* distinguishes carefully ' between the data or
deliverances of consciousness considered simply *in themselves,
as apprehended facts or actual manifestations,* and those deliverances considered *as testimonies to the truth of facts beyond
their own phenomenal existence* ;' but in so doing neither sufficiently distinguishes the state of the case in external perception
from that in internal perception, nor sets clearly before himself
the difference between the logical and metaphysical problems.[3]]

C.—The Combination of Internal and External Perception.

§ 41. *The knowledge of the outer world* depends upon
the *combination of external with internal perception.* Our
corporeal circumstances, sensibly perceived by ourselves,
are in orderly coherence with circumstances belonging
to our internal perception. In consequence of this coherence, that association grows up within us, by means
of which we presuppose, along with the sense-perception
of corporeal circumstances analogous to our own, a
mental (psychic) existence also analogous. This combination, which is at first carried on instinctively, as it were,
without any conscious reflection upon the mental laws

[1] *Neue Grundlegung zur Metaphysik,* p. 10, 1822.
[2] *System der Metaphysik,* pp. 68–75, 1840 ; *Lehrbuch der Psychol.*
§ 129, p. 121, 1845 ; cf. W. F. Volkmann, *Grundriss der Psychologie,*
Halle, p. 169, 1856.
[3] [Cf. Hamilton's ed. of *Reid's Works,* p. 743 ff.; *Lect.* i. 138 ; cf.
Mill's *Exam. of Sir W. Hamilton's Philosophy,* 3rd ed. pp. 234–43.]

of logical development, if logically developed, takes the form of a reasoning from analogy—as our corporeal phenomena are to our mental reality, so other corporeal phenomena are to a strange mental reality (here accordingly presupposed). As to the *logical correctness* of the presupposition of a plurality of personal essences after the analogy of our own existence, it is generally undoubtedly certain, that, by this combination of the content of external perception with that of internal, we make the first a moment, which belongs to reality, although it does not present itself in the external sense according to its nature. The proof for this lies partly in the consciousness, that the species and connection of external phenomena under consideration are not wholly conditioned by the mere causality of our own individual mental (psychic) life, partly in the thorough-going positive confirmation which the presupposition has from experience.

It does not belong to Logic to explain further the psychological side of this matter. Logic has to do with what is psychological only in the form of an hypothesis to be established in some other place. On the other hand, it does belong to Logic to prove the logical right, or to decide upon the question, whether the assertion originally and necessarily formed according to psychological laws has truth, i.e. agreement with existence. This follows from the general notion of both sciences. See §§ 2, 6, and 36.

Schleiermacher was the first to recognise correctly that in the knowledge of existence external to us we first affirm a plurality of animate subjects. *Beneke* follows him in this, but expresses the psychological relation more definitely. He finds in it the essential foundation of Metaphysics.[1]

[1] *Grundleg. der Metaphys.* p. 23; *Syst. der Metaphys.* pp. 76–90;

§ 42. Extending his consideration of the external world, man recognises the *internal characters of other things*, chiefly by means of the related sides of his own inner existence. He copies in himself the existence of *higher* and *lower* objects; for he partly raises, partly lowers, the corresponding moments of his own mind, and in this fashion gives a supplementary meaning to the content of the external perception of what appears at the time. By such a reproductive process, developed, trained, and fitted for a deeper self-knowledge, he imitatively seeks to recognise in gradually higher proportion the inner nature of other essences. The *truth* of these elements of knowledge modifies itself according to two relations: (1) in objective relation according to the distance of the then present objects of knowledge from our own existence; (2) in subjective relation according to the discrimination between nearer and more remote analogy, and to the suitable application of this discrimination to phenomena.

The foregoing propositions contain the logical principles for determining a series of important questions in different spheres of real science. In the gradual series of earthly existences the law holds good that the higher essence takes up into it the character of the lower as a moment.[1] The animal, while it is raised above the plants by consciousness, contains the vegetative

Lehrbuch der Psych. 2nd ed. § 159, p. 149 f.; cf. Herbart, Werke, v. 137; vi. 501 f.

[1] This law was perhaps, if the fragments of the writing ascribed to Philolaus are genuine (cf. § 11), hinted at symbolically by the Pythagoreans. It was recognised more distinctly by Plato and Aristotle in their doctrines of the parts or powers of the Soul. It was raised by Schelling to be the principle of his Nature-Philosophy, and determined the whole course of the Hegelian Dialectic.

powers as the ground in which the peculiar animal life takes
root; and in the same way man unites in himself, along with
the activities of reason, the powers of vegetative and animal
life. By this he is capable of acquiring an approximately true
judgment of the life of animals, and, with reference to their
working powers generally, of the essential nature of plants and
of nature as a whole, since he reflects upon the lower in himself, and reduces its character in his conception to an inferior
power. A modern searcher into nature says rightly on this
matter: ' As the investigation of nature was originally produced by the feeling of the inner kinship of nature with the
essential being of man, it is also its aim to lay hold of this
coherence in its whole depth, and bring it to knowledge.'
' The history of nature gains its highest significance when it
is connected with the history of the development of man.'[1] On
the other side, man apprehends the higher and divine by
idealising his peculiar inner nature, and that in the form of
faith and presentiment, since he cannot bring adequate powers
of knowledge to bear upon it. If one defines the relation of
faith, in the more general sense, to knowledge as that of *nice
perception* (tact) *to proof*,[2] then this wider notion of faith includes the more special one of immediate trust in a higher Being,
and the recognition of his authority. This trust must take the
form of nice perception (tact), because what is lower cannot
completely copy the higher, and therefore cannot test it (or
prove it) scientifically. But in proportion as our own mind
developes by advances in intelligence and morality, and becomes
higher, the higher without us can be recognised by us in a more

[1] Braun, *Betrachtungen über die Verjüngung in der Natur*, pt. xi.
p. 13, 1850.

[2] *Tact* is the ability to reach a definite result by means of an irre-
flective combination of manifold elements without clear consciousness
of the individual members combined. *Proof* or *Analysis* brings the
individual members into consciousness, and separates the true from the
false. Cf. Beneke, *Lehrbuch der Psychologie*, § 138; *Psych. Skizzen*,
ii. 275 ff.; *Syst. der Logik*, i. 268 f.; Lazarus, *Das Leben der Seele*,
ii. 286; cf. § 101.

and more adequate way, and faith become scientific knowledge
or vision. Hence, within certain limits, according to the
different stages of mental development, the same content of
knowledge, which is only an object of faith for the one, is for
others an object of knowledge. But as often as knowledge
completely annexes to itself one province, a higher province of
faith reveals itself. It must be noted, with regard to the subjective criterion or discrimination between nearer and further
analogy, that the uneducated consciousness is at the same time
liable to the two opposite faults, of raising the lower too nearly
up to, and of dragging the higher too nearly down to, its own
peculiar nature. For, since our own peculiar existence is the
only one immediately given to us, what first necessarily presents
itself, until the phenomena refute this first hypothesis, is a
multiplication of such existences. ' Man refers his own peculiar essence to Nature, and throws into the world of things the
conception of human relations ' (Trendelenburg). The capability both of fully idealising and of in the right way dividing
and depotentialising our own nature is only attained gradually
and amidst fluctuations hitherto by no means completely overcome even by the sciences. The tendency to anthropomorphism
does not allow people living in a state of nature either to reach
the pure ideal above, or the abstract categories of scientific
physics beneath. It appears in numberless expressions of the
poets and of the earlier philosophers. The well-known astronomical axiom of Heraclitus, the ancient equivalent of the
modern theory of gravitation, belongs to this way of looking at
things—' The sun will not transgress its bounds, for if it did so
the Furies, the servants of Dike, would find it.' Timoleon
erected an altar to Automatia, to the personified might of accident, moulding his notion to the very opposite of self-conscious
personality. The exaltation of Christianity over Judaism
appeared to the Gnostics to be the exaltation of the God of
the Christians over the God of the Jews. Clement of Alexandria thought that the Greek philosophy had been given by
God to men by the lower angels. Up to the present time this
anthropomorphism continues to exercise its influence, not only

in the thousand forms of popular superstition, down to spirit-
rapping, but also in a way less evident perhaps, but all the
more prejudicial because it checks the development of the
sciences, in ' a course of symbolising myths, which were considered real theories,'[1] and in the hypostatising or quasi-per-
sonification of the faculties of the soul, of the animal and
vegetable powers, of the Ideas, and of the Categories, &c.
Kepler's Pythagorean theory of heavenly harmony, which
barred against him the way to Newton's great discoveries,
since it did not let him know the actual powers, depends upon
this way of looking at things, as much as the Ancient and
Aristotelian-Scholastic personification of the stars or their
moving principles as gods or angels.

Auguste Comte, the French philosopher, in his Philosophie
positive, expresses this relation of personification, mere quasi-
personification, and adequate description, by the distinction of
Theology, Metaphysics, and Positive Philosophy; for he believes whole doctrines to embody the logical mistakes which
explained lightning by an angry Jove, and fire by Phlogiston.
On the other side, the polemic of science against these childish
conceptions has not seldom mistaken the limits beyond which
it becomes unscientific, when it denies the really existing
analogy, and favours a false dualism. Into this error fell the
Anaxagorean physics, and still more the Cartesian natural-
philosophy, which, seeking only pressure and resistance in
nature, refused recognition to Gravitation and to the animal
and vegetable powers. The same mistake of scientific endeavour
induced Spinoza and many others to combat all Teleology,
true or false.

Final decision upon all these questions is only possible by
the help of considerations which belong to the Positive
Sciences. It belongs to Logic, however, to explain them
so far as the grounds of determination lie in the essential
nature of the human power of knowledge in general. A
Logic which leaves this problem untouched, leaves its task
unfulfilled in many essential relations.

[1] Alex. v. Humboldt, *Kosmos*, ii. 399; cf. i. 66 f.

That the same and the similar in things are recognised by the same and the similar in us is a doctrine agreed upon by the ancient *Oriental*, and by almost all the *Greek Philosophers* except *Anaxagoras*: cf. *Arist.* De Anima, i. 2, § 20. In modern times the same view comes back in the *Leibnizian* Monadology; in the *Kantian* view, that the end and aim of Nature is the analogue of the moral law; in the theory of *Herbart*, which traces back everything that has 'really' happened, or every change of the inner circumstances of a simple real existence (monad), to the analogy of conceptions, or of 'preservations of self' (Selbsterhaltungen), and to the relations of the conceptions of the human mind (Seele); in *Schelling's* Nature-philosophy; and in the *Hegelian* doctrine of the identity of thinking and being. *Schleiermacher* taught that the powers of essences in nature were to be looked at as the lower analogues of the human will, and the whole of nature as a fainter Ethic (Dial. p. 150). Man is a microcosm since he has in himself all grades of life, and hence constructs his conceptions of the external existence (Dial. p. 109). *Schopenhauer* forms his 'panthelematism' on the identification of the notions of power and will, but has not sufficiently noticed the distinction between a blind impetus and will consciously directed to an end. *Günther's* 'dualism' arises from the thought that the analogy between the categories, according to which nature and mind (Geist) respectively develope themselves, is not to be understood as Identity, but as involving an essential Opposition. He was fond of laying stress upon the opposition. *Beneke* has explained in the fullest and most satisfactory way [1] the problems of the theory of knowledge, which depend on this consideration. [2]

§ 43. In other phenomena, which cannot be looked on as merely subjective because of the consciousness

[1] *System der Metaph. und Religionsphil.* especially pp. 102–5, 110–13, 495–511.

[2] Cf. Trendelenburg, *Log. Untersuch.* 2nd ed. p. 460; 3rd ed. ii. 198 f.; *Hist. Beiträge zur Philos.* ii. 123–24.

that they are not merely dependent on our own mental causality, the transference of the analogues of our own mental (psychic) life, by means of which we know with proximate truth the psychic life both of other men and of animals, does not seem to hold good. These phenomena lead to the admission of a material (Stoff), which we call *Matter*, remaining in itself in dead stillness, and capable of change only by outer impulse. But the notion of matter so acquired cannot correspond with its actual existence. Every phenomenon objectively founded, as this very act of becoming a phenomenon itself testifies, and as the scientific investigation of the laws of nature makes evident, is to be traced back to some active power as its real basis. In all matter—and if there are atoms, in every atom—there must lie some internal conditions or *qualities*, which if they become mutually related in the immediate contact, or in the partial or total interpenetration of matters (Stoffe), become *powers* by their opposition in reference to each other.

The notions of *Matter* and *Power* denote two ways of comprehending things; on the one side by sense-perception, on the other by the analogy of the internal perception of our own power of will. *Helmholtz* rightly says,[1] 'Matter and power are abstractions from the actual; science calls the objects of the outer world matter (substance) according to their mere existence there, without regard to their effects on other objects, or on our organs of sense, but we attribute power to them considered as acting.' What *Herbart* taught of the qualities of his supposititious point-essences, which he calls 'simple real essences,' holds true of the qualities of extended things: they act in contact as powers.

[1] *Erhaltung der Kraft*, p. 4 f., Berlin, 1847.

§ 44. The co-existence and co-operation of a multiplicity of powers necessarily involve some real order of coherence and succession, or some real *existence in space* and *in time*. This cannot be of a kind different from the space and time of sense; for if the reality of development in time is recognised (§§ 40–43), then on the supposition that such a space of three dimensions as mathematics require really exists without our mind, and on it alone, the psychical-physiological facts which have place in our sense-affections are fully explained by natural laws. *Therefore the order in space and time belonging to real objects mirrors itself in the order in space and time of External and Internal Perception. Sense-qualities, however, colours, sounds, &c. are, as such, subjective only. They are not copies of motions, but are regularly and connectedly related to determinate motions as their symbols* (cf. § 38).

From the truth of Internal Perception (§ 40) it follows that succession in time at least is not a mere phenomenon, but a reality.[1] The reality of extension in space in three dimensions follows from the reality of time, and must be ascribed to things-in-themselves, and not merely to our apprehension of things. For the order in time empirically given in us—the change of night and day, the change of the seasons, &c.—is embodied in

[1] It follows not only that we apprehend the mental occurrence in the form of time, but that the mental occurrence itself goes on in us in time, and therefore also in other animate beings, and further by analogy that there is in real things a succession in time. A 'fallacy' occurs only in the unjustifiable transference of a 'form of intuition' only mentally (psychically) real in us to the external reality; for a subjective form of intuition could of course refer to 'an order of things quite incomprehensible to us,' but succession in time is a mental reality in us, and inference from us to other emances is logically correct.

mathematico-physical laws, which, according to the principles of Mechanics, can *only* exist on the supposition of an external space which agrees with the space of sense-perception in all essential relations.   For our senses are affected at certain times by certain things which exist in themselves outside of our consciousness.   The succession of phenomena conditioned by their affections is to be explained not by the mere internal connection between acts of consciousness, but by the wider connection which comprehends both the subject and the things-in-themselves which affect us.   The natural laws which belong to *this* connection relate to a space of three dimensions.   Newton's law in particular, according to which the intensity of gravity for unchanged masses is in inverse ratio to the *square* of the distance, necessarily presupposes a real space of three dimensions.   For in a space of only two dimensions the intensity must be inversely proportional to the distance itself; in a space of three dimensions, to the square of the distance; and in every other space to another function of the distance.   For since, on the hypothesis of two dimensions, the effect in any given distance is distributed on the circumference of the circle whose radius is the distance, and since, on the hypothesis of three dimensions, the effect is distributed on the surface of the corresponding sphere, and so on; and as the circumferences are to each other as the radii, and the superficies of the spheres as the quadrates of the radii, therefore the part of the whole effect which belongs to every individual point is in each case in the inverse ratio.[1]   In all physical phenomena, causes and effects are exactly commensurate as soon as they are reduced to motions in space, and a clear scientific insight into their real connection can be attained.   And this justifies the fundamental thought of this paragraph, which makes the perception-picture in its position in space and time strictly parallel with the existence in space and time properly belonging to objective reality.[2]

[1] As Halley (1656–1742) has shown; cf. my treatise on the fundamental contradiction in the Kantian view. *Altpreuss. Monatschrift*, 1869.

[2] In the foregoing argument, a 'brain really extended in three

The relation of sense-qualities, such as sounds and colours (Locke's 'secondary qualities'), to vibrations resembles that

dimensions' has not been presupposed. What has been already proved in the preceding paragraphs—that there is a plurality of real essences, that many exist outside of the consciousness of one essence, and that these may stand in certain changing relations to each other—serves only as a starting-point. The connection among phenomena which are in the consciousness of the perceiving essence—e.g. among astronomical events, as they occur in the firmament—is not exclusively conditioned by the subjective manner in which they are perceived. It also depends upon the way—by no means chaotic, by no means presenting a matter (*Stoff*) to be set in orderly arrangement à priori by the subject alone in each particular—in which it is affected by things lying outside its consciousness. If now these latter are conformable to other laws which are to be understood from space knowable geometrically to the essence perceiving, this essence would be able to attain to a *pure* geometry harmonious with itself, but could never be able to attain to an *applied* geometry harmonious with itself, nor to a geometrico-*physical* explanation adapted to phenomena conditioned by sense-affections. By means of the projection of the external into the internal any arrangement held objective by the percipient subject would arise, on whose basis certain expectations finding confirmation in experience are created. But this orderly arrangement, in part conditioned by a conformability to law different from the form of the intuition of the subject, would not be able to be understood from the peculiar nature of this form of intuition, as the decrease of gravity in inverse ratio to the *square* of the distance is from the *three* dimensions of space. For example, in a projection from an objective space which has $m \pm a$ dimensions into a subjective space of m dimensions, every relation of intensity of gravity to the distance understandable by the subject would vanish; and the subject confined to this form would construct deceptive laws, since it receives as objective the course of nature intuitively perceived by it, but cannot fully explain it according to the nature of its phenomenal space. Physical phenomena find throughout their most complete explanation in the supposition, that things-in-themselves exist in a space of three dimensions as we know it. It is at least very doubtful that any other supposition could be so brought into agreement with the facts. We have, therefore, every ground for believing that our conception of substances extended in space in three dimensions does not in some way symbolise things which exist in themselves in quite another way, but truly repre-

of sounds to letters.[1]   It is a constant relation (in the one case
following by natural necessity, in the other arbitrary), and
a sameness of combinations without similarity of elements.

The sceptical thought (cf. § 37) which asserts that our knowledge of the outer world is impossible, or at least unreliable,
because it cannot be compared with its objects, is finally overcome by this, that the consideration of the causal relation gives
a sufficient equivalent for the immediate comparison which is
wanting (just as the mathematical reckoning of distances
makes up for the want of direct measurement).   Des Cartes'
proof from the Véracité de Dieu, and Delboeuf's[2] from the
veracity of our thoughts, are expositions of our faith, not
strict proofs.[3]

It has been already seen that the *Kantian* Dualism, which
makes 'things-in-themselves' affecting us the exclusive source
of the material content of perception, and the subject the
exclusive source of its form and intuition-in-time and-in-
space, is untenable.   But *Fichte's* assertion still remains
possible, that matter and form have both a purely subjective
origin.   So does the *intermediate* assertion (which has found
supporters quite lately) that an element is present in the

sents things as they actually exist in three dimensions. Our conception
of things and their motions is, therefore, the result of such 'an organisation of the situation of our sensations' as effects the harmony, not discrepancy of things and their phenomena as to size and form or as to the
'primary qualities.' (Cf. my *Grund. der Gesch. der Phil.* iii. § 10.)
From the impossibility that motion can change itself in consciousness,
follows the necessity of accepting a latent consciousness, which, aroused
by definite motions, strengthened by combination and concentration,
can arise out of its latency.

[1] [Cf. Berkeley, *Theory of Vision*, Coll. Works, vol. i., Fraser's Ed.;
cf. also Editor's preface to the *Theory*, and Fraser's *Life and Philosophy
of Berkeley*, ch. x.]

[2] *Log.* pp. 73–78.

[3] [The same may be said of Sir W. Hamilton's appeal to the veracity
of consciousness (*Lect. on Metaph.* i. 264 ff.); edition of *Reid's Works*,
note A, p. 773 ff.; cf. Mill's *Exam. of Hamilton's Philos.* 3rd ed.
p. 72 f.]

things-in-themselves which, when it affects us, originates in us the forms of space and time, but that this element has a character essentially different from these forms. The possibility of such an assertion can be disproved, and the real truth of the forms of space and time can be proved, by reflecting upon internal perception and its co-operation with external. One must not presume to rise above the necessity of this scientific demonstration by a mere axiom, by which the agreement of our forms of intuition with those forms of existence is *called* something immediately certain—a postulate of reason, a necessity of thought, a something lying in the very notion of knowledge (since the validity of this notion, so understood, has first to be proved). Such dogmatic axioms, which make too comfortable pillows, will always lead back to scepticism and critical doctrines which they cannot confute. For example, in modern times, *Schopenhauer*, following Kant, says: 'One must be forsaken by all the gods to imagine that this visible world there outside as it fills space in three dimensions, is completely objectively real, and exists as it does without our co-operation.'[1] This is true as regards colour, sound, &c., but as regards extension and space it is false. And since we do not want for arguments to support our position, we need not care much about being forsaken by Schopenhauer's gods. The assertions of students of Nature of the Kantian School that the investigation of Nature has to do *always* and *above all* with phenomena, are to be corrected by what we have said above. They are true so far as regards the *results* of the sense-affections, but false as regards their *causes*. These causes, the things-in-themselves, the metaphysical bases of phenomena, are themselves objects in space and time. The thesis—the world of phenomena accommodates itself to things-in-themselves; and the antithesis, it accommodates itself to the organs of sense—are both one-sided and half-true. The world of phenomena is the common result of the two factors whose contributions can and must be adjusted. 'Secondary qualities'

[1] *Ueber die vierfache Wurzel des Satzes vom zureichenden Grunde,* 2nd ed. § 21, p. 51.

(sound, colour, heat, &c.), *as such*, are purely subjective; and they are symbols of motions. Time and space are both subjective and objective at the same time.

Schleiermacher rightly teaches[1]—' Space and time are not only conceptions of ours, they are the kind and way in which things themselves exist.' ' Space is the-being-the-one-outside-the-other of existences, Time the-being-the-one-outside-the-other of actions.' Schleiermacher further held[2] that if the contents of sense were conditioned by sense alone, there would result only a chaotic manifold of impressions. ' Organic function,' as such, has to do only with the ' chaotic material,' or the formless boundless manifold of what fills space and time. Schleiermacher distinguishes[3] *perception* from *organic function*. He defines the perception to be the unity of the organic and intellectual function with a preponderance of the organic. In *thought* proper intellectual function prevails, and in *intuition* both functions have equal prominence. Schleiermacher, however, has not made clear enough *what* the intellectual element is which enters into perception. If we hold that it is ' orderly arrangement in space and time,' we may make our theory agree with Schleiermacher's, and consider it to be its completion and more definite statement; but we cannot admit that the activity of sense or the ' organic function ' has not got this orderly arrangement. The senses seize upon all those forms of existence, as yet in unsettled unity and in ' chaotic' commixture, on whose separation the different forms of thought rest (e.g. the essential and the non-essential, on whose separation depends the formation of the notion; substantiality and inherence, which are the basis of the subject and the predicate of the judgment). They do not apprehend chaotically, but in distinct separation, those forms which make *their special* object, the relations of existence in space and time, or the external arrangement of things, in which the internal distinctly expresses itself. The *physiological* consideration of the senses of Sight and Touch shows that the capability to apprehend distinct positions is established in their organisation.

[1] *Dial.* p. 305 C.   [2] Ibid. §§ 108, 118, 185.   [3] Ibid. § 115.

The eye, it is true, does not see three dimensions; but mere sensation suffices to distinguish positions on a superficies, on which distinction rests all further discrimination of the actual form of what is seen, and is so far by no means chaotic. If one believed (with *Herbart* and *Lotze*) that all separation in space of parts of the organic image of sight and of the affections of the nervous vanishes in the spacelessness of the simple mental monads, in order to be reproduced in consciousness in a new way, out of the quality of sensation in general, or, according to *Lotze,* out of certain ' signs of place,' even on this hypothesis (which is not admissible from Schleiermacher's standpoint) it must be recognised that the production of every definite position of the picture conceived in space and time is conditioned by the position in space and time of each organic affection, and this again, on its side, by the position of the external thing affecting. The organic function even in this case would be by no means chaotic.

Again, Schleiermacher's view of the nature of the sense-activity may be refuted *directly* from his own dialectical principles. For Schleiermacher distinguishes, in existence generally, ' *Power* ' (Kraft) and ' *Action,*' and refers the former to existence-for-itself, and the latter to existence in connection with others. But the arrangement of real objects affecting our senses, and the organic function itself, fall under the notion of co-existence and co-operation or of ' Action.' The kind of this co-operation, however, can only be determined by the ' System of *Powers,*' and since, according to Schleiermacher, this is known to be undoubtedly conformable to reason, the co-operation must also be orderly. Hence organic function as ' The " Action " of things in us "[1] is not a chaotic but an orderly manifold of impressions. The same thing can also be proved *indirectly.* If the organic function, as such, produces a mere chaos of sensations, the function of reason could not stand in essential relation to it, but could only come after it, as something original and independent of it. Schleiermacher, in consequence of this opinion, ascribes to organic function this

[1] *Dial.* p. 56.

significance only, that it excites the intellectual to self-activity. He thinks that ' the system of all notions constituting science is given in a timeless way in one reason dwelling in all.'[1] These actual notions are always realised ' in connection with organic function;'[2] but organic function is not a co-operating factor in the formation of notions, it is only an exciting element, on occasion of which the notions, lying in the universal reason in individuals and in races of men, develope themselves in consciousness more fully and more purely.[3] Schleiermacher thus only allows organic function, as follows from the presupposition of its chaotic character, to influence the becoming conscious, not the formation and development of notions. But then he explains that ' pure thought ' in the Hegelian sense, or the self-sufficiency of intellectual power wholly freed from any intermixture with organic function, is impossible. He is right, but scarcely consistent; for the impossibility of pure thought of any kind contradicts throughout Schleiermacher's presuppositions about organic function, and the system of notions. Why should pure thought be impossible if these presuppositions are true? The mere excitement of intellectual activity might as well have happened from some other side than that of sense-activity,—from the will or the resolve to keep itself thinking, and from the living power of deliberation. Schleiermacher says, because ' the activity of the reason, when it is set up, apart from all activity of the organisation, is no longer thinking,'[4] or, because ' apart from all organic function no *ground of partition* can be found for the unity of existence.'[5] But this only proves that no system of *notions* can ever be given in the human reason in itself, which only needs successive awakening to consciousness; for every system of notions presupposes a *partition* of indeterminate abstract existence. If the doctrine of the impossibility of that pure thought, and the corresponding doctrine of the impossibility of partitioning the unity of existence into a plurality of distinct notions by means of mere intellectual

[1] *Dial.* p. 101.   [2] Ibid. p. 105.   [3] Ibid. p. 106 ff. § 177.
[4] Ibid. § 109, p. 57.   [5] Ibid. § 168, p. 96.

function, be held correct, the view of the chaotic character of
organic function, and the corresponding assertion that the system of notions is given in intellectual function, must be given
up. The content of perception reached by means of organic
affection must be recognised to be a co-operating factor in the
process of the formation of notions. The notion is by no
means reduced on this view to a 'merely secondary product of
the organic function'—a doctrine Schleiermacher rightly opposes;—an essential part in the formation of notions is attributed
to organic function. This part is to be more closely defined
by this, that by it the *external orderly arrangement* in space
and time is brought to consciousness. Then thinking led
from the *signs* contained in it to *the internal orderly arrangement, makes it signify* the moments constituting the essence of
things. This is also the way in which the *individual sciences*
actually proceed in the construction of their notions and judgments. The system of notions is not given in a lasting way
in the general subjective reason. It exists in the absolute
reason which comprehends all mere subjectivity and adjusts
it to objectivity. It is therefore as essentially requisite for
the subject, in order to reach science, to advance by means
of organic function, which is more powerful in relation to
objectivity, as to verify its results by means of its own intellectual power, which works more independently in the service
of the end and aim of knowledge.

This also presupposes that organic function is not a 'chaotic
manifold of impressions,' but is orderly, the mirroring of the
orderly arrangement in space and time which belongs to things,
and can warrant a sure starting-point for thought. Schleiermacher himself almost expressly recognises this, when he
makes the correspondence between thought and (external)
existence to be brought about by the real relation in which the
totality of existence stands to the organism;[1] for this presupposes
that this higher significance belongs to organic function. The
ascription of a chaotic character to organic function can only
be viewed as a remaining part of the Kantian subjectivism not

[1] *Dial.* § 106.

yet overcome, which supposes that all orderly arrangement
originates in the spontaneity of the subject, and must consequently be quite different from organic affection. The opposite expressions of Schleiermacher, on the other hand, rest
on the deeper and truer thought of a conformability to law
dwelling in the external reality, according to which organic
affection, as the immediate action of things in us, or as ' our
existence in so far as it is identical with the existence established
without us,'[1] must bear the character of an arrangement conformable to reason.[2]

[The reality of Space and Time appears to be a necessary
element in the Hamiltonian Philosophy of Common Sense, but
we do not find Sir *Wm. Hamilton* giving thoroughly consistent
utterances on this subject. He sometimes unreservedly assents
to the Kantian doctrine ; at others he insists upon adding to
the à priori and subjective Space and Time of Kant an à
posteriori and objective Space and Time acquired in perception ;[3] while his doctrine of the primary qualities of matter

[1] *Dial.* p. 56.

[2] In connection with this whole paragraph, cf. the Author's tract,
*Zur logischen Theorie der Wahrnehmung und der zunächst an die
Wahrnehmung geknüpften Erkenntnisswreisen*, in Fichte's *Zeitschrift
für Phil.*, New Series (Halle, 1857), xxx. 191–225 (especially
pp. 222–24, on the Reality of Space) ;—also my tract, *Zur Theorie der
Richtung des Sehens*, in Henle's and Pfeuffer's *Zeitschr. für rationelle
Medicin*, 3rd Series, 1858, v. 268–82 (especially on the distinction of
the objectively-real space from the space of the field of vision). Cf. also
my notes to my translation of Berkeley's *Principles of Human Knowledge*, Berlin, 1869.

The argument stated above for the extension of ' things-in-themselves'
in three dimensions, has been combated by Alb. Lange in his *Geschichte des Materialismus*, pp. 497–99, Iserlohn, 1866. I have answered
it partly in my *Grundr. der Geschichte der Philos.* 1st ed. iii. 279,
Berlin, 1866 ; p. 303, 2nd ed. 1868 ; and partly in this edition of my
Logik, in the notes appended to this section. Cf. my tract *Der Grund-
gedanke des Kantischen Kriticismus nach seiner Entstehungszeit und
seinem wissenschaftlichen Werth* in the *Altpreuss. Monatschrift*, 1869,
vi. pp. 215–21.

[3] [Cf. Hamilton's edition of *Reid's Works*, p. 126, note : *Reid's*

implies that space is known à priori and as objective. As the doctrine of the primary qualities is most essential to his system of philosophy, and most carefully elaborated by Hamilton, we may take it as his final deliverance. The primary qualities are all derivable from Space. They are, in fact, forms of Space. They are known as objective, and they are known à priori. Hence Hamilton must be held to believe in the objective existence and à priori nature of Space. He has not so explicitly expressed his opinion with regard to Time.[1]

Mr. Mill and *his School* deny the objective reality of Space and of Time. They are sensations worked up into permanent possibilities of sensation. All that they possess of reality, i.e. permanence, and objectivity, i.e. power to affect not one perceiving subject but several at the same time, they owe to the laws of association.[2] *Berkeley* and *Prof. Fraser*, while they refuse to believe in any other Space and Time than Sensible Space and Sensible Time, recognise: (1) An externality to our present and transient experience in *our own* possible experience past and future, and (2) An externality to our own conscious experience, in the contemporaneous, as well as in the past or future experience of other minds; and therefore admit the reality of space and time as far as that is contended for in this section.[3]]

Works, p. 641; *Discussions*, p. 273; *Lect. on Metaph.* i. 403; ii. 114, 166–70.

[1] Cf. for a very severe criticism of Hamilton's theory, Dr. J. H. Stirling's *Philosophy of Perception*, pp. 69–87 and passim.

[2] Cf. J. S. Mill's *Examination of Sir Wm. Hamilton's Philosophy*, 3rd ed. pp. 258–304; Bain's *Senses and Intellect*, 2nd ed. pp. 111, 197, 250, 370, 637. Cf. for an analogous doctrine, Herbert Spencer, *Psychology*, pp. 52, 241, 309.

[3] Cf. the *Life and Letters, &c. of Bishop Berkeley*, by Prof. Fraser, Oxford, Clarendon Press, 1871, ch. x.]

PART SECOND.

THE INDIVIDUAL CONCEPTION OR INTUITION IN ITS RELATION TO THE OBJECTIVE INDIVIDUAL EXISTENCE.

§ 45. THE *INDIVIDUAL CONCEPTION* OR *INTUITION* (representatio or conceptus singularis) is the mental picture of the individual existence, which is (or at least is supposed to be) objective.

External orderly arrangement, or that in Space and Time, which is represented by perception, is to be explained by the thought of the internal orderly arrangement, in which it is reflected. The first step towards the solution of the problem is naturally the discrimination of *individuals* by means of *individual conceptions.*

The word *conception* is not used here to mean a *perception reproduced,* nor to mean a *mental product generally.* It means the *mental picture of an individual existence,* whether presented in perception or reproduced in memory. A conception may be either an *individual conception* or *intuition,* which has to do with one individual (or with what belongs to one individual), or a *general conception,* which refers to a mutually-related group of individuals (or of what belongs to individuals), and forms the approximate mental (psychic) basis for the notion. In this section we shall explain what belongs equally to both kinds of conception.

§ 46. *Individual intuitions* gradually arise out of the original *blur* of perception, when man first begins to recognise himself, an *individual essence* in opposition to the outer world. This form of *individual existence* or *individuality* is transferred to any external existence whose appearance betokens that it can be isolated or set over against other phenomena. The *logical correctness* of the application of this form of knowledge is to be tested by the same criteria as the truth (cf. § 42) of all those elements of knowledge which originate in our internal, and go to complete our sense-perception. For: (a) (cf. § 40) In reference to one's own person, self-consciousness directly warrants the reality of our individual existence. (b) (cf. § 41) An existence analogous to our own must be attributed to all other persons, and therefore the form of existence as an individual essence. (c) (cf. § 42) The analogy of things without us to our own essence decreases gradually, but never vanishes wholly at any point. Hence we may allow ourselves to believe that the partition of the totality of impersonal existence into relatively independent individuals actually takes place, and is not brought by us by means of a merely subjective necessity. The sense-phenomena, however, taken along with the analogous gradations in the department of mental life, prove that the boundary, the individual determinate existence, and its development into a greater whole, becomes more indistinct and indefinite the lower any object stands on the gradual series of essences. (d) On the other side, the most complete individual independence, together with the widest and most intimate community of life and action, is to be found along with the greatest mental and moral height in the scale of being.

The intuition, or the individual conception, like perception (§§ 41–42), is correctly formed in proportion as the gradations in question have been observed.

The problems here treated often come up in the positive sciences of Botany and Zoology in particular cases. Their full solution cannot be reached by the special means which these sciences have at their disposal, but only by reference to general considerations belonging to Logic or the theory of knowledge. *Aristotle* does not enter very deeply into these questions either in his physical or in his metaphysical and logical writings. He calls individual essences the first substances (πρῶται οὐσίαι), without submitting to a stricter investigation the knowableness, essence, and limits of individuality. Questions such as the following first arose in modern times, and received full attention as scientific problems:—Is the true individual the plant or the single shoot (eye, bud, &c.; 'gemmae totidem herbae,' Linnaeus; cf. *Roeper*, Linnaea, p. 434, and other later botanical writings), the coral stem or the single coral insect? How far is the life of the embryo individual and independent, and how far part of the life of the mother, &c.? In natural science it has been seen that the individual cannot pretend to more reality than belongs to the genus, species and individual; that the individual is characterised not by unity of sensible appearance, but by unity in the course of development; that the individual plant is far inferior to the individual animal in internal unity. Cf. Rud. Virchow, Atome und Individuen, a lecture delivered in 1859,[1] where the individual is defined to be 'a single community where all parts co-operate to a similar end or act according to a definite plan.'

[1] Published in *Vier Reden über Leben und Krankheit*, pp. 35–76, Berlin, 1862.

In other provinces also the consciousness of the gradations of individuality is an essentially scientific demand, and a condition without which a solution of many important questions of debate cannot be reached. For example, the Homeric question between unitarians and separatists can only be got rid of by the scientific view (already attained by Aristotle) that the epic poem, because of its nature as an earlier and lower stage in the development of poetry, does not possess the strict comprehensive unity of the Drama, and yet does not exclude a certain poetic unity. The individual epic poet of that early age, belonging to an associated company of minstrels, had less independent individuality within his circle than the dramatist. The question to be asked is not, therefore, whether the poem is to be ascribed to one or to many, but *what part* of it is to be ascribed to the one and what to the many?—or, more particularly, what is to be presupposed as the pre-Homeric foundation? what is to be considered as the work of one master, who, trained in intimacy with the smaller poems of the earlier minstrels who sung the history and tales of the people, seized on and realised the thought of the greater epic? and what has been added by post-Homeric poets, and what praise or blame belongs to the rhapsodists, to the collectors, and, lastly, to the grammarians who arranged and made emendations and explanations?

The doctrine of *Spinoza* reduces all individuality to the same dead level of meaninglessness. The *Leibnizian* and *Herbartian* doctrine of monads, with equal incorrectness, transfers that full comprehensive individuality which belongs to the personal human spirit to the lowest bases of organic and inorganic life which they believe to be independent individual essences without extension in space. The *Kantian* critical philosophy believes that it has found the true mean between these two extremes, in the doctrine of the impossibility of settling the problem in question theoretically. It enumerates among the subjective elements of knowledge the categories of Unity, Plurality, and Totality, which, founded on the organisation of our means of knowing, are necessarily transferred by us to the world of

I

phenomena, but find no application to real existences or to things-in-themselves. *Schelling, Hegel,* and *Schleiermacher,* on the other hand, believe that these forms have a real validity. But when they come to determine the different gradations of individuality, Schelling and Hegel approach very closely the doctrine of Unity founded by Spinoza, and Schleiermacher, in certain considerations, almost adopts the individualism of Leibniz and Herbart.

[In Mr. Mill's system of philosophy, where all independent and objective reality depends only on association, where all external and internal things are only congeries of possibilities of sensation, there seems no place for a theory of individuality. But the fact that, so far as regards mind, there always remains a final inexplicability unable to be resolved into a series of feelings affords a basis for our own existence as an individual. And Mr. Mill's theory of inseparable association, i.e. that when certain sensations have been thought of together in certain ways they *cannot be thought* as existing apart, combined with his theory of the chemical composition of causes, according to which a whole of association may have a character which *is* quite different from the sum of the characters of the associated parts, affords ground for the individual existence of things.[1]]

§ 47. As the individual conception corresponds generally to the individual existence, so *its different kinds* or *forms* correspond to the *different kinds* or *forms* of *individual existence.* The individual existence is first recognised in independent objects. When the object of a conception makes up a whole, in which different parts, attributes, and relations may be distinguished, the different elements of such a conception may be considered singly to be conceptions. We must distinguish two cases here. Either the form of objective independence

[1 Cf. *Exam. of Sir Wm. Hamilton's Philos.* pp. 234–43, 305–27; and *Logic.* 7th ed. 405–12.]

is attributed to the objects of these conceptions, with the consciousness that this independence is only imagined not real, or these objects are absolutely perceived to be not independent. On these relations are based the forms of the *substantially concrete*, the *substantially abstract*, and the *verbal, attributive*, and *relative conception*. The forms of the individual conceptions and of their verbal expression, in their relation to the corresponding forms of existence (and these last themselves metaphorically), are the *Categories* in the *Aristotelian* sense of the word.

All these Categories are transferred from objectively valid conceptions to those whose objects are mere fictions (e.g. to mythical beings).

As the (*logical*) forms of conception correspond to the (*metaphysical*) forms of individual existence, so the (*grammatical*) forms or parts of speech correspond to the *logical*. A word is the expression in speech of a conception. The conception of an independently existing object is expressed by the *concrete substantive*, to which must be added the *substantive pronoun*, which denotes a person or thing in its relation to the speaker. The conception of that which does not exist independently, but is intuitively perceived under the borrowed form of individual existence, is denoted by the *abstract substantive*. The conception of that which does not exist independently, as such, whether an act, property (or quality), or relation, is expressed by the *verb*, the *adjective* with the *adjective pronoun*, and the *adverb*, and by the *preposition* with the *forms of inflection*. *Numerals* can only be understood on the basis of the formation of notions; for they presuppose the subsumption of similar objects under the same notion. *Conjunctions* can only be comprehended on the basis of the formation of judgments and inferences; for they bind together sentences and parts of sentences, whose opposite references express the corresponding relations of conceptions to each other, which on their side again must rest on relations between real combinations. (*Prepositions*, on the other hand, by means of the relations between single words and complexes of words, which express the corresponding relations between single conceptions, denote the relations of single things, actions, &c. to each other.) *Interjections* are not properly words, but only direct expression of feelings not developed into conceptions or thoughts.

'The construction of all language proves that the oldest form was essentially that which is preserved in some languages of the simplest construction (e.g. in the Chinese). All languages have started from significant sounds, simple sounds picturing intuitions, conceptions, and notions, which do duty in every relation, i.e. as every grammatical form, without requiring for each function an audible expression—so to speak, an organ. In this earliest stage in the growth of languages neither verbs nor nouns, conjugation nor declension, are to be distinctively distinguished. The oldest form for the words which now sound *deed*, *done*, *do*, *doer*, *doing*, was, when the Indo-Germanic stem-language arose, *dha*; for this *dha* (i.e. to set, to do—Old Indian *dha*, Old Bactrian *dha*, Greek θε, Lithuanian and Slavonic *de*, Gothic *da*, High German *ta*) appears to be the common root of all these words. In a somewhat later stage of the development of the Indo-Germanic language, in order to express distinct references, they repeated the roots twice, not yet supposed to be words, along with another root, and linked them together into a word. In order, for example, to denote the first person of the present, they said *dha-dha-mi*, from which, in the later stage of the growth of the language, by fusion of the elements into one whole, and by the consequent possibility of change, came the root dhadhâmi (Old Indian dádhâmi, Old Bactrian dadhâmi, Greek τίθημι, Old High German tôm, tuom, tětâmi, New High German thue). In that earliest form *dha* there lay, as yet unseparated and undeveloped, the different grammatical references, their whole verbal and nominal modifications; and this can still be observed in languages which have remained in the stage of simplest development. This example, selected by accident, represents all the words of the Indo-Germanic language.'[1]

The logical consciousness of the different forms of conception originally developed itself with and in the grammatical consciousness of the different parts of speech, and with the metaphysical consciousness of the different forms of existence.[2]

Plato recognises the grammatical opposition of the ὄνομα and ῥῆμα.[3] The author of the dialogue Sophistes[4] refers them to the opposition between the corresponding forms of existence—Thing and Action—and refers these last to the more general opposition of Rest and Motion, which he immediately subserves together with that of Identity and Difference under the universal unity of Being.

Aristotle developes the division of the parts of speech by adding the σύνδεσμος or Particle (the more special meaning of conjunction was first given to this word by later grammarians). He taught that the word, the ὄνομα and the ῥῆμα, corresponds to the conception, the νόημα:—ἔστι μὲν οὖν τὰ ἐν τῇ φωνῇ τῶν ἐν τῇ ψυχῇ παθημάτων σύμβολα.—τὰ οὖν ὀνόματα αὐτὰ καὶ τὰ ῥήματα ἔοικε τῷ ἄνευ συνθέσεως καὶ διαιρέσεως νοήματι (De Interpr. 1). The ὄνομα is a conventional designation which does not include a reference to time, but the ῥῆμα does. The σύνδεσμος, according to Aristotle, is a dependent φωνὴ ἄσημος, e.g. μέν, ἤτοι, δή.[5] In the Poëtics (c. xx.) the ἄρθρον is also named; but the reading is uncertain, and the genuineness of the passage doubtful. Aristotle calls single conceptions and words τὰ ἄνευ συμπλοκῆς, τὰ κατὰ μηδεμίαν συμπλοκὴν λεγό-

[1] Aug. Schleicher, *Die Darwin'sche Theorie und die Sprachwissenschaft*, pp. 21-23, Weimar, 1863.

[2] Cf. Classen, *De Gramm. Graecae Primordiis*, Bonn, 1829; L. Lersch, *Die Sprachphilosophie der Alten*, Bonn, 1838-41; Bd. ii. (*die Sprachkategorien*), Bonn, 1840; G. F. Schömann, *Die Lehre von den Redetheilen nach den Alten*, Berlin, 1862; H. Steinthal, *Geschichte der Sprachwiss. bei den Griechen und Römern* (with special reference to Logic), Berlin, 1863.

[3] *Theaet.* p. 206 D; cf. *Cratylus*, p. 399 B.   [4] P. 261 E sqq.

[5] *De Interp.* c. ii. ff.; *Poët.* c. xx. (cf. notes to my ed. and transl.).

μένα,[1] i.e. the uncombined elements, into which the proposition or judgment (λόγος) dissolves when analysed. Aristotle divides conceptions according to their *formal* points of difference. In this division he proceeds on the fundamental thought that conceptions as elements of thought must correspond with the elements of what actually exists objectively, and their differences of form to the differences of form in what is conceived. Every conception, and so also its verbal expression or word, must denote either: 1. a substance; 2. a quantity; 3. a quality; 4. a relation; 5. a where; 6. a when; 7. a position; 8. a habit; 9. an action; or 10. a passion: —

Τῶν κατὰ μηδεμίαν συμπλοκὴν λεγομένων ἕκαστον ἤτοι οὐσίαν σημαίνει ἢ ποσὸν ἢ ποιὸν ἢ πρός τι ἢ ποῦ ἢ ποτὲ ἢ κεῖσθαι ἢ ἔχειν ἢ ποιεῖν ἢ πάσχειν (De Categ. iv. 1 B, 25). The Aristotelian examples are: 1. ἄνθρωπος, ἵππος; 2. δίπηχυ, τρίπηχυ; 3. λευκόν, γραμματικόν; 4. διπλάσιον, ἥμισυ, μεῖζον; 5. ἐν Λυκείῳ, ἐν ἀγορᾷ; 6. ἐχθές, πέρυσιν; 7. ἀνάκειται, κάθηται; 8. ἀναδέδεται, ὥπλισται; 9. τέμνει, καίει; 10. τέμνεται, καίεται.

The Categories are stated in this completeness in the Topics,[2] where the first, as commonly happens, is called τί ἐστιν. Single categories are mentioned in many places. Anal. Post. i. 22, Phys. v. 1, Metaphys. v. 7, leave out κεῖσθαι and ἔχειν. In Anal. Post. i. 22, οὐσία is opposed to συμβεβηκότα.[3] Aristotle calls these ten forms τὰ γένη or τὰ σχήματα τῆς κατηγορίας or τῶν κατηγοριῶν. The shorter and more convenient designation, κατηγορίαι, occurs repeatedly.

With Aristotle κατηγορία means originally assertion or predication, and so the expression τὰ γένη τῶν κατηγοριῶν or αἱ κατηγορίαι may be translated the kinds of assertion or of predicates. If, then, Category means that which naturally takes the place of predicate, this meaning would suit most of the last nine forms, but would not suit the first, for the first naturally takes the place of the subject. It is only the conceptions of genera or of the so-called second substances of Aristotle, not the indi-

---

[1] *Cat.* c. ii. 1 A, 16; c. iv. 1 B, 25.   [2] i. 9, 103 B, 20.

[3] Prantl (*Gesch. der Logik*) gives a very good tabular scheme of the places where they are mentioned.

vidual conception which belongs to the individual substance, to substance in the first and fullest sense of the word, that take easily and naturally the place of the predicate. The individual substance, on the other hand, can only be asserted as predicate in combination with a subject not determined according to its proper nature; as, e.g. in the sentences—'This wise man is Socrates,' 'This one who approaches is Callias.'

But since Aristotle has also included individual substances under the designation κατηγορίαι, he cannot mean predicates in general, but predicates of certain propositions. The full designation κατηγορίαι τοῦ ὄντος, or τῶν ὄντων, shows what propositions Aristotle has in view. Every ὄν (in the widest sense of the word) is either an οὐσία or a ποσόν or a ποιόν, &c. All definite conceptions, whether substantive, adjective or verbal, &c., are predicates of their objects, the things, properties, actions. &c. in a proposition whose subject is formed of this object conceived only indistinctly as any kind of ὄντα in general. Τοῦτο τὸ ὄν, or τὸ προκείμενον,[1] or τὸ ἐκκείμενον,[2] is to be thought of as subject. By a well-known and not uncommon grammatical analogy the plural denotes the kinds; the κατηγορίαι τοῦ ὄντος[3] are the kinds or different forms of categories, i.e. of predications, and also conceptions, of the existent so far as they correspond to the kinds or different forms of the existent, and by metonymy are these last themselves. The notion, kinds or forms, may be expressed not only by the plural, but also by a word added to κατηγορία or κατηγορίαι, such as σχήματα or γένη. Τὸ σχῆμα τῆς κατηγορίας is the kind of assertion about the existent, of predication of the existent, or form of conceiving the existent, whether the conception be substantive, i.e. denoting what is substantial, or adjective, i.e. denoting a quality, &c.[4] The first Category, that of substance, belongs, according to Aristotle, partly to his so-called first substances (πρῶται οὐσίαι), i.e. individuals, partly to second substances (δεύτεραι οὐσίαι), i.e. kinds and genera. In the first substances Aristotle distinguishes matter (ὕλη or

[1] According to *Top.* i. 5, p. 102 a, 31.   [2] Ibid. i. 9, p. 103, b, 30.
[3] *Metaph.* ix. 1, 1015 b, 28.   [4] Ibid. v. 28, § 7.

ὑποκείμενον), form (εἶδος or μορφή or τὸ τί ἦν εἶναι, or ἡ κατὰ
λόγον οὐσία), and the whole (τὸ ἐκ τούτων ἀμφοῖν or τὸ σύνολον).
Aristotle comprehends[1] the nine remaining kinds of conception under the common name of τὰ συμβεβηκότα.   He sometimes distinguishes[2] three chief classes, οὐσία, πάθη, and πρός
τι.[3]

[1] *Analyt. Post.* i. 22, 83 a, 25.
[2] *Metaph.* xiv. 2, 1089 a, 23.
[3] It is not certain how this doctrine of the Categories may have
developed itself in the mind of Aristotle. Trendelenburg [*] believes that
Aristotle had been led to it by the consideration of grammatical relations—viz. of the parts of speech—whose characteristics were embodied
in the terms (πτώσεις). The *relationship* of the doctrine of the Categories to the grammatical doctrine of the parts of speech has been
thoroughly, acutely, and evidently exhibited by Trendelenburg. But
it is at least doubtful that the *origin* of the doctrine of the Categories
was a consideration of the *parts of speech* and their distinction according
to πτώσεις. The Aristotelian division of the parts of speech (see above)
is too little developed to favour this assertion. ὄνομα and ῥῆμα correspond well enough to οὐσία and συμβεβηκός, but cannot supply a basis
for the ten categories. Moreover, Aristotle adds to the πτώσεις † forms
of verbal inflection on which he has based no verbal categories (as the
tenses ὑγίαινεν and ὑγιανεῖ). When he further adduces a substantive
(καιρός) as an example of a logical πρός τι, this is evidently independent
of the distinction of the parts of speech, and rests on essentially different grounds.

Aristotle, as Trendelenburg himself recognises, has distinguished not
so much parts of speech as parts of the sentence (subject and predicate,
and different forms of the predicate). He defines: ὄνομα ἐστι φωνὴ
σημαντικὴ κατὰ συνθήκην ἄνευ χρόνου '—ῥῆμα δέ ἐστι τὸ προσσημαῖνον
χρόνον;‡ but adjectives (such as ἴσκιος, λευκός), as far as they are
predicates with ἐστίν, are considered to be ῥήματα ;§ although elsewhere
λευκός is called ὄνομα, because it does not connote time. In the distinction of ὀνόματα and ῥήματα, and in the distinction of τὰ κατὰ μηδεμίαν συμπλοκὴν λεγόμενα, Aristotle seems to have kept to the empirically
given forms of sentences, such as ' Socrates is wise, Socrates disputes, in

[*] *De Arist. Categ.* 1833 ; *Geschichte der Kategorienlehre*, pp. 11–13,
1845.
   † *De Interp.* c. iii. 16 a, 16.   ‡ Ibid. c. i. and ii.   § Ibid. c. i. and x.

The Stoics reduced the ten Aristotelian Categories to four, which they call τὰ γενικώτατα (the most universal kinds), and refuted,' &c. The distinction of ὀνόματα and ῥήματα seems to have been the basis of that of οὐσίαι and πάθη, and the distinction of the parts of speech seems to have been the basis of that of the nine kinds of συμβεβηκότα.

Still Aristotle in his construction of the doctrine of the Categories may have been influenced by definite philosophical references, and especially by his polemic against the Platonic doctrine of ideas. Aristotle sought to recognise the universal in the particular. He based his speculation on the empirical, and tested the truth of the doctrine of ideas in its relation to the actual existence presented to him. In this critical endeavour it could not have escaped his quick glance that all phenomena are not to be considered in the same way as pictures of ideas. Some contradicted this view in formal reference. When he came to account for this inconsistency, he must have found its cause in this, that Plato thought his ideas, and could only think them as ideas, under a single form of existence, the form of substantiality; while what actually exists is represented under different forms. The idea of the good, e.g. must be of substantial existence, and at the same time must be the common ideal for everything which actually appears good. But this latter is only in part something substantial, as God, the νοῦς (thought substantial by Aristotle). It is partly something predicative or accidental—an action, a property, a relation; as, a good deed, the goods of the mind, the usefulness of means to an end, &c. This formal difference contradicts the formal unity of the common ideal accepted by Plato.[*] The methodical and systematising mind of Aristotle, led to pay attention to the difference of the forms of existence by considerations of this kind, would soon attempt to draw up a comprehensive series of these. In his investigation into the Categories, he had positive points of connection with the investigations, carried on by Plato or a Platonist in the Sophistes, upon the Existent generally, about thing and action, resistance and motion, identity and difference, unity, indefinite greatness and smallness, and in the further discussions[†] upon relative notions, upon ποιεῖν and πάσχειν, as kinds of γένεσις.[‡] But these would assist him only in a small degree, because with Plato the question of the forms of the individual existence is entirely subordinated to the question of the relation of the

---

[*] *Arist. Eth. Nic.* i. 4; *Eth. Eud.* i. 8; *Metaph.* i. 9, xiii. 4, xiv. 2.
[†] As in *De Rep.* iv. 438.   [‡] *Soph.* p. 218.

believe to be forms of objective reality. They are—1. The Substrate (τὸ ὑποκείμενον); 2. The (essential) Property (τὸ ποιόν); 3. The (unessential) Quality (τὸ πὼς ἔχον); 4. The Relation (τὸ πρός τι πὼς ἔχον).[1] They subordinate all these Categories to the most universal of all notions, to that of ὄν or (probably later) to that of τί. The Stoics also develope the doctrine of the parts of speech. They define the ἄρθρον as a species of word, the article namely, and they afterwards add the adverb (πανδέκτης or ἐπίρρημα), and divide the ὄνομα into κύριον and προσηγορία.[2] The ἐπίρρημα serves for the extension of the predicate, and the σύνδεσμος for the combination of the chief parts of discourse with each other. The doctrine of the eight parts of speech first arose in the Alexandrine era. The constituent parts of the thought, and therefore of speech, had been separated by philosophers from the logical point of view. The grammarians undertook to arrange the empirically given material of language. They joined to single definite parts of speech the terms used by philosophers in a wider sense, and they introduced new terms for the others. The σύνδεσμος, which

individual to the universal. The elaboration of the Categories is rather to be considered as the independent work of Aristotle.

Cf. Bonitz, *Sitzungsberichte der phil.-hist. Classe der Wiener Akad. der Wiss.* Bd. x. pp. 591–645, 1853; Brandis, *Gesch. der Gr.-Röm. Phil.* ii. 2 a, p. 375 ff.; Prantl, *Gesch. der Logik*, i. p. 182 ff., 1855; Wilh. Schuppe, *Die Aristotelischen Kategorien, im Jubiläumsprogramm des Gleiwitzer Gymnasiums*, Gleiwitz, 1866. [Cf. also Manuel, in his edition of *Aldrich*, Appendix, Note D, p. 175, where he follows Trendelenburg.]

[1] These categories correspond to the three classes of categories placed together by Aristotle (*Metaph.* xiv. 2, 1089 a, 23)—τὰ μὲν γὰρ οὐσίαι, τὰ δὲ πάθη, τὰ δὲ πρός τι—the first and second to the first, the third to the second, and the fourth to the third.

[2] Diog. Laert. vii. 57; Charis. ii. 175. Cf. *Priscian*, ii. 15, 16: Partes igitur orationis secundum dialecticos duae, nomen et verbum; quia hae solae etiam per se conjunctae plenam faciunt orationem; aliae autem partes syncategoremata, hoc est consignificantia appellabant: secundum Stoicos vero quinque sunt ejus partes—nomen, appellatio, verbum, pronomen sive articulus, conjunctio.

had denoted both conjunction and preposition, from this time
denoted the former only, and the preposition[1] was called the
πρόθεσις. The ἀντωνυμία (the pronoun) was separated from
the noun. The participle (μετοχή) came in between the verb
and the noun. Adjectives and numerals were added to
the noun. The interjection was not reckoned an actual
part of speech. Priscian, in his enumeration of the 'octo
partes orationis,' followed in the footsteps of Apollonius Dys-
colus. His theory remained the standard one for following
times, while the Aristotelian doctrine of the Categories prevailed in the Middle Ages.

The formal metaphysical notions of *Des Cartes* and *Spinoza*
—substantia, attributum, modus; those of *Locke*—substance,
mode, relation; those of *Wolff*—ens, essentialia, attributa,
modi, relationes extrinsecae—are related to the Stoical doctrine
of the Categories. The *Leibnizian* five universal divisions of
essence (cinq titres généraux des êtres)—Substances, Quantities, Qualities, Action or Passion, and Relations—come
nearer the Aristotelian division.

The *Kantian* Categories, or 'pure stem-notions of the understanding,' do not serve as the metaphysical basis of forms of
conception, but of relations of judgments.

Herbart considers the forms of common experience—Thing,
Property, Relation, Negation; and the categories of the
internal apperception—Sensation, Science, Volition, Action—
to be the results of the psychological mechanism, and without
metaphysical or logical significance.

Hegel understands by the Categories, the universal, intelligible essentialities which enmesh all actuality.

Schleiermacher founds his formal division of notions into
'subject and predicate notions,' which he makes parallel with
the grammatical division of words denoting notions into nouns
and verbs, on the distinction of the forms of existence, of
being set for itself, and of co-existence, or of things and actions.
Abstract nouns are substantives which make the action sub-

---

[1] Perhaps Aristotle's ἄρθρον is the preposition and also the article;
cf. my transl. of the *Poetics*, Berl. 1869, note 95.

stantive in order to use it as a subject. Co-existence divides into activity and passivity, doing and suffering. The adjective which expresses the quality—i.e. the result of an activity already embodied in substantial existence, must be thought to arise by means of participles and other verbals out of the verb (Dial. p. 197).

Lotze[1] divides the manifold notions we find in our consciousness into three great groups of object-notions, predicative (i.e. verbal and adjectival) notions, and relation-notions. In each the peculiarity of the central point, as the point of distribution of the attributes, conditions the whole configuration of the parts.

[*Hamilton* thinks that the doctrine of the Categories belongs to Metaphysics, not to Logic. He regards the Categories of Aristotle as a classification of existences, and thinks them liable as such to many objections. He would substitute for them: 1. The Supreme Category Being ($\tau\grave{o}$ $\mathring{o}\nu$, ens). This is primarily divided into, 2. Being by itself (ens per se), and 3. Being by accident. Being by itself is the first Category of Aristotle. Being by accident includes his other nine.[2]

J. S. Mill thinks the Categories of Aristotle an enumeration of nameable things, and as such ' a mere catalogue of the distinctions rudely marked out by the language of familiar life, with little or no attempt to penetrate, by philosophical analysis, to the rationale even of those common distinctions.' As ' a substitute for this abortive classification of existences ' Mr. Mill offers the following:—1. Feelings, or States of consciousness. 2. The Minds which experience these feelings. 3. The Bodies, or external objects, which excite certain of those feelings, together with the powers or properties whereby they excite them. 4. The Successions and Co-existences, the Likenesses and Unlikenesses, between feelings or states of consciousness.[3]]

Cf. *Trendelenburg*, Gesch. der Kategorienlehre, Berl. 1846.

---

[1] *Log.* p. 77 ; cf. pp. 42, 50. [2] [*Lect. on Metaph.* i. 197-201.
[3] *Logic*, 7th ed. i. 49-81.]

§ 48. A conception is *clear* (notio clara in opposition to notio obscura) when it has sufficient strength of consciousness to enable us to distinguish its object from all other objects. It is *distinct* (notio distincta in opposition to notio confusa) when its individual elements are also clear, and consequently when it suffices to distinguish the elements of its object from each other.

The *Cartesian* criterion of truth (s. § 24) gave rise to a closer enquiry into the essential nature of clearness and distinctness. The definitions given above are those of Leibniz (§ 27). They are to be found in all the Logics of the Wolffian and Kantian period, where a fundamental significance is often attached to them. Some of the later logicians, on the other hand, have undeservedly disregarded them. Clearness and distinctness were overrated in the seventeenth and eighteenth centuries, but were undervalued in the first half of the nineteenth.

§ 49. An *Attribute* (nota, τεκμήριον) of an object is everything in it, by which it is distinguished from other objects. The conception of an attribute is contained in the conception of the object as *a part of its conception* (representatio particularis).

Attributes are attributes of things, of an *object* which is real (or conceived as if it were real). One can only speak correctly of the attributes of a *conception* in so far as it is considered to be something objective, i.e. as it is the object of thinking directed upon it. ' To receive an attribute into a conception ' is a shorter expression for ' to bring into consciousness the attribute of a thing by means of the corresponding part-conception, or to receive into the conception an element by means of which the attribute of the thing under consideration is conceived.

§ 50. The individual attributes of an object do not
make a mere aggregate, but stand to each other and to
the whole in definite relations, on which depend their
grouping together, their peculiar character, and their
very existence. This real relation must mirror itself
in the relation of the part-conceptions to each other and
to the whole conception. The sum total of the part-
conceptions is the *content* (complexus) of a conception.
The analysis of the content of a conception into part-
conceptions, or the statement of the individual attributes of its object, is called *partition*.

So far as the subjectively-formal Logic leaves unnoticed
that real relation, it can only apprehend the combination of
marks under the inexact scheme of a sum, or under the inadequate, and still insufficient, picture of a product. If one
of the numbers to be added is removed, this does not affect
the other numbers to be added, and the sum is lessened only
by the value of the number removed. If a factor is = 0, then
the whole product is = 0. But the removal of an attribute
ought neither to leave the other attributes undisturbed nor
annihilate the whole. Both can happen in certain cases, but
in general the other attributes are partly removed, partly
modified by the removal (real, or thought to be real) of an
attribute, and the whole is not removed with it.

The expression *Content* has been formed after ὑπάρχειν.[1]
The expression *mutual determination* of attributes, which
Lotze[2] uses to designate the dependence of the attributes on
each other, would be convenient if the term *determination*
were not already used in another cognate sense (see below, §
52).

[1] Arist. *Anal. Post.* i. 4: ἐνυπάρχειν ἐν τῷ λόγῳ τῷ τί ἐστι λέγοντι
or ἐνυπάρχειν ἐν τῷ τί ἐστιν.   [2] *Log.* p. 58.

PART THIRD.

*THE NOTION ACCORDING TO CONTENT AND EXTENT
IN ITS RELATION TO THE OBJECTIVE ESSENCE AND
TO THE GENUS.*

§ 51. WHEN several objects agree in certain attributes and their conceptions in part of their content
(§§ 49–50), there may result the *GENERAL CONCEPTION*
(allegemeine Vorstellung, Schema, notio sive representatio communis, generalis, universalis). It arises by
attention to the similar attributes and *abstraction* of the
dissimilar, in consequence of the psychological law of
the mutual arousing of similar mental (psychic) elements and the reciprocal strengthening of the similar
in consciousness. The more general conception arises
in the same way from several general conceptions which
agree in part of their content.

The *general* conception (in opposition to the individual conception) is not to be confounded with the *abstract* (in opposition to the concrete, s. § 47). The divisions cross each other.
There are concrete and abstract individual conceptions, and
concrete and abstract general conceptions. The usage of some
logicians, which identifies *abstract* and *general*, is not to be
recommended.[1] Grammar distinctly distinguishes the two.

[1 Cf. Mill's *Logic*, 7th ed. i. 29.]

Wolff's terminology agrees with the grammatical. He[1] defines the 'notio abstracta' as that 'quae aliquid, quod rei cuidam inest vel adest (scilicet rerum attributa, modos, relationes) repraesentat absque ea re, cui inest vel adest;' but the 'notio uuiversalis'[2] as that 'qua ea repraesentantur, quae rebus pluribus communia sunt.'

Aristotle noticed that one experience embracing them all together in it may arise from several similar perceptions if memory preserves them; for the universal remains in the mind and as it were finds a resting-place there, and this universal is the one amongst the many, which dwells in the many as the same :—Ἐνούσης δ᾽ αἰσθήσεως τοῖς μὲν τῶν ζῴων ἐγγίνεται μονὴ τοῦ αἰσθήματος, τοῖς δ᾽ οὐκ ἐγγίνεται. Ὅσοις μὲν οὖν μὴ ἐγγίνεται,— οὐκ ἔστι τούτοις γνῶσις ἔξω τοῦ αἰσθάνεσθαι. ἐν οἷς δέ, ἔνεστιν αἰσθομένοις (or, according to Trendelenburg's Conjecture, μὴ αἰσθανομένοις, The Codices have mostly αἰσθανομένοις without μή, one, D, ἢ μή) ἔχειν ἔτι ἐν τῇ ψυχῇ.—Ἐκ μὲν οὖν αἰσθήσεως γίνεται μνήμη, ἐκ δὲ μνήμης πολλάκις τοῦ αὐτοῦ γινομένης ἐμπειρία, ἐκ δὲ ἐμπειρίας ἢ ἐκ παντὸς ἠρεμήσαντος τοῦ καθόλου ἐν τῇ ψυχῇ, τοῦ ἑνὸς παρὰ τὰ πολλά, ὃ ἂν ἐν ἅπασιν ἓν ἐνῇ ἐκείνοις τὸ αὐτό, τέχνης ἀρχὴ καὶ ἐπιστήμης.[3] Aristotle calls Abstraction ἀφαίρεσις.[4] The opposite of ἀφαίρεσις is πρόσθεσις.[5]

The functions of Attention and Abstraction, which were ascribed by earlier writers for the most part to the 'understanding,' to a quasi-personifying general power, within the whole personality of the mind, have more recently by *Herbart, Beneke* [*Hamilton* and *Mill*] been reduced to psychological laws.[6]

[1] *Log.* § 110. [2] Ibid. § 54.
[3] Arist. *Anal. Poster.* ii. c. xix. 99 a, 36 ; *De An.* iii. 2, 425 a, 24.
[4] *Anal. Post.* i. c. xviii. 81 a, 3 ; cf. *De Anim.* iii. 4, § 8, ibique comm. Trendelenburg.
[5] *De Coelo,* p. 299 a, 16 ; *Anal. Poster.* i. c. xxvii. 87 a, 34. Cf. Plato's *Rep.* vii. 534 b : ἀπὸ τῶν ἄλλων πάντων ἀφελὼν τὴν τοῦ ἀγαθοῦ ἰδέαν, separating the iden of the good from all others.
[6] Cf. Berkeley's remarks on Abstraction in the introduction to his *Prin. of Hum. Knowl.,* and note 5 to my translation. [Fraser's edition of Berkeley's *Collected Works,* i. 140 f.]

Herbart also rightly remarks that a pure separation of the like elements from the unlike may be a logical ideal, which can easily be postulated by a definition, but can be actually realised only approximately by a process of abstraction. We determine to leave out of our consideration that kind of difference which is not connected with a certain course of thoughts, but it can never be quite rooted out of consciousness in the actual conception. The purest separation possible comes about when conscious scientific insight is superadded to the unconscious activity of the psychological law.[1]

Before Kant's time the grammatical rule in use was,—to abstract the common attributes. Thus, e.g. *Lambert* says,[2] ' We abstract the common attributes from those which belong specially to each individual, in order to get at those which, when so abstracted, make a general or abstract notion.' *Kant*[3] finds fault with this usage, and thinks the only valid expression is,— to abstract the dissimilar elements in the conception in order to attend to the similar. On his authority this latter rule has become the prevailing one, and cannot well be given up again. It is, however, open to the grammatical inconvenience that it does not agree with the procedure of the *abstract* participle, and to the actual defect that it lays too much stress on what is only an action of less importance. For (as Kant himself recognises) it is not the becoming unconscious of dissimilar elements, but the concentration of consciousness on the similar, that is the essential thing in what is called the process of abstraction.

[*Hamilton* adopts the phraseology of Kant. He explains further that Attention and Abstraction are only the same process viewed in different relations—the positive and negative poles of the same act. He generalises the action of Attention and Abstraction into the rule,—Pluribus intentus minor est ad singula sensus. The points of resemblance among things are discovered by Comparison, and by Attention constituted into

---

[1] Cf. I. H. Fichte, *Grundzüge zum System der Philosophie*, I. Abth. *Das Erkennen als Selbsterkennen*, § 86 ff.

[2] *N. Org.* i. § 17.   [3] *Log.* ed. by Jäsche, p. 116.

K

exclusive objects; by the same act they are also reduced in
consciousness from multitude to unity; for objects are the
same to us when we are unable to distinguish their conceptions.[1]]

The process of Abstraction is reciprocally related to the
designation of many similar objects by the same *word*. This
sameness of designation is possible by the process of Abstraction, and the result of this process is itself secured and made
permanent by the sameness of designation. Extreme Nominalism is wrong, however, when it seeks to reduce the process of
Abstraction to a mere identity of verbal relation.[2]

§ 52. *DETERMINATION* (πρόσθεσις) means the formation of less general conceptions out of the more general.
The content of these last is increased by the addition
of new elements of conception appropriate to the object
conceived, and what remained undetermined in the
more general notion becomes more closely determined
(determinatur). The formation of new valid conceptions implies an insight into the real relation of
dependence among the attributes.

Subjectively-formal logic, from the essential demand of its
principles, is not able to lay down the rule, that, in the addition
of new elements of content, reference must be had to the real
relation of the characteristics to each other and to the whole.

§ 53. The *EXTENT* (Ambitus, Sphaera, sometimes
extensio) of a conception is the totality of those conceptions whose similar elements of content (cf. § 50) make

---

[1] [*Lect. on Logic*, i. 123 ff.; cf. *Lect. on Metaph.* i.; cf. Mill, *Exam.
of Sir Wm. Hamilton's Philos.* 3rd ed. pp. 364 ff.; Mansel, *Proleg.
Log.* 2nd ed. p. 65, where he distinguishes, as above, the unconscious
psychological process from the conscious scientific procedure.

[2] As Hobbes did; see *Computatio sive Logica*, c. ii.; *Leviathan*,
pt. i. ch. iv.]

up its content. The enumeration of the parts of the extent of a general conception is called *DIVISION* (Divisio). The general conception, in relation to those conceptions which fall within its extent, is the *higher* or *superordinate*; they in relation to it are the *lower* or *subordinate* (Relation of Subordination). Conceptions which are subordinated to the same higher one are *co-ordinate* (Relation of Co-ordination). *Aequipollent* or *Reciprocal* (notiones acquipollentes or reciprocae) conceptions are those whose spheres are identical with each other, without their content being exactly the same. *Identical* conceptions have the same extent and content. Those conceptions are *opposed to* each other *as contraries* (notiones contrarie oppositae) which, within the extent of the same higher notion, are most different from each other, and furthest removed from each other when both have a positive content; when one notion contains only the denial of the contents of the other, both are said to be *opposed to* each other *as contradictories*. A notion which merely denies is called notio negativa seu indefinita (ὄνομα ἀόριστον, ῥῆμα ἀόριστον). The Spheres of different notions *intersect* when they fall partly within, partly without each other. Conceptions are *compatible* (notiones inter se convenientes) when they can be combined in the content of the one and the same conception (consequently when their spheres fall wholly or partly within each other); in the opposite case, they are *incompatible*. Conceptions are *disjunct* when they fall within the extent of the same higher, especially if it be the next higher, conception (and consequently have some identical elements of content), but *have no part of their own extent common* (and consequently are not combined in the content of one and the same notion).   They are *disparate*, on the other hand, when they do not fall within the extent of the same higher, or at least of the same next higher, conception (and consequently *have not common elements of content*), while they sometimes have a part of their own extent common (or are combined in the content of one and the same notion).   All these relations of conceptions exist not only in substantive, but also in verbal, adjectival, and relative conceptions.   The formal relation of the subordination of several conceptions under the same higher one leads to the notion of *number*, which is originally (as whole number) the determination, by means of the unit, of the plurality of the individuals of the extent.

Geometrical figures, especially the circle (Ellipse, &c.) and parts of the circle, serve as a very convenient aid for the clear representation of the relations of extent.

The *relation of subordination* between the conceptions, of the superordinate A (e.g. man) and the subordinate B (e.g. European), is illustrated by two circles, the one of which falls wholly within the other :—

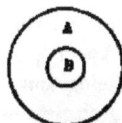

The *Co-ordination* of two conceptions, A and B, both of which are subordinated to a third, C (e.g. A = valour, B = prudence, C = duty), is illustrated by the following figure :—

In *Arquipollence* the two circles coalesce. The spheres are denoted by A (e. g. founder of scientific Logic), and by B (e.g. tutor to Alexander the Great):—

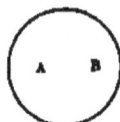

The relation of *contrary opposition* between A and B (e.g. white and black, or in reference to the widest difference in the circle of colours, red and green, yellow and violet, blue and orange) may be expressed in the following way:—

In *contradictory opposition*, between A and non-A (e. g. between white and not-white), the positively definite notion A is denoted by the space of the circle, the conception B or non-A is negatively definite, but with reference to its positive content, left indefinite by the unlimited empty space outside the circle:—

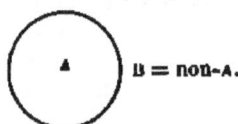

B = non-A.

The relation of *Intersection* between the conceptions A and B (e.g. negro and slave, Apocrypha and ungenuine writings, regular figures and parallelograms, red and bright) is symbolised by two intersecting circles:—

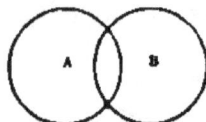

The schema of the *Compatibility* (e.g. red and coloured, redness and colour of the smallest number of the vibrations of aether, redness and brightness) is made by combining the schemata for Subordination, Acquipollence, and Intersection.

The schema for *Incompatibility* (e.g. red and blue) is the complete separation of the circles:—

Disjunct conceptions (e.g. Athenians and Spartans, motion and rest) belong to opposing ones. They are only distinct because they are comprehended under one and the same higher conception. Their schema is therefore:—

There is no sufficient schema for the relation of *disparate* exceptions (e.g. spirit and table, red and virtuous, long and sounding), because the negative determination, that their spheres do not fall within the extent of any conception superordinate commonly to both (excepting of course the quite general and indefinite conception of Anything), cannot be represented by a figure. The positive relation of their spheres, however, remains so far indefinite, that it can be that of intersection or that of complete separation.

The relations of judgments and inferences may be symbolised in a similar way: see under § 71; § 85 ff.; § 105 ff.; and for the history of this symbolising cf. § 85.

For the corresponding doctrines of *Plato* and *Aristotle*, cf. §§ 51 and 56. According to Plato the individual good has part in (μετέχει) the idea of the good, the individual beauty in the idea of the beautiful, and so every individual in its corresponding idea. Within the world of Ideas, according to the author of the Sophistes,[1] the lower (the logically subordinate) is compre-

---

[1] *Soph.* p. 250 B.

hended (περιέχεται) by the higher. With Aristotle the more universal is the πρότερον φύσει (cf. § 139). He uses the expressions, πρῶτος, μέσον, and ἔσχατος ὅρος[1] of notions which stand in the relation of subordination, and says of the subordinate notion, in reference to its extent, that it is wholly comprehended in the higher, or included in it (ἐν ὅλῳ εἶναι τῷ μέσῳ,—τῷ πρώτῳ, and so on). The representation of the relations of conceptions by means of circles is connected with these Aristotelian expressions. It was first applied in the Nucleus Log. Weisianae, 1712, written by *J. Ch. Lange.* Cf. § 85. For *contrary opposition* cf. (Plat. ?) Soph. p. 257 b, where ἐναντίον and ἕτερον are distinguished; *Aristotle*, Metaph. x. 4, where the opposition is defined to be the μεγίστη διαφορά between species of the same genus. The Aristotelian expression,[2] ἐστὶ μὲν ταὐτά, τὸ δὲ εἶναι οὐ ταὐτό, refers to conceptions of the same extent but different content. The expression *disjunct* is connected with the Aristotelian ἀντιδιῃρημένον,[3] and more closely with the later term διάζευξις (cf. § 123).

[*Hamilton* supplemented the list of relations of conceptions, in reference to their extent, by a list of their relations in reference to content. The great stress he laid upon the equal importance of content and extent in logical forms led him to make the two lists as far as possible parallel. The relations in content cannot be symbolised by figures. Hamilton's list is chiefly taken from the Logics of Esser and Krug.[4]]

§ 54. The higher conception has a *narrower content* but *a wider extent* than the lower; for it contains only those elements of content which agree in several lower conceptions. The lower conception has a fuller content but a narrower extent. The extent, however, is by no means increased or lessened by *every* lessening or increase of a given content; nor, on the

---

[1] *Anal. Pr.* i. 1, 4.　[2] *Eth. Nic.* v. 3, 1130 a, 12.　[3] *Top.* vi. 6.
[4] [Cf. *Lectures on Log.* i. lect. xii.]

other hand, is the content increased or diminished
with *every* decrease or increase of a given extent. Still
less does the law of a strict inverse ratio [as *Hamilton*
says] regulate those cases, in which the decrease of content produces an increase of extent, and an increase of
content a decrease of extent.

[*Hamilton* asserts expressly—' these two quantities of comprehension (content) and extension (extent) stand always in an
inverse ratio to each other; for the greater the comprehension of
a concept the less is its extension, and greater its extension the
less its comprehension.' [1]]

Drobisch[1] seeks to express mathematically the relation
which exists between the increase of the content and the
decrease of the extent. He proves that the content is not in
the inverse ratio of the extent, but that other relations exist.
He shows (to mention only the most important) that, under the
simplest presupposition—i.e. when in the series of subordinations
the number of conceptions, which are immediately subordinate
to any one or are richer by *one* element of content, is always
the same, and when, at the same time, the extent is mea-
sured exclusively according to the number of the conceptions of the lowest rank—the size of the extent decreases
according to geometrical progression, while the size of the content increases according to arithmetical progression.   Drobisch
further expresses this theorem by these two other assertions.
On the above presupposition, the extent of a conception is
inversely proportional to that power whose base is formed by
the number of conceptions immediately subordinate to any one
conception, and whose exponent is formed by the number of
the elements of the contents of that notion.   Under the same
presupposition, the difference between the greater number of
elements of the content of one of the lowest conceptions,
and the (lesser) number of the elements of the content of any

[1] [Cf. for a thorough discussion of the matter, *Lect. on Logic*, i. 146 ff.]
[1] *Logik*, 2nd ed. pp. 196–200.

conception, is directly proportional to the logarithm of the number which expresses the present size of the extent. The application of this investigation (which is valuable as a mathematico-logical speculation) is rendered useless in most cases, by the circumstance that peculiar limitations, which cannot be brought under general rules, underlie the possibility of attributes existing together. For example:

(Rectilineal) Triangle

acute | right-angled | obtuse
equilat. | isosc. | scal. | (equilat.) isosc. scal. | (equilat.) isosc. scalene.

Drobisch computes as follows: *Triangle*, cont. = a, ext. = 9 = 3^2. *Acute* triangle, cont. = a + 1, ext. = 3 = 3^1. Equilat. tr., cont. = a + 2, ext. = 1 = 3^0. But this computation is imaginary, because two of the nine combinations are not valid, according to the geometrical relations of dependence between the sides and angles of a triangle. Where conceptions refer to natural objects and relations of mental (geistige) life, the application of these laws is still more limited.[1]

The universal conception adjusts itself[2] to the delineation, well marked in some fundamental features only, in which the outlines do not waver in the Whole; but in the individuals there is room for a freer play of the phantasy which fills in the outlines. The common picture within the fundamental outline which makes its limit, is elastic and can take a manifold formation. If we call[3] this indeterminateness and elasticity a quantity of attributes or generalities of attributes, indefinite but able to be made definite, as numerous as those embraced

---

[1] In the 3rd ed. of his *Logik* (p. 211), Drobisch expressly says, that the theory holds good only on the presupposition that every species of any order is to be determined by every specific difference of the following order. It is true that this presupposition is sometimes realised, but it is realised completely in very few cases. Subjectively-formal logic, as such, cannot take into consideration the limited validity of the presupposition, for that depends upon real relations of dependence.

[2] Trendelenburg, *Log. Unters.* 2nd ed. ii. 220 ff.; 3rd ed. ii. 243 ff.

[3] With Lotze, *Log.* pp. 71 ff., 79.

in the lower conception, definitely and simply; then, there stands
opposed to the old doctrine, that the higher conception has the
widest extent and narrowest content, the new doctrine, that
the content of the higher conception does not come behind the
content of the lower in number of attributes; and this has a
certain degree of correctness. But the terminology is artificial,
and not to be justified. A richer content must manifest itself
in reference to the extent;[1] but the way in which it mani-
fests itself is not by widening the extent, but by the developing consolidation of thoughts around a definite object;
and this is accomplished not by extending but by limiting the originally unsettled possibility. The sum total of
individual conceptions is contained only potentially in the
general conception. Their actual existence is accomplished by
the entrance of other elements. There are in the nature of
things, besides this or that specific connection of a common
attribute with a definite group of dissimilar attributes, other
combinations, into which the common attribute can also enter.
The smallest number of (logical) elements of content and of
(real) characteristics or attributes corresponds to the widest extent, only potentially asserted; the greater number, to a smaller
(in the individual conception, to the smallest) extent, actually
asserted. The widest content possible has to do with actual
existence only by combining the greatest number of elements
of content in the whole of the individual conceptions. [Cf. also
in this reference Mr. Mill's very valuable observations upon
connotative and denotative names, Logic, i. 31 ff.]

§ 55. Since the relation of subordination and of superordination is repeated continuously by an abstraction
which goes on until one simple content is reached, the
sum total of all conceptions can be thought of, as arranged according to the relations of extent and content
in an organic *gradual succession.* The summit or upper

---

[1] As Trendelenburg demands, *Log. Unters.* 2nd ed. p. 226 ff.

limit is found by the most general conception *something*.
Immediately under it lie the categories. The basis, or
under limit, is formed by the infinite number of individual conceptions.

The gradual succession of conceptions may be compared to a
Pyramid. But this picture is only approximately true, because
the subordination of conception is not carried on with strict
uniformity. The highest conception is not the conception of
Being (Sein), but of *Something* (Etwas), because *Being* falls
under one of the Categories, viz. under that of Attributive
(predicative) Existence, and is opposed to *Being* as substantive.
Something, on the other hand, comprehends all the Categories
(an action or passion, property or relation, as, e.g. by, near to,
&c., is *Something*). The highest *material* opposites, such as
Real or Ideal, Natural and Spiritual, are connected with the
Categories, which are the highest *formal* divisions. They are
divided according to another principle of division, and repeat
themselves in every one of the Categories.

§ 56. The NOTION (Begriff, notio, conceptus) is that
conception in which the sum total of the *essential* attributes, or the *essence* (Wesen, essentia) of the object
under consideration, is conceived. By the phrase—
attributes (Merkmale, notae) of the object, we include not
only the outward signs by which it is known, but all its
parts, properties, activities, and relations,—in short,
whatever belongs in any way to the object. The *essential*
(essentialia) are those attributes which (a) contain the
common and persistent basis for a multitude of others;
and on which (b) the subsistence of the object, its worth
and its meaning, depends. This meaning belongs to it
partly because it is a means to something else, and
partly and principally to itself, as a final end in a
gradual course of objects. In a wider sense also,

these attributes are called essential, which are *neces-sarily* united to marks essential in the stricter sense, and whose presence, therefore, indicate with certainty the presence of those others. The essential *charac-teristics,* in the strictest sense, are called the *funda-mentally essential* (essentialia constitutiva); the others, which are only essential in a lower sense, *derivatively essential* (essentialia consecutiva) or *attributes in the stricter sense* (attributa). The other characteristics of an object are called non-essential (accidentia, modi). The *possibility* of modi or the capability to take this or that modification must have its foundation in the essence of the object. Under the essential determina-tions are those which the notion has in common with notions super-ordinate and co-ordinate with it, the *common ones* (essentialia communia), and those by which it is separated from these notions, the *proper* or *peculiar* (essentialia propria). The *relations* belong generally to the non-essential, but with relative notions they are essential attributes. In the proportion that the fundamentally essential characteristics are unknown, the formation of the notion is ambiguous. With another grouping of the objects, other determinations may ap-pear to be common and essential, and the whole pro-cedure cannot raise itself above a relativity which rests on accidental subjective opinions. In proportion, how-ever, as the really essential characteristics are known, the conceptions acquire a scientific certainty and an objective universal validity. In perfect knowledge notions are valid only as they correspond to the types of the real groups of their (natural or mental) objects.

When the formation of the notion is not made in the purely scientific interest, but is conditioned by any external purpose (even were it the purpose of a superficial view of any part of the subject), that one which has for its aim the widest reference appears to be the most essential. Several different constructions of a notion can exist alongside of each other, each of them being often relatively correct; one only, however, is absolutely correct, that, viz. which constructs the notion, purely according to objective laws, on the basis of what is most essential for the object in itself.

After that *Socrates* had first shown that he was conscious of the value of the notion in knowledge, *Plato* sought to solve the question of the real and peculiar object of notional knowledge. He defined it to be the Idea (ἰδέα or εἶδος), and strictly distinguished the real thing, which is known through the notion, from the notion itself (the λόγος), its corresponding subjective picture in our minds.[1] We seek in vain throughout the whole extent of Plato's writings for one single passage where εἶδος or ἰδέα even partially denotes the subjective notion, or where this meaning has not rather been introduced by interpreters. Plato rightly sought an objective correlative to the subjective notion. He failed because, instead of recognising this correlate in the essence indwelling in things, he hypostatised an objective existence outside of things and separate from them; in other words, because he ascribed to the idea an existence independent and for itself. The Platonic doctrine of Ideas is the fore-

---

[1] *De Rep.* v. 477, vi. 509 sqq., vii. 533 sqq.; *Tim.* pp. 27 D, 29 C, 37 A, C, 51 D, E; cf. § 14. The *Parm.* p. 132 A, was quoted in the first ed. of this book. It represents very clearly the relation of the subject to the object, of notional knowledge to ideal existence. It cannot, however, serve as a proof of Plato's views, if, as I have sought to prove, the *Parmenides* is not genuine. Cf. *Plat. Untersuch.* (pp. 175-181, Wien, 1861) and *Ueber den Dial. Parm.* in the *Jahrbuch f. class. Phil.* (p. 97 ff., Leip. 1864). The genuineness of the *Sophistes* and *Politicus* is very doubtful, as Schaarschmidt has shown (in the *Rhein. Mus. f. Philol.* New Series, xviii. pp. 1-28, 1862; xix. 63-96, 1864; *Ueber die Platonischen Schriften,* Bonn, 1866, pp. 181-245).

shadowing of the logical metaphysical truth in a mythical form. Hence also *Aristotle*[1] rightly compared the Platonic ideas to the anthropomorphic gods of Mythology.[2] *Aristotle* battled against the Platonic χωρίζειν of ideas, i.e. against the supposition that ideas exist in real separation from the individual existences as particular substances; but he does not reject the doctrine of a real correlate to the subjective notion. He did not place the forms of thought outside of all relation to the forms of being. He recognised a thorough-going parallelism between both (cf. § 16). According to Aristotle the *essence* corresponds to the *notion*, and is therefore called by him ἡ κατὰ λόγον οὐσία. The essence is immanent in the individual existence. Aristotle says[3]—εἴδη μὲν οὖν εἶναι ἢ ἕν τι παρὰ τὰ πολλὰ οὐκ ἀνάγκη—εἶναι μέντοι ἐν κατὰ πολλῶν ἀληθὲς εἰπεῖν ἀνάγκη.[4]—ἐν τοῖς εἴδεσι τοῖς αἰσθητοῖς τὰ νοητά ἐστιν.

This *one* in the many, this intelligible in the sensible, is called by Aristotle the *form*, the *what is*, and, with a terminology quite peculiar, the *being what a thing was*—μορφή, εἶδος, ἡ κατὰ λόγον οὐσία, τὸ τί ἐστι, and τὸ τί ἦν εἶναι. The expression τὸ τί ἦν εἶναι is explained by Aristotle himself to be the term for the matterless essence.[5] τὸ τί ἦν εἶναι corre-

---

[1] *Met.* iii. 2, 997 a, 10.

[2] It is an apprehension historically true in the main, and agreeing with Plato's own declarations, especially in his later writings, and not, as some would have it (Ritter, *Gesch. der Philos.* iii. 120, 1811), an open misrepresentation, when Aristotle thinks that ideas are hypostatised by Plato, and made to exist separately from the sensible things. Aristotle has only defined, somewhat more dogmatically than it is in the conception of the poet-philosopher, the representation which in Plato vacillates between figurative and real meaning. He has done it in strict accordance with Plato's own later constructions and with the doctrines of many Platonists. The desire to combine philosophy with poetry, which Schleiermacher with a too-sweeping generalisation finds to be the characteristic of the Hellenic Philosophy, is certainly the characteristic not only of Platonic representation, but also of Platonic thinking. Aristotle deserved commendation, not blame, when he in his own doctrines strips off this form, and thereby founded *scientific* Logic and Metaphysics.

[3] *Anal. Post.* i. c. xi.   [4] *De Anima*, iii. 8.   [5] *Metaph.* vii. 7.

sponds, therefore, to the *abstract* form of the notion (and consequently to the substantivum abstractum). (Cf. in this reference the difference, explained by Plato in the dialogue Phaedo,[1] of the inherent characteristic from the thing in which it inheres.) It does not, however, amount to the mere general characteristic of genus, still less is it concerned with the non-essential qualities. It is the whole collected essentiality (everything which must enter into the definition), and includes both the characteristics of the genus and the specific difference. The τί ἐστι of Aristotle is of wider and less definite use. It can denote both the matter[2] and the matterless essence,[3] and, lastly and most commonly, the union of the two, the σύνολον ἐξ εἴδους καὶ ὕλης.[4] In this last case it corresponds to the concrete form of the notion (and so to the substantivum concretum). The non-essential determinations or the mere accidents (συμβεβηκότα), e. g. mere qualities (ποιά) or quantities (ποσά), cannot serve as answers to the question τί ἐστι; at least, not when, as usually happens, the question is about the τί ἐστι of *a thing*. Aristotle recognises, that not only with things (substances), but also with Quantities, Qualities, Relations—in short, in every category—the question τί ἐστι or the τί ἦν εἶναι can be asked, and the essential separated from the non-essential; but he teaches that the τί ἐστι is present in things in an original and pre-eminent way. In dependent existences (in the συμβεβηκότα) it is present only derivatively:[5] ἐκεῖνο δὲ φανερὸν ὅτι ὁ πρῶτος καὶ ἁπλῶς ὁρισμὸς καὶ τὸ τί ἦν εἶναι τῶν οὐσιῶν ἐστιν. οὐ μὴν ἀλλὰ καὶ τῶν ἄλλων ὁμοίως ἐστί, πλὴν οὐ πρώτως. By this remark the two meanings of οὐσία, *Essence* and *Substance*, are placed in inward relation to each other. Unfortunately, however, the number of the meanings of this word, which denotes—now Substance in the sense of substrate or material basis of existence (τὸ ὑποκείμενον or ἡ ὕλη, *subjectum*); now the essence corresponding to the notion (ἡ κατὰ λόγον οὐσία, εἶδος, μορφή, τὸ τί ἦν εἶναι, *essentia*); now the whole,

---

[1] *Phaedo*, p. 103 B.
[2] E.g. *Metaph.* viii. 3.
[3] E.g. *De Anima*, p. 403 A, 30.
[4] E.g. *Metaph.* viii. 2.
[5] Ibid. vii. 4.

or what exists (τὸ σύνολον, τὸ ἐξ ἀμφοῖν, *ens*), and in this third case both the individual existence (τόδε τι, *individuum*) and the sum total of the objects belonging to one genus, or to one species (τὸ γένος, τὸ εἶδος, *genus, species*, materialiter sic dicta), —from then till now has been the cause of numberless cases of vagueness and error. A defect still more felt lies in this, that with Aristotle there are no criteria of Essentiality. The difference often brought forward in the treatise on the Categories —that what belongs to the essence can be predicated *of* the subject, but cannot be *in* the subject, while the accident is *in* the subject (e.g. Socrates is man, but man is not in him; Socrates is wise, and wisdom is in him), is not sufficient. It substitutes the opposition of substantive and adjective apprehension of the predicate notion for essentiality and non-essentiality. Now the two divisions are not parallel, but cross each other (e.g. Socrates is gifted with life and reason; Socrates is a wise man). Aristotle, not usually, nor yet in his logical writings, but now and then in single places, makes this criterion hold good for essentiality and non-essentiality: That is an essential part of the whole whose removal or alteration influences the whole.[1] But here, of course, the amount of influence on the totality of the remaining parts remains undefined. What lies in the definition belongs, in its totality, to the object of the definition only, or is peculiar to it; but single parts of the definition may belong to other objects;[2] and besides the *essence* given in the definition, something else may be peculiar to the object of the definition. This is the ἴδιον in the narrower sense.[3] Predicates which follow necessarily from the essence are called συμβεβηκότα ταῖς οὐσίαις by

---

[1] ὥστε μετατιθεμένου τινὸς μέρους ἢ ἀφαιρουμένου διαφέρεσθαι καὶ κινεῖσθαι τὸ ὅλον, *Poët.* c. viii. 1451 a, 33; in the words following, ὁ γὰρ προσὸν ἢ μὴ προσὸν μηδὲν ποιεῖ ἐπίδηλον, μηδὲν is the grammatical subject. Cf. my translation of the *Poetics*, Berlin, 1869, p. 102; cf. *Top.* vi. 12: ἕκαστον γὰρ τὸ βέλτιστον ἐν τῇ οὐσίᾳ μάλιστα.

[2] *Anal. Post.* ii. 13.

[3] *Top.* i. c. iv. 101 a, 22; ibid. c. v. 102 a, 18.

Aristotle,[1] or (more commonly) συμβεβηκότα καθ' αὑτό.[2] These last were later called the consecutively essential or attributes. They too belong to the καθόλου; for the καθόλου is everything[3] which belongs to what is denoted in the whole extent of its notion (κατὰ παντὸς and καθ' αὑτό or ᾗ αὑτό), in distinction from what is common in any way (κοινόν). The καθόλου is a κοινόν, but every κοινὸν is not a καθόλου. According to the doctrine of the *Stoics*, notions exist only as subjective creations in the mind. The κοινὸς λόγος, the reason of the universe separated into a plurality of λόγοι, dwells in external things. But the Stoics do not expressly make these λόγοι denote what is known by the subjective notion.

In the *Middle Ages* the Realists paid homage partly to Plato, and partly to Aristotle's opinions,—'universalia ante rem,' and 'universalia in re.' The *Nominalists* allowed no other existence to the 'universalia' (universal objects or universal predicates) than an existence in the word (strict Nominalists), or in the thinking mind also (Conceptualists)—'Universalia post rem.' The manifold defects in Platonic and Aristotelian Realism called forth Nominalism, its extreme opposite, and gave a relative correctness to it. Among modern philosophers Descartes, Leibniz, as well as Bacon and Locke, belong to Nominalism, or rather to Conceptualism. This logical and metaphysical problem, discussed by Scholasticism, was scarcely affected by the psychological question, chiefly discussed by modern philosophers, about the origin of our notions, viz.—Are notions really innate? Is development in common life limited to a gradual coming more and more distinctly into consciousness? or, are all notions, in content and form, products of a mental development conditioned by outward influences? *Kant* and *Herbart*, like the earlier Nominalists, concede to notions a subjective meaning only.

[1] *De Anima*, l. c. i. 402 a, 18.
[2] *Metaph.* v. c. xxx. 1025 a, 30 : ὅσα ὑπάρχει ἑκάστῳ καθ' αὑτὸ μὴ ἐν οὐσίᾳ ὄντα.
[3] According to *Anal. Post.* i. 4.

L

Herbart uses ' universalia ' to denote all general and individual
conceptions, so far as they are looked at, not on their psychological side, but in reference to what is represented by them.
Yet Herbart says,[1] in a passage where he is not expressly
teaching Logic, but makes a logical remark accidentally—
' Definition becomes a significant expression of the result of
this whole deliberation only after the first attempt to separate
the *essential* from the *accidental.*' Now, since the notion is
determined by what is essential, and not what is essential by
the notion, there is here presupposed a difference of the essential and accidental lying in the objective reality, and the
dependence of the genuine formation and explanation of
notions—i. e. a formation and explanation, which corresponds
to scientific and didactic laws—upon this objective difference
is recognised.

Subjectively-formal Logic, which should identify the notion
with the general conception, so far as it at all explains the category of essentiality, calls those attributes essential without
which an object could not be what it is, nor remain what it is,
nor be subsumed under the same notion. In other words,
those attributes are essential which belong to the object in the
whole extent of its notion or make up its content.[1] This explanation is unsatisfactory, for it argues in a circle. The
notion is explained by the essence, and then the essence by the
notion. If Logic[2] is to settle the normal laws of thought, it
must answer the question,—according to what marks are objects to be grouped together and their notions formed? For
example, are plants to be grouped according to the shape and
divisions of the corolla (Tournefort), or according to the
number of their stamens and pistils (Linneus)? They are
to be grouped according to their essential attributes. What
attributes are essential? Those which belong to the object

[1] In his discourse at the opening of his *Vorlesungen über Pädagogik*,
1803. *Werke*, Bd. xi. 63, Leipzig, 1851.

[2] Cf. Drobisch, *Log.* 3rd ed. § 31. [Sir Wm. Hamilton's account is
the same; cf. *Lect. on Logic*, i. 217.]

[3] According to Drobisch, *Logik*, § 2.

in the whole extent of its *notion*, those which lie in its notion, and to which the name belongs. If then we seek first the correct notion and name, how shall we determine it? By the essential attributes. What are the essential? Those which lie in the notion; and sic in infinitum. The consequence is, that the formation of the notion remains quite arbitrary. He who arranges plants according to the shape and divisions of the corolla, and thereby forms his botanical notions—for him the shape and divisions are essential. He who arranges them according to size—for him size is essential; and so on. At the best, the common use of words, as yet uncorrected by science, gives a starting-point; no way is pointed out; and we are left to the most elementary and wholly unscientific modes of forming notions.[1] When we once know what objects, according to their nature, belong to each other, and make up the extent of the one and the same notion, we can set ourselves right by this, in our search after the essential properties. But how can we scientifically know that reciprocal dependence, and determine rightly the limits of the extent, so long as we are unable to distinguish the essential from the non-essential attributes? Does the whale belong to the extent of the notion fish? Is the Atomic philosophy within the sphere of the notion of Sophistic? Does the mode of thought shown in the Pseudo-Clementine Homilies fall within the sphere of the notion of

[1] Drobisch confesses this in the third edition of his *Logic*, in a remark appended to § 119 (p. 137), inasmuch as he explains that his distinction can only be fully justified and established when the reference is to the analytical definition of a notion which is given by its commonly used designation, when we only seek the notion which corresponds to a given name. But my assertion points to this, that subjectively-formal Logic, unless it goes beyond its principle, can only bring forward its laws for the solution of certain merely elementary and propædeutic problems, and can only produce a small part of the laws of thought, and not, as is promised in Drobisch's *Logic* (3rd ed. § 2, p. 3), the normal laws of thought. The consideration of the 'synthetic forms of thought' can only be scientifically satisfactory when it is based on the relation to the forms of existence (e.g. of the ground of knowledge to the causal relation, of the notion to the real essence).

Gnosticism? Does Joannes Scotus (Erigena) belong to the
Scholastics? Tiedmann says [1]—' Scholastic philosophy is that
treatment of objects à priori, where, after statement in syllogistic form of the greatest number of reasons for or against,
decision is made from Aristotle, the Church Fathers, and the
prevailing system of belief.' It follows from this definition
of the notion that Scholasticism proper had its beginning at
the commencement of the thirteenth century, after acquaintance
with the metaphysics, physics, and ethics of Aristotle, which
did not take place until the close of the twelfth century
(before this the Logic only was known). Whether this definition of the notion is to be agreed to, can be settled only
from a consideration of the essentiality of the attributes, independent of the previous settlement of the extent. Every question of this kind can only be settled scientifically, when, before
and independently of the limitation of the extent, the essentiality, or degree of the essentiality, of the attributes has been
settled. *Now, wherein lie the criteria?* Subjectively-formal
Logic, when it takes the forms of thought apart from their relation to forms of existence, and will not treat them as forms
of *knowledge*, proves itself to be inadequate to give rules for
that formation of notions which the positive sciences require.

The somewhat common explanation of the essential attributes as the *lasting* and *persistent* properties is not more satisfactory.[2] In its reference to the amount of time of duration,
this definition does not prove a just one. The highest and
most essential form, the most pre-eminent, is often the point
of culmination of a life which swiftly passes away. If it only
denotes inseparability from the object, so long as the object
remains what it is, or while it is subsumed under the same
notion, and can be called by the same name, the reasoning in a
circle again results.

The principle of grouping objects together according to the
most *important* properties, or those which are of the *greatest
similarity* or *natural relationship* (on which *Mill*[3] would

---

[1] *Geist der spec. Phil.* iv. 358.
[2] E.g. in Ritter's *Logik*, 2nd ed. p. 67.   [3] *Logic*, ii. 264.

base the formation of notions), leaves the question undecided.
For, What similarity or relationship is the greatest? A
similarity in many, and even in most, determinations would
by no means justify comprehension together and subsumption under the same notion, provided that the many were the
least significant. A similarity in the significant, important,
and essential would. But then we come back to the question,
What are to be considered the essential?

II. Taine's definition of the essential characters is to be cri-
ticised in the same way[1] :—' The essential characteristic is a
quality from which all the other, or at least most other qualities, derive according to a settled mutual interdependence.'
The genetic consequence, without regarding the degree of value
of each attribute, is scarcely sufficient for the determination of
what is essential. Besides, one moment of an object ought
not to come from another, but the sum total of the attributes
from earlier original circumstances. The connection belong-
ing-to-each-other, and the dependence, ought to be reciprocal,
and give no criterion to decide what attributes are essential
among those which belong to each other.

Schelling's Nature-Philosophy, while it seeks to blend the
Platonic doctrine of ideas (modified in the Aristotelian sense)
with Spinoza's doctrine of substance, finds the real antitype of
the notion in the *ideas*, the creative types, or characters of
genera, the media between the unity of substance and the endless number of individual existences.

Hegel does not seek a real antitype of the notion, but holds
that the notion is as much the fundamental form of objective
reality as of subjective thought. He defines the notion to be
the higher unity and truth of being and essence, to be the substantial power existing for itself, and therefore the freedom
and truth of the substance.[2] But the notion as a form of
human thought is not sufficiently characterised by this.

According to *Ulrici*,[3] the logical notion is universality as

[1] *Philosophy of Art*, p. 51, translated into English, 1867.
[2] *Logik*, ii. 5 ff. in the ed. of 1834 ; *Encycl.* § 158 ff.
[3] *Log.* p. 452.

the category of separative thinking. But the mere category of universality will not sufficiently distinguish the notion from the general conception.

Schleiermacher distinguishes the sensible and intellectual sides of the notion. The former is the *Schema*,[1] or common picture, i.e. sense-picture of the individual object represented confusedly, and therefore become a general picture from which several particular pictures, co-ordinate to each other, could quite well arise. With respect to the intellectual side, Schleiermacher recognises[2] in the system of notions, that creation of the thinking reason, or of the 'intellectual function,' to which the system of 'substantial forms' corresponds in real existence, or of powers and phenomena, in opposition to the system of judgments as the correlate of the system of 'actions.' This definition of Schleiermacher's, when it places the notion as a form of knowledge in relation to a form of existence, is the right mean between the mutually opposed one-sided views of the subjectively-formal and the metaphysical Logics. It labours under the defect that it does not distinguish sharply enough between *substance* meaning *existence, thing, ens*, and *substance* meaning *essence, essentiality, essentia*. This seems to be a consequence of the Aristotelian vagueness in the use of the word οὐσία. Every conception of a *thing* is not a notion, nor does every *notion* rest upon a thing. The conception is a notion when the *essential* is represented in it, whether it be of a thing, an action, a property, or a relation.[3] Schleiermacher makes the opposition of the higher and lower notion parallel with the opposition of power and phenomenon, or universal thing (Genus and Species), and individual existence; so that (e. g.) the power of sight of the eye is to be thought of, in analogous relation to the single eye as a phenomenon of this power, as the universal notion of the eye is to the individual notion of the single eye. This theory has its root in the Aristotelian doctrine of the active power (ἐντελέχεια) as the essence,—ἡ ὄψις οὐσία ὀφθαλμοῦ ἡ κατὰ τὸν λόγον.[4]

---

[1] *Dial.* §§ 110 ff., 260 ff.   [2] Ibid. § 175 ff.

[3] Schleiermacher himself partly recognises this, *Dial.* pp. 197, 110, 545.   [4] *Arist. de Anima*, ii. 1.

Beneke [1] considers the notion or general conception to be a form of ' analytical thinking.' He incorrectly believes that its correspondence with the essence as the ' synthetical form ' is merely accidental.

Ritter's definition of the notion corresponds with Schleiermacher's:[2]—' the form of thinking, which represents the enduring basis of the phenomenon;'[3] ' the existence which is represented in the notion is an enduring one, but one which can show itself in changing activities, now in one way, now in another—such an existence we call a living thing or a substance;'[4] ' when the understanding strives to think the individual thing as the lasting foundation of many phenomena (or, according to p. 5, as substance), its thought must take a form in which the meaning of many phenomena is comprehended or conceived—every such thought we call a notion, and when it comprehends this meaning in the thought of an individual, an individual notion;'[5] ' the general notion represents the totality of the particular essences with their activities.'

Trendelenburg [6] understands by the notion, the forms of thinking which correspond to the real substance as its mental copy.

In a similar way *Lotze* [7] calls a notion, that content which is thought of not merely as the conception in the mutually inter-dependent totality of its parts, but whose multiplicity is referred to a logical substance, which brings to it the method of combining its attributes. But the reference to a substance belongs to every substantive conception, and is not the distinguishing character of the notion. It cannot be granted that Logic has nothing to do with the essential;[8] not, at least, from the stand-point of Logic as the doctrine of knowledge.

[*Mill's* doctrine of the essence cannot be wholly summed up by

---

[1] *System der Log.* i. 253 ff.   [2] *Log.* 2nd ed. p. 50.

[3] Ibid. p. 56.   [4] *Syst. der Logik und Metaphysik*, ii. 13.

[5] Ibid. p. 297.   [6] *Log. Unters.* ii. §§ 14, 15.

[7] *Log.* p. 177 ff.   [8] As Lotze thinks, *Log.* p. 82.

saying that objects have the same essence, or are to be subsumed under the same notion, which have similar properties, or
are most naturally related to each other. He knows that the
further question arises—What objects are naturally related,
and so serve as the basis of the formation of a notion? and
would say that this latter question cannot be answered in a
sentence, but is the one question of Inductive Logic. It is the
business of induction to find out methods for discovering and
testing the relations of properties, and so finding out whether
they are so related that they can form the bases of notions.
The inductive methods show what properties are essential.
The portions of Mr. Mill's Logic which refer to this question
in debate are the most instructive in the whole book; cf.
especially, vol. i. pp. 131-170, and vol. ii. pp. 169-201, p. 216 ff.,
pp. 262-285. Essentiality, however, does not depend upon Inductive Methods; Inductive Methods depend upon Essentiality;
and thus Mr. Mill fails to solve the problem of Essence.]

§ 57. We *recognise* and distinguish the essential—

(a) In ourselves, immediately by feeling and mediately by ideas. Feeling is the immediate consciousness of the relation of our activities and conditions to
the present existence and development of our whole
life, of its single sides and organs, or of the life of other
beings related to us. What aids is felt with pleasure ;
what hinders, with uneasiness and pain. In the ethical
feelings, more especially, the gradation of the worth of
different developments reveals itself, according as they
are sensible or mental, more passive or active, isolated
or connected, limited to the individual or extended
to a wider community, or consist in that relation on
which the law of human will and action rests. The
ethical ideas are developed (by abstraction) out of
feelings. The knowledge of our own essence depends

both on the consciousness of the ethical ideas, and on the amount of our actual existence in them.

(b) By means of the knowledge of the essence in ourselves we recognise the essence of persons beyond us, more or less adequately, in proportion to their relationship with ourselves. The relation between the knowledge of ourselves and of others is a reciprocal one. The clearness and depth of the knowledge of our own essence depend upon intercourse with others, upon living in connection with the whole mental development of the human race (just as one can say in theology, that the understanding of the revelation of God within us depends as much on the understanding of the historical revelation, as this does upon that).

(c) The essence or the inner purpose of nature in animals and plants is the analogue of the ethical duty of man, and is to be known in the proportion of this analogy. The analogy is limited but not destroyed by a threefold opposition:—that the powers of the impersonal essence are of a very different and lower kind; that they do not strive to win to their end by means of a free conscious activity, but by unconscious necessity actually realise the tendency indwelling in them; and that the significance of their existence as ends in themselves is outweighed by the significance of their existence for others.

(d) With the inorganic objects of nature, existence as an end in itself, and self-determination, come after existence as a mean for another, and the mechanically becoming determined by another. Hence the possibility of knowing their inner essence is thrown into the background by the knowledge of their outward relations.

(e) The essence of what exists not in the form of independent existence or substantiality, and of what has only a fictitious independence, the result of art, is known partly according to its analogy with the life of independently-existing individuals, partly and chiefly according to the significance which belongs to it as a mean to something else.

Material truth is to be reached in our notional knowledge of the essential from the same grounds, and undergoes the same limitations and gradations, as in the case of perception (§§ 41–42) and of the individual conception (§ 46).

The essential relation of the activity of knowledge to the whole of the mental and ethical life depends upon this.

The question whether human notions are present à priori (if the phrase, according to Kant's use, is applied to what is derived from the subject as such) in the mind (Geist) as innate possessions, or are raised up in it à posteriori by means of the senses, by way of gradual development, may be decided in the following way. Every notion contains an ' à priori' element, not only in the sense in which this is true of every conception, but, more particularly, because the knowledge of the essential in things can only be reached by means of a knowledge of the essential in us (though this knowledge is often not developed into full consciousness). *Schleiermacher*[1] rightly places the development of the whole system of notions in relation to our self-consciousness. Man, as the microcosm, has in himself all the degrees of life, and thereon constructs his conceptions of outward existences. In *this* sense it may be rightly said that the system of all notions is originally contained in the reason or ' intellectual function;' only we must not make the mistake of supposing that the actual system of human notions is independent of the objective reality and quite different from it.

[1] *Dial.* § 178.

When correctly constructed it represents the proper essence and arrangement of the objects.

But the formation of any notion referring to the outer world is conditioned by the outer or 'à posteriori' factor just as much as by the subjective or 'à priori' element; for if notional knowledge is to have truth, the completion of the contents of perception by analogues of our essence must conform to the phenomena, and can only be references of the outer phenomena of things to their inner essence. The à priori element is only à priori as regards the outer world, and is by no means independent of inner experience.[1]

It is impossible to admit the existence of notions, which, although unknown, may have been present as notions in us from the beginning. On any acceptation, this admission would contradict the course of human development. And the end which would induce us to make this unpsychological admission, the objective validity of notions apparently involved in it, is not satisfied by it. A pure subjectivism may connect itself with the presupposition of an à priori character; and, in fact, Kant's critical philosophy has so connected itself. The truth lying at the bottom of this doctrine is,[*] that the human mind is able to reach a knowledge of objective reality. Cf. § 140.

§ 58. Those individuals which have the same essential properties make a *class*, or *genus*, in the universal sense. The genus is as much the real antitype of the extent as the essence is of the content of the notion. The essence has different degrees, and different circumscribing groups of marks can serve as the basis of determining the formation of the notion. In a similar way several classes or genera encircling each other can be distinguished, which are denoted successively by the

[1] Cf. Schleiermacher's *Ethik*, ed. by A. Twesten, § 46, p. 55.
[*] As J. Hoppe has rightly remarked in his *Gesammte Logik*, i. § 54, p. 45, Paderborn, 1868.

terms, *Kingdom* (regnum), *Sphere* (orbis), *Class* (classis), *Order* (ordo), *Family* (familia), *Genus* (genus), *Species* (species). *Group* (cohors) is sometimes inserted between Kingdom and Sphere; *Tribe* (tribus) between Family and Genus; *Subdivision* (sectio) between Genus and Species, and in other places; and *Subspecies* and *Variety* (varietas) between the Species and Individual. The notion of *Race* is specially applied, in definite cases only, to the most general division of men in natural history. It might be referred to Subspecies. The opposition of *Genus* and *Species* is frequently used to denote the relation of any higher class to any lower, which is proximately subsumed under it without any intervening members.

Objects are *generically* different when they belong to different genera; *specifically* different when they belong to different species of the same genus. They are *gradually* different when they differ only according to quantity or intensity. They are *numerically* different when they, although wholly similar in essence, are not identical, but are several objects.

The characteristic of the species in natural history, maintained by earlier investigators, was continuous fruitful procreation. Later research has made this criterion a relative one. But this characteristic, so far as it holds good, is to be looked at only as *consecutively*, not as *constitutively* essential; for the possibility or impossibility of continuous fruitful procreation must depend upon the whole character of the organisation. The true characteristic attribute of the species is not procreation, but the *type*. By *type* is to be understood, neither the mere outer form and figure, nor the peculiarity of any one given standard form, but the whole character of the organisation—the Platonic idea, not in its historical but in its true sense, the Aristotelian form, the Kantian 'Urbild der Erzeugungen,'[1] or[2] 'the image which is afterwards realised.' The possibility of reproduction only serves as a mean to recognise the correspondence in the type. Formations belong to a kind, if they, so far as their like stages of development are compared with each other, show correspondence in all essential attributes. *Comparison* is the function of the knowing *subject* only; *essentiality* of the marks compared is the *objective* moment which gives real meaning to the notion of species. Individuals which have been correctly arranged under a *species* (or any class) must agree with each other, not only in those marks which make up the content of the notion, but also in many secret relations. Hence it is seen that the notion of species (and every notion of class founded upon essentiality) is based upon the objective reality itself. *George Henry Lewes*[3] says, 'What is the aim of a zoological classification? Is it not to group the animals in such a manner, that every class and genus may tell us the degree of *complexity* attained by its organisation, so that the outer form may explain the inner structure?' But the degree of complexity on its part tells us the degree attained by every object in the scale of perfection. Cf. § 63.

It is an inconsequence to recognise the real existence of the individual and then to deny the reality of species; and it would be an inconsequence to recognise the natural reality of species, and then to deny the natural reality of genus, family, and other wider divisions in which the narrower are included. For the reality of *species* depends upon the reality of *essentiality*. Certain elements must be recognised, not only to be eminently useful as fulcra for the determination of notions, but as eminently important and decisive for determining the existence and significance of real objects. If this be once allowed, the recognition of the graduation of essentiality, and with it the recognition of the reality of the graduated division of

---

[1] *Krit. der Urtheilskraft.*

[2] According to Spring, *Ueber Gattung, Art und Abart.*

[3] *Aristotle: a Chapter from the History of Science, &c.*, p. 277, § 323, 1864

external existence, cannot be well denied.   *Braun* says rightly[1]
— ' As the individual appears to be a member of the species,
so the species appears to be a member of the genus, the genus
to be a member of the family, order, class, and kingdom.'   The
recognition of the organism of nature and its regular division,
as objective facts witnessed to by nature herself, is an essential
requisite for placing natural history in a higher position.[2]

Aristotle made species and genera δεύτεραι οὐσίαι, just as individuals were οὐσίαι in the fullest sense of the word,[3] and
so recognised them to be real.   He saw in the natural classes
a graduated series of ascending perfection.   *Linneus* rightly
believed the classes and orders of artificial systems to be a
make-shift for the natural until they are known, but considered
the true species and genera, when known, to be objective
works of nature.[4]   The knowledge of natural genera, families,
and orders is always more uncertain than that of the species.
The acceptation of an objective validity of natural division
does not exclude the recognition of a certain relativity in the
notion of species; as little as the objective existence of the individual excludes the partial indefiniteness of the limits of
the individual.   In a genetic view of nature (such as the
Darwinian,[5] whose fundamental thought Kant had already
expressed hypothetically in his Kritik der Urtheilskraft),
which is founded on the supposition of a gradual origin and
partial transformation of species, the objectivity of the species
for the world as it now exists can still be accepted.   For a
realised tendency of nature to construct definite forms may be
recognised, and *objectivity* does not mean *absolute stability*.   On
the basis of the Darwinian theory of species, inasmuch as its
notion is referred to organisms existing contemporaneously
at any given time, an objective validity in the full sense of
the word can always be vindicated, because the systematic
table of the classes of organisms rests on their genealogy, and

[1] *Verjüngung in der Natur*, p. 343.
[2] Cf. Rosenkranz, *Logik*, ii. 48 ff.   [3] *Cat.* v.
[4] *Philos. Botan.* § 161 sqq.
[5] Charles Darwin, *On the Origin of Species*, Lond. 1859.

so unites the genetic point of view of common origin with the teleological point of view.[1] 'The difficulty of natural-history treatment does not now lie in the determination of the species, but in this, that every systematic category is considered to be a natural unity which represents the starting-point of a great historically developing movement. The genus and the higher notions (as much as the species) are not abstractions but concrete things, complexes of connected forms which have a common origin.'[2] As it is in the province of natural history, so is it in that of ethics. We must seek out the essential in the grouping of the relations presented, and consequently in the formation of the notion, which is thus not left to the subjective arbitrary choice, but is connected with objective law. The distinction of wider and narrower spheres rests throughout on the gradations of essentiality.

§ 59. In those cases where individuals which belong to the same species are separated from each other by *essential* peculiarities, they form INDIVIDUAL NOTIONS. The individual notion is that individual conception, whose content contains in itself the whole of the essential properties or attributes, common and proper, of an individual. A certain universality belongs to an individual notion also, inasmuch as it contains under it the different stages of the development of the individual. The conception of an individual living in time is not purely individual, unless it represents the individual in a single moment of its existence.

The schoolmen's question about the 'principium individuationis,' formed by the opposition of Aristotelianism and

[1] Cf. for the logical treatment, Trendelenburg, *Log. Unters.* 2nd ed. ii. 225 ff., 3rd ed. ii. 248 ff.; cf. ii. 78 ff.

[2] Carl Nägeli, *Entstehung und Begriff der naturhist. Art*, 2nd ed., München, 1865, p. 34.

Platonism,[1] rests on the presupposition that the universal is
not only a notional, but also a real *prius* of the individual.
It loses significance, whenever it is seen, that to descend
from the general to the particular can only be done by the
thinking subject; and that, in objective reality, the essence
cannot exist before the individual in any such way that
the individual must form itself upon it.   The Nominalists
(who went too far on the other side) have recognised this
when they explain that what exists is, as such, an individual.
After them Leibniz and Wolff explain that to be individual
which is determined on all sides (res omnimodo determinata,
or ita determinata, ut ab aliis omnibus distingui possit), and
assert that the universal, as such, exists only in abstraction.
Individuality is constituted not by one determination (such as
Matter, Space, Time), but by the sum total of all.   This does not
prevent the distinction of essential and unessential, and of degrees of essentiality, from existing in the objective reality itself.

So far as properties, which belong to this or that individual,
have essential significance, there are individual *notions*.   From
§ 46, it follows that individual notions are chiefly formed from
the highest essences under the *personal*.

§ 60. The DEFINITION or *determination of the notion*
(Definitio, ὁρισμός) is the complete and orderly statement of its content (§ 50).   All the essential elements
of the content of the notion, or all the essential properties of the objects (§ 49) of the notion, must be stated
in the definition.   It is the expression of the essence
of the objects of the notion.   The essential elements
of content are, partly those shared by the notion
to be defined along with co-ordinate notions and so
form the content of the superordinate notion, and partly
those by which the notion is distinguished from the co-
ordinate and superordinate notions.   But since (§ 58)

[1] Cf. Arist. *Metaph.* i. 6.

the opposition of genus to species serves to indicate, generally, the opposition of any higher class to any lower, in so far as the latter is immediately subordinated to the former, the essential elements of the content of the notion to be defined can be separated into *generic* and *specific*. On this rests the postulate—*that the definition contain the superordinate or genus-notion and the specific difference or what makes the species distinct.* The statement of the genus-notion serves also to determine the *form* or *category* of the notion to be defined (whether it be substantive or adjectival, &c.). Simple notions, in which the totality of attributes is reduced to one attribute only, cannot have a regular definition (cf. § 62).

Plato finds in Definition (ὀρίζεσθαι) and in Division (διαιρεῖν, κατ' εἴδη διαιρέσεις) the two chief moments of Dialectic,[1] but does not develope its *theory* more thoroughly. He does not expressly say that the Definition must contain the Genus and Specific Difference, but actually proceeds according to this axiom; e.g. in the Gorgias,[3] in the definition of Rhetoric; in the Republic, in the definition of the co-ordinate virtues (Wisdom, Courage, Temperance, and Justice); for he adds to the statement of their generic character the specific peculiarities. In the Dialogue Euthyphro, the ὅσιον is defined to be a μέρος of the δίκαιον, and then it is asked, ποῖον μέρος? whereon Euthyphro answers—τὸ περὶ τὴν τῶν θεῶν θεραπείαν. Socrates had already proceeded in this way, e.g. in the definition of the φθόνος[3] as the λύπη ἐπὶ ταῖς τῶν φίλων εὐπραξίαις. In the Platonic Dialogue Theaetetus,[4] the διαφορά or διαφορότης, or the σημεῖον ᾧ τῶν ἁπάντων διαφέρει τὸ ἐρωτηθέν, is distinguished from the κοινόν, as when, e.g. the ἥλιος is said to be τὸ λαμπρότατον τῶν κατ' οὐρανὸν ἰόντων περὶ γῆν. Plato combats the assertion, that a characteristic sufficient to

[1] *Phaedr.* p. 265 sqq.   [3] Ibid. p. 463 ff.
[3] Xenophon's *Memorab.* iii. 9, 8.   [4] *Theaet.* pp. 208, 209.

distinguish science from mere (though correct) opinion is afforded
by the consciousness of the διαφορά. In the Philebus[1] generic
identity is distinguished from the διαφορότης of the μέρη (species);
the latter may be increased up to the most complete opposition.
The remark that simple notions do not admit of definition is
introduced and examined in the Theaetetus :[2]—ἀδύνατον εἶναι
ὁτιοῦν τῶν πρώτων ῥηθῆναι λόγῳ, οὐ γὰρ εἶναι αὐτῷ, ἀλλ' ἡ
ὀνομάζεσθαι μόνον, ὄνομα γὰρ μόνον ἔχειν· τὰ δὲ ἐκ τούτων ἤδη
ξυγκείμενα ὥσπερ αὐτὰ πέπλεκται, οὕτω καὶ τὰ ὀνόματα αὐτῶν ξυμπλακέντα λόγον γεγονέναι. In the Dialogue Politicus[3]
the term διαφοραί signifies rather the species themselves,
which are contained in the genus, and into which it can be
divided, than the specific elements of content which must be
added to the generic in the *Definition* of the species-notion.
Definition is based on Division in the Dialogue Sophistes.[4]
In the Platonic Leges[5] are distinguished—ἡ οὐσία, τῆς οὐσίας
ὁ λόγος, and τὸ ὄνομα. By λόγος Plato here means both the
notion and the definition of the notion, as, e.g. the λόγος of
that which bears the name ἄρτιον is ἀριθμὸς διαιρούμενος εἰς ἴσα
δύο μέρη.

Aristotle teaches,[6] ὁρισμὸς οὐσίας τινὸς γνωρισμός·[7] ὁρισμός
ἐστι λόγος τὸ τί ἦν εἶναι σημαίνων·[8] ἐν ᾧ ἄρα μὴ ἐνέσται λόγῳ
αὐτό, λέγοντι αὐτό, οὗτος ὁ λόγος τοῦ τί ἦν εἶναι ἑκάστῳ : i.e.
whatever expression does not contain the object (by its name),
while it denotes it (in fact), is the assertion of the essence (or
the definition) of any thing [9]—ὁ ὁρισμὸς ἐκ γένους καὶ διαφορῶν
ἐστιν.

The phrase *Specific Difference* (differentia specifica) is the
translation (due to Boethius) of the Aristotelian διαφορὰ
εἰδοποιός.[10]   Later logicians[11] demand 'definitio fiat per genus
proximum et differentiam specificam.' It must also be pos-

[1] Pp. 12, 13.   [2] P. 202.   [3] P. 285.
[4] P. 219 sqq.   [5] P. 895.   [6] Analyt. Post. ii. 3.
[7] Topic. vii. 5.   [8] Metaph. vii. 4.   [9] Top. i. 8.
[10] Ibid. vi. 6 : πᾶσα γὰρ εἰδοποιὸς διαφορὰ μετὰ τοῦ γένους εἶδος ποιεῖ.
[11] Founding on Arist. Top. vi. 5, p. 143 A, 15, where μὴ ὑπερβαίνειν
τὰ γένη is demanded.

tulated that what can be said in few words should not be expressed in many. But the postulate cannot be universally applied. For example, the definition which would subsume the circle under the proximate genus *conic section*, would in the majority of cases be less useful and convenient than that which subsumes it under the more general notion of *plane figure*, and in elementary geometry would be quite inadmissible. Cases of this kind may be generally reduced to the following formula:—The notion to be defined, A, falls under the proximate genus-notion B, and both under the proximate genus-notion C. A differs from B by the Specific Difference *a*; B from C by the Specific Difference *b*. Now, it may happen that the two differences (*a* and *b*) cannot be easily defined by themselves, but easily coalesce into one whole difference *a′*, in which both are implicitly contained. When this happens, the Definition by a remoter genus-notion is easier and simpler than the Definition which contains the proximate genus-notion, and is therefore to be preferred, save in single cases where the purpose requires the more difficult definition.

Modern *Dogmatic Philosophy since Des Cartes* lays great stress upon Definition; and *Kant* also, although he believed the knowledge of the essence of the thing to be unattainable, holds the stricter form of Definition to be important. *Leibniz* teaches that the genus and the difference making the species are often interchangeable, for the difference may become the genus, and the genus the difference: this opinion, if, in accordance with Aristotle's view, a real relation is represented in the reciprocal relation of the elements of content, must be limited to the case where several definitions are equally essential; as (e.g.), adulari can be as well defined to be mentiri laudando as laudare mentiendo, ut placeas laudato.[1]

The *Hegelian* philosophy merges the Definition of the notion in its dialectical genesis.

[1] Trendelenburg discusses the Element of Definition in the Leibnizian Philosophy in the *Monatsber. der Berl. Akad. d. Wiss.* Juli 1860, republished in his *Hist. Beitr. zur Philos.* iii. 48–62, Berl. 1867; cf. *Log. Unters.* 2nd ed. ii. 221 ff.; 3rd ed. ii. 217 ff.

[According to *J. S. Mill*, a Definition is a proposition declaratory of the meaning of a word, and so must directly or indirectly include its whole content or connotation, or express the sum total of all the *essential* propositions which can be framed with that name for their subject. All names can be defined which have meaning. Even those whose meaning is summed up in a single abstract quality may be defined by their causes. Complete definition is not brief enough, and is, besides, too technical for common discourse. Hence arise incomplete definitions. Of these the most noteworthy is per genus et differentiam. Such definitions are useful abbreviations, but may be, and are continually set aside in the progress of science.[1]]

§ 61. DEFINITIONS are DIVIDED according to various points of view. We distinguish—

1. *Substantial* and *Genetic* (Definitio substantialis and genetica sive causalis). The content of the notion to be defined is in the one case taken from the present existence, in the other from the origination of its object.

2. *Nominal* and *Real* Definitions (definitio nominalis et realis). The former defines what is to be understood by an expression. The Real Definition has to do with the internal possibility of the object denoted by the notion, and thus with the real validity of the notion; for it either contains the proof of its real validity in the statement of the way in which the object originated, or was based upon such a proof.

3. The *Essential Definition* and the *Distinctive Explanation*, or the *Explanation of the Essence* and *Explanation* by *Derivative Determinations* (Definitio essentialis; Definitio attributiva vel accidentalis sive

[¹ Cf. *Logic*, i. 150-178.]

declaratio distinguens). The one gives the constitutively essential marks; the other the secondary, and
consequently the attributes or different possible modes,
but in the number and connection in which they belong
exclusively to all the objects falling under the notion
to be defined, and therefore sufficient to distinguish
these objects from all others.

4. *Analytically-formed* and *Synthetically-formed* Definitions (Definitio analytica and synthetica). The one
is formed in conformity with the existing use of speech,
or according to the way of conception at present in use
among the sciences; the other is formed anew and
freely, independent of any demand of agreement with
present use and want.

5. *Description* (descriptio), *Exposition* (expositio),
and *Explication* (explicatio) are less strict forms of
explaining what belongs to the content of a notion, and
so are related to Definition. These forms, along with
Definition, may all be comprehended under the wider
word *Explanation* (declaratio). *Illustration* (illustra-
tio, exemplificatio), giving examples which are taken
from the extent, is rather related to *Division*.

There can only be one essence to the same object. Hence
it might be expected that there can only be one definition to
the same notion. *Different definitions of the same notion* are
possible in as far as a reciprocal dependence of the constitutively and consecutively essential attributes exists; so that,
when any one or any group of them is stated, the sum total of
the others cannot be separated from it. For example, we
might define the circle by the curve of the straight line
which produces it, or by the equidistance of every point of
the circumference from the centre, or by the section parallel to

the base of the right cone, or by the formulae of analytical geometry ready to our hand; each of these attributes is so necessarily linked to the rest by mathematical laws, that the defined notion (of the circle) is the same in each. It is none the less undeniable, however, that only one definition fulfills the task of the definition in the fullest sense, viz. the definitio essentialis. Johannes Scotus (Erigena) said correctly :[1] quamvis multae definitionum species quibusdam esse videantur, sola ac vere ipsa dicenda est definitio, quae a Graecis οὐσιώδης, a nostris vero essentialis vocari consuevit.— Sola οὐσιώδης id solum recipit ad definiendum, quod perfectionem naturae, quam definit, complet ac perficit.

From the definitions given above several axioms may be derived about the relation which exists *between the members of those different divisions.* The substantial definition, at least when it stands alone by itself, is generally a nominal definition; the genetic, unless where the pretended genesis is impossible, is always a real definition. The nominal definition seems to be related to the accidental, or to the distinctive explanation; and the real definition to the essential. But it is by no means the case that every nominal definition is merely an accidental definition. A nominal definition may be an essential, and an essential a nominal. When, e.g. *Wolff* defines truth to be the agreement of thought with the existence which is thought, he himself correctly explains this definition to be nominal, because it does not show the possibility of such a correspondence, and consequently does not warrant the real validity of the defined notion. Yet it is the essential definition of truth because it states its essence or fundamentally essential character. (If the essence were the ground of the thing, as some define it, every essential definition would at the same time be a genetic, and consequently also a real, definition; but the essence is only the ground of the other attributes of the thing, not the ground of the thing because it is not the ground of itself.) Every real definition is not at the same time an essential definition. It may also be an

[1] *De Divis. Nat.* l. 13.

accidental definition, and an accidental may be a real definition. (The possibility of the thing may be warranted in a more external way, perhaps, by reference to some genesis which does not follow from the essence itself: in this case we have a real definition which is not an essential definition.) The division of definitions into analytically- and synthetically-constructed definitions has no definite relation to the other divisions.

The terms *Nominal* and *Real Definition* are not thoroughly expressive; for every definition defines not the name, nor the thing, but the *notion*, and with it the name and the thing so far as this is possible. But so long as the real validity of the defined notion is not warranted, it is always possible that a notion may have been defined which is only apparently valid, and is in truth only a mere name or a feigned notion corresponding to nothing real. On the other hand, the definition of an objectively-valid notion serves at the same time to give a knowledge of the thing denoted by the notion. Considered in this sense these terms justify themselves.

Some logicians distinguish from the Real and Nominal Definition a third kind, the *Verbal Definition* or explanation of words, by which they mean the mere statement of the meaning of terms. This co-ordination of the so-called verbal definition with the other kinds is inadmissible. In the statement of the meaning of a word it is the *object* of the explanation, not the *kind* of explanation which is peculiar. The so-called verbal definition, if it be a definition at all, is either the Nominal or Real Definition of the notion of a word.

Definitions formed *synthetically* are only admissible where science actually requires new notions. The intermixture of determinations, which are admitted into a synthetic definition of a notion according to the individual judgment, with the elements of the content of that notion, which, according to the universal use of language, bears the same name, has always been one of the most inexhaustible sources of errors and mistakes. Many of Spinoza's definitions serve as examples—his definition of Substance, for instance, of Love, &c.; and not a few of Kant's, of knowledge à priori for instance, and of

the Idea, of Freedom; the moral definitions of faith also, in
their relation to its actual reference, which is also conformable
to the use of language, to the acceptance as true of distinct
propositions; or, reciprocally, the definitions enunciated in this
last sense, in their relation to another use of the word, in
the sense of trust in God and Men, &c.[1] (The terms *synthetic* and *analytic definition*, introduced by Kant, are particularly useful to point out the distinct kind of quaternio terminorum, which rests on the confusion mentioned above. On
the other hand, one must remember that the distinction
denoted does not so much concern the character of the
definition itself as the kind of its origin in the subject. It is
rather a psychological than a logical distinction.)

Aristotle teaches: ὁ ὁριζόμενος δείκνυσιν ἢ τί ἐστιν ἢ τί σημαί-
ει τοὔνομα.[2] He calls the latter kind of Definition λόγος
ὀνοματώδης,[3] the former is called by Aristotelians ὅρος πραγ-
ματώδης (realis) or ὅρος οὐσιώδης (essentialis). We can also
give a definition of notions which have no real validity, as, for
example, τραγέλαφος. But we can only know the essence or the
τί ἐστι of what is, and of which we know that it is. Hence,
e.g. we cannot know the essence of τραγέλαφος, τί δ' ἐστὶ τραγέλαφος, ἀδύνατον εἰδέναι.[4] Knowledge advances from existence to essence and reason—ἔχοντες ὅτι ἐστι, ζητοῦμεν διὰ τί
ἐστιν. The full knowledge of the τί ἐστι includes the knowledge of the διὰ τί ἐστιν, and is distinct from it, only in a
formal relation. In other words, the knowledge of the essence
of the thing must found itself on the knowledge of its origin.
The essential explanation must either include the cause of the
object along with the genetic demonstration, or must presuppose the knowledge of the cause along with the conclusion of
the demonstration. This postulate falls to the ground only in
the definition of causeless self-evident principles.[5] The Aristotelian notion of the essential explanation, or ὁρισμὸς τὸ τί
ἐστι σημαίνων, unites in itself these two moments—the state-

[1] Cf. § 160.   [2] *Anal. Poster.* ii. 7.
[3] Ibid. ii. 10.   [4] Ibid. ii. 7.   [5] Ibid. ii. 10.

ment of the *essential* attributes, and the proved *reality* of the object.

Leibniz distinguishes ' Definitiones *nominales*, quae notas tantum rei ab aliis discernendae continent, et *reales*, ex quibus constat rem esse possibilem.'[1] He thus, on the one hand, includes in the notion of definitio realis a moment less than Aristotle does in the corresponding notion of ὁρισμὸς τὸ τί ἐστι σημαίνων. He does not expressly demand a statement of the essential marks (for the essence is not identical with that by which the possibility and the genesis of the object is known). On the other hand, he includes a moment more than Aristotle does. He does not admit, as Aristotle does, that the real definition contains either the proof of the reality and of the genesis of the notion, or founds itself on a previous demonstration. He only asserts that it gives the proof of the internal possibility.

Starting from these definitions of Leibniz, *Wolff* distinguished more strictly the two elements which lay combined in the Aristotelian notion of ὁρισμὸς τοῦ τί ἐστι, and separated the simple Aristotelian opposition into the double one of, on the one side, the definitio nominalis and realis; and, on the other, of definitio accidentalis and essentialis. He says:—
' definitio, per quam patet rem definitam esse possibilem, *realis* vocatur:[2] definitionem *essentialem* appello, in qua enumerantur essentialia, per quae definitum determinatur; *accidentalem* dico, in qua enumerantur vel attributa, vel quae per modum attributorum insunt, modorum ac relationum possibilitates, quibus definitum determinatur.'[3]

Kant, on the other hand, recombined the two moments. In his explanation of nominal and real definitions, he includes the characteristics of accidental and essential definitions.[4]

The post-Kantian logicians have partly followed Wolff or

[1] *Acta Erudit.* p. 540, 1684.   [2] *Log.* § 191.

[3] *Log.* § 192.   The older logicians distinguished after Boëthius the definitio secundum substantiam, quae proprie definitio dicitur and the definitio secundum accidens, quae descriptio nominatur.   Cf. Abælard, *Dial.*, in Cousin, *Œuvr. inéd. d'Ab.* § 493; Joh. Scotus, as above.

[4] *Log.* ed. by Jæsche, § 106.

Kant,[1] and have partly[2] referred the distinction of nominal
and real definition to that distinction which Wolff expressed
by the terms accidental and essential definition.[3] This terminology is, however, not advisable, partly because the meaning of the words used refers more to the distinction between
the subjectively arbitrary, and objectively or really valid,
determination of the notion, than to the non-essential and essential attributes; and partly and chiefly because it is foreign to
prevailing use and wont in mathematics and other sciences.[4]
Those mathematical definitions, e.g. which are brought forward
by Euclid to prove the construction of required figures,
whether they contain constitutively essential or secondary attributes, are to be called Nominal definitions; but definitions
which contain only secondary determinations, as, e.g. that of
the straight line, as the shortest distance between two points
(since the essence of straightness is rather continuous direction), although it may prove its objective validity, are to be
called Accidental or Attributive Definitions, or Distinctive

---

[1] Herbart, *Lehrb. zur Einl. in die Philos.* § 42, following Wolff and
Aristotle, finds the characteristic attribute of the real definition in the
validity of the notion.

[2] Schleiermacher, *Dial.* § 266; and Drobisch, *Log.* 2nd ed. § 109.

[3] In the 3rd ed. of his *Logic*, in §§ 115, 116, which correspond to
§§ 109, 110 of the 2nd ed., Drobisch uses the expressions, 'distinctive
explanation' and 'definition,' in the sense of accidental and essential
definition; and in § 120 introduces as the common use and meaning of
the term real definition, which he means to disregard, that explanation
by which the possibility, or more correctly the validity, of a notion is
made clear.

[4] Drobisch has himself followed the use which he exclaims against
in the 2nd ed. of his *Logic*, in his *Empirische Psychologie*, e.g. at
p. 292, where he says of the prevailing explanations of the mental
faculties, 'they are only explanations of names which do not warrant
the reality of their objects.' A discrepancy between the terminology in
Logic and in the other sciences is always a misfortune; and should be
the less admissible because it may be avoided without innovations, by
a simple reference to definitions given by Wolff after Aristotle and
Leibniz.

Explanations. When the penal code distinguishes felony
and misdemeanour, and defines felony as 'a crime punished
by forfeiture either of the fee or of the goods and chattels of the
criminal,' this is an Attributive Explanation (Distinctive
Explanation); but when 'trial' is defined to be the proving
of the resolve to commit a felony or misdemeanour, by deeds
which contain a beginning of the procedure in this felony or
misdemeanour, this is an essential explanation. Both explanations are equivalent, so far as the distinction between Nominal.
and Real Definitions goes.

. [*J. S. Mill* reduces all definitions to Nominal Definitions.
No definition is intended to explain the nature of a thing.
All definitions are of names, and of names only. In some
definitions, however, it is clearly apparent that nothing is
intended save to explain the meaning of a word; while in
others, besides explaining the meaning of the word, it is intended to be implied that there exists a thing corresponding
to the word. There is a real distinction between definitions of
names and what are erroneously called definitions of things;
but it is, that the latter, along with the meaning of a name,
covertly asserts a matter of fact. This covert assertion is not
a definition, but a postulate. On this doctrine of definition
Mr. Mill bases his hypothetical theory of demonstration, since
the certainty of the so-called necessary sciences depends on
the correctness of the hypothesis which connects their definitions with real things. Definitions, however, are not arbitrary, and though of names must be grounded on a knowledge
of the corresponding things.[1] In this theory of Definition
Mr. Mill seems to contradict the doctrine enforced with so
much vigour when treating of propositions in general, that
propositions express not a relation between two names, but
between matters of fact. Had Mr. Mill only applied this
same doctrine to that class of propositions called definitions,
he would have hesitated ere he reduced all definitions to definitions of names, and might have been led to a theory of
demonstration more consistent with fact, than that which makes

[1 Cf. *Logic,* i. 160–178, ii. 216–220.

him say that there may be any number of sciences as necessary as geometry if only suitable nominal definitions are combined with a few real axioms.

Mansel gives a very good resumé of Aristotle's views upon Definition. He does not recognise Definition so far as it has to do with material truth or correctness, or so far as it gives information about the meaning of words we were previously ignorant of. Logical definition has to do only with the subjective *distinctness* of a notion.[1]

Sir Wm. Hamilton gives the common division of definitions, but, refusing to introduce them into pure Logic, relegates the discussion to applied Logic.[2]

Aug. De Morgan divides Definitions into nominal and real. Nominal definitions substitute for a name other terms. A real definition so explains a word that it suffices to separate the thing contained under that word from all others.[3]]

§ 62. The most noteworthy FAULTS of DEFINITIONS are:—

(1) Too great *width* or *narrowness* (definitio latior, angustior suo definito). The definition is of greater or less extent than what is defined, and the rule is broken that the definition be adequate (definitio adaequata), or that the definition and what is defined be reciprocal notions.

(2) *Redundancy* (definitio abundans). Along with the fundamentally essential determinations are given derivative ones, which belong only to the development of the notion.

(3) *Tautology* (idem per idem). The definition explicitly or implicitly repeats the notion to be defined.

---

[1] Cf. his ed. of Aldrich's *Log.* 4th ed., Appendix, pp. 181–197.
[2] *Lect.* ii. 22–36.
[3] Cf. *Formal Logic; or, the Calculus of Inference*, p. 36, 1847.]

(4) The *Circle* or *Diallelon* (circulus sive orbis in definiendo). A is defined by B, and B again by A; or A is defined by B, B by C, C by D, and D or any following member is again defined by A. This commonly happens in consequence of an ὕστερον πρότερον, i.e. of an attempt to define a notion, whose scientific presuppositions are not known, by means of those notions which already presuppose it.

(5) Definition by *figurative expression*, by *mere negations*, by *co-ordinate* and *subordinate* notions. The negative definition is legitimate with *negative* notions, and in *simple* notions their mere separation from their state of confusedness among other notions, and explanation by means of the statement of their extent, is scientifically correct.

The following definition of the infinitely little (which is to be found in a recent text-book on the Differential Calculus) is an example of too great width:—'A quantity which we think as a fraction, with the numerator always remaining the same, but the denominator continually increasing, we call the infinitely little.' The definiens has here a wider extent than the definiendum, for the denominator steadily increases when it advances in the following way:—10, 15, 17½, 18¾ . . . and yet the fraction is not in this case infinitely little. The limitation is needed—the series of fractions must also be of such a kind that whatever number be given, one member of the series can always be found, which is smaller than its whole value, or stands nearer zero; in other words, the series must have zero as its limit of value. Cato's definition of an orator is *too narrow*, —'Orator est vir bonus dicendi peritus;' for individuals can be thought of which belong to the extent of the definiendum, and do not belong to the extent of the definiens. K. H. Becker's definition is also *too narrow*,—' Thought is that act of the intelligence, by which notion an activity and a substance are perceived to be one (congruent);' for it includes one kind of thinking only. The definition, which is *too narrow*, is false as a proposition and as a general reference. The definition, which is *too wide*, is true as a proposition, but its converse is false. (In the converse the subject becomes predicate and the predicate subject; cf. § 85—The Doctrine of Conversion.) An adequate definition is true conversely, for the definitum and the definiens must be reciprocal notions. Conversion can therefore serve as a *means* of *testing* definitions.

Redundancy is exhibited in the explanation,—Parallels are lines which have the same direction, and always keep the same distance from each other. But there is only an apparent redundancy when, in the definition of the similarity of rectilineal plane triangles, the equality of the angles, as well as the proportionality of the sides, is taken into consideration; for though in the triangle one of these two conditions can be deduced from the other, the two, when united, express the full essence of similarity, since the general definition of similarity of rectilineal plane figures can be established only on the union of the two attributes.

Tautology occurs in the answer given by Callicles to the question of Socrates : τίνας λέγεις τοὺς βελτίους ;—τοὺς ἀμείνους ἔγωγε, whereon Socrates replies: ὀνόματα λέγεις, δηλοῖς δ' οὐδέν. The same fault occurs when living power is explained to be the inner ground of life. But no tautology occurs when, if a species-notion is to be defined which has no peculiar name, but is denoted by the addition of an adjective to the name of a genus, the name of the genus is repeated in the definition. This procedure is not confined to Nominal Definitions (as has sometimes been asserted); for if the species is to be defined, the genus in every case must belong to the notions already previously defined, and therefore to be presupposed as known. Thus, e.g. the definition—a straight line is a line with a direction constant in itself—is without fault as a real and essential definition; for the definition of a line (as a construction formed by the motion of a point) must be presupposed, if the notion of the species *straight line* is to be defined.

An *Hysteron proteron* is contained in the explanation of size as the capability of increasing and diminishing. It leads to a *circle explanation*; for increase is only addition to size, and diminution is only taking away from size. The definition which I. G. E. Maass gives of pleasure[1] is really a *circle.* He says: ' A feeling is pleasant when it is desired because of itself.' ' We desire only what we in some way represent to be good.'[2] ' The sensibility takes that to be good which warrants or promises pleasure, and affects us pleasantly ;—the desires rest on pleasant feelings.'[3] The pleasant feeling is here explained by the desire, and the desire again by the pleasant feeling. (If this circle is to be avoided, we must refer in the definition of feeling to the notion of futherance of life, which forms its scientific presupposition. The feeling of the pleasant is the immediate consciousness of the futherance of life.)

When Plato calls the idea of the good the sun in the kingdom of ideas, he did not mean this *figurative* designation to be a definition; for he believed the good, as a simple and highest notion, to be indefinable. But we cannot presuppose that the Pythagoreans had the same logical consciousness when they defined things to be numbers,—justice, for example, to be a square number, ἀριθμὸν ἰσάκις ἴσον; nor that Jacob Böhme had it when he said,—' the new birth is the disentanglement of the heavenly essence in the centre of the animal soul.' ' Nature (Heaven and earth, and all that is therein) is the body of God,' &c. Explanations, too, like the following—Justice embodies the ethical idea; the state is man writ large; the Church is the body of Christ; Conscience is the internal court of justice, which has taken up its abode in every man; and such like—which contain figuratively true thoughts, require the explanation of the parable in its peculiar sense, in order to become scientific definitions. The figurativeness in Zeno's definition of πάθος as the ἄλογος καὶ παρὰ φύσιν ψυχῆς κίνησις,[4] where the meaning of ' motion' wavers between feel-

[1] In his *Versuch über die Gefühle*, i. 39.   [2] Ibid. p. 243.
[3] Ibid. p. 241.
[4] *Diog. Laert.* vii. 110; cf. Cic. *Tusc.* iv. 6: averss a recta ratione contra naturam animi commotio.

ing and desire, is more indirect, and therefore more injurious in Science. The same fault of indirect figurativeness injures Wundt's explanation—'Sensation is the inference which the mind draws from a series of signs lying in the nerve-processes.' Under the figure of inference the difficulty is concealed, whether and how a sensation can be the *result* of motions, and what kind of connection does actually exist.

Euclid's definition—' Parallel lines are straight lines in the same plane, which, produced infinitely, will never meet '—characterises parallel lines by a determination merely *negative*, and only *derivative*, not *fundamentally essential.* It leads to confusion, which does not occur in definitions formed upon the notion of direction (cf. § 110). The definition—περιττόν (ἐστι) τὸ μονάδι μεῖζον ἀρτίου—may be taken, with Aristotle, as an example of a faulty definition formed by means of *co-ordinate* notions.

In formal reference it is always more correct to define co-ordinate notions by means of the genus-notion and their specific differences. For example, the even number is a number which is divisible by 2 without remainder; the odd is a number which, divided by 2, has a remainder of 1. It would, however, amount to a formal rigorism, if one were wholly to despise the shortness and comprehensiveness which can be reached, in many cases, by reference to a foregoing definition of a co-ordinate notion; for example, after the definition of the even number has been granted, not to allow the definition,—the odd number is that which is distinguished from the even by unity.

The enumeration of the members of the extent of a notion (e.g. the conic section is that mathematical figure which divides into these four forms—circle, ellipse, parabola, hyperbola) is useful to illustrate this notion, if it goes before or comes after definition. When it stands in the place of the latter, it becomes the faulty definitio per divisionem or per disjuncta.

Since simple notions, as has been already remarked (§ 60), admit of no proper definition, but can be brought into consciousness and distinctly distinguished from other notions only by abstraction and isolation, the highest scientific strictness possible in this case is reached by the form of the accidental definition. For example, the notion of the point is to be defined by a progressive series of limitations, which find scientific expression in the following accidental definitions—Space is what remains over from the sum total of sense-intuition, after the abstraction of matter (i.e. of what is unchanged in motion); mathematical body is a finite part of infinite space, or a limited space; surface is the limit of body, the line of surface, and the point of the line. After that the simplest element has been reached in this way, the other constructions can be genetically reconstructed from them, and defined by the explanation of the essence.

§ 63. DIVISION (divisio, διαίρεσις) is the complete and orderly statement of the parts of the extent of a notion, or the separation of the genus into its species. The species-notions are distinguished from the genus-notions by this, that the more indistinct features of the genus-notion, by the addition of the specific differences, have *actually* taken the different forms or modifications of which they are capable. Hence, in the division of the genus-notion, the formation and arrangement of the species-notions must be founded on these modifications of the characteristics of the genus. Accordingly different divisions are produced, in any genus-notion, which unites in itself several characteristics able to be modified, when the species are distinguished according to the differentiations of the one or the other. That attribute of the genus, on whose modifications the formation and arrangement of the notions of species is based, is called the GROUND OF DIVISION or PRINCIPLE OF DIVISION (fundamentum sive principium divisionis); the

N

species-notions themselves, the MEMBERS OF DIVISION (membra divisionis, less strictly membra dividentia). Division is *Dichotomy, Trichotomy, Tetrachotomy, Polytomy,* according to the number of the members in division. The formal postulates of Division are:—that the spheres of the members of division, taken together, exactly correspond to the sphere of the notion to be divided, and therefore fill it without *hiatus* ;—that they in no way overpass it ; and,—that they do not cross but completely exclude each other. In the arrangement of the members of division, those which are the most closely related to each other should be placed together. Division determined by the modifications of a single attribute is called *artificial division.* It has scientific value in the proportion in which the presupposition is true, that by means of some causal connection the modifications of this attribute are linked to the corresponding modifications of the whole essential attributes. The most perfect Division founds itself on the essential modifications of the essentially constitutive attributes. It depends on the essential definition of the notion to be divided. It is called *Natural Division* in the same sense as the system which results from a continuous series of such divisions is to be called a natural system. Divisions of this kind cannot be formed in any way according to an external uniform scheme. It is incorrect to look for an equal number of members of division in all cases in divisions of this kind so far as they correspond to the ideal demand. A strict *Dichotomy* may always be attained by means of a negative species-notion ; but then it labours under the

defect that the species classed under the negation are
left indefinite. When there are several of them the
dichotomy will show itself to be illusive, as soon as they
come to be specified according to their positive attributes.
Such a division therefore can only serve as an introduction in the formation and testing of divisions. *Trichotomy* usually finds application where a development
occurs which is independent and rests on internal
causes; because such a development is accomplished
in the form of an opposition of two members and
their fusion in a third. Mere trichotomy, however,
not unfrequently falls short of the domain of actual
existence; for actual existence in its higher grades does
not usually advance in simple series. The higher unity
to be brought about often results from a great number
of cross oppositions.

By the natural method of division *Cuvier* means (Règne
animal, Introduction), ' An arrangement in which existences
of the same kind will rather be neighbours of each other than
of those of other kinds, kinds of the same order of each other
than of those of other orders—and so on.' Cuvier explains
this to be the ideal which natural history must aim after; for it is
' the exact and complete expression of the whole of nature.' Cf.
§ 58.

The doctrine of Divisions, whose scientific value *Plato* had
already recognised, formed with *Aristotle* an integral part of
Analytic. *Plato* preferred Dichotomy. Every opposition has
two members.[1] The parts must be *species* (εἴδη), i.e. formed
according to essential differences,[2]—κατ' ἄρθρα, ᾗ πέφυκεν—εἰς
ἓν καὶ ἐπὶ πολλὰ πεφυκότα ὁρᾶν.[3] In his later period Plato was
fond of adding to the two members of the opposition, as a
third, τὸ ἐξ ἀμφοῖν μικτόν. He did not, however, recognise in

[1] *Prot.* p. 332.　　[2] *Phaedrus*, 265.　　[3] Cf. *Polit.* 262 sqq.

this third member (as Hegel does) the highest but intermediate element.[1] In the dialogue Sophistes[2] dichotomy is traced back to the general point of view of ταὐτόν and ἕτερον.[3] Tetrachotomy results from the combination of two grounds of division.

Aristotle treats of the doctrine of the grounds of division in Top. vi. 6, and De Part. Anim. i. 3, where he more especially notices the passing from one ground of division to another. He explains[4] the advantages and disadvantages of dichotomy formed by negation. We do not find that he had the modern preference for a distinct number of positive members of division; this is, for the most part, a consequence from the Kantian doctrine of the Categories. *Kant* believes that he can, according to his table of categories, which contains completely and systematically all the elementary notions of the understanding, determine à priori every moment of every speculative science and their arrangement.[5] Hence the scheme of the categories has served him, and still more his disciples, as a leading principle in the treatment and division of the varied scientific material. Goethe himself was once induced by Schiller to attempt the thankless task of dividing his doctrine of colours according to the Kantian Categories. One of the 'singular reflections' which Kant attached to his table of categories has proved very rich in consequences. He says that every other à priori division of notions must be a dichotomy (A is partly B, partly not D); but a trinity of Categories appears in every class, and in each case the third arises from the union of the first and second. This remark of Kant's has led to that scheme of thesis, antithesis, and synthesis, which, on all points, conditions the methodical course in *Fichte's* constructions, and still more in the *Hegelian* dialectic. These trichotomies are not purely arbitrary, but rest on a true insight into the essence of development. Yet they cannot be recog-

---

[1] See *Phileb.* 23; *Tim.* 35 A; cf. the author's article in the *Rhein. Mus. für Philologie,* N. S. part ix. p. 64 ff., 1853.

[2] P. 253.   [3] Cf. *Polit.* 287.

[4] *Anal. Post.* ii. 13; *De Part. Anim.* i. 2, 3.

[5] *Krit. der r. Vern.* § 11.

nised to be the only valid, and everywhere predominating, form
of division; not merely because now and then the phenomena
of nature fall behind the notion, as Hegel says, and because
dialectic thought is not yet thoroughly the lord of things; but
because the simple uniformity of trichotomy of itself is not
enough to represent the fulness of the phenomena of natural
and mental life. In many cases this fulness corresponds more
to the intertwined double method of *Schleiermacher's* tetrachotomy, which starts from two cross dichotomies. Schleiermacher endeavours to prove the unity which is above the
double opposition. (For example, he divides the sciences into
the speculative and empirical knowledge of reason, and the
speculative and empirical knowledge of nature, or into ethics,
science of history, physics, and natural science, according to the
oppositions of reason and nature, force and phenomenon, and
finds in Dialectic, which starts from their common principles,
the vital point of unity.) But this fourfold or fivefold combination cannot be suitably applied to every matter, any more
than the ninefold division of *George*, which combines the principles of Hegel's and Schleiermacher's methods of division, or
other schemes published by others. The only general rule
which can be established is,—every natural division must be
conformable to its objects.[1]

The doctrine of Division owes to *Herbart* the remark, that,
as the division of a notion depends upon the division of an
attribute, which forms the ground of division, all divisions in
the last resort return necessarily to certain fundamental divisions, in which only a single attribute of the notion to be
divided is the ground of division; but this notion is itself the
ground of division, and the series of species or individuals must
therefore be given immediately. For example, the series of
colours, sounds, numbers, &c.[2]

---

[1] Cf. Trendelenburg, *Log. Unters.* 2nd ed. ii. 233; 3rd ed. ii. 256;
cf. Johan. Scotus (Erigena) in Prantl, ii. 32, and Plato, *Phaedr.* p. 265.

[2] See Herbart, *Lehrbuch zur Einleitung in die Phil.* § 43; cf. Drobisch, *Logik*, 3rd ed. § 123.

§ 64. When the single members of division are again divided into their subspecies, *Subdivision* results. When one and the same notion is divided according to two principles, *Co-division* arises. The same ground of division, on which a co-division of the genus-notion rests, can generally serve as a ground of division for the subdivision or partition of species into subspecies, under the limitations which result from the mutual relations of the dependence of the attributes.[1] *Progressive* division must proceed continuously by species and subspecies without hiatus (divisio fiat in membra proxima). It contradicts the laws of complete formal strictness if the subdivisions into which a co-ordinate species may be divided are placed directly beside the species, so that the subspecies may come in instead of whole species. It is a licence sometimes convenient however, in cases where the limit between the different ranks of species and subspecies is indistinct, and by no means to be rejected unconditionally, especially in a widely ramified division of a very comprehensive material. Only do not let the possibility of survey be lost, nor the division, in this reference, fail in its design.

For example, it would be an unjustifiable rigorism not to admit the division of natural objects into *Minerals, Plants,* and *Animals* (instead of, I. Inorganic objects or minerals; II. Organic objects: *a.* Plants; *b.* Animals); more especially because if the capacity of consciousness be the ground of the principal division, minerals and plants may be taken together as subspecies under the chief species—inanimate objects of nature, and animals alone make up the second chief species. In the case of simple co-ordination the gradual sequence of

[1] Cf. §§ 50, 54.

internal value appears as a ground of division. When *Epicurus* divides the desires in their ethical reference into three
classes,—naturales et necessariae, naturales et non necessariae,
nec naturales nec necessariae—the gradation in the proportion
of its correctness forms the ground of division which may
justify this kind of co-ordination. In any case the fault of
superfluity is not justifiable which *Cicero*[1] expresses against
this division when he says, 'hoc est non dividere, sed frangere
rem; — contemnit dissecrendi elegantiam, confuse loquitur.'
Cicero reproaches Epicurus with counting the species as a
genus in this division ('vitiosum est enim in dividendo partem
in genere numeraro '), and on his side only admits the division—1. Naturales: *a.* Necessariae; *b.* Non necessariae; II.
Inanes. In this last division the naturales necessariae and the
naturales non necessariae are only species, and the inanes, on
the other hand, a genus. But this is not the case from the
Epicurean point of view, which really makes the three classes
co-ordinate with each other.

Division can only descend to such groups as are not essentially separated from each other. Subdivisions are not
formed for the sake of very small differences. *Seneca* warns
against the extravagances which the usages of rhetorical
arrangement seem to have introduced into the rhetorical
schools of the ancients, in the words—'quidquid in maius
crevit, facilius agnoscitur, si discessit in partes; quas vero
innumerabiles esse et minimas non oportet; idem enim vitii
habet nimia, quod nulla divisio; simile confuso est, quidquid
usque in pulverem sectum est.'[2] *Quintilian* says the same
of partitio: 'quum fecere mille particulas, in eandem incidunt
obscuritatem, contra quam partitio inventa est.'

§ 65. The most important DEFECTS *in* DIVISIONS
are:—

(1) Too great *width* or *narrowness.* (The latter occurs
chiefly by overlooking transition-forms.)

---

[1] *De Fin.* ii. c. ix. [2] *Epist.* lxxxix.

(2) The placing side by side species-notions, which do not *purely exclude* each other, whose spheres fall wholly or partly within each other.

(3) *The confusion of different principles of division.* (This fault is often connected with the others.)

The defects in Division are nearly allied to those in Definition (§ 62).

In too great *width* the spheres of the members of division, taken together, exceed the sphere of the notion to be divided (membra dividentia excedunt divisum; divisio latior est suo diviso). The Stoical division of passions (πάθη) into four chief forms—laetitia, libido, aegritudo, and metus—is too wide, if, according to the definition recognised in that school, πάθος is taken to mean ὁρμὴ πλεονάζουσα.[1] The member of division goes beyond the sphere of (positive and negative) desire, and embraces the feelings also.

Divisions of men into good and evil, of systems into true and false, of actions into voluntary or not voluntary, or of temperaments into the four well-known fundamental forms, are too *narrow*, because they disregard the endless number of transition forms. The division of natural objects into simple and compound overlook the third possibility of organic unity, in which we can as little speak of a combination, which presupposes an original separation and an external conjunction, as we can of simple punctual unity. The same fault occurs often in *disjunctions* which are divisions of possibilities.

A modern division of affections into self-love, affection for others, and mutual affection, may serve as an example of faulty division whose *spheres do not thoroughly exclude each other.* Mutual affections are those affections for others which are returned. They are a subdivision of the second, not a new third kind.

A confusion of different principles of division exists in the division of the tenses of the verb into principal and historical tenses, used more especially in Greek grammar. The motive

[1] Appetitus vehementior, Cic. *Tusc.* iv. G.

for this illogical division lay, undoubtedly, in the well-founded dislike to call the historical tenses merely secondary tenses, which would have been actually false, and in the dislike, also well-grounded, to denote the one class, by a merely negative designation, the non-historical tenses. The tendency, arising from a false love of system, to place on either side an equal number of classes of tenses, was unjustifiable. It should rather have been recognised that the one group of rules hold good for *one* class of tenses, for the historical, namely ; and the other group in an essentially similar way for *two* classes of tenses, viz. for the present and future tenses. These two classes, however, were not to be opposed to the historical under one positive notion, but were to be named in connection with each other.

§ 66. The *formation* of valid *notions* and of adequate definitions and divisions can only attain to scientific perfection in *connection* with all the other *processes of knowledge.*

For the formation of *general conceptions* there is needed the combination of particular conceptions only, not of judgments, inferences, &c. The combination of the elements of the content of the conception does not need to be produced by judgments which include them ; it is already originally contained in the perceptions and intuitions. Nor does the separation of the content need negative judgments. It results by means of the processes of attention and abstraction, which in no way presuppose the forms of the judgment. Those who mean by *notion* only a general conception, or a conception with an objective reference, are not correct if they make the structure of the notion depend on a previous structure of judgments. The formation of the notion, however, in its fuller sense (as a knowledge of the *essence*) depends upon the formation of judgments. In order to decide what makes an *essential*, or what makes up the universal and lasting basis for the most, and the most important, attributes, one must ascertain on what conception the most universal, most exception-

less, and most scientific *judgments* are based. For example,
the completion of grammatical notions depends upon an investigation, requiring ever to be renewed, whether a consistent
system of universal rules can rest upon the notions we already
have. The dependence is reciprocal, however. The scientific judgment also presupposes the scientific notion. For
example, it is impossible to reach a system of grammatical
rules in any way satisfactory if a happy tact in forming grammatical notions had not already prepared the way. The
history of Grammar shows a gradual mutual development of
notion and rule. In this sense *Schleiermacher* [1] says rightly—
the judgment presupposes the notion according to its essential
existence, and the notion the judgment. The notion which,
according to the measure of its form, agrees with the object,
must have before it a whole system of judgments. The
formation of the notion stands in like reciprocal relation
to the syllogistic and inductive *formation of inferences*, to
knowledge of *principles*, and to the formation of complete
systems. Notions like *Entelechies, Monads, Stages-of-develop-
ment, Stages-of-culture, Differential* and *Integral, Gravitation,
Chemical Affinity,* and the like, presuppose whole scientific
systems. They again, on their side, condition the development of the systems. We may say [2]—the notion must be the
starting-point, and also the end and aim of all thinking,
provided that it is not explained with a one-sided exaggeration, and with unjust disregard of the other function, and of
their logical analysis, to be 'the single product of the mind.'
Any one function, in the degree of its own development,
furthers the development of other functions, and is furthered
by them. In science at least the mutual advancement of
every member is no empty delusion.

But the doctrine of the Notion as 'the simpler form must
precede the doctrines of Judgments, Inferences, and Systems,
without detriment to a real reciprocal relation, and must now
be brought relatively to a close.

[1] *Dial.* pp. 82, 83, 402.
[2] With J. Hoppe, *Die gesammte Logik*, p. 20, Paderborn, 1868.

PART FOURTH.

THE JUDGMENT IN ITS REFERENCE TO THE OBJECTIVE
FUNDAMENTAL COMBINATIONS OR RELATIONS.

§ 67. THE JUDGMENT (iudicium, ἀπόφανσις, as a part
of the inference it is called propositio or πρότασις) is the
consciousness of the objective validity of a subjective
union of conceptions, whose forms are different from,
but belong to each other. It is the consciousness,
whether or not the analogous combination exists between
the corresponding objective elements. As the individual
conception corresponds to the individual existence, so
the judgment in its various forms corresponds to and is
the subjective copy of the various objective relations.
A judgment expressed in words is an *Assertion* or *Proposition* (enuncitatio, ἀπόφανσις).

In the formation of *judgments* we advance from single conceptions and their elements to the combination of several.
The progress here (as it is also in the combination of judgments and inferences) is *synthetic*, while the progress made
from perception to the formation of individual conceptions and
notions was *analytic*. The judgment is the first whole which
has been again reached by synthesis. Logical theory, however, must not begin (as some logicians say) by attention
to *this* (derivative) whole, but must first attend to the immediately given (primitive) whole, i.e. to the perception.

Neither single notions (absolute or relative), nor mere combinations of notions, are judgments. Conviction conceiving the happening or not happening of what is thought, is Judgment. The Judgment is distinguished from the merely subjective combination of conceptions by a conscious reference to what actually exists, or, at least, to the objective phenomena. The reference of thought to actual existence gives the judgment its character of a *logical* function. Where the consciousness of the objective validity is wanting there is no judgment ; where it is *erroneous* the judgment is *false.*

The formation of a combination of conceptions, and of the consciousness of its validity, can be contemporaneous ; but the combination of conceptions (e.g. of the conception of this criminal with the conception of the deed laid to his charge, and of his unlawful intention, which makes him guilty) may be accompanied for a time by the consciousness of the uncertainty of its objective validity, until sufficient grounds of decision present themselves, which lead to the consciousness of its correspondence or non-correspondence with objective reality, i.e. to the (affirmative or negative) judgment.

In mathematical judgments the reference to objectivity is never wanting. Our conception of space corresponds to objective existence in space, and the *geometric* judgment is the consciousness of the accordance of a (subjective) assertion with an (objective) relation of a construction in space. The true axiom in actual construction, whether this is realised in us or in nature, must prove itself to be objectively valid, in each case, in proportion as it is the more exactly constructed. The notion of a number, also, although number does not exist without our consciousness, has its basis on objective reality, viz. on the quantity of the objects, and on the existence of genus and species, which compel the subsumption of many objects under one notion. The true *arithmetical* axiom must accord with the objective relation of quantity, that when the presupposition (hypothesis) is realised the assertion (thesis) is realised also. If I take 30*l.* from 100*l.*, and then add 20*l.*, 90*l.* must remain in the cash-box ; for in the abstract the equation is $100 - 30 + 20 = 90$; and the validity of the equation is its applicability to all numerical objects possible. Numbers can be detached by abstraction from this reference, and can be raised to be themselves objects of thought, but in this way they attain only a relative independence.

The assertion made [by Hamilton, Mansel, and others] that thought is to be called *formal* only in so far as it can be considered from the side of its form, without reference to the matter, is not correct. It is not the thinking, which is considered from the side of its form, that is formal, but the logical treatment which has to do with the form of the thinking, just as it is not language grammatically considered, but its grammatical consideration that is formal. Thinking in Logic itself is something formal, i.e. it is thinking which has to do with the form of thinking. Thinking considered and legislated for by Logic, is logical thinking when it is logically correct or in accordance with the logical laws. It is not a special kind of thinking coordinate with other kinds. Every operation of thought is logically or formally correct when it corresponds with the logical laws. Now, in so far as the logical postulate, which has to do with the judgment, is concerned—that it may be *true*—formal correctness and material truth coincide in the *individual* judgment. The former can also be limited to the mere correctness of the structure (of the conjunction of subject and predicate); but it is a proceeding of very little value to do so, and to say, for example, that the materially false proposition, ' all trees have leaves,' is formally correct. So far as the *derivation* of a judgment from data (which are possibly false) corresponds to the logical laws which are valid for it, this derivation is formally correct; and the derived judgment has then been *derived* with formal correctness, though it may not be materially true. The logical correctness of the sum total of all the operations of external and internal perception aiming at knowledge, though not *identical* with the material truth (which is the result aimed at by it), is *necessarily connected with* the material truth (whether in the fullest or in a limited sense of the word). Logic, as such, cannot decide upon

the truth of a judgment, because it only enunciates *rules*, and
does not itself carry out their *application*. Its problem is
legislative only.   Logic, as such, has ' no exception to take'
against the judgment, 'all trees have leaves.'   But it is a
mistake when this is understood to mean,[1] that the proposition
is recognised to be ' a judgment logically correct according to
form.'   Logic takes no exception to it, because it has not to
do with this judgment any more than with any other.   The
application of the logical postulate, that it must have a subject
and predicate, is to be put into execution by means of a merely
logical knowledge, but the logical postulate, that it must be
true, by means of knowledge of natural science, which forces the
falsehood to appear.   ' Formal correctness ' is limited to ' freedom from contradiction ' only when the logical rules aim solely
at this absence of contradiction.[2]   But even in this case Logic,
as the legislative science, would not decide upon the correctness (in this sense not at all involving the material truth) of
any one given judgment, nor expose the single contradictions,
but would only enunciate the rules for this judicial function.

As the forms of conception were originally recognised in
and by kinds of words, so judgments are in and by propositions.   Plato explains the λόγος to be the revelation of thought
(διάνοια) by the voice (φωνή) by means of ῥήματα and ὀνόματα ;
for thought is, as it were, coined into the sounds which stream
from the mouth.[3]   In the Dialogue Sophistes (more probably

---

[1] By Dr. Cal, in his *Lehrb. der propäd. Log.*, § 8, Vienna, 1865
[and Mansel, in his *Proleg. Log.* p. 258 ; *Rudimenta*, 4th ed. prof. 69].
Against these statements, cf. J. Hoppe, *Die gesammte Logik*, § 29,
Paderborn, 1868.   Hoppe believes thinking to be the function of
translating the objective reality into subjective conceptions.   His own
opposition between ' notional' and ' formal' thinking is defective.
Thinking, in Logic, is both ' formal' because it considers the forms of
thought, and ' notional' because it attains to notions about them.

[2] Cf. § 3.

[3] *Theaet.* p. 206 D: τὸ τὴν αὐτοῦ διάνοιαν ἐμφανῆ ποιεῖν διὰ φωνῆς
μετὰ ῥημάτων τε καὶ ὀνομάτων, ὥσπερ εἰς κάτοπτρον ἢ ὕδωρ τὴν δόξαν
ἀπεικονιζόμενον εἰς τὴν διὰ τοῦ στόματος ῥοήν.   Shorter and less strictly,
p. 202 a: ὀνομάτων γὰρ συμπλοκὴν εἶναι λόγου οὐσίαν.

the work of an early Platonist than of Plato [1]) the proposition
(λόγος), which is the verbal expression of the thought (διάνοια) [2]
in its simplest fundamental form (e.g. ἄνθρωπος μανθάνει),
explains the combination of substantive and verb as that
which corresponds to the combination of thing and action
(ξυμπλοκή or ξύνθεσις ἔκ τε ῥημάτων γιγνομένη καὶ ὀνομάτων,
—ξυντιθέναι πρᾶγμα πράξει δι' ὀνόματος καὶ ῥήματος).

Aristotle [3] defines the Judgment (ἀπόφανσις or λόγος ἀπο-
φαντικός) to be a combination of conceptions in which there is
truth or falsehood (σύνθεσις νοημάτων, ἐν ᾗ τὸ ἀληθεύειν ἢ
ψεύδεσθαι ὑπάρχει), or, with reference to the verbal expression,
as an assertion about existence or non-existence : [4] ἔστιν ἡ
ἁπλῆ ἀπόφασις φωνὴ σημαντικὴ περὶ τοῦ ὑπάρχειν ἢ μὴ
ὑπάρχειν. Aristotle, [5] agreeing with Plato, makes the ὄνομα
καὶ ῥῆμα the elements of the simple judgment.

In accordance with the Platonic and Aristotelian definitions, *Wolff* defines a judgment as [6] 'actus iste mentis, quo
aliquid a re quadam diversum eidem tribuimus vel ab ea
removemus, iudicium appellatur.' The judgment is formed
by means of the union or separation of conceptions.[7] The
proposition or assertion (enunciatio sive propositio) is the
combination of words, corresponding to the conceptions,
which are the elements of the judgment denoting the union
and separation of the conceptions and what belongs or does
not belong to the thing.[8] Wolff, accordingly, demands, as
Plato and Aristotle had done, three series parallel to each
other—the combination in things is to correspond with the
union of conceptions, and this last with the expression.
Several logicians after Wolff, in order to get rid of the disjunction, ' combination or separation,' in the definition of the

[1] *Theaet.* p. 262 E; 263 D, E.
[2] Soph. 263, E. A not very happy abbreviation of Plato's definitions in the *Theaet.*: τὸ ἀπὸ τῆς διανοίας ῥεῦμα διὰ τοῦ στόματος ἰὸν μετὰ
φθόγγου. The διάνοια is the ἐντὸς τῆς ψυχῆς πρὸς αὑτὴν διάλογος
ἄνευ φωνῆς γιγνόμενος.
[3] *De Interp.* c. iv.　　[4] Ibid. c. v.　　[5] Ibid. c. v. x.
[6] *Log.* § 39.　　[7] Ibid. § 40.　　[8] Ibid. § 41.

judgment, use the expression, The judgment is the conception of a relation between two notions.

Kant defines the judgment [1] to be the conception of the unity of the consciousness of different conceptions, or the conception of their relation so far as they make up one notion, or, more definitely,[2] the way to bring given cognitions to the objective unity of the apperception. By *objective* unity Kant understands the mutual connection of cognitions according to those categories which the Ego evolves from itself by the original activity of its own spontaneity, and by which, as à priori forms of thought, the Ego fashions the whole content of perception. Objectivity in this sense evidently does not denote a reference to a real external world, but only to a kind of activity of the ego. Hence this doctrine of judgments, in spite of the expression of objectivity which it contains, reveals throughout the subjective character of the Kantian philosophy. The view which regards the judgment as merely a process of subsuming the special under the universal is very prevalent among logicians influenced by Kant. In this sense *Fries* teaches,[3] the judgment is the knowledge of an object by notions, since the notion is added to the object as a characteristic, and the object is thereby rendered able to be understood.

Herbart[4] believes the judgment to be the deciding upon the capability of uniting given notions.

Hegel[5] understands by the judgment, the determination given to the notion by itself, or the notion making itself particular, or the original self-division of the notion into its moments, with distinguishing reference of the individual to the universal and the subsumption of the former under the latter, not as a mere operation of subjective thought, but as a universal form of all things. Here again, as in the notion, reference to reality is taken to be identity with reality. Hegel distinguishes judgments from propositions which do not refer

---

[1] *Log.* § 17.   [2] *Kritik der r. Vern.* § 19.
[3] *Syst. der Logik*, § 28.   [4] *Lehrbuch zur Einl. in die Phil.* § 52.
[5] *Logik*, ii. 65 ff.; *Encycl.* § 166 ff.

the subject to a universal predicate, but only express a
circumstance, a single action, &c. But in fact every (assert-
tory) proposition must express a logical judgment.

Beneke[1] distinguishes the logical judgment, as the analytic
act of the subsumption of the particular under the universal,
from the synthetic bases of the judgment or the combinations
of conceptions by which knowledge is advanced, which are
accompanied by those analyses. In common life we generally
have to do with the syntheses only, which precede the judgment proper; the logical element is the analytic subsumption of the less general subject-notion (or subject-conception)
under the more general predicate notion. For example, in
the judgment, A is a coward, the combination of the notion of
A with the notion of his deeds is the basis of the judgment;
its subsumption under the notion of cowardice is the judgment
proper. *Ulrici* in a similar way teaches that the judgment in
the logical sense is the subsumption of the particular under the
general,[2] and distinguishes from it the grammatical proposition
as the mere expression of a perception or a remark.[3] But the
reference to objectivity is, however, essential to every judgment. It is true or false, according to this reference, but not
according to a merely subjective subsumption. How the view
of the subsumption can be united with this, cf. 68.

Schleiermacher explains the judgment to be that product
of the intellectual function or of the thinking reason, which
corresponds to the community of existence or the system
of the reciprocal influences of things, i.e. of their co-existence,
their actions and passions. Subject and predicate are related
as noun and verb. The one corresponds to the permanent
existence or to an existence contained in itself; the other
expresses a circumstance, deed, or suffering—an existence
contained in another. The notion of the predicate is contained in the subject only in judgments improperly so called.
The judgment proper proceeds upon a fact, and asserts something which is contained only potentially in the notion of the

[1] *System der Log.* i. 156 ff., 960 ff.
[2] *Log.* p. 182 ff. [3] Ibid. p. 187.

o

subject. The primitive judgment asserts mere action; the incomplete mere reference to the acting subject; the complete a reference also to the object of the action under consideration.[1] Schleiermacher's definition makes justly prominent the relation of the subjective element to the objectively real. It is defective in this only that it keeps in view too exclusively the predicative and the objective relation. The definition of judgment, without being *vague*, i.e. without effacing the limits between the judgment and other forms, must be *wide* enough to embrace all the forms of judgment.

The same may be said of the opinions of *Trendelenburg and Lotze.*

Trendelenburg[2] recognises the judgment to be the logical form, to which action corresponds as the analogous form of existence. In the incomplete judgment the action alone is originally considered. In the complete judgment, however, the subject represents the substance, and the predicate the action or the property which carries the fundamental notion of the action.

Lotze[3] also gives in the same way a too narrow explanation of the judgment, when he calls it a conjunction of conceptions, whose material is worked up in the logical forms, which correspond to the metaphysical presuppositions concerning Substance, Accident, and Inherence.

[*J. S. Mill* asserts that a proposition is not the mere expression of a relation between two ideas, nor of a relation between the meanings of two names, nor the referring or excluding something from a class. It is the assertion of a matter of fact that the set of attributes connoted by the predicate *constantly accompany* the set of attributes connoted by the subject. But as sets of attributes may be classed under heads, the proposition really asserts or denies a sequence, a co-existence, a simple existence, a causation, or a resemblance. Propositions whose terms are abstract are no exception. The abstract terms stand for attributes which really exist,

[1] *Dial.* p. 301 ff.
[2] *Log. Untersuch.* ii. 208, 2nd ed.; 231, 3rd. ed.   [3] *Log.* p. 36.

and the real ground of the proposition is that when the real
states connoted by the subject are found, they are always
accompanied by the real states connoted by the predicate.
Co-existence and immediate succession, not subsistence and
inherence, are, according to Mr. Mill, the real analogues of
the relation of the subject and predicate in the judgment.[1]

Boole[2] divides propositions into primary and secondary.
The primary express relations among things, the secondary
among propositions. The former are also called ' concrete,'—
The sun shines; and the latter ' abstract,'—It is true that the
sun shines. The difference between the two kinds is one of
interpretation, not form, and therefore they require different
methods of expression.]

§ 68. *Judgments* are both *simple* and *complex.* In
simple judgments the following relations are to be distinguished :—

(1) The *predicative*, or the relation of subject and
predicate, i.e. the subjective representation of the real
relation of *Subsistence* and *Inherence.* It comprehends
under it the following :—

(a) The relation of the thing to the action or to
the passion.

(b) The relation of the thing to the property,
which is, as it were, an action become permanent (*with this must be reckoned the relation of the thing to the sum total of those
attributes which make the content of the superordinate notion*).

(c) The relation of the action or property (thought
as subject) to its nearer determination.

[1 Cf. *Logic*, i. 96–118, especially pp. 107–110, 115–118.
2 *Laws of Thought*, 1854 ed., p. 32 ff.]

In the so-called judgments without subjects (which are expressed by sentences with 'impersonal' verbs) the sum total of the existence surrounding us, thought of indefinitely, or an indefinite part of it, takes the place of the subject. In the substantial judgments the being conceived as inhering, or the existence, takes the place of the predicate.

(The *verbal* designation of the predicative relation is the grammatical *congruence* between the subject and predicate in the inflection of noun and verb. In the case, (a) the grammatical subject is a substantivum concretum and the predicate a verb; (b) the subject is again a substantivum concretum, and the predicate either an adjective or a substantive, with the auxiliary verb *to be*; (c) the subject is a substantivum abstractum, and the predicate is either a verb, adjective, or substantive, with the auxiliary verb. The copula in *every* case lies in the form of inflection. *The auxiliary verb to be belongs to the predicate*, and is not, as usually but erroneously happens, to be considered as itself the grammatical copula. The grammatical *agreement* of its inflection with the inflection of the subject, by means of which the forms *is, are*, &c. come from the infinitive *to be*, is the copula, or the expression of the relation of inherence between the predicate and subject.)

(2) The *object-relation* of the predicate to its object, i.e. the representation of the real relation of the *action to the objects* towards which it is directed. The change of reference to others is contained immediately in the essence of the action as the proper change of the subject. (Here also the real relation is expressed in the

logical, and the logical in the grammatical.) The object either *completes* or makes more *determinate.* The object which completes the predicate corresponds to the immediate object of the action, the object which makes more determinate or is adverbial corresponds to an object which stands in some mediate relation to the action. These relations are those of space, time, modality, causality, conditional and concessive, instrumental, consecutive, and final.

(The *oblique* cases are the *verbal* expression of the various fundamental forms of the object-relation. The accusative, as it appears, originally denoted distance, and so the whither or aim of the action ; the genitive, the whence, and the wherefrom, or the starting-point of the action ; and the dative, the where, wherein, and whereby, or the place, determination, and means of an action. The causal relation was thus originally confused with the local, just as in the formation of individual conceptions, notions, &c., and in all logical operations generally, the elements which arise from internal perception are confused with the time- and space-form. Some other cases, and *prepositions* joining themselves to the cases, serve to denote the manifold modifications of those fundamental forms.)

(3) The *attributive* relation. It is a *repetition* of the *predicate,* and mediately also often a *repetition of the object-relation* as a mere member of a judgment whose predicate is another member.

(The grammatical *agreement* in the inflection of nouns and verbs is the *verbal* expression of this relation. When the object-relation is added, the use of *cases* and *preposi-*

tions must be combined with this agreement. Sometimes the cases and prepositions alone (e.g. the Genetivus possessivus) serve to express the relation; for the participial determination added in thought—arising, being, &c.—is not to be expressed.)

The *multiple* or *complex* judgment arises from simple judgments (as complex propositions from simple propositions), which are *co-ordinate* or *subordinate* to each other. *Co-ordination* belongs both to complete judgments (and propositions) and to simple parts of a judgment (and proposition). It may be copulative, divisive, and disjunctive, comparative, adversative, and restrictive, concessive, causal, and conclusive. *Subordination* rests on this, that a judgment (and proposition) is joined to another judgment (or proposition) either as a whole or with one of its parts. The subordinate judgment is: (a) according as it enters into its superordinate, either as a whole or with only one of its elements, either an infinitive or relative judgment (and accordingly its verbal expression, the subordinate proposition, is either an infinitive or relative proposition; the 'conjunctional proposition' is logically classed with the former, and the 'pronominal proposition' with the latter); (b) according to the place which it or the part of it entering into the whole judgment (proposition) takes, It is a judgment (or proposition) either subjective, predicative, attributive, objectively completing or objectively determining. The objectively determining or adverbial judgments (and propositions) divide again into local, temporal, comparative, causal, conditional (or hypothetical), concessive, consecutive, and final. Several

judgments (propositions) which are subordinated to
the same principal judgment (or sentence) may be co-
ordinate or subordinate to each other, and may be formed
(e.g.) copulatively-hypothetical, disjunctively-hypothe-
tical judgments (propositions), &c.

(Language denotes the relations, co-ordinate and subordinate sentences, partly by conjunctions and relative
pronouns, partly by peculiar syntactical forms.)

Logic has hitherto paid attention to a few cases only out of
the great number of these relations, while Grammar, more
accustomed to correct itself by the consideration of individual cases, has recognised them for a long time in greater
completeness, and (by means of the researches of *Karl F.
Becker*) has learned to know them more thoroughly.[1] False
explanation and a one-sided exaggeration of the logical character of language are always to be rejected. But, to deny the
assertion of a logical basis of grammatical relation itself, is a
perverseness which cannot be logically justified, however easily
it may be psychologically explained. Strenuous battling against
one extreme easily impels us to the opposite.

Aristotle discussed the so-called (by later logicians) categorical judgments exclusively (he himself understood by the
categorical judgment the affirmative). The earlier *Peripatetics* and *Stoics* soon brought hypothetical and disjunctive
judgments within the circle of their logical investigations.

Kant[2] based the division of judgments into categorical,
hypothetical, and disjunctive, on the *Category of Relation*—
Subsistence and Inherence, Causality and Dependence, Community or Reciprocity. But this division is by no means

---

[1] Although many points of Becker's doctrine are seen to be false
from the stand-point of the historical investigation of the development
of language, the doctrine itself is very serviceable for the logical understanding of language, and is especially useful for that of the structure
of sentences

[2] *Kritik der r. Vern.* §§ 9-11 ; *Proleg.* 2 ; *Metaph.* § 21 ; *Log.* § 23.

complete, and referring the disjunctive to real reciprocity is a mistake. Besides, the Kantian Categories of Relation may be naturally compared with the Aristotelian Categories. For the latter proceed upon the formal kinds of *individual existence*, and the former on the formal kinds of *relations* which arise between the different forms of individual existence and groups of similar individual existences. The comparison extends similarly to their application to Logic. The Aristotelian Categories denote *forms of conception*, but the Kantian Categories of relation establish *forms of judgments*. The defects of the Kantian division have been partly, but not sufficiently, recognised and avoided by later logicians. The logical meaning of the grammatical relations of the sentence has seldom been rightly appreciated.[1]

Schleiermacher gives some hints about the mutual dependence of relations in simple judgments worthy of consideration. The existence which corresponds to the judgment is, according to him, the co-existence of things, by means of which every one thing is in every other, and acts and is acted on by it.[2] The first moment of judging, or the *primitive* judgment, asserts mere action without reference to a subject which acts, or to an object which endures. The place of the subject is occupied by the chaotically established sum total of existence. The primitive judgment is verbally expressed by the impersonal verb.[3] The advancing construction of the judgment is a passing over from the more indefinite to the more definite. If reference to

---

[1] We may say " Logic means by *predicate* the verb together with its objective relations, if such are present. For example, in the proposition, A strikes B, it is not the mere striking, but the striking B, that is the logical predicate. But we must, in the predicate so defined, distinguish the purely predicative from the objective relation, and give to the latter a particular consideration ; which consideration belongs to Logic and not to Grammar, because it *depends* upon a special *real* fundamental relation ; *mere grammar* has to do with the *mere* form of the *verbal* expression.

[2] *Dial.* § 139. [3] *Ibid.* § 304.

[4] With Trendelenburg, *Log. Unt.* 2nd ed., ii. 253.

the acting subject merely is affirmed the primitive judgment passes over to the *incomplete*: if, further, the fact can be traced back to its two co-operating factors, the *complete* judgment results, which must, besides the predicative, include also the objective-relation.[1] An *absolute* judgment is developed from the sum of all complete judgments, whose subject is the world, or the orderly whole of existence.[2] The *Adjective* as Epitheton (or Attribute) is the result of an earlier judgment, which is already contained as an element in the subject-notion.[3]

The division of Judgments[4] into *Judgments of Content and of Extent* presupposes that the judgment, as if it were a dependent form, is to be estimated only according to its relation to the forms of the notion (though Trendelenburg himself attributes to it a *peculiar* 'antitype in the actual'—the action of the substance). This estimation does not wholly include the essence of the judgment, and the division falls short of its multiplicity of its relations. The judgment, with its flexible form, may be of service in the formation of notions; but this is not its whole significance. The so-called '*judgments of content*' denote as categorical judgments a *relation of inherence*, and the designation is convenient when the inherence of the *essential* marks is under consideration. *Every* relation of inherence is not to be thought of as a relation of content (e.g. the inherence of mere *modi* and *relations* is not). As hypothetical judgments they depend upon *a relation of causality*, whether they denote the connection of a cause with its effect, or the connection of several effects with the same cause, or the connection founded on the real causal relations of several

---

[1] *Dial.* § 305.   [2] Ibid. §§ 306–7.   [3] Ibid. § 250, p. 197 ff.
[4] Cf. Trendelenburg, *Log. Unt.* 2nd ed., ii. 237 ff.; 3rd ed., ii. 261 ff. Categorical and Hypothetical Judgments are called 'judgments of content' by Trendelenburg; and Disjunctive Judgments, 'judgments of extent.' For example, the proposition: Conic sections are regular curves, is a judgment of content; but the proposition: Conic sections are either circles or ellipses or parabolas or hyperbolas, is a judgment of extent.

objects of knowledge. In any case they correspond to special
relations of existence, and their meaning does not merely
express the relation of content. The so-called *judgments of
extent* may be reduced to the 'judgments of content,' and are
recognised to be designations of the relation of what subsists
to what inheres; provided only that the true predicate is not
sought for in the predicate substantive, but (as must happen)
in the connection of this substantive with existence, and the
copula not in the auxiliary verb, but in the logical connection
of subject and predicate and its verbal expression in the grammatical form of inflection. (The so-called 'judgment of
extent,'—' Every man is by race either a Caucasian, Mongolian,
Ethiopian, American, or Malay'—is equivalent to the judgment,
' Every man has either the sum total of marks which charac-
terise the Caucasian, or &c.' The true predicate is being a
Caucasian. The expression of the copula lies in the inflection
only, according to which the form ' is ' has resulted from the
form ' to be.') This reduction exempts us from the necessity
either of comprehending under the one notion, or at least
under the one name of judgment, operations of thought which
are quite distinct, or with *Fries, Hegel, Ulrici,* and others, of
considering subsumption to be the only valid form of judgment, and so taking this relation out of its natural connection
with the rest.

[Sir W. Hamilton, starting from the thought that judgment
is the subsuming one class under another, and that the predicate and subject are respectively greater as the notions are
taken in their extent and content, divides judgments into two
classes, according to the relation of Subject and Predicate, as
reciprocally whole and part. If the subject, or determined
notion, be viewed as the containing whole, we have an *Inten-
sive* or *Comprehensive Judgment*: if the Predicate notion be
viewed as the containing whole, we have an *Extensive Judgment.* On this distinction the Comprehensive and Extensive
forms of Syllogism are afterwards based. [1]

J. S. Mill, who proceeds upon the thought that the most

[1] *Lect. on Logic,* i. 231.

important relation of the notion is its connotation of a set of attributes, bases on this his *attributive theory* of propositional forms. All propositions express an actual relation between two sets of attributes, so that when the one is present the other is present or absent. The attributes, e.g. connoted by the word 'man,' are always accompanied by the attributes which are connoted by the word 'mortal,' and so we say 'all men are mortal.' Mr. Mill's *attributive theory* of propositional forms agrees to some extent with the *comprehensive* judgments of Hamilton; though it has an entirely different point of view. It is more nearly related to Trendelenburg's Judgments of content as modified by Ueberweg. Mr. Mill has noticed the ambiguity which results when the copula is taken to be the auxiliary verb 'is,' and tries to get rid of it by distinguishing between 'is' when a *mere* sign of predication, and when it signifies *existence*. In the proposition, 'Socrates is just,' the word 'is' may mean either that the quality *just* may be affirmed of Socrates, or that Socrates *is*, that is to say, exists. But the difficulty is better got rid of while the thought that the relation of subject and predicate in the judgment actually mirrors a corresponding relation in real things, and in turn is mirrored by the verbal relation in the proposition, is better expressed by saying that the real copula is not 'is,' but the form of inflection which changes 'to be' into 'is.' For example, in 'man is mortal' the real copula is that form of inflection which changes the 'to be' into 'is,' so that, instead of the unconnected notions, 'man' and 'to be mortal,' we can say 'man is mortal.' ']

The question of debate between *Localists* and *Causalists*, in reference to the original meaning of the *cases*, might be decided in this way, that the *unity* of the causal relation with that of space (and that of time analogous to it) must be held to be the original, and that the stricter *separation* of the meanings is later. This principle of the original unity of the causal relation with the local is not contradicted but established by the historical proof that the nominative in the Indogermanic

¹ Cf. *Logic*, i. 85–87, 107–10.]

languages was probably originally formed by an s = sa = this (or here) added to the stem; and the accusative by an m = amu = you (or there) (which was dropped in neuters); so that, e.g. Rex donum dat is = This here king gives that there gift.[1] The *predicate proposition* has been named among the subordinate complex propositions. They are such sentences as— Nonnulli philosophi sunt *qui dicant*, and the like. That the relative proposition here—*qui dicunt*, is, according to its logical nature, a predicative sentence, is clear from the transposition— multi sunt dicentes, and is especially apparent in cases where a proposition of the same kind as a co-ordinate member comes in beside a simple predicate, e. g.[2] Est hic—animus lucis contemptor et istum qui vita bene credat emi—honorem. It is here as certain that *qui credat* is the *predicate sentence*, as that *contemptor* is the *predicate* to the corresponding proposition. It is only the *copula* as the expression of the connection between subject and predicate, not the *predicate*, that cannot be changed in a subordinate proposition.

A judgment (and proposition) can never altogether want a subject. There may be no distinct subjective conception, and in its stead a mere something (it) may enter. Cf. ὕει and Ζεὺς ὕει. The indefinite conception of the subject may have been the earlier form.

The view, that *hypothetical* and *categorical* judgments are opposed to each other as conditioned and unconditioned is combated by some logicians.[3] Judgments such as—God is just, the soul is immortal, do not, they say, involve the assertion, there is a God or a soul. But it is a fact that he who does not accept the presupposition must add clauses to these propositions, which will make them hypothetical;— if there be a (one or several, personal) God, if there be a (substantial) soul. A proposition such as—True friends are

[1] Cf. the Dissertation of G. Curtius, *Ueber die localistische Casus-theorie*, to the Philological Association of Meissen, 1863.

[2] Virgil's *Aen.* ix. 205 sqq.

[3] Herbart, *Einl. in die Phil.* § 53 ; Drobisch, *Log.* 3rd ed. p. 59 f.; Beneke, *Log.* i. 165.

to be esteemed, rests on the supposition that there are true friends. This presupposition is contained in the indicative. Languages have created other forms for expressing its doubt and denial (the Greek, the fullest and strictest). Such a clause is superfluous, only when the connection of the whole (as in a novel) or the well-known sense of the word (as Zeus, Sphinx, chimera) refers to an actual existence merely imaginary. Cf. § 85 and § 94. The grammatical question, concerning the meaning of a categorical proposition spoken in the indicative, is to be strictly distinguished from the logical question about the meaning of the categorical judgment. Affirmative judgments and such negative ones as only take away a distinct predicate from the subject (as—this criminal is not guilty) are not co-ordinate with (formal or only actually) negative judgments of such a kind, that the subject-notion is itself thereby abolished (as—An absolutely greatest number is impossible). The stricter expression for judgments which deny the subject itself would be the negation of the objective validity of the conceptions and words under consideration (e.g. the word magic is an empty sound), or some turn of expression such as—there is no absolutely greatest number. The presupposition of the reality of the subject is already contained (with the above exception) in the categorical expression, and the affirmation of mere existence in the predicate would amount to a tautology. This affirmation can only come in expressly to oppose a doubting or denial of the existence of the subject (as when it is said—God is, the soul exists). It would then, however, be an artificial form quite different from the common use of language. The natural mode of expression, when existence is to be asserted, prefers other forms—as, e.g. There is a God, equivalent to *Es* (i.e. etwas, something) *ist ein Gott* – where the indistinctly conceived totality of existence, or an indefinite part of it, comes in as subject (just as in the sentences it rains, it snows, &c.); or where we affirm of the existing subject, its existence as something (sunt aliquid Manes), or its existence there, its entrance into our neighbourhood, or within the sphere of our observation, and more than its mere existence in general. For this last is itself implicitly asserted by positing the subject.

§ 69. The kind of reference of the combination of judgment to actual existence furnishes a basis for the *division* of judgments according to *quality* and *modality*. We must be conscious in the judgment, as we have defined it, whether or not the combination of conceptions corresponds with the reality. The Quality of the Judgment rests on the result of the decision, the Modality on the degree and kind of its certainty. According to *quality*, judgments are affirmative or negative. The notion or idea of *affirmation* is the consciousness of the agreement of the combination of conceptions with actual existence; the notion of *negation* the consciousness of the want of agreement of the combination of conceptions with actual existence. According to *modality*, the judgment is problematic, assertory, or apodictic. Its *problematic* character lies in the uncertainty of coming to a decision upon the agreement of the combination of conceptions with actual existence. Its *assertory* character lies in the immediate (based on one's own or another's perception) certainty; and its *apodictic* character in the mediately acquired (based on demonstration, ἀπόδειξις) certainty of coming to such decision.

(Negative particles form the *verbal* expression of the negation; the moods of verbs and corresponding particles, e.g. perhaps, certainly, &c., which all belong to the copula, not to the predicate, express modality.)

Aristotle divides[1] the Simple Judgment (ἀπόφασις) into Affirmation (κατάφασις) and Negation (ἀπόφασις). A co-existence is predicated in affirmation, a separate existence in

---

[1] *De Int.* c. v., vi.

negation (κατάφασίς ἐστιν ἀπόφανσίς τινος κατά τινος, ἀπόφασις ἐί ἐστιν ἀπόφανσίς τινος ἀπό τινος). A negative subject-notion (ὄνομα ἀόριστον) or a negative predicate-notion (ῥῆμα ἀόριστον) may enter into the affirmation or negation.[1] The negation which negatives the judgment itself, and not a single notion in the judgment, belongs to the copula. Hence the Schoolmen enunciated the Canon—In propositione negativa negatio afficere debet copulam.

Wolff also only distinguishes the classes—affirmative and negative judgments, and teaches that when the subject or predicate only, and not the copula, is affected by the negation, the judgment appears to be negative, but is not so. He calls such judgments propositiones infinitas. In the same way *Reimarus* speaks of 'propositiones infinitae ex parte subiecti vel praedicati.'[2]

Kant divides judgments according to *Quality* into affirmative, negative, and limitative or infinite, according to the three *Categories* of Quality, Reality, Negation, and Limitation. He understands by the limitative or infinite judgment one in which the negation is connected, not with the copula, but with the predicate. (He has not noticed judgments with negative subjects.) Judgments of that kind belong rather partly to affirmative and partly to negative judgments, as the union of the subject with the negative predicate is affirmed or denied. Kant has been led to this triple division by his love for the schematic regularity of his Table of Categories.[3]

The division of judgments from the point of view of *modality* into assertory, apodictic, and problematic, has been founded on the Aristotelian division:[4] πᾶσα πρότασίς ἐστιν ἢ τοῦ ὑπάρχειν ἢ τοῦ ἐξ ἀνάγκης ὑπάρχειν ἢ τοῦ ἐνδέχεσθαι ὑπάρχειν. But this division has to do with the analogous objective relations rather than with the subjective degree of certainty. Such a determination as ἐξ ἀνάγκης, and also ταχέως, &c., is called τρόπος by Amnonius, *modus* by Boëthius.

[1] De Interpr. c. x.   [2] Vernunftlehre, § 151.
[3] Kritik der r. Vern. §§ 9-11; Proleg. § 21; Log. § 22.
[4] Anal. Pr. i. 2.

Kant[1] bases the division according to modality upon his *modal categories*—Possibility and Impossibility, Existence and Non-Existence, Necessity and Accidentality. In this, however, the combination of Impossibility, which is a negative necessity, with Possibility and also Accidentality, which denotes existence not recognised to be necessary, with Necessity, is inexact. The knowledge of Impossibility is not a problematic, but a (negatively) apodictic judgment (which Kant in the application has himself recognised, since, in his Krit. der r. Vern. p. 191, he considers the formula—*it is impossible*, to be the expression of apodictic certainty). The knowledge of the accidental is not an apodictic but an assertory judgment. Besides, Kant has not sufficiently distinguished the subjective and objective element in the Categories of Quality and Modality.

The *Relation* of the *subjective* and *objective elements* in the act of Judgment is not the same in Quality and Modality as it is in Relation. The Categories of Relation are notions of forms of existence and of relations between objective existences which are mirrored in the corresponding relations of the judgment. Quality and Modality, on the other hand, have to do with the various relations which exist between the combination of conceptions and what actually exists. Non-existence does not exist as a form of what is. What is thought in a true negative judgment does not exist. The notion of non-existence may be applied to what is represented as existing without actually existing, only in so far as the subjective picture does not correspond to the objective fact. In this sense Aristotle rightly says—οὐ γάρ ἐστι τὸ ψεῦδος καὶ τὸ ἀληθὲς ἐν τοῖς πράγμασιν ἀλλ' ἐν τῇ διανοίᾳ—ἡ συμπλοκή ἐστι καὶ ἡ διαίρεσις ἐν διανοίᾳ, ἀλλ' οὐκ ἐν τοῖς πράγμασιν.[2] Cf. Trendelenburg.[3] ' The Logical negation roots itself in thought only because it never can find itself pure and without support anywhere in nature.'[4] ' Pure negation belongs to thought only.' But we cannot wholly agree with Aristotle, when[5] he seeks a

[1] *Kritik der r. Vern.* §§ 9–11 ; *Proleg.* § 30 ; *Log.* § 30.
[2] *Metaph.* vi. 4, §§ 1–6.   [3] *Log. Unters.* 2nd ed. i. 41.
[4] Ibid. ii. 118.   [5] *Metaph.* ix. 10, § 1.

form of existence as a correlate to negation, and thinks that
separation in things corresponds to it. Separation actually
takes place (and the state of separation is a real occurrence),
and is rather to be expressed in a positive judgment. A
negative judgment does not therefore imply a separation in
things. (The sum of the angles of a plane-rectilineal triangle
is neither more nor less than two right angles, the diagonal
of a square is not commensurable with its side; but the
former does not therefore *separate* itself from a sum which is
greater or less than two right angles, nor the latter from com-
mensurability.) In real things which are the objects of our
thought there is a positive opposition or strife between contrary opposites; but conceptions and negations exist only
in so far as mental essences, which themselves conceive and
think, form the object of our conceptions and judgments;
and analogues of conceptions and negations exist only in
so far as the tendencies motions and desires, which dwell in
inanimate objects, bear in themselves, as it were, a picture of
what shall be, and this picture in consequence of hindrances does
not arrive at realisation (e.g. an arrested motion or a blighted
flower). In such a case the picture comes into objective comparison with the external actual existence, and is not merely
placed in comparison with it by us. When our combination
of conceptions is established by an objective tendency which
in consequence of hindrances is never realised, it becomes most
conformable to nature; for example, Your letter has not
reached me; This flower does not bloom. It is not limited,
however, to this one case.

The negative judgment, when its construction does not
result from caprice, presupposes that the question to which it
may be considered the answer is not absurd;—that some
motive may be thought for the affirmation;—and in general
that at least the genus-notion, under which the questioned predicate notion falls, belongs to the subject as predicate.

The case of *Modality* is analogous. The modality on which
the distinction of problematic assertory and apodictic judgments rests, exists only in the comparison of our combinations

P

of conceptions with reality. Our decision of affirmation and
negation rests either upon perception, or upon authentic
witness which does instead of one's own perception, or upon an
inference from another judgment. In the first case we judge
assertorically. In the last we know either the whole of the
moments on which the decision must be based, when we can
give an *apodictic judgment*; or only a part of them, in which
case we attain to a merely *problematic judgment*. Possibility, as
something objective, must always be distinctly separated from
subjective uncertainty, and is done so in common language.[1]
The Greek language (e.g.) denotes by δύνασθαι (to be capable)
possibility in the objective sense, and by ἴσως (perhaps), or by
the optative with ἄν, the (subjective) uncertainty, or the problematic character, of the judgment, while ἐνδέχεσθαι denotes the
objective possibility on the side of its external conditions from
their negative side,—i.e. it agrees with the circumstances, it leads
to nothing impossible, or nothing prevents that it should be.[2]
Possibility in the objective sense rests on this, that among the
moments upon which realisation depends there is established
an essential separation, not merely subjective by our knowledge
of the one and ignorance of the other, but also objective by the
nature of the case. The sum total of these circumstances, or
the total cause, is generally divided into the (internal) reason
and the (external) conditions. For example, the total cause of
the growth of a plant divides into the organic power which
lies in the seed—the (internal) reason, and the chemical and

---

[1] Cf. Trendelenburg, *Log. Unt.* ii. 137.

[2] Waitz says (*Ad Arist. Org.* i. 376) τὸ δυνατόν is the physically
possible, τὸ ἐνδεχόμενον the logically possible, the problematical. This
definition, so far as it refers to δυνατόν, is correct, but not strict as
regards ἐνδεχόμενον. Waitz himself admits that it does not quite harmonise with Aristotle's actual usage when he thinks that Aristotle
'saepius alterum cum altero confundit.' Our definition given above
may correspond better. Cf. Arist. *Anal. Pr.* i. 13, p. 32 A, 18:
λέγω δὲ ἐνδέχεσθαι καὶ τὸ ἐνδεχόμενον, οὗ μὴ ὄντος ἀναγκαίου τε-
θέντος δὲ ὑπάρχειν, οὐδὲν ἔσται διὰ τοῦτ' ἀδύνατον. The δύνασθαι
denotes the presence of the internal reason, the ἐνδέχεσθαι the presence
of the external conditions and the absence of hindrances.

physical powers of air, earth, and light—the (external) conditions. When the reason is present alone, or the conditions alone, possibility arises; where both are present together, there is necessity in the objective sense. In this sense the possibility (or capability) of the existence of the oak is contained in the acorn. The historical genesis depends on the advance from an objective possibility (potentia) to actuality. It is possibility in the objective sense that Buhle speaks of, e.g. when he[1] explains the opinion to be erroneous, that acquaintance with the pure Platonic and Aristotelian philosophy was again brought about by learned Greeks crossing over into Italy and by their literary activity, and says, ' They only brought about its *possibility* because they brought with them the *works* of Plato and Aristotle, and taught people to understand them in the original language, so that sooner or later an un-prejudiced person who studied them *could* remark the difference between the kind of philosophy taught in each and the kind which had been formed from them.' Again, it is the re-establishment of the conditions and the objective possibility, not a ' perhaps' (subjective uncertainty), that is meant when we say to a boy—I know that it is *possible* to solve this problem; you *can* solve it (you have the ability to solve it). The assertion that possibility is something objectively real does not contain the contradiction that the same thing is called both merely possible and also actual. For the occurrence is possible ; but its possibility actually exists in the object of our thinking as a real complex of causal moments, which is objectively separated from the others whose presence makes the occurrence necessary. This real possibility, however, as such, is not expressed in a problematic, but most commonly in an assertory judgment, by means of the verbs—can, is capable, &c.; just as the real necessity in an assertory judgment is expressed by means of the verbs—must, is necessary, &c. (which then belong to the predicate, and not, like the ' perhaps,' to the copula).

But a problematic judgment may be based upon our know-

[1] *Gesch. der neuern Philos. seit der Epoche der Wiederherstellung der Wiss.* ii. 123, Gött. 1800.

ledge of an objective possibility, and an apodictic judgment
upon our knowledge of an objective necessity; for what is possible may perhaps occur, and what is necessary will certainly
occur. A negative judgment is most conformable to nature
when it is based on an objective negation in the sense given
above, or on a tendency which is never realised; but it is not
confined to this relation. In the same way the problematic
judgment is most conformable to nature where the subjective
uncertainty about any occurrence, property, &c., rests on a
known objective possibility—i.e. when the subjective separation
of the part of the total cause known and of that unknown to
us (or of what is kept in view by us and of what has not, at
first at least, been brought into consideration) corresponds
strictly with the objective separation of the internal cause
and the conditions. Wherever we know assertorically that
the occurrence can happen or has objective possibility, we
naturally use the problematic judgment about the occurrence,
that it perhaps will happen. The application of the problematic judgment, however, is not limited to this one relation,
but occurs wherever we have any ground of probability and no
absolute hindrance, i.e. know no cause of impossibility. In the
same way, the apodictic judgment is most complete, and yields
the highest satisfaction to the mind in its search after knowledge, when it rests on an insight into the real genesis from
the internal cause and the external conditions. Wherever we
know the presence of this objective necessity of an occurrence, we ought to express the subjective necessity, that it will
happen, in an apodictic judgment. The application of the apodictic judgment goes beyond this one relation, however, and
embraces all subjective mediate certainty, even when it has been
reached in another way (e.g. by indirect proof). The assertion
of an objective possibility, or of an objective necessity, belongs
to the matter or content of the judgment because it belongs to
the predicate, but the problematic or apodictic character belongs
to the form of the judgment. *Aristotle*, in his De Interpretatione and in his Analytics, treats of such 'modal' modifications
of judgments as really belonging to their matter or content, and

do not cóncern the logical theory of judgments. The modal difference, however, of problematic, assertoric, and apodictic form does concern logical doctrine.

In a monograph of *Gustav Knauer* [1] Affirmation and Negation are traced to Modality. Both are, in fact, to be regarded from the same point of view. They have not to do, as Relation has, with the different objective relations which are mirrored in the judgment, but with the various relations of the subject to the object. Accordingly, Knauer calls negation in a negative judgment 'modal negation,' and distinguishes it from ' qualitative negation,' which rests on the opposition—not of reality and negation, but—of the positive and the negative contrarily opposed to it, as black to white, vice to virtue. (This distinction corresponds to that of Trendelenburg, between ' logical negation ' and ' real opposition.') In a similar way, Knauer understood by the ' limited judgment,' one in which the predicate is saddled with a limiting determination, which can be expressed either by a positive adverbial addition (as in bright red, dark red, half right), or by a ' qualitative not,' strictly to be distinguished, however, from the ' modal not.' But Knauer has overlooked this, that the logical division of judgments has to do with differences which belong to the form of the judgment, as such, and not with differences belonging to any form whatever of notions entering into the judgment. Whether man or not-man, red or bright-red, &c., is the predicate of a judgment, makes a difference in the form of the notions under consideration, and in the content of the judgment. It makes no difference in the form of the judgment with which the logical division of judgments has alone to do. Accordingly, the rectification of the Kantian Table of Categories attempted by Knauer—the substitution of Positive and Negative for Reality and Negation — contradicts the general point of view, according to which the Categories con-

---

[1] *Conträr und contradictorisch, nebst convergirenden Lehrstücken, festgestellt und Kant's Kategorientafel berichtet,* Halle, 1868. Well worthy of attention, although making some mistakes in what is new, and often erroneously believing a correct statement to be new.

dition the various functions of judgment. Reality and Negation are not, of course, like Substantiality and the other Categories of Relation, valid as forms of actual existence. They
only denote a relation between our thoughts and actual existence. This, however, only justifies the attack upon the Kantian
table of Categories, not Knauer's own doctrine. On the other
hand, the axiom of Knauer's is correct (in which he recognises
the 'master of Stagira' as his ally, but which is not a new
doctrine, even in the sense that it had been lost sight of since
Aristotle, and was first brought to light again by Knauer), that
necessary contradiction exists only between affirmation and
negation of the same thing, and not between judgments
whose predicates are opposed contradictorily. See §§ 77–80.

[*Sir W. Hamilton*, with *Mansel* and *Thompson*, refuse to
recognise the modality of judgments as any part of their logical
treatment. The mode, they say, belongs to the matter, and
must be determined by a consideration of the matter, and
therefore is extralogical.[1]]

§ 70. QUANTITY is the extent in which the predicate
is affirmed or denied in the sphere of the subject-notion.
Some logicians divide judgments according to Quantity
into *Universal, Particular,* and *Singular.* Singular judgments are to be subsumed under the other two classes :
under the first when the subject is definite and individually designated (e.g. Caesar, or this man); under the
second when the subject is indefinite and designated only
by a general notion (e.g. a man, or a great general).
For in the first case the predicate is affirmed or denied
of the *whole* sphere of the subject (which in this case is
reduced to an individual), and in the other case of an
indefinite *part* of the sphere of the subject-notion.

[[1] Cf. Hamilton's *Lect. on Log.* i. 257; Mansel's Aldrich's *Rudimenta,* 4th ed. p. 46 n.; *Proleg. Log.* 2nd ed. Note II.]

Aristotle distinguishes Universal, Particular, and Indefinite Judgments: πρότασις—ἡ καθόλου, ἡ ἐν μέρει, ἡ ἀδιόριστος.[1] The Judgment Indefinite according to quality, which Aristotle makes co-ordinate with the Universal and Particular, is not properly a third kind, but an incomplete, or incompletely expressed, judgment.[2] *Kant* recognised three kinds—Singular, Particular or Plurative, and Universal Judgments—and traces them to the three *Categories of Quantity*—Unity, Plurality, and Universality. He teaches that singular judgments belong to the same class as the universal.[3]

Herbart says, that individual judgments are only to be reckoned along with universal ones when they have a distinct subject. When the meaning of a general expression is limited by the indefinite article to any individual not more definitely designated, those judgments are to be reckoned with the particular.[4] This manner of reduction shows itself to be the correct one, partly in itself, *because it does not depend upon the absolute number of subject-individuals, but on the relation of this number to the number of individuals falling under the subject-notion generally;* partly in its application to the forms of inference.[5]

The subject of the particular judgment is any part of the sphere of the subject-notion, and *at least any single* individual falling under this notion. Its limits may be enlarged up to coincidence with the whole sphere, *so that the particular judgment does not exclude, but comprehends, the possibility of the universal.*

The rule that the judgment, *indesignate* in reference to quantity, is universal if affirmative, and particular if negative, is more grammatical than logical, and not unconditionally valid.

[1] *Anal. Pri.* i. 1.
[2] [Cf. Hamilton's *Lect. on Log.* i. 243.]
[3] *Krit. d. r. Vern.* §§ 9–11; *Proleg.* § 20; *Logik*, § 21.
[4] *Lehrbuch zur Einl. in die Phil.* § 62.
[5] Cf. below, § 107.

§ 71. By *combination of the divisions of judgments*
according to QUALITY and QUANTITY four kinds arise:—
1. Universal Affirmative of the form—All S are P.
2. Universal Negative of the form—No S is P.
3. Particular Negative of the form—Some S are P.
4. Particular Negative of the form—Some S are
not P.

Logicians have been accustomed to denote these forms
by the letters a, e, i, o (of which a and i are taken from
affirmo, e and o from nego). It will be seen from a
comparison of spheres, that in every universal judgment
the subject is posited universally, and particularly in
every particular judgment; but the predicate is posited
particularly in every affirmative judgment, or, if universally, only by accident (for, according to the form of
the judgment, both in a and i its sphere can lie partly
outside of the subject), and universally in every negative judgment (for in e the sum total of S, and in o the
part of S concerned, must always be thought as separated
from the whole sphere of the predicate).

The judgments of the form a (S a P—All S are P) can be
represented in a scheme by the combination of the two following figures:—

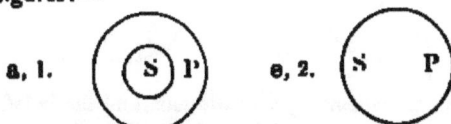

a, 1.   e, 2.

The following scheme is for judgments of the form e (S e P
—No S is P):—

e.

Judgments of the form i (S i P—At least a part of S is P) require the combination of the four following figures (of which 1 and 2 are peculiar to the form i, but 3 and 4 repeat the schema of the form a):—

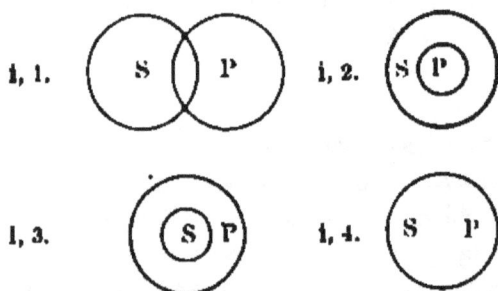

i, 1.   S   P   i, 2.   S P

i, 3.   S P   i, 4.   S   P

Judgments of the form o (S o P—At least one or some S are not P) are to be represented by the combination of the three following figures (of which 1 and 2 are peculiar to the form o, while 3 repeats the schema of the form e :—

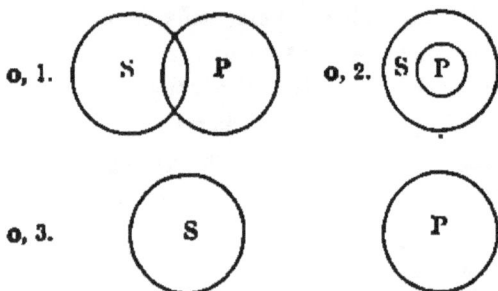

o, 1.   S   P   o, 2.   S P

o, 3.   S   P

If the definite be denoted by a continuous, and the indefinite by a dotted line, the symbol of judgments of the form a may be reduced to the one figure :—

S P

The Symbol for the judgments of the form **i** under the same presupposition :—

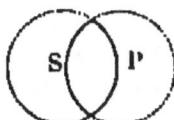

And for judgments of the form **o** :—

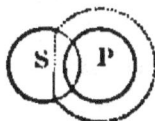

The use of these Schemata is not confined to that apprehension of the judgment which finds it to be only a subsumption of the lower subject-notion or conception under the higher predicate-notion, and which, therefore, requires that the predicate-notion be made substantive in cases where this is actually unsuitable. If the predicate-notion is the proper *genus-notion* of the subject, it is quite natural to take it for substantive, but not when it denotes a *property* or *action*. This last case does not require to be reduced to the first for the sake of a comparison of spheres. It is not necessary (although in many cases very convenient) to attach such a meaning to the circle P as to make it embrace the *objects* which fall under the substantive predicate-notion. The sphere of an adjective or verbal conception can be also understood by the sphere P. It may mean the sum total of the cases in which the corresponding property or action occurs, while S may denote the sphere of a substantive conception— the sum total of the objects in which the corresponding property or action occurs. On this presupposition the coincidence of the circles or parts of the circles is not to be taken to be the symbol of the *identity* of objects, but as the symbol of the co-existence of what subsists and what inheres. Cf. § 105.

In **a**, 1 all S are only a part of P, but in **a**, 2 all S are all P; in **i**, 1 some S are some P, &c. The *Quantification of the Predicate* consists in paying attention to these relations. It has been carried out by *Hamilton* on the basis of assertions of Aristotle,[1] and according to partial precedents in the Logique ou l'Art de penser,[2] and in *Beneke.*[3] Cf. § 120. For the use of these Schemata as aids in the demonstration of the theorems which have to do with inference, cf. § 85 and § 105 ff.; cf. also § 53.

§ 72. *Two judgments*, of which the one precisely affirms the very thing which the other denies, are CON-TRADICTORY to each other, or *are contradictorily opposed* (iudicia repugnantia sive contradictorie opposita). *Contradiction* is the affirmation and denial of the same thing. Judgments are *opposed to each other diametrically*, or as CONTRARIES (contrarie opposita), which, in reference to affirmation and negation, are as different as possible from each other, and, as it were, stand furthest apart. Judgments should be called SUBCONTRARIES, the one of which particularly affirms what the other, agreeing with it in other respects, particularly denies. Judgments are SUBALTERN (iudicia subalterna), the one of which, affirmatively or negatively, refers a predicate to the whole sphere of the subject-notion, while the other refers the same predicate in the same way to an indefinite part of the same sphere. The former is called the subalternant (iudicium subalternans), the latter the subalternate judgment (iudicium subalternatum).

Aristotle defines[4]—ἔστω ἀντίφασις τοῦτο· κατάφασις καὶ ἀπόφασις αἱ ἀντικείμεναι. He distinguishes contradictory opposition (ἀντιφατικῶς ἀντικεῖσθαι· ἡ ἀντικειμένη ἀπόφανσις) from

---
[1] *De Interp.* c. vii.   [2] *Par.* 1664.
[3] Cf. upon this Trendelenburg, *Log. Unters.* 2nd ed. ii. 304–307, and Appendix B.
[4] *De Interp.* c. vi.

contrary (ἐναντίως ἀντικεῖσθαι· ἡ ἐναντία ἀπόφανσις). Judgments with the same content of the forms **a** and **o** (S **a** P and S **o** P) stand to each other in the relation of contradictory opposition, and so do judgments of the forms **e** and **i** (S **e** P and S **i** P). Judgments of the form **a** and **e** (S **a** P and S **e** P) stand in the relation of diametrical or contrary opposition. The relation between the forms of judgment **i** and **o** (S **i** P and S **o** P) Aristotle calls only apparently analogous,[1] κατὰ τὴν λέξιν ἀντικεῖσθαι μόνον. Later logicians call such judgments προτάσεις ὑπεναντίας, iudicia subcontraria. Aristotle arranged the four forms of judgment,[2] πᾶς ἐστιν ἄνθρωπος δίκαιος (**a**), οὐ πᾶς ἐστιν ἄνθρωπος δίκαιος (**o**), πᾶς ἐστιν ἄνθρωπος οὐ δίκαιος (**e**), οὐ πᾶς ἐστιν ἄνθρωπος οὐ δίκαιος (**i**), according to the annexed scheme:—

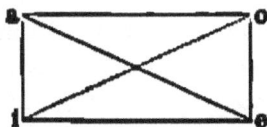

The judgments **a** and **e**, which stand furthest apart from each other, according to their mutual relations, and in the same way the judgments **i** and **o**, are thus set at the opposite ends of the diagonal or διάμετρος. In this scheme all the above-mentioned relations of judgments are thus arranged:—

Modern Logicians represent these relations in the following scheme (which is found in *Boëthius*, and, with some difference

<hr>

[1] *Anal. Pr.* ii. 15.   [2] *De Interp.* x. 19 **a**, 32–36.

of terminology, but with the same position of the forms of judgment, in *Apuleius*):—

a   opposit. contraria   e

subalt.   opposit.   contradict.   subalt.

     opposit.   contradict.

i   opposit. subcontrar.   o

This is less convenient because contraries do not lie at the opposite ends of the diameter, but in another view is better.

§ 73. The *matter* or content of our judgments is obtained immediately through external and internal perception, mediately by inference. In the act of judgment the *forms*, which are designated by the *Categories of relation*, are imposed upon this matter. We recognise these forms:—

(a) First and immediately in ourselves by means of internal perception. For example, the relation of what inheres to what subsists is recognised in the relation of the individual perception or individual feeling or volition to the totality of our existence or to our ego, the relation of causality to dependence in the relation of our will to its expression, &c.

(b) In the personal and impersonal essences without us, on the ground of its analogy to our own internal existence.

The notional apprehension of these forms, in their separation from the content, with which they are combined, comes afterwards, by means of abstraction.

The objective validity of these forms is warranted by the same moments, and lies under the same limitations and gradations, as the truth of internal perception and its analogues (§ 41 ff.), as the truth of the conception of individuals (§ 46), and as the notional knowledge of the essential (§ 57).

Kant believed these forms to be à priori, or originally inherent in the human understanding (Stammbegriffe des Verstandes). Before his time *knowledge à priori* meant, agreeably to the *Aristotelian* idea, *knowledge from causes* which are the *prius natura* (πρότερον φύσει), and *knowledge à posteriori, knowledge from effects* which are the *posterius natura* (ὕστερον φύσει), and therefore knowledge from immediate experience and by testimony (for this knowledge is a kind of knowledge from effects).

Leibniz identifies[1] connaître à priori and par les causes. He calls[2] ratio à priori that reason which is the cause not merely of our knowledge, but of the truth of things themselves. He distinguishes 'prouver à priori par des démonstrations' (which, of course, is sufficient only when 'démonstrations' mean syllogistic deductions from known real reasons), and 'à posteriori par les expériences.' He recognises the Axiom of Identity and Contradiction (the element à priori) to be the only 'principe primitif' for all knowledge co-ordinate with experience (the à posteriori element);[3] but later adds the Principle of Sufficient Reason.[4] The same use of the terms is also found in Leibniz, applied to mathematics, in a very instructive passage of his Epistola ad Jacobum Thomasium,[5] in Leibniz's edition of the work of Nizolius, De veris principiis et vera ratione philosophandi:[6] 'Si rem cogitemus curatius, apparebit demonstrare eam (sc. geometriam) *ex causis*. Demonstrat enim figuram

[1] *Theod.* i. § 44, e.g. [2] *Nouv. Ess.* ii. 17.
[3] *Réflexions sur l'Essai de Locke*, 1696.
[4] *Theod.* i. § 44, 1710; *Monad.* § 32, 1714. [5] Published in 1669.
[6] *Opera Phil. Leib.*, ed. Erdman, p. 51.

ex motu, e.g. ex motu puncti oritur linea, ex motu lineae
superficies, ex motu superficiei corpus. Ex motu rectae super
recta oritur rectilineum. Ex motu rectae circa punctum im-
motum oritur circulus, &c. Constructiones figurarum sunt
motus; iam ex constructionibus affectiones de figuris demon-
strantur. *Ergo ex motu, et per consequens à priori et ex causa.*'
Wolff says, very insufficiently : ' utimur in veritate proprio
Marte eruenda vel solo sensu ; vel ex aliis cognitis ratioci-
nando elicimus nondum cognita : in priori casu dicimur veritatem eruere *à posteriori*, in posteriori autem *à priori.* He
adds that experience has to do with the individual only, but
yet supplies us with the principles from which those individual cognitions, which are not to be reached by immediate experience, must be derived à priori. Only by such a
' connubium rationis et experientiae ' can the trifling Scholastic formulae be avoided, and be taught ' non ex proprio ingenio
conficta, sed naturae rerum consentanea.'
Kant[2] holds that knowledge which has been reached by a
general rule, if this rule be itself derived from empirical
sources, is only relatively to be considered knowledge à priori.
He, for his part, will ' not understand such knowledge to be à
priori which is independent of this or of that experience, but
only knowledge which is absolutely independent of all experience. Opposed to it is every kind of empirical knowledge, or
knowledge possible only à posteriori, i.e. by experience.' Kant
has narrowed the notion *à posteriori* in its relation to the
Aristotelian *knowledge from effects,* or from the ὕστερον φύσει
(but has done so in accordance with the use prevailing in
Leibniz and Wolff). He understands by it, knowledge from
one kind of effects (viz. from those which affect our senses).
He has given an entirely new meaning (which has since come
to be the prevailing one) to the expression *à priori* (partly
determined by Wolff and Baumgarten, and partly on the other
side by Hume). He denotes by it, not the opposite of knowledge from effects, but the opposite of knowledge from experience. By combining the distinction of knowledge à priori and

¹ *Log.* § 663.   ² *Kritik der reinen Vern., Einl.* i.

à posteriori with the division of judgments into synthetic and
analytic (cf. § 83), Kant finds three kinds of judgments—
1. *Analytic judgments,* or explanatory judgments, which, as
such, are all judgments *à priori*; 2. *Synthetic judgments à
posteriori,* or enlarging judgments, which are founded on
experience; 3. *Synthetic judgments à priori,* which found
themselves on the pure forms of intuition or the pure notions
of the understanding, and ideas of reason. But those judgments which Kant calls synthetic judgments à priori are not,
in fact, formed independently of experience, but are made in
this way, that we complete the sense-perception by the presupposition of a causal interdependence (cf. § 140). Kant
teaches rightly—That an element arising from within, and in
this sense à priori, is added to the sensible or à posteriori, but
wrongly—1. That the à priori element is independent of
internal experience; and 2. That it does not belong to things
in themselves.

The Kantian use of the expressions à priori and à posteriori,
which at present prevails, has done more damage than good.
Kant's mysterious fiction of a ' knowledge à priori,' which he
took to be absolutely independent of experience, and his use of
the term ' à priori,' often confounded with the old meaning of
the term, has produced numberless obscurities and paralogisms,
from which the Kantian and almost the whole post-Kantian
Philosophy suffers. A return to Aristotle's meaning were better.

Schleiermacher teaches that the pure à priority of the
Hegelian Dialectic and the pure à posteriority of Empiricism
are alike one-sided and untenable. He says,[1] ' The judgments
(together with the system of notions) which constitute science
are developed in every individual identically, in proportion to
the activity of his intellectual function, because of the relation
between organic function and the outer world, which exists in
all men.' Schleiermacher, accordingly, traces all scientific
judgments to the co-operation of an inner and an outer factor,
which are equally necessary for the formation of any judgment
in the sense given above.

[1] *Dial.* §§ 189–192.

PART FIFTH.

INFERENCE IN ITS REFERENCE TO THE OBJECTIVE CONFORMABILITY TO LAW.

§ 74. INFERENCE (ratio, ratiocinatio, ratiocinium, discursus, συλλογισμός) in the widest sense is the derivation of a judgment from any given elements. Derivation from a single notion or from a single judgment is IMMEDIATE INFERENCE or (immediate) *consequence* (consequentia immediata). Derivation from at least two judgments is MEDIATE INFERENCE, or *inference in the stricter sense* (consequentia mediata).

As the conception represents the individual existence and what is to be distinguished in it, and the notion represents the essence, so the judgment and inference represent the relations of single existences. The judgment has to do with the primary and nearest relations; the simple judgment with a fundamental relation; and the complex judgment with a placing side by side of several relations. Inference has to do with such a repetition of similar or dissimilar relations as give rise to a new reference. The possibility of the formation of inference, and of its objective validity (as will be proved afterwards), rests upon the presupposition of a real interdependence of things conformably to law. This is to be said of mediate inference only, however, for immediate inference is a mere transformation of the subjective form of thought and expression (though not of the expression alone).

' To *derive from* ' means to accept because of something else, so that the acceptation of the validity of the one depends upon the acceptation of the validity of the other, i.e. is received therefore and in so far, because and in as far as the other is received.

The ' *immediateness* ' in the so-called ' immediate inference ' is relative. It implies that this kind of inference does not require, as mediate inference does, the addition of a second datum to the first, but at once and of itself yields the derived judgment, which is nevertheless another judgment and not merely another verbal expression. There is no Immediateness, in the full sense, that no activity of thought is required to reach the derived judgment; but since the term is traditional, and holds good in a relative sense, it is not advisable to change it. When a change in terminology is not absolutely essential, it does harm, produces unintelligibility, and gives occasion to error.

In *Plato*, συλλογίζεσθαι and συλλογισμός do not occur in the sense of later logical terminology. They have a wider and more indefinite meaning—to draw a result from several data, taking them all into consideration; and, more commonly—to ascertain the universal from the particular.[1]

Aristotle defines :[2] συλλογισμὸς δέ ἐστι λόγος, ἐν ᾧ τεθέντων τινῶν ἕτερόν τι τῶν κειμένων ἐξ ἀνάγκης συμβαίνει τῷ ταῦτα εἶναι. This definition is not meant by Aristotle to include immediate inference. It comprehends the two kinds into which mediate inference divides—inference from the universal to the particular, and inference from the particular to the universal. In this sense, Aristotle distinguishes between ὁ διὰ τοῦ μέσου συλλογισμός and ὁ διὰ τῆς ἐπαγωγῆς, or ὁ ἐξ ἐπαγωγῆς συλλογισμός.[3] Syllogism, in the strict sense, is inference from the universal to the particular. Aristotle says, in this sense,[4] τρόπον τινὰ ἀντίκειται ἡ ἐπαγωγὴ τῷ συλλογισμῷ·—ἅπαντα πιστεύομεν ἢ διὰ συλλογισμοῦ ἢ ἐξ ἐπαγωγῆς.

Wolff, in agreement with Aristotle, and, like him, referring

---

[1] *Theaet.* 186 D; cf. *Phileb.* 41 c.   [2] *Anal. Pri.* i. 1, 24 a, 18.
[3] Ibid. ii. 23.   [4] Ibid.

to mediate inference only, defines it ;[1] est ratiocinatio operatio mentis, qua ex duabus propositionibus terminum comununem habentibus formatur tertia, combinando terminos in utraque diversos; syllogismus est oratio, qua ratiocinium (seu discursus) distincte proponitur.

Kant[2] defines inference to be the derivation of one judgment from another. This happens either without an intermediate judgment (iudicium intermedium), or with the help of such. On this is based the division of immediate and mediate inference. Kant calls the former inferences of the understanding, and the latter inferences of the reason.

Hegel[3] sees in inference the re-establishment of the notion in the judgment, the unity and truth of the notion and judgment, the simple identity into which the formal distinctions of the judgment have returned, the end and aim towards which the judgment in its various kinds advances gradually, the universal which by means of particularity has coalesced with individuality. He thinks inference the essential basis of all truth, the intellectual and all intellectual, the return upon itself of the mean of the moments of the notion of the actual. Hegel here also identifies the logical and metaphysical relation, or the form of knowledge and existence.

Schleiermacher[4] defines inference to be the derivation of one judgment from another by means of a middle premise. He does not recognise inference to be an independent third form, co-ordinate with notion and judgment, and denies that it has a real correlate of its own. He therefore does not believe that it has any scientific value for the production of knowledge; but thinks its worth didactic only, for the transmission of knowledge already existing. We believe this view to be erroneous, and will seek to show (§ 101) the real correlative of inference, and its significance as a form of knowledge.

[*J. S. Mill*[5] defines inference to be the setting out from known truths to arrive at others really distinct. He refuses the name to the so-called 'immediate inferences,' because in

[1] *Log.* §§ 50, 332.   [2] *Kritik der r. Vern.* p. 360; *Log.* § 44 ff.
[3] *Log.* ii. 118 ff; *Encycl.* § 181.   [4] *Dial.* p. 268.   [5] [*Log.* i. 185.]

them the progression from one truth to another is only
apparent, not real, the logical consequent being a mere repetition of the logical antecedent. He divides inference into three
kinds, from generals to particulars, from particulars to generals, and from particulars to particulars. The third kind,
though not generally recognised by logicians, is not only valid,
but is the foundation of both of the others. It is the inference
of every-day life, and in its finer forms corresponds to the
ἰδιασμός of Aristotle, which plays such an important part in the
formation of our judgments in matters of taste and morality—
the delicate imperceptible ingathering of instances gradually
settling and concreting into opinions. It is the recognition
and discussion of this third kind of inference in all its manifold
forms, but more especially in its formation of religious beliefs,
which gives so much logical value to *J. H. Newman's* Grammar
of Assent, 2nd ed., Lond. 1870.]

§ 75. The PRINCIPLES OF INFERENCE are the axioms
of *identity* and *correspondence*, of *contradictory disjunction* (or of Contradiction and Excluded Third) and of
sufficient reason. The derivation of a judgment from a
notion rests on the first, the derivation of a judgment
from a judgment on the first and second, and the derivation of a judgment from several judgments on the
first, second, and third.

Logic considers these principles as *rules* of our thinking
(which is also an act of knowing). It leaves to *psychology* to
discuss in how far these laws are, or are not, so simple and
evident in their application that they *cannot* be altered in clear
thinking, and in this sense attain the character of *natural laws*
for our thinking.

Aristotle does not place these axioms at the head of Logic,
but discusses them, in so far as he enunciates them in scientific
form at all, partly and occasionally as laws of the formation
of inferences, and partly and more particularly in the Meta-

physics,[1] where he holds the axiom of Contradiction to be πασῶν βεβαιοτάτη ἀρχή.

Leibniz[2] holds them to be the principles of our *inferences* (raisonnements); *Wolff* does as Aristotle.

Daries and *Reimarus* were the first to find the *principle* of Logic in some or other of those axioms. *Reimarus* places[3] the essence of reason in the power to reflect upon conceived things according to the two rules of consistency and contradiction, and holds that by the right use of reason the knowledge of truth is to be attained. He defines the 'doctrine of Reason' to be a science of the right use of reason in the knowledge of truth,[4] and truth in thinking to be the agreement of our thoughts with the things we think about.[5] He seeks to prove the proposition, 'When we think according to these laws of consistency and contradiction, our thoughts must also correspond to the things themselves, and so be true;' 'these laws are sufficient to give truth and correctness to all our thoughts.'[6]

Kant, on the other hand, reduces formal Logic to the doctrine of the laws which flow from the principles of Identity and Contradiction, in this sense, that by their observance the agreement of thought with itself, or the absence of contradiction, will be attained. He does not believe possible an agreement of the contents of thought with actual existence or with things in themselves.

Fries remarks[7] that these axioms should not be placed at the head of Logic, since they can only be understood in their true meaning when one has learned to know the notion and the relation of subject and predicate in the judgment. This remark is correct, for these axioms express the relation of several judgments to each other, and so have their first distinct influence upon the doctrine of inference.

Delboeuf[8] places at the head of the whole of Logic three axioms which partly take the place of those given above. These

---

[1] *Met.* iv. 3.
[2] *Monad.* § 31.
[3] *Vernunftlehre*, § 15.
[4] Ibid. § 3.
[5] Ibid. § 17.
[6] Ibid. § 17 ff.
[7] *System der Logik*, § 11.
[8] *Log.* pp. 91 sqq., 101 sqq., 113 sqq., and 130 sqq.

axioms are—1. We must conclude from the representation
of phenomena to phenomena themselves ; 2. We must posit
the results as identical by abstraction of the differences ;
3. The logical concatenation of ideas corresponds to the real
concatenation of things. He derives them from the 'first
postulate of the reason'—'that certainty is possible,' by the
following argument. If certainty is to be given, truth must be
given; if truth be given, our conceptions must be able to
be true; if they can be true then—1. The mind must be able
to conceive phenomena as they are. 2. The causes which
produce them must remain identical with themselves in the
various combinations into which they enter. 3. The logical
power of deduction must also correspond to actual objective
existence, the mental analysis be a true (though converse)
picture of the real synthesis. By means of the first principle
we advance, says Delboeuf, from the conception to the actual
existence, by means of the second from conceived identity to
actual identity, by means of the third from conceived connection to actual connection. Delboeuf finds the warrant for
the agreement of a thought with what actually exists in a
thorough-going logical harmony in the operations,—observation, conjecture, and verification (p. 85). Understood in this
sense—that the agreement of thought with objective existence
is attainable by man and guaranteed by the observation of
the sum total of the logical laws (s. § 3)—the first of those
three principles coincides with the principles of this system
of Logic and of every Logic which is a doctrine of knowledge. The second principle has chiefly to do with the process
of abstraction (s. § 51). Delboeuf recognises the third principle
to lie at the foundation of inferences (raisonnements) (cf. § 81).
He calls these three principles '*principes réels*,' and makes the
first two correspond to the principle of Identity, and the last to
that of Sufficient Reason. He places beside them as '*principes
formels*' the axioms of Contradiction and Excluded Third.[1]

[Hamilton, Mansel, Thompson, and that school of formal
logicians make Logic the science of these laws of thought and

[1] *Log.* p. 165 ff.

their application. They push Kant's doctrines to an extreme
which he himself would have scarcely contemplated. But
Hamilton, on the side of metaphysics, asserts that the three laws
of Identity, Non-contradiction (as he calls it), and Excluded
Middle are ' laws of things ' as well as ' laws of thought,' and
hold good of things-in-themselves.[1] They reject the law of
Sufficient Reason because it either has to do with the matter,
not the form of thought, or else is no law of thought, but
only the statement that every act of thought must be governed
by some law or other.[2] Mansel has tried to show how Logic
should be merely a statement of these three fundamental laws
—the laws of the thinkable—the deduction from them of the
laws of thinking in the stricter sense—viz. those of conception, judgment, and reasoning, and their thorough-going application to produce in thinking, consistency with itself.[3]
J. S. Mill refuses to place these laws at the head of Logic,
and considers them of little or no value in the science. He
severely criticises the views of Mansel and Hamilton in his
Exam. of Sir Wm. Hamilton's Phil.[4]]

§ 76. The AXIOM OF IDENTITY (principium identitatis)
should be thus expressed: A is A, i.e. *everything is
what it is,* or—omne subiectum est praedicatum sui.
The axiom of consistency (principium convenientiae),
which is allied with it, should be thus expressed: A
which is B, is B; i.e. every attribute which belongs to
the subject-notion may serve as a predicate to the same.
The reason of the truth of the axiom lies in this, that
the attribute conceived in the content of the notion

[1 Cf. *Lect. on Logic*, i. 98.
[2] Cf. Mansel, *Proleg. Log.* p. 214, and Hamilton, *Disc.* 2nd ed.,
Appendix.
[3] *Prolegomena Logica*, 2nd ed. p. 190 ff. Cf. also Hamilton's
Lect. ii. 244 for an elaborate list of authorities.
[4] 3rd ed. pp. 130–180.]

inheres in the object conceived through the notion, and
this relation of inherence is represented by the predicate.
The sentence—Not-A is Not-A, is only an application
of the axiom of Identity to a negative notion. It is not
a new axiom. In the same way: A, which is Not-B, is
Not-B, is only an application of the axiom of consistency.
The latter formula furnishes a basis for the application
of this thought to negative judgments in the *axiom of
negation* (principium negationis)—A, which is not B,
is not B.

In a wider sense the axiom of Identity may apply to
the agreement of all knowledge with itself, as the
(necessary though insufficient) condition of its agreement with actual existence.

The axiom of Identity was not, as some think, discovered by
a Schoolman (perhaps the Scotist Antonius Andreæ, quoted
by Polz, and after him by Bachmann and others, who enunciated the formula—ens est ens). Still less is it due to modern
logicians. *Parmenides,* the Eleatic, is its author. He expresses it in its simplest form—ἔστι;[1] further, χρὴ τὸ λέγειν τε
νοεῖν τ'· ἰὸν ἔμμεναι· oportet hoc dicere et cogitare: *id quod
sit, esse,*[2] and ἔστι γὰρ εἶναι[3] (cf. § 11).

Heraclitus thought that anything is and is not, at the same
time, and that all fleets. *Parmenides* thought that only Being
exists; Not-Being is not; everything lasts. *Plato* seeks to
overcome this opposition by his distinction between the invariable world of Being or Ideas, whose every essence is always
like to itself, tale, quale est, ἀεὶ κατὰ ταὐτὰ ὂν (Tim. p. 27,
and elsewhere), and the changeable world of Becoming or of
sensible things. Science or true knowledge has to do with
existence, and consists in this, that what exists is known as

[1] Parm., *Fragm.* ed. Mullach, vs. 35, 58.
[2] Ibid. p. 43.   [3] Ibid.

existing[1]—οὐκοῦν ἐπιστήμη μὲν ἐπὶ τῷ ὄντι πέφυκε γνῶναι ὡς ἔστι τὸ ὄν;[2] ἐπιστήμη μὲν γέ που ἐπὶ τῷ ὄντι (πέφυκε) τὸ ὂν γνῶναι ὡς ἔχει.[3]—λόγος—ὃς ἂν τὰ ὄντα λέγῃ ὡς ἔστιν, ἀληθής, ὃς δ' ἂν ὡς οὐκ ἔστι, ψευδής. The admission, that a mere agreement of conceptions with each other is a criterion of their truth, is expressly rejected by Plato.[4]

Aristotle defines[5] τὸ μὲν γὰρ λέγειν, τὸ ὂν μὴ εἶναι ἢ τὸ μὴ ὂν εἶναι, ψεῦδος· τὸ δὲ, τὸ ὂν εἶναι καὶ τὸ μὴ ὂν μὴ εἶναι, ἀληθές.[6]— ἀληθεύει μὲν ὁ τὸ διῃρημένον οἰόμενος διαιρεῖσθαι καὶ τὸ συγκείμενον συγκεῖσθαι· ψεύσται δὲ ὁ ἐναντίως ἔχων ἢ τὰ πράγματα. When he[7] requires from truth thorough-going agreement with itself— δεῖ γὰρ πᾶν τὸ ἀληθὲς αὐτὸ ἑαυτῷ ὁμολογούμενον εἶναι πάντῃ—this does not amount to the mere tautological oneness, which the axiom of Identity in its stricter sense requires, it also means the agreement of the consequences with the reasons.[8]

Leibniz[9] enunciates as the first affirmative truth of reason, or as the first identical truth, the sentence ' everything is that which it is,' or A is A.

In a similar way *Wolff*[10] considers the most universal identical judgment to be the axiom—idem est illud ipsum ens, quod est, seu omne A est A.

The Wolffian *Baumgarten*[11] used the formula: omne possibile A est A, seu quidquid est, illud est, seu omne subiectum est praedicatum sui, and calls this axiom ' principium positionis seu identitatis.'

Schelling[12] declares the axiom inadmissible in scientific Logic, and very properly draws attention to this, that propositions sounding identical do not belong, according to their sense, to the merely analytical principle, A is A.

Hegel[13] makes the correct remark against the axiom of Identity in the form A is A, that no consciousness thinks,

[1] *Rep.* v. 477 a.   [2] Ibid. p. 478 a.   [3] Cf. *Cratyl.* 385 b.
[4] Ibid. p. 436.   [5] *Metaph.* iv. 7, § 2.
[6] Ibid. ix. 10, § 1.   [7] *Anal. Pri.* i. 32 ; cf. *Eth. Nicom.* i. 8.
[8] Cf. *De Interpret.* c. xi.   [9] *Nouv. Essais,* iv. 2, § 1.
[10] *Log.* § 270.   [11] *Metaph.* § 11, 1739.
[12] *Phil. Schr.* i. 407.   [13] *Log.* i. 2, 32 ff ; *Encycl.* § 115.

nor conceives, nor speaks according to this law. Speech conducted according to it would be absurd:—A plant is—a plant; the planet is—the planet.

Schleiermacher[1] thinks that the axiom, in order not to be an empty formula, must either express the identity of the subject as the condition of science, or the identity of thought and existence as the form of science.

Some *more recent logicians*[2] make the axiom express the sure and self-identical nature of human knowledge, especially notional knowledge, and make the principle of Contradiction its negative form. But this is too far removed from the meaning and application which has been given to these axioms in Logic, and especially in the doctrine of Inference and Proof, since the time of Aristotle. The doctrine of the notion has also another metaphysical principle, in the doctrine of *Essence*, whose significance is by no means exhausted by mere necessary identity with itself (cf. § 56). When men proceed to say that the axiom must contain the principle of all Logic, a corresponding meaning must be given to it. It must assert the postulate, that knowledge in general be *true*, i.e. consistent with existence. But why should not this postulate be signified distinctly, by means of the adequate expression, *Idea of truth*, rather than concealed under the ambiguous formula, $A = A$.

Delboeuf recognises the axiom of Identity, interpreted either by the postulate that every judgment be true, i.e. in agreement with actual existence (which meaning was given in the first edition of this work), or by the first or second of his three logical principles (cf. § 75).

[*Hamilton* and *Mansel* say that the law of Identity expresses the fact that every object of thought, as such, is conceived by limitation and difference, as having definite characteristics, by which it is marked off and distinguished from all others; as being,

[1] *Dial.* § 112.

[2] Weisse, *Ueber die philos. Bedeutung des Grundsatzes der Identität*, in Fichte's *Zeitschrift für Philosophie u. spec. Theol.* iv. 1, 1 ff. 1839; I. II. Fichte, *De principiorum contradictionis, identitatis, exclusi tertii in logicis dignitate et ordine dissertatio*, pp. 10 ff., 26, 1840.

in short, *itself* and no other; and that an object is in any other way inconceivable. It is the law of logical Affirmation and Definition.[1] *J. S. Mill*[2] expresses the law of Identity thus—'Whatever is true in one form of words is true in every other form of words which express the same meaning.' He calls it an indispensable postulate in all thinking, and says that it is of value in Logic,—providing for (e.g.) the whole of Kant's 'Inferences of the Understanding.']

§ 77. The AXIOM OF THE (avoidance of) CONTRADICTION (principium contradictionis) is—*Judgments opposed contradictorily to each other* (as—A is B, and A is not B) *cannot both be true.* The one or the other must be false. From the truth of the one follows the falsehood of the other. The double answer, Yes and No, to one and the same question, in the same sense, is inadmissible. The proof of this axiom comes from the definitions of truth (§ 3), of the judgment (§ 67), and of affirmation and negation (§ 69). According to these definitions, the truth of the affirmation is equivalent to the agreement of the combination of conceptions with actual existence, and consequently to the falsehood of the negation. The truth of the negation is equivalent to the absence of agreement between the combination of conceptions and actual existence, and consequently with the falsehood of the affirmation. Hence, when the affirmation is true the negation is false, and when the negation is true the affirmation is false—which was to be proved.

The axiom of Contradiction may be applied to an

[1 Cf. Mansel's *Proleg. Log.* pp. 195-96, 2nd ed.; Hamilton's *Lect. on Log.* i. 81.
3 *Exam. of Sir Wm. Hamilton's Philos.* 3rd ed. p. 466.]

individual notion (notio contradictionem involvens sive
implicans), to the combination of a notion with a single
attribute (contradictio in adiecto), and further to the
repugnance (repugnantia), i.e. to the mediate contradiction which first appears by inference in corollaries,
in so far as these forms can be resolved into two judgments opposed contradictorily to each other.

Although the axiom of contradiction is so simple and obvious
in itself, many questions and discussions have clustered round
it in the course of the centuries during which it has been considered to be the first principle in Logic and Metaphysics,
and require to be strictly examined. These have to do chiefly
with its expression and signification, its capability for proof,
its validity, and the sphere of its application.

Its Expression.—The formula most commonly used is,—
Judgments opposed contradictorily cannot be true at the same
time. This must be rejected as inexact. It leaves it uncertain
whether the relation of time which lies in the 'at the same
time' refers to the judgments themselves as *acts of thought*,
or to their *content*. If the former (which the verbal sense of
the formula implies), then, because of the relation of time, the
law says too little. It does not suffice for the avoidance of the
contradiction that its one member is *thought* now, and the other
then. Can it have been true in the eighteenth century that
the works of Homer proceeded from one poet, while it is true
in the nineteenth that they have several authors? If, however, the formula bears the second meaning — Judgments
opposed contradictorily cannot both be true so far as their
content has reference to one and the same time—then (1) the
words of the formula strictly taken do not mention this, and the
expression, which must be as strict as possible in formulas of
this kind, suffers from grammatical inexactness, and (2) the law
is burdened by a superfluous addition. One judgment which
agrees with another in other things, but differs in the determination of time (although this difference does not enter into the

verbal expression, but only lies implicitly in the reference
to the presence of the person who judges at a particular time),
is no longer the same judgment. Hence its denial does not
make the contradictory opposite of the other judgment. Hence
the law of Contradiction, which has only to do with judgments
contradictorily opposed, cannot be applied to judgments of that
kind, and it is not necessary, in order to state this inapplicability, that the formula should contain a determination of time.
The determination of time has no more right to admission than
a determination of place, and than all other adverbial determinations, none of which require particular mention for the same reason, that judgments in which they differ cannot stand opposed
to each other in contradictory opposition. If the ' at the same
time ' does not denote a relation of time (*simul*), but the being
true together, or community of truth (*una*), it is better to avoid
the double sense which has led so many not insignificant
logicians astray by the expression,—They cannot *both* be true.

ITS MEANING.—Perfect *sameness of sense*, both in the
single terms of the two judgments and in their *affirmation* and
negation, is the condition without which no contradictory
opposition can take place. Hence, in given judgments, which
according to sound appear to be opposed contradictorily, the
relation of thought is to be strictly tested in these references.
When judgments contradict each other in words only, and not
in sense, or when they appear to be logical judgments, but
are really, because of the indefiniteness of their sense, mere
rudimentary thoughts, *yes* and *no* very often can, and must
rightly, be answered to the same question. For example, it
can be both affirmed and denied, without any real contradiction existing between the answers apparently contradictorily
opposed, that Logic is part of Psychology, if the word psychology, in the affirmative answer, be used in its widest sense (as
equivalent to mental science), and in the negative answer in
a narrower sense (as, e.g. that given in § 6). The logical
demand, that a choice be made between yes and no, interposes
in force after that the possibility of a simple answer has been
established by the strict statement of the ambiguous sense of a

question and the correction of its somewhat erroneous presuppositions. Not a few empty disputed questions, and not a few
obstinate mistakes and deceptive sophisms, have been connected with the neglect of this precaution.

The possibility of a different sense in the way in which the
affirmation and negation is to be understood rests on this, that
the combination of conceptions contained in the judgment may
be compared, either with existence in the absolute sense or with
the mere objective phenomenon (as it is conditioned by the
normal function of the senses), and with this latter in various
ways. For example, the question whether the sun moves on
in space must be affirmed, denied, and again affirmed, as it
refers to the first sensible phenomenon, to the system of the
sun and the planets revolving round it (looked at from the
distance of their centre from the centre of Gravity), or to the
relation of the sun to the system of the fixed stars. Finally, he
who (with Kant) believes that all existence in space is merely
phenomenal, conditioned by the peculiar nature of man's sense-
intuition, and refers the question to the sun as 'a thing-in-
itself,' or to the transcendental object, which, since it affects
us, causes the appearance of the sun in space, must give a
denial to the question, from this critical stand-point.

ITS PROOF.—The possibility and necessity of *proving* the
axiom of Contradiction may be disputed, because it is a *first
principle*, and so cannot be derived from another. At the most
it can only be proved in the indirect way, that no thinker can
avoid recognising its validity in any individual case. But it
is doubtful whether this axiom is absolutely first and underivable. It has been often denied by Sceptics, Empiricists,
and Dogmatists. And we ourselves believe that the highest
logical principle is not the axiom of Contradiction, but rather
the idea of truth, i.e. the consistency of the content of perception and thinking with existence (cf. §§ 3, 6). The desirability
of a proof can scarcely be denied now, when there are so many
discussions of its correct formula, validity, presupposition, and
the probable limits of its application. These can never find a
settlement which will be generally recognised without some

proof which will make clear the true meaning of the axiom. The fact that in some treatises the very truth of the axiom is seriously questioned contradicts in the most forcible way the vague assertion of its innateness, which would by anticipation prevent every philosophical investigation and recommend blind submission to the incomprehensible authority of the axiom. The possibility of proof rests on sufficient definitions of truth, of the judgment, and of affirmation and negation. If these are premised, then it is (as an analytically-formed proposition) deduced without difficulty from the mere analysis of the notions. Accordingly, the proposition correctly bears the name of *fundamental proposition* (axiom) only in so far as it has a fundamental significance for a series of other propositions, those, viz. in the doctrine of inference and proof, but not in the sense that it is itself underivable.

Several *objections* of course arise against the general possibility of proving the axioms of contradiction, and against the special deduction given above. The deduction, it may be said, *presupposes the validity of the axiom.* To deduce it from the definitions is only possible on the presupposition that the contradictory cannot be true. But this objection proves too much or nothing at all. The same thing may be said of all logical laws—the thinking which deduces them rests upon them. If on this account demonstrations become fallacious reasonings in a circle, all scientific representation of Logic must be abandoned. But it is not so. For though these laws *carry with them their own validity*, and they are (at first unconsciously to us) *actually present* in our actual thinking *even in that which deduces them*, yet this deduction does not rest upon a *scientific knowledge* of these laws; and this knowledge is to be carefully distinguished from their actual validity (cf. § 4). The deduction of the axiom of Contradiction, as of any other logical law, would be a reasoning in a circle, if the proposition to be proved is itself, explicitly or implicitly, presupposed as *known*, and as one of the means of proof, as a *premiss*; but this does not happen in the above deduction. This fallacy does not occur because the thinking, which makes the deduction, is correct, i.e. by its being *conformable* to the law to be derived as well as to the other logical laws.[1]

It may be objected to our *proof* and to the *validity of the axiom*, that the deduction given above presupposes *real existence to be the steady standard of thinking.* This, however (one may say), can only happen upon the metaphysical presupposition of the unchangeable *persistency* of all actual existence. Under the opposite metaphysical presupposition, and in reference to the objective phenomenal world, that very standard of change may be brought under the influence of time and become itself changeable. And in this way the necessary truth of the axiom is destroyed, or at least narrowed to a very limited sphere. We do not accept the metaphysical presupposition, however, for we (§ 40) have recognised the *reality of change in time* independent of human comprehension. History shows that most famous thinkers of the past and of the present, *Parmenides* and *Herbart*, and in a certain reference *Plato* himself and Aristotle, have held the validity of this logical principle to be connected jointly and separately with that of the metaphysical doctrine; and that, on the other hand, *Heraclitus* and *Hegel*, who concede reality to Becoming and Change, also allow the axiom of Contradiction to disappear in the vortex of the universal flux. Nevertheless, we maintain our two theses equally firmly, Motion and Change have reality; but this does not exclude the universal validity of the proposition that judgments opposed contradictorily to each other cannot both be true. The appearance that one of these theses excludes

---

[1] This conformability appears to me to exist only in the *division* of the possible relations of thought to actual existence, into agreement and want of agreement (cf. § 69), on which division the above proof rests (p. 235). This division is a dichotomy, because, in constructing the notions of *Negation* and *Falsehood*, we comprehend whatever is not agreement under one other notion. If we believed (as Delboeuf, *Log.* p. 61 ff. does) that the principle of Contradiction enters into the *premises* of the proof given above, and that it is therefore not valid as an actual proof, the discussion would still have significance because showing the relation of that principle to the fundamental definitions (and so Delboeuf accepts it).

the other is due to that one-sided view of the judgment which
sees in the subject and predicate its only essential constituent
parts, while all the different parts of the proposition which
grammar distinguishes have a logical significance, and correspond to just as many parts in the judgment (§ 68). The
determination of time does not belong to the formula of the law,
but to the judgments to which the law finds application, if these
refer to something which belongs to a section of time. If
the objective existence with which the judgment has to do is
a changing one, it is postulated that the same change enters
into the combination of conceptions, and that it may come into
consciousness along with the contained element of time. To
this section of time the conception generally must be referred,
and the simple elements of the conception to those points of
time which are within this section. In this way, in spite of
the continuous change, the conception of what has happened
finds its steady, i.e. sure, standard in what has actually happened. An historical fact, e.g. the assassination of Caesar,
belongs as a whole to a definite section of time, and in every
moment during its occurrence must bear the character of that
which continuously happens. Nevertheless, the law of truth,
excluding the contradictory opposite, for the judgment which
relates to it, is :—The judgment is true if the real motion in
the occurrence is truly mirrored by the corresponding ideal
motion in the combination of conceptions, so that our conception of the occurrence takes its place in our conception of the
universal connection of historical occurrences in our consciousness, just as the occurrence has its place in this connection in
actual existence ; and the conception of each of its elements is
arranged in the conception of its whole course, as each element
is arranged in the actual and real course of the event. Historical judgments affirming and denying the same about an
occurrence in time, e.g. Socrates was born 469 B.C., and
Socrates was not born 469 B.C. (but 470 or 471), are as
strictly opposed to each other as contradictories, and can as
little be both true as the mathematical judgments which refer
to unchangeable existence—the sum of the angles of any rec-

R

tilineal triangle is, and is not, equal to two right angles. *Hegel* and *Herbart* assert that *motion* and *change* are *in themselves contradictory*, and *Hegel* teaches that motion *is* THE *existing contradiction.* Every moment of passing over from the one circumstance into the other (e.g. the beginning of day) unites in itself predicates which are opposed as contradictories to each other. *Hegel* asserts that these contradictory judgments are both true in reference to the same moment; but *Herbart* thinks that that is impossible according to the irrefragable law of Contradiction, and that the passing over into, and the becoming another, have no reality.[1] Both opinions are false. The semblance of contradiction results from the indefiniteness of the sense, and disappears as soon as every individual expression is referred to distinct notions. By means of strict definition of notions secure points of limitation are at once reached. For example, if the beginning of day be defined to be the moment in which the centre of the sun's disc appears above the horizon, the time of passing over into, which unites in itself the predicates opposed as contradictories, must now signify either a finite or an infinitely small section of time, or none at all. If the first be the case, the parts of the finite section of time lie either on the negative or on the positive, or upon different sides of the boundary. In the first case (when the time of dawn is called the passing over of night into day, or the beginning of day), the negative judgment, and it only, is true. The time of the passing over into, or the beginning, in this sense, is not the present existence (the dawn is not day). In the second case, when all parts lie on the positive side (when the first time after the passing over into is called the beginning of day), the affirmative judgment, and it only, is true. The beginning, in this sense, belongs to the time of present existence (to the day). In the third case, where the parts of the section of time, which forms the passing over into, fall on different sides (e.g. when the time between the

[1] Hegel, *Wiss. der Logik*, i. 2, p. 69, ed. 1834; cf. i. 1, p. 78 ff.; *Encycl.* § 88, p. 106, 3rd ed. 1830; Herbart, *Einl. in die Phil.* § 117; *Metaph.* ii. p. 301 ff.

transit of the upper, and the transit of the under edge of the
sun's disc is considered as the time of passing over into, or
as the beginning of day), the difference holds good of the
different parts of the subject, and the two judgments now
stand as co-ordinate to each other. The one part of the beginning in this sense belongs to the time of the present existence (to
the day), and the other does not. But no contradiction exists
in this any more than in the co-ordination in space of different
attributes in one subject. With reference to the undivided
subject, however, the negative judgment, and it alone, is
true (the time of the passing over into, in this third sense,
considered as a whole, is not a part of the day). This does
not prevent it, that the affirmative judgment, and it alone, is
true of one part of the subject. If an infinitely small section
of time be taken to denote the passing over into and beginning of, it must either fall on the one side, or on the other
side of the boundary point, or divide itself on either side. In
all these three cases, however, and for the same reasons, there
is no more contradiction than in the supposition that the
passing over into and the beginning of, is denoted by a finite
section of time. Lastly, no contradictory judgments arise
under the third supposition, that the boundary point itself,
without any reference to extension in time, denotes the passing over into. For this boundary point is a nothing of
time. Its extension in time is supposed to be equal to zero.
There are, therefore, no positive predicates at all which can
be predicated of it. In actuality, present existence is joined
to non-existence immediately, i.e. without any intervening
(finite or infinitely little) time. (For example, the ended
transit of the centre of the sun's disc through the horizon to
the time anterior to the transit.) The boundary point, so far as
it is represented as something existing, or as a real intervening
time which is also a nothing of time, is a mere fiction, which
for mathematical purposes cannot be dispensed with, but
which is destroyed in logical reference by the contradiction
which it bears in it.[1] If this non-existent be feigned to exist,

[1] This fiction rests on the abstraction, which holds fast and modifies

R 2

and be made the subject of a positive assertion (the point of
time of the beginning belongs to the time of present existence
—the point of the beginning of day belongs to day), this
assertion is false, and what is opposed to it as contradictory is
true; not in the sense that this feigned point of time belongs
to the time of what is about to exist, but in the sense that it
does not belong to time at all. It is no part of time, neither
finite nor infinitely little. It is a nothing of time. We may
say of this judgment what Aristotle said of the judgment—
τραγέλαφός ἐστι λευκός. It is false, and its denial true; not
in the sense that the sting-goat had another colour, but because
there is no such existence, and its conception is a mere fiction.
We cannot, therefore, agree with *Trendelenburg,* who says
that a contradiction is present in motion,[1] and yet allows that
motion has reality, because the axiom of contradiction, although
of irrefragable validity within its own limits, cannot be applied to motion, which only conditions and creates the objects to
which it applies.[2] The axiom of contradiction may be applied
to the notion of motion if we do not confine our attention to the
proposition which is without difficulty—' Motion is motion;' but
analyse the notion and go back to the elements which are fused
together in it, as Trendelenburg himself has done in the
statements given above, that 'motion (why not rather that
which moves itself?) is and is not at the same point at the
same time.' According to our previous explanations, this

the second of two really inseparable predicates—to be extended, and to
occupy a place—while it completely sets aside the first. The Leibnizian monadology, and the Herbartian assertion of simple real essences,
involve the mistake of taking for real the separability of the two
predicates, which exist only in abstraction, and of hypostatising the
existence of a point.

[1] *Log. Uters.* 2nd ed. i. 187; 3rd ed. i. 189: ' Motion, which by means
of its notion is and is not at the same point at the same time, is the living
contradiction of dead identity;' 2nd ed. i. 271; 3rd ed. i. 276: ' The
point first carries that contradiction which was present in motion as
soon as the elements contained in it were separated.'

[2] Ibid. 2nd ed. ii. 151; 3rd ed. ii. 175.

being and not being, at the same point at the same time, is a mere fiction. *Motion is not impossible because it is not contradictory.*

Yet it would appear as if the axiom of Contradiction, at least in one special case, admits of an *exception*, which is not excluded, but confirmed by the above argument. The actual existence to which the judgment refers, and in which it finds its measure of truth, whether it be external or internal (mental, psychic), is in both cases generally opposed to the judgment itself as another thing. The truth of the judgment depends upon it, but it, on its side, is not dependent upon the truth of the judgment. Now, there is one case in which the dependence is mutual. The actual existence to which it refers becomes another thing by the judgment (and that not mediately by an action connected with the judgment, but immediately by the judgment become a thought). Hence the judgment appears able to become false because of its own truth. It is evident that this case happens when, and only when, the *truth of the judgment* is itself *the object of the judgment*, or belongs to the object of the judgment. The ancients have empirically discovered this case, without (so far as we know) giving an account of its logical nature. What is called '*The Liar*' represents it. Epimenides, the Cretan, says, all the Cretans are liars (Κρῆτες ἀεὶ ψεῦσται). No logical difficulty exists if the invariable practice of lying refers only to the majority of cases, or rather to a prevailing inclination to lie; and this is the meaning of the sentence spoken by anyone who wishes to depict the Cretan character. It is also undoubted that the assertion, if the invariable habit of lying be strictly understood, is actually false, and false only. It may be granted, however, that apart from this assertion of the Cretan Epimenides, the proposition—All Cretans are always in all things liars—is true in all cases without exception. This assertion, although actually inadmissible, contains no internal contradiction, and *in this sense* is not impossible. But now it may be asked whether, on this presupposition, the axiom of contradiction has or has not validity when applied to the assertion of Epimenides, and whether this assertion, together with its contradictory opposite, can or cannot be true? Here is a logical problem which must be solved scientifically, and must not, as too commonly happens with modern logicians (the ancients, at least, tried earnestly to solve it), be evaded by one or other way of escape, least of all by an appeal to the pretended innateness and absolute character of the axiom. If, on the above presupposition, the assertion of Epimenides universally comes to pass, and is true; then if a stranger had asserted it, its contradictory (Cretans are not always in all they say liars, but sometimes speak the truth) would be, and remain, false. But since Epimenides, who has made this true assertion about the Cretans, is himself a Cretan, there is this one true assertion spoken by a Cretan. Hence the proposition that Cretans always lie about everything has become false by its own truth; and its contradictory opposite is just as true as itself. This may also be put thus:—If the general statement about the Cretans is true, it must also be true of Epimenides the Cretan, and of his assertion. He must in this statement have told a falsehood. The statement has proved itself false by its own truth, and its contradictory must be true. The two propositions then—This expression is true, and It is not true, are both true, contrary to the principle of contradiction. (Our first consideration had for its basis the truth of the assertion of Epimenides as its logical predicate. This must help to serve to constitute the objective matter of fact, and we infer from this matter of fact to its untruth in its content. The second proceeds from the meaning of the truth of the assertion in its content, and infers, back from it to a matter of fact to which it belongs, that the attribute to be untrue belongs to its assertion.) If we first take the expression to be false, we find ourselves equally compelled to conclude that it must also be true. For all other assertions of the Cretans, according to the above presupposition, are falsehoods. If this assertion of Epimenides be untrue, they are all absolutely untrue. But then, because of this matter of fact, the assertion is true that all Cretans are always liars; the pro-

position has become true by its untruth. The same may be
shown in the following way :—If the assertion is untrue that
all Cretans are always liars, then, that at least one example must be given where a Cretan speaks the truth. But
according to the above presupposition, all their other assertions
are untrue, and the assertion of Epimenides cannot be untrue,
but must form a single exception, and be true ; and so has
given us the statement of its truth from its untruth. The
propositions, This expression is not true, and It is true, are
again both true. (In this statement, as in our previous one,
our first consideration has for its basis the untruth of the
assertion of Epimenides as its logical attribute. Let this now
be taken along with the matter of fact, and from the matter
of fact, the truth of the assertion, in its content, follows. The
second, on the other hand, proceeds from the meaning of the
untruth of the statement in its content, and infers from it back
to the matter of fact to which it belongs, that to-be-true
belongs as a predicate to the same assertion.) But yet, in
spite of this apparent confirmation, it would be too hasty a
decision to grant that there is here an actual exception to the
axiom of Contradiction. Under the simple grammatical expression two different logical judgments are comprehended,
the second of which cannot at all be thought, nor can exist as
an actual judgment, unless the first has been previously
thought. The first judgment has to do with all other assertions of the Cretans. It is true, and only true, on the presupposition on which we have here gone, that they are all of
them untrue. Its contradictory is false, and false only. The
second can only be formed with reference to this first judgment. In the second a similarly sounding statement is made
with such universality that it also refers to the first judgment
and its truth. But since the true assertion lies in the first
judgment, the proposition in this enlarged sense is not more
generally true, but false, and false only. Its denial or contradictory is true, and true only. If that complete strictness
of thought and of expression of thought prevails, without which
all these investigations are useless, we cannot assert that the

248   § 77. *The Axiom of Contradiction.*

same judgment, by the truth belonging to it, may change the matter of fact with which it has to do, and thereby become false. We must correct our statement in this way—By the truth of the first judgment the second becomes false, whose ideal presupposition is formed by the first. Hence the axiom of contradiction, in spite of this very deceptive appearance of an exception, asserts its exceptionless validity.

To absolutely shun contradiction is a task demanding so harmonious a thorough construction of thought, and at the same time such a purity and freedom of intention, that to fulfil it remains an ideal which is ever to be reached proximately only. Not merely gaps in our investigation, but every kind of ethical narrowmindedness, the tenacity of national, religious, political, and social prejudices, lead to contradictions. The difficulty of overcoming contradictions reveals itself in antithetic propositions. Cf. § 136.

Its History.[1]—We make the following remarks on the history of the axiom.

Parmenides, the Eleatic, placed the positive axiom, ἔστιν, or ἐὸν ἔμμεναι, or ἔστι γάρ εἶναι, by the side of the negative, οὐκ ἔστι μὴ εἶναι,[2] or, οὔτε γάρ οὐκ ἐὸν ἔστι,[3] or, οὐ γάρ φατὸν οὐδὲ νοητόν ἐστιν ὅπως οὐκ ἔστι,[4] or, οὐ γάρ μήποτε τοῦτό γ' ἔη (φανῇ?) εἶναι μὴ ἐόντα.[5] In these expressions, and especially in the last,[6] lies the germ of the axiom of Contradiction. They decline to assert that, what is, is not; and they deny the co-existence of the truth of the judgments—This is and This is not.[7] These expressions in Parmenides, however, have rather a metaphysical than a logical meaning.

[1] Cf. the Articles of Weisse and I. II. Fichte referred to in § 76.
[2] *Parm. Fragm.* ed. Mullach. vs. 35.
[3] Vs. 106.   [4] Vs. 64–65.   [5] Vs. 52.
[6] The forms given above partly depend upon conjectures in the (Plat.?) *Sophist.* p. 237. Bergk supposes τοῦτ' οὐ Δὰν ἦ; cf. my *Hist. of Philos.,* translated by G. S. Morris, New York, 1871 (4th Germ. ed. 1871), i. § 19.
[7] The axiom did not originate, as Weisse thinks, in the opposition of Aristotle to the Stoics, nor yet, as I. II. Fichte (cf. as above, p. 17) supposes, in the Platonic Doctrine of Ideas.

Socrates says:[1] ὃς ἂν βουλόμενος τἀληθῆ λέγειν μηδέποτε τὰ αὐτὰ περὶ τῶν αὐτῶν λέγῃ, ἀλλ' ὁδόν τε φράζων τὴν αὐτὴν τοτὲ μὲν πρὸς ἕω, τοτὲ δὲ πρὸς ἑσπέραν φράζῃ, . . . δῆλος ὅτι οὐκ οἶδεν.

Plato, when he is engaged with the metaphysical problem of establishing the relation between Being and Becoming, distinguishes intelligible and sensible things. Every sensible thing unites in itself the oppositions,—what is large is at the same time little, what is beautiful is at the same time ugly, &c. We cannot establish the thought that it is what it is, nor yet that it may be the opposite, or is not, for all sensible things are in continual change. Hence, they have not existence, but vacillate between existence and non-existence: ἅμα ὄν τε καὶ μὴ ὄν —ἐκεῖνο τὸ ἀμφοτέρων μετέχον τοῦ εἶναί τε καὶ μὴ εἶναι. On the other hand, the axiom of Parmenides about Being is true of the *Idea.* It is ἀεὶ κατὰ ταὐτὰ ὡσαύτως ἔχουσα.[2] In the *Phaedo*, Plato mentions, besides ideas and sensible things, a third class, viz. the qualities which inhere in sensible things. He there does not attribute persistent sameness to ideas only, but asserts of the *qualities of sensible things* also, that they, so long as they remain that which they are, can never become nor be at the same time the opposite:[3] οὐ μόνον αὐτὸ τὸ μέγεθος οὐδέποτ' ἐθέλειν ἅμα μέγα καὶ σμικρὸν εἶναι, ἀλλὰ καὶ τὸ ἐν ἡμῖν μέγεθος οὐδέποτε προσδέχεσθαι τὸ σμικρὸν οὐδ' ἐθέλειν ὑπερέχεσθαι, ἀλλὰ δυοῖν τὸ ἕτερον, ἢ φεύγειν καὶ ὑπεκχωρεῖν—ἢ ἀπολωλέναι.[4] οὐκ ἐθέλει—οὐδὲν τῶν ἐναντίων ἔτι ὂν ὅπερ ἦν ἅμα τοὐναντίον γίγνεσθαί τε καὶ εἶναι.[5] αὐτὸ τὸ ἐναντίον ἑαυτῷ ἐναντίον οὐκ ἄν ποτε γένοιτο, οὔτε τὸ ἐν ἡμῖν, οὔτε τὸ ἐν τῇ φύσει.[6] ξυνωμολογήσαμεν ἄρα—μηδέποτε ἐναντίον ἑαυτῷ τὸ ἐναντίον ἔσεσθαι. Plato says of sensible things, however, the opposite always comes from the opposite, and that opposite qualities are in them at the same time:[7] οὑτωσὶ γίγνεται πάντα, οὐκ ἄλλοθεν ἢ ἐκ τῶν ἐναντίων τὰ ἐναντία.[8] ἐκ τοῦ ἐναντίου πράγματος τὸ ἐναντίον πρᾶγμα

[1] In *Xenophon Memorab.* iv. 2, 21.
[2] *Plat. de Rep.* v. 478 sqq. [3] *Phaedon*, p. 102 b.
[4] Ibid. p. 102 e. [5] Ibid. p. 103 a. [6] Ibid. p. 103 c.
[7] Ibid. p. 70 d. [8] Ibid. p. 103 b.

250   § 77. *The Axiom of Contradiction.*

γίγνεσθαι.¹ ἆρ' οὐ—λέγεις τότ' εἶναι ἐν τῷ Σιμμίᾳ ἀμφότερα, καὶ
μέγεθος καὶ σμικρότητα; ἔγωγε. Cf. the words in an already
quoted passage of the Rep. p. 479 B: ἀνάγκη—καὶ καλά πως
αὐτὰ αἰσχρὰ φανῆναι καὶ ὅσα ἄλλα ἐρωτᾷς·—ἀεὶ ἕκαστον ἀμφοτέρων ἕξεται. In another passage:² οὐκοῦν ἔφαμεν τῷ αὐτῷ
ἅμα περὶ ταὐτὰ ἐναντία δοξάζειν ἀδύνατον εἶναι;—from which it
is proved that the λογιστικόν whose ἔργον it is to measure, &c.
is different from the lower parts of the mind: τὸ παρὰ τὰ
μέτρα ἄρα δοξάζον τῆς ψυχῆς τῷ κατὰ τὰ μέτρα οὐκ ἂν εἴη ταὐτόν
—the union of different parts of the contradiction in the object
is not taken into consideration, but the existence of the contradiction in the thinking subject is. This copious quotation is
needed to make clear in how far it is an incorrect expression
to say (as is often done) that Plato has enunciated the axiom of
Contradiction (particularly in the words,³ μηδέποτε ἐναντίον
ἑαυτῷ τὸ ἐναντίον ἔσεσθαι). The axiom of Contradiction has
to do with contradictory opposition exclusively ; the passage
quoted from the Phaedo refers, in the first instance at least, to
predicates opposed as contraries. The difference between Contrary and Contradictory Opposition was not enunciated by
Plato with the distinctness which is a necessary condition of
the pure apprehension of the axiom. Thus he believes that,
when he finds contraries combined in things, he must ascribe
to them Contradictory Opposition. The *change* of predicate
—the same thing has now, and then has not now, the same
predicate—seems to him rather a *contradiction* in things.
(The thought that, because the second point of time is
another one, and therefore the second judgment in the affirmative a new judgment, and its negative form not the contradictory of the first, would have solved the difficulty, but lies beyond
Platonism.) Accordingly, Plato excludes sensible things from
the domain of this axiom (in both senses) because they are,
what is and at the same time is not. He places under its
authority the εἰλικρινῶς ὄν, that which is uniform and unchangeable—Ideas and Mathematical objects. The axiom least

¹ *Phaedon*, p. 102 A.   ³ *Plat. Rep.* 603 A.
² *Phaedon*, p. 103 C.

entangled in ideological relations, and approaching most closely
to the logical form in Aristotle, is stated in the Euthydemus,[1]
where it is said to be impossible that any existing thing may
not be what it is (τὶ τῶν ὄντων τοῦτο, ὃ τυγχάνει ὄν, αὐτὸ τοῦτο
μὴ εἶναι).

Aristotle, developing Plato's doctrines, expresses the axiom
of Contradiction as a *metaphysical axiom* in the following carefully circumscribed formula,—It is impossible that the same
can and cannot belong to the same in the same reference:[2] τὸ
αὐτὸ ἅμα ὑπάρχειν τε καὶ μὴ ὑπάρχειν ἀδύνατον τῷ αὐτῷ
καὶ κατὰ τὸ αὐτό.[3] In a parallel passage[4] he makes the expression of contemporaneousness ἐν τῷ αὐτῷ χρόνῳ co-ordinate
with the ἅμα οὕτω καὶ οὐχ οὕτων. By adding to the significance of the ταυτό, Aristotle expresses the same axiom in
the shorter formula,—The same cannot be and not be:[5] τὸ
αὐτὸ ἅμα εἶναι τε καὶ οὐκ εἶναι—ἀδύνατον.[6] ἀδύνατον ἅμα εἶναι
καὶ μὴ εἶναι.[7] Aristotle joins to this the corresponding *logical*
axiom,—It is not to be *asserted* that the same is and is not;
Contradictory expressions cannot both be true:[8] βεβαιοτάτη
δόξα πασῶν τὸ μὴ εἶναι ἀληθεῖς ἅμα τὰς ἀντικειμένας φάσεις.[9]
ἀδύνατον τὴν ἀντίφασιν ἀληθεύεσθαι ἅμα κατὰ τοῦ αὐτοῦ.[10] ἀντι-
φάσεις—οὐχ οἷόν τε ἅμα ἀληθεῖς εἶναι. Cf.[11] καὶ ἔστω ἀντίφασις τοῦτο· κατάφασις καὶ ἀπόφασις αἱ ἀντικείμεναι.[12] μὴ ἐνδέχεσθαι ἅμα φάναι καὶ ἀποφάναι.[13] ἀδύνατον ὄντινοῦν ταὐτὸν
ὑπολαμβάνειν εἶναι καὶ μὴ εἶναι. We can recognise the influence
of the Platonic thought in Aristotle's statement, that nothing
can be true if all things are in motion;[14] and that in order

---

[1] P. 293 B.   [2] *Metaph.* iv. 3, § 13 Schw.

[3] The statement of the axiom reminds us of the passage quoted in
another sense from Plato, *Rep.* iv. 436: δῆλον, ὅτι ταὐτὸν τἀναντία
ποιεῖν ἢ πάσχειν κατὰ ταὐτόν γε καὶ πρὸς ταὐτὸν οὐκ ἐθελήσει ἅμα.

[4] In the *Metaphysics,* iv. 5, § 39.   [5] *Anal. Pri.* ii. 2, 53 B, 15.

[6] *Metaph.* iii. 2, § 12.   [7] Cf. Ibid. iv. 4, § 1.

[8] Ibid. iv. 6, § 12.   [9] Ibid. § 13.   [10] Ibid. p. 8, § 3.

[11] *De Interpr.* p. 6.   [12] *Anal. Post.* i. 11.   [13] *Metaph.* iv. 3, § 14.

[14] *Metaph.* iv. 8, § 10: εἰ δὲ πάντα κινεῖται, οὐθὲν ἔσται ἀληθές, πάντα
ἄρα ψευδῆ: cf. iv. 5, § 27, and ix. 10, § 4.

to completely secure the validity of the axiom of Contradiction, Aristotle thinks he must state that there is an existence unchangeable throughout.[1] But he does not, like Plato, hold the axiom to be absolutely invalid with reference to the changeable. By means of his distinction between δύναμις and ἐντελέχεια or ἐνέργεια, he more correctly shows that the same object may at the same time possess the capacity or possibility for opposites, but cannot contain the opposites in actuality or in their developed existence:[2] δυνάμει ἐνδέχεται ἅμα ταὐτὸ εἶναι τὰ ἐναντία, ἐντελεχείᾳ δ᾽ οὔ.[3] This last proposition, however, has to do with contraries rather than with contradictories. Besides, Aristotle does not hold the axiom of Contradiction (as modern Formal Logic does) to be a sufficient foundation for a whole logical system. So far from this, he makes mention of it only occasionally in his logical writings, and considers it to be a principle of Demonstration only; and this not without the distinction that the axiom of Excluded Middle has a more intimate connection with indirect than the axiom of Contradiction has with direct Demonstration.[4]

Aristotle sought to deduce the logical form of the axiom from the metaphysical (by a course of reasoning which is not stringently correct);[5] and, conversely, from the supposed truth of the logical to prove the truth of the metaphysical.[6] He thus placed the two in the strictest reciprocal relation. But he explains that it is impossible to deduce its truth from a higher principle by direct proof, for the reason that the axiom (in its metaphysical form) is itself the highest and most certain of all principles:[7] φύσει γὰρ ἀρχὴ καὶ τῶν ἄλλων ἀξιωμάτων αὕτη (ἡ δόξα) πάντων. βεβαιοτάτη[8] αὕτη τῶν ἀρχῶν πασῶν. The validity of the axiom itself can only be proved indirectly, viz. by showing that no one can help recognising it in actual thinking and acting, and that were it destroyed all distinctions of thought and existence would perish with it.[9] According to

[1] *Metaph.* v. §§ 10, 33.　　[2] Ibid. iv. 5, § 9.
[3] Cf. Ibid. ix. 9, § 2.　[4] *Anal. Post.* i. 11.　[5] *Metaph.* iv. 3, § 13.
[6] Ibid. iv. 6, §§ 13–14.　[7] Ibid. iv. 3, § 16.
[8] Ibid. p. 4, § 2.　[9] Ibid. iv. 1.

the statements we have given above, a direct proof is impossible only when distinct definitions are wanting. The proof of the axiom in its metaphysical form may be put thus:—If the thought, or whatever is defined to be a copy (picture) of actual existence, differs from its real original, then the notions of *untruth* and *non-existence* find application, conformably to the definitions enunciated above. The notion of *untruth* is to be referred to the supposed image or picture. The notion of Existing-but-not-in-this-manner is applied to what the copy was defined to correspond to; and the notion of Non-Existence is applied to what was falsely thought to be the real correlate to the elements which do not agree with it. Truth and falsehood, like affirmation and negation, are only in the image in so far as the image can be referred to the thing, and are in the domain of actual existence only in so far as images exist in it. The notion of the *Existence* exists independently of that of the image (while, on the other hand, the notion of *reality* implies that the existence has become known by means of an act of thought different from it, and may be applied to thinking itself, only in so far as this thinking has itself become the object of thought to another act of thinking reflecting upon it). *Non-Existence* is neither in the image (although it may be in its denial) nor in the object (although the existence of the object in a judgment, which is therefore false, may be denied), but simply does not exist. The *notion of non-existence*, however, is primarily in the negative judgment in which we *think* the discrepancy between image and actuality. It can always be used to denote what does not exist, but is falsely conceived to exist; never to denote what does exist. In other words—It is not true, that the same thing which is, also is not; or (as Aristotle says)—It is impossible that the same thing is and also is not.[1]

The Aristotelian doctrine, in spite of many attacks, remains the prevailing one in antiquity, in the middle ages, and in modern times.

[1] Cf. Trendelenburg. *Log. Unters.* il. § 11: *Die Verneinung.*

In Antiquity.—The axiom of Contradiction was attacked by the *Sceptics*, who believed that the one of the two contradictory opposites was not truer (οὐδὲν μᾶλλον), or at least not more able to be proved true, than the other. *Epicurus* also attacked it. He did not wish to abolish it absolutely, but only to make it as indefinite as some things themselves are. The bat (νυκτερίς), e.g. is a bird and yet is not a bird. The stem of the broom (νάρθηξ) is and yet is not wood, &c.[1] (Plato had said the same thing in reference to the world of sense.[2]) But this exception is false. In such intermediate forms, which according to the notions of natural science do not belong to a definite class, the negative, and this only, is true. If a more extended notion is enunciated which includes it, then the affirmative is true. But then the judgment (in spite of the identity of words) has materially become another, and this affirmation is not the contradictory of the former negation.

In the Middle Ages.—The *Thomists* followed Aristotle unconditionally; but in the School of the *Scotists*, doubt began to attack, not the axiom itself, which Aristotle, the highest authority in philosophical matters, had declared to be most certain, but its outworks. The question was raised, whether the axiom had the originality of a highest principle. The Scotist *Antonius Andreae* appears to have been the first who denied its originality and the impossibility of its direct proof. He sought to derive the axiom of Contradiction from the axiom ens est ens, which he thought was the positive and earlier. Somewhat later the Thomist *Suarez* defended the Aristotelian doctrine, and discussed the formula, ens est ens, in order to show that it could not, because of its emptiness and barrenness, be the highest principle and ground of metaphysics.[3]

In Modern Times.—The axiom has experienced bolder attacks. *Locke*[4] despised it as a meaningless abstraction, an artificial

[1] *Ioann. Sic. schol. ad. Hermog.* vi. 201, ed. Walz, republished by Prantl, *Gesch. der Log.* i. 360; cf. Cic. *De Nat. Deorum*, i. 25.
[2] *De Rep.* v. 479.   [3] Cf. Polz, *Comm. Metaph.* pp. 13, 21, 61 sqq.
[4] *Essay*, iv. 7.

construction of the Schools yielding no food for actual thought.
But the reputation of the axiom was more firmly established
after that *Leibniz* undertook to vindicate it, and combated
Locke's objections. Leibniz held it to be an innate principle,
which does not arise from experience, and indispensable as a
rule for scientific knowledge.[1] He says,[2] that on the strength of
this principle we hold to be false what contains a contradiction,
and believe to be true what is opposed as its contradictory
to what is false. The last case, however (though Leibniz
did not recognise it) presupposed that judgments may be
known to be false in another way than by an internal contradiction. Every contradiction must be represented in the
form of two judgments which are opposed to each other as
contradictories, the one or other of which is necessarily false.
But we cannot know, merely by means of the axiom of Contradiction, which of the two is false. We only know, according to this axiom, that it is false that both are true. But to
this falsehood nothing is opposed as its contradictory save the
axiom—The two members which a contradiction contains in
itself are not both true. The axiom is correct enough, but
does not teach us how to find out which of the two members
is the true one ; and this is the problem. It is only when we
know in some other way the falsehood of a definite one of the
two members, that the axiom, that the contradictory opposite
of the false is true, satisfies the demands of our knowledge and
comes to have a real value.

Wolff, like Aristotle, considers the metaphysical axiom to
be self-evident,—fieri non potest, ut idem praedicatum eidem
subiecto sub eadem determinatione una conveniat et non conveniat, immo repugnet,[3] or: si A est A, fieri non potest, ut
simul A non sit A ;[4] and deduces from it, by means of the
definition of Contrary and Contradictory Opposition, the
logical axiom of truth and falsehood,—duae propositiones con-
trariae non possunt esse *simul* verae ;[5] propositionum contra-

[1] *Nouv. Essais,* iv. 2, § 1.   [2] *Monadol.* § 31.   [3] *Log.* § 529.
[4] Ibid. § 271.   [5] Ibid. § 529.

dictoriarum — *altera* necessario falsa.[1]   Wolff also followed
Aristotle in not considering the axiom of Contradiction to be
the one principle of the whole of *Logic* (although he bases his
Ontology upon it), and in mentioning it only occasionally in
Logic.

Baumgarten says, in his Metaphysic:[2] nihil est A et non-A:
haec propositio dicitur principium contradictionis et absolute
primum.

Reimarus[3] formularises the law of Contradiction (principium
Contradictionis) thus,—A thing cannot be, and at the same
time not be.

Kant[4] considers the axiom of Contradiction to be the principle
of *Analytic* judgments.   It is sufficient to establish their truth,
and it furnishes a universal, though negative, criterion of all
truth; for contradiction completely does away with and abolishes
all knowledge.   In *Synthetic* knowledge, according to Kant, it
is inadmissible to act contrary to this inviolable principle; but it
is no test of the truth of a synthetic judgment. It is the conditio
sine qua non, but not the ground of the determination of the
truth of our synthetic knowledge; for even if a cognition be
not self-contradictory, it may yet be contradictory to its object.
Kant defines the expression of the axiom therefore—' A predicate does not belong to a thing which contradicts it.'   He
rejects the Aristotelian-Wolffian formula,—It is impossible
that something is and is not— partly because apodictic certainty,
which should be understood from the axiom itself, is super-
fluously brought in (in the word *impossible*), partly, and more
particularly, because the axiom is affected by the condition of
time.   It is a merely logical axiom, and its expression must not
be limited to the relation of time (or rather, the notion of contradictory opposite already includes identity of relation of time
in the two members, so far as a reference to time exists in the
case under consideration).   Kant comprehends the axiom of
Identity and the axiom of Contradiction under the common

[1] *Log.* § 532.   [2] *Metaph.* § 7.   [3] *Vernunftlehre*, § 14.
[4] *Krit. der r. Vern.* p. 190 ff.; cf. p. 83 ff.

designation, *Axiom of Contradiction and Identity.*[1] Those who
have worked at Formal Logic since Kant generally share his
views about the axiom of Contradiction, but think differently
of its relation to the axiom of Identity. Some seek to deduce
the latter from the former, or the former from the latter; while
others consider each to be a separate and independent axiom.
The question only amounts to how each of these axioms is to
be taken. According to different ways of expression and
comprehension they are to be considered either the positive and
negative form of one and the same law, or two different laws.

Fichte[2] believes the axioms of Identity and Contradiction to
be the basis of our knowledge of the primary activity of the
Ego (positing itself and the Non-Ego): and finds this action
of the Ego to be the real basis of these axioms.

Hegel[3] expresses the axiom of Contradiction in this way—A
cannot be A and at the same time not be A. He considers it
to be the negative form of the axiom of Identity, according to
which A = A, or everything is identical with itself. He therefore
thinks that this axiom, instead of being a true law of thought,
is only the law of the reflective or 'abstract' understanding.
The form of the proposition itself contradicts it. A proposition
promises a distinction between subject and predicate, but this
law does not perform what its form demands. It is, moreover, invalidated by the following so-called laws of thought
(the axiom of Difference, the axiom of Opposition or of Excluded Third, and the axiom of the Reason). The truth of
these laws is the unity of the identity and the difference,
which finds its expression in the Category of the Reason.
Thought as *understanding* lets things stand in their strict determinateness and distinction from others: its next higher stage
is the self-elevation of those finite determinations and their
passing over into their opposites, wherein lies their *Dialectic* or
negative-intellectual moment. Lastly, the highest stage is the

[1] *Logik*, ed. by Jäsche, p. 75.
[2] *Grundlage der Wissenschaftslehre*, p. 17 ff.
[3] *Logik*, i. 2, p. 36 ff.; 57 ff.; *Encycl.* § 115; cf. 119 and
§§ 79–82 : 'A kann nicht zugleich A und nicht A sein.'

unity of the determinations in their opposition, the *speculative* or *positively-intellectual* moment, in which both the dualism of the understanding and the one-sided monism of the negative power of the reason reach their right position as the mutually dependent elements of free speculative truth. These Hegelian doctrines are not without truth (cf. § 80) in reference to *contrary opposites*; but their transference to the relation of *contradictory* opposition is based, as *Trendelenburg* has proved in his 'Logische Untersuchungen,' so clearly that we need only refer to his work in this place, upon the substitution of real opposition for logical negation. Chalybäus, too, says,[1] 'it must be granted that in the Hegelian system it would be more correct to say opposite instead of contradiction.' Cf. § 31 and § 83, on the dialectic method ; § 42, on the recognition of the gradation of things as the true mean between the two extremes, which lie in the dualistic or 'abstract-understanding' separation, and the monistic or 'negative-rational' identification ; and also the deduction of the law of excluded middle in the next paragraph. As regards Hegel's charge, that the axiom of Contradiction does not pay attention to the difference of predicate from subject, this has to do only with the form of sentence selected by him to express it, which so far from being essential to it is rather an expression very unsuitable and deviating from the true meaning. The true expression pays attention to predicate and subject, and to every relation of the judgment.

Herbart[2] reduces the axiom of Contradiction to the formula —' What is opposed is not one and the same.' He not merely asserts the validity of the axiom, but exaggerates its significance. He makes it exclude not merely the possibility of uniting contradictory opposites, or the affirmation and negation of the same, but also the possibility of uniting contraries, and of uniting a mere plurality of predicates in the same subject (unless it is an aggregate without true unity), and therefore the impossibility of thinking a thing with several changing

1 *Die hist. Entwickelung der speculativen Philosophie von Kant bis Hegel*, 2nd ed. p. 821 ; English translation by Edersheim, p. 419.
2 *Lehrbuch zur Einl. in die Philos.* § 39.

§ 77. *The Axiom of Contradiction.* 259

qualities. Both extremes, the Hegelian and the Herbartian,
are only expressions, from different sides, of the same fundamental error—the substitution of contradictory and contrary
opposition. Hegel transfers what is true of the latter to the
former; Herbart, what is true of the former to the latter.

[*Hamilton* [1] thus states the axiom of Contradiction, or, as he
calls it (after Krug), Non-Contradiction—What is contradictory
is unthinkable. The logical import of the law lies in this, that
it is the principle of all logical negation and distinction, and
that it, together with the law of identity, regulates the categorical syllogism. He does not make it, as some other formal
logicians do, the only primary law of Logic; but makes the
law of Identity and the law of Contradiction co-ordinate and
reciprocally relative, and says that neither can be educed as
second from the other as first. In every such attempt at derivation the supposed secondary is always necessarily presupposed.
The two are, in fact, one and the same law, differing only by a
positive and negative expression. [2]

Boole, [3] in his attempt to reduce all logical to mathematical
relations, to explain every possible operation and combination
of thoughts by mathematical principles, and express them in
mathematical notation, asserts, as his Fourth Proposition—
‘ That the axiom of Metaphysicians which is termed the principle of contradiction, and which affirms that it is impossible
for any being to possess a quality, and at the same time not to
possess it, is a consequence of the fundamental law of thought,
whose expression is, $x^2 = x$.’ He proves his proposition very
simply and elegantly from his mathematical premisses, but cannot be said either to have explained or derived the logical law.
To prove his whole theory, as well as this particular part of it,
Boole must show that the fundamental mathematical relations
are (1) simpler, and also (2) of more extensive application than
the logical. If this be shown, then he may go on to show that

[1] *Lect. on Logic*, i. 81–2 ; cf. Mansel's *Proleg. Log.* p. 193 ff.
[2] For a list of authorities upon this law of Contradiction cf. ib.
ii. 246.
[3] *Laws of Thought*, p. 49.

s 2

the less simple relations of Logic, which have a narrower sphere of application, may be reduced to those of mathematics, and Logic become part of the latter science. But in fact the mathematical relations which Boole assumes (e.g.) to prove the law of contradiction are neither more simple nor of more extensive application than the logical axiom proved by them.[1]

J. S. Mill[2] says that the law of Contradiction is a principle of reasoning in the sense that it is the generalization of a mental act which is of continual occurrence, and which cannot be dispensed with in reasoning. He would express the law thus—The affirmation of an assertion and the denial of its contradictory are logical equivalents, which it is allowable and indispensable to make use of as mutually controvertible.

A. Bain[3] makes the law of Contradiction, with those of Identity and Excluded Middle, take rank among the maxims by which we attain *consistency* in thinking. Consistency requires that when we affirm a definite fact, we do not at the same time deny it; having made an assertion, we are to abide by that. As by the law of Relativity everything that may be thought of, and every affirmation that can be made, has an opposite notion or affirmation, thoroughgoing consistency requires that we must be prepared to deny the counter notion or affirmation. The maxim of consistency which provides for this is the law of Contradiction.]

§ 78. THE AXIOM OF EXCLUDED THIRD OR MIDDLE (principium exclusi tertii sive medii inter duo contradictoria) is thus stated: Judgments opposed as contradictories (such as A is B, and A is not B) can neither both be false nor can admit the truth of a third or middle judgment, but the one or other must be true,

[1] Cf. the whole of Chapters II. (of signs and their laws) and III. (Derivation of the laws of the symbols of Logic from the laws of the human mind), pp. 26–51.

[2] *Examin. of Sir W. Hamilton's Philos.* 3rd ed. p. 471.

[3] *Deductive Logic*, p. 16.]

and the truth of the one follows from the falsehood of the other. Or,—The double answer, *yes and no*, cannot be given to one and the same question understood in the same sense. The validity of this law also follows from the definitions of truth (§ 3), judgment (§ 67), and affirmation and negation (§ 69). These definitions assert, that the falsehood of the affirmation is equivalent to the want of agreement between the combination of conceptions and the reality it represents, and consequently to the truth of the negation; and that the falsehood of the negation is equivalent to the agreement of the combination of conceptions with the reality it represents, and consequently to the truth of the affirmation.

The remarks made under the law of Contradiction upon the entrance of a determination of time into the notion of contradictory opposition, and the other references to the distinctness of the sense in the judgments, to the possibility of proving the axiom, to its presuppositions, and to the case of apparent exception, are all applicable to the law of Excluded Middle. They are, indeed, to be more carefully attended to because this law is even more liable to be misunderstood.

Various *objections*, partly against the *value*, partly against the *truth* of the law, are founded upon false ideas of its aim and meaning.

The VALUE of the law has been denied. It has been said to be devoid of meaning and to be superfluous. (The attacks have been made from the mutually opposite stand-points of the purely Speculative and of the Empirical Philosophy.) Its legitimate existence in Logic has been denied. It does not distinguish, it is said, between cases where the denial is proper, and those where it is not proper. It does not distinguish between partial and total negation. It is, consequently, a meaningless and barren formula.[1] But the strength of

[1] Hegel's *Encycl.* § 119; Beneke's *Logik*, I. 101 ff.

these objections lies in this, that they demand from the axiom
what does not belong to it. The axiom, rightly understood,
does not say that we may search after predicates of any given
subject by a sort of 'mounting to the sky,' and then find it
able to be defined either by the positive notion or its contradictory opposite. It does not say that in order to know the
predicates of Spirit, e.g., we may and do bring forward the
notions of the qualities green and not-green, wooden and not-
wooden, &c., and then rejoice in the certainty that in every case
the one predicate must be applicable if the other is not. This
would be absurd. The axiom presupposes a suitable question.
It does not show what question is suitable. That follows from
the essence of affirmation and negation (§ 69). There must
be a motive for the affirmation. And usually the genus-notion,
to which the predicate is subordinate, already belongs to the subject. If the question be unsuitable, the axiom of Excluded
Third gives an unsuitable, but not a false, judgment. (It is not
false that Spirit is not blue, nor that a table does not think,
&c.; indeed, while the craze of table-turning and spirit-rapping
lasts, this latter judgment is not even unsuitable.) The axiom
is valid, without exception, in every case in which the question
is distinctly unequivocal; and therefore is not to be limited by
annexing any condition which will embody the demands made
above.[1] The axiom itself has nothing to do with its unsuitable
application. It must be admitted, however, that the misinterpretation of the axiom has been apparently sanctioned by the
name which some logicians have given to the axiom of Excluded
Third, and by the formula in which it is expressed. It has been
called the 'Axiom of the determinability of every object by
every predicate;' and has been expressed in the formula—The
one of all possible pairs of contradictory predicates must belong
to every object.

The application of the axiom in indirect proof shows that it is
not valueless. The scientific postulate of systematic completeness demands that it be placed as the essential complement of

[1] As I. II. Fichte, *De Princ. Contrad. &c.* p. 30, and Ulrici,
Logik, p. 125, demand.

the axiom of contradiction; and would demand the same in cases where it could not be applied.

The TRUTH of the law has been denied. Objections are directed not merely against the value and productiveness of the axiom of Excluded Third, but also against its truth. Some logicians have limited it by certain exceptions. Others would entirely abolish it. The former think that the axiom is not valid when the subject is a general notion. For example, the triangle in general is neither rectangular nor not-rectangular.[1] But it is only the indefiniteness of the sense which causes the appearance of invalidity. If the sense of the sentence be—Every triangle is rectangular, the negation, and it only, is true. If the sense be—There are right-angled triangles which are objects of mathematics, the affirmation, and it only, is true.

Others refuse to acknowledge the validity of the axiom at all.[2] The mean between the contradictory predicates, they say, is often the true predicate. All development rests on the union of opposites. Between 'guilty' and 'not-guilty' there is 'not-proven.' Between full imputation and no imputation there is partial imputation. It would be a dangerous error to exclude this third case. It would often give judges the painful alternative of unjust acquittal or unjust condemnation, and give effect to expressions of only half truth in spite of better knowledge and desire. Absolute recognition or rejection, the simple division of the character into good and evil, leaving out of consideration all the intermediate grades, the partition of systems into true and false without making allowance for the gradual advance of knowledge, the separation of statements into credible or incredible and forged without including the myth or poetic truth,—all denote a certain crudeness of thought. The cultivated man knows how to recognise the finer ramifications of truth and error, and to draw the elements of truth, scattered everywhere, from under the coverings of error, as gold is drawn from dross.

---

[1] Krug, *Denklehre*, § 19, teaches this.

[2] Hegel and his school, and Fr. Fischer, *Logik*, p. 40 ff.

Hegel says,[1] ' a philosophy of history has to seek a moment of spiritual truth in the most languishing constitutions.' *Aristotle*[2] and, more distinctly, *Leibniz*[3] speak of elements of truth lying hidden in systems the most different and contradictory to each other, which the careful glance of him who searches most deeply may everywhere recognise. *Leibniz*[4] remarks (in opposition to Bayle) that the reason, when it recognises two views opposed to each other to be both false, thereby promises a deeper insight. But neither Aristotle nor Leibniz have explained themselves more definitely upon the relation of that relativity to the absolute validity of the logical laws of Contradiction and Excluded Middle, which is recognised by both philosophers. The opposition is established by later philosophers. ' If the knowledge of truth is not comprehended in a development,' *Erdmann* says, in *Hegel's* sense,[5] ' everything is either wholly truth or wholly not-truth. Truth becoming, or developing itself, is both or neither the one nor the other.' The strict maintenance of the laws of Identity and Excluded Middle, principles of the ' heathen Aristotle,' is even explained, humorously, but with all earnestness, to be unchristian,[6] because the reconciliation of opposites is the fundamental thought of Christianity (guilt removed, a ' felix culpa '), while the persistency in opposition is heathenish. These observations, however correct in themselves, and worthy of attention, so far as they are to be considered as warnings against a false apprehension and application of the axiom of Excluded Third, prove nothing against the validity of the axiom rightly understood. They can only be held to be exceptions to it by exchanging contradictory for contrary opposition. Whoever[7]

[1] *Philos. der Geschichte*, ed. of 1837, p. 202.
[2] *Metaph.* i. 10 ; cf. ii. 1.
[3] In his third letter to Remond de Montmort, p. 701 of Erdmann's edition.
[4] *De Conform. fid. et rat.* § 60.
[5] *Gesch. der neueren Philos.* i. 2, 171.
[6] Fichte's *Zeitschrift für Phil.* &c. xxviii. pp. 8, 9, 1856.
[7] Like Fr. Fischer, *Logik*, p. 40 ff.

first explains that by Non-A he means something else than
other logicians do, viz. contrary, and not as they do, contradictory opposition, and then upbraids them with the incorrectness of their axiom because it does not hold good under his
terminology, acts no way differently from the man who, first
of all explaining that he deviates from Euclid's usage, and
understands, or at least comprehends, under 'triangle' the
spherical triangle, then turns round and blames Euclid because
he teaches that the sum of the angles of a triangle are always
equal to two right angles. The stricture, however, is to a
certain degree legitimate when opposed to the formula—A
notion or *its opposite* is to be predicated of every object. But
if one keeps strictly to the notion of *contradictory* opposition, its opposing members denote only the presence or absence
of a strict agreement of the combination of conceptions with
the actual existence they represent. No one can really and at
bottom doubt but that one of these two members must always
be true, and that the axiom of Excluded Middle, which only
asserts this universally, is true also. It is already implicitly
given in the definitions of truth and falsehood, and affirmation
and negation. According to these definitions, to explain the
negation to be false, is equivalent to the denial of the want
of agreement with what actually exists, and equivalent to the
affirmation of the truth of the affirmation. To explain the
affirmation to be false, is equivalent to denying the presence
of agreement with what actually exists; and this is again
equivalent to the recognition of the truth of the negation.
The negation cannot be interchangeable with the affirmation of the predicate opposed as a *contrary.* Not guilty
is not equivalent to guiltless or pure. Not mortal (which
may be said of a stone) is not equivalent to immortal or
eternal. Not good ('no one is good but God') is not equivalent to bad or wicked (the new-born child is not morally
good. It requires education and the growth of personality in
order to become good. But this is not to say that it is morally bad); and so in all like cases. The truth of the negation, which excludes the agreement of the positive statement

with actual existence, does not exclude any degree whatever
of *approximation* to this agreement. The question—Is this
criminal guilty of this distinct crime?—must be denied if
only partial blame can be attached to him; because in this
case the presupposition of blame conformable to the actual
state represented does not occur. But the denial of this
question does not make further questions, whether there
has been any, and if so, what degree of approximation to full
guilt, superfluous. It rather makes them necessary. The contradictory disjunction, guilty or not guilty, is not to be charged
with the error of denying the possibility of half guilt or
partial insanity. The error lies in making reciprocal the
negation of this definite guilt with the affirmation of perfect
innocence. The denial of guilt, as the accusation puts it,
leaves open the possibility of a certain degree of guilt. In the
same way the negation of a full ability to manage one's own
affairs is always true, when its affirmation is false; but this
negation is not equivalent to the assertion of complete incapa-
city to manage one's own affairs. Forms of transition between
different kinds of the same genus are a mean between existences positively distinct. They do not stand to each other
in the relation of Being and Not-Being, but in that of Being
so and Being otherwise. Such transitions are not excluded
by the law of Excluded Third between the affirmation and
negation of the same. Grey is not a mean between white and
not white, but between white and black; and belongs as well
as black to not-white. The partially good character is not a
mean between good and not good, but between good and bad;
and belongs to the not-good character. A gradual development
in knowledge and a gradual approximation to perfect truth are
not excluded by this axiom. Partial views which are opposed
to each other as contrary opposites, are generally both false;
but are not without an element of truth, for they both diverge
from truth on the two opposite sides. In cases of this kind the
application of the law of Excluded Middle requires much care.
It is so very easy to confuse judgments whose predicates are
contradictions, with judgments whose predicates are contraries;

so very easy to make the negation, which should denote only the want of a strict agreement in everything or the presence of some divergence, denote a full divergence. This is more especially the case when practical motives get mixed up with the discussion. The negation then both leads on those who frame the judgments to a full divergence on all points, and is so interpreted by others. When the one party combats the conclusion, the denial appears to be inseparable from the contrary. In such relations, when the practical interest is considered, he who is mentally free from the party errors which both sides fall under may be induced, in accordance with Solon's law, to accept the partial error which is supportable, or at least rest content with not opposing it. He will thus avoid the isolation of negation, and will not give up the kernel with the shell, the thought with its inadequate expression. It is a logical duty, however, in theoretical reference, to make clear to one's self and to those who seek the truth for its own sake, the falsehood of both extremes, and instead of the simple yes or no, to seek that construction of notion and judgment which makes possible a statement of the question more conformable to the state of the case. Dr. Richarz says forcibly,[1] 'The impossibility of answering certain categorical questions, about health or sickness, capacity for managing one's own affairs and the want of such capacity, categorically, by a short yes or no, is often made matter of reproach against the science of medicine, and given as a sign of the inferiority of its stand-point. This is often done by jurists, who always require for their decisions concise expressions of the relations of circumstances. But most unjustly; for, while he who investigates nature proceeds on his course, and as his circle of vision widens he abundantly discovers new and wider conditions and relations in phenomena and notions which have hitherto seemed only simply related, which the plain affirmation and negation given to questions arising from the practical wants of life, are no longer sufficient to express.' (It is with sanity and insanity as with

[1] In the writing *Reiner Stockhausen, mit Gutachten von M. Jacobi, F. W. Böcker, C. Hertz, Fr. Richarz,* Elberfeld, 1855, p. 131 ff.

being of age and being under age; observation from the stand-point of natural science and instruction finds a gradual development. Practical necessity first imposes strict limits, which are to be defined only according to laws imposed by jurists.) In the questions about Homer, the adherence to extreme views marks the starting-point of investigation. A maturer scientific treatment seeks to investigate, not *whether*, but *how far*, the poems are to be referred to one or to more authors. A modern philologist says, ' People should at length cease to settle the Homeric question by a yes or no.'[1] The question — Was Thales a theist? cannot be affirmed; but neither can it be denied in the sense that he was an atheist. His stand-point lies without and is below the opposition of the clearly defined pure Theism or Atheism. The same is to be said to the question — Did he subscribe to the mechanical or dynamical theories of natural philosophy? The statement that Socrates was an upholder of the old morality and ancient simple faith of his people, must be denied; so must the assertion that he was a partaker in the philosophical movement to which the Sophists belonged. His stand-point was *already above* these two opposites. It was the higher point in which they became one. His old accusers made the legitimate denial of the first statement the ground for affirming the second ; and not a few ancient and modern defenders have made the legitimate denial of the second the ground for affirming the first. Both were led astray in different ways by the same misapprehension — a misapprehension which finds easy entrance, and is inevitable, so long as the peculiarity of the higher stand-point is not recognised. In the naive sayings of children and of persons of kindly feeling, who are not accustomed to put things to the test of objective fact, there is often truth. They express their actual subjective feelings. But the conceptions in which this truth is embodied do not strictly agree with the external actual fact. Now if the truth of these assertions be enquired after, and if the answer be limited to yes or no, the axiom of Excluded Third appears to justify this procedure ;

[1] G. Curtius in the *Zeitschrift für die østr. Gymn.* p. 115, 1854.

and does indeed justify it in so far as the negation is understood in the purely logical sense that a complete correspondence with fact in every particular does not exist. But it does not justify the negation in so far as it means a complete divergence from fact. It very often happens in this reference, that it is more difficult to formulate the question than to give the answer. In criminal cases the answer, guilty or not guilty, is left to the jury, but the statement of the question is entrusted to well-trained judges. A philosophical system may be partly true, when it contains true judgments along with false, and also when every individual judgment may approach more or less nearly to truth. And if a similar character pervades the whole system in strict connection, the very kind and degree of approximation to truth which exists in the principles of the system may be found in every individual proposition. The different systems which have appeared in the course of history may, in this sense, be looked upon as different stages in the development of human knowledge, and as degrees of approximation to perfect knowledge. He who now-a-days, in presence of this historical development of scientific notions, can put questions such as the following—Is the human soul free or is it not? Is freedom a true good or is it not? Do the New Testament writings contain the whole of the Christian Revelation or do they not? Has the idea of philosophy embodied itself in Plato, or has it not? and the like;—he who puts such questions, and demands a simple yes or no as answer, only proves that he has never studied the problems in hand, at least *fundamentally.* If he had, he would have first asked—*What* is freedom? *What* is revelation? *What* is truth? &c. In what sense and measure does the affirmation hold good, and in what sense and measure the negation? The conceptions, which exist *before* the scientific investigation, cannot be here presupposed to be self-evident. It is not their objective validity only that must be put to proof. In the form which they have *before* investigation, they are not absolutely valid, nor are they absolutely invalid. The chief task consists in finding the truly valid notion. This task does not indeed

promise ease. Thinking must strain itself to the highest
degree possible. That restless bustle of action, which, with a
ready yes or no, will proceed to external action, to stablish or
revolutionise, but never will shake itself free of the bonds of
those hurtful opposites, is not attainable by it. The true
freedom of the mind is the stipulated reward of a disinterested
resignation to pure thinking. Every false repose on a superficial affirmation or negation must be decidedly opposed. But
we must hold as decidedly by the persuasion that there may be
pure truth, in whose attainment the gradual succession of
approximations find their end and aim, which finds its fulfilment
in adequate science ; for then only the question rightly stated,
which has already included the determinations which correspond
to the facts, can be answered by yes or no. In its limited
province, mathematics has almost thoroughly reached this end
(and natural science has in great part). Its development requires only upbuilding, never or seldom rebuilding. It is foolish to explain this excellence to be a defect in mathematics ;
saying that it is a subordinate science, in which the laws of the
reflective understanding yet hold good. The attainment of
pure truth was an easier task for mathematics, because of the
simpler nature of its problems, than it is to philosophy and to
several of the other sciences. All, however, each in its sphere,
are destined to reach the same goal by a gradual advance.[t]

HISTORY OF THE AXIOM.—As the logical consciousness
of the axiom of Contradiction was developed by Parmenides,
in his polemic against the common affirmation of contradictory
opposites by Heraclitus, so the origin of the doctrine of the
Excluded Third is apparent in *Aristotle's* opposition to the
Platonic assertion of a Third or mean between Being and Not-
Being.

Plato set on one side Ideas, as that which *is*, on the opposite
side, matter, as that which *is not* (but nevertheless made it the

[t] [This thought runs through the late Prof. Grote's *Exploratio
Philosophica*. Professor Grote had, apparently, in a quite independent
way, reached many of the conclusions of those modern German philosophers who are supporters of the Ideal-Realismus.]

substratum of sensible things), and between the two as the Third, sensible things. They are, he said, an indefinite manifold, and are in continuous becoming and change. As such, they neither truly are, nor yet are not. Their true place must be considered to be the mean between Being and Not-Being:[1] καὶ γὰρ ταῦτα ἰναμφοτερίζειν, καὶ οὔτ' εἶναι οὔτε μὴ εἶναι οὐδὲν αὐτῶν δυνατὸν παγίως νοῆσαι οὔτ' ἀμφότερα οὔτ' οὐδέτερον. Ἔχειν οὖν—ὅποι θήσεις καλλίω θέσιν τῆς μεταξὺ οὐσίας τε καὶ τοῦ μὴ εἶναι;

Aristotle, on the other hand, allowed no mean between the members of the contradiction, between Being and Not-Being :[1] ἀλλὰ μὴν οὐδὲ μεταξὺ ἀντιφάσεως ἐνδέχεται εἶναι οὐθέν.[1] ἀνάγκη τῆς ἀντιφάσεως θάτερον εἶναι μόριον ἀληθές—ἀδύνατον ἀμφότερα ψευδῆ εἶναι. Cf.[1] ἀντίφασις δὲ ἀντίθεσις, ἧς οὐκ ἔστι μεταξὺ καθ' αὑτήν. The assertion of a mean term, Aristotle thinks, would lead to the absurd consequence that Existence would be one-and-a-half-ply, made up of the Being and the half-Being which is between it and not-Being. Then between these two another mean must be taken, and so on ad infinitum.[3] ἔτι εἰς ἄπειρον βαδιεῖται καὶ οὐ μόνον ἡμιόλια τὰ ὄντα ἔσται ἀλλὰ πλείω. *Wolff* teaches, like Aristotle[4]—inter contradictoria non dari medium;[7] propositionum contradictoriarum altera necessario vera.[1]

Baumgarten uses the formula[9],—omne possibile aut est A aut non A, seu omni subiecto ex omnibus praedicatis contradictoriis alterutrum convenit—a formula which is liable to the misapprehension stated above, that it authorises a universal comparison of any possible subject-notion with any possible predicate-notion.

---

[1] *Rep.* 479 c.　　[9] *Metaph.* iv. 7, § 1.　　[3] Ibid. §§ 5–6.
[4] *Analyt. post.* i. 2.　　[5] *Metaph.* iv. 7, § 9.　　[6] *Ontolog.* § 52.
[7] *Log.* § 532.

[8] It is singular, since these words of Wolff are only a translation of the Aristotelian, that some think, such as Bachmann, *Log.* p. 62, that the axiom of Excluded Third is first found as principle of science in modern times and in Wolff.

[9] *Metaph.* § 10.

Kant[1] explains the axiom, which elsewhere he incorrectly calls the axiom of *Excluding Third*, to be the basis of the logical necessity in *apodictic* judgments; but does not determine the formula more closely.

Kiesewetter, following Kant, says,—'The one or other of two attributes, contradictory to each other, must *necessarily* belong to every logical object.' (The necessity lies only in the choice which must not be refused. The axiom does not teach at all, still less with apodictic certainty, which of the two members of the contradictory opposition is to be chosen. Hence the apprehension of the axiom, as a principle of *apodictic* judgments, rests on a misunderstanding.)

Krug,[2] who disputes the possibility of applying the axiom in its common form to genus-notions,[2] chooses the formula,—' Of opposed determinations of one thing you can only affirm one, and if you have affirmed this one you must deny the other ' —which is rather a formula for the axiom of Contradiction ; and ' Every possible attribute must either belong or must not to every object thought as thoroughly determined ;' in which formula both axioms are comprehended.   Krug calls this axiom the principle of reciprocal capacity for determination.

Fries[4] uses the formulae,—' A notion or its opposite belongs to every object.'—' Any notion belongs either affirmatively or negatively to any thing.'   He chooses the name,—Axiom of the determinability of any object by any predicate.   The misapprehension of the axiom, already contained in Baumgarten's formula, is still more provoked by this.

Hegel's strictures[5] are justifiable against such a false apprehension of the axiom, but not against the axiom itself.   He says, ' Difference in itself gives the axiom,—Everything is essentially different ; or as it is also expressed,—Of two contradictory attributes only the one belongs to anything, and there is no third.' (This is, however, not strict enough.   The definition, *only* one predicate and not the two together belongs

[1] *Logik*, p. 75.
[2] *Denklehre*, § 19.   Following Polz, *Comment. Metaph.* p. 107 sqq.
[3] Cf. p. 263.   [4] *Log.* § 41.   [5] Ibid. i. 2, 66 ff. ; *Encycl.* § 119.

to the same object, has rather to do with the axiom of Contradiction. The axiom of Excluded Third, on the other hand, says—*in every case* the one predicate, and not both of the two, belongs to the same object, and Hegel himself recognises this.[1] He calls the axiom in that form—*the axiom of the opposite*, or *of opposition*, or the *axiom of Excluded Third*. He thinks that this axiom contradicts the axiom of Identity. He combats it more especially by the assertion, that there is always a third between $+$ A and $-$ A, viz. A in its absolute value; and O is a Third between $+$ and $-$. But here Hegel identifies the logical relations with the mathematical, from which, in spite of some similarity, they are to be essentially distinguished. Contrary not Contradictory opposition exists[2] between positive and negative size in the mathematical sense. The negative quantity $-$ A is by no means identical with the logical denial of $+$ A. A quantity need not be either $= +$ A or $= -$ A. It may be either $= +$ A or not $= +$ A, and also either $= -$ A or not $= -$ A. And looked at apart from the signs, according to its absolute value, it may be either $=$ A or not $=$ A.

Herbart and his school rightly hold firmly by the validity of the axiom of Excluded Middle.[3]

[*Hamilton*[4] gives the formula—' Of contradictory attributions we can only affirm the one of a thing; and if one be explicitly affirmed the other is denied. *A either is or is not B.*' This law differs from the Laws of Identity and Contradiction by warranting the conclusion from the falsehood of one contradictory proposition to the truth of another. Its logical significance

---

[1] *Logik*, i. 2, p. 67.
[2] Kant noticed this in his *Versuch, den Begriff der negativen Grössen in die Weltweisheit einzuführen*, 1763; *Sämmtliche Werke*, ed. by Hartenstein, ii. 69 ff.
[3] Herbart, L. z. Einl. in die Phil. § 39; *Commentatio de principio logico exclusi medii inter contradictoria non negligendo*, Gotting. 1833; cf. Hartenstein, *Diss. de methodo philosophica logicae legibus adstringenda, finibus non terminanda*, Lips. 1835; Drobisch, *Logik*, 2nd ed. § 57, 3rd ed. § 60.
[4] [*Lectures on Logic*, i. 83.

T

lies in this, that it limits the sphere of the thinkable in relation to affirmation. It determines that of the two forms given by the laws of Identity and Contradiction, and by these laws affirmed as those exclusively possible, ' the one or other must be affirmed as necessary.' Hamilton seems to have fallen into the error of supposing that the law of Excluded Middle is a principle of Apodicticity, and gives necessary results. It necessitates the *affirmation* of one or other of the opposed contradictories. It does not affirm *the one or other* to be necessary. Besides, the formula which Hamilton uses is really the formula for the joint axiom of Contradiction and Excluded Middle, and does not express the latter purely. Cf. § 79.

J. S. Mill[1] thinks that this law is one of the principles of all reasonings, being the generalisation of a process which is liable to be required in all of them. It empowers us to substitute for the denial of two contradictory propositions the assertion of the other two. He denies in his Logic[2] the necessity and universality of the law, and says that it is not even true without a large exception. A predicate must be either true or false, *provided* that the predicate be one which can in any intelligible sense be attributed to the subject. Between the true and the false there is always a third possibility—the unmeaning. There are many valuable remarks in the pages Mr. Mill has given to the discussion of these laws, and had he not been hampered by his empirical theory of the origin of all knowledge, and his consequent theory of the supposititious nature of demonstrative science, he would have approached very nearly to the doctrine laid down in the text. Had he only pursued the theory laid down in discussing propositions—that they express real relations, he would have arrived at it. But there always seems to be a double view of Logic before Mr. Mill, and he shifts from the one to the other. On the one view Logic is a theory of knowledge, on the other it is almost a theory of naming.

[1] *Examination of Sir W. Hamilton's Philos.* 3rd ed. p. 473.
[2] i. 309.

The two views come out most clearly in the chapters on propositions. Propositions in general describe facts, but Definitions describe names. In what is said of the laws of thought in his Logic the former view predominates; in what is said in the Examination, &c., the latter.

A. Bain [1] confuses the opposition of predicates as contradictories, with the so-called contradictory opposition of judgments, to the extent that he makes the one grow out of the other; while they are in no way related. He thus makes the law of Excluded Middle an 'incident of partial or incomplete contrariety;' and says: 'It is too much honoured by the dignity of a primary law of thought.']

§ 79. The axiom of Contradiction and the axiom of Excluded Middle may be *comprehended* in the formula: A is either B or is not B. Any predicate in question either belongs or does not belong to any subject; or—of judgments opposed as contradictories to each other, the one is true and the other false; or—To every completely distinct question understood always in the same sense, which has to do with the possession of a definite attribute by a definite subject, yes or no must be answered. These formulae contain the axiom of Contradiction, for they posit *two contradictory members*, and assert that the affirmation and denial of the same *cannot both be true*; A is *either* B, *or* is not B. They also contain the axiom of Excluded Third, for they posit *only two* mutually exclusive members, and assert, that any third besides affirmation and negation is inadmissible, and that *both are not false*, but one of the two is true,—A is either B or *is not* B; there is no third. The comprehension of the axioms of Contradiction and Excluded Third in the foregoing formula may be called the PRINCIPLE OF CONTRADICTORY DISJUNCTION (principium disiunctionis contradictoriae).

A suitable statement of the question is again the natural presupposition of the *application* of this principle.

The transference of the denial to the predicate ' A is either n or non-B,'—is not false, provided that, by non-n, only contradictory opposition be understood. It is a useless artifice, however, and easily gives rise to a false meaning in the contrary opposite.

The simplest metaphysical formula of the principle of Contradictory Disjunction is found as early as in *Parmenides*,[1] ἔστιν ἡ οὐκ ἔστιν. It is here used only in the sense of the axiom of Contradiction to reject the common truth of the assertion of Being and Not-Being. Being and Not-Being cannot exist together, the one excludes the other.

Aristotle, on the other hand, uses the comprehensive formula mostly in the sense of the axiom of Excluded Third.[2] ἀλλὰ μὴν οὐδὲ μεταξὺ ἀντιφάσεως ἐνδέχεται εἶναι οὐθέν, ἀλλ' ἀνάγκη ἢ φάναι ἢ ἀποφάναι ἓν καθ' ἑνὸς ὁτιοῦν.[3] πᾶν ἢ φάναι ἢ ἀποφάναι ἀναγκαῖον.[4] ἐπὶ τῆς καταφάσεως καὶ τῆς ἀποφάσεως ἀεί—τὸ ἕτερον ἔσται ψεῦδος καὶ τὸ ἕτερον ἀληθές.[5] τὸ δ' ἅπαν φάναι ἢ ἀποφάναι ἡ εἰς τὸ ἀδύνατον ἀπόδειξις λαμβάνει. Aristotle tried to deduce the axiom from the definitions of truth and untruth, on the ground of the presupposed impossibility that the same could be and not be. Every judgment (because it is a subjective assertion about objective existence) must fall under one of four forms of combination: denying what exists, affirming what does not exist; affirming what exists, denying what does not exist. The first two of these are false, the last two are true (for in the former the thought does not correspond with the actual fact; in the latter it does). The one assertion is true and the other false on presupposition of Being, and also so on presupposition of Not-Being. And in

---

[1] *Fragm.* vs. 72, ed. Mullach; *ap. Simplic. ad Arist. Phys.* fol. 31 a.
[2] *Metaph.* iv. 7, § 1.
[3] Ib. 8, § 6.
[4] *Categ.* c. x. 13 a, 27.
[5] *Anal. Post.* i. 11.

every case either the affirmation or the negation is true, and, therefore, since truth is what we aim at, ἢ φάναι ἢ ἀποφάναι ἀναγκαῖον. Both cannot be false and a Third or Middle true. No place is left for a Middle. For a Middle, if it be true, or even thinkable, and have the reference to truth and falsehood, which belongs essentially to every judgment, must itself be one of that combination of members, which it cannot be according to its very notion. For in the Middle neither what exists nor what does not exist is affirmed or denied. It is in this way that the incompletely expressed reasoning of Aristotle against the Middle or Third must be completed.[1]

Leibniz[2] places the negative form—'A proposition is either true or false,' by the side of the affirmative form of the primitive, identical, rational truth—'Everything is what it is.' He calls this axiom the principle of Contradiction, and divides it into the two axioms which he includes in it—'That a proposition cannot be true and false at the same time;' and—'That there is no mean between the true and the false,' or rather—It is not possible that a proposition can be neither true nor false. In the same way Leibniz[3] calls, 'Principe de la Contradiction,' the one 'which asserts that of two contradictory propositions the one is true and the other false.' Leibniz, therefore, understands by the Principle of Contradiction that axiom which includes both what is usually called the Axiom of Contradiction and the Axiom of Excluded Third.

Wolff[4] enunciates the formulae 'quodlibet vel est, vel non est;' 'propositionum contradictoriarum altera necessario vera, altera necessario falsa,' and says, 'patet per se, eidem subiecto A idem praedicatum B vel convenire, vel non convenire.' Many, both of the earlier and of the later logicians, have wrongly believed the formula—A is either B or not B, which includes both the axiom of Contradiction and of Excluded Third, to be the proper and simple expression of the axiom of Excluded Third.[5]

[1] *Metaph.* iv. 7, §§ 2, 6. [2] *Nouv. Ess.* iv. 2, § 1.
[3] *Theod.* i. § 44. [4] *Ontol.* § 52; *Log.* § 532.
[5] Cf. upon the whole question, Katzenberger, *Grundfragen der Logik*, Leipzig, 1858.

§ 80. The foregoing Axioms are *not* to be applied to *judgments whose* PREDICATES *stand to each other in the relation of* CONTRARY *opposites* (like positive and negative quantities). In this relation it is possible under certain presuppositions, that (a) both judgments be false ; and that (b) both judgments be true.

Both may be false :—

1. When that notion which is superordinate to the two predicates opposed to each other as contraries as their common genus-notion does not belong to the subject as its predicate.   (Kant called this relation *Dialectical Opposition.*)

2. When that genus-notion belongs to the subject, but comprehends under it, besides the two predicates opposed as contraries to each other, other species-notions. In this last case *the axiom of the Third lying as a mean between two contrary opposites* finds application (principium tertii intervenientis inter duo contraria).

Both may be true :—

When the subject denotes an object, which is neither absolutely simple nor yet a mere aggregate, but is a synthetic unity of manifold determinations. When some of these determinations or attributes stand in the relation of contrary opposites to each other, the axiom of Coincidence may be applied to them (principium coincidentiae oppositorum). All development by strife and union of opposites rests on this principle.

Judgments, whose *predicates* are opposed *to each other* as contraries (§ 53)—e.g. Caius is happy, Caius is sad—are to be strictly distinguished from judgments which are contrarily opposed *to each other as judgments* (§ 72)—e.g. all men are learned, no men are learned. The former may not only both be false, but in a certain sense may both be true. For example, both joy and sorrow are contained in the feeling of yearning. The latter cannot both be true, but both may be false (§ 97). From both of these relations we must distinguish the relation of Contradictory Opposition, whose members cannot both be true nor both false (§ 79); for example—Caius is happy, Caius is not happy; all men are learned, some men are not learned.

Plato teaches that one and the same thing may unite in itself qualities which are different and even opposed to each other, although the quality itself is never identical with its opposite.[1] In a similar way, *Aristotle* explains that the object may change because it may take properties which are opposed to each other, but that the property itself always remains the same in its notion.[2] Since Aristotle says distinctly, that *only* contradictory opposites exclude every mean, he makes a mean possible in contrary opposites[3] (ἐπὶ γὰρ μόνων τούτων ἀναγκαῖον ἀεὶ τὸ μὲν ἀληθὲς, τὸ δὲ ψεῦδος εἶναι).

Later logicians have seldom thought the relations of judgments with predicates opposed as contraries worthy of more particular attention.

Augustine says, in his short doctrinal epistle to Laurentius:[4] —Omnis natura etiamsi vitiosa est, in quantum natura est, bona est, in quantum vitiosa est, mala est. Quapropter in his contrariis, quae mala et bona vocantur, illa dialecticorum regula deficit qua dicunt nulli rei duo simul incsse contraria. Nullus enim aër simul est et tenebrosus et lucidus, nullus cibus aut potus simul dulcis et amarus, nullum corpus simul ubi album ibi et nigrum . . . . sed mala omnino sine bonis et nisi in bonis esse non possunt, quamvis bona sine malis possint. But he does not strictly distinguish Contrary from Contradictory opposition.

Nicolaus Cusanus, and after him Giordano Bruno, were the

---

[1] *Phaedon.* p. 103 a; cf. *Soph.* p. 257 a, where the ἐναντίον is distinguished from the ἕτερον.
[2] *Metaph.* iv. 5, § 40.   [3] Ibid. iv. 7, § 1; cf. *Categ.* x. 13 a, 2.
[4] *De Fide Spe et Caritate*, c. v.

first to enunciate expressly the principium coincidentiae oppositorum.

Kant rigorously distinguishes the opposition of contrary predicates from contradiction. Judgments of the first kind can both be false. For example, it is equally incorrect to attribute the predicates of limited and unlimited to what has no existence in space; beginning in time, and beginningless, endless duration in time, to the timeless. The opposition here is only 'dialectic,' or apparent.[1]

Hegel and *Herbart,* as has been shown above, make no distinction between the oppositions, but do this in opposite ways. The insight that the *form* of all development in the life of nature and mind (Geist) is the development of (contrary) opposites out of the indifferent or the germ, and their union in a higher unity, is to be recognized as an abiding result of the speculation of Schelling and Hegel.

In the same sense, *I. H. Fichte,*[2] while he condemns the exchange,[3] says quite correctly,[4] ' est enim ubertas rei quaedam, si opposita ad se referre et in se copulare possit;' and *Trendelenburg,* who shows the dialectic method of Hegel to be an exchange of logical negation for real opposition,[5] recognises that[6] 'solet quidem natura, quo maiora gignit, eo potentius, quae contraria sunt, compleeti."[7]

If contrary opposites could not unite in any way there could be no multiplicity or development. Everything would be as *Parmenides* believes, ' The One alone truly exists;' or as *Herbart,* in a milder way, expresses it, ' Each one of the many is

[1] *Krit. der r. Vern.* 2nd ed. p. 531 ff.

[2] *De Princ. Contrad.* 1810; cf. *Ontol.* p. 159, 1836, where he incorrectly makes ' Unterschied' (Difference) and ' Gegensatz ' (Opposite) equivalent to ' Contrary ' and ' Contradictory,' p. 166 ff.

[3] P. 25.   [4] P. 28.

[5] *Log. Unters.* 2nd ed. i. 43 ; 3rd ed. i. 43.

[6] *Elem. Log. Arist.* ad § 9, p. 65, 3rd ed.; cf. *Log. Unt.* 2nd ed. ii. 234 ; 3rd ed. ii. 257.

[7] Cf. also the work mentioned above (§ 69), Gustav Knauer, *Contrár und Contradictorisch,* Halle, 1868.

simple and unchangeable, unalterable, persisting in its simple quality.'—If contrary opposites were not relatively independent (or if contradictory opposites even could be united), there could be no unity nor persistence. Everything would be as *Heraclitus*, and in a more logically definite way *Hegel*, believes.—' Everything fleets. Everything is like and also not like itself. Nothing is definable by a permanent notion.' In reality both unity and plurality, persistence and change, exist together. And the one not exclusive of the other, as *Plato* represents by Ideas and Sensible Things, or as *Kant* almost similarly represents by his ' Ding an Sich ' and phenomena. They exist, as was partly taught in antiquity by *Aristotle* and the *Stoics*, and in our time has been taught by *Schleiermacher* in a purer and deeper way, *in, with, and through each other*; so that the uniting essential form and force dwells in the multiplicity of phenomena, and inviolable law rules the change of actions.

§ 81. THE AXIOM OF THE (*determining or sufficient*) REASON subjects the deduction of different cognitions from one another to the following rule:—A judgment can be derived from another judgment (materially different from it), and finds in it its sufficient reason, only when the (logical) connection of thoughts corresponds to a (real) causal connection. The perfection of the knowledge lies in this, that the ground of knowledge is coincident with the real ground. The knowledge of a real interdependence of things conformable to law is reached, as (§§ 42–42 ; 46 ; 57 ; 73) the knowledge of the inner nature of things in general, and more especially of the individual existence, of the essence, and of the fundamental relations are reached. The external invariable connection among sense-phenomena is with logical correctness explained by an inner conformability to law, according to the analogy of the causal connection perceived in ourselves, between volition and its actual accomplishment (whose existence we learn for the most part by striving against what resists us).

The real conformability to law reveals itself in the simple regularity of external and especially inorganic nature in a way more evident and more fitted to arrest the attention, than in the manifoldly complicated psychic processes. Yet these are the only cases, in which the peculiar character of that conformability to law as the realisation of the internal powers, is immediately accessible to observation. So long as the man has no presentiment of an internal conformability to law, what happens externally is also referred to the lawless caprice of imaginary agents.

A genetic treatment finds a thoroughgoing causal conformability to law in the (objectively real) relations with which mathematics has to do. The objective interdependence between quantities and between forms exists in and for itself, when not recognised by the subject. On this objective interdependence the physical processes rest, which exist independently of the knowing subject, and condition the possibility of existence of knowing subjects. *On the objective nature of quantity and of space that conformability to law is established, which Kant referred falsely to a subjective origin.*

The *logical* form of axiom given above only asserts that the combination of judgments, by which a new one is derived from given ones, must rest on an objective causal nexus. *Whether* and in *what* sense *everything* objective stands in causal relations is to be decided elsewhere (in Metaphysics and Psychology).

Plato and *Aristotle* make the thoroughgoing agreement (ὁμο-λογία, ξυνᾷδειν, ξυμφωνεῖν) of cognitions with each other and with their grounds, an essential condition of their truth.

Plato teaches :[1] πᾶν τὸ γιγνόμενον ὑπ' αἰτίου τινὸς ἐξ ἀνάγκης γίγνεσθαι· παντὶ γὰρ ἀδύνατον χωρὶς αἰτίου γένεσιν σχεῖν.[2]

---

[1] *Tim.* p. 28 A.

[2] Cf. *Phaedon,* pp. 100 A, 101 D; *De Rep.* vi. 511.

Aristotle places the essence of science in the adequate knowledge of causes. The syllogism warrants this knowledge, since the middle notion corresponds to the real ground.[1] Aristotle distinguishes, in his Metaphysics, four principles or causes (ἀρχαί or αἰτίαι): Matter, Form, Cause, and End;[2] but with reference to our knowledge he distinguishes the grounds of Being, Becoming, and Knowing.[3] πασῶν μὲν οὖν κοινὸν τῶν ἀρχῶν τὸ πρῶτον εἶναι ὅθεν ἢ ἔστιν ἢ γίγνεται ἢ γιγνώσκεται· τούτων δὲ αἱ μὲν ἐνυπάρχουσαί εἰσιν, αἱ δὲ ἐκτός.

The axiom, ' Nihil fit sine causa' was in use among the ancients as an axiom of Physics. *Cicero* quotes it against Epicurus,[4] ' Nihil turpius physico, quam fieri sine causa quid quam dicere.'

Suarez.[5] ' Omnia alia, praeter ipsum (Deum), causam habent.'

Jacob Thomasius[6] distinguishes ' Omne ens, quod fieri dicitur, habet causam *efficientem* ;'—' Christiania omnino statuendum est, canoni praesenti locum esse quoque universaliter in causa *finali.*'

Leibniz was the first who expressly placed the *axiom of Determining* (or as he afterwards called it) *of Sufficient Reason,* side by side with the axiom of Contradiction, as a principle of inference. He says,[7]—' It is necessary to remember that there are two great principles of our reasoning; the one is the principle of Contradiction ; the other, that of " la raison déterminante," which is, that nothing can be concluded, without it has a determining cause, or at least reason.'[8] ' Our intellectual inferences rest on two great principles : the principle of Contradiction, and the principle of Sufficient Reason, in virtue of which we know that no fact can be found real, no proposition true, without a sufficient reason, why it is in this way rather than in another.' In his Second Letter to Clarke

[1] *Arist. Anal.* pt. I. 32 ; *Eth. Nicom.* i. 8 ; *Anal. Post.* i. 2 ; ii. 2.
[2] *Metaph.* i. 3, § 1 and elsewhere.   [3] Ibid. v. 1, § 9.
[4] *De Fin.* i. 6, 19, and elsewhere.   [5] *Metaph.* i. 235.
[6] *Dilucid. Stahlianae,* § 127.   [7] *Théol.* i. § 44.
[8] *Monadologie (Princip. Phil.),* § 30 sqq.

Leibniz also calls this principle, 'Principium Convenientiae.'
At the end of the fifth letter to Clarke he makes the same
threefold distinction as Aristotle:[1] 'This principle is that of a
sufficient reason, why a thing exists, an event happens, a truth
has place.' The first and second references belong to Metaphysics, the third to Logic.

Wolff[2] and *Baumgarten*[2] seek to deduce the axiom of the
Reason from the axiom of Contradiction, because they believe
that the latter is the only absolutely à priori principle (which
is to be combined with Experience however). If the ground
of a thing lies in nothing, then nothing is the ground or reason
itself. But this contains the *contradiction*, that nothing, as an
actual principle, is also something. The mistake in this deduction (the misinterpretation of the expression 'nothing is
the ground,' because of a false realisation of 'nothing') was
pointed out by contemporaries. *Wolff*,[4] following *Leibniz*,[5]
explains the axiom of Contradiction to be the ground of
necessary, and the axiom of Sufficient Reason, the source of
accidental truth.

Kant[6] thus enunciates the '*Law of Causality:*' 'All
changes happen according to the law of the connection of
cause and effect.' He considers this to be a synthetic axiom
à priori, and a ground of possible experience, or of the objective knowledge of phenomena, in view of their relation in the
course of succession in time. He does not allow that it is
applicable to 'Things in-themselves.' In Logic, Kant explains the '*axiom of sufficient reason*' to be the principle of
assertory judgments.[7] He gives it[8] the form—'Every proposition must have a reason.' He makes this *logical* principle
not co-ordinate with, but subordinate to the axiom of Contradiction. On the other hand, the transcendental or material

[1] *Metaph.* v. 1, § 9.   [2] *Ontol.* § 70 sqq.; cf. *Metaph.* § 30 ff.
[3] *Metaph.* § 20.   [4] *Annot. ad Met.* p. 9 ff.
[5] *Princ. Phil.* § 30 sqq.; *Epist.* ii. ad Clarc.
[6] *Krit. der r. Vernunft*, p. 232 ff.   [7] *Log.* ed. by Jäsche, p. 73.
[8] In the treatise *Ueber eine Entdeckung*, &c. Works, ed. by Hartenstein, vi. 1 ff.

principle, 'every thing must have a cause,' is in no way derivable from the axiom of Contradiction.

On the basis of the Kantian theory *Arthur Schopenhauer*[1] asserts that the principium rationis sufficientis essendi, fiendi, agendi, and cognoscendi, are the four fundamental forms of synthesis à priori.

Hegel (following Fichte and the Neoplatonists) resolves the law of the Reason,—'Every thing has a sufficient Reason,' into the law of the combination of opposites,—' The reason is the unity of Identity and Difference.'[2]

Herbart[3] seeks to explain the real (causal) nexus by means of his theory of the *self-conservation* of simple essences, in opposition to their disturbance by conflict with others; and to solve the question of how antecedent and consequent may be connected, by his so-called 'method of references,' i.e. by the *hypothetical completions* of what is given, which prove themselves necessary by the fact that the law of Contradiction remains unviolated only when they are accepted.

According to *Schleiermacher*,[4] the (causal) necessity rests on the inter-dependence of the system of the co-existence of Being, or on 'Actions,' just as freedom does upon its existence in and for itself—as 'power.' The true view is contained in the definitions of Hegel, Herbart, and Schleiermacher. It is that *the whole cause is made up of the inner ground and the outward conditions.*[5] A more exhaustive representation and proof of this doctrine would lead us away from the province of Logic into that of Metaphysics.

Delboeuf, agreeing with the views laid down in this paragraph, enunciates as the principle which makes legitimate all our inferences (raisonnements) the axiom, 'The logical concatenation of the ideas corresponds to the real concatenation of things.'[6]

[*J. S. Mill*[7] says that the most valuable truths relating to phenomena are those which relate to the order of their succes-

---

[1] *Ueber die vierfache Wurzel des Satzes vom zureichenden Grunde.*
[2] *Logik*, i. 2, p. 72 ff.; *Encycl.* § 121.
[3] *Allg. Metaph.* ii. 58 ff.   [4] *Dial.* p. 150 and elsewhere.
[5] Cf. § 69.   [6] Cf. § 75.   [7] *Logic*, i. 360.

sion. In order to know such truths we must endeavour to
find some law of succession which has the same attributes, and
is therefore fit to be made the foundation of processes for discovering, and of a test for verifying all other uniformities of
succession. This fundamental law is the ' *Law of Causation* '
—' every fact, which has a beginning, has a cause.' The notions
which are combined in this formula, along with the law it
expresses, are gained by experience. Invariability of succession is found by observation to obtain between every fact in
nature and some other fact which has preceded it. The succession is not usually between one antecedent and its consequent. The processes of nature are complicated. ' The cause
is the sum total of the conditions, positive and negative taken
together; the whole of the contingencies of every description,
which being realised, the consequent invariably follows.' On
this law every inductive truth rests, and to it every inductive
process must be referred.

A. Bain[1] believes that there must be some guarantee for
every *real* inference, and that the sole guarantee is the Uniformity of Nature. Now uniformities of Nature are either of
co-existence or *succession*. The evidence for uniformities of co-
existence is special observation of each separate uniformity.
In uniformities of succession the labour has been shortened by
the discovery of a *law* of uniformity—the law of Causation. It
may be expressed thus:—' Every event is uniformly preceded
by some other event.' The most important form of the law of
Causation is what Mr. Bain calls the ' law of the conserva-
tion of force which encompasses and pervades all the natural
sciences, each one of which is but a partial development of it.'

Sir W. Hamilton, in his lectures,[2] enounces a law of Reason
and Consequent, which he says is the foundation of the Hypothetical Syllogism. He expresses it, ' Infer nothing without a
ground or reason.' In the Appendix to his Lectures, however,
and in his Discussions, he refuses to admit this law, saying that,
(1) inasmuch as it is not material it is a derivation of the three
formal laws of Identity, Contradiction, and Excluded Middle;

[1] *Deductive Logic*, pp. 18–20.   [2] P. 65.]

and (2) inasmuch as it is material, it coincides with the principle of Causality and is extralogical.]

The *Leibnizian* principium identitatis indiscernibilium[1] can only be expounded in Metaphysics, not in Logic.

§ 82.

The Forms of *Immediate Inference* are : partly —*The derivation of a judgment from a notion,* i.e. the analytical formation of notions ; and partly—*The derivation of a judgment from a judgment.*

There are seven kinds of this latter derivation, viz. : (1) Conversion ; (2) Contraposition ; (3) Change of Relation ; (4) Subalternation ; (5) Aequipollence ; (6) Opposition ; (7) Modal Consequence.

Conversion has to do with the position of the elements of the judgment within its Relation, and often indirectly with the Quantity.

Contraposition has likewise to do with the position of the elements of the judgment in its Relation with the Quality, and often indirectly with the Quantity.

Change of Relation has to do with the Relation itself.

Aequipollence refers to Quality ; *Opposition* to Quality and indirectly to Quantity.

Modal Consequence has to do with the Modality of the judgment.

All these deductions rest on the axioms of Identity and Contradictory Disjunction.

Aristotle discusses Conversion (ἀντιστρέφειν, ἀντιστρεφή), which he places at the service of Syllogistic,[2] the relation of Opposition (ἀντικεῖσθαι),[3] and Modal Consequence.[4] He

---

[1] *Princ. de la Nature et de la Grâce,* § 9 ; *Epist.* iv. *ad Clarc.,* non dantur duo individua plane indiscernibilia.

[2] *Anal. Pri.* i. 2 ; 13 ; 17.   [3] *De Interp.* c. vii. ff.

[4] Ibid. c. xiii.

recognises Subalternation only as an element of the syllogistic formation of inferences, not as an independent form. He says[1] the proposition not-man is not just, is equivalent to the proposition no not-man is just. This contains qualitative Aequipollence.

The name Aequipollence (referred to equivalent judgments in a wider sense) was first introduced by *Galen*, the author of a work περὶ τῶν ἰσοδυναμουσῶν προτάσεων. Galen distinguished between ἀντιστρέφειν, by which he understood *Contraposition*, and ἀναστρέφειν, by which he meant *Conversion*. He applied both terms to categorical and also to hypothetical judgments.

Appuleius seems to have been the first to use the Latin term aequipollens in his definition : ' Aequipollentes autem dicuntur (propositiones), quae alia enunciatione tantundem possunt et simul verae fiunt aut simul falsae, altera ob alteram scilicet.'

Boëthius calls equivalent judgments indicia convenientia or consentientia. He uses the phrase conversa per contra positionem for Contraposition, and calls Conversion in the strict sense Conversio Simplex. Simple Conversion is accomplished either principaliter, i.e. without change of quantity, or per accidens, i.e. with change of quantity. In other respects, the terminology employed by Boëthius is the same as that of the Scholastic and of modern formal logic.[*]

Wolff does not call immediate inferences ratiocinatio (because he means by ratiocinatio the deduction of a third judgment from two given ones only). He calls them consequentiae immediatas.[*] He explains them to be abbreviated hypothetical syllogisms ;[4] and accordingly discusses them after Syllogism.

Kant,[*] and most modern logicians along with him, have reversed the order. Kant founds the division of immediate inference on his table of Categories. Subalternation, according to his view, rests on *Quantity*; Opposition on *Quality* (Aequipollence is only a change of the expression in words, and not a form of judgment); Conversion on *Relation* ; and

[1] *De Interp.* c. x. 20 ▲, 39.

[*] Cf. Prantl, *Gesch. der Logik*, i. 568 ff.; 583, 692 ff.

[*] *Log.* § 459.   [4] Ibid. § 460.   [*] *Log.* § 41 ff.

Contraposition on *Modality*. The later logicians have mostly kept by the principle of the Kantian division, but have sought to remedy, with greater or less success, many insufficiencies which lie in the Kantian statement.

The *Analytic Construction of Judgments* should not be reckoned among immediate inferences (and was not in the first edition of this Logic); but belongs to this species of inference.

§ 83. The *Analytic Formation of Judgments* rests on the axiom (§ 76) that every attribute may be posited as a predicate. The distinction between *Synthetic* and *Analytic Judging* belongs to the *genesis* of judgments. Every judgment is so far synthetic, that it, according to the definition, is the consciousness of the real validity of a combination (*synthesis*) of conceptions. But the synthesis of the members of the judgment may originate in different ways, either immediately by the *combination* of the conceptions presented, or mediately by the *analysis* of a whole conception earlier formed, in which the members of the judgment are already contained in an undeveloped form. In the former case the construction of the judgment is *synthetic*, in the latter it is *analytic*. The judgment derived analytically from the notion of the subject, is valid only on the presupposition of this subject-notion. The validity of the subject-notion can never be inferred from it.

In *every* judgment the subject is the conception otherwise definite, but in reference to the predicate still indefinite. In the propositions—This accused man is guilty, This accused man is not guilty—the subject is the conception of the accused person, so far as he is a distinct person who stands under an accusation; while the connection of the conception of guilt with the conception of the subject still remains an open question, i.e. an indefiniteness, which may be made definite, and is made definite by the acceptation or rejection of the predicate notion. In the judgment—The earth is a planet—the case is the same. The subject, the earth is on other sides definite, perhaps as γῆ εὑρύστερυος, πάντων ἕδοι ἀσφαλὲς αἰεί; but in reference to what the predicate asserts it is still indefinite. The judgments—Iron is metal, every body is extended, the quadrate is a parallelogram—have sense and meaning only in so far as he who judges has left a place in his notion of the subject for the determination given in the predicate, but does not yet know this determination. He conceives iron perhaps by immediate sense intuition. He understands by body the perceivable thing, about which it is not quite determined whether it is always extended or not. He conceives the square as an equilateral rectangular four-sided figure, without being conscious that the opposite sides are parallel. The subject of a definition denotes the thing only as that to which the name belongs. The predicate brings the closer determination, which was left indefinite in the conception of the subject. Thus *all* these *judgments*, according to their character, are *synthetic*. It is only the *mode* of making the synthesis of the parts of the judgment that is different. Recourse to the definition of the subject-notion, in the *analytical* construction of judgments, means to call into one's consciousness the moments which would not have been thought along with the name alone. In the *synthetic* construction of notions the synthesis may be accomplished either by perception or by an inference. The inference rests either on circumstances known otherwise (as in the proof by witnesses of the guilt of the person accused), or upon attributes thought expressly in the notion of the subject itself. The necessary connection of the attributes thought in the predicate is recognised from these because of a causal relation of dependence (e.g. from the equality of sides, the equality of angles in a triangle). The last named way often exists where Kant speaks of a 'synthesis à priori.'

Thomas of Aquino[1] and others explain identical propositions

[1] *Summa Theol.* i. 2, I

to be absolutely certain, on the basis of the *Aristotelian* axiom of Contradiction.[1]

Locke's remarks on 'frivolous propositions,' whose predicate only repeats the notion of the subject or single parts of it,[2] and Hume's distinction[3] between '*relations of ideas*' and '*matters of fact*,' paved the way for the Kantian distinction.

Leibniz[4] held that all the primitive intellectual truths are identical propositions.

Wolff's[5] notion of the *Axiom*—propositio theoretica indemonstrabilis — embraced, besides the identical propositions, those also which were derived from identical propositions by analysis and combination.[6] The difficulty, which Kant afterwards indicated by the distinction between analytic and synthetic judgments, is concealed behind the indefiniteness of his expression, in those places in his Logic[7] where Wolff mentions the relation in question. He says,[8] 'propositio illa indemonstrabilis dicitur, cuius subjecto convenire vel non convenire praedicatum terminis intellectis patet.' He tries to make the phrase 'terminis intellectis patet' evident by examples. He explains it partly in this way, that we are to understand by it the warrant that those predicative determinations which do not belong to the notion of the subject, as it is exhibited in the definition, are yet inseparably connected with it: 'ea, quae praedicato respondent, ab iis, quae ad subiecti notionem referimus sive quae ad definitionem eius pertinent, separari non posse animadvertimus.' Wolff does not state the reason of this inseparability. Hence he is not conscious of the difficulty that if the predicate be found by merely going back to the definition of the subject, and to the definitions of single notions which are found in the definition of the subject, the judgment is then merely an analytical judgment, which has indeed apodictic certainty, but does not extend our knowledge. (His examples are

---

[1] Cf. *Arist. De Interp.* c. xi. [2] *Essay* iv. 8; cf. 3, 7.
[3] *Enquiry* iv.; cf. Locke, *Ess.* iv. 4, 6.
[4] *Nouv. Ess.* iv. 2; *Monadol.* § 35. [5] *Logik*, § 267.
[6] Ibid. §§ 268, 270, 273; cf. 264. [7] Ibid. § 261 ff.
[8] Ibid. § 262.

v 3

specimens: The whole is greater than a part; Radii of the
same circle are equal to each other, &c.; and the case appears
to be universally the same, according to the Leibnizo-Wolffian
axiom that all primitive intellectual truths are identical propositions.) Nor does he see that if to go back to the definition of
the subject is not sufficient, and if the predicate constitutes an
essentially new determination, which is not contained in the
content of the subject-notion given in the definition, as far as
analysis leads us, our knowledge may be enlarged, but we
want a ground of certainty for this enlargement. This is the
point where Kant, who got his impulse from other sides also
(viz. from the investigations of Locke and Hume), finds the
first motive to an advance beyond the stand-point of Leibniz
and Wolff.

Kant[1] rightly distinguishes the analytical and synthetical
formation of judgments, however wrongly he may transfer the
distinction to the judgments themselves.

He calls *Analytical Judgments* those in which the connection
of the predicate with the subject rests on the relation of identity
(e.g. $a=a$, or, All bodies are extended; which depend on the
definitions : equality is identity of size; body is extended substance). These do not assert in the predicate anything beyond
what is already thought in the notion of the subject, although
not with the same clearness or strength of consciousness. They
are merely explanatory judgments.

He calls *Synthetic Judgments* those in which the connection
of the predicate with the subject does not rest upon the relation
of Identity (e.g. the straight line is the shortest between two
points; or, every body is heavy. These examples proceed on
the presupposition that shortness does not enter into the definition of the straight line, nor weight into the definition of body.
If the notion of the subject were already so defined and limited
the judgments would be analytic). In these judgments there
may be a necessity, belonging to the subject, to think the predicate along with it; but the predicate is not actually, nor in a

---

[1] *Krit. der r. Vern., Einl. iv.; Proleg. zu einer jeden künftigen Metaph.*
§ 2; *Log. § 36.*

covert way, thought in the subject. Synthetical judgments are ampliative judgments.

Hegel, by his dialectic method, seeks to do away with the distinction of analytic and synthetic judgments by means of the notion of *development*. He says,[1] ' Dialectic progression is the established judgment of the Idea ;—this progression is both *analytic*, because by the " immanent " Dialectic that only is posited which is contained in the immediate notion, and *synthetic*, because the distinction has not yet been posited in this notion.'

This method is itself untenable. A smaller content has no power in any way to make itself increase to a larger content. The genuinely scientific formation of notions demands that the subject should be regarded as the germ out of which the different predicates grow. For example, the notions of circle, of gravitation, &c., may be looked upon as the germ, the capacity, the dynamis, in which lie unfolded the rich manifoldness of geometrical propositions or judgments in the doctrine of the circle, in astronomical knowledge, &c. But the germ, the dynamis, that which Hegel calls the In-itself-ness (Ansichsein), is only the inner ground of the development. The external conditions must be added if the development is to be more than a mere analysis, and is to lead not only to the bringing into stronger consciousness the content already present, but to an enlargement of content. In the above examples, straight lines, such as sines, tangents, secants, &c., must come into relation with the circle ; the masses and distances of the heavenly bodies into relation with the principle of gravitation. In short, elements must enter which, in relation to this subject at least, are separately acquired, and are not to be obtained or (to use Kant's word) ' picked out ' (herausklauben) of it. Without this external element the methodic procedure would be analytic (the mere assertion of what already lies in the subject), not synthetic (no enriching the content, no advance to new predicates). With this external element it is synthetic, but no longer analytic. The point of view of development in the construction of the judgment,

[1] *Encycl.* § 239.

and in all provinces of philosophical thinking, is essential; but the dialectic method has not been able to do away with the necessity of the Kantian distinction.

Schleiermacher [1] explains the distinction between the analytic and synthetic judgments to be a fleeting and relative one. The same judgment can be analytic and synthetic, according as what is said in the predicate has or has not yet been included in the notion of the subject. But the distinction holds in reference to any single subject standing by itself. The incomplete judgment (which contains only the subject and predicate) is more analytic, the complete (which contains the object also) is more synthetic, the absolute judgment (whose predicate is the world) is again analytic. It must be urged, however, against Schleiermacher that the distinction of the analytic and synthetic character of the judgment is not connected with its completeness or incompleteness.

Delboeuf says [2] the advance of science consists in this, that synthetical judgments change to analytic, i.e. predicates subjoined empirically into those which exhibit necessity. This thought, in itself quite correct, is not so in relation to Kant's distinction. The meaning which Delboeuf gives to the expression is essentially different from the Kantian terminology, according to which an apodictic connection, which rests on a known causal relation, is synthetic.

[*J. S. Mill's* distinction of propositions into *verbal* and *real*; those which 'assert of a thing under a particular name, only what is asserted in the fact of calling it by that name,' and those which predicate 'some attribute not connoted by that name;' corresponds very nearly to Kant's distinction between analytic and synthetic propositions. [3]]

§ 84. CONVERSION is that change of form, by means of which the parts of a judgment change their place in reference to its relation.

[1] *Dial.* §§ 155, 308–9; *Beilage, E.* lxxviii. 5.
[2] *Prolég. philos. de la Géom.* p. 46 ff. and *Log.* p. 108.
[3] Cf. *Logic,* i. 119 ff.

In the categorical judgment the subject becomes predicate and the predicate subject ; and in the hypothetical judgment, the conditioning proposition becomes the conditioned, and the conditioned the conditioning.

The conversion of the *categorical* judgment is *internally correct*, only when the notion of the predicate can itself become substantive, i.e. when the sum total of the objects, to which what is designated by the predicate-notion belongs, are all of the same kind, or are a class or genus (in the sense of § 58). For in this case, these objects only can be comprehended under a substantive notion, which can become a subject-notion (according to § 68), while the earlier subject-notion, from its connection with the auxiliary notion of existence, may refer to a relation of inherence, and so take the predicative form (cf. § 68).

The *internal correctness* of the *hypothetical* judgment, generally, lies under no limitation, because it denotes only a causal nexus, whether in the direction of from cause to effect, from effect to cause, or from effect to effect. When relations of time come into consideration, the first presupposition is the most natural, and therefore the consequent, because the antecedent in Conversion is frequently to be expressed in the form of a final judgment (If it be—then must, &c.).

The question of the internal correctness of Conversion was not discussed by *Aristotle*. The Aristotelian principle, that the elements of thought generally correspond to actual existence, and that the subject and predicate especially, which find expression in the ὄνομα and ῥῆμα, must correspond to the thing, and to the action or quality, forms the basis for such a discussion ; but Aristotle did not apply it to Conversion.

The possibility of making the predicate substantive [1] is a tacit presupposition, but is not further discussed. The post-Aristotelian and the modern formal Logic have still more neglected metaphysical relations referred to. *Schleiermacher* [2] has hinted at it, and *Trendelenburg* [3] has remarked that in Conversion ' The Accident is raised to be Substance,' (or rather) that the substance in which it inheres becomes the object thought of instead of the attribute inhering; but it does not follow from this, that Conversion, if we except the case of the universal negative judgment, is ' a mere artifice of formal Logic,' and can lead to no sure result. Logic, as a doctrine of knowledge, can and ought to investigate what and how much follows by conversion [4] from a single given judgment, presupposed to be

---

[1] *Anal. Prior.* i. 2.   [2] *Dial.* § 325.
[3] *Log. Unters.* 2nd ed. ii. 300; 3rd ed. ii. 336.
[4] The stand-point of logical treatment is completely mistaken, and numerous mistakes are inevitable in particular cases, when this investigation is supposed to be undertaken in order to ' teach and make possible an arbitrary thinking, according to artificial rules and formulae,' or to ' reduce thinking to a mechanical schema, in order to proceed arbitrarily according to this schema, so that we require to think according to the schema only, and not according to the notions.' [*] One might as well reproach the mathematico-mechanical procedure with being one-sided and arbitrary, if it investigates what follows simply from certain simple presuppositions, and looks at these apart from other data, from which they can never be actually separated. If, for example, the path and position of a projectile be computed solely on the ground of gravitation and inertia, without taking into consideration the influence of the resistance of the air, the concrete intuition will apparently determine the result more strictly and more accurately than the computation. But if mathematical mechanics did not use this abstract procedure the *laws* of motion could not be known, and the science would be ruined. It is true that there is commonly more than merely one judgment given to us, and that we ought to know more about the relation of the spheres of its subject and predicate *from other sides* than that only which the judgment, considered purely in itself, shows. If the given judgment be: All men are

---

[*] J. Hoppe, *Die gesammte Logik*, Paderborn, 1868.

internally correct. It must also show on what this internal correctness depends.

The conversion of the *disjunctive* judgment, whether categorical or hypothetical, does not require special rules any more than the conversion of the copulative or any other co-ordinated judgment. Its rules come directly from the laws of the Conversion of simple judgments. The *hypothetical* judgment is also the *type* for the cognate kinds of judgments.

§ 85. By Conversion there follows—

I. From the *Universal affirmative categorical judgment* (of the form **a**): Every S is P,

The particular affirmative judgment (of the form **i**): At least one or some P are S (at least a part of the sphere of P is S).

From the *Universal affirmative hypothetical judgment*: whenever A is, B is,

The particular affirmative: At least once or sometimes, when B is, A is (at least in part of the cases, where B is, A is).

The *proof* lies in the comparison of the spheres.

mortal, or: All men are sensible-intellectual dwellers on earth, we know in other ways that there are also other mortal beings, but that there are no other sensible-intellectual inhabitants of earth. He who keeps to the example, and adds the other knowledge got in another way, can, without the trouble of abstraction, attain a completer result than the judgment which results according to the rules of Logic *from a single given judgment*, and so can very easily, on the ground of supposed 'notional' procedure, triumph over the logician, who troubles himself and others with his abstract schemata. But this procedure does not abolish a false logic for the sake of a better; it destroys the possibility of a methodically progressive logical knowledge of the laws of thought. It is only after the investigation, What follows from one datum? is finished—that the scientific theory of thinking requires to subjoin the consideration of other data.

The given *Categorical* judgment: All S are P', presupposes (§ 71) the relations of the two spheres, which
are signified by the Schema—

a, 1. (Ⓢ P)   a, 2. (S   P)

i.e. the action or quality, which the predicate-notion P
denotes, is (a, 2) found in all the objects which the
subject-notion S denotes, while it remains uncertain
whether it is also found in others (a, 1) or is not so
found (a, 2). Under the first present position it may
only be said of part of the objects to which the action
or quality denoted by the former predicate-notion P
belongs, that they are S, under the second it may be
said of all of them. It cannot be decided, from the
given judgment alone: All S are P, when other data
are excluded, which of the two presuppositions holds
good in any case. But this decision is not required.
The inference: At least some P are S, is true on both
presuppositions. And this is what was to be proved.

In the same way the *hypothetical* judgment: Whenever A is, B is, presupposes two relations of spheres,
whose Schema is—

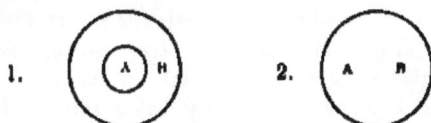

1. (Ⓐ H)   2. (A   B)

i.e. the relation denoted by B is found everywhere where
A is ; while it remains uncertain whether it is found in

other cases (1), or is not so found (2). But under both
presuppositions the inference: At least in a part of the
cases where ɒ is, ᴀ is, is equally true. And this is what
was to be proved.

There are cases, therefore, where the Converse: All
P are S, or: Whenever ɒ is, ᴀ is, holds good in the
universal judgment. But at each time a special proof
is necessary to show that the case before us is such a
case, and this proof can only be given when other data
besides the judgment to be converted are present.
[Cf. Appendix B.]

Conversion without change of Quantity is called by
modern logicians *Simple* Conversion (*Conversio Simplex*), Conversion which is accompanied by change of
Quantity is called *Conversion per accidens*. These universal affirmative judgments, which admit simple or
pure Conversion, are called *reciprocal.*

If the judgment given is only problematically valid,
or if it is apodictically certain, the same *modality* belongs to the judgment reached by Conversion. For the
degree and the kind of the probability or certainty, which
the given judgment has, must pass over to the judgment which follows from it. The validity of the second
is entirely dependent upon the validity of the first.

Examples.—If the proposition is true: Every true duty
must harmonise (not only with objective laws but also) with
one's own moral consciousness,—the other must also be true:
Something which harmonises with one's own moral consciousness is a true duty, but it does not follow that: Whatever
harmonises with one's own moral consciousness is a duty. If
the proposition is true: Whenever an action is evil in the full
sense, it must contradict one's own moral consciousness (or,

If it is evil, it contradicts, &c.); the axiom is also true: In some cases (at least), if an action contradicts one's own moral consciousness, it is evil. But the converse does not *follow* for *all* cases. From the proposition: Whenever the predicate in Greek has the article, the spheres of the subject and of the predicate-notions coincide with each other, the proposition follows: In some cases, at least, where the spheres of the subject and predicate-notions coincide with each other, the predicate in Greek has the article (in those cases, namely, where this coincidence not only exists, but is expressly denoted. But it must be known from other data that the converse proposition holds good with *this* limitation). The validity of the converse follows from the given proposition only, 'in some cases, at least.' We cannot learn from the given proposition whether the converse holds good *only* in some or in all, and if true in some only, in *what* cases.

Simple convertibility is one condition of the correctness of Definitions.[1] The definition is adequate only when the definiendum (S) and the definiens (P) are reciprocal notions, and have the same extent; and in this case P can be as universally predicated of S, as S of P. But definitions are not the only cases in which universal affirmative judgments admit of simple conversion. Almost all geometrical propositions are universally true in the converse form; but this must be shown in every case by special mathematical proof. It does not follow from the logical laws of Conversion. The proposition: All coincident triangles have an equal content, can only be converted *per accidens*: Some triangles of equal content are coincident. In the same way, the proposition: All parallelograms having equal base and height are parallelograms of equal content, is to be converted: Some parallelograms of equal content have equal bases and height. It must be observed with reference to algebraical propositions, that the mathematical notion of equality is not identical with the logical copula. The simple converse of: All a = b, is not: All b = a, but: Whatever is *equal* to a *is* A. But Logic does not warrant this simple con-

<hr>

[1] As has already been noticed, § 62.

version, and mathematical considerations lead only either to the proposition: All b = a, or to the proposition: Whatever is equal to b, *is equal* to a. Equal quantities are, with reference to quantity, identical; but we cannot make them absolutely identical, while the different relations which lie in the different expressions, have meaning.

These rules for Conversion would be false if *Herbart's* opinion,[1] shared by *Drobisch*[2] and *Beneke*,[3] were correct. He believes that the truth of the affirmative categorical judgment is not conditioned by the actual existence of the object, thought in the notion of the subject, but that every kind of judgment is valid only hypothetically, on the hypothesis of the affirmation of the subject. Herbart himself feels the difficulty arising from this, but knows better how to state it than to overcome it.[4] His example is: The wrath of the Homeric gods—if there are any—is terrible. But they are merely poetic, and have no real existence, and hence, though many a terrible thing actually exists, the truth of the converse does not follow: Some terrible thing—if there be any—is the wrath of the Homeric gods. But, in fact, the truth of the affirmative categorical judgment always includes the truth of the hypothesis, that the object designated by the subject exists. If we refer that assertion about the wrath of the Homeric gods to external actual existence, then, because that wrath does not exist, it is as false as the converse. But if we allow to the world of the Homeric gods an ideal actual existence, both the proposition and its converse are equally true in this sense; and the rules of conversion are warranted to be correct in this application also.

The rules for the Conversion of the *Hypothetical* judgment and their proof enunciated in this and the following paragraphs, are correct, only on the hypothesis that the conditioning proposition denotes cases which actually exist. The hypothetical proposition expressed by ' Whenever,' involves this hypothesis, just as the categorical judgment involves the

[1] *Lehrbuch zur Einl. in die Phil.* § 53.
[2] *Log.* 3rd ed. p. 59 ff.   [3] Ibid. i. 165.   [4] *Lehrb.* § 59, Anm.

presupposition of the existence of the subject, provided that
the nexus does not refer to a merely hypothetical actual existence, and the clause ' if this at all happens ' is not to be added
in thought. Cf. §§ 68, 94.

As to *Modality*, the judgment: All S are P, may be uncertain, and yet the judgment: Some P are S, be certain.
This happens, when it is certain that some S are P, and when
the uncertainty of the universal judgment refers only to the
other S. The certainty of the converse follows not from the
uncertainty of the universal affirmative, but from the certainty
of the particular affirmative judgment (§ 86), and therefore
from a datum reached in another way. If we only know that it
is uncertain whether all S are P, we are uncertain whether
some or perhaps none S are P; and it also remains uncertain
whether some P are S.

The *use of circles* as an aid in the demonstration of the
doctrine of Syllogism, especially in Syllogistic proper, has
been referred by modern logicians (e.g. by Maass, J. D.
Gergonne, Bachmann, and Bolzano) to *Euler*.[1] But Drobisch[2]
[and Hamilton[3]] have rightly remarked that, according to the
testimony of Lambert,[4] *Joh. Chr. Lange*, in his ' Nucleus
Logicae Weisianae,' 1712, uses circles, and that *Christ. Weise*,
rector of the Gymnasium at Zittau (d. 1708), (on whose doctrines
many of the thoughts in this compend are based,) was probably
the inventor. [According to Hamilton, Lambert's method of
' sensualising the abstractions of Logic ' by parallel lines of
the different lengths, is to be found in the ' Logicae Systema
Harmonicum,'[5] of Alstedinos, published in 1614.] Demonstration by means of direct comparison of spheres could only
come into use after that the authority of the Aristotelian
methods of reduction had been impugned (more particularly
by Cartesianism).[6] These methods prevailed unconditionally,

[1] *Lettres à une princesse d'Allemagne sur quelques sujets de physique
et de philosophie*, 1768–72, ii. 106.
[2] *Log.* 3rd ed. p. 96.   [3] [*Lect. on Log.* i. 256.]
[4] *Architectonic*, i. 128.   [5] [P. 395.]
[6] Cf. below, §§ 105, 113 ff.

if we except some attempts at independent proofs among the Earlier Peripatetics and by the Neoplatonist Maximus,[1] in the latter period of Ancient Philosophy, and during the Middle Ages. The ' Logique, ou l'art de penser,'[2] belonging to tho Cartesian School, teaches certain reductions, but enunciates along with them a general principle,[3] according to which the validity of any syllogism may be immediately determined. The principle is, that the conclusion must be *contained* (*contenu*) in one of tho premises, and that the other premise must show that it is contained, cf. § 120. This thought is not far removed from an attempt at a sensible representation by means of circles. Among tho German logicians *Thomasius* rejected the reductions. The tendency of that age to treat Logic mathematically, which *Leibniz* was partially influenced by, and the didactic requirement of clear and sensible representation, may have led to the use of these schemata.

Prantl[4] derides, not quite correctly, this sensible representation, as serving only to ' train stupid heads.' It is, however, no more necessarily antagonistic to the consideration of the distinctive logical and metaphysical references, and to the scientific character of Logic, than the sensible representation of geometrical proofs in the figures denoting them need be prejudicial to mathematical accuracy.

Figures of another kind, which represented sensibly only the three different positions or fundamental relations of the middle notion to the two other notions, in the three Aristotelian figures of the Syllogism, were used in Logic in antiquity.[5]

Lambert's symbolical notation of the relations of extent between the subject and predicate by means of the relations of the extent of lines partly continuous partly dotted,[6] may be justified against the accusations of *Maass*[7] and *Bachmann*.[8]

---

[1] Cf. Prantl, *Gesch. der Log.* i. 362, 639.

[2] Which appeared in 1662.

[3] *Logique, ou l'Art de Penser*, iii. 10.   [4] *Gesch. der Log.* i. 362.

[5] Cf. Barthélemy Saint-Hilaire in tho Appendix to his work, *De la Logique d'Arist.* 1838.

[6] *Neues Organ. Dian.* § 171 ff.   [7] *Logik*, Vorrede, p. 11.

[8] *Log.* p. 142 ff.

They wrongly believe that the mere subordinate reference of
the upper or under position of the lines is the principal point of
view. But Lambert's notation is neither a very easy nor a
sure way of representation. The notation by triangles adopted
by *Maass* is not so convenient as that by circles.

Gergonne[1] symbolises the relations of circles by simple
signs—the identity of two spheres by ı, the complete separation
by ıı, the crossing by x, the comprehension of the sphere of
the subject in that of the predicate by c, and, lastly, the comprehension of the sphere of the predicate in that of the subject
by ᴐ. By the use of these signs the representation attains
brevity and elegance, but loses immediate intuitiveness.

[*Mansel* objects to the use of any sensible representations
whatsoever. He thinks that to represent the relation of terms
in a syllogism by that of figures in a diagram is to lose sight of
the distinctive mark of a concept,—that it cannot be presented.
The diagrams of Geometry, he says, furnish no precedent, for
they illustrate the *matter*, not the *form*, of thought. This last
statement is scarcely correct.

Hamilton employs, in his Lectures on Logic, the circle
notation of Euler, and also a modification of Lambert's linear
method. The notation (linear) which he afterwards adopted is
very intricate, and while free from the objection that it con-
founds logical with mathematical extension, does not intuitively
represent the logical relations.[2]

For a history and criticism of various methods of logical
notation, cf. Hamilton's Lectures on Logic, i. 250 and ii. 460 ff.]

§ 86. By Conversion follows—

I. From the *particular affirmative categorical*
judgment (of the form i): Some S are P,
The particular affirmative judgment (also of
the form i): At least some P are S.

[1] *Essai de Dialectique rationnelle* in the *Annales des Mathématiques*,
tom. vii. 189-228, 1816-17.

[2 Cf. *Lect. on Logic*, ii. Appendix, p. 469 ff., and *Discussions*,
pp. 657-661.]

And from the *particular conditional* judgment:
If A is, B sometimes is,
The particular conditional follows: Sometimes
at least if B is, A is.

The *proof* results from the comparison of the spheres.
The given categorical judgment: Some S are P, when
the predicate P belongs *only* to some S, presupposes
two relations of spheres, which are denoted by the
Schema:—

i, 1. (S)(P)   i, 2. (s (P))

But since the possibility is not excluded, that the
same predicate P belongs also to other S, the two following relations of the spheres also exist:—

i, 3. ((S) P)   i, 4. (S   P)

These Schemata are to be taken in the same sense
as in § 85. Now in i, 1 and i, 3 some P only are S;
and in i, 2 and i, 4 all, and therefore at least some P
are S. But this is what was to be proved.

In the corresponding *hypothetical* judgments the relations of the spheres are the same and the result equivalent.

The Conversion of the particular affirmative and of
the particular conditional judgment is therefore a *Conversio simplex.* For both the given judgment, and the

x

judgment arising from the conversion, take the form of the particular affirmative (i).

The *Modality* of the given judgment and of its converse is the same.

Examples of i, ·1 are: Some parallelograms are regular figures;—of i, 2: Some parallelograms are squares;—of i, 3: Some parallelograms are divided by a diagonal into two coincident triangles;—and of i, 4: Some parallelograms are divided by both diagonals into two coincident triangles. The relation of spheres i, i admits of many other modifications. If two spheres are of unequal size, it can happen that most S are P, and relatively very few P are S, or a few S are P, and most P are S. Although the number of S which are P, and of P which are S, is in itself necessarily the same, yet the relation of the sum total of individuals is a different one in each of the two spheres. For example, some, and relatively not a few, planets belonging to our system are heavenly bodies which may be seen by us with the naked eye; but only a very few of the heavenly bodies visible to the naked eye are planets of our system. This conversion is not, therefore, conversio simplex, in the stricter sense that the quantity remains the same in each reference. It is so only in the more general sense, that the judgment remains a particular one, and does not pass over to any other of the four classes of judgments designated by a, e, i, o.

§ 87. By Conversion follows—

III. From the *universal negative categorical judgment* (of the form e): No S is P,
The universal negative judgment (also of the form e): No P is S.
And from the universal negative *hypothetical* judgment: If A is, B never is,
The similarly universal negative hypothetical judgment: If B is, A never is.

The validity of these rules may be *directly* proved by the comparison of spheres. The Schema of the universal negative *categorical* judgment is the complete separation of the spheres :—

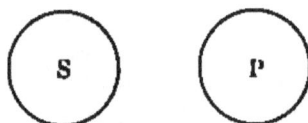

i.e. The action or quality which the notion of the predicate P denotes, is to be found in no object which the subject-notion S denotes, and, if it really exists, only in other notions. Hence the judgment: No objects in which the predicate P is found, and which may therefore be denoted by the notion P made substantive, are S. And this is what was to be proved.

The same may be proved indirectly. For if any one P were S, then (according to § 86) some one S would be P ; but this is false according to the axiom of Contradiction (§ 77), for it is opposed contradictorily (§ 72) to the given judgment : no S is P. Hence the assertion is false, that any one P is S, and it is true that no P is S; which was to be proved.

The corresponding *hypothetical* judgment presupposes the analogous relation of spheres :—

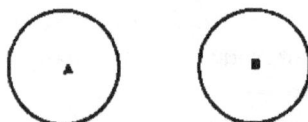

i.e. The case denoted by B is never found where A is present. Whenever B happens, it takes place under other conditions. The case B does not occur together

x 2

with the case A; and the case A does not occur with the case B. If B is, A never is; which was to be proved.

The *indirect* proof may be led here as well as in the universal negative categorical judgment. For if it once happened that when B is, A is also, then (according to § 86) the converse would be true that, once, when A is, B is; this would contradict the given presupposition, that when A is, B never is, and is therefore false. Hence it is false, that when B is, A is once; and the proposition is true: when B is, A never is; which was to be proved.

The converse of the universal negative judgment is therefore not accompanied with any change of quantity, and is throughout *simple* conversion.

The rule also holds good without exception that *Modality* remains unchanged in the conversion. If it is apodictically certain that no S is P, the same kind of certainty passes over to the judgment, that no P is S. If that is only probable, or is true only perhaps, and the assertion remains possible, that, perhaps at least some one S is P, then (according to § 86) there is the same possibility for the assertion that, perhaps at least, some one P is S. It does not follow: no P is S; but only: Probably or perhaps, no P is S.

The following are *examples* of the conversion of the universal affirmative *categorical* judgment. If the judgment be given as true: No innocent person is unhappy, it follows with equal truth: No unhappy person is innocent. If the proposition be proved: No equilateral triangle is unequiangular, it follows without further mathematical demonstration, by logical conversion: No unequiangular triangle is equilateral (every unequiangular triangle has sides of different sizes). If it is proved that: No unequilateral triangle is equiangular, it follows by mere logical conversion, that: No equiangular triangle is unequilateral (every equiangular triangle is equilateral). No square has a diagonal commensurable with one of the sides; and no figure, with a diagonal commensurable with one of the sides, is a square. We may take the theory of parallels as an example of the conversion of the corresponding *hypothetical* judgment. The proposition may be proved (it may be known without the aid of the eleventh axiom of Euclid): If two straight lines (in one plane) are so intersected by any third that the corresponding angles are equal to each other, or that the interior angles on the same side of the intersecting line are together equal to two right angles, these lines will never meet in any one point. It follows, by mere conversion, without the necessity of going back upon the mathematical construction: If two straight lines (in one plane) meet in any point, they are never so intersected by any third that the corresponding angles are equal to each other, or that the interior angles, on the same side of the intersecting line, are together equal to two right angles. (In other words: Two angles in any triangle are never together equal to two right angles. But it cannot be asserted in this way that these two angles together with the third make two right angles; nor that, when the intersected lines do not meet, the corresponding angles are equal to each other.)

Aristotle holds that the universal negative *judgment of possibility* does not admit of altogether simple conversion: Anal. Pr. i. c. iii.: ὅσα δὲ τῷ ὡς ἐπὶ πολὺ καὶ τῷ πεφυκέναι λέγεται ἢ δέχεσθαι—ἡ μὲν καθόλου στερητικὴ πρότασις οὐκ ἀντιστρέφει, ἡ δ' ἐν μέρει ἀντιστρέφει· cf. c. xiii.; c. xvii.: ὅτι οὐκ ἀντιστρέφει τὸ ἐν τῷ ἐνδέχεσθαι στερητικόν. If the judgment is given: τὸ A ἐνδέχεται μηδενὶ τῷ B, it does not necessarily follow that τὸ B ἐνδέχεσθαι μηδενὶ τῷ A. Aristotle understands the first proposition in this sense: Every B, each by itself, is in the state of possibility to have or not to have A for a predicate. He understands the second proposition similarly, in this sense:

Every A, each by itself, is in the state of possibility to have or not to have B for a predicate (cf. § 98). Now the case may occur, as Aristotle rightly remarks, where all B are in that double state of possibility, while some A are in the state of necessity, *not* to have B for a predicate. Hence the Schema is:—

In cases of this kind the first judgment (τὸ A ἐνδέχεται μηδενὶ τῷ B) is true, and the second (τὸ B ἐνδέχεται μηδενὶ τῷ A) is false. Hence the second is not the necessary consequence of the first. In this sense Aristotle's doctrine is well founded. But it does not contradict our proposition (which *Theophrastus* and *Eudemus* had recognised[1]), that universal negative propositions of any modality, and consequently the problematical, are converted with Quantity, Quality, and Modality unchanged. The contradiction is not overcome by the circumstance that the Aristotelian ἐνδέχεσθαι does not denote subjective uncertainty like the *perhaps* of the problematic judgment, but the objective possibility of Being and Not Being, more especially (in distinction from δύνασθαι) in the sense of there being nothing to hinder it. For the argument of Aristotle remains correct, if subjective uncertainty be substituted for the objective possibility. If it is uncertain of all B, whether they are or are not A, it does not follow that it must be uncertain of all A, whether they are or are not B. The certainty that they are *not* B may exist of some A. But this does not prejudice the above demonstration that from the proposition: Perhaps no B is A, the proposition follows: Perhaps no A is B. For this last proposition is not equivalent to that, which can not be deduced: It is uncertain of *all* A, and of each one by itself, whether they are or are *not* B. It is equivalent to the following: It is uncertain whether *all* A are *not* B, or whether there be at least *any one* A which *is* B. And this proposition can very well exist along with the certainty that some A are not B. Similarly, from the proposition: It is (objectively) possible that *no* B *is* A, the proposition follows necessarily : It is (objectively) possible that *no* A *is* B (while it is also possible that at least *some one* A *is* B). Conversion in the Aristotelian way, according to which *the possibility not to be* B is adjudged to *every individual* A, holds good (as Aristotle himself shows[1]) in two cases — (1) when by διδέχεσθαι is understood what might be expressed by it όμωνύμως : to be *at least* in the state of possibility, *without exclusion* of the necessity ; and (2) where *all* necessity whatever *is excluded, and with it necessity in the direction from* A *to* B, so that *no* A are present which are in the *state of necessity not to be* B. The apparent contradiction between the doctrine enunciated in the text of this paragraph and the Aristotelian is solved in this way.[2]

§ 88. Nothing follows from the conversion of the *particular negative* judgment. The particular negative *categorical* judgment asserts, that some S have not the predicate P, without saying anything definite about the rest of S. Its Schema is accordingly the combination in the three figures :—

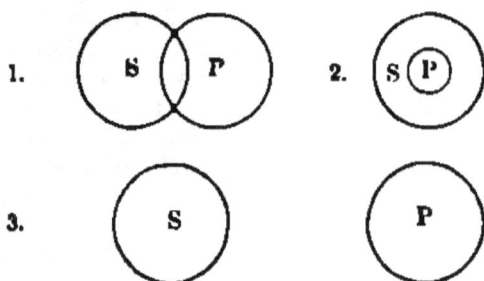

or in the one figure, which, comprehending the three

[1] *Anal. Pr.* i. c. iii.   [2] Cf. Prantl, *Gesch. der Log.* i. 267, 364.

possible cases, denotes the definite by the continuous, and the indefinite by the dotted lines:—

According to this, it can happen that when some S are not P: (1) Some P are not S, and other P are S;— (2) All P are S; and (3) No P are S. Nothing can be said universally of the relation of P to S in a judgment whose subject is P.

Similarly, the Schema of the particular negative *hypothetical* judgment: Sometimes when A is, B is not, is the following:—

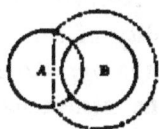

It may happen that when B is, (1) A sometimes is and sometimes is not; (2) A always is, and (3) A never is. Hence the general relation of B to A is quite indefinite.

Examples of these different possible cases are the following:—
Of the particular negative *categorical* judgments of the form 1: Some parallelograms are not regular figures. Of the form 2: Some parallelograms are not squares; or: Some rectilineal plane figures, which are divided by a diagonal into two coincident triangles, are not parallelograms. Of the form 3: (At least) some parallelograms are not trapezoids; or: (At least) some rectilineal plane figures, which are divided by a diagonal into two triangles not coincident, are not parallelograms.
Of the particular negative *hypothetical* judgment of the

?

form 1: Sometimes, when the accused has confessed himself to
be guilty, the accusation is not established. Of the form 2:
Sometimes, when unestablished accusations are raised, there is
not calumny (only error). Of the form 3: At least sometimes,
when the advocate of a higher ideal principle is condemned to
death by the advocates of a principle which is less in accordance
with reason, but has become an historical power, the right and
wrong have not been shared equally by both parties.

§ 89. *Contraposition* is that change of form, according to which the parts of the judgment change places
with reference to its relation, but at the same time one
of them receives the negation, and the quality of the
judgment changes. Contraposition in *categorical* judgment consists in this, that the contradictory opposite of
the predicate notion becomes the subject, and in this
transference the quality of the judgment passes over
to its opposite. In the *hypothetical* judgment, it consists in this, that the contradictory opposite of the
conditioned becomes the conditioning proposition, and
there is, instead of an affirmative nexus between the
two parts of the judgment, a negative one, and instead
of a negative an affirmative one.

The *internal correctness* of Contraposition is to be
decided by the same axioms as that of Conversion
(cf. § 84).

The term 'conversio per contrapositionem,' used by *Boëthius*
(§ 82), where 'contrapositio' means the change of one member
into its contradictory opposite, is in itself unobjectionable, if
the notion of conversion is sufficiently widely understood and
defined. But then a term would be needed to designate the
first kind of Conversion in the wider sense, or Conversion in
the stricter sense. Boëthius (cf. § 82) calls it 'conversio

simplex.' But modern Logic cannot well adopt this term, since it denotes by this expression Conversion without change of quantity. Hence it is more convenient for us to use the notion 'conversio' in the narrower sense only.

Schleiermacher[1] adduces the following example of a contraposition ('Umwendung'): 'All birds fly; not everything that flies is a bird' (instead of: What does not fly is not a bird). This, however, rests on a mistake, and not on a peculiar though admissible terminology. For the Contraposition, however differently in other respects its notion may be defined, must in every case fall under the higher notion of immediate consequence. If the judgment is given: All S are P, the judgment: Not all P are S, or: Some P are not S, cannot be derived from it by any kind of consequentia immediata. Now Schleiermacher himself, in his example, asserts as a new presupposition, the perception that other animals fly, and makes this the basis of the judgment to be derived.

§ 90. By Contraposition follows—

I. From the *universal affirmative categorical judgment* (of the form a): Every S is P,

The universal negative judgment (of the form e): No not-P is S (Everything that is not P is not S).

And from the universal affirmative *hypothetical* judgment: Whenever A is, B is, there follows,

The universal negative: When B is not, A never is (It always happens that when B is not, A is not also).

Proof may be given *directly* by comparison of spheres. The sphere of P in the *categorical*, and the sphere of B in the *hypothetical*, judgment, either includes the sphere

[1] *Dial.* p. 286.

of S, and that of A, or is exactly coincident with it.
These relations are to be explained in the same way
as § 85. In both cases, whatever lies outside of the
spheres of P and of B, must also lie outside of the
spheres of S and of A; i.e. whatever is not P, is also not
S, and it always happens, when B is not, that A is not;
which was to be proved.

The *Modality* remains unchanged in Contraposition
in this and in the other forms (§§ 91 and 92), for the
same reasons as in Conversion.

The expressions, 'contrapositio simplex' and 'contrapositio per accidens,' are used as in Conversion with
reference to *Quantity.*

Examples.—Every regular figure may be inscribed in a circle
(so that all its sides become chords): Every figure, therefore,
which cannot be inscribed in a circle is not regular. Every
rectangular triangle may be inscribed in a semicircle (so that its
one side becomes the diameter, and the other two chords):
Every triangle, therefore, which cannot in this way be inscribed
in a semicircle is not rectangular. Wherever there is a good
conscience, there will be correct conduct : Wherever, therefore,
there is not correct conduct, there is not a good conscience.
Wherever there is perfect virtue, there is also complete internal
satisfaction : Wherever, therefore, there is not complete internal
satisfaction, there is not perfect virtue. Every sin contradicts
the moral consciousness : What does not contradict the moral
consciousness, is not sin. Whenever the predicate in Greek
has the article, the spheres of the subject and predicate notions
coincide : When the spheres of the subject and predicate notions
do not coincide, the predicate in Greek has never the article.

The *universality* with which *Contraposition* holds good of a
general affirmative judgment is worth noticing, in opposition to
the merely particular validity of the judgment reached by conversion. *Four universal judgments* (of the forms a and e)

may always be enunciated, *two* of which are *valid* or *invalid* of each other. The first pair may be valid without the second, and the second without the first. If the judgment is true: Every S is P, it follows that: What is not P is not S. But it does not follow: Every P is S, nor, what is equivalent to this: What is not S is not P. If the judgment is valid: If A is, B is, it follows: If B is not, A is not; but it does not follow: If B is, A is, nor, what is equivalent to this: If A is not, B is not.

For example, if the judgment is recognised to be valid: That in which consists the essence of an object is, in its fluctuations, the measure of the completeness of the object, the judgment of equal universality follows by Contraposition: Whatever in its fluctuations is not the measure of the completeness of an object does not contain the essence. But it does not follow: Whatever (only some at least) is, in its fluctuations, the measure of the perfection of an object contains its essence. Nor does the equivalent proposition follow: Whatever does not contain the essence of an object, is not in its fluctuations the measure of its completeness. (Certain external marks may very well fluctuate in strict proportion with the essence.) If the proposition is true: Every good thing is beautiful, it follows: What is not beautiful is not good. But it does not follow: Every beautiful thing is good, nor: What is not good is not beautiful. The propositions: Where there is not a very comprehensive memory, there is not a very comprehensive understanding, and: Where there is a very comprehensive understanding, there is a very comprehensive memory, are equivalent. But the propositions: Where there is not a comprehensive understanding, there   not a comprehensive memory, and: Where there is a comprehensive memory, there is a comprehensive understanding, are essentially different from these, although equivalent to each other. The two first propositions are both true, the two latter are both false. The propositions: Whoever does not recognise a state to be independent, does not recognise its rights of embassy, and: Whoever recognises the right of embassy of a state, recognises also its independence, are equivalent. The two following propositions, which are equiva-

lent to each other, may be false without detriment to the truth
of the former: Whoever recognises a state to be independent,
recognises also its rights of embassy, and: Whoever does not
recognise the rights of embassy of a state, does not recognise it
to be independent. (England in 1793 recognised the French
Republic to be independent, but it did not admit its rights of
embassy.) In like manner the proposition: Whenever desire
has gained its utmost height, all pain is removed, admits of
simple Contraposition, but only of Conversion accompanied by
change of Quantity. On the other hand a proposition which
is a definition or corresponds to a definition in this, that the
spheres of the subject and predicate notions coincide, admits
both of simple Conversion and of simple Contraposition. For
example: Every calumny is an untruthful statement of deeds
which are false and defamatory: Every such statement is a
calumny; and: What is not such a statement about such
deeds (e.g. a false and defamatory account of actions which are
true) does not fall under the notion of a calumny.

§ 91. By Contraposition follows—

II. From the *universal negative categorical judgment* (of the form e): No S is P,

The particular affirmative judgment (of the
form I): At least some not-P are S (At
least something, which is not-P, is S).

And from the universal negative *hypothetical*
judgment: if A is, B never is,

The particular affirmative: (At least) in
some cases, if B is not, A is not.

For the universal negation both in the *categorical* and
in the *hypothetical* judgment presupposes a complete
separation of the spheres, and S and A must be found
outside of the spheres of P and B; i.e. S belongs to what
is not-P, and A exists in those cases where B is not.

And so some not-P is S, and in some cases where B is not, A is. The possibility that *every* not-P is S, or that if B is not, A *always* is, is not excluded; but happens only when S and P, or A and B, taken in their whole extent, include everything existing.

Examples.—Nothing good is ugly: Something not-ugly is good. Nothing ugly is good: Something not-good is ugly. No animate essence is lifeless: Something not-lifeless is animate. No animate essence is inanimate: (At least) some not-inanimate is animate. The divine is not finite: (At least) something not-finite is divine. The finite is not divine: (At least) something not-divine is finite.

§ 92. By Contraposition follows:—

III. From the *particular negative categorical judgment* (of the form o): (At least) some S are not P,

The particular affirmative judgment (of the form i): (At least) some not-P are S (At least, something which is not P is S);

And in the same way from the particular negative *hypothetical* judgment: (At least) sometimes, if A is, B is not,

The particular affirmative: (At least) in some cases, if B is not, A is.

For particular negation presupposes, that (at least) part of the spheres of S or A lies without the spheres of P or B, without making any definite statement about the other part; and so that some of what lies outside of the spheres of P or of B, are S or A; i.e. some not-P are S; sometimes, if B is not, A is. The case: *All* not-P are S: If B is not, A *always* is, may exist, not only when no S is P, and when if A is, B never is (as is possible according to the given judgment) (cf. § 91); it may also occur when *only* some S are not P, and when it *only* sometimes happens that if A is, B is not. The latter case occurs more especially when S or A refer to the sum total of all existence, and P or B to a part of it. But, whichever of these different possible cases exists, anyhow the proposition is true: At least some not-P are S, and: At least in some cases, if B is not, A is.

Examples.—Some parallelograms are not regular figures: Something which is not a regular figure is a parallelogram. Some parallelograms are not squares: Some not-squares are parallelograms. (At least) some parallelograms are not trapezoids: Something, which is not a trapezoid, is a parallelogram. Some living thing is not animate: Something not-animate is living. Some real essences are not animate: (At least) something, which is not animate, is a real essence.

§ 93. No conclusion follows by Contraposition from the *particular affirmative judgment.* The particular affirmative *categorical* judgment has, in general, two forms (i, 1 and i, 2), which correspond to the presupposition: *only* some S are P, and two forms (i, 3 and i, 4), which correspond to the presupposition: at least some, but in fact the other S also, are P. If the first two forms were the only ones, it might follow (§ 92): Some not-P are S. But this consequent has no universal validity, because it is not suitable to the last two forms. The consequent: (At least) Some not-P are not S, which contains the proper contraposition, is true on the hypothesis of the last two forms, where all not-P are also not S (§ 90). It may be applied fre-

quently and almost in the greater number of examples
to the first two forms also.   But in case of the first two
forms, it can happen that it is false.   The form 1, 2 is
represented by the figure :—

It is usually the case that besides the Not-P which are
S, there are some Not-P which are not S; but it may
happen that S comprehends the sum-total of existence,
and then all not-P will be S.   It will not then happen
that there are some not-P which are not S, and *that*
consequent will be invalid.   The schematic representation of the form 1, 1 is given in the figure :—

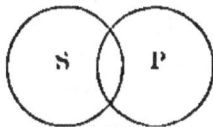

There are commonly some Not-P which are not S, besides the Not-P which are S, but the opposite case can
also occur.   The form 1, 1 (which is distinguished from 1,
3 and 1, 4 by the fact that some S are P, and others are
not, and form 1, 2, by the fact that some P are not S)
exists, when the case represented by the following
figure occurs :—

Where P extends from the centre to the periphery of
the second circle, and S from the periphery of the first to
the periphery of the third circle. If the sphere of S is a
limited one, there will be many not-P which are also
not S; but if its sphere is unlimited outwards, i.e. if S
comprehends all existence with the exception of that
part of P which is denoted by the smallest circle, there
are no longer some not-P which are not S, but all not-P
are S. This relation frequently occurs where S is a
notion designated by a negation (S = Not-I, where I
stands for the innermost circle); and it can also occur
with an S positively designated. Hence the consequence:
Some not-P are not S would be false. (The like holds
good, if in the above figure S and P change places, when
the sphere of P is unlimited towards the outside.)

There are cases when the judgment: Some S are P,
is true, where (at least) some Not-P are S, and there
are also cases, where No Not-P is S. There are cases
where (at least) some Not-P are not S, and also cases,
where all not-P are S. Hence where that one judgment only is given, nothing can be universally asserted
of the relation of the Not-P to S in a judgment whose
subject is Not-P.

The corresponding *hypothetical* judgment, since all its
relations of spheres are similar, just as little admits any
universal inversion.

It is enough to give *examples* of the two cases where all
Not-P are S, and where therefore the judgment proves false,
which would correspond to the universal form of Contraposition: Some Not-P are not-S. 1. Some reality is material
(inanimate). It does not follow from this that: Some thing not-

Y

material (psychic) is not real; for every not-material (psychic) is real. 2. Some living essences are inanimate. It does not follow from this that: Something not-inanimate (animate) is not a living essence; for everything which is animate is living. The first example corresponds to the form 1, 2, where the sphere of S extends to the infinite. The second example corresponds to that case of 1, 1, which is sensibly represented by means of the three concentric circles. The inmost circle (s) is, in this example, formed by the inorganic or elementary essences; the first enclosing ring (A_1) embraces plants, and the outer ring (A_2) animated essences; $P = I + A_1 =$ inanimate essences; and $S = Not\text{-}I = A_1 + A_2 =$ animate essences.

The *proof* for the inapplicability of Contraposition to the particular affirmative judgment is commonly given in another way. The judgment: Some S are P, is *reduced* to the particular negative to which it is equivalent: Some S are Not-P. And since the latter cannot be converted (according to the laws of Conversion), so the former cannot be transposed.[1] But this demonstration is beside the mark, unless it is shown that the proof of the impossibility of converting the particular negative judgment, which is constructed for the case where P is a positive notion, holds good for a negative predicate Not-P. If this is not specially proved, then that proof may, without anything further, be transferred to the case of a negative predicate-notion, just as little as in mathematics, e.g., a proof, which has been given of a positive whole exponent, holds good directly for a negative fractional exponent. The transference must obviously submit to a strict test, for the whole power of the proof, that P o S does not follow from S o P, rests on the possibility that in S o P the sphere of S wholly comprehends that of P, and that all P are S. But if this relation is found naturally with a positive predicate, its possibility is not at all directly evident if the predicate is a negative notion and consequently of unlimited extent. The doubt rather demands attention, whether this unlimited sphere may be completely included by the sphere of S, which, when

[1] Cf. e.g. Drobisch, *Log.* 2nd. ed. § 77, p. 66.

S is a positive notion, appears to be limited. If it cannot, the proof loses its validity for this case, and with it is lost the validity of the proof by Reduction of the impossibility of Contraposition in S 1 P.[1]

Twesten says,[2] 'Particular affirmative judgments cannot submit to contraposition. If some *a* are *b*, it remains undecided whether *a* is partly or not at all without the sphere of *b*, and partly or not at all within the sphere of not-*b*.' This is no proof. At the most, it is an introduction to a proof. For, from what is given, it follows at once that it is uncertain whether some *a* are not-*b*, and whether some not-*b* are *a*; it does not follow so immediately, that it is also uncertain whether some not-*b* are not-*a*. And the inadmissibility of the consequence: (At least) Some not-*b* are not-*a*, is what was to be shown. It should have been said: If some *a* are *b*, it remains undecided whether not-*b* lies wholly or at least partly without the sphere of *a* (or, wholly or at least partly within the sphere of not-*a*).

§ 94. If in Conversion and Contraposition the position of the individual members of the judgment can be

[1] Drobisch, in the 3rd ed. of his *Logic*, § 82, p. 88, has sought to show that the proof for the inconvertibility of the particular negative judgment holds good for a negative (Not-P) as well as for a positive predicate (P); but his proof is not sufficient. He only proves that the proposition: Some Not-P are S, cannot be inferred, because the case exists in which the contradictory opposite judgment: No Not-P is S, is true. What was to be proved, that it cannot be concluded that: Some Not-P are *not* S, does not in the least degree follow; for this judgment may be recognised to be true when some Not-P are S, as easily as it is true when no Not-P are S. When, according to circumstances, the one or other of two judgments contradictorily opposed to each other may be true, it is only implied that neither the one nor the other of these two judgments is true in *every* case. Another judgment which coexists with both may be true in *every* case. Judgments contradicting each other (No Not-P is S, and Some Not-P are S) may both be *uncertain*, and a third judgment (Some Not-P are not S) may be certain. Drobisch's reasoning is not sufficient.

[2] *Log.* p. 79.

x 2

exchanged while their relation remains unaltered, there may also be *a change in the Relation itself.* This occurs when an hypothetical is formed from a simple categorical judgment (which is always possible), or when several hypotheticals are formed from a disjunctive categorical judgment, or when the converse of both cases happens. The possibility of this change of form rests on this:—

1. The relation of inherence always includes a certain dependence of the predicate upon the subject, which may always be made conspicuous when it is treated by itself, and is expressed in an hypothetical judgment.

2. The disjunctive judgment is the comprehensive expression of several hypothetical judgments, and may be resolved into them as easily as these mutually-related hypothetical judgments may be reduced to a disjunctive judgment.

From the judgment: A is B, the judgment: If A is, B is, may be deduced. But the categorical judgment is not always correct, when the hypothetical is; for the latter does not proceed upon the hypothesis of the existence of A, but only on the fact that B stands in a relation of inherence together with A. From the judgment: Every A, which is B, is C, follows the judgment: If A is B, A is C; and the latter, which presupposes the existence of such A which are B, may be reduced to the former. The judgment: A is either B or C, divides into the mutually connected hypothetical judgments: If A is B, it is not C, and If A is C, it is not B; If A is not B, it is C, and If A is not C, it is B. And the latter may be again reduced to the former.

The possibility of this Change of Relation does not prove [1] that difference of Relation is *only verbal,* and has no logical or

[1] As several modern logicians believe—viz. Herbart, *Einleit.* §§ 53, 60 Rem.; Beneke, *Log.* i. 163 ff.; Dressler, *Denklehre,* 199 ff.

metaphysical significance. If this view were correct, the change of form could be accomplished, without alteration of the material constituent parts of the judgment, equally well by changing the hypothetical judgment into a categorical as by changing the categorical into an hypothetical. But this is not the case. The transformation of the hypothetical judgment into a categorical is only admissible, in so far as a relation of inherence is connected with the relation of dependence, and the existence of the subject is ensured, as it is in the cases adduced above. It is not possible whenever the hypothetical judgment is given: If A is B, C is D; for the fact that A is B does not stand in the same relation to the fact that C is D, that A does to B or C does to D. The former is not the latter, nor can it be considered to be a *kind* of the latter. But the A *is a* B, and can be held to be a *kind* of B. There is not only a verbal, but a logico-metaphysical difference, which reveals itself indeed in language, the flexible garment or rather the organic body of thought, but belongs originally to thought itself. One fundamental relation exists between the parts of the hypothetical judgment, and another between those of the categorical. The two are essentially related and connected with each other,[1] but they are not to be thought identical. Cf. §§ 68, 85.

§ 95. *Subalternation* (Subalternatio) is the passing over from the whole sphere of the subject-notion to a part of it, and conversely from a part to the whole. By Subalternation follows :—

1. From the *truth of the universal categorical judgment* (S a P or S e P) the truth of the corresponding particular (S i P or S o P), but not conversely the former from the latter.

---

[1] Cf. Trendelenburg, *Log. Unters.* 2nd ed. i. 313; 3rd ed. 351 : ' The settled product of causality is substance ; ' 2nd ed. i. 355 ; ii. 246 ; 3rd ed. l. 363 ; ii. 270.

2. From the *falsehood of the particular* the falsehood of the universal judgment, but not conversely the former from the latter.

The *proof* for the correctness of the first consequence lies in this, that the subalternate judgment repeats an assertion lying in the subalternant, and only asserts as true what is already recognised to be true. The second consequence is founded on this, that, if the universal judgment be true, then (according to 1) the particular is true, which contradicts the hypothesis. The converse consequences, however, are not universally valid, because the truth of the particular judgment may co-exist along with the falsehood of the universal, because it may happen that Some S are and others are not P.

The same laws hold good of *hypothetical* judgments (If A is, B always is—At least in some cases, if A is, B is also).

The consequence from the universal to the particular is called consequentia or conclusio *ad subalternatam* propositionem, that from the particular to the universal conclusio *ad subalternantem*.

The older logicians were accustomed to express the law of consequence, ad subalternatam propositionem, in the *dictum de omni et nullo*, in the following way : ' quidquid de omnibus valet, valet etiam de quibusdam et singulis; quidquid de nullo valet, nec de quibusdam vel singulis valet.'

§ 96. By (qualitative) AEQUIPOLLENCE (aequipollentia) modern Logic means the agreement in sense of two judgments of different Quality. This agreement becomes possible by the fact that the predicate notions stand in the relation of contradictory opposition to each other. Consequence per acquipollentiam proceeds from the judgment: All S are P, to the judgment: No S is not-P, and vice versâ; from the judgment: No S is P, to the judgment: Every S is a Not-P, and vice versâ; from the judgment: Some S are P, to the judgment: Some S are not Not-P, and vice versâ; and lastly from the judgment: Some S are not P, to the judgment: Some S are Not-P, and vice versâ.

The *proof* for the correctness of these consequences lies in the relation of the spheres, according to which every S, which does not fall within the sphere of P, is outside it, and must lie in the sphere of Not-P; and whatever falls within this cannot lie within the sphere of P.

Every sin contradicts the conscience; there is no sin which does not contradict the conscience. Nothing sinful is in harmony with the ethical consciousness; whatever is sinful is not in harmony with the ethical consciousness.

The earlier logicians[1] understand by ἰσοδυναμοῦσαι προτάσεις, iudicia aequipollentia sive convenientia, every kind of equivalent judgments, i.e. those which with material identity are necessarily true or false together because of their form. (Cf. the expression ἀντιστρέφειν found in *Aristotle*.[2])

Kant[3] and some modern logicians with him will not allow the inferences of Aequipollency to be inferences proper, because there is no consequence, and the judgments remain unchanged even according to form. They are to be looked at only as substitutions of words which denote one and the same notion. But since in Aequipollency the Quality of the judg-

---

[1] Cf. § 82.   [2] *De Interpret.* c. xiii. p. 22 a, 10.
[3] *Log.* ed. Jäsche, § 47, Rem.

ment passes over to its opposite, however trivial the change
may be which here exists, it evidently concerns the form of
the judgment itself, and not its mere verbal expression.

§ 97. *Opposition* (oppositio) exists between two judgments of different Quality and different sense with the
same content.

By Opposition follows (cf. §§ 71 and 72) :—

1. From the *truth* of one judgment the falsehood of
its *contradictory* opposite, since according to the axiom
of contradiction (§ 77) judgments opposed contradictorily cannot both be true ;

2. From the *falsehood* of a judgment the truth of its
contradictory opposite, since according to the axiom of
Excluded Third (§ 78) judgments opposed as contradictories cannot both be false ;

3. From the *truth* of one judgment the falsehood of
the *contrary* opposite (but not conversely from the falsehood of the one the truth of the other), according to the
axiom that judgments opposed as contraries cannot both
be true (though both may be false). Otherwise the
assertions opposed as contradictories, which (according
to § 95) are contained in them and may be deduced by
Subalternation, must both be true, and the axiom of
Contradiction does not admit this (but their common
falsehood includes neither the truth nor the falsehood of
assertions which are opposed to each other as contradictories) ;

4. From the *falsehood* of a judgment the truth of its
subcontrary (but not conversely from the truth of the
one to the falsehood of the other), according to the
axiom, that subcontrary judgments cannot be both false

(but may both be true), because otherwise (according to 2) their contradictory opposites, which stand to each other in the relation of contrary opposition, must both be true, and also (according to 3) cannot both be true.

According to 1, there follows by an inference *ad contradictoriam propositionem.*

> From the truth of S a P, the falschood of S o P;
> From the truth of S e P, the falsehood of S i P;
> From the truth of S i P, the falschood of S e P;
> From the truth of S o P, the falsehood of S a P.

According to 2, there follows by an inference *ad contradictoriam propositionem :—*

> From the falsehood of S a P, the truth of S o P;
> From the falsehood of S e P, the truth of S i P;
> From the falsehood of S i P, the truth of S e P;
> From the falsehood of S o P, the truth of S a P.

According to 3, there follows by an inference *ad contrariam propositionem :—*

> From the truth of S a P, the falsehood of S e P;
> From the truth of S e P, the falsehood of S a P.

According to 4, there follows by an inference *ad subcontrariam propositionem :—*

> From the falsehood of S i P, the truth of S o P;
> From the falsehood of S o P, the truth of S i P.

The like consequences hold good in the corresponding *hypothetical* judgments.

Although the transformations given in this paragraph are so simple that they seem to need no *examples* or illustration, yet one may be given to show that attention should be paid to these relations not merely for the sake of logical theory, but also for their practical application, which is not unimportant. The truth of the affirmation is equivalent to the falsehood of the negation, and the truth of the negation to the falsehood of the affirmation. Affirmation is opposed to ignorance, inattention, or negation. Negation is (according to § 69) only suitable where a motive for affirmation can at least be thought, and more especially where an affirmation has actually been made by others. Hence in the interpretation of an affirmation the sense of the negation must be kept in mind, and in the interpretation of a negation the content and form of its corresponding affirmation. According to this rule, if Heinrich Düntzer's conjecture[1] in Hor. Epod. v. 87, ' venena magna,' be accepted, an explanation different from Düntzer's must be given. Düntzer translates: ' Strong charms may perpetrate intentional transgression; they cannot change a man's condition.' But the first part of this sentence (if we suppose that Horace expressed these thoughts by these words) is languidly directed against the witches. The negation which in the natural construction refers to the whole of the sentence is opposed to an affirmation made by the witches. They believe that a change in human nature (convertere humanam vicem, the change from hate or indifference to love), unattainable by weaker charms, may be brought about by stronger (venena magna); and they believe those charms to be strong (as Düntzer remarks) for whose preparation crimes are necessary. But they have not avowed to themselves nor to others the whole nefas; the fear of the knowledge of the crime still remains to some extent, even when the fear of the crime itself has departed; and so the perpetrators assure themselves and others that the scrupulous distinction between fas and nefas vanishes only in ' more potent' means, and that in means of that kind fas and nefas are equivalent. They declare: venena magna (ac?) fas nefasque (i.e. venena magna per fas nefasque adhibita) valent convertere humanam vicem; and the boy whom they threaten denies this assertion. The truth of the negation which he asserts is equivalent to the falsehood of what the witches affirm.

[1] *Philol.* xxvii. 184.

§ 98. MODAL CONSEQUENCE (consequentia modalis) is change of modality. By modal consequence follows (cf. § 69):—

1. From the *validity* of the *apodictic judgment* the validity of the assertorical and of the problematic, and from the *validity* of the *assertorical*, that of the problematic judgment; but from the validity of the problematic that of the assertorical and apodictic does not conversely follow, nor from the validity of the assertorical that of the apodictic;

2. From the *inadmissibility* of the *problematic* judgment follows that of the assertorical and apodictic, and from the *inadmissibility* of the *assertorical* that of the apodictic judgment; but from the inadmissibility of the apodictic judgment does not follow conversely that of the assertorical and problematic, nor from the inadmissibility of the assertorical that of the problematic judgment.

The *first* consequence depends (in the same way as Subalternation) on the fact that the judgment deduced only repeats a moment which is contained in the given judgment. Apodictic certainty, when we abstract the reason of the certainty, justifies us in stating the judgment in its assertorical form, as simply true, and therefore still more in attributing to it at least probability. In the same way the immediate certainty which the assertorical judgment expresses, includes probability as a moment. On the other hand, the certainty of the higher degree is not conversely contained in that of the lower degree.

The *second* consequence rests on this, that where the

lower degree of certainty is wanting, the higher must
also be absent. On the other hand, it is not to be
concluded conversely, that, where the higher degree is
not present, the lower must also be absent.

Since Modality treats of the degree of (subjective) certainty,
the terms: *validity* or *admissibility*, and *invalidity* or *inadmissibility*, must be used, and the notion of *truth* or *falsehood*
must not be uncouditionally substituted for them. For example,
if the assertorical judgment: A is B, is inadmissible, the reason
may consist in this, that we have not the (subjective) conviction of its truth, while the judgment in itself may be
true. In this case the problematic judgment: A is perhaps
B, may remain thoroughly admissible or valid. But if the
assertorical judgment: A is B, is false, then according to the
axiom of Excluded Third (§ 78) its contradictory opposite: A
is not B, is true; and if this is once established, the problematic
judgment: A is perhaps B, is no longer correct.

The same postulate holds good in this relation which is true
of the particular judgment, that the assertion of the less (there
of *some*, here of *perhaps*, &c.) is to be understood not in the
exclusive sense (*only* some, *only* perhaps, &c.), but in the sense
of containing the possibility of the greater (*at least* some, *at
least* perhaps).

Analogous laws are valid with reference to *objective* possibility, actuality, and necessity, but their explanation belongs
rather to Metaphysics than to Logic. *Aristotle* has treated of
them in his logical writings, especially in De Interp. o. xiii. He
finds a difficulty in the question, whether possibility follows
from necessity. On the one hand, it appears to do so. For if
it were false that what is necessary is possible, it must be true
that what is necessary is impossible, which is absurd. But on
the other hand, it appears that the proposition must also be
valid : What has the possibility to be has also the possibility
not to be, and so what is necessary, if it were something possible, would have a possibility both to be and not to be, which
is false. Aristotle solves this difficulty by the distinction, that

the notion of the possible is used partly in a sense in which
necessity is not excluded (*at least* possible), in which sense it
may be applied to those energies which include the dynamis,
partly in a sense which excludes necessity (*only* possible), in
which sense it may be applied to the dynamis which are not
energies. In the former sense the necessary is a possible, in
the latter it is not. (In reference to possibility in the narrower sense, which excludes necessity, Aristotle says[1] that the
μὴ ἐνδέχεσθαι, since it denies possibility on both sides equally,
finds application not merely where the thing is impossible, but
also where it is necessary.) Later logicians, since they apprehend the judgment of possibility according to the analogy of
the particular, and accordingly presuppose the meaning: *at
least possible*, enunciate the rule: 'ab oportere ad esse, ab
esse ad posse valet consequentia: a posse ad esse, ab esse ad
oportere non valet consequentia.'

§ 99. MEDIATE INFERENCE divides into two chief
classes: *Syllogism* in the stricter sense (ratiocinatio, discursus, συλλογισμός), and *Induction* (inductio, ἐπαγωγή).
Syllogism in the stricter sense, in its chief forms, is inference from the general to the particular or individual,
and in all its forms inference proceeding from the
general. Induction is inference proceeding from the
individual or particular to the general. Inference by
Analogy, which proceeds from the individual or particular to a coordinate individual or particular, is a third
form distinct from both, though able to be reduced to
a combination of the other two.

If it is proved universally that only two tangents can be
drawn to any conic section from one and the same point, and
it is then inferred: The Hyperbola is a conic section, for this
proposition holds true of it, the reasoning is a *Syllogism*. But
if, on the contrary, it is first shown of the circle, that from one

[1] *Analyt. Pr.* i. 17.

and the same point only two tangents can be drawn to its circumference, and then the like is inferred of the ellipse, parabola, hyperbola, and it is concluded: this proposition holds good
of all conic sections whatever, the reasoning is an *Induction.*

Kepler and his followers proceeded *inductively* in the establishment of the laws named after him, for they generalised the
truth of the results proved of Mars, and extended them to the
other planets. But the converse procedure accomplished by
Newton is *syllogistic*; for he proved, on the ground of the
principle of gravitation, that every planet must move round its
central body, or rather round the common centre of gravity,
in a path which is a conic section, and such that the radius
vector sweeps over equal areas of the plane of the orbit in equal
times, and that when several bodies move around the same
centre of gravity, the squares of their periods must be proportional to the cubes of their mean distances; and he applied
these axioms to planets, moons, and comets. The molten condition of the interior of the earth is proved *inductively* from
the connection of volcanic phenomena, *deductively* or *syllogistically* from the process of the earth's formation (probable on
astronomical grounds).

The Syllogism in reference to its most important and, for
positive knowledge, most productive ·forms, may be called
' *the inference of subordination*' (with J. Hoppe,' who also calls
it ' inference by analysis of notions'); Induction (with Hoppe),
the ' *inference of superordination*;' and inference by Analogy
(Hoppe does not recognise Analogy as a special form), ' inference of coordination.' [2]

---

[1] *Die gesammte Logik*, I. Paderborn, 1868.

[2] The remarks made above (§ 84) upon Hoppe's charge of schematism in the logical treatment of immediate inferences may be repeated
of what he calls the ' schematic and mechanic procedure' of Syllogistic.
If it is supposed that over and above the given judgment we know the
particular kind of knowledge involved, the particular kind of union of
predicate with subject, and which of the different relations of the predicate with the subject actually exists in the individual case, then of
course more may be concluded than is admissible according to the
' schematic procedure ;' but the number of the legitimately presupposed
data has been exceeded.

The Syllogism has ever experienced much childish trifling at the hands of its advocates, and much perversity from its opponents. But he who fairly compares both, will find the greater misunderstanding on the side of the opponents. Its advocates possess at least a certain degree of acquaintance with the matter, while many of its opponents, with equal ignorance and arrogance, abuse what they do not understand.

§ 100. The syllogism is SIMPLE (simplex), when from two judgments, which are different and have a common element, a third judgment is derived. It is COMPOSITE (compositus), when more than three elements of judgments, or more than two judgments, serve to establish the conclusion. The common element mediates the inference, and is accordingly called the *middle* (mediating) *notion* or *middle term* (medium, terminus medius, nota intermedia, τὸ μέσον, ὅρος μέσος). It comes, as the name tells, into each of the premises, but not into the conclusion. The given judgments, from which the new one is derived, are called *premises* (propositiones praemissae, iudicia praemissa, posita, προτάσεις, τὰ προτεινόμενα, τὰ τεθέντα, τὰ κείμενα, also sumptiones, acceptiones, λήμματα), and the judgment deduced, the *conclusion* (conclusio, iudicium conclusum, illatio, συμπέρασμα, ἐπιφορά). The one premise, which contains the subject, or the subordinate propositional member (e.g. the hypothesis) of the conclusion, is called the *Minor Premise* (propositio minor, assumptio, πρόσληψις); the other, which contains the predicate or the superordinate propositional member (the axiom or principal sentence), is called the *Major Premise* (propositio major, λῆμμα).

The component parts of the syllogism or the members of
the judgments contained in it, are comprehended under
the name, *Elements of the Syllogism* (Syllogismi Elementa, τὰ τοῦ συλλογισμοῦ στοιχεῖα). The *Relation* of
the syllogism is determined by that of its premises, i.e.
the syllogism is copulative, disjunctive, hypothetical, &c.,
or mixed, according to the form of the premises. If the
premises are of different forms, the Relation of the
Syllogism should, by preference, be that of the Major
Premise.

From two judgments, which have nothing in common, no
new relation can be established, and no conclusion deduced.
If a third follows from two judgments, they must either have a
common element, or can receive it by a mere change of form.
The latter case exists, when one element of the one judgment
is the contradictory opposite of an element of the other. This
case can be enumerated among simple syllogisms only if the
notion of such syllogism be defined in this way, that every
syllogism which is founded on two given judgments independent of each other, without a third not produced by a mere
change of form being brought in, is to be called *simple*; and
that that only is *compound* which presupposes more than two
judgments given. But in the course of exposition this definition would lead to many mistakes. Several of the rules which
syllogistic must enunciate (e.g. the axiom: ex mere negativis
nihil sequitur, cf. § 106; the statements about the number
and form of the valid moods, &c.) would not hold good, and
would require to be superseded by others less simple and
evident. In internal correctness also this terminology would
be inferior to that enunciated in the text of this paragraph.
For in the case, when two elements of the two premises stand
to each other in the relation of contradictory opposition, the
conclusion cannot be reached unless a judgment which follows
by aequipollence from one of the given judgments is added in
thought. Hence the inference is actually compound,—com-

pounded, viz. of an immediate consequence and a simple syllogism.

The expressions ὅρος and πρότασις are explained by *Aristotle*.[1] He also defines the middle notion (τὸ μέσον).[2] The name συμπέρασμα is often found.[3] The terms λήμματα and ἐπιφορά belong to the Stoics.

§ 101. The *possibility of the syllogism as a form of knowledge* rests on the hypothesis, that a *real conformability to law* exists, and can be known, according to the *axiom of Sufficient Reason* (§ 81). Perfect knowledge rests on the coincidence of the ground of knowledge with the real cause. Hence *that syllogism is most valuable, in which the mediating part (the middle notion, the middle term), which is the ground of the knowledge of the truth of the conclusion, also denotes the real cause of its truth.*

The doctrine stated in this paragraph is the most important in the whole of syllogistic. The decision of its most important question of debate depends on the reference in the syllogism to a real conformability to law. Is the syllogism a mean to *knowledge*, and is it to be set side by side with the notion and judgment as a form equally correct in this sense, or is syllogistic procedure to be reckoned a mere combination of notions, which may perhaps serve to give greater clearness to the knowledge we already possess in an undeveloped way, and may have some worth for the purpose of communicating our knowledge to others? If the conviction of the universally valid truth of the premises is not founded on the presupposition of a real conformability to law, but is first reached by comparison of all individual cases,—then it is evident that those cases which are asserted in the conclusion must also be included in the cases compared, that the truth of the conclusion must already be established ere the truth of the premises can be

[1] *Anal. Pri.* i. 1.   [2] Ibid. i. 4.   [3] Ibid. i. 9.

z

recognised, and that we really fall into the fallacy of the Circle
when we attempt again to deduce the conclusion from the
premises. This last deduction can, at most, have the value of
a 'deciphering of our notes' (Mill), and can serve only to
recall to our recollection, to make clear, or to communicate to
others. And in fact, syllogistic does no more in many cases.
For example, if the syllogism is enunciated: Every body
describing an elliptical orbit round our Sun is of itself a dark
body; Vesta is a body describing an elliptical orbit round our
Sun; therefore Vesta is in itself a dark body,—it is evident
that I can recognise the universal validity of the premises only
when I know that Vesta belongs to the bodies describing an
elliptical orbit round our Sun, and that it possesses no light of
its own. So little can I know the truth of the conclusion from
the truth of the premises, that, on the contrary, the conviction
of the truth of the first premise must be founded on the previously established conviction of the truth of the conclusion,
and that if the conclusion is shown to be uncertain or false, the
first premise shares the same fate. The proposition, that all
planets are always seen within the zodiac (which is true of all
the planets known to the ancients) loses its apparently universal
validity, so soon as any one is found (among the asteroids)
which passes beyond the zodiac. It cannot be inferred from
the general proposition, as if this proposition were established
previously to and independent of a complete enumeration of
the particulars, that there can be no planet which passes
beyond these limits. The planet Pallas actually passes beyond
them. But all cases are not of the same kind. So far as a
definite conformability to law can be established with reference
to any relation to be explained, the universal may be recognised
to be true *before* a thorough investigation of the sum total of
all the individuals, and therefore the truth of the individuals
can be arrived at from its truth by syllogistic deduction. For
example, since Newton's time we can know that the laws of
Kepler have universal validity, without first testing their
application to all planets and satellites, and whenever a new
body of this kind is discovered, those laws may be syllogistically applied to it with perfect assurance. The certainty of

the laws derived from the principle of gravitation is so firmly established, that when the observed orbit of Uranus appeared to contradict them, this observation did not raise an objection to their certainty; it rather justified the inference of the presence of some planet hitherto unobserved, and affecting this orbit,—an inference which led to the discovery of Neptune. In this way, in all cases in which our thinking rests on the foundation of a definitely known real conformability to law, the syllogism is a completely correct form of knowledge, to which we owe valuable extensions of science.

If the middle term in a syllogism which makes a real addition to our knowledge is the expression of the *real cause*, it must not be forgotten that the real cause can only accomplish the effect in combination with the corresponding external conditions. For example, in the inference: What lengthens the pendulum increases the times of its swing; Heat lengthens the pendulum, and so increases the times of its swing,—the lengthening of the pendulum by heat is the real cause of the increase of the time of its swing, but is so only because of the attraction of the earth and the motion of its parts according to the laws of the case. Cf. § 69, and § 81, upon the combination in every cause of the (internal) ground and (external) conditions.

Aristotle expresses the doctrine stated in this paragraph with perfect distinctness when he demands that the *middle term* must express the *real cause*:[1] τὸ μὲν γὰρ αἴτιον τὸ μέσον. Aristotle does not here ' trace the real back to the formal,' as Drobisch says,[2] but conversely gives depth to the formal by showing its reference to the real. For although the expression quoted admits of two meanings, because both subject and predicate have the definite article, and the sentence is reciprocal, only one meaning corresponds to the context. In order to be sure of existence, says Aristotle, and in order to recognise essence, we must have a *middle term*. If we have this, we know the *cause*, and have found with it what was

<hr/>

[1] *Anal. Post.* ii. 2, 90 a, 6.   [2] *Log. Prrf.* 2nd ed. p. xi.

especially sought, and what we must seek; for the certainty
of the (real) cause evidently ensures the certainty of the
existence. And the meaning of our proposition is: The significance of the middle term lies in this, that it corresponds to
the cause.[1] The opposite thought: The essence of the αἴτιον
lies in this, that it is the middle term of an inference, would
not correspond to the context. For from the propositions:
the αἴτιον ensures the existence, and: the essence of the αἴτιον
lies in this, that it is the middle term of an inference, what
Aristotle wishes to prove, that whenever we have the middle
term the existence is ensured, would not follow. It would
be a fallacious universal affirmative syllogism in the third
figure. *Waitz* says in his Commentary:[2] 'Quum omnis
quaestio iam in eo versetur, ut *rei* subiectae naturam sive
causam, per quam *res ipsa* existat vel ob quam aliud quid de
ea praedicetur, exploramus, *quam quidem cursum terminus
medius exprimere debet.*' The examples, which Aristotle
adduces here and in other passages, show that he does not
mean to resolve the real into the formal, but to comprehend
the form in its relation to the content. The real ἀντίφραξις of
the earth between the sun and the moon is the αἴτιον of the
eclipse of the moon. Now it is evident that the essence of that
real position of heavenly bodies with regard to each other does
not lie in this, that it is the middle term of a syllogism, but on
the contrary, the essence of the middle term lies in this, that it
denotes the real cause. (An opaque body which comes between
a luminary and a body, which, dark in itself, is light by means of
the other, causes an eclipse of the latter. The earth is an opaque
body, which at certain times comes between the luminary, the
sun, and the moon which is dark in itself and made luminous by
the sun. Hence at certain times the earth causes an eclipse of
the moon.) In the same sense *Aristotle* teaches[3] that the four

---

[1] This does not conflict with what Aristotle says (*Anal. Post.* ii. 12,
Init.): τὸ γὰρ μέσον αἴτιον. Becoming and having become, &c., have
the same mean; but the mean is the cause,—therefore they have the
same cause.

[2] *Ad Anal. Post.* ii. 2, 380.   [3] c. xi.

metaphysical *airiai*: Essence, Condition, Moving Cause, and
Final Cause, are all denoted by the middle term, and are to
be so denoted, not because they are all reduced to a single
formal reference, and their real metaphysical character destroyed, but, on the contrary, because the real reference of the
metaphysical *airiai* is represented in the middle term. Aristotle
remarks,[1] that in what actually happens, there is partly a strong
causal necessity and universality, but partly only an ὡς ἐπὶ
τὸ πολύ, and adds: τῶν δὴ τοιούτων ἀνάγκη καὶ τὸ μέσον ὡς ἐπὶ
τὸ πολὺ εἶναι. The nature of the middle term is evidently
determined by the nature of the case, the ‘formal’ by the
‘real,’ and not conversely. The Aristotelian postulate, that
(human) thinking must conform to existence, proceeds also
upon this. It was reserved for a modern philosopher, Kant,
despairing, in consequence of so many failures made by dogmatic philosophers, of establishing a knowledge of ‘things-in-
themselves,’ to grasp the converse principle, that the real (the
world of phenomena) must adapt itself to the forms of our
human capacities of knowledge, and accordingly to attempt to
‘trace the real back to the formal.’ Aristotle admits that there
are also syllogisms, in which the actual cause is not apprehended, and that the effect, because it falls within sense-perception and is therefore able to be known by us, serves for the
middle term, and that we infer back from this to what causes.
We may do this when the effect can have one cause only, and
the judgment, in which the causal-nexus is thought, is therefore to be converted simply—ἀντιστρέφον.[2] He refers the following example to this last case: What does not twinkle is near;
the planets do not twinkle, therefore they are near. But syllogisms of this kind are of less value and are not valid in the most
strictly scientific manner. The scientific or apodictic syllogism
must derive the conclusion from the true and proper cause.[3]

[1] c. xii. pr. fin.   [2] *Anal. Pr.* i. 13.
[3] *Anal. Post.* i. 2, 6, and *passim.* Drobisch says in the third edition
of his *Logic*, p. 170, that the Aristotelian axiom, τὸ αἴτιον τὸ μέσον,
appears to have the meaning, that *when* the syllogism is applied to real
objects, the middle notion has the meaning of cause, or the cause is

In so far as the true and proper ground of a thing lies in its essence (οὐσία or τί ἐστι), to this extent the syllogism rests upon the essence,[1] and since the definition gives the essence, syllogistic knowledge stands in the most intimate reciprocal relation to knowledge by definitions, in spite of their undeniable difference. The definition is the principle of the syllogism in so far as it supplies the major premise, and the syllogism leads to definition in so far as its middle notion reveals the essence in the cause.[1]

Later logicians, and among them the *Stoics*, neglected to refer the middle term to the real cause, and syllogistic thinking generally to the real conformability to law, and confined their attention too exclusively to the easier technical parts of the Aristotelian syllogistic. Hence we need not wonder that the *Sceptics* of antiquity combated the syllogistic procedure in general by the assertion, which has often been repeated in modern times, that the premises so far from being able to establish the truth of the conclusion, presuppose it. *Sextus Empiricus*[2] says that the major premise can only be made certain by induction, and that induction presupposes a complete testing of every individual case; for a single negative instance (the crocodile moves not the under, but the upper jaw) can destroy the truth of the universal proposition (all animals move the under jaw). On the other hand, if the testing has completely included every individual member, we

knows by it, but not that it is the cause. It seems to me that, according to Aristotle, the middle notion (is not, but) expresses the real cause and corresponds to it, that the cause is recognised by it. But I cannot appropriate the expression that the middle term, in its application to the real, receives the meaning of cause. Since the middle term brings the real cause (independent of it and existing before it), or as Drobisch says, the 'chief cause,' within our knowledge, it follows that in a syllogism of this kind the 'formal,' or the manner of knowing, is conditioned by the 'real,' or the objective causal relation. This holds good also in mathematical inferences.

[1] *Metaph.* vii. 9, § 7, ed. Schw.
[2] *Anal. Post.* i. 8; ii. 3, sqq.; *De Anima,* ii. 2, § 1.
[3] *Pyrrhon. Hypotyp.* ii. 194 ff.

argue in a vicious circle, when we deduce the individual from
the universal syllogistically.

In modern times it has often been made a matter of reproach
against the logicians of later antiquity, and of the Middle
Ages, that they have spun out with great subtlety the technical
part of the Aristotelian logic. It must be admitted that the
charge is justifiable, inasmuch as they, wholly devoted to the
technical, let the deeper elements pass unobserved. But it is
intolerable in the mouth of those who do not regard the relations of the formal to the real any more than the Schoolmen did,
and seek their own renown and pre-eminence over them only
because they disdain and neglect the technicalities of their
science. Is the superficiality and heedlessness, which in modern times has become only too frequent (many logical text-
books especially, especially from the Kantian period, swarm
with logical blunders), to be preferred to the Scholastic accuracy
and acuteness? Or does not exactness in these matters, as in
everything, deserve praise? The very didactic artifices of the
Schoolmen, although we look on them as trivialities, deserve at
least excuse, because they serve their immediate purpose so
well. The mathematician *Gergonne* says rightly:[1] ' Le grand
nombre de conditions auxquelles on avait cherché à satisfaire
dans la composition de ces vers artificiels (dont chaque mot
rappelait une des formes syllogistiques concluantes), aurait
peut-être dû en faire excuser un peu la dureté qui a été dans
ces derniers temps le sujet d'une multitude de plaisanteries
assez mauvaises.'

Coming to *modern philosophers,— Bacon of Verulam* did not
absolutely declare the syllogism incapable of furthering knowledge, though he greatly preferred induction. He thought
that it did not come up to the subtlety of nature, and that its
proper place was among the more superficial disciplines (cf.
§ 23).

Des Cartes goes much further. In the proud consciousness
of his own fresh mental power, he would throw overboard at
once, as if it were merely ballast impeding the course of his own

[1] *Essai de Dial. rat.*, *Annales de Math.* vii. 227.

mental discovery, syllogistic and with it all the Aristotelian and Scholastic Logic, the whole logical heritage of more than two thousand years, and would put in its place four simple rules which refer to one's own subjective disposition in the investigation of truth (cf. § 24). And yet Des Cartes himself in his mathematico-physical investigations has made a most extensive, and, for the furtherance of the science, a most productive use of the despised syllogism.

It is easily understood how the empiricism of *Locke* makes the syllogism of less value than external and internal experience, induction, and common sense.[1]

Leibniz, on the other hand, recognises the logical rules, whose value he has learned to estimate in their application to mathematics, to be the criterion of truth (cf. § 27). He says more especially of syllogistic:[2] 'The discovery of the syllogism is one of the most beautiful and greatest ever made by the human mind; it is a kind of universal mathematic whose importance is not sufficiently known, and when we know and are able to use it well, we may say that it has a kind of infallibility :—nothing can be more important than the art of formal argumentation according to true logic.' This well-grounded judgment, however, when maintained in a one-sided way, occasioned the formalism of *Wolff* in the Leibnizian School, which frightened *Kant* into the belief that he must hedge in the syllogism within narrower bounds. He first cut off the second, third, and fourth figures as useless appendages (cf. § 103), and then made the syllogism, thus supposedly purified from a false subtlety, no longer a means to extend knowledge, but only to make clear by analysis what we have already known.

Fries, Herbart, and *Beneke* have adhered to Kant's opinion.

Hegel not only restored the syllogism to its former rights, but also explained it to be the necessary form of everything intelligible.[3] He gave to it, when he identified it with the circular course of the dialectical adjustment of the moments of

---

[1] *Essay,* iv. 7.   [2] *Nouv. Ess.* iv. 17, § 4.   [3] *Log.* ii. 119; *Encycl.* § 181.

the actual, a meaning so essentially changed, that the restoration did scarcely any good to the Aristotelian syllogism. Hegel has properly made it conspicuous that a distinction should be drawn between the 'syllogism of totality' as a 'syllogism of attention,' and 'the categorical syllogism' as a 'syllogism of necessity.' The major premise of the one has for its subject particular determinateness, the middle term has only empirical totality or the sum total of all concrete individual subjects, and therefore the conclusion, which should have that for its presupposition, itself presupposes it. The 'terms' of the other 'according to their substantial content stand in identical reference to each other as existing in and for themselves,' and, therefore, this inference does not, like the syllogism of reflection, presuppose its conclusion in its premises.' *Trendelenburg* has very acutely proved in his 'Logische Untersuchungen'[2] that the Hegelian Logic itself is not free from inaccuracies and errors.

Schleiermacher asserts:[3] 'The syllogistic procedure is of no value for the real construction of judgments, for the substituted notions can only be higher and lower;—nothing is expressed in the conclusion but the relation of two terms to each other, which have a common member, and are not without, but within each other. Advance in thinking, a new cognition cannot originate by the syllogism; it is merely the reflection upon the way in which we have attained, or could attain, to a judgment, —the conclusion;— No new insight is ever reached.' But a new insight must always occur when two notions are combined in one judgment, which were previously separated from each other, and when united to any third, belonged to two different judgments. It did not escape Schleiermacher that an important instance against his opinion is furnished by mathematical procedure, which evidently originates knowledge. But what he remarks against it is insufficient. He says, mathematical knowledge is not reached by means of the syllogistic form. All depends upon the discovery of the

[1] *Log.* ii. 151, 162; *Encycl.* §§ 190, 191.   [2] ii. 326-59.
[3] *Dial.* § 327, p. 285; cf. p. 287 ff.

construction. He who has it, has the proof, and only analyses the construction by means of the syllogism. 'The true mathematicians do not depend upon the syllogism, but refer everything back to intuition.' These expressions upon the nature of mathematical knowledge are certainly untenable. The force of the proof does not lie in the construction, but in the application, which it renders possible, of propositions previously proved, and, in the last instance, of axioms and definitions, to the proposition to be proved, *and this application is in its essence a syllogistic procedure.*[1] The construction is only the way of learning, not the way of knowing, the scaffolding not the foundation. The proof rests (as *Leibniz* has rightly remarked) on the force of the logical form (cf. § 27). It is no mere illusion that the enlargement of mathematical knowledge and its certainty is founded on the syllogism. This truth always lies at the basis of Schleiermacher's remarks, that the cognition of syllogistic rules is not sufficient to find out the suitable syllogisms, but that there is needed a peculiar mathematical sense, a faculty of divining, and that this faculty, while it can, at a glance, penetrate through whole series of interwoven relations, need not prefer the broad form of completely developed syllogisms. There is in mathematics, as in common life, a *tact* or *quick-sightedness*, an ἀγχίνοια, which *Aristotle*[2] rightly defined to be εὐστοχία τις ἐν ἀσκέπτῳ χρόνῳ τοῦ μέσου, and on this gift depends the art of discovery. The essence of this ἀγχίνοια lies in the psychological relation, that the middle members of that series of thoughts, which lead to the result sought for, are thought in quick combination with complete objective truth, but with only a slight subjective strength of consciousness, while the last member of the series, or the result, is thought in the full strength of consciousness. The elevation of the individual members to complete clearness in consciousness is of little value for the discovery, but is of great importance to the certain scientific insight and for instruction.[3] If then the peculiar nature of

[1] [Cf. Translator's preface.]   [2] *Anal. Post.* i. 34.

[3] Cf. Beneke's excellent analyses of *tact* in his *Lehrbuch der Psy-*

this quick-sightedness belongs not to logic but to psychology, it is evident that no objection can be raised from the side of the mathematical ἀγχίνοια against the foundation of mathematical certainty on syllogistic procedure. The mathematic vision passes over, in its flight, the same syllogisms, without being conscious of them individually as syllogisms, which mathematical analysis goes through in detail, and brings before consciousness. The logical essence of mathematical knowledge and the foundation of its certainty remain the same in both cases.

Trendelenburg, who espouses the Aristotelian doctrine of the parallelism of the productive cause in the reality, and the middle notion in the logical syllogism, and advocates it very successfully,[1] when he approaches Schleiermacher's opinion, expresses himself in the following way. Syllogism infers from the *fact* of the universal to the individual. The synthetic procedure, on the other hand, constructs the phenomena as a consequence from the general *cause* (reason, ground). The fact, on which the syllogism proceeds, may be the result of its internal foundation; but the universal fact comes solely *into consideration* for the subsumption. The necessary reason clothes itself in the expression of a universal fact, and becomes in this form the middle notion of the syllogism. The power of the syllogism is *formal* only, not *real,* like the synthesis. Geometry gives to every advance the *appearance* of a syllogistic subsumption, but the *synthetic elements,* which lie in the *construction* and *combination,* work throughout by means of every syllogism and act *creatively.* The syllogistic procedure proceeds side by side with the synthetic, protecting it, and is its *external representation.* Thought in the synthetic procedure is itself conscious of its accuracy, *and in this way is for itself immediately certain.* But if it wishes to represent to itself, or to others, what it has in its grasp, the connecting

chalogie, § 158; *Psychol. Skizzen,* ii. 275 ff.; *System der Logik,* i. 267 ff.; and German's work, *Die alte Streitfrage: Glauben oder Wissen?* Cf. also above, § 42.
[1] *Log. Unters.* 2nd ed. ii. 354–58; 3rd ed. ii. 388–393.

subordinating syllogisms serve to represent visibly the invisible course of thought. The individual *vision of the synthesis* is related to the *syllogistic development*, as measurement with the eye is to the surveyor's chain.[1] The same objection which held good against Schleiermacher's, holds good against this opinion. It is true that in mathematics only a very few propositions, and a few corollaries, can be proved by a simple syllogistic subsumption under others, and that for the most part in the constructions special 'synthetic elements' are introduced; and also that the discovery and combination of syllogisms leading to the end in view presuppose a mathematical 'vision,' which is essentially different from the capacity to understand and appreciate the given syllogisms. But we cannot admit that the 'synthetic' *combination* is other than the combination of the judgments in syllogisms, and of the syllogisms in courses of inference; nor that the *force of the proof* and the certainty of the thoughts can lie in any other ' synthetic elements,' than in the *complex of syllogisms.* For new knowledge can only be reached by deduction from the universal already known, and this deduction in its nature is necessarily syllogistic, for it can only happen by *subsumption* under the universal, however its syllogistic character may be concealed under the form of enthymemes. The synthetic combination cannot be ' *individual*' or ' *immediate*' in *the* sense that it does not subordinate the singular or particular in the case in hand to the general law, axiom, and previously proved theorems, and that it warrants to the thoughts in themselves an accuracy and certainty, as if by means of a hidden force. The truth is that the distinction of the ways of knowledge lies only in the measure of the strength of consciousness of the intervening members, in the

---

[1] *Log. Unters.* 2nd ed. ii. 281 ; 3rd ed. ii. 314, where I am accused of the misunderstanding of which I believe myself to be free, of thinking that ' the universal of facts' must be, as facts, *always derived from experience.* I have only said, and argued from this, that, according to Trendelenburg, the fact only and not the reason is to be *taken into consideration.* For the other side, see Trendelenburg's *Log. Unters.* 2nd ed. ii. 354 ff.; 3rd ed. ii. 388 ff.

permanence in consciousness of the individuals, or in their swift passage through it, in the completely stated or enthymematic form of the syllogisms. But above all it is not to be granted, that the syllogism and the complex of syllogisms does *not produce new knowledge*, but only serves to be the external representation for one's own subjective certainty, and the means by which others may recognise what is already present, and, in another way, known certainly in itself and thought accurately without syllogisms; nor is it to be allowed that for the syllogism as such *the universal fact alone comes into consideration.* For if the syllogism rests only on the universality of the fact, the objection of the Sceptics cannot be got over. The major premise cannot be established before the conclusion, and cannot serve as its foundation, and the Aristotelian doctrine of the middle notion is, at least for the syllogism as such, of no validity. If, on the other hand, the *thought is essential for the syllogistic procedure* that the ' universal of the facts ' must rest on the ' universal of the reason '—and this is actually the case,—then the Aristotelian doctrine is valid. But then it is also false that, for the syllogism, only the universal fact *comes into consideration,* and that a ' synthetic' procedure, other than that which completes itself in and by syllogisms, is required for the creative establishment of knowledge; and that the syllogism has only a ' formal ' and didactic value. It must rather be recognised that syllogistic procedure is essentially 'synthetic,' and that all the other 'synthetic elements' to be included in the concatenation of syllogisms, are of use only for the discovery and application of suitable syllogisms. The ' real ' power of the syllogism to produce knowledge shows itself not only in the mathematical, but in all the other fields of knowledge. Every intellectual apprehension of an individual fact of history results necessarily from a universal law according to a syllogistic form of thought, although it is seldom expressed syllogistically. When, for example, in his ' History of the Thirty Years' War,' Schiller explains the duration and violence of this religious contest, he points to a universal conformability to law, according to which religious wars are

carried on with the greatest pertinacity and bitterness, because
every man may take the one side or the other with a personal
self-determination, and not, as in national wars, in consequence
of the merely natural determination of birth, and thus in a
syllogistic form of thought subsumes the individual fact under
this universal law. The view that the ' power of the syllogism is only formal and not real like the synthesis,' is true
only when limited to incomplete and unscientific syllogisms
(whether of the first or of the other figures). It cannot be
applied, if the Aristotelian doctrine of the middle term is true,
to complete or specially scientific syllogisms, in which the ground
of knowledge coincides with the ground of reality. The distinction, correct in itself, between the ' universal of the reason '
and the ' universal of the fact ' cannot serve as the basis for a
distinction between ' synthesis' and ' syllogism,' but only for a
distinction between two *formations of the syllogism*, and in reference to the complete syllogism, between its ' real ' and ' formal '
side. There are *three essentially different opposites* : 1. Reason
and fact. 2. Tact and analysis. 3. Constructions and inferences. It is not necessary that the reason is apprehended
only in the form of tact or vision, and is accompanied by constructions, any more than that the opposed members, fact,
analysis, and inference exist together; and accordingly it does
not appear correct to comprehend the three first members
under the common name of ' synthetic elements,' nor to oppose
reason and tact or vision to the syllogistic procedure, as if
it were antagonistic to them. ' Synthetic ' procedure is rather
of syllogistic character, and the complete or truly scientific
syllogism of ' synthetic ' character.

§ 102. THE SIMPLE CATEGORICAL SYLLOGISM consists
of three categorical judgments, of which two form the
premises and the third the conclusion. They contain *three
chief notions* ; that which is the subject in the conclusion
is the *minor notion* (terminus minor, ὅρος ἔσχατος, τὸ
ἔλαττον sc. ἄκρον); that which is the predicate in the

conclusion is the *major notion* (terminus major, ὅρος πρῶτος, τὸ μεῖζον); the two together are the *extreme notions* (termini extremi, τὰ ἄκρα); and the common element mediating the inference is called the *middle notion* (terminus medius, ὅρος μέσος, τὸ μέσον).

The premise which contains the major notion (terminus major), is the *major premise* (cf. § 100), and that which contains the minor notion (terminus minor), the *minor premise.*

This terminology was established by Aristotle. He defines:[1] ὅρον δὲ καλῶ εἰς ὃν διαλύεται ἡ πρότασις, οἷον τό τε κατηγορούμενον καὶ τὸ καθ' οὗ κατηγορεῖται.[2] καλῶ δὲ μέσον μὲν ὃ καὶ αὐτὸ ἐν ἄλλῳ καὶ ἄλλο ἐν τούτῳ ἐστὶν, ὃ καὶ τῇ θέσει γίνεται μέσον · ἄκρα δὲ τὸ αὐτό τι ἐν ἄλλῳ ὂν καὶ ἐν ᾧ ἄλλο ἐστίν·— λέγω δὲ μεῖζον μὲν ἄκρον ἐν ᾧ τὸ μέσον ἐστὶν, ἔλαττον δὲ τὸ ὑπὸ τὸ μέσον ὄν. In the same passage and elsewhere, Aristotle uses also the names: ὁ ἔσχατος ὅρος (terminus minor), and ὁ πρῶτος (terminus major). He formed this terminology having regard to that form of the syllogism in which the relation of the spheres of the three notions agrees with the verbal meaning of the names: μεῖζον or πρῶτον (the wider or higher), μέσον (the middle), and ἔλαττον or ἔσχατον (the narrower or lower notion). He then transfers it[3] to the other forms, where the relation of sphere is otherwise, and correspondingly modifies its meaning. If the definitions are given as equally applicable to all cases (which is a scientific demand that cannot be refused), the relation of spheres cannot come into consideration. The middle term is in some cases in the first form or figure of the syllogism only the *mean* according to extent; it must generally be defined as that which *mediates* (the inference). The other two terms cannot be distinguished from each other in an equally universally valid way, if their relation as *subject* and *predicate* in the *conclusion* be not attended to. Their relation of spheres (although a specially

[1] *Anal. Pri.* i. 1.   [2] Ibid. i. 4.   [3] Ibid. i. 5, 6.

fixed one in the fundamental form of the first syllogistic figure) is one which in general is completely indefinite. It might appear then as if the reference to the conclusion were a fallacious ὕστερον πρότερον, and as if every attempt at a general distinction of the major and minor terms must necessarily miscarry.[1] Syllogistic would then lose much of its scientific definiteness, and a thoroughgoing distinction of moods would be impossible. But in fact, there is no fallacy whatever in that reference to the conclusion. It is only the universal form of the conclusion (S P, i.e. either A B, or B A, if A and B are the extremes) which is by hypothesis brought under consideration. There is no reference either to the distinct formation (S a P or S e P, &c.) which the conclusion may take, or to the question whether a conclusion of that form can at all exist;—all that is to be found out by further investigation. The general form (either A B or B A) can without harm be presupposed, and the designation of the different notions in the premises founded upon it.

§ 103. Simple Categorical Syllogisms divide into *three chief classes*, which are called SYLLOGISTIC FIGURES (figurae, σχήματα); and the first of these divides into *two subdivisions*, which are also designated *Syllogistic Figures*. The *division into three chief classes* rests on the relation of the middle term in the premises as subject or predicate to the other two notions, without reference to the distinction of major and minor term, and consequently without reference to the form of the conclusion, on which the general distinction of these two terms from each other is founded. The middle notion is either subject in the one premise and predicate

---

[1] Trendelenburg, *Log. Unters.* 2nd ed. ii. 309 ff., finds this fallacy in the distinction ; and Drobisch, *Log.* 3rd ed. p. 92, asserts, that the distinction, whether A or B is the subject of the conclusion, is an arbitrary anticipation.

in the other, or predicate in both premises or subject in both. In the first case the *first chief class* or *First Figure in the more comprehensive sense* results. The second case gives the *Second*, and the third case the *Third* chief class or *Figure* of the Categorical Syllogism. The *subdivision* rests on an included reference to the distinction between the major term (that notion which is predicate in the conclusion) and the minor term (that notion which is subject in the conclusion). This subdivision establishes *two sections in the first chief class*: in the *first*, the middle term is subject to the major term and predicate to the minor; in the *second*, it is predicate to the major and subject to the minor. The first section of the first chief class is *the First Figure in the narrower sense*. The second section of the first chief class is the so-called *Fourth* or *Galen's Figure*. In the second and third chief classes, the distinction of major and minor term gives no analogous subdivision, for in both the relations of the major term and of the minor term to the middle are the same. Both in the second figure take the place of subject in the two premises, and in the third figure that of predicate; and their exchange, therefore, does not alter the general relation.

According to what is said above *three or four Syllogistic Figures* may be spoken of *with equal correctness*, as the name *figure* is used in the more comprehensive or more limited sense. We may say that there are three because there are *three chief classes*. We may say that there are four, because the first class has two sections; each of the others coincides with a section, and so there are in all *four sections*. The uncritical confusion of the two divisions is fallacious. The *first method of division* (into three Figures with two divisions in the first) has always a greater formal accuracy, just as the division of bodies according to their condition as aggregates into—

I. Flowing bodies, (*a*) fluid, (*b*) liquid;
II. Solid bodies.—is to be preferred in formal reference to the division into (1) fluid, (2) liquid, and (3) solid bodies;

but it is a pedantic rigorism which attaches too much weight to this (cf. § 64). On the other side, the *second method of division* (into four Figures) has its value in didactic and scientific reference. It is simpler, and more thoroughly separates the artificial and complicated methods of inference, which belong to the Fourth Figure (or to the second division of the First Figure in the wider sense), from the simple and natural forms of the First Figure in the narrower sense. Schematic representation may make both methods of division sensibly evident. If we call the middle notion (terminus Medius) M, and the other two notions, without previously regarding their distinction as major and minor term, A and B, then, according to the *first method* of *division*, the *Schema of the three chief classes* is the following:—

I.	II.	III.
M A	A M	M A
B M	B M	M B

The form of the conclusion (B A or A B) remains out of consideration; but if we distinguish the major and minor terms, and call the minor, because it becomes the subject in the conclusion (Subiectum conclusionis), S, and the major, because it is predicate in the conclusion (Praedicatum conclusionis), P, the *first chief class* or the *First Figure* in the *wider* sense, in which the word is used in the *first method of division*, divides into its *two divisions*, while the *Second* and *Third* remain undivided, according to the following Schema:—

I, 1.	I, 2.	II.	III.
M P	P M	P M	M P
S M	M S	S M	M S
S P	S P	S P	S P

In the *second method of division* S, P, and M again find application. But since the expression *figure* is now understood in the narrower sense, *four Figures* result, the *first* of which corresponds to the first division of the First Figure in the wider sense, the *second* to the Second Figure, the *third* to the Third Figure, and the *fourth* to the second division of the First Figure in the wider sense, according to the following Schema:—

I'.		II'.		III'.		IV'.	
M	P	P	M	M	P	P	M
S	M	S	M	M	S	M	S
S	P	S	P	S	P	S	P

It is self-evident that the conclusion in all cases must take the form S P, for the meaning of S is that it denotes *that* term which becomes the subject of the conclusion, and the meaning of P is that it denotes the predicate of the conclusion. It would not be necessary even to allude to this if it were not that in some logical works the question, which shows a complete misunderstanding, has been asked, Why should one so one-sidely always come to the conclusion S P, and why is not the conclusion P S also admissible?[1] It is certain that if the terms outside of M are immediately, without any further distinction, called A and B, the general inference to B A is as admissible as to A B; but if the conclusion has the one form, then B is the S (Subiectum conclusionis) and A the P (Praedicatum conclusionis): if it has the other form, then A is the S, and B the P. The relation of the major term to the minor in the conclusion is a definite one; in the premises it is indefinite. Hence their position in the conclusion must serve as the foundation of their distinction, and therefore their designation in the conclusion should not change.

The *succession of premises* is in all cases without influence on the determination of the Figure. It is useful to place the

---

[1] Bachmann, who has otherwise stated Syllogistic very well, says (*Log.* p. 226), 'Another fancy of the Aristotelians was to draw the conclusion S P for all Figures; but this is not at all necessary.'

major premise first, and it is practically convenient to keep to
the one definite succession of premises in the logical explanation of syllogistic relations in order to guard against over-
sights, and prevent errors. But this does not mean that the
procedure in the syllogism is *linked to this one method of succession.* *The other is quite as admissible,* in which the above
Schemata take the following form :—

I, 1 or I′.	I, 2 or IV′.	II or II′.	III or III.′
S M	M S	S M	M S
M P	P M	P M	M P
S P	S P	S P	S P

This succession of premises is easier and more convenient in
the First Figure, at least (the position of the subject before
the predicate is presupposed in single propositions), and occurs
oftener in actual inferences. But it is not necessary, in
logical explanation, to depart from the mode of representation
in use since Aristotle's time. It is rather advisable, in
didactic reference, to keep to it, although too much weight
should not be given to it, because it only concerns the expression. The essential thing is this, that the succession in the
expression of the premises is not to be recognised as limitative,
and that the mere change of external position does not establish a change of the form or figure of the conclusion. For
example, the syllogism—

S M	or	A M
M P		M B
S P		A B

is called a syllogism of the Fourth Figure ; or it is said that the
premises here stand in the 'inverse order,'[1] or that there are
in all[2] eight forms (one fundamental form, and seven secondary
forms, or seven 'Figures'), by means of a combination of the
above Schemata I′, II′, III′, IV′, and of those following there-
from : I, 1, or I′, &c.

[1] Prantl, *Geschichte der Logik*, I. 587.
[2] As the Kantian Krug thinks.

Aristotle usually preferred to place the predicate before the subject in those judgments which form the syllogism. For example, a syllogism of the First Figure, according to him, is stated in the following way :—

εἰ τὸ Α κατὰ παντὸς τοῦ Β,
καὶ τὸ Β κατὰ παντὸς τοῦ Γ,
ἀνάγκη τὸ Α κατὰ παντὸς τοῦ Γ κατηγορεῖσθαι.

In this way the terms from the most universal (the πρότερον φύσει) to the most special (the ὕστερον φύσει) follow each other successively, and their arrangement is conformable to nature in this reference.

In this way Aristotle uses the ὑπάρχειν: e.g. εἰ τὸ Μ τῷ μὲν Ν παντὶ τῷ δὲ Ξ μηδενὶ, οὐδὲ τὸ Ν τῷ Ξ οὐδενὶ ὑπάρξει (on the other hand the expression, ἐντεῖναι, e.g. τὸν ἔσχατον ὅρον ἐν ὅλῳ εἶναι τῷ μέσῳ καὶ τὸν μέσον ἐν ὅλῳ τῷ πρώτῳ ἢ εἶναι ἢ μὴ εἶναι, has the meaning: to be contained in the *extent* of the wider or higher notion as a subordinate notion, and in the judgment to form the *subject* to that).

The following is an old Scholastic example of the Four Figures:[1] 1. Every virtue is praiseworthy; Eloquence is a virtue: Eloquence is praiseworthy. 2. No vice is praiseworthy; Eloquence is praiseworthy: It is not a vice. 3. Every virtue is praiseworthy; every virtue is useful: Something useful is praiseworthy. 4. Every virtue is praiseworthy; everything praiseworthy is useful: Something useful is a virtue.

Aristotle divides syllogisms into *three* Figures (σχήματα), the first of which he explains at length in the Prior Analytics i. c. iv., the second, ib. c. v., and the third, ib. c. vi. He calls the syllogism of the First Figure *perfect* (συλλογισμὸς τέλειος),[2] because in it the result follows from the premises immediately (without the aid of sentences coming in between, which according to his view is required in the other Figures). The syl-

[1] According to Lambert and Rosenkranz, *Log.* li. 153.
[2] *Anal. Pri.* i. 1.

logisms of the two other Figures are *incomplete* (συλλογισμοὶ ἀτελεῖς). The thought also influences him in this terminology, that a universal affirmative conclusion can result, and the ground of knowledge coincide with the real cause, in the First Figure only.

The relation of this Aristotelian division to the division into *Four Figures* which was common in the latter part of the Middle Ages, although some very valuable researches have already been directed towards this point, requires stricter investigation. The common account is, that the three Aristotelian Figures coincide with the first three of the later division (the above I′, II′, III′), and that the fourth (IV′) was *added* by *Cl. Galenus*. On the other hand, *Trendelenburg*[1] has sought to show that the Aristotelian division is as complete as the later, but rests on a different—and really better—principle. ' *Aristotle* distinguishes three Figures, according as the *middle term in the series of subordinate notions* takes the *middle* place (First Figure), or forms the *highest* (Second Figure), or *lowest* notion (*Third* Figure). When we look at the *subordination of the three notions* necessary to a syllogism, *three figures* result. When *four figures* came to be enunciated, another ground of division was followed: the possibility of the different *positions* which the middle notion may have in the two premises. Aristotle saw the *internal* relation of the three terms present in the inference ; the external relation which was afterwards looked to consisted in the position of the middle term as subject or predicate in the two premises. Aristotle *did not take the succession of premises into consideration*; but one succession only is allowed by modern logicians, according to which the notion, that is the subject in the conclusion, is always referred to the minor premise. This order is an arbitrary arrangement, and the inverse of the natural relations ; for the conclusion following from the premises can in no case influence its grounds (the premises): ' Qui *terminorum naturam* spectant, eos *tria* figurarum genera, qui *externam enunciationum formam*, eos *quatuor* constituere

---

[1] *Log. Unters.* 2nd ed. ii. 308 ff. ; 3rd ed. ii. 311 ff. ; cf. *Elem. Log. Arist.* § 28, and Explanations of the Elements, same paragraph.

necease est. Quare Galenus *non addidit*, ut vulgo putant, quartam tribus prioribus, sed tres Aristotelis in quatuor novas *convertit*; nituntur enim *plane alio dividendi fundamento.*[1] In order to settle this question of debate, we must, with direct reference to *Aristotle*, distinguish between the principle of his division and its application.

So far as the principle is concerned, one thing is undoubted, that the relation of a successive subordination among the three notions requisite to the syllogism exists in the First Figure only; and even there not everywhere, for it does not exist in negative and particular judgments. In the Second Figure, as *Trendelenburg* himself remarks,[1] and mostly in the Third, this relation 'is more an assertion of an anology than strictly true, for the negation breaks the connection of the subordination.' It follows from this as certainly, that Aristotle,. *if* he attempted the division of syllogisms into figures upon the internal relations of the *subordination of terms*, on a relation which actually exists in the first of these figures only (and not even in this throughout), made a decided *blunder*, and that if the Aristotelian Syllogistic is free from this incorrectness, it ought to be recognised to be free from it. The relation between the terms which actually exists, is the *judgment* relation, that the middle notion is either *subject* in the one premise and *predicate* in the other, or *predicate* in both, or *subject* in both. If Aristotle selected, as the ground of division, this relation, which is also an internal and essential, apart from the distinction between the two other notions, his procedure would be justifiable, and his three principal σχήματα would coincide with our three *chief classes*. *Trendelenburg*[2] founds his opinion: (1) On the Aristotelian Definitions of the single figures;[3] (2) On the Aristotelian reduction of the Second and Third Figures to the First; and in the first edition of his work,[4] he also (3) makes the explanation of Aristotle[5] equivalent to:

---

[1] *Log. Unters.* 2nd ed. ii. 314; 3rd ed. ii. 347.
[2] Ibid. 2nd ed. ii. 310; 3rd ed. ii. 343.   [3] *Anal. Pri.* i. c. iv.-vi.
[4] ii. 238, in a note which is left out in the later editions.
[5] *Anal. Pri.* i. c. v.

the middle notion in the Second Figure is ' the highest ' (πρῶτον τῇ θέσει).

As to the first point, it is correct that the Aristotelian *definition* of the *First Figure* rests on the principle of successive subordination which is true in its fundamental mood. This definition is : ' ὅταν ὅροι τρεῖς οὕτως ἔχωσι πρὸς ἀλλήλους ὥστε τὸν ἔσχατον ἐν ὅλῳ εἶναι τῷ μέσῳ, καὶ τὸν μέσον ἐν ὅλῳ τῷ πρώτῳ ἢ εἶναι ἢ μὴ εἶναι, ἀνάγκη τῶν ἄκρων εἶναι συλλογισμὸν τέλειον, and to it are annexed the definitions of the μέσον and the ἄκρα given in the former paragraph. The definition of the *Second Figure*, however (or rather of the second possible way of combining the premises, the question whether a valid inference results or not being previously abstracted), is as follows : ² ὅταν δὲ τὸ αὐτὸ τῷ μὲν παντὶ τῷ δὲ μηδενὶ ὑπάρχῃ, ἢ ἑκατέρῳ παντὶ ἢ μηδενί, τὸ μὲν σχῆμα τὸ τοιοῦτον καλῶ δεύτερον. This definition evidently does not presuppose the principle of *subordination*, but only the *judgment* relation that the middle term is *predicate* in both premises ; for Aristotle adds the words : μέσον δὲ ἐν αὐτῷ λέγω τὸ κατηγορούμενον ἀμφοῖν, ἄκρα δὲ καθ᾽ ὧν λέγεται ταῦτα. The same is true of the definition of the *Third Figure* (or rather of the *third* way of combination), which is as follows: ³ ἐὰν δὲ τῷ αὐτῷ τὸ μὲν παντὶ τὸ δὲ μηδενὶ ὑπάρχῃ, ἢ ἄμφω παντὶ ἢ μηδενί, τὸ μὲν σχῆμα τὸ τοιοῦτον καλῶ τρίτον. Aristotle adds: μέσον δ᾽ ἐν αὐτῷ λέγω καθ᾽ οὗ ἄμφω τὰ κατηγορούμενα, ἄκρα δὲ τὰ κατηγορούμενα, so that here the judgment relations are specially taken into consideration.

Secondly, as to the *Reduction* of the individual ways of inference in the Second and Third Figures to that of the First, it serves the purpose of proving the validity of the deduced inference. It does not follow from this kind of *demonstration* that according to the view of Aristotle the Second and Third Figures must rest on the principle of successive subordination, which is partially true in the First.

At the most, the *third* point seems to favour the view that Aristotle looks upon the relation of the terms in all three figures as a relation of successive subordination. He says of

¹ *Anal. Pri.* i. 4.　　² C. v.　　³ C. vi.

the *middle notion* of the First Figure : ¹ ὃ καὶ τῇ θέσει γίνεται
μέσον ;² of the second : τίθεται δὲ τὸ μέσον ἔξω μὲν τῶν ἄκρων,
πρῶτον δὲ τῇ θέσει ; and of the third : ³ τίθεται δὲ τὸ μέσον ἔξω
μὲν τῶν ἄκρων, ἔσχατον δὲ τῇ θέσει. He also says ⁴ the μεῖζον
ἄκρον (terminus maior) is τὸ πρὸς τῷ μέσῳ κείμενον in the Second
Figure, but the ἔλαττον (terminus minor) τὸ πορρωτέρω τοῦ
μέσου, and ⁵ the converse relation exists in the Third Figure.
All these assertions conform very well to the view that a successive subordination of the terms exists in *all three figures,*
and if it were shown on other grounds that Aristotle entertains
this view, that they are to be explained by it. It is another
question, however, whether they can be explained *only* on
this view, and whether they justify an inference back to it.
For this view, as has been shown, is a wrong one, and is
to be attributed to Aristotle in his syllogistic only, if his words
admit of no other natural explanation, and only in proportion as the words necessitate it. These expressions, however, always admit of a more favourable meaning (which
Waitz has followed in his commentary on c. v. p. 26, b. 37).
The expression θέσις may be understood of the *position* or
arrangement of the terms *in the premises,* which rests on the
relation of subject or predicate, and of the position hereby
conditioned in the shorter Aristotelian Schema. The fundamental form of the First Figure is the following :—

τὸ Α κατὰ παντὸς τοῦ Β,
τὸ Β κατὰ παντὸς τοῦ Γ,
τὸ Α κατὰ παντὸς τοῦ Γ.

The θέσις, positio, collocatio, of the middle notion Β is the
mean betwixt Α and Γ, and Aristotle therefore places the terms
of the *First* Figure shortly together in the following order :—

Α Β Γ,

or, as we (with Trendelenburg) ⁶ might write it, if we denote
the middle notion by the capital letter :—

a Β γ.

¹ *Anal. Pri.* i. c. iv.   ² C. v.   ³ C. vi.
⁴ C. v.   ⁵ C. vi.   ⁶ *Erläut.* p. 52.

In this figure the relation of its *extent* may coincide with the relation of the terms in the premises, and with the external position resting on this relation; but this does not prevent the most immediate meaning of θέσις from denoting the *judgment* relation, and this meaning from being the only one in the remaining figures. The fundamental form of the *Second Figure* is, according to the Aristotelian way of representation:—

$$\text{τὸ Μ κατὰ μηδενὸς τοῦ Ν,}$$
$$\text{τὸ Μ κατὰ παντὸς τοῦ Ξ,}$$
$$\overline{\text{τὸ Ν κατὰ μηδενὸς τοῦ Ξ.}}$$

The middle term here, or the part mediating the inference, M, is the first in position, πρῶτον τῇ θέσει, because as the predicate it precedes the other notion in both premises. The shorter Schema is:—

$$\text{M N Ξ,}$$

or, as above, to distinguish the middle term from the other two:—

$$\text{M ▪ ξ.}$$

If the assertion of Aristotle about the middle term in this figure is easily explained from its predicative relation in the premises, without the false presupposition of a successive subordination of the terms, the wider question always includes and accounts for the fact that Aristotle separates the major term, τὸ μεῖζον, from the minor, τὸ ἔλαττον. He says (see above) the major is here the nearer to the middle notion, the minor the further from this. This coincides with the position in the Schema:—

$$\text{M ▪ ξ.}$$

But on what does this rest, and on what, more especially, does the placing ν before ξ rest? We may easily go back a step further to the previous more detailed Schema, in which likewise the N follows immediately after the first M, because that one of the two premises which contains the N should be placed before the other by Aristotle. But how does this happen? What is the reason for this preference of one premise to the other?

It appears as if we should be here obliged to return to the opinion, that Aristotle had entertained that false presupposition of a relation of logical subordination existing between ν and ξ, and all the more because the terminology μεῖζον and ἔλαττον brought over from the First Figure favours this view. And in truth this much must be granted, that Aristotle, *in this terminology,* has allowed himself to be guided by an analogy which does not always hold good, but which was excusable in *the* circumstance because he recognised (with complete correctness) the First Figure to be the form most important scientifically, and looked on the others (in this going too far) as dependent forms of less value. He made the ν however parallel to the major of the First Figure, and the ξ parallel to the minor, and gave the precedence to the premise which contains the ν, and so we must seek for the cause, but not necessarily in an erroneous opinion upon the internal relation of these terms. Aristotle may have come to a determination (more unconsciously) by the same reflection upon the form of the *conclusion* which the later logicians expressly explain to be the reason for the distinction of the major and minor term, as well as of the major and minor premise, although he does not introduce this consideration into his *division* of the figures of the syllogism. (The passage in the Anal. Pri. i. 23, where Aristotle proceeds from the conclusion, and defines according to its form that of the premises, also favours this.) All those expressions of Aristotle may be explained in a natural way without recourse to the hypothesis of an error. The *Third Figure* is to be explained in the same way. The Schema of its fundamental forms is, according to the Aristotelian representation, the following :—

τὸ Π κατὰ παντὸς τοῦ Σ,
τὸ Ρ κατὰ παντὸς τοῦ Σ,
τὸ Π κατὰ τινὸς τοῦ Ρ.

The shorter Schema is :—

Π Ρ Σ,

or (according to the above manner of representation) :—

π ρ Σ.

The notion mediating the inference, the Σ, ἔσχατον τῇ θέσει, is here the subject both times, and is, accordingly, in the shorter Schema placed last. In this figure, when both premises are affirmative and universal, the middle notion is logically subordinate to the other two notions. This relation, however, does not exist in other modes of inference in this figure, investigated by Aristotle no less carefully, so that we must here also explain the position, θέσις, of Σ from its *judgment-* (or as it happens to be subject-) relation. Besides, a definite relation of subordination does not necessarily exist between π and ρ in *the* case where both premises are affirmative and universal, much less in all inferences of the Third Figure; and when Aristotle calls that term in this figure the minor, which is nearer the middle notion, and that term the major, which stands further from the middle notion, this position and the connected terminology are to be explained in the same way as in the Third Figure.

Trendelenburg's three arguments do not prove that Aristotle has endeavoured to establish the division of syllogisms into three Figures on an imaginary threefold relation of subordination between the three terms. Aristotle expressly enunciates the principle of his division :[1] ἐὰν μὲν οὖν κατηγορῇ καὶ κατηγορῆται τὸ μέσον, ἢ αὐτὸ μὲν κατηγορῇ, ἄλλο δ' ἐκείνου ἀπαρνῆται, τὸ πρῶτον ἔσται σχῆμα· ἐὰν δὲ καὶ κατηγορῇ καὶ ἀπαρνῆται ἀπό τινος, τὸ μέσον. ἐὰν δ' ἄλλα ἐκείνου κατηγορῆται, ἢ τὸ μὲν ἀπαρνῆται τὸ δὲ κατηγορῆται, τὸ ἔσχατον·—τῇ τοῦ μέσου θέσει γνωριοῦμεν τὸ σχῆμα. According to this the *position, θέσις,* of the middle notion in the premises, settles the figure; but this position rests in its turn on the relation of the middle notion as *subject* or *predicate* in the premises. *In this division the distinction of major and minor term does not come into consideration.* The unambiguous principle of division here laid down by Aristotle is not a secondary point of view, but is fully identical with that principle, which, according to the above explanation, lies at the basis of the definitions of the three figures (or rather of the three syzygies condition-

[1] *Anal. Pri.* i. c. xxxii.

ing the figures) in chapters iv., v., and vi., and to which Aristotle himself refers in c. xxxii. in the words: οὕτω γὰρ εἶχεν ἐν ἱκάστῳ σχήματι τὸ μέσον. (Cf. Anal. Pri. i. 23, p. 41 A, 14: ἢ γὰρ τὸ Α τοῦ Γ καὶ τὸ Γ τοῦ Β κατηγορήσανται ἢ τὸ Γ κατ' ἀμφοῖν ἢ ἄμφω κατὰ τοῦ Γ, ταῦτα δ' ἐστὶ τὰ εἰρημένα σχήματα.) So far as we keep to *what is general and principal*, that either *firstly* the middle notion is predicate in the one premise (κατηγορῇ), and at the same time subject in the other (κατηγορῆται unusually for τοῦτο ᾗ καθ' οὗ κατηγορεῖται, praedicato exornetur, sustains predication),[1] or *secondly* is predicate in both, or *thirdly* subject in both,—this Aristotelian distinction of the different *judgment relations of the middle term in the premises* establishes a complete division of all simple categorical syllogisms into three figures, and in this respect we can assert as the result of our investigation up to this point, that *the Aristotelian principle of division of syllogisms agrees with the principle of our above-mentioned division into three chief classes.*

Another question arises,—Is the *application* of this principle *in Aristotle complete,* or *does it break down in the second division of First Figure?* It is a fact that Aristotle does not divide his First Figure into two sections, and that he does not formally explain the particular way (or moods) of inference which belong to its second section or to the later so-called Fourth Figure, at least not in the same manner as he does the other ways of inference; and he has not placed them on a level with these others. They were first *added* (cf. below) by other logicians to the Aristotelian Moods. It is also evident that in the nearer determination of the First Figure,[2] according to which the subordinate notion falls within the extent of the middle notion, and the middle notion either falls within or is completely excluded from it, the extent of the superordinate notion only belongs to the first section of the First Figure, or to the First Figure in the more limited sense (I'). It is evident also that the definition in c. xxxii., so far as it has to

[1] Cf. Trendelenburg, *Elem. Log. Ar.* at § 28, and Waitz on the passage.

[2] *Anal. Pr.* l. c. iv.

do with the First Figure in the more comprehensive sense, does not expressly take into consideration the distinction of the major and minor terms,—that according to its fundamental thought it would comprehend all the moods of both sections, —that it may be applied in its single determinations not merely to those of the section, but also to some moods of the second (viz. Bamalip, Calemes, Dimatis, of which more below) —and that in consequence of the limiting determination, according to which the premise which contains the middle notion as predicate can only be affirmative, it cannot apply to the rest of the ways of inference in the second division (viz. to Fesapo and Fresison).

Aristotle has, however, given in two passages *indications* which only need to be followed out, in order to find the Moods belonging to the second section of the First Figure. He says[1] that if a special syllogism cannot be constructed, a conclusion may be found in a certain position of the premises, in which the minor term (τὸ ἔλαττον) is the predicate, and the major (τὸ μεῖζον) the subject. This case occurs, if the one judgment affirms universally or particularly, and the other denies universally. When (according to the way of combination in the First Figure) A belongs to every or Some B, and the B to no Γ, it results necessarily, when the premises are converted, that some A are not Γ. (Conversion brings it to the Syllogism: Ferio of the First Figure: some A is B; no B is Γ; Some A is not Γ. In the application of the expressions: μεῖζον and ἔλαττον, Aristotle has, in this case, been led by analogy only to use the designations which he uses in the syllogisms recognised by him to be completely valid.) The moods here signified (as the old exegetes have remarked) are identical with those which were afterwards considered to be the last two of the five moods of the second division of the First Figure (I, 2) or of the Fourth Figure (IV'), viz., Fesapo and Fresison. Aristotle remarks in the same place, that the same happens in the other figures also; for a conclusion is always reached by Conversion (ἀντιστροφή) of the premises. But the moods, accord-

[1] *Anal. Pri.* i. c. vii.

ing to which inferences can be made in the other Forms, are
not new ones, but coincide with distinct kinds or moods of
inference already explained by Aristotle. (These are Cesare,
Camestres, and Festino of the Second Figure, which by Conversion of both premises pass over into Ferison of the Third,
and Felapton and Ferison of the Third, which pass over into
Festino of the Second.) Aristotle says further,[1] that all those
syllogisms whose conclusion universally affirms, universally
denies, or particularly affirms, yield a second result, if the conclusion be converted, while a particular negative conclusion,
according to the universal rule of conversion, admits of no conversion. Aristotle does not distinguish the cases in which the
inference reached by the conversion of the conclusion coincides
with one of the already explained moods or methods of inference (such as Cesare, which passes over into Camestres by this
conversion, and Camestres into Cesare, Disamis into Datisi, vice
versa; while an inference in Darapti only passes over into another
inference of the same mood) from those cases where a new result
is attained which is not attained by any other way of inference.[2]

[1] *Anal. Pri.* ii. c. i.
[2] Waitz has not appreciated this essential distinction when he says:[*]
'Apulei librum nullius fere pretii esse facile inde coniicitur, quod
ubi de prima figura disputat, Theophrastum imitatur in convertendis
propositionibus, in tertia vero eum reprehendit, quod opinatus sit duos
modos nasci ex conversione conclusionis.' In the same way, Prantl[†]
calls the procedure of Apuleius 'simple.' On the contrary, the true
view lies at the foundation of the assertion of Apuleius, that the syllogism with a converted conclusion in the First Figure belongs to
another division, and therefore to another mood; but in the Third
Figure, Darapti is only another example of inference in the same
mood. The mood is determined by its essential attributes, which enter
into its definition. The relation, in which the conclusion of the syllogism under consideration stands to that of another, does not belong to
this; consequently nothing prevents the conversion of the conclusion
of a syllogism in one case (viz. when a change of essential attributes is
connected with it) leading to a new Mood, and in another case not.

[*] *Org.* i. 886.   [†] *Gesch. der Log.* i. 370.

If, however, these last cases were singled out, they are those (as the old commentators remarked) which afterwards became the *first three* of the five Moods of the second division of the First Figure (1, 2) or of the Fourth Figure (IV'), viz. Bamalip, Calemes, and Dimatis, and which may be produced from the three corresponding moods of the First Figure, Barbara, Celarent and Darii, by Conversion of the conclusion, although they need not necessarily originate in this way. Cf. below.

The disciples of Aristotle, *Theophrastus* and *Eudemus*, have added *the five ways of inference*, which result as a new acquisition from those Aristotelian indications, to those modes of inference recognised to be fully valid and strictly explained by Aristotle himself. They number them from the *fifth to the ninth mood of the First Figure*, in the order which remained in use afterwards (viz., 5. Bamalip, 6. Calemes, 7. Dimatis, 8. Fesapo, 9. Fresison). Alexander of Aphrodisias, the Commentator, and Boëthius attest this.[1] The former says: αὐτὸς μὲν (ὁ 'Αριστοτέλης) τούτους τοὺς ἐγκειμένους συλλογισμοὺς δ' ἔδειξε προηγουμένως ἐν τῷ πρώτῳ σχήματι γινομένους, Θεόφραστος δὲ προστίθησιν ἄλλους πέντε τοῖς τέσσαρσι τούτοις οἰκέτι τελείους οὐδ' ἀναποδείκτους (i.e. not as the first four moods, evident without proof) ὄντας, ὧν μνημονεύει καὶ 'Αριστοτέλης—τῶν μὲν τριῶν τῶν κατ' ἀντιστροφὴν τῶν συμπερασμάτων γινομ. ὧν τοῦ τε πρώτου ἀναποδείκτου καὶ τοῦ δευτέρου καὶ τοῦ τρίτου ἐν τῷ δευτέρῳ κατὰ τὰς ἀρχάς[2]—τῶν δὲ καταλειπομένων δύο ἐν τούτοις[3] οἷς λέγει ὅτι – ἐν ταῖς ἀσυλλογίστοις (συζυγίαις) ταῖς ἐχούσαις τὸ ἀποφατικὸν καθόλου καὶ οὔσαις ἀνομοιοσχήμοσι (i.e. where the premises are of different quality) συνάγεταί τι ἀπὸ τοῦ ἐλάττονος ὅρου πρὸς τὸν μείζονα· αὗται δέ εἰσιν ἐν πρώτῳ σχήματι δύο συμπλοκαὶ ἥ τε ἐκ καθόλου καταφατικῆς τῆς μείζονος (sc. προτάσεως) καὶ καθόλου ἀποφατικῆς τῆς ἐλάττονος, καὶ ἡ ἐξ ἐπὶ μέρους καταφατικῆς τῆς μείζονος καὶ καθόλου ἀποφατικῆς τῆς ἐλάττονος·—ὧν τὸν μὲν ὄγδοον, τὸν δὲ ἔνατον Θεόφραστος λέγει.[4] Boëthius[5] says, habet enim prima figura

[1] Alex. *Ad Anal. Pri.* f. 27 b.   [2] *Anal. Pr.* ii. c. i.
[3] Ibid. i. c. vii.   [4] Cf. ibid. 42 b–13 a.
[5] *De Syll. Categ. Oper.* ed. Basil. 1516, p. 591.

sub se Aristotele auctore modos quatuor, sed Theophrastus
vel Eudemus super hos quatuor quinque alios modos addunt,
Aristotele dante principium in secundo priorum Analyticorum
volumine;[1] hoc autem, quod nuper dixiuus (viz. the conversion of the conclusion in Darii, Celarent and Barbara)
in secundo priorum Analyticorum libro ab Aristotele mon-
stratur, quod scilicet Theophrastus et Eudemus principium
capicutes ad alios in prima figura syllogismos adiicicudos
animum adiccere, qui sunt eiusmodi, qui κατὰ ἀνάκλασιν vocantur, i.e. per refractionem quandam conversionemque pro-
positionis (according to which Boëthius numbers the moods
V—IX).[1]

It is these five Moods which were afterwards separated from
the First Figure, and collected together under the *Fourth* or
Galen's Figure. Galen's own writings, so far as we have
them, do not show that he was the author of this mode of representation. All logicians of note in the whole of the later
antiquity down to Boëthius have followed the method of Theophrastus, and reckoned these five as moods of the First Figure.
There is no mention in the whole of ancient literature, with
the exception of two single notices discovered lately (of which
anon), that there is any other mode of representation. All
accounts of the much-talked of discovery by Galen, those two
notices excepted, go back to the testimony of the Arabian
philosopher *Averroës*, which in the old Latin translation is as
follows:[3]—Sin autem dicamus: A est in C, quoniam C est in B
et B in A, res erit, quam nemo naturaliter faciet;—et ex hoc
planum, quod figura quarta, *de qua meminit Galenus*, non est
syllogismus, super quem cadat naturaliter cogitatio.—Ad-
ducitur deinceps terminus medius, qui praedicetur de praedicato quaesiti et subiiciatur subiecto quaesiti, secundum quod
existimavit Galenus hanc figuram quartam esse, secundum quod

[1] Boëth. *De Syll. Categ. Oper.* ed. Basil. 1546, p. 595.
[2] Cf. Philop. *Ad Anal. Pri.* f. xxi. B; οἱ καλούμενοι ὑπτιανακλώμενοι.
Cf. Prantl, *Gesch. der Log.* i. 365 ff., 700).
[3] *Averr. Prior. Resol.* i. 8, f. 63 B, ed. Venet. 1553.

B B

refertur ad quaesitum. Of those two lately discovered passages, the modern Greek *Minnides Minas* has found the one in an unedited anonymous commentary on the Aristotelian Analytic, and has published it in his edition of the Pseudo-Galen's Εἰσαγωγὴ διαλεκτική.[1] The words are:—Θεόφραστος δὲ καὶ Εὔδημος καί τινας ἑτέρας συζυγίας (synonymous with τρόπους) παρὰ τὰς ἰντεθείσας τῷ 'Αριστοτέλει προστεθείκασι τῷ πρώτῳ σχήματι·—ἂν καὶ τέταρτον ἀποτελεῖν σχῆμα τῶν νεωτέρων ᾠήθησάν τινες ὡς πρὸς πατέρα τὴν δόξαν τὸν Γαληνὸν ἀναφέροντες. Minas has given nothing more exact about the Commentary, and so the time from which the extracted notice dates remains very uncertain.[2]

Prantl gives us the other passage in the second volume of his History of Logic in the West,[3] from a work of Johannes Italus (a later contemporary of Psellus), the Διάφορα Ζητήματα:[4] τὰ δὲ σχήματα τῶν συλλογισμῶν ταῦτα· ὁ Γαληνὸς δὲ καὶ τέταρτον ἐπὶ τούτοις ἔφασκεν εἶναι, ἐναντίως πρὸς τὸν Σταγειρίτην φερόμενος. It is certain that the *discoverer of this figure did not add it* as one 'lately found out' to those earlier known, but only presented what was already known in his time in a new form. He *divided* the nine moods of the First Figure, in the wider sense of Aristotle and Theophrastus, into two figures, the First in the stricter sense and the now so-called Fourth Figure. Galen in his endeavours to represent Logic as far as possible in a mathematical way:[5]—ἀκολουθῆσαι τῷ χαρακτῆρι τῶν γραμμικῶν ἀποδείξεων—might be led to this separate representation of the Fourth Figure.

The view which Trendelenburg asserts in a passage quoted above, that the division of Figures into four rests on the *external form* and *position* of the propositions, and presupposes *a settled course of succession* in the premises, is untenable. This principle would rather have led to a division into eight, a position to which Krug only has fallen (cf. above, p. 356). The division

[1] Paris, 1844.   [2] Προθεωρ. pag. νς'.
[3] Cf. Prantl, *Gesch. der Log.* i. 532 f.
[4] *Gesch. der Logik im Abendlande*, ii. 295.   [5] Fol. 330.
[6] *De Prop. Libr.* x. xix. 40 u.

into four rather involves complete freedom of external position and succession, and the principle of the division is distinguished from that of Aristotle and Theophrastus only by directly taking into consideration the universal distinction between the major and minor term, and the distinction between major and minor premise, which rests on the former. It neither depends on nor conditions an absolutely fixed external succession. The *Scholastic* term ' metathesis praemissarum ' signifies chiefly the *change of internal relation*, by which the premise which was the major premise (in the sense established by the definition) becomes the minor premise, and the former minor premise passes over into the major, the *external transposition of the propositions* being connected with this only as a useful formula to represent it.

The *Scholasticism of the Middle Ages*, which appropriated the syllogistic procedure, perhaps not with entire and thorough-going comprehension, but all the more with the most unbounded faith, allowed itself to be robbed of no Figure and of no Mood. The division of Theophrastus remains in use co-ordinate with the so-called Galen's division. Many of the *Humanists* and *Modern Philosophers*, on the other hand, in the first heat of the struggle against a form of culture which had outlived itself, threw overboard without distinction the whole (actual or imaginary) rubbish of Scholastic subtlety, amongst which many included Syllogistic. Others again, especially in later times, took a middle course; but, because for the most part they lacked the deeper understanding, they were led to an external via media rather than to a true mean. The syllogism was not abandoned because it was seen to be indispensable; but in order not to fall under the scorn of the ' Illumination,' and in order to make things more comfortable, its wings were clipped, as it were, and a certain respect only was paid to it. This uninteresting, dry, redundant treatment gradually increased, and brought syllogistic completely into contempt. Even Wolff, to whom strictness of syllogistic form was a desire of his heart as strong as that of the most zealous

Scholastic, and who himself eminently deserved the title of a
' demonstrator optimus,' which he gave to Joachim Jungius, the
author of the Logica Hamburgensis, an earlier logician, believed
that the tendency of the time had to be so far considered that
in his lesser Logic, written in German, he treated of the First
Figure only, and in his ampler Latin works the first three
figures, leaving unmentioned the moods of Theophrastus.
Wolff teaches[1] that the syllogisms of the First Figure are the
most natural, because they contain direct application of the
Dictum de omni et nullo. They are sufficient to establish all
possible conclusions. The First Figure is therefore *figura
perfecta*. The other two are *figurae imperfectae*, because they
contain only indirect applications of that axiom, and cannot
establish all kinds of conclusions, especially not the universally
affirmative, which is the most important for science. Their
moods do not all lead to a knowledge of the reason why the
predicate belongs to the subject, ' non continere rationem, unde
intelligitur, cur praedicatum conveniat subiecto.'[2] To this,
which agrees in all essentials with Aristotle's doctrine, Wolff,
going further, adds,[3] ' syllogismi *secundae*—syllogismi *tertiae*
figurae sunt syllogismi *cryptici primae* ;—apparet adeo, *non
opus esse, ut peculiares pro iis figurae constituantur.*'

In opposition to the preference which Wolff gives to the First
Figure, because it alone follows from the Dictum de omni et nullo,
Lambert, in his Neues Organon,[4] places the four figures on an
equality. He founds the Second Figure on a Dictum de Diverso :
' Things which are different do not belong to each other ;' the
Third on a Dictum de Exemplo: ' When one finds things A
which are B, then there are A which are B ;' the Fourth on a
Dictum de Reciproco : ' If no M is B, no B is this or that M ; if
C is or is not this or that B, there are B which are or are not C.'
With the help of diagrams (which, limited to straight lines and
points, are greatly inferior in didactic value to the circle sym-
bols) he seeks to show that the other figures are as capable of

¹ *Log.* § 378 sqq.   ² Ibid. § 399.
³ Ibid. §§ 385, 397.   ⁴ Leipzig, 1764.

immediate derivation from the nature of the axioms as the First. The First Figure is naturally and unconsciously used to prove qualities, the Second to prove differences, the Third to prove examples and conceptions, and the Fourth to prove reciprocities.

Kant, who did not much like the syllogistic form, advanced in some degree beyond the Wolffian axioms. In his treatise ' proving the false subtlety of the four syllogistic figures' (1762), he enunciated the axiom that *pure* rational inferences are possible in the First Figure only, and *mixed* inferences (ratiocinia *hybrida* or impura) in the other three,[1] and that division into figures generally, in so far as they contain simple pure inferences, without a medley of auxiliary judgments, is therefore false and impossible. It is not, as Kant in his treatise thinks, ' indisputable that all the figures, with the exception of the First, determine their consequences by a circumlocution and a medley of inferences coming in between.' The conclusion in the other figures may be directly found (as will afterwards be shown) without the need of reduction to the First. Even if that reduction was needed for the purpose of proving their correctness (as Kant, in agreement with older logicians, believed), they would as little lose their position as new and independent syllogistic figures, as would a mathematical axiom, which must found itself on an axiom proved earlier, necessarily sink to the place of a dependent corollary. The syllogisms of the last three figures would remain ' *simple*' syllogisms even if their *proof* had to be established by means of an auxiliary judgment, for the definition which makes the *simple* syllogism to be an inference from three terms only in two given judgments would be no less applicable. Hence they must be co-ordinate with syllogisms of the First Figure, as the other *kinds* of *simple syllogisms* (or, if one would question the correctness of this terminology, as *kinds* of *syllogisms from three terms*). The Aristotelian recognition of the less scientific value of these syllogisms is not incompatible with this co-ordination. The charge which Kant adds [2] is quite peculiar : If it happened that a number of inferences, which were blended together under the principal judgments, became so mixed up with them that when some were expressed others were unexpressed, it would take a great deal of art to judge of their agreement with the rules of inference, and one would be able to contrive not only more figures, but still more puzzling inferences, fit to break one's head. But the aim of Logic is not to confuse, but to solve, to advance something not in a concealed way but openly. Hence these four kinds of inference should be simple, not hybrid nor mixed up with secondary inferences, or else they cannot be allowed to appear in a logical statement as forms of the most significant representation of an 'inference of reason.'

This assertion rests on a complete misconception of the nature of the case. The charge resembles that which might be brought against Astronomy, if one were to blame it because it imagines such complicated cases, and enunciates such difficult calculations, that they rack the brains of learners instead of remaining stationary at the simplest and easiest statements. Since the heavenly bodies are not polite enough to wheel in circles, nor yet to avoid perturbations in order to spare the astronomer's headaches, his calculations must be adjusted to all the cases present. In the same way the problem of the logical doctrine of inference is to consider exhaustively the different cases which occur in actual thinking. When two judgments of definite form, having one notion common to both, are presented in the thoughts with which logical laws have to do, they are not always actually so placed as is most convenient for the purpose of forming an inference; they may have all different kinds of relations to each other. The different cases are not contrived by logicians, nor are they examples for the illustration of the notion of an inference of reason unhappily chosen and very confused; they represent the various possibilities which, although not all equally frequent, are yet realised in actual thought. For example, the historical critic lights upon the following testimonies of Aristotle. They come to him in a certain form which he cannot alter as he might in an artificial example

chosen according to one's fancy : ' Those natural philosophers
who affirm an existence between water and air to be the principle, account for the existence of individual essences by
rarefaction and condensation ; ' ' Anaximander on his principle
accounts for the existence of individuals not by rarefaction
and condensation, but by separation.' These propositions do
not belong to the scheme of the First Figure, and yet they
lead naturally to a definite and valuable conclusion. It belongs
to positive thinking to determine in every single case, whether
there is a valid inference or not, and it belongs to Logic to
lay down completely in an exhaustive division the different
relations possible, and to enunciate their universal laws.
Drobisch justly remarks in this reference [1] that it absolutely
belongs to the strictly scientific demands to develope *completely*
the possible forms of inference, because the *critical enquiry
into the value* of the single modes of inference can only depend
upon an *exhaustive survey.*

When several modern logicians, like *Hegel* and *Herbart*, and,
in spite of the assertion quoted above, *Drobisch* also, reject
the modes of inference of the Fourth Figure (or the moods of
Theophrastus), or, like *Trendelenburg*, reject the Third Figure
also or certain of its moods, we may recognise *this* truth,
that the scientific value of the debated modes of inference is
less in comparison with the others, but we may not for this
reason proceed to reject them altogether. The ambiguity and
danger of going wrong, which Trendelenburg says attaches to
them, although it does exist in most of them, and might exist
in Darii and Ferio of the First Figure, vanishes when we
strictly and accurately settle what belongs to the notion of the
particular judgment.

We cannot approve of Hegel's plan of making the Second
and Third Figures change places. The exchange is not
warranted by any internal necessity, and departure from use
and wont in these things only creates confusion.

[*Hamilton's* New Analytic of Logical forms makes Figure
only an unessential circumstance. For if the predicate be

[1] *Log.* 2nd ed. pref. xiii.

rigidly quantified, then the copula marking the relation of
subject and predicate may be dispensed with, and the algebraical sign of equality (=) may be used instead. When this is
done, we may have terms which are not related as subject and
predicate, and inferences which do not belong to any Figure.
Hence syllogisms are either: (1) *Unfigured*, where the terms
are both subject or both predicate, or either indifferently;
where there is no order of terms, for they may be enounced
first or second indifferently; and where all difference of major
and minor term or proposition is abolished. For example,
One who practically adopts the utilitarian theory of Ethics in
solving difficulties in morals, and one who acknowledges this
theory, are equivalent; Kant and one who practically adopts
the utilitarian theory of Ethics in solving difficulties in morals
are equivalent: therefore Kant and one who acknowledges
this theory are equivalent (Mill's argument).—(2) *Figured*
where two forms of syllogism result by different orders of
terms:—(*a*) First Figure, where two forms of conclusion are
possible. For here the middle term is subject of the one
extreme and predicate of the other, and there is a determinate
major extreme and premise, and a determinate minor extreme
and premise: consequently, also, one proximate indirect, and
one remote or indirect conclusion,—the latter by the conversion of the former.—(*b*) *Second and Third* Figures are the
reverse of the first. They have no major and minor extreme
and premise, both extremes being subjects or predicates of the
middle: consequently, in the inference, as either extreme
may be indifferently subject or predicate of the other, there are
two indifferent conclusions, that is, conclusions neither of which
is more direct or indirect than the other. Hamilton abolishes
the Fourth Figure as a hybrid and as useless.[1]

De Morgan adopts the four figures because the external
combination of three terms in two propositions (the premises)
gives four combinations. He seems to say that the Fourth
Figure is the more natural.[2]]

[[1] *Lect. on Log.* ii. 404.   [2] *Formal Logic,* p. 130.]

§ 104. Each of the two premises of the categorical syllogism in reference to quantity and quality may be of four different forms;—of the form:

    a, i.e. All A are B;

or of the form:

    e, i.e. No A is B;

or of the form:

    i, i.e. At least a part of A is B

      (At least one or some A are B);

or of the form:

    o, i.e. At least a part of A is not B

      (At least one or some A are not B).

Hence in each of the two divisions of the first class and in each of the other classes there are sixteen, in all sixty-four, *forms of combining the premises.* If the *first* letters symbolise the form (quantity and quality) of the *major premise* (which contains the major term, i.e. that notion which forms the predicate in the conclusion whose existence we prove), and the *second* letters the form of the *minor premise* (which contains the minor term or subject of the conclusion), the sixteen combinations may be represented in the following Schema:—

a a	e a	i a	o a
a e	e e	i e	o e
a i	e i	i i	o i
a o	e o	i o	o o

These forms of combination lead only partially to valid syllogisms. The single modes of inference or kinds of

syllogistic figure which rest on the different forms of
combination of the premises in reference to quantity
and quality, are called *moods* (modi, τρόποι τῶν σχη-
μάτων).

The repeated reference to the meanings of the symbols:
a, e, 1, o, and of the expressions *major premise* and *minor premise*, is justified by the fact that embarrassing mistakes so
frequently arise about them.

The *procedure by combination* borrowed from Mathematics
(which was probably first brought into use by the Peripatetic
Aristo of Alexandria)[1] has been very much condemned. It
has been called mechanical and irrational. *Prantl*[2] calls it a
'Game of Mosaic' which 'fundamentally disavows the Aristotelian middle notion,' and compares it to what he calls the
'combination-game of the childish imbecile Stoics,' &c.; but
incorrectly. It is true that the chief matter of interest
for syllogistic does not lie in the single figures and moods, but
in the universal principles of syllogistic. But the *principle*
itself expands into the system. If it be justly considered that
something valuable has been done when natural science, by
empirical collection of the discoverable species to any one
genus, has reached complete cognition, how much higher must
the gain be when we succeed in reducing the forms possible to
a universal principle, and in proving with mathematical accuracy the completeness of the enumeration? Syllogistic is able
to do this in its province; and procedure by mathematical
combination is an indispensable instrument. The nature of
the thing demands this, and it is quite in conformity with
reason. The charge of 'mechanism' and its external appearance need not alarm us. He who will have nothing to do
with 'mechanism,' where it properly exists, is in danger of
giving himself up to mere abstractions, as Hegel does in the
physical, and more especially in the astronomical parts of his
natural philosophy. Is then 'the mechanical' a necessary
and unavoidable presupposition in all the departments of

[1] Cf. Prantl, *Gesch. der Logik*, i. 557, 500.   [2] Ibid.

organic and spiritual life? The expression of Lotze's which is the fundamental conception of his ' Mikrokosmos '[1] gives the true answer : ' *The mechanism is nowhere the essence of the thing ; but the essence never presents itself in any other form of finite existence than that which is supplied by the mechanism.*'

§ 105. The *testing* whether a given combination leads to valid inferences, and the *proof* of the validity or invalidity, must depend upon the *comparison of the spheres*, within which, according to the premises, the notions under consideration find application. These spheres suitable for that comparison are made apparent to the senses by geometrical figures (especially by circles), whose reciprocal relations agree with the relations of the spheres of the notions to each other in all relations essential for demonstration.

It has been already remarked above[2] that this kind of comparison of spheres in no way presupposes a thorough-going making substantive predicate notions. The possibility remains of placing the whole procedure (as *Aristotle* does),[3] under the point of view of a subsumption of lower notions, under similar higher ones,—or (as *Kant* does, who explains the axiom : ' nota notae est nota rei ipsius ; repugnans notae repugnat rei ipsi,'[4] to be the principle of all categorical inferences of the reason)[5] of regarding it from the point of view of an advance in thought from attribute to attribute, or from predicate to predicate[6];— or, lastly (as *Trendelenburg* does),[7] of uniting both points of view

[1] *Mikrok.* L 437 ; 2nd ed. L 451.   [2] § 71.
[3] *Anal. Pri.* l. c. iv. sqq.
[4] Which Aristotle had already enunciated and with a more accurate apprehension. Cf. *Categ.* c. iii.
[5] *Die falsche Spitzfindigkeit d. vier Syllog. Fig. erwiesen*, § 2 ; *Log.* § 63.
[6] [Which is almost Mr. Mill's opinion. See *Log.* L 201.]
[7] *Log. Unters.* 2nd ed. ii. 315 ff.; 3rd ed. ii. 348 ff.

and recognising in the conclusion a reference of the content to
extent, and of the extent to the content.[1] In the different
single examples, where the syllogistic form is the same, sometimes the one, sometimes the other, and sometimes the third
view, will be the more suitable, according as the predicate
denotes (a) in both the *genus* of the subject, or (b) in both an
action or *property*, or (c) in the major premise an action or
property, and in the minor the *genus*. The three following
syllogisms are all categorical of the First Figure (and the
mood Barbara), and yet they fall naturally successively under
the view of subsumption, of inherence, and of the (subsuming)
subjection of the particular under the (inhering) predicate or
law of the universal:—(1) Every planet is a heavenly body ;
the earth is a planet ; Therefore it is a heavenly body.—(2)
All right-angled triangles have such a relation of their sides
that the square of the hypothenuse is equal to the sum of the
squares of the other two sides ; All triangles which may be
inscribed in a semicircle, so that one side is the diameter, are
right-angled ; Hence they have this relation of sides discovered
by Pythagoras. (Triangles in order to be inscribed in a
semicircle are not to be subsumed as a *species* under the *genus*
right-angled triangles, but are identical with them ; the inference proceeds from *property* to *property*.)—(3) All similar
triangles have the same relation of sides : those triangles, into
which the right-angled triangle is divided by the perpendicular
from the vertex of the right angle to the hypothenuse, are
similar to each other (and also to the whole, which has been
divided) ; therefore they have the same relation of sides.

Aristotle makes the relation of spheres the foundation for
syllogisms of the First Figure, reduces those of the other
figures to the First, and proves the invalidity of the forms of
combination not suitable for inference, by producing examples,
in which a conclusion is yielded and supposed to be valid,

[1 As Hamilton substantially does, with the difference that he does
not unite the two opinions and make them the basis of one syllogistic
procedure, but separates it into two orders of syllogisms, those in
Extension and those in Comprehension.]

while its material falsehood is recognised in some other way. This demonstration is convincing in so far as the hypothesis of the validity is overthrown by the falsehood of one of its consequences. It lies under a twofold difficulty, however: (1) that for the sake of the proof, a datum more than was demanded must be added; (2) the ground of the knowledge of the invalidity does not correspond to its real ground.

Later logicians base the rules for the rejection upon certain fundamental axioms (viz. that the middle notion may not be particular in both premises, and must not stand in a merely negative relation to the other terms, and that no term is to be taken in the conclusion in a more universal extent than in the corresponding premises), which result from a comparison of spheres, and this comparison of spheres is applied by means of the definitions in § 71. But the immediate comparison of spheres in each of the individual rules is the more convenient.

[*Hamilton*, by a thorough-going application of the quantification of the predicate, gets rid of the ordinary rules of syllogism, and shows the validity of several moods which are commonly rejected. No syllogism can be formally wrong in which: (1) Both premises are not negative; and (2) The quantifications of the middle term, whether as subject or predicate, taken together exceed the quantity of the term taken in its whole extent. These two simple rules being obeyed, no syllogism can be bad. Its premises hold good in any mutual subordination, and may be of any figure. The result is an increase of the logical moods. For the doctrine of the quantification of the predicate gives eight instead of four propositional forms to begin with; and when these eight forms are combined according to position, quantity, and quality, they give *thirty-six valid moods* (twelve affirmative and twenty-four negative); and these thirty-six are valid in each figure.][1]

The history of the comparison of spheres by means of *geometrical schemata* has already been explained at § 85, p. 234 f.

[[1] Cf. Hamilton's *Lect. on Log.* ii. 359-57, 457-60, 475, 476; and Prof. Baynes' *New Analytic of Logical Forms*, p. 74.]

§ 106. On application of this means of testing, we
find that in all the figures of the categorical syllogism
no inference can be drawn from merely negative premises.
‘Ex mere negativis nihil sequitur.’ For—

(a) If *both* premises are *universally negative,* then the
middle notion (M), which (according to §§ 100 and
102) must enter once into each of the two premises as
subject or predicate, must be thought to be completely
separated from the other two premises (A and B); and
the relation of these to each other remains wholly undetermined. The premises admit of the three possible
cases: (1) that the sphere of the one of the two extremes is quite separate from that of the other; (2) that
the one lies partly within and partly without that of the
other; and (3) that the one falls quite within that
of the other. This is represented by the following
Schema:—

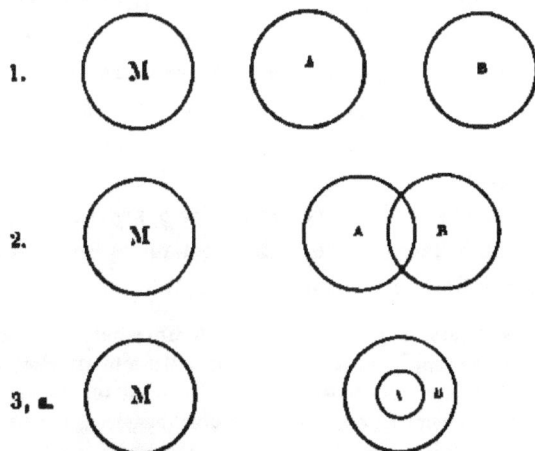

3, b. (M) ((B) A)

3, a. (M) (A   B)

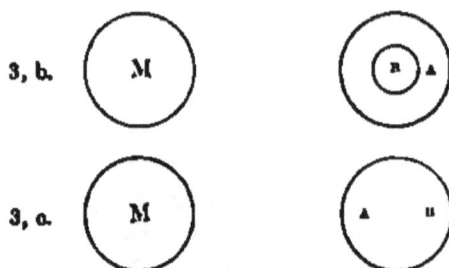

Hence there is no definite relation between A and B, which can be expressed in a valid conclusion.

(b) If the *one* premise be *universally* and the other *particularly denied*, then M must be thought to be quite separated from one of the two terms and (at least) partly separated from the other. But the partial validity of the negation, according to the logical notion of the particular judgment (§§ 70 and 71), never excludes the possibility of the universal negation, and does not necessarily include the validity of the particular affirmation. Hence the whole indeterminateness, which exists between two universally negative premises, remains, and is still more increased by the additional possibility of other relations. Consequently a definite result is still less given.

(c) If *both* premises are *particularly negative*, then, for the same reason, the indefiniteness is increased. Hence no definite conclusion can result.

If the particular negative judgment meant: *only* some are not, but others are, it would then yield a definite conclusion, provided the other premise was universally negative. It would then not be the consequence of the double negation, however, but of the particular affirmation implicitly thought along with it.

The axiom: *ἐν ἅπαντι (συλλογισμῷ) δεῖ κατηγορικόν τινα τῶν ὅρων εἶναι* was enunciated by *Aristotle*.[1] Now there is of course a case in which a valid conclusion may be obtained from two *negative premises*. If the premises are given: What is not M is not P; and: S is not M—the inference follows: S is not P. But this inference does not fall under our above-given definition of the *simple* syllogism (§ 100), as a syllogism from three terms; for there are here four terms: S, P, M, and not-M (that, which is not M). If this is reduced to a simple syllogism, the minor premise must (by means of an immediate inference per acquipollentiam, cf. § 96) take the form: S is a not-M. But then it is according to quality an *affirmative* judgment (§ 69), and the rule, that from merely negative premises nothing can follow in a simple syllogism, may remain unchanged. This reduction is not an artificial mean, contrived in order to violently reconcile an actual exception to a rule falsely considered to be universally valid. We only arrive naturally at the conclusion, when we think the minor premise in the form: S falls under the notion of those beings which are not M.

The *old logicians* have already noticed this case, and have sought to solve the difficulty by this very reduction. Boëthius says:[2] 'Sed fuerunt, qui hoc quum ex multis aliis, tum ex aliquo Platonis syllogismo colligerent;—in quodam enim dialogo Plato huiusmodi interrogat syllogismum: sensus, inquit, non contingit rationem substantiae; quod non contingit rationem substantiae, ipsius veritatis notionem non contingit; sensus igitur veritatis notionem non contingit. Videtur enim ex omnibus negativis fecisse syllogismum, quod fieri non potest, atque ideo aiunt, infinitum verbum, quod est: *non-contingit*, pro participio infinito posuisse, id est: *non-contingens est*;—et id quidem *Alexander Aphrodisieus* arbitratur ceterique complures.' It is not improbable that the doctrine of qualitative *Acquipollence* between two judgments owes its origin to the explanation of the syllogistic case.

[1] *Anal. Pri.* i. 21.
[2] *Ad Arist. de Interpr.* p. 403; Prantl, *Gesch. der Log.* i. § 555.

In the Middle Ages *Duns Scotus* combated the universal validity of the rule: Ex mero negativis nihil sequitur, on the ground of that case.

Wolff enunciates the axiom:[1] si terminus medius fuerit negativus, propositio minor infinita est (negandi particula non refertur ad copulam, sed ad praedicatum),[2] and remarks:[3] equidem non ignoro, esse qui sibi persuadeant, steriles esse nugas, quae de propositionibus infinitis aliisque aequipollentibus in doctrina syllogistica dicuntur, eum in finem excogitatas, ut per praecipitantiam statutae regulae salventur; but justly repels this view because his doctrine necessarily follows from the notions of the terms. The later logicians have superficially passed over this question.

According to the rule established in the foregoing paragraphs, the premises in the following forms of combination cannot lead to valid inferences :—

e e   o e
e o   o o

The sixteen possible forms of combination are therefore already reduced (§ 104), in so far as the combination consists of those only from which an inference can be obtained, to the following twelve :—

a a   e a   i a   o a .
a e   i e
a i   e i   i i   o i
a o   i o

According to other criteria 'certain other forms must be eliminated.

§ 107. In all figures of the simple categorical syllogism, *no valid inference results if both premises are particular.* 'Ex mere particularibus nihil sequitur.' For—

Log. § 377.   [2] Ibid. § 208.   [3] Ibid. § 877.

c c

(a) If both are *particularly affirmative*, then only an indefinite part of the sphere of the middle notion is united with an indefinite part of the spheres of either of the two remaining terms. If the middle term is the subject in any one of the premises, or in both, the assertion holds good, according to the particular form of the judgment for an indefinite part only of the sphere of the middle notion. If it is predicate, the same indefiniteness arises from a more universal reason, because in every affirmative judgment it remains unexpressed whether the sphere of the predicate wholly or only partially coincides with the sphere of the subject (cf. § 71). Hence it remains indefinite whether the same part of the middle notion or a different part is united with the two other terms in the two premises, and it is also uncertain in what relation they stand to each other. Hence no conclusion is obtained.

(b) If the one premise is *particularly affirmative* and the other *particularly negative,* it is also indefinite with what part of the sphere of the middle notion the one extreme is particularly connected, and from what part of this sphere (if the middle notion is the subject in the other premise) the other extreme is separated, or whether the middle notion (if it makes the predicate in the other premise), while it is quite separated from a part of the sphere of the other extreme, is also, wholly, in part, or not at all, separated from the other part of this sphere. If it is also uncertain, whether the two extremes have any definite relation to one and the same part of the middle notion or not, the relation in which they stand to each other is the more uncertain. Hence, again, no definite conclusion can be reached.

(c) If *both premises* are *particularly negative*, then, partly because of the indefiniteness which lies in the particularity of both premises, and partly because of the negative nature of both premises (§ 109), no valid inference results.

Since the ground of the proof of the invalidity lies in the *indefiniteness* of the parts of the spheres, it follows that one can apply to it the axiom of the paragraph on those *singular* judgments whose subject is something denoted by its universal notion, but is an individual left indeterminate, i.e. those singular judgments which (§ 70) fall under the wider notion of the particular. This indefiniteness, however, has nothing to do with those judgments whose subject is an individual designated individually (e.g. by a proper name), i.e. with those which are not to be reckoned individuals but generals.

Aristotle expressed the axiom that no syllogism can be without a universal premise in these words:[1] ἐν ἅπαντι συλλογισμῷ δεῖ τὸ καθόλου ὑπάρχειν. Later logicians have more universally based the proof which Aristotle adduced in examples of individuals only, on the relations of the spheres.

The forms of combination which must be rejected according to this rule, besides o o, which has been already eliminated by the rule of the preceding paragraph, are the three following:—

$$\begin{matrix} \text{i i} & & \text{o i} \\ \text{i o} & & \end{matrix}$$

So that according to this the following nine forms remain:—

$$\begin{matrix} \text{a a} & \text{e a} & \text{i a} & \text{o a} \\ \text{a e} & & \text{i e} & \\ \text{a i} & \text{e i} & & \\ \text{a o} & & & \end{matrix}$$

But all of them do not lead to valid conclusions.

[1] *Anal. Pr.* i. 24.

c c 2

§ 108. Lastly, in all figures *the combination of a particular major premise with a negative minor premise does not lead to a valid inference.* For—

(a) If the *major premise is particularly affirmative*, and the *minor premise universally negative*, the middle notion M, according to the major premise, whether it form its subject or predicate, is connected with an indefinite part of the sphere of one extreme A (cf. § 71; cf. 107), but, according to the minor premise, is completely separated from the other extreme B, according to the following Schema:—

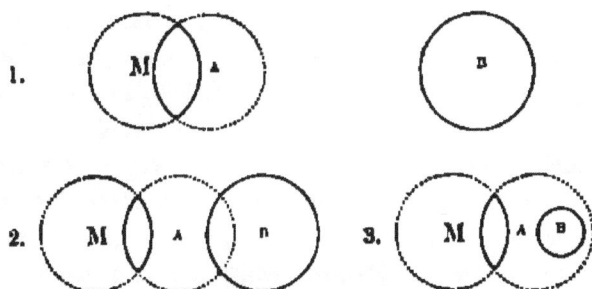

Here there is a conclusion whose subject is A and whose predicate is B: (At least) some A, viz. those which coincide with M, are not B, because it is quite separated from all M, and must, therefore, also be separated from those A which coincide with M. There is no conclusion, however, whose subject is B and whose predicate is A, because it remains undetermined, according to the premises, whether B is also quite separated from the remaining A, and therefore from the whole sphere of the notion A, or partly coincides with it, or finally falls wholly within it. In other words, it is quite undetermined whether no в are A, whether some в are A and others are not, or, lastly, whether all в are A. The particular negative conclusion which is actually drawn : Some A are not в, does not, according to the general rule (§ 88), admit of Conversion. In order to reduce these two relations, the validity of the inference from A to в and the impossibility of an inference from в to A, to one short general expression, that logical terminology must be applied, which designates the two extremes (A and в) in their distinction from each other according to the presupposed universal form of the conclusion, whose possibility is yet to be tested. This terminology calls that notion, which is to be the subject in the conclusion, the minor term (S), and that which is to be the predicate, the major term (P); and in this way determines the major and minor premises. According to this terminology, if the universal form A в is taken for the conclusion, and the validity of such an inference, as well as the more determinate form which the valid conclusion must take (whether a, e, i or o), is tested, A is the minor notion (S), в the major notion (P), and that premise which contains the A is the minor premise, and the other the major premise. Now if, according to the presupposition, the premise with A is particularly affirmative, and that with в particularly negative; the valid inference (some A are not в) is here attained from a particular affirmative *minor* premise and a universal negative major premise. But if the opposite from в A is laid down as the basis of the conclusion, and the investigation carried on, whether a similar con-

clusion in any more definite form (a, e, i or o) results
from the premises, then A may all the more be designated the major term (P), and the premise which
contains A the major premise, and D the minor premise
(S), and the premise which contains D the minor premise. This testing has now shown that no valid conclusion of the form B A results from the above premises.
The result may also be expressed: The combination of
a particular affirmative *major premise* (the premise
with A) and of a universal negative *minor premise* (the
premise with D) does not lead to a valid inference. And
this is what was to be proved.

(b) If the *major premise is particularly negative*, no
valid conclusion results because of the negative character
of both premises (§ 106).

(c) If the *minor premise is particularly negative*, no
valid conclusion results because of the particularity of
both premises.

This demonstration could have been reduced to a shorter
form by the immediate introduction of the signs S and P. It
seems important, however, because many misunderstandings
have owed their origin to these designations, to state thoroughly
the actual relation of the case, and to prevent the charge
(however unfounded) of an *hysteron-proteron*, which might
have been made. If the artificial expressions: *major notion,
minor notion, major premise, minor premise,* are to be avoided,
the paragraph might be headed: from the combination of
a particular and of a negative premise no inference of such
a form can result, that the notion, united in the particular
premise with the middle notion, is the predicate of the conclusion, and the notion united with the same in the negative
premise is the subject of the conclusion. But there is no
tenable reason for avoiding that terminology. Etymology

does not define the meaning of scientific expressions; Definition does. According to this definition the heading of the paragraph only asserts in a more precise form what the axiom just enunciated does; for it substitutes their definitions for the logical technical expressions under consideration.

According to the preceding paragraph, in every figure four forms of combination are rejected, viz. i e, i o, o e, and o o, if the last three were not already excluded by the former rules. There is, therefore, added to the earlier eliminations one new one, viz.:—

i e

So that there remain the following forms only:—

a a   e a   i a   o a
a e
a i   e i
a o

Among these eight forms of combination of the premises there is none which would be absolutely incapable of leading to a valid conclusion in any figure, and therefore must, in universal reference, be eliminated. But some of the eight forms of the preceding schemes are to be excluded in each of the figures according to the especial rules of these figures.

The rules for the relation of the form of a valid conclusion to the form of the premises (e.g. to the rule: ‘conclusio sequitur partem debiliorem’) must, if they are to be proved with full logical strictness, be established on a comparative survey of the individually valid modes of inference, and are therefore to be mentioned below (§ 118).

§ 109. *The First Figure in the stricter sense*, or the *first division of the first principal class* of the *First Figure in the wider sense*, does not lead to a valid inference when the *major premise* (M P) is *particular* and when the *minor premise* (S M) is *negative*. For—

(a) When the *major premise* is *particular and affirma-*

tive, or *particular and negative*, then the predicate P is affirmed or denied of a *part* of the sphere of the middle notion M; and the minor premise, which in this case according to the general rules (§§ 106–108) must be universally affirmed, asserts that the sphere of S falls wholly within the sphere of M, without determining in *what part of the sphere* of M. Hence it remains uncertain whether S falls within that part of M of which the major premise has affirmed or denied the predicate P, or within the other part of which nothing has been determined, or partly within the one and partly within the other part of M.

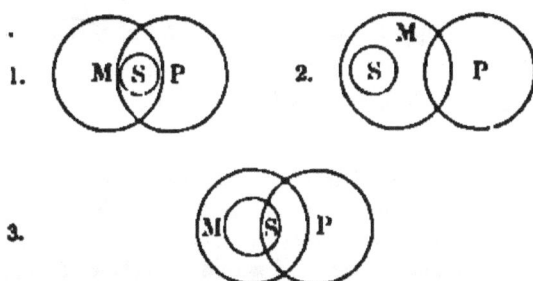

Therefore the relation subsisting between S and P also remains quite indeterminate.

(b) When the *minor premise* is *negative*, then, whether it is universal or particular, S is wholly or (at least) partly separated from M. But M is subsumed under P by the major premise, which must be both affirmative (§ 106) and (§ 108) universal, while it is left undetermined whether, and how far, the sphere of P stretches beyond that of M. Hence it remains also indeterminate in what relation S stands to P, and no conclusion can result from the form S P. The Schema for the case relatively conformable to the least indeterminate, and, in particular premises, the case always possible, is the following:—

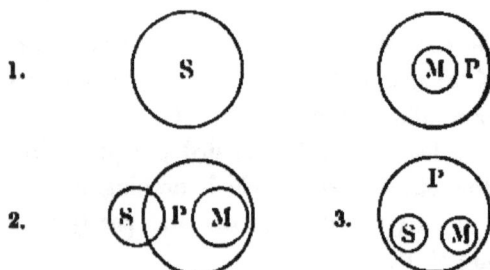

Hence it may happen that no S is P, and also that some S are P, others not, and, lastly, that all S are P. Hence nothing definite can be asserted of the relation of S to P.

If we look on S and P as indifferent signs only of the two extremes, and use them as A and B, the following valid inference will always result from the last Schema: (At least) some P (those namely which fall within the sphere of M) are not S, or: Some B are not A. But this conclusion does not properly belong to the First Figure in the stricter sense, or to the first division of the first chief division, but to its second division, or to the so-called Fourth Figure. For the first P or B in relation to this form of the conclusion is now become the minor notion (S), and the first S or A the major notion (P). Hence, if the first minor notion is become the major notion, and the major the minor, the external position or succession may remain unchanged, and the middle notion is now predicate to the major, or is in the major premise, and subject to the minor, or in the minor premise. Consequently the Fourth Figure (in the moods Fesapo and Fresison) arises.

The forms of combination, which accordingly fall outside of

the First Figure, are 1 a, 0 a; a e, a o. Hence there
remain the four following only :—

$$a\ a \qquad\qquad e\ a$$
$$a\ i \qquad\qquad e\ l$$

It must now be shown that these necessarily lead to valid
inferences.

§ 110. The First Mood of the First Figure has the
form a a a, i.e. its premises are a universal affirmative
major premise, a universal affirmative minor premise,
and its conclusion is likewise a universal affirmative
judgment.   Hence the universal Schema of the First
Figure :

$$\begin{array}{cc} M & P \\ S & M \\ \hline S & P \end{array}.$$

takes here the more definite form—

$$\begin{array}{ccc} M & a & P \\ S & a & M \\ \hline S & a & P \end{array}$$

This mood bears the scholastic name *Barbara*, which
is formed so that its initial letter, as the first *consonant* of the alphabet, shows it to be the first mood,
and the *vowels* of the three syllables (a, a, a) denote in
their succession the logical form of major premise, minor
premise and conclusion.   The other letters are inserted
for the sake of euphony.   The comparison of spheres
shows the validity of this mood.   For every universal
affirmative judgment presupposes (according to § 71)
one of two relations of spheres whose Schema is—

1.   2.

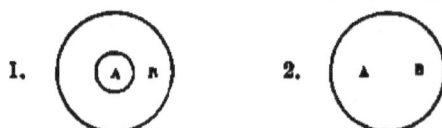

i. e. the predicate в is always present where the subject A is, while it is left undetermined whether other existences besides have or have not the same predicate. Hence the Schema of the two combined judgments—

$$\text{M} \quad \mathbf{a} \quad \text{P}$$
$$\text{S} \quad \mathbf{a} \quad \text{M}$$

is the following :—

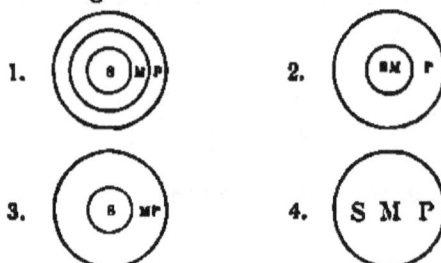

1.   2.

3.   4.   S M P

It remains generally undetermined which of these four relations belongs to a given single example; but since in every one of the four possible cases such a relation exists, that the predicate P belongs to every S, the conclusion—

$$\text{S} \quad \mathbf{a} \quad \text{P}$$

follows in a strictly necessary way from the premises; which was to be proved.

This is the mood which is used most frequently, and in the most important cases, in the sciences and in common life, though commonly in an abbreviated (enthymemic) form, and without logical consciousness.

The comparison of spheres by means of circles as little presupposes that the notions compared are made substantives, as it did in the case of single judgments (see above, § 71). The different ways of apprehending, represented by *Aristotle*, *Kant*, and *Trendelenburg* (see above at § 105), may exist coordinately with it.

The four following syllogisms may serve as *examples* of the *four relations of extent possible.* The comparison is made easier and more evident by the fact that they have been so chosen that the middle term (M) (viz. Triangles, in which the angles of the one are equal to the angles of the other each to each) is the same in all of them. The premises will take the position which is here the most natural, tho *minor premise* always *precedes the major.*

1. Those triangles, into which the right-angled triangle is divided by the perpendicular from the vertex of the right angle on the hypothenuse, are triangles whose angles are equal each to each. All triangles whose angles are equal each to each other are figures which are similar to each other. Hence those parts of the right-angled triangle are figures which are similar to each other.

2. All triangles, the relations of whose sides are equal each to each, are triangles whose angles are equal each to each. All triangles whose angles are the same each to each, are figures which are similar to each other. Hence all triangles, the relations of whose sides are equal each to each, are figures which are similar to each other.

3. Those triangles, into which a right-angled triangle is divided by the perpendicular from the vertex of the right angle to the hypothenuse, are triangles whose angles are equal each to each. All triangles whose angles are equal each to each, are triangles in all respects similar. Hence those triangles which are made by that division of a right angle are triangles in all respects similar.

4. All triangles, the relations of whose sides are equal each to each, are triangles whose angles are equal each to each. All triangles whose angles are equal each to each, are similar to each other. Hence, all triangles, the relations of whose sides are equal each to each, are similar to each other.

The second and fourth cases occur more especially when the middle notion is an individual notion, and when either a universal or an individual predicate is attached to it in the major premise. The first German teacher of the differential calculus is Leibniz. Leibniz is the author of the system of Monadology. Therefore, &c. He who founded syllogistic was Aristotle. Aristotle was the most influential tutor and trainer of Alexander the Great. Therefore, &c.

In order to show the significance of this first mood of the First Figure in scientific knowledge, the following examples from the different sciences may be given.

Direct mathematical demonstrations for affirmative theorems are given exclusively in syllogisms of this mood. The logical analysis in such demonstrations and attempts at demonstration, where an oversight easily occurs, has a special interest, and we will therefore choose as an example a course of reasoning having to do with the well-known *eleventh axiom of Euclid.* This axiom asserts, that two straight lines (A B and C D), thought as infinite, in the same plane, which are intersected by a third line (F F), so that the two interior angles on the one side of the intersecting line (B G H and D H G) are together less than two right angles, must intersect each other on this side.

It was early recognised that this axiom is not so evident as the others. It does not assert something about a self-contained figure, which is at once presented in the very intuition. In the axiom that two straight lines which cut each other diverge continually from the common point, it is only requisite for

intuition to follow the construction from distance to distance,
each time as far as it directly witnesses for the assertion, in the
faith that what now holds good will hold good from this distance onwards; but more is needed here. It is demanded that
an intersection which, in a very small divergence of the sum
of the interior angles from two right angles, does not exist
at a very great distance, does exist at a position lying at an indefinite distance further off, where immediate perception cannot be sure that it is correct, while the axiom is recognised to
hold good for all cases on the ground of this intuition. This
undeniably requires proof. The eleventh axiom of Euclid
may be divided into an axiom and a theorem annexed. It may
be taken as an axiom, that if any third line (E F) which intersects the two lines (I K and C D) makes the corresponding
angles equal, then any other line (O L) which intersects the
two makes the corresponding angles equal. From this follow
the theorems, that the external angle of a rectilineal plane triangle is equal to the sum of the two interior and remote angles,
and that the sum of the three angles of a triangle are equal to
two right angles. It also follows conversely that if one of
these axioms be taken to be an axiom, the axiom from which
they are deduced would also follow from them. On the basis
of these axioms a stringent proof may be led for what is asserted
in the eleventh axiom of Euclid. But the proposition given,
which approaches nearer the axiomatic character than the
eleventh axiom of Euclid, is too complicated to be considered a
perfect axiom. What it affirms is conditioned by the nature
of the straight line and of the angle. The true element, to
which the special task in the construction of the axiom is to be
referred, must lie in this nature. But this reference is accomplished most conveniently by the introduction of a *notion* (new
to the representation of Euclid)—the notion of *direction*. The
straight line is defined to be a line originating by the motion
of a point in a constant direction, the angle is defined to be the
distinction of directon of two straight lines intersecting each
other, and parallels are defined to be lines of the same direction.[1]

[1] It is to be understood, that the notion of *direction*, which is con-

On the basis of this definition it is to be proved, that the line A B, if the sum of the angles D G H + D H G < 2 R, must at an indefinite distance intersect the line C D on the side of E F on which B lies.

Let the straight line I K be drawn through the point G in the same direction as C D. The following syllogisms may then be constructed:—

1. Like directions have like distances of direction; the directions of G K and H D, of G H and H F, are like directions; hence they have like distances of direction, i. e. angle K G H = D H F.

2. Adjacent angles are together equal to two right angles; the angles D H F and D H G are adjacent angles; therefore D H F + D H G = 2 R.

3. Equal magnitudes may be substituted for each other;

ditioned by the tendency of the motion (but is not *identical* with the notion of straight line), is not itself capable of a definition of such a kind, that proofs *led in the way of Euclid* may be built on it. The argument has rather the character of a philosophical explanation of notions, and in mathematical consideration falls short of an axiomatic. This will not be concealed by a notion newly introduced, but will be introduced in the most elementary form possible. The course of thought: the angle is a quantity of turning, therefore advance in a straight line is without influence on the sum of the angles, therefore the sum of the external angles of a triangle = 4 R, and the sum of the angles of a triangle = 2 R, is essentially the same as the above. A demonstration built on this course of thought would have this preference to the one given above (which may be expressed in fewer syllogisms), that the notion of equality of direction may be used without definition as something immediately understandable only when applied to the constancy of the direction of the motion of a point advancing in a straight line, and of the motions of two lines proceeding from different points. If it is used with this application, the attribute of the equality of the angle which the lines make with an intersecting line is contained in it, and so is the axiom referred to above, that the angles which the lines then make with any other line intersecting them are equal to each other. This axiom (aequipollent with the proposition that the three angles of a triangle = 2 R) is the natural prius of the eleventh 'axiom' of Euclid.

the angles K G H and D H F are equal magnitudes (according to 1): therefore they can be substituted for each other.

Let us substitute accordingly in an inference like No. 2 K G H for D H F then K G H + D H G = 2 R.

4. According to the hypothesis B G H + D H G < 2 R. If now the proposition about substitutions is taken as the major premise, and the result reached above, that K G H + D H G = 2 R, is taken as the minor premise, and the conclusion drawn, it follows that B G H + D H G < K G H + D H G.

5. The subtraction of an equal from a less leaves a less. The subtraction of the angle D H G from the sum of B G H + D H G is the subtraction of an equal from a less in comparison with the subtraction of the angle D H G from the sum of K G H + D H G; hence a less remains, i.e. B G H < K G H.

6. Two unequal angles in one plane, which have the vertex and one line common, and lie on the same side of the common line, must so lie that the other line of the lesser angle projects from the vertex between the two lines of the greater. (For the greater difference of direction corresponds to the wider turning of the side of the angle around the vertex, and the smaller to the smaller.) The angles B G H and K G H are two angles of this kind. Hence they must lie so that G B falls between G H and G K. (The diagram shows it immediately: It could not, however, as self-evident, exempt us from the necessity of a proof.)

7. Vertical angles are equal to each other: the angles D H F and C H G are vertical angles, and therefore equal to each other.

If K G H were substituted for D H F (according to 3) then we should have K G H = C H G. And since the propositions which establish the conclusion contain nothing which would not be quite as true for every position and distance of lines of the like direction (I K and C D) and of the intersecting one (E F), this result may be universally expressed: Reciprocal angles in lines of the like direction are equal to each other.

8. Reciprocal angles in lines of the like direction are equal to each other; the angles K G L (K G L₁, K G L₂, &c.) and

II L G (II L$_1$ G, II L$_2$ G, &c.) are reciprocal angles in lines of a like direction, and therefore of a like direction.

The points L$_1$, L$_2$, L$_3$, &c. may be so defined that II L$_1$ = II G, L$_1$ L$_2$ = L$_1$ G, L$_2$ L$_3$ = L$_2$ G, and so on ad infinitum. We may then further conclude :—

8. Isosceles triangles have equal angles at the base. (The proof of this is independent of the eleventh axiom of Euclid.) The triangle II L$_1$ G is isosceles. Hence it has at the base (G L$_1$) equal angles, i.e. the angles II L$_1$ G = II G L$_1$. Hence it follows that the angle II L$_2$ G = L$_1$ G L$_2$, II L$_3$ G = L$_2$ G L$_3$, &c.

10. Two magnitudes which are equal to a third are equal to each other. The angles K G L$_1$, K G L$_2$, K G L$_3$, &c., and II G L$_1$, L$_1$ G L$_2$, L$_2$ G L$_3$, &c. are two quantities, which are equal to a third (viz. II L$_1$ G, II L$_2$ G, II L$_3$ G, &c. according to 8 and 9). Hence they are equal to each other, each to each ; i.e. K G L$_1$ = II G L$_1$, K G L$_2$ = L$_1$ G L$_2$, K G L$_3$ = L$_2$ G L$_3$, &c. In other words: the angle K G II and the angle K G L (K G L$_1$, K G L$_2$, K G L$_3$, &c.) are always bisected by the next straight line.

11. The sum of the series $\frac{1}{2} + \frac{1}{4} + \frac{1}{8} + \frac{1}{16} + \ldots$ approaches unity (according to an arithmetical axiom here presupposed) in such a way that, what and however small magnitudes be given, the difference of the sum from unity in infinite advance of the series must continually become less. The angles II G L$_1$, II G L$_2$, &c. are the successive sums of angles (II G L$_1$, L$_1$ G L$_2$, &c.) which are parts of the angle II G K according to the progression $\frac{1}{2}$, $\frac{1}{4}$, $\frac{1}{8}$, $\frac{1}{16}$, &c. (according to 10). Hence they approach the unity or the whole angle of this angle (II G K) in such a way that what and however small a magnitude of an angle (K G B) may be given, the difference of the angle II G L$_x$ from II G K must be less than this magnitude K G B. Let us denote *the* point on the line II D (to be thought of as infinite) where this diminution commences, G L$_x$, it follows that II G L$_x$ > II G B.

12. If the major premise of 8 be applied to this case, then

in the same way it follows that the line о в must fall between
о ii and о L₁.

13. An infinite straight line can proceed but from a figure
bounded on all sides in the same plane on two sides only by
means of intersecting the boundaries. The line A B is an
infinite straight line, which (according to 12) lies partly
within the triangle ii L₁ о which is bounded on all sides.
Hence it can only pass through it on two sides only by means
of intersecting the limits.

The one intersection is at о, the other not yet determined.

14. Two straight lines which do not quite coincide can have
only one point in common. о в and о ii are two such straight
lines. Hence they can have only one point in common (the
point о only, and no other). The like holds good of о в and
о L₁.

15. The infinite straight line о в (or A в), in order to
go through beyond the enclosed space of the triangle ii L₁ о
in the direction of в, must intersect one of its three sides in
this direction (according to 13). But it cannot (according to
14) intersect in this direction о ii or о L. Hence it must
intersect the line ii L₁ (or C D); which was to be proved.[1]

[1] If the major premise of 13 is not used, it must be asserted further
that the straight line L_{k-1} (to be thought of as infinite), if it is turned
about the point о at the coincidence with L₁ in the plane determined
by the three points о, L_{k-1} and L₁, may pass through all points of the
line L_{k-1} L₁ and also through all points of the triangle о L_{k-1} L₁, and
consequently may have a second point besides о, common with the line
о в (or A в), and then must wholly coincide with it, so that its point of
intersecting, L_{k-1} L₁, belongs also to the line A в, and hence that this
intersects C D; which was to be proved.

In mathematical reference the author's article on the principles of
Geometry, scientifically explained in the *Archiv für Philol. und Pädagog.*
(founded by Jahn), xvii. pt. i. 20–54, 1851, may be compared. The
notions here applied are there explained in their more universal scientific
connection. This treatise was republished with an introduction altered
by myself in a French translation in Joseph Delboeuf's *Prolégomènes
philosophiques de la Géométrie*, pp. 269–305, Liège, 1860. Delboeuf's
foundation of geometry on the one fundamental character of space,

Only the syllogism under 15 is of a form which cannot be reduced to the mood Barbara (a form of a disjunctive kind), and that under 14 is to be added in so far that the ' only ' (' *only* the point o, and no other ') implicitly contains a negation.

which he calls homogeneity, that the form is independent of the magnitude and therefore may be united to every magnitude (which may be traced back to the relativity of all extension), is in my opinion the true scientific apprehension. It does not lead to the Kantian subjectivity of space, but to the subjective recognition of that objectively real relation. Cf. my critical notice in Fichte's *Zeitschrift für Phil.* xxxvii. pt. i. 1860. Cf. among others a treatise by John Prince Smith, *Ueber die Grundbegriffe der Geometrie,* Berlin, 1860. Cf. further H. Helmholtz, *On the Facts which lie at the Basis of Geometry,* in the *Nachrichten der K. Gesellsch. der Wiss.* pp. 193–221, at Göttingen, June 3, 1868, where, following Riemann (*On the Hypotheses which lie at the Basis of Geometry,* in *Abh. der K. Gesellsch. der Wissensch.* zu Göttingen, 1867), such a system of simple facts is enumerated as amounts to a determination of the relations of quantity of space. Helmholtz with Riemann defines the space of n dimensions as an n-fold extended multiplicity, i.e. such an one that the individual in it is determined by n changeable magnitudes (co-ordinates). The capacity of space for measuring is founded on the existence of steady bodies. By means of the free motion of bodies steady (in themselves), certain systems of points can be brought to be in congruence. This is independent of the place and direction of the congruent systems of points and of the way in which they have been brought to each other. If a steady body turns itself about its n − 1 points, and these are so chosen that its position depends only on something independently changeable, then the turning returns, without reversion, to the point of beginning. Space has three dimensions. Space is infinitely extended. In the above-mentioned treatise Geometry is founded on following (still more simple) experimental facts of statics, which we take axiomatically to be of an absolutely strict validity, and idealising, by means of hypothesis, the testimony of the senses. A material steady body: 1. If it is not fixed at any point, may be taken to any free place of space; 2. When fixed at a point, cannot be taken everywhere; 3. If fixed at a second point, cannot perform all the motions which are still possible when fixed at one point, but can still always be moved (only a certain row of points which stand in unbroken connected succession between each other and the two fixed points remain unmoved); 4. If it

All the syllogisms of the first thirteen numbers fall under
the first mood of the First Figure.

This syllogistic concatenation is the spinal cord of mathematical demonstration. The mathematician shortens *the form*
is fixed at one of the points hitherto remaining moveable, all motion is
taken from the body.

In the treatise by Tiberghien, a follower of Krause (*Logique, la Science
de la Connaissance,* Paris, 1865), the anti-Kantian opinion expressed
in the above-quoted tractate, that the certainty of mathematical axioms
is compatible with an empirical origin of the conception of space, is
combated. I there said, that Kant's demonstration for the à priority of
the intuition of space is only an indirect one, which is grounded on the
disjunction : given by experience or independent of all experience (empirical or à priori) ; and the demonstration is fallacious because of the
incompleteness of the disjunction, for there is a third possibility, viz.
the intellectual working up the empirical data according to logical laws
without the à priori (i.e. independent of all experience) elements of
knowledge. If we do not reach mathematical knowledge by direct
observation, it does not follow that it is absolutely independent of all
observation. The mathematical *fundamental axioms* are partly analytical judgments (§ 83), but are partly, so far as they are synthetical
judgments, like physical judgments, e.g. the law of gravitation based
immediately on observation, the geometrical on the observation of the
relations of space, and the arithmetical on the observation of objects of
the same kind leading to the notion of number. From these fundamental axioms the theorems are derived by means of a syllogistic
deduction, which does not follow purely subjective laws, but is
founded on the presupposition of an *objective arrangement,* which our
thinking only *reproduces,* and this presupposition itself rests on the combined external and internal experience (cf. §§ 28, 41 ff., 79, 81, and
several of the remarks to §§ 137, 138 ff.). Tiberghien answers
(p. 244 f.) with the question, Why does Kant leave the third possibility
unnoticed ? and answers it thus : ' It is because the *critique of pure
reason had shown* that there is no knowledge without elements à priori,
and that thus the elaboration proposed is manifestly absurd.' But this
answer involves an error in reference to Kant's actual course of demonstration. It is only necessary to read Kant's work to be convinced that
Kant *proceeds* upon this disjunction in his reasoning, that he employs
it *as premise,* and not, as Tiberghien asserts, as a *result* or *conclusion* of
a demonstration independent of it. The third possibility is to be called

of expression, but the syllogistic *form of thought* cannot be removed without destroying the force of the demonstration itself.

Physics also can explain particular phenomena from syllogistic rules only in a syllogistic form of thought. Every application of a mathematical formula to a given case is made by means of a syllogistic subsumption of the special under a universal relation of magnitude or situation. The province of the syllogism, and more especially of the mood Barbara, in Physics extends beyond that of the mathematical formula. The law that the warm body must radiate part of its warmth out through the atmosphere towards a colder surrounding it, if it is not separated from it by protecting media, and so must grow cold, adds to our meteorological knowledge by means of syllogistic subsumption, without being brought to a mathematical form.

an 'evident absurdity,' if the subjective presupposition is thought to be an unalterable truth, that all orderly arrangement has its origin in ourselves only. But this itself is first deduced from this disjunction, whose completeness is what is questioned, and therefore the argument undeniably proceeds in a vicious circle. If Tiberghien on his side believes this hypothesis to be controvertible, there is not even the appearance of justice for that designation. Kant's rejection of the weightiest of all objections which have been raised against his doctrine, by a mere jest ('Ex pumice aquam!' *Kr. d. pr. V.,* pref.), whose application involves the Kantian hypotheses, may be explained and excused from Kant's subjective isolation at his own stand-point, but not accepted. Lastly, so far as the infinitude of space goes, which Tiberghien lays so much stress on, this can only be understood by us in the *negative* sense, that the possibility of advance to any other place is not taken away, and only this notion is mathematical. Reimann and H. Helmholtz, in the above-quoted articles, recognise the empirical basis of Geometry as settled. Cf. Boncke, *Syst. d. Log.* ii. 51 ff.

[Another side of the Logic of Geometry stated in this paragraph, that the major premise so defines the geometrical notion that the intuitions from the construction may be dispensed with in the proof, is combated by Prof. W. R. Smith in two papers read before the Royal Society of Edinburgh (*Transactions,* vol. xxv.), 'On Mr. Mill's Theory of Geometrical Reasoning,' and 'Hegel and the Metaphysics of the Fluxional Calculus.' Cf. Translator's Preface.]

The superficies of the earth by night, under a clear sky, is warmer than the surrounding space, and is not separated from it by a cloud-covering protecting it from cooling. It therefore must radiate a part of its warmth, and become cooled (until the warmth of the sun makes reparation). The explanation of the formation of dew rests on the syllogism: Every cooling object whose temperature is below that of the so-called point of dew, attracts to itself out of the atmosphere a part of the watery vapour contained in it, and causes it to precipitate itself on it; the superficies of the earth, and especially of plants, are colder in clear nights than the atmosphere, in consequence of the radiation of the heat to the space around; and, therefore, when the cooling exceeds a certain limit, they attract a portion of the watery vapour contained in the atmosphere, and make it precipitate itself on them.

The application of *grammatical* laws to individual cases is a syllogistic process of thought. The verbs (verba sentiendi et declarandi) which denote an intellectual activity (the recognition an *existence* of what *is*) require in Latin the construction of the accusative with the infinitive; persuadere with the meaning *to convince* (that something is) denotes an intellectual activity, and requires this construction. Verbs which refer to a striving (after something which *is to be*) take the construction of ut; persuadere in the meaning of *to persuade* (to do something) belongs to this class, and, with this meaning, takes the construction of ut.

The like holds good of the application of the *laws of justice.* Theft is the crime in which a moveable thing belonging to another is taken from his possession or custody. The deed which this accused person has done is a crime of this kind. Therefore it is theft. Theft requires a severer punishment than the appropriation of something found (which was not in the possession or custody of another, if the former possessor had lost or abandoned it). The deed done by this accused person is theft. Therefore it requires severer punishment. In the application of a law to a given case the major premise is established by laying down the law; the minor premise has to

do with facts, and is found out by actual sight, avowal, testimony or circumstantial evidence. If an authentic interpretation lies between the law and its enforcement, then in this
case the law is the major premise, and a delivery of the court,
by which the meaning of an expression used in the law is
stated (e.g. whether the erroneous subjective view, that something may have happened which has not happened, be an
'opinion' in the sense of law or not), is the minor premise, and
a rule directly applicable to one of the individual cases present
(or directly excluding this applicability) is the conclusion.

In the province of *Ethics* the particular is known from
the general syllogistically, however much the *expression* may
despise syllogistic prolixity. This prolixity indeed is not
required, because the ethical relations lie so near the universal human consciousness. But the course of ethical *thinking* is syllogistic, if we, e.g. affirm of a definite person, whom
we have known to be faithful to duty, that he is worthy of
esteem. For we subsume the individual case under the universal law that fidelity to duty establishes the ethical claim to
esteem.

The like holds good of the understanding of *historical* phenomena. Besides the explanation given by Schiller of the
vehemence and length[1] of the Thirty Years' War—that in religious wars, and more especially in later times, the individual
takes his side from personal conviction—the following example
may bear witness to the force of this form of thought. Those
individuals who have freed the elements of culture, separately
acquired by the noblest and best endowed peoples of antiquity,
from their national limitations, and made them extend over all
peoples of the earth capable of civilisation, are among the men of
antiquity who are of most world-wide importance. Men who recognised the elements universally true for man in the rich treasury
of Grecian Art and Science, of Roman law and policy, acquired
by the labour of centuries, and, in a still greater degree in
religious ideas jealously guarded by the Jewish people, who
have freed their eternal truths from the temporal and transient

---

[1] Already quoted, § 101.

veil of national restriction, who have advanced them to a
new and purer position, and have prepared the way for their
universal diffusion,—they are, each in his province, men who
have freed elements of culture, &c. Hence, they are the men
of antiquity who are of the most world-wide importance. If
this conclusion is referred to individual persons, in whose
effects on the history of the world that character has shown
itself, this reference in its logical form takes the same mode
of inference. If the major premise of the first syllogism requires verification, this is to be done only in a like syllogistic
form of thought, viz. by presenting a universal law of development, which mankind, as one whole ethical organism, must
obey.

§ 111. The *three remaining moods of the First Figure*
in the stricter sense have the forms e a e, a i i, e i o, and
take the names *Celarent, Darii, Ferio.* In these names
the place in the alphabet of the initial consonant signifies the order of the moods, and the vowels in their
succession signify the characteristic logical form of the
major and minor premises and of the conclusion.

In the mood **Celarent** a universally negative conclusion (No S is P) is derived from a universally negative
major premise (No M is P) and a universally affirmative minor premise (Every S is M), according to the
following scheme :—

$$\begin{array}{ccc} M & e & P \\ S & a & M \\ \hline S & e & P \end{array}$$

The proof of the validity lies in the relation of spheres.
If M is quite separated from P, and S contained in M,
then S must be quite separated from P.

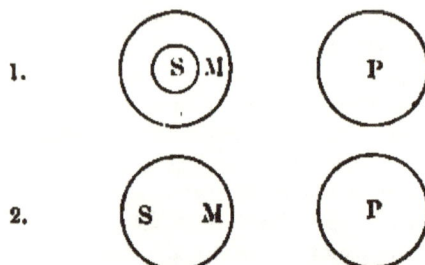

The mood *Darii* has the form—

$$
\begin{array}{ccc}
\text{M} & \text{a} & \text{P} \\
\text{S} & \text{i} & \text{M} \\
\hline
\text{S} & \text{i} & \text{P}
\end{array}
$$

The same relation of spheres exists here between P, M, and those (some) S which are M, as in the mood *Barbara* (§ 110) between P, M, and all S. Hence it must be true of those (some) S which was there true of all S, that they are P. It remains uncertain of the remaining S whether they are P or not. If they are M they must also be P. If they are not M they may still be P, but they can also be not P. This easily results from a comparison of spheres. The conclusion has the meaning: *At least* some S are P.

Lastly, the mood *Ferio* has the form—

$$
\begin{array}{ccc}
\text{M} & \text{e} & \text{P} \\
\text{S} & \text{i} & \text{M} \\
\hline
\text{S} & \text{o} & \text{P}
\end{array}
$$

The same relation of spheres exists here between P, M, and those S which are M, as between P, M, and all S in the mood *Celarent* (see above). Hence, as there all S are *not* P, here at least some S are *not* P. It remains undecided of the remaining S whether they are P or not. If they are M it follows that they are not P. If they are not M, however, then they can have any conceivable relation to P. Hence the conclusion has the meaning: At least some S are not P.

No. 14 of the larger mathematical example in the foregoing paragraph is an *example* of *Celarent.* The '*only*' of the major premise contains the denial of a second common point. The following are other examples from other provinces of thought : (1) No form of knowledge, which corresponds to a peculiar form of existence, is of merely didactic value ; Syllogism is a form of knowledge which corresponds to a peculiar form of existence (viz. to the real conformability to law). Hence the syllogism is not of mere didactic worth. (2) What is involuntary cannot be overcome by laws which entail punishments. Theoretical convictions are involuntary. Hence no theoretical conviction can be overcome by laws which entail punishment. (3) No just decision upon happiness is independent of moral restraint. The divine decision is correct. Hence it is not independent of moral restraint.

Darii.—(1) What has proceeded from a pure moral consciousness must be allowed to be moral. Some deviations from the common rules of Ethics have proceeded from a pure moral consciousness. Hence some deviations from the common rules of Ethics must be allowed to be moral. In this case *only* some, those namely which are under the middle notion. In other examples the predicate of the conclusion is true of a part of the sphere of the notion of the subject conformable to the premises, but besides this of the other parts also, about which nothing can be inferred from the premises. All squares are rectilineal plane figures. Some (and *only* some) parallelograms are squares. Some (*in fact however the other also*) parallelograms are rectilineal plane figures. The *value* of this mode of inference, as well as of all other in the various figures, which are in the same case with it, is limited but not destroyed by this indefiniteness. For everything is not indefinite, only that about which nothing can be concluded from the premises. It is always something gained to know that some S belong to P (or in other moods with particular negative conclusions, that some S do not belong to P). This gain is not to be despised because, so far as results from the premises, something further, the condition of the other S, remains unknown. ‘ *Too little* ’ may result for our desire of knowledge; but it does not follow that it is ‘ *too little* ’ in the sense that the inference leads to a fallacious limitation of the predicate to some S. A fallacy can never originate by this mood of inference, nor by any like it, if correctly applied, provided only the meaning of the particular judgment is strictly defined.

Ferio.—No human weakness can belong to God. Some attributes imputed to the deity by mythology are human weaknesses. Hence (at least) some attributes imputed to the deity by mythology cannot belong to Him. The remarks made upon the importance of the particular conclusion in Darii are also true in Ferio.

§ 112. In the *Second Figure,* whose general scheme (cf. § 103) is the following :

$$\frac{\begin{array}{cc} P & M \\ S & M \end{array}}{\begin{array}{cc} S & P \end{array}}$$

(1) The *major premise must be universal,* and—

(2) *One of the two premises must be negative.* For—

1. If P and M are connected particularly (P i M, which corresponds to M i P) while the relation of the remaining part of their spheres remains undefined, and if S falls wholly within M (S a M), then it remains uncertain whether S falls within that part of M which coincides with part of P, or within that part to which P has no defined relation, or partly in the former,

partly in the latter. Hence nothing definite results
about the relation of S to P. If P, however, is particularly separated from M (P o M), and if S falls
within M (S a M), the consequence would then be that
some P, viz. those which are not M, are also not S; but
in this inference the *particular* premise would be the
minor. On the other hand, nothing follows concerning
the relation of S to P, for the sphere of P, the sphere
of M, and, moreover, the sphere of S, which lies quite
within M, may include, cross, or, lastly, wholly exclude
each other, so that sometimes all S are P, sometimes
some are but others not, and, lastly, sometimes no S
are P. All other forms of combination with a particular
major premise are already excluded by the general rules
(§§ 106–108).

2. If both premises are affirmative no valid inference
can be attained, because both P and S wholly or partly
fall within the sphere of M, and nothing results about
their mutual relation.

Of the eight forms of combination whose validity is not
destroyed by the general rules (§§ 106–108), viz.:

a a	e a	i a	o a
a e			
a i	e i		
a o			

i a and o a are rejected in the Second Figure, according to
the rule of the universality of the major premise, and (besides
i a) a a and a i according to the rule that both premises cannot be affirmative. Hence the four following remain :

e a   a e   e i   a o

Their validity is still to be proved.

§ 113. *The valid moods of the Second Figure* have the forms **e a e**, **a e e**, **e i o**, and **a o o**. They take the names *Cesare, Camestres, Festino,* and *Baroco*. In these names the vowels of the three syllables in their succession denote the form of the major and minor premises and conclusion. The initial consonants refer to those moods of the First Figure to which the Schoolmen, following Aristotle, sought to reduce them in order to prove their validity. Some of the remaining consonants show the manner of this reduction (of which below). The comparison of spheres proves the validity of these moods directly.

The universal scheme of the Second Figure—

$$
\begin{array}{cc}
P & M \\
S & M \\
\hline
S & P
\end{array}
$$

in the mood *Cesare* has the more definite form—

$$
\begin{array}{ccc}
P & e & M \\
S & a & M \\
\hline
S & e & P
\end{array}
$$

The major premise asserts a complete separation of the spheres of P and M, the minor a complete comprehension of the sphere of S in that of M. The symbol is therefore—

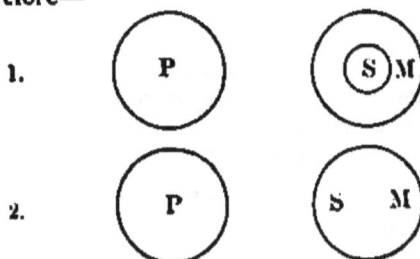

1.

2.

In both cases the complete separation of M from P has, as a necessary consequence, a complete separation of the S which is in M from P.

In the mood **Camestres** the scheme of the Second Figure takes the form—

$$
\begin{array}{ccc}
\text{P} & \text{a} & \text{M} \\
\text{S} & \text{e} & \text{M} \\
\hline
\text{S} & \text{o} & \text{P}
\end{array}
$$

In this mood, when compared with *Cesare*, P and S have exchanged the parts they play; P lies wholly within M, S wholly without M. Hence follows that between M and P there is a relation of complete separation.

An inference may each time be made from the same premises in *Cesare* and *Camestres*. The Conversion of the (universal negative and therefore simply convertible) conclusion accomplishes the transference from the one mood to the other (which is not universally necessary, and is not the case in *Darapti* of the Third Figure), because the exchange of the major and minor premise conditioned by this has for its consequence a form of the major premise now present, which is changed when compared with the previous major premise; the same is true of the minor.

The mood *Festino* has the form—

$$
\begin{array}{ccc}
\text{P} & \text{e} & \text{M} \\
\text{S} & \text{i} & \text{M} \\
\hline
\text{S} & \text{o} & \text{P}
\end{array}
$$

The proof of its validity lies in this, that those (some)

S which are M, must here stand in the same relation to
P which is wholly separated from M, as all S in *Cesare,*
that is (at least) these S, and hence (at least) some S
are not P. (When *all* S are M, then *all* S are *not* P;
when *only* some S are M, and others are not, then the
two cases can enter; *only* some S are *not* P, while others
are P, and *all* S are *not* P.)

The mood *Baroco* has the form—

$$
\begin{array}{ccc}
\text{P} & \text{a} & \text{M} \\
\text{S} & \text{o} & \text{M} \\
\hline
\text{S} & \text{o} & \text{P}
\end{array}
$$

Here some S, those, namely, which are not M, stand to
P, which falls wholly within M, in the relation of
separation, as all S did in *Camestres.* Hence (at least)
some S are not P. (When no S is M, then no S is P;
but when *only* some S are *not* M, then sometimes *only*
some S, sometimes *all* S are *not* P.)

The following are examples of *Cesare.* It is inferred in
the Platonic dialogue Charmides: Bashfulness is not something thoroughly good; Modesty is something which is
thoroughly good; Hence Modesty is not Bashfulness. Aristotle concludes :[1] the πάθη make men neither noble nor base,
worthy of praise nor worthy of blame ; the ἀρεταί do this; the
ἀρεταί are not πάθη. Further : The affections do not rest upon
purpose ; Virtues depend upon purpose ; Hence they are not
affections. In the same manner, Erdmann concludes :[2] The
author of the essay on the relation of the Nature-Philosophy
to philosophy generally[3] had not the consciousness that specu-

[1] *Ethic. Nic.* ii. 4.

[2] *Gesch. der neueren Phil.* iii. 2, 694.

[3] In the critical *Journal der Philos.*, edited by Schelling and Hegel,
1802-3.

lative Logic takes a special place in the list of philosophical sciences. Hegel, however, had this consciousness before the date of the essay. Hence Hegel is not its author.

Camestres.—Aristotle shows[1] that the virtues are not δυνάμεις (original capacities, dispositions, or faculties) by the following inference: The δυνάμεις are natural gifts; virtues are not natural gifts, but acquired properties or facilities; Hence they are not δυνάμεις. Aristotle concludes:[2] Every knowledge of essence is affirmative; no conclusion in the Second Figure is affirmative; Hence no conclusion in this figure is a knowledge of an essence. Further: Every knowledge of an essence is universal; no conclusion in the Third Figure is universal; Hence the Third Figure does not lead to a knowledge of an essence. On the basis of the Aristotelian account of the Ionic natural philosophers, later historical criticism constructed the following criticism: According to the testimony of Aristotle,[3] all those philosophers who define the one material principle as a mean existence between water and air have thought that things originate from this principle by condensation and rarefaction. According to the testimony of the same Aristotle,[4] Anaximander thought that the particular kinds of matter arise from the primary matter not by condensation and rarefaction (but by repulsion). Hence, Anaximander (if both Aristotle's testimonies are strictly accurate) does not belong to those philosophers who define the one material principle as a mean between water and air. The proof which historico-literary criticism has produced against the authenticity of Macpherson's Ossianic poems may be comprehended, in so far as it rests on internal reasons, in the following syllogism: Every real natural poem is naïve; those poems of Ossian which Macpherson pretended to discover are not naïve (but sentimental). Hence they are not real natural poems. Origen, the Neo-Platonist, according to the witness of Porphyry,[5] wrote only two works: περὶ δαιμόνων and ὅτι μόνος ποιητὴς ὁ βασιλεύς. Origen the

[1] *Ethic. Nicom.* li. 4. [2] *Anal. Post.* i. 11.
[3] *De Cœlo,* iii. 5. [4] *Phys.* i. 4.
[5] *Vit. Plot.* c. iii.; cf. ibid. c. xx.

Theologian has written many other works, which Porphyry knew of, so that the assertion cannot be true of him that he wrote these and only these writings. Hence Origen the Theologian was not Origen the Neo-Platonist. On the other hand, nothing would follow from the two affirmative premises : The Neo-Platonist Origen was (according to Porphyry) a scholar of Ammonius Saccas : The theologian of the same name was[1] a scholar of Ammonius Saccas. The astronomer Leverrier concluded : The sum total of the worlds belonging to our solar system must completely determine the orbit of Uranus ; the known worlds of our solar system do not fully account for the orbit of Uranus : Hence the whole of them are not known—a negative knowledge which prepared the way for the positive discovery of the existence, place, and size of Neptune.

Festino.—The realisation of a blind (thought of as determined according to the method of Epicurus, and not originally by end and aim) physical causality and chemical force of nature does not lead to organisms ingeniously articulated and reproducing themselves. Some processes of nature lead to such organisms. Hence (at least) some natural processes are not a realisation of a purposeless physical causality and chemical natural force.

Baroco.—Whatever is true must thoroughly agree with itself and with undoubted facts. Some theorems of the Kantian system do not thoroughly agree with themselves nor with undoubted facts. Hence (at least) some theorems of the Kantian system are not true. All regular plane figures (in the strictest sense of this notion) may be inscribed within a circle. Some parallelograms cannot be inscribed within a circle. Therefore some parallelograms are not regular plane figures. All who are morally disposed do what is right with right intention. Some, who act in accordance with law, do not do what is right with right intention. Therefore, some who act legally are not morally disposed.

The *ways* in which the Schoolmen, following Aristotle, *reduce* the moods of the Second, Third, and Fourth Figures to

---

[1] According to Porphyry in *Euseb. Church History*, vi. 19, 3.

E E

the corresponding mood of the First, is denoted in their names
by the consonants **s, p, m,** and **c.**

s conversio simplex,
p conversio per accidens sive in particul. propositionem,
m metathesis praemissarum,
c conversio syllogismi,' or ductio per contradictoriam pro-
       positionem sive per impossibile.

Accordingly, in *Cesare* (where the **s** is to be regarded as the
consonant of inference in the *first* syllable) the *first* or major
premise is changed by conversio simplex from P e M to M e P,
and the inference becomes *Celarent* :—

$$\begin{array}{ccc} M & e & P \\ S & a & M \\ \hline S & e & P \end{array}$$

This reduction is of course perfectly capable of proof, and as
little to be found fault with in itself as the demonstration of a
mathematical theorem which is deduced from an earlier theorem
by means of an auxiliary proposition, for the procedure does
not destroy its authority to be considered as a new and peculiar
theorem. But since proof may be led by means of a comparison of spheres without reduction, and a stronger conviction
reached by sensible representation, the direct way is to be preferred. In the comparison of spheres there lies a general
principle, which makes it possible to test immediately in each
given case whether a valid conclusion results and what figure
it must take, without first requiring a special recollection of
the figure and mood.

The like holds good and true of the other Reductions.

In *Camestres* there must be a change of the internal relation
of premises, by which the major premise becomes the minor,
and vice versâ (which is symbolically denoted by the external
change of place), then the negative premise is converted
simply, and last, the conclusion is simply converted. Thus :

$$\begin{array}{ccc} P & a & M \\ S & e & M \end{array}$$

---

[1] According to Aristotle, *Top.* viii. 14, 163 a, 32 : ἀντιστρέφειν.

becomes first :

$$S \quad e \quad M$$
$$P \quad a \quad M$$

then :

$$M \quad e \quad S$$
$$P \quad a \quad M$$

from which, according to *Celarent* in the First Figure follows :

$$P \quad e \quad S$$

from which, lastly, by conversio simplex, comes :

$$S \quad e \quad P$$

Instead of this Reduction, modern logicians (as for example Wolf[1]) used another, by the Contraposition of the major premise. It is to be preferred because it does away with the Conversion of the minor premise, which is unnatural in many cases. It is, however, inferior in value to the direct comparison of spheres.

In *Festino,* as in *Cesare,* the major premise only is converted, and the conclusion is drawn in *Ferio.*

In *Baroco* the ductio per impossibile or the apagogical demonstration is applied. In order to prove that from the premises :

$$P \quad a \quad M$$
$$S \quad o \quad M$$

the conclusion :

$$S \quad o \quad P$$

necessarily follows, it is shown that the contradictory opposite of the conclusion, viz. S a P, could not co-exist with the premises. For if S a P is thought along with the major premise P a M, S a M follows in the First Figure according to *Barbara,* which is the contradictory opposite of the given minor premise, and therefore must be as false as S o M is true. Hence the admission which led to this false result must also be false, i.e. S a P must be false. Hence the contradictory

---

[1] *Log.* § 381; cf. § 399.

opposite S o P must be true; which was to be proved. This Reduction is not so unnatural as it at first may appear to be. If (according to *Trendelenburg*) thought at first sight deduces from the given judgments: all squares are parallelograms: some regular rectilineal figures are not parallelograms, the inference: some regular rectilineal figures are not squares—analysis might discover in this process of thought the implied hidden reflective consciousness, which, only slightly modified, is brought to the light of consciousness by the Aristotelian-Scholastic Reduction:—for if they were squares they would be parallelograms, which they are not. This Reduction is at least as natural as the *Wolffian*, by the Contraposition of the major premise—e.g. in that example: What is not a parallelogram is not a square.

Baroco may also be referred to *Camestres* and *Festino* to *Cesare*, when those (some) S of which the minor premise is true be placed under a special notion and denoted by S'. Then the conclusion must hold good universally of S', and consequently particularly of S. Aristotle calls such a procedure *Ἔκθεσις*.[1] Cf. § 115. Demonstration of every kind of reduction by the immediate comparison of spheres is to be preferred. [For *Hamilton's* views upon Reduction, cf. App. A.]

§ 114. In the Third Figure, whose general scheme is the following (§ 103)—

$$
\begin{array}{cc}
\text{M} & \text{P} \\
\text{M} & \text{S} \\
\hline
\text{S} & \text{P}
\end{array}
$$

the *minor premise* must be affirmative. For if it is negative (M e S or M o S) where, according to the general rules (§§ 106–108), the major premise must be universally affirmative (M a P), then it remains uncertain whether the S, which (in M e S) is thought to be separated from

[1] Arist. *Anal. Pri.* i. 6.

the whole sphere of M, or at least (in M o S) from a
part of that sphere, may perhaps fall within another
part of the sphere of P' (perhaps as a species-notion co-
ordinate with M under the genus P'), whether it crosses
the sphere of P', or whether it lies wholly without that
sphere. (If S and P' were understood to be only the
indifferent signs of the two Extremes both in M e S
and in M o S, an inference of the form P S, viz. P o S,
would result. But then, in reference to this conclusion,
the *negative* premise is no longer the *minor* but the
major premise. For the S has become the major notion,
the praedicatum conclusionis, and the universal affirmative premise is the minor premise. It occurs in the
moods *Felapton* and *Bocardo*.)

The forms of combination which are rejected by this are:

a e   and   a o

Hence of the eight combinations whose validity stands the test
of the general rules (§§ 106–108), the following six remain
over:

a a   e a   i a   a i   o a   e i

It must now be shown that these lead to truly valid inferences.

§ 115. *The valid moods of the Third Figure* have the
forms a a i, e a o, i a i, a i i, o a o, o i o. They take
the names *Darapti, Felapton, Disamis, Datisi, Bocardo,
Ferison*. The vowels in them denote in succession the
form of the major and minor premises and the conclusion. The consonants refer to the Aristotelian-Scholastic
Reduction. Here also the proof of the validity results
on immediate comparison of spheres.

The general scheme of the Third Figure—

$$
\begin{array}{cc}
M & P \\
M & S \\
\hline
S & P
\end{array}
$$

takes in the mood *Darapti* the more definite form:

$$
\begin{array}{ccc}
M & a & P \\
M & a & S \\
\hline
S & i & P
\end{array}
$$

According to the premises the sphere of M is a common part of the spheres of P and S. Hence these latter must also coincide with each other in this part; while the relation of their other parts, if there be any, remains indefinite. Hence the conclusion holds good: At least one part of the sphere of S belongs to the predicate P.

In every example where both extremes may be made substantive, a double inference may be deduced from the same premises; e.g. when these terms are A and B, A i B as well as B i A. But since in both cases the major premise in each is of a universal affirmative form, and the same thing is done with the minor premise in each, there result, as has been remarked above (§ 113), two different examples of the same syllogistic mood, not, as in *Cesare* and *Camestres*, two different moods.

The mood *Felapton* has the form—

$$
\begin{array}{ccc}
M & e & P \\
M & a & S \\
\hline
S & o & P
\end{array}
$$

The proof of its validity lies in this, that those S with which M coincides must together with M itself be separated from P. Hence (at least) some S are not P.

The form of the mood *Disamis* is the following :—

$$\begin{array}{ccc} M & i & P \\ M & a & S \\ \hline S & i & P \end{array}$$

If the spheres of M and P are partially united, and if M falls wholly within S, then S must also be partially united with P, viz. in that part at least with which the portion of M falling within P coincides. (If *only* some M are P and others not, *all* S cannot be P, but in this case also *only* some S are P; cf. under *Bocardo*.)

The mood *Datisi* is of a wholly similar kind. The conclusion is made from the same premises as in *Disamis*. The proposition which is the converse of the conclusion of *Disamis* is taken as the conclusion. The particular proposition which there was major premise is here the minor, and the universal proposition is the major premise. The form of this mood is—

$$\begin{array}{ccc} M & a & P \\ M & i & S \\ \hline S & i & P \end{array}$$

Those S with which a part of M coincides, because this part along with the whole sphere of M falls within the sphere of P, must be included with it in this same sphere. Hence at least some S must have the predicate P. (If *only* some M are S, all S may yet be P.)

The mood *Bocardo* has the form—

$$
\begin{array}{ccc}
\mathrm{M} & \mathrm{o} & \mathrm{P} \\
\mathrm{M} & \mathrm{a} & \mathrm{S} \\
\hline
\mathrm{S} & \mathrm{o} & \mathrm{P}
\end{array}
$$

If some M are not P, and all M are S, then any one part of the sphere of S co-exists (according to the minor premise) with every part of M, and, consequently, with that part which (according to the major premise) is separated from P. Hence a part of the sphere of S is separated from the sphere of P, i.e. one or some S are not P. (It may happen that those S which do not coincide with M are separated from P; on the other hand, even if no M is P, still some S may be P. But if *only* some M are *not* P, and others are, it is impossible that *no* S are P. In this case if *only* some S are not P, others are always P, according to *Disamis*.)

Forison, lastly, has the following form:—

$$
\begin{array}{ccc}
\mathrm{M} & \mathrm{e} & \mathrm{P} \\
\mathrm{M} & \mathrm{i} & \mathrm{S} \\
\hline
\mathrm{S} & \mathrm{o} & \mathrm{P}
\end{array}
$$

Those S at least with which a part of M coincides must with it be separated from P, because this part along with the whole of M is separated from P. Hence it remains uncertain whether the sphere of S has also parts which lie without M, and, if it has, what relation they have to P. Therefore perhaps all, and at least some, S are not P. (If *only* some M are S, and also if *all* M are S, the case may occur in which *some* S are P and *others are not*; but the case may also occur in which *all* S are *not* P. It is always certain, however, that at least some S are not P.)

Examples to Darapti.—All whales are mammalia; all whales are water animals: Hence some water animals are mammalia. Or: All cetaceous animals are water animals; all cetaceous animals are mammalia: Hence some mammalia are water animals. The verb iubeo takes the construction of the accusative and infinitive; the verb iubeo is a verb which has to do with what is to be (not with what is): Hence at least a part of the verbs which have to do with what is to be (and not with what is) take the construction of the accusative and infinitive. (The singular judgment is to be considered as an universal, because the subject is a definite individual. Cf. § 70.)

To *Felapton.*—Iubeo is not a verb sentiendi vel declarandi; iubeo takes the construction of the accusative and infinitive: Hence at least one or some Latin verbs which take the construction of accusative and infinitive are not verbs sentiendi vel declarandi.

To *Disamis.*—Some pronouns of the French language take case-inflection; all French pronouns are words of the French language: Hence some words in the French language take case-inflection.

To *Datisi.*—All inferences in Darapti belong to one and the same mood; some inferences in Darapti are inferences from the same premises with conclusions which are the converse of each other: Hence some inferences from the same premises, with conclusions which are the converse of each other, belong to one and the same mood. All inferences, the one of which is concluded in Cesare and the other in Camestres (and also those in Disamis and Datisi), belong to two different moods; some inferences of this kind are inferences from the same premises, with conclusions the converse of each other: Hence some inferences from the same premises, with conclusions which are the converse of each other, belong to two different moods.

To *Bocardo.*—Some persons accused of witchcraft have not believed themselves to be free from the guilt laid to their charge; all those accused of witchcraft were accused of a merely feigned crime: Hence some who were accused of a merely feigned crime have not believed themselves free from the guilt laid to their charge.

To *Ferison.*—No syllogistic mood can be passed over in a scientific syllogistic; some syllogistic moods are moods which are inferior in scientific value to the principal moods of the First and Second Figures: Hence (at least) some moods which are inferior in scientific value to the principal moods of the First and Second Figures cannot be passed over in a scientific syllogistic.

The Aristotelian-Scholastic method of Reduction is here also denoted in the name of the mood.

In *Darapti,* the *D* and the p denote: By conversion of the universal affirmative minor premise M a S into the particular affirmative S i M, the mood *Darii* of the First Figure results, which gives the sought-for conclusion S i P.

In like manner *Felapton* is reduced by the conversio particularis of the minor premise to *Ferio.*

In *Disamis* the minor premise cannot be converted, for then there would be two particular premises. Hence the (particular affirmative) is converted simply, and the premises transposed, and there now results an inference in *Darii* not of the form S P but of the form P S. It is an inference of the kind that the proposition originally given as major premise serves rather as minor premise, and that given as minor premise as major, and a metathesis praemissarum is the necessary (a reciprocal change of the internal relation of the premises, whether the external position, which is the symbol of this relation, is changed or not). Lastly, by a conversio simplex of the conclusion, *the* conclusion proper to this mood is reached.

Reduction is easier in *Datisi,* where only the conversio simplex of the minor premise is needed in order that the inference according to *Darii* may take directly its own proper form.

All these moods, as *Aristotle* has correctly remarked,[1] may

[1] *Anal. Pri.* i. c. vi.

also be shown to be valid indirectly or apagogically. *Disamis* and *Datisi* may also be reduced to *Darapti* by ἐκθέσει, i.o. by exclusion of a part; in *Disamis* those (some) M which are P, and in *Datisi* those M which are S, are excluded from the sum total of all M, and placed under a special notion, and accordingly denoted by a special letter, say N. Now since what was true of all M must be true of these N, N may be placed instead of M in the other premise, so that in both moods the premises take the form: N a P; N a S: from which, according to *Darapti*, follows S i P.

The validity of the mood *Bocardo* is apagogically proved (as the validity of *Baroco* in the Second Figure was) by Aristotle and the Schoolmen. If the proposition were false, that some S are not P, and if its contradictory opposite were true that all S are P, then when we think this proposition and the given minor premise, according to which all M are S, it follows in *Barbara*, in the First Figure, that all M are P. This contradicts the given major premise which asserts that some M are not P. Hence the proposition which led to this contradiction cannot be true, viz. that all S are P. Hence some S are not P; which was to be proved. Aristotle remarks, that this mood may be proved without apagogical procedure, by the ἐκθέσθαι or λαμβάνειν of that part of the middle notion which is true of the major premise. If we denote this part by N, then (as above) we get the premises: N e P; N a S: from which follows in *Felapton* S o P; which was to be proved.

The mood *Ferison*, lastly, as the characteristic letters *F* and *s* show, is reduced by conversio simplex of the minor premise to *Ferio*, according to which form M e P and S i M follows S o P; which was to be proved. This mood may also be reduced to *Felapton* by ἐκθέσει.

§ 116. The *Fourth Figure* (or *second division of the First Figure in the wider sense*), whose general scheme (§ 103) is the following:—

$$
\begin{array}{cc}
\text{P} & \text{M} \\
\text{M} & \text{S} \\
\hline
\text{S} & \text{P}
\end{array}
$$

cannot have a particular negative premise. The combination of a universal affirmative major premise with a particular affirmative minor is also excluded. For if a premise is particular negative, the other premise must be universal affirmative, according to the general rules (§§ 106–108); so that the two forms result—

I. P   o   M   2. P   a   M
   M   a   S   M   o   S

But (according to 1), P is particularly separated from M, and M falls wholly within S. Hence it is uncertain what relation M, thought as subject, has to P, when P is thought as predicate; for the particular negative judgment does not admit of conversion (§ 88). Now it remains uncertain (according to the minor premise) whether, and how far, the sphere of S projects beyond that of M, and, therefore, the relation between S and P is quite indistinct, and no decision can be come to about the relation of S to P. (If the meaning of the premise P o M were that *only* some P are not M and others are, then from the judgment P i M thought implicitly along with M a S a definite conclusion S i P in the mood *Dimatis* would result; but this is not the sense of the particular judgment.)

If (according to 2) M is particularly separated from S, but wholly includes the sphere of P, the relation of P to S and of S to P remains quite indeterminate. For P may quite as well fall within the part of M separated from S, as either wholly or partly in the part of M which may coincide with S, and this again either so that S falls wholly or partly within P. (This relation would remain

indefinite even if the sense of M o S were: *only* some
M are not S. See below.)

In the combination **a i**—

$$\text{P } \mathbf{a} \text{ M}$$
$$\text{M } \mathbf{i} \text{ S}$$

in which P falls wholly within M, and M partly within
S, it remains undetermined which part of M falls within
S, whether it is a part which coincides with P or with
a part of P, or only a part that lies outside of P. Hence
the relation between S and P remains quite undetermined. (This relation would also remain indeterminate
if the meaning of M i S were: *Only* some M are S, and
others not. See above.)

Since accordingly the forms of combination :

$$\mathbf{o\,a}\qquad \mathbf{a\,o}\qquad \mathbf{a\,i}$$

are rejected, there remain for the Fourth Figure of the eight
combinations warranted by the general rules (§§ 106–8) the
following five which lead to valid inferences :—

$$\mathbf{a\,a}\qquad \mathbf{a\,e}\qquad \mathbf{i\,a}\qquad \mathbf{e\,a}\qquad \mathbf{e\,i}$$

§ 117. The *valid moods of the Fourth Figure* (or of
the *second division of the First Figure in the wider sense*)
have the forms **a a i a e e i a i e a o e i o**. They
take the names *Bamalip, Calemes, Dimatis, Fesapo,
Fresison*. In these the vowels in their succession denote
the form of the major and minor premises and Conclusion, and the consonants refer to the Aristotelian-
Scholastic Reduction. The ground of validity lies here
also in the relation of spheres, and proof may be given
by a direct comparison of spheres.

The universal scheme of the Fourth Figure—

$$
\begin{array}{cc}
P & M \\
M & S \\
\hline
S & P
\end{array}
$$

takes in the mood *Bamalip* the more definite form—

$$
\begin{array}{ccc}
P & a & M \\
M & a & S \\
\hline
S & i & P
\end{array}
$$

According to the premises the terms have here the same relation to each other as in the mood *Barbara* of the First Figure, only P and S exchange characters; the sphere of P falls wholly within the sphere of M, which is either identical with it or more extended, and this again wholly within the sphere of S, either identical with it or more extended. The judgment P a S follows at once from this relation of spheres, and just as directly follows the judgment S i P. In the case of the identity of all three spheres *all* S are P, in all other cases *only* some S are P. If this case does exist in a given example, it cannot be decided that it does so from the given premises unless something further is given. But nothing further is required to attain with certainty the conclusion S i P, in the sense: At least some S are P; which was to be proved.

The mood *Calemes* has the form—

$$
\begin{array}{ccc}
P & a & M \\
M & e & S \\
\hline
S & e & P
\end{array}
$$

The relation of terms is here the same as in *Celarent*, in the First Figure, only that P and S again exchange the parts they have to play. There is required here, as little as in *Bamalip*, a Conversion of the conclusion P e S which results according to the First Figure, in order to reach S e P. The judgment: S is wholly separated from P, or: No S is P, may be established directly on the relation of spheres, according to which M and S are wholly separated from each other, while P lies wholly within M.

The mood *Dimatis* has the following scheme:—

$$
\begin{array}{ccc}
P & i & M \\
M & a & S \\
\hline
S & i & P
\end{array}
$$

The relation of the spheres is the same as in *Darii*, when the extremes exchange places: M coincides in its whole extent with S or with a part of S, and at least in part of its extent with part of the extent of P. Hence it follows that S and P must coincide with each other, at least particularly, in that part, namely, which they both have in common with M. Consequently, at least some S are P; which was to be proved. (If *only* some P, as well as if *all*, P are M, the case may occur that *only* some S are P, and also the other, that all S are P.)

The form of the mood *Fesapo* is—

$$
\begin{array}{ccc}
P & e & M \\
M & a & S \\
\hline
S & o & P
\end{array}
$$

According to the premises, P and M are quite separated from each other, while M falls wholly within S. Hence those S at least which coincide with M must also be separated from P: At least some S are not P. No corresponding mood exists in the First Figure in the stricter sense, because from the given premises nothing definite can be obtained about the relation of P to S. The sphere of S may project itself over that of M in such a way that at the same time all P, or that some P, may fall within it; but it may be so limited that it remains quite separate from P and P quite separate from it.

The mood *Fresison*, lastly, has the following form:—

$$
\begin{array}{ccc}
P & e & M \\
M & i & S \\
\hline
S & o & P
\end{array}
$$

This mood is distinguished from *Fesapo* by the particular character of the minor premise. Those S which coincide with part of M, because this part along with the whole of M is separated from P, must be separated from P. Hence at least some S are not P. (When *only* some M, as well as when *all* M, are S, the case may occur that *only* some S are *not* P, and also the other case, that *all* S are *not* P, or that no S is P.) Here also as in *Fesapo* the sphere of P may have every conceivable relation to that of S; and for this reason, no analogous mood can exist in the First Figure in the stricter sense.

Inferences from the same premises, from which inferences in *Barbara*, *Celerent*, and *Darii* may be constructed, may serve as

examples to *Bamalip, Calemes,* and *Dimatis,* where each of
the two extremes may naturally take the place of the subject
as well as that of the predicate. From the premises : Good non-
conductors of heat retain heat longer ; woollen clothes are good
non-conductors—it is concluded in *Barbara* of the First Figure :
Therefore woollen clothes retain heat longer. If we first think
of the end of preserving warmth, and if we then seek for means
to attain to this end, we advance naturally from the same premises to the conclusion in the form of the mood *Bamalip* :
Some things which retain heat longer (some of the means to
retain heat longer) are woollen clothes. From the premises :
All squares are parallelograms ; no parallelogram has converging opposite sides—the conclusion is naturally drawn, according
to *Celarent,* and not according to *Calemes,* because the predicate—having converging sides—does not properly take the
form of a substantive predicate-notion. But if the second premise is : No parallelogram is a trapezoid, both inferences are
equally natural : No square is a trapezoid, and : No trapezoid
is a square. From the premises : Some parallelograms are
squares ; all squares are regular figures—follows, according to
Dimatis : Some regular figures are parallelograms, and according to *Darii* : Some parallelograms are regular figures.

No mood in the Fourth Figure corresponds to *Ferio* in the
First, which is based on the particular negative form of the
conclusion, nor on the other hand the moods *Fesapo* and *Fresison* find correlates in the First.

The following is an inference in *Fesapo.* None of those
inferences which fall under the definition enunciated by Aristotle[1] of inferences in the First Figure is a conclusion of the
form Fesapo (nor of the form Fresison) ; every inference of the
form Fesapo (and of the form Fresison) is an inference of the
Fourth Figure ; consequently, (at least) some inferences of the
Fourth Figure do not fall under Aristotle's definition of inferences in the First Figure. (It cannot be determined from the
given premises only, without reference to other data, whether
only some do not, or perhaps *all* do not; yet the result inferred

[1] *Anal. Pr.* i. 32.

F F

from that has a distinct scientific value in and for itself. It is
an essential moment in the explanation of the relation of the
Aristotelian syllogistic to the later doctrine of the four syllogistic figures.) In the foregoing example, if instead of the
moods themselves the attribute is given which prevents
them falling under that definition, an inference in the mood
Fresison occurs. None of those inferences which fall under the
Aristotelian definition of the First Figure has a negative premise in which the middle notion is the predicate ; some inferences
with a negative premise in which the middle notion is predicate
are inferences of the Fourth Figure : Therefore some inferences
(at least) of the Fourth Figure do not fall under the Aristotelian definition of the First.

Earlier logicians proved the validity of these moods, as they
had done the validity of the moods of the Second and Third
Figures, by *Reduction* to the moods of the First Figure in the
stricter sense.

In the mood *Bamalip*, the conclusion P a S in *Barbara* is
first drawn by the reciprocal change of the internal relation of
the premises symbolised by that (m) of their external position,
and then this conclusion is converted by conversio per accidens
sive in particularem propositionem (p) to S i P.

In *Calemes*, the conclusion P e S is first formed, according
to *Celarent*, with metathesis praemissarum (m), and then is
changed to S e P by conversio simplex (s).

In like manner *Dimatis* is reduced to *Darii*, and the conclusion simply converted.

Fesapo, reduced to *Ferio* by conversio simplex (s) of the
(universal negative) major premise, and the conversio in partic.
propos. (p) of the (universal affirmative) minor premise.

Fresison is converted to *Ferio* by a conversio simplex (s) of
the major and minor premises.

Those Scholastic logicians who, following Theophrastus,
reckon the five moods under consideration as indirect moods
of the First Figure, consider the subject of the conclusion in
these moods to be the major extreme or the major term, and
the predicate of the conclusion the minor. They designate and

arrange the premises in a corresponding manner. Those logicians give the following names: *Baralip* (or Baralipton), *Celantes, Dabitis, Fapesmo, Frisesom* (or Frisesomorum). In this mode of designation there undeniably lies an inconsequence because the general principle of distinguishing the major and minor notion, and accordingly the major and minor premise, according to the form of the conclusion, which has been followed in the designation of all other moods, is here abandoned without reason. The mistake in the last two moods is especially striking. They cannot be caused or conceived by a conversion of a conclusion derived from the First Figure, and the relation of spheres of the terms in themselves, where they are not viewed in their position as subject and predicate in the premises, can as little justify the admission that here the S is the (higher) major notion, and P the (lower) minor notion.

§ 118. From a *comparative survey* of the valid moods we find that the *conclusion* in all the figures—

(a) can only be *affirmative* if *both premises are affirmative* (cf. Barbara, Darii; Darapti, Disamis, Datisi; Bamalip, Dimatis);

(b) must be *negative* if *one premise* is *negative* (cf. Celarent, Ferio; Cesare, Camestres, Festino, Baroco; Felapton, Bocardo, Ferison; Calemes, Fesapo, Fresison);

(c) is sometimes *universal* if both premises are *universal,* viz. in the First and Second Figure, and in part of the Fourth (cf. Barbara, Celarent; Cesare, Camestres; Calemes); sometimes *particular,* viz. in the Third Figure and in part of the Fourth (cf. Darapti, Felapton; Bamalip, Fesapo);

(d) must be *particular,* if *one premise* is *particular* (cf. Darii, Ferio; Festino, Baroco; Disamis, Datisi, Bocardo, Ferison; Dimatis, Fresison).

The *First Figure* admits conclusions of all forms

(a, e, i and o), the *Second* only negative (e and o), the *Third* only particular (i and o), the *Fourth*, particular affirmative, universal negative and particular negative conclusions (i, e and o).

A *universal affirmative* conclusion (a) can be deduced in the First Figure only (and in *one* mood only, Barbara); a *universal negative* (e) in the First, Second and Fourth Figures (in the *four* moods, Celarent; Cesare, Camestres; Calemes); a *particular affirmative* (i) in the First, Third and Fourth Figures only (in the *six* moods, Darii; Darapti, Disamis, Datisi; Bamalip, Dimatis); lastly, a *particular negative* (o) in all the figures (in the *eight* moods, Ferio; Festino, Baroco; Felapton, Bocardo, Ferison; Fesapo, Fresison).

The corresponding particular may be obtained from every universal conclusion by *Subalternation*. But in so far as the particular conclusions may be obtained immediately on the basis of premises by the comparison of the spheres, these modes of inference may be called Special moods. They take the names *Barbari, Celaront; Cesaro, Camestros; Calemos.* If these five moods are added to the previous ones, *each of the four Figures has an equal number of six valid moods.* But these new moods are meaningless, because only a part of what really results from the premises is taken. Besides the rules, given for the form of the conclusion in general, remain valid when these moods are under consideration.

Universal affirmative conclusions have the highest *scientific value*, because they advance our knowledge in a positive manner and admit of reliable application to the individual. The *universal negatives* come next; they guarantee only a negative but a distinctly definite view. Then come the *particular affirmatives*, which promise a positive advance, but leave us helpless in the application to individual cases. Lastly, the *particular negative* conclusions are of the lowest value. Particular propositions, however, are by no means without scientific meaning. Their special service is to ward off false generalisations. The universal negative or affirmative judgment, falsely held to be true, is proved not true by the particular affirmative or negative conclusion, which is its contradictory opposite.

Aristotle teaches,[1] that what is universal follows only from the universal, but sometimes something not universal follows from the universal, and either both or at least one premise must in reference to quality agree with the conclusion. Later logicians say : Conclusio sequitur partem debiliorem. This formula recommends itself by its apparent simplicity and clearness. It is not, however, minute nor distinct enough, but is incomplete and apt to mislead. For if a, e, i, and o are successively 'weaker,' i.e. are forms of successively lower scientific value, then, according to this rule, a conclusion from the premises of the forms a and e must necessarily come second as the pars debilior, and thus take the form e; but in Felapton and Fesapo it has the form o, which is weaker still. Hence the rule must rather run : Conclusio non sequitur partem fortiorem, sed aut sequitur partem debiliorem aut debiliore debilior est. If the meaning of the formula is more closely defined in this way, that the conclusion in reference to Quantity must be particular with a particular premise, and in reference to Quality negative with a negative premise, this definition is not false, only incomplete. For it is not said what form the conclusion may take, if both premises are either of

1 *Anal. Pri.* i. 24.

the same form (a a), or agree only in reference to Quantity
(a e), or only in reference to Quality (a i). More particularly
attention is not drawn to the different relations of Quantity
and Quality, according to which both a and i, but not e nor
o, can follow from a a, both e and o from a e, but not both i
and o from a i.

The versus memoriales (mnemonic verses) may be here inserted. They contain the names of the whole of the moods of
the Four Figures, and are not without value as an aid to the
memory.

> Barbara, Celarent primae, Darii Ferioque.
> Cesare, Camestres, Festino, Baroco secundae.
> Tertia grande sonans recitat Darapti, Felapton,
> Disamis, Datisi, Bocardo, Ferison. Quartae
> Sunt Bamalip, Calemes, Dimatis, Fesapo, Fresison.

The scholastic *names of the moods* were brought into common
use by Petrus Hispanus (who died Pope John XXI. in the
year 1277). He made use of them in his Compendium
'Summulae Logicales.' (Prantl believes this to be a Latin
translation from the work of Michael Psellus, who lived from
1020-1106, Σύνοψις εἰς τὴν Ἀριστοτέλους λογικὴν ἐπιστήμην.
The converse is rather true, as Thurot has proved; the Σύνοψις
is a translation of the Compendium of Petrus Hispanus. See
above, § 31.)[1]

In Petrus Hispanus (and also in his predecessors William
Shyreswood and others) the words run as follows: Barbara,
Celarent, Darii, Ferio; Baralipton, Celantes, Dabitis, Fapesmo,
Frisesomorum; Cesare, Camestres, Festino, Baroco; Darapti,
Felapton, Disamis, Datisi, Bocardo, Ferison.[2] The incon-
sequence in the designation of the five Theophrastic moods
induced later Latin logicians to change the names into Bamalip,
Calemes, &c.[3] The Greek reproduction of the Summulae

---

[1] [Cf. Prantl, ii. 275; Mansel's edition of *Aldrick's Rudimenta*, 4th
ed. p. 84; Hamilton's *Discussions*, 2nd ed. p. 669.]

[2] See Prantl, *Gesch. d. Log.* ii. 275; iii. 15 f.

[3] Cf. the remarks at § 117, p. 435.

(Σύνοψις, &c.) has (according to the Augsburg MS. collated by Pmntl) the following mnemonic words.[1] For the four principal moods of the First Figure: γράμματα, ἔγραψε, γραφίδι, τεχνικός (which taken together have the meaning: Letters were written with the pen of a master); for the other five (Theophrastic) moods of this figure: γράμμασιν, ἔραξε, Χάρισι, πάρθενος, ἱερόν (by an inscription dedicated to the graces, a virgin, a temple); for the four moods of the Second Figure: ἔγραψε· κάτεχε μέτριον ἄχολον; for the six moods of the Third Figure: ἅπασι σθεναρός, ἰσάκις ἀσπίδι ὁμαλός, φέριστος. Joh. Hospinianus, in a work upon the moods of the Categorical Syllogism,[2] enunciates the moods which are added by subalternation. Leibniz does so also in his De Arte Combinatoria,[3] and in his Nouv. Essais.[4]

§ 119. If both premises are *apodictic*, or both *problematic*, the conclusion has a like MODALITY, because the measure of its certainty is entirely dependent on the measure of the certainty of the premises. In all other respects the same rules hold good which are true of assertorical premises, because the relations of spheres are the same.

If the *modality* of one premise *differs* from that of the other, the conclusion follows that which has the least certainty. For—

(a) If the relation between the middle notion and the one term is of *apodictic* or *assertorical* certainty, and the relation between it and the other is *problematic* only,

---

[1] They are copies of the Latin, but have not the signs of reduction. The same Greek words, with the exception of the names of the Theophrastic moods, are also added, apparently by a later hand, to the Ἐπιτομή of Nicephorus Blemnides, published in 1250.

[2] Basel, 1560.

[3] Erdmann's edition of the *Philosophical Works*, pp. 13, 15.

[4] Erdmann's edition, p. 395.

there exists co-ordinate with the last, and because of its
problematic character, the opposite possibility. But
this, when in combination with the unchanged (apodictic
or assertoric) premise, does not lead by any form of
combination to a conclusion absolutely the same, but in
all cases excludes at least the certainty that the judgment contradictorily opposed to the conclusion is false.
Hence the conclusion has only a *problematic* validity.

(b) If one premise is of *apodictic* and the other of
assertoric certainty, then the contradictory opposite of
the latter is excluded only with assertoric not with
apodictic certainty. Now this, connected with a premise apodictically valid, would make it uncertain at
least whether the judgment opposed to the conclusion
as its contradictory be not true ; and thus this uncertainty is excluded only assertorically, not apodictically.
Hence the conclusion is true with *assertorical* certainty,
not apodictically.

Subjective uncertainty includes the consciousness that perhaps
the opposite admission is true, and so *real possibility* as such is
accompanied by the possibility of the opposite. *Assertoric
certainty* excludes the opposite with assertoric certainty only,
and the *apodictic* with apodictic certainty, and so *actual existence*, in so far as it does not prove itself to be founded on a
universal conformability to law, excludes its opposite only as
far as facts warrant, while *necessary existence* on the other
hand necessarily excludes its opposite. Real relations must
be mirrored in our consciousness, and so the knowledge of the
real possibility or of the actual present capacity establishes a
problematic judgment about its actual occurrence which has
to do with its possibility, and knowledge of the real necessity a
corresponding apodictic judgment. But because it is not true
conversely, that reality adapts itself to our knowledge, a real

possibility does not always present itself where subjective uncertainty exists, and the real cause is not always to be recognised where a sufficient ground of knowledge makes strict demonstration possible, and therefore warrants apodictic certainty. Accordingly, the cases where a problematic conclusion is obtained from problematic premises, in no way coincide with those where a judgment of possibility can be inferred from a judgment of possibility. Hence, for example, in the Second Figure from the premises: P is perhaps M ; S is perhaps not M—the conclusion follows ; S is perhaps not P. But from the premises: P has a possibility to be M ; S has the possibility not to be M—the conclusion does not follow: S has the possibility not to be P. For the real possibility of a definite existence and of a corresponding non-existence is in itself the same, and therefore P and S have actually the same predicate. And thus there are two affirmative premises in the Second Figure, from which, according to the universal rules of the Second Figure, nothing definite in the relation between S and P can be deduced. The judgments, however, in which any real possibility (or capacity) is adjudged to any subject are not necessarily problematic (which they become by a ' perhaps' added in thought), but are in themselves assertoric (although the judgment originating from them upon the actual existence, *which* in them is thought as possible or exists in capacity, is problematic). Consequently the inferences formed from them fall under the general laws of conclusions from assertoric premises, and do not form a special form of inference, and so do not require a special representation.

Aristotle [1] explains the manifold relations of forms of inference which arise from the different modes of combination of the judgments of real possibility, real actual existence, and real necessity. He holds that under certain conditions, from the combination of a judgment of necessity with a judgment of actual existence, there results a judgment of necessity, and from a combination of a judgment of necessity with a judgment of possibility there results a judgment of actual existence.

[1] *Anal. Pri.* l. c. viii.–xxii.

442 § 120. *Substitution of one Notion for another*

Theophrastus and Eudemus, however, teach that in these references the conclusion always follows the weaker premise. Alex. Aphrod. says:[1] οἱ δέ γε ἑταῖροι αὐτοῦ οἱ περὶ Εὔδημόν τε καὶ Θεόφραστον οὐχ οὕτως λέγουσιν, ἀλλά φασιν ἐν πάσαις ταῖς ἐξ ἀναγκαίας τε καὶ ὑπαρχούσης συζυγίαις, ἐὰν ὦσι κείμεναι συλλογιστικῶν, ὑπάρχον γίγνεσθαι τὸ συμπέρασμα. Philop. says:[1] οἱ μέντοι περὶ Θεόφραστον καὶ ἐπὶ ταύτης τῆς συζυγίας (sc. τὸ Α τῷ Β ἐξ ἀνάγκης οὐδενὶ ὑπάρχει, τὸ δὲ Β ἐνδέχεται παντὶ τῷ Γ) ἐνδεχόμενον λέγουσιν εἶναι τὸ συμπέρασμα (sc. τὸ Α ἐνδέχεται τῷ Γ οὐδενὶ) ἵνα καὶ ἐνταῦθα τῇ χείρονι τῶν προτάσεων ἔπηται τὸ συμπέρασμα. Theophrastus and Eudemus are certainly correct here, for in syllogisms which refer to real relations of possibility, actuality, and necessity, every limitation which lies in one of the two premises passes over to the conclusion.[2]

§ 120. It is not necessary to the validity of the inference that in both premises the relation of subject and premise should exist between the terms. The conclusion may also be formed, when for any one notion of the one premise (or *fundamental judgment*) which stands in an *objective* and *attributive* relation, another notion is SUBSTITUTED which is supplied by the second premise (or the *auxiliary judgment*). Instead of the sphere of the higher notion, taken universally, the sphere (or even part of the sphere) of a lower notion, which coincides with a part of the former, may be substituted, and in place (of the whole sphere or) of the indefinite part of the sphere of a lower notion, the indefinite part of the comprehending sphere of a higher notion may be substituted. The form of the conclusion must strictly correspond to the form of that premise (or fundamental judgment) in which the new notion is substituted.

[1] *Ad Anal. Pri.* f. 49 A. [2] Ad eundem locum, f. 51 A.
[3] Cf. §§ 87, 98, and Prantl, *Gesch. d. Logik*, i. 278 ff., 370 ff.

The following inference may serve as *an example*, in which
the notion for which another is substituted is apprehended
universally, and takes the place of the *object* in the fundamental judgment: The earth attracts the whole of the bodies
contained in its neighbourhood; the moon is a body existing
in the neighbourhood of the earth: Hence the earth attracts
the moon. Or: [1] Love craves the beautiful; the Good is
beautiful: Therefore Love craves the Good. In the following
inference the *attributive* relation occurs: Abuse of the regulations
of those in authority deserves legal punishment; the political
measures of the Government are regulations of those in authority: Hence abuse of the political measures of the Government
deserves legal punishment. In the following inference a
higher notion is substituted for a notion taken *partially* in an
attributive relation: The peculiar motion of (at least) some
double stars is undoubted; all double stars are fixed stars:
Hence the peculiar motion of some fixed stars is undoubted.

The inferences from two *simple* (containing only the predicative relation) categorical judgments may be placed under the
same point of view, for the one may generally be considered as
a *fundamental judgment* (in which the substitution is made),
and the other as an *auxiliary judgment* (by means of which the
substitution is made). According to § 71, the *subject* is universal in every *universal* judgment. Hence another subject-
notion may be substituted for it whose sphere coincides with
(at least) part of the sphere of the first subject. In every
particular judgment the subject is particular, and so the indefinite part of another subject-notion, the sphere of which
comprehends the sphere of the first subject, may be substituted for it. The *predicate* in every *affirmative* judgment is
particular, and hence a higher predicate-notion may be substituted for it. Lastly, the predicate in every *negative* judgment is universal, and therefore a lower predicate-notion may
be substituted for it. This mode of consideration is less
convenient in inferences of this kind because the distinction of
both premises as fundamental and auxiliary judgment is not

[1] *Plat. Sympos. c. xxi.*

thoroughly established in the nature of the case. In many cases also each of the two premises may be considered as the fundamental judgment, and each as the auxiliary judgment, and in a complete representation, according to this principle, a part of the mould must submit to a double construction. Hence the immediate comparison of spheres leads to the end in view in a simple and natural way.

The Aristotelian-Scholastic Logic attempted a thorough explanation of inferences from simple categorical syllogisms only. The inferences, where a term is substituted by another in an attributive or objective relation, are left unnoticed. The first work which strictly takes up the question is the Logique ou l'Art de Penser, produced by the Cartesian School. It first appeared in 1662, and its principal author was probably *Ant. Arnauld.* It calls syllogisms of this kind *syllogismes complexes,* and endeavours both to prove (only by examples, however) how they may be reduced to *syllogismes incomplexes,* and also to enunciate a principle according to which the force of inference in all syllogisms may be at once estimated without reduction. The principle is : 'that one of the two propositions must contain the conclusion, and the other show that it contains it;' the term of the conclusion substituted for it must be contained either in the extent or content of the middle term. The judgment which contains the conclusion may be called *proposition contenante,* and the one which proves that it is contained, *applicative.* In simple affirmative syllogisms each of the two premises may generally be conceived to be the *contenante,* because each in its way contains the conclusion, and each is *applicative.* In negative syllogisms the negative premise is the *contenante.* In the *syllogismes complexes* it is the premise whose form determines the form of the conclusion.[1] The application of this principle to special cases would have led to a succession of special rules. But they are not developed in that logical treatise; individual examples only are analysed.

Beneke has founded on this principle a complete theory of

[1] *Log.* pt. iii. c. ix.-xi.

syllogism. He expounds this in his Logic.[1] Beneke calls *substitution* the deepest fundamental relation in analytic inferences. In a given judgment (the fundamental judgment) we substitute for one of its elements another on the occasion of a second judgment (the auxiliary judgment), which shows the relation between the former and the new element. *What is substituted* may be a *part* of that for which it is substituted, or the *same* thing conceived in a different way. It is a part when the *extent* of the term is divided. This case can only occur where the universal notion is true *in the whole of its extent* ('*ambitum* dividi posse, ubi *totus* adsit; non posse ubi non nisi pars eius inveniatur'), i.e. in the subjects of every universal, and in the predicate of every negative judgment. It is the *same* in another apprehension when the *content* of a term is divided. This case can only occur when a notion is true *in a part of its extent* only ('*complexus* partem poni non posse, nisi quantitate data *particulari*'), because the part of the narrower sphere must also be a part of the wider in which the narrower lies; hence, in the subject of every particular and in the predicate of every affirmative judgment.

> ' Quod vero ad singulas formas attinet, in aperto est:
> in forma **a** ambitum subiecti et complexum praedicati,
> in forma **e** ambitum subiecti et ambitum praedicati,
> in forma **i** complexum subiecti et complexum praedicati,
> in forma **o** denique complexum subiecti, et ambitum praedicati partitionem admittere.'

Beneke's exposition of syllogistic, according to this principle of substitution, is very valuable. The principle of the immediate comparison of the spheres of the three terms in simple

[1] *Lehrbuch der Logik*, p. 110 ff., 1832; in his *Syllogismorum analyticorum origines et ordinem naturalem demoustravit Frid. Eduard. Beneke*, Berol. 1839; and in his *System der Logik*, I. 201–245, 1812: cf. Drewler, *Prakt. Denklehre*, pp. 290–320, 1852; [and Prof. W. Stanley Jevons in his *Substitution of Similars the true principle of Reasoning*, Lond. 1869.]

categorical syllogisms, according to which the relation of
spheres between the two extremes may be directly sought on
the basis of their relation to the middle-notion, without the
fiction ('alteram *finge* fundamentalem sive priorem, alteram
accedentem sive posteriorem') of a fundamental and auxiliary
judgment, is to be preferred as the simpler and more natural.
The expressions, '*partition of extent*,' and '*partition of content*,'
however, are inexact and misleading. In the so-called ' partition of extent' a notion is indeed substituted whose sphere
coincides with a part of the sphere of the former notion, and in
the ' partition of content ' a notion, whose sphere partly coincides with the former notion, and which, therefore, if it belongs
at all to its content in a special sense, belongs to part of it
only ; but that coincidence need not always denote a (partial)
identity ; it may also denote a *connection*. Cf. §§ 71, 85, 105.

It appears better to enunciate the rules belonging to the
cases as we have done above, and thus avoid the expressions,
' partition of extent ' and ' partition of content,' which are not
appropriate in many and in the most important cases. Least
of all can we agree to the consequence deduced by Beneke
from that incorrect expression ' partition : ' ' syllogismos, qui
per tot saecula numeris omnibus absoluti habiti sint, nihil
ad scientiam humanam valere neque amplificandam neque
provehendam.' ' What we gain is only division and clearness.'
This assertion is true of syllogisms formed from the Kantian
' analytic ' judgments, but false of syllogisms formed from synthetic judgments. Syllogisms of this latter kind, in so far as
they rest on the foundation of real conformability to law, are
the most essential means of extending and advancing human
knowledge. Cf. § 101.

Hamilton, like Beneke, but more definitely, founded the
analysis of inferences on the ' quantification of the predicate.'
See above, § 71 [cf. also Appendices A and B].

§ 121. All of the modes of inference which are found
in categorical judgments are repeated in the *subordinately
complex*, and especially in the HYPOTHETICAL judgment.

The proofs of their validity may be obtained in the same way by a comparison of spheres, provided that the coincidence and separation of spheres is made to signify not the relation of inherence, but the corresponding relations of complex judgments, and more particularly the relation of dependence in hypothetical judgments.

The thorough-going analogy of these relations with those of categorical inference, renders it unnecessary to do more than give individual examples of the different figures.

The following is an hypothetical inference of the *First Figure* in the *Mood Barbara* (its minor precedes the major premise): If the earth is in motion, then the light of the fixed stars, so far as they do not lie in the (momentary) direction of the motion of the earth, must be perceived by means of another direction of the telescope and of the eye from that in which their position lies; If this is the case, the apparent position of the fixed stars, so far as they do not lie in the momentary direction of the movement of the earth, must be different from their true position. Hence, if the earth moves, the visible position of those stars must be different from their true position.

The following inference belongs to the *Second Figure* and to the *Mood Cesare* (its minor premise is also placed first): If decided characters exist, then persons may be found who strive after great and noble ends, with real faithfulness and persistence. If the Kantian notion of transcendental freedom is true, no persons can be found who strive after such aims in such a manner. Hence, if decided characters exist, the Kantian notion of transcendental freedom has no truth.

The following inference belongs to the *Third Figure* and to the *Mood Disamis*: In certain cases, if a magnet approaches a non-electrified conductor, or recedes from it, an electric current originates in the latter. In all cases, whenever this experiment is made, magnetic powers only are directly called into operation. Therefore, sometimes, when magnetic forces only are directly set in operation, an electric current is produced.

A conclusion is made in the *Fourth Figure* and in the *Mood*

Bamalip, if the premises of the example given above under the mood *Barbara* are not applied, as there, to explain the phenomena from the real cause, but in the opposite sense to get at the knowledge of the real cause from the actual phenomenon, or at least to pave the way for this knowledge. In some cases at least, and under certain presuppositions, if the apparent position of the stars, which do not lie in the (momentary) direction of the earth, deviates from their true position, the earth moves. The particular form of the conclusion, which is necessary according to the general laws of this mood of inference, has not here the meaning, that sometimes (at certain times) only, the cause of the aberration of light lies in the motion of the earth, but denotes the uncertainty which attaches to the inference from the effect to the cause. It is only when the further proof has been given that the real cause received, which is sufficient to explain the phenomenon in consideration, is also the single reason possible, or the conditio sine qua non, that the problematical admission passes over into certain and universal knowledge. In the given example, the proof, that if the earth did not move, the aberration would not occur in the way that it does actually occur in astronomical observation, must also find a place.

Aristotle does not recognise the scientific correctness of inferences, which he calls *hypothetical* (οἱ ἐξ ὑποθέσεων συλλογισμοί, in opposition to the δεικτικοὶ συλλογισμοί), because science does not result from inference from uncertain presuppositions (ὑποθέσεις), but only from inference from sure principles.[1] He understands by ὑπόθεσις a proposition conceded, which is neither proved nor is yet immediately certain, and of which it is affirmed that it either contains what is to be supposed to be true (διὰ συνθήκης ὡμολογημένον) and what is yet to be proved a truth or an untruth. The judgment passed by Aristotle may be justified in propositions of this kind, but does not at all concern hypothetical judgments in the later use of the phrase. For what is asserted of these in the premises and in the conclusion is not the actual existence of what conditions and what is conditioned, but the *nexus* or *relation of dependence*

[1] *Anal. Pri. l. 11.*

between the conditioning and the conditioned. *And this is not to be received as an arbitrary hypothesis, but as a scientific truth.* It is an unquestionable fact, in spite of the contradiction of Waitz[1] and of Prantl,[2] that Aristotle did not formally comprehend under his notion of inferences ἐξ ὑποθέσεων, hypothetical inferences in the later sense, and that his syllogistic therefore required this enlargement. He reckoned indirect proof among the syllogisms hypothetical in his sense—τοῦ δ' ἐξ ὑποθέσεως μέρος τὸ διὰ τοῦ ἀδυνάτου[2]—because in it a false proposition, viz. the contradictory opposite of the proposition to be proved, is hypothetically taken as true, in the meaning of the (real or feigned) opponent who might assert it, and so serves as an ὑπόθεσις, and forms the basis of a syllogism by means of which something evidently untrue is inferred, – because its contradictory is already recognised to be true, with the aim and in order to destroy the false hypothesis itself by showing the falsehood of its consequence.

The remark of Aristotle:[4] πολλοὶ δὲ καὶ ἕτεροι περαίνονται ἐξ ὑποθέσεως, οὓς ἐπισκέψασθαι δεῖ καὶ διασημῆναι καθαρῶς, appears to have induced *Theophrastus* and Eudemus to reconstruct more accurately the theory of hypothetical inference. Boëthius says[3] that, in the doctrine of the hypothetical syllogisms, ' Theophrastus rerum tantum summas exsequitur, Eudemus latiorem docendi graditur viam.' Theophrastus treats in particular of the *thoroughly hypothetical* syllogisms, in which the premises are of the same form with each other and with the conclusion (οἱ δι' ὅλου or δι' ὅλων ὑποθετικοί, διὰ τριῶν ὑποθετικοί, called also by Theophrastus συλλογισμοὶ κατ' ἀναλογίαν), and have three syllogistic figures like categorical syllogisms. He appears to have made the hypothetical proposition (εἰ τὸ Α, τὸ Β) parallel with the categorical (τὸ Α κατὰ τοῦ Β), the condition (εἰ τὸ Α) with the predicate (τὸ Α), and what is conditioned (τὸ Β) with the subject (κατὰ τοῦ Β). This at least is the only explanation of the fact[6] that he considered

[1] *Ad Arist. Org.* i. 433. [2] *Gesch. der Log.* i. 272, 205.
[3] *Anal. Pri.* i. 23. [4] *Ibid.* i. 44. [5] *De Syl. Hyp.* p. 606.
[6] According to the accounts of Alex. *Ad Anal. Pri.* fol. 134; cf. Prantl, *Gesch. der Log.* i. 381.

450 § 121. *Syllogism from Subordinately Complex*, etc.

that form of inference to be the Second Figure of the hypothetical syllogism, in which the premises beginning with the same condition end with a different conditioned: εἰ τὸ Α, τὸ Β· εἰ μὴ τὸ Α, τὸ Γ· εἰ ἄρα μὴ τὸ Β, τὸ Γ; and that to be the Third Figure in which the premises beginning with a different condition and ending with the same conditioned: εἰ τὸ Α, τὸ Γ· εἰ τὸ Β, οὐ τὸ Γ· εἰ ἄρα τὸ Α, οὐ τὸ Β. Theophrastus contrives to find, by this way of paralleling, the most complete analogy between the First Figure of the Hypothetical inference and the First Figure of the Categorical, according to the following position of the premises: εἰ τὸ Α, τὸ Β· εἰ τὸ Β, τὸ Γ· εἰ ἄρα τὸ Α, τὸ Γ. This opinion of Theophrastus may have determined his choice of the letters, since the early logicians, and Aristotle himself, made the letter which stood first in the alphabet denote the most general term, or what stands in the same relation as the general term.

But this way of paralleling the two kinds of inference is false. The condition is rather to be considered as analogous to the subject of the categorical proposition, and what is conditioned to the predicate. For the sphere of the cases in which the condition exists is not equal to the sphere of the predicate, which is the wider, but is equal to the sphere of the subject, which is either narrower or equal to the sphere of the conditioned.

Alexander of Aphrodisias showed the true relation.[1] He properly recognised the Third Figure in that hypothetical inference which Theophrastus made the Second, and the Second in that which he made the Third.

The *Stoics* have paid special attention to hypothetical syllogism.

Boëthius (in his writing De Syllogismo hypothetico) represents the possible forms of conditional inferences with superabundant detail.

Kant refers hypothetical inference, as well as the hypothetical judgment, to the category of *Dependence*.

[*Hamilton*, in his earlier writings, followed Kant's opinion;

[1] *Ad Arist. Anal. Pri.* fol. 131.

latterly he believed that all hypothetical inference could be classed under immediate inference.[1]]

We agree with the opinion that the logical distinction between the categorical and hypothetical mode of inference rests on the metaphysical distinction between the categories of inherence and dependence. It is not to be considered, as some *later logicians* have done, only or almost only a difference in the verbal expression. Cf. §§ 68, 85, and 94.

§ 122. MIXED INFERENCES are those whose premises are judgments which have different relations. HYPOTHETICO-CATEGORICAL inferences belong to this class. From the *combination of an hypothetical* premise with a *categorical*, which either asserts the fact of the condition or denies the fact of the conditioned, there follows in the first case the categorical affirmation of what is conditioned (modus ponens), in the other case the categorical negation of the condition (modus tollens). The modus ponens corresponds to the First Figure of categorical inferences, the modus tollens to the Second. Different modifications, which correspond to the moods in the first two figures, result by the admission of negation into the second member of the hypothetical premise, as well as by that of the distinction of quantity (in some cases—in all cases). If the negation occurs in the first member of the hypothetical premise, the case corresponds to categorical inferences of the same figures which have a negative subject-notion in the major premise. No form of these inferences can agree with the Third and Fourth Figures of the categorical syllogism (in whose minor premise the middle

[1 Cf. *Lectures on Logic*, ii. 376 ff.]
u o 2

notion is subject). For the condition in the hypothetical corresponds to the subject of the categorical judgments, and the subject does not occur in the minor premise where a categorical takes the place of a conditioned assertion. Hence in such an assertion the part mediating the inference would be wanting.

The *Scheme* of the *modus ponens*, in the fundamental form which corresponds to the mood Barbara, and is more accurately called the modus ponendo ponens,[1] is: If A is, B is; A is: Therefore B is. Its formula was, as given by the older Logicians: posita conditione ponatur conditionatum. The modus ponendo tollens corresponds to the mood Celarent; If A is, B is not; A is: ∴ B is not. These moods pass over into Darii and Ferio, if the minor premise is: Sometimes or in some cases A is, and accordingly the conclusion is: ∴ B is in certain cases, and B is not in certain cases. If the major premise runs: If A is not, B is, or B is not; and the minor premise: A is not, the existence or non-existence of B follows by a modus tollendo ponens or tollendo tollens. The scheme of the *modus tollens* in its fundamental form, which corresponds to the mood Camestres, and may more strictly be called modus tollendo tollens, is: If A is, B is; now B is not: ∴ A is not. Its formula is as follows: sublato conditionato, tollatur conditio. The modus ponendo tollens corresponds to the mood Cesare: If A is, B is not; B is: ∴ A is not. The moods Baroco and Festino can in this case be formed in a way quite analogous to the construction of Darii and Ferio. When the negation occurs in the first member of the hypothetical major premise, a modus tollendo ponens: If A is not, B is; now B is not: ∴ A is; and a modus ponendo ponens: If A is not, B is not; now B is: ∴ A is—may be formed. A conclusion from the conditioned to the condition is unjustifiable: If A is, B is; now B is: ∴ A is (just as a categorical inference in the Second Figure from two affirmative premises is false); for the sphere of the cases where B is may be more extensive than the sphere of the case where A is,

[1] Drobisch, 3rd ed. § 98.

so that B can exist where A is not. For the same reason the inference: If A is, B is; now A is not: ∴ B is not, is false (just as a categorical inference in the First Figure with a negative minor premise is not valid).

In this case also, because of the thorough-going analogy, a few examples will suffice. Böckh[1] concludes, in opposition to Gruppe, in the *modus ponendo ponens* (and in the *modus ponendo tollens*) after the manner of the First Figure: If Plato in the Timaeus teaches the daily motion of the heavens from the east to the west, he must deny the daily rotation of the earth on its axis from west to east (and so cannot teach the rotation of the earth on its axis); but he teaches the former: Therefore he must deny the latter (and cannot teach it). With equal correctness, Böckh, in the same book, in opposition to Stallbaum, argues in the *modus tollendo tollens* after the manner of the *Second* Figure: If Plato teaches the rotation of the earth about the axis of the universe, he must also accept the rotation of the earth round its own axis (for the one axis is only the lengthening of the other); but he denies the latter rotation: Therefore he denies the former also.

Inferences of this kind, though only one of the premises is hypothetical and the other categorical, are commonly called hypothetical inferences, and so explained. The *older Peripatetics* (more particularly Theophrastus and Eudemus) have already made use of this opinion. They call the hypothetical major premise τὸ συνημμένον, its conditioning member τὸ ἡγούμενον, the conditioned τὸ ἑπόμενον, the categorical minor premise μετάληψις, because it repeats categorically, or changes to this form, what was already asserted in the hypothetical major premise as a member, and, lastly, the conclusion συμπέρασμα.

The *Stoics* change the terminology without, as it appears, essentially advancing the doctrine. They call the hypothetical major premise τὸ τροπικόν, or the major premise generally τὸ λῆμμα, its members τὸ ἡγούμενον and τὸ λῆγον, the categorical minor premise πρόσληψις, and, lastly, the conclusion, as in general, ἐπιφορά.[2]

---

[1] In his *Untersuchungen über das Kosmische System des Plato*, 1852.
[2] Cf. Philop. *Ad Anal. Pr.* fol. lx. A.

454 § 122. *Mixed Inferences, etc.*

Boëthius[1] gives a detailed enumeration of the forms here possible.

Kant[2] holds that hypothetical inference of this kind is not properly 'an inference of the reason,' that is, is not a mediate but an immediate inference, because it has only two terms and no middle notion. In point of fact, however, it does not belong to the notion of immediate but to that of mediate inference, because the conclusion does not follow from one premise only, but from the combination of the two. The member which corresponds to the middle notion of categorical inference is not wanting; but what would correspond to the minor notion is absent. Hence the First and Second Figures find place, but not the Third nor Fourth.

Reimarus,[3] *Herbart,*[4] and *Drobisch*[5] have proved that these forms of inferences are parallel to the categorical.

Herbart, however, incorrectly believes that he is able to enunciate a wholly analogous form of the categorical inference in two terms : A is B ; now A is : ∴ B is. For the categorical judgment, in distinction from the hypothetical, always includes the presupposition of the existence of the subject ; and if the speaker asserts this in his own name, this existence, according to his own opinion, is presupposed ; but if it is expressed in the sense of another, or in following up a circle of thought which proceeds upon an actual existence which is feigned, it is presupposed in this sense. Cf. above, § 85. But if the mode of the existence of the subject is more closely defined in the minor premise (e.g. A has not a mythical but a real existence) in order to vindicate for the predicate the same mode of existence in the conclusion ; or if the present in the minor premise, and accordingly in the conclusion, has to do with the future of the person judging, more than two terms are present. The determination of the existence or of the time gives a third term.

[1] *De Syllog. Hypoth.* 614 sqq.   [2] *Log.* § 75.
[3] *Vernunftl.* § 198.
[4] *Lehrb. zur Einleit. in die Philos.* § 64 ff.   [5] *Log.* §§ 94, 98.

§ **123.** All forms of *co-ordinate compound* judgments may occur as premises in inferences. In these inferences the same figures are to be distinguished as in categorical inferences. Their validity may be proved by reduction to the corresponding simple inferences. The like holds good of those judgments in which several of the elements subordinate to the principal proposition are co-ordinate to each other, as well as of those in which the relations of *co-ordination* and *subordination* of judgment are somehow connected with each other.

The CATEGORICAL-DISJUNCTIVE and the HYPOTHETICAL-DISJUNCTIVE inferences are to be taken as examples of mixed inferences. The most prominent example is *disjunctive inference in the stricter sense*, or inference to the validity of a definite part by means of the exclusion of all the rest (modus tollendo ponens), and inference to the invalidity of the others by proving the validity of a definite member (modus ponendo tollens). Other examples are given in hypothetical inferences of the First and especially of the Second Figure from a conjunctive (copulative or remotive) and a disjunctive premise, the *Dilemma*, *Trilemma*, and *Polylemma* (or the Syllogismus cornutus or Complexio). In these inferences it is shown that, whichever of the members of the disjunction may be true, the same conclusion results (that the opponent, whichever of the different possible cases he may choose, must find himself in every case forced to the same conclusion). These dilemmata, &c., which turn against what they themselves enunciate, or which can be applied as a proof of the opposite (δίλημμα ἀντίστροφον, reciprocum), must of necessity contain a fallacy either in the premises or in the form of inference. In the last case the fallacy originates in the identification of two conclusions which are different although contained in the same words.

Disjunctive inferences in the wider sense may be formed in all figures. A disjunctive inference takes the following form:—

<table>
<tr><td>In the First Figure.</td><td>In the Second Figure.</td></tr>
<tr><td>M is either P₁ or P₂, &c.</td><td>P is either M₁ or M₂, &c.</td></tr>
<tr><td>S is M :</td><td>S is neither M₁ nor M₂, &c.:</td></tr>
<tr><td>∴ S is either P₁ or P₂, &c.</td><td>∴ S is not P.</td></tr>
</table>

In the First Figure.

M is either P_1 or P_2, &c.

S is M :

∴ S is either P_1 or P_2, &c.

In the Second Figure.

P is either M_1 or M_2, &c.

S is neither M_1 nor M_2, &c.:

∴ S is not P.

In the Third Figure.

M is either P_1 or P_2, &c.

M is S :

∴ Some S is either P_1 or P_2, &c.

In the Fourth Figure.

P is M ;

M is either S_1 or S_2, &c.

∴ (At least) something which is either S_1 or S_2, &c. is P.

Disjunctive inferences strictly so called are those which contain one of the two following forms:—

A is either B or C.

(1) But A is B :

∴ A is not c

or:

But A is c :

∴ A is not D

(2) But A is not B :

∴ A is c

or :

But A is not c :

∴ A is D

or which take one of the analogous forms which can be formed from more than two members of disjunction.

Disjunctive inferences of this kind essentially agree with those hypothetical inferences explained in the foregoing paragraphs; for the disjunctive major premise is only the comprehension of the following hypothetical judgments:—

If A is B it is not c, and | If A is not B it is c, and
If A is c it is not B. | If A is not c it is B.

The *modus ponendo tollens* follows the scheme of the *First Figure*, the *modus tollendo ponens* can be reduced both to the

First and the *Second* Figures. The *Third* and *Fourth* Figures, however, do not come into application for the same reason as in hypothetical inferences.

The DILEMMA, in the stricter and special sense, is an inference of the *Second* Figure, with an hypothetico-disjunctive premise (which is sometimes major, sometimes minor premise) and with a remotive premise. In the wider sense of the term, inferences with a categorico-disjunctive premise and inferences in the *First* Figure with a disjunctive and a copulative or remotive premise are also attributed to it. The like holds good of the Trilemma, Tetralemma, and Polylemma. The forms of the Dilemma in the *Second* Figure—

(*a*) with *categorical* premises, are :

(1) A is either B or C ;   (2) A is neither B nor C ;
     D is neither B nor C :   D is either B or C :
  ∴ D is not A.   ∴ D is not A.

(*b*) with *hypothetical* premises :

(1) If A is, either B or C is ;   (2) If A is, neither B nor C is.
If D is, neither | Neither B nor   If D is, either | Either B or C
 B nor C is ı | C is :   B or C is: | is ı
∴ If D is, A is | ∴ A is not.   ∴ If D is A is | ∴ A is not.
 not. | not. |

An inference in the First Figure may be considered to be a Dilemma, whose major premise is conjunctive—either copulative : A as well as B is C, and in the hypothetical form : If A is, as well as if B is, C is,—or remotive : Neither A nor B is C, and hypothetically : Neither if A is, nor if B is, is C ; and whose minor premise is disjunctive : D is either A or B, and hypothetically : If D is, either A or B is—or : Now either A or B is ; from which the conclusion is to be drawn according to the moods Barbara and Celarent. These inferences of the First Figure, however, both in the categorical and hypothetical forms, are to be denoted as *inferences of induction.* Hence, if they are to be called Dilemmata, they must be subsumed under both of those logical notions whose spheres partially coincide. This

458	§ 123. *Mixed Inferences with*

relation must always be avoided if the construction of the terminology could result purely according to a scientific point of
view. But the name Dilemma, in its transmission, has been
inseparably connected with certain examples which can only
naturally be represented in the hypothetical forms of the First
Figure.

Modern logicians waver between more limited and wider
definitions of the term. *Herbart*, for example,[1] limits them to
the Second Figure, but denotes by the term categorical as
well as hypothetical disjunctive inferences.

Twesten[2] gives the name Dilemmata to inferences in the
hypothetical form only, but reckons among them hypothetical
inferences of the First Figure, with negative major premise and
conclusion (whose scheme follows the analogy of the mood
Cesare, but is called Diprese by Twesten, following Lambert).

With *Drobisch*[3] only hypothetical inferences are Dilemmata,
but they include positive as well as negative inferences of the
First Figure.

[*Hamilton* defines the Dilemma to be a hypothetico-disjunctive reasoning whose major premise is both hypothetical and
disjunctive, and whose minor denies the *whole* of the disjunctive
consequents, e.g.: If A is B, either C is D, or E is F; but neither
C is D, nor E is F: Therefore A is not B.

Mansel defines the Dilemma to be a syllogism having a conditional major premise with more than one antecedent, and a
disjunctive minor. Its different forms are :—

I. Simple Constructive.

If A is B, C is D ; and if E is F, C is D ;
But either A is B, or E is F ;
∴ C is D.

II. Complex Constructive.

If A is B, C is D ; and if E is F, G is H ;
But either A is B, or E is F :
∴ Either C is D, or G is H.

---

[1] *Lehrbuch, etc.*, § 69.	[2] *Logik*, § 150.
[3] *Logik*, 3rd ed. § 101.

III. Destructive (always complex).

If A is B, C is D; and if E is F, G is H;
But either C is not D, or G is not H:
∴. Either A is not B, or E is not F.[1]]

Others proceed in other ways.

The Dilemma, Trilemma, &c. is a perfectly correct form of knowledge, when used scientifically. It is no objection to its significance in Logic that from antiquity down to the present day it has been used constantly for rhetorical ends, and to display one's wit. *An example of its scientific value* is given in the mathematical inference which is true of parallelograms of equal height but of unequal and incommensurable bases. If the content of the first is not related to the content of the second, as the base of the first to the base of the second, they must either be related as the base of the first is to a line which is greater than the base of the second, or as it is related to a line which is smaller than the base of the second. But neither the one nor the other proportion is probable. Hence the relation of the content must be equal to the relation of the bases. In the same way the foundation of the Leibnizian Optimism is a scientifically justifiable trilemma. If the actually existing world were not the best of all possible worlds, then God did not either know the best, or could not create and preserve it, or did not wish to create nor preserve it. But (because of the divine wisdom, omnipotence, and goodness) neither the first, second, nor third is true. Hence the actual world is the best of all possible worlds.

Disjunctive inferences were originally subsumed as a species under the notion of the *hypothetical.*

Alexander of Aphrodisias says:[1] ἐξ ὑποθέσεως γὰρ καὶ οἱ διαιρετικοί, οἳ καὶ αὐτοὶ ἐν τοῖς κατὰ μετάληψιν ἐξ ὑποθέσεων.

Philoponus,[2] where he gives an account of the older Peripatetics and Stoics, distinguishes in those hypothetical syllogisms whose conclusion is a categorical judgment (and which thus

---

[1 *Artis Logicæ Rudim.* p. 108 x.]
[2 *Ad Arist. Anal. Pr.* fol. 133 a.   [3] *Ad Anal. Pr.* fol. ix. b.

form the opposite of the δι' ὅλου or διὰ τριῶν ὑποθετικοί) the
ἀκολουθία and the διάζευξις.

Boëthius[1] refers the following division of hypothetical syllogisms to *Eudemus*: ' aut talo acquiritur aliquid per quandam
inter se consentientium conditionem, quod fieri nullo modo
possit, ut ad suum terminum ratio perducatur (the apagogical
method of inference), aut in conditione posita consequentia vi
coniunctionis (the συνημμένον or the ἀκολουθία) vel disiunctionis
(the διάζευξις) ostenditur.' But it is very doubtful whether the
older Peripatetics, and Theophrastus and Eudemus more especially, enunciated in a similar way, as the Stoics did later, five
fundamental forms of the ' hypothetical ' syllogisms leading to
a categorical conclusion.[2]

The Stoic *Chrysippus*[3] placed five συλλογισμοὶ ἀναπόδεικτοι
at the head of his Logic. The two first of these agree with the
modus ponens and *modus tollens* of inferences formed from an
hypothetical and a categorical premise. If the first is, the
second is ; but the first is : Therefore the second is—and : But
the second is not : Therefore the first is not. The *third* of
these syllogisms has a conjunctive major premise of a negative
form. There is not at the same time the first and the second
—from which, by means of an affirmative (but not by means of
a negative) πρόσληψις, an inference can be formed, viz. : Now
the first is : ∴ the second is not. The *fourth* and *fifth* inferences rest on a disjunctive major premise : Either the first is
or the second—from which in two ways, by means of an affirmative and also by means of a negative πρόσληψις—(1) Now
the first is : ∴ the second is not ; or (2) Now the second is
not : ∴ the first is.

The *Dilemma* was first explained by the rhetoricians.

Cicero says:[4] complexio est, in qua utrum conecsseris,
reprehenditur.

[1] *De Syllog. Hypoth.* p. 607.
[2] Prantl imagines they did, *Gesch. der Log.* i. 379 ff., 385 ff. ; cf.
473 ff.
[3] According to *Sext. Emp. Adv. Math.* viii. 223 ; cf. *Hyp. Pyrrh.*
ii. 157 sqq.
[4] *De Invent.* i. 29, 45.

Quintilian teaches: [1] fit etiam ex duobus, quorum necesse est alterutrum, eligendi adversario potestas, efficiturque, ut, utrum elegerit, noceat.

The rhetorician *Hermogenes* has the term: διλήμματον σχῆμα [2]—διλήμματον δὲ σχῆμά ἐστι λόγος ἐκ δύο προτάσεων ἐναντίων τὸ αὐτὸ πέρας συνάγων.

The most noted examples transmitted of rhetorical sophistical dilemmas are the anecdote of Korax and Lisias about instruction in the art of persuasion: [3] ὦ Κόραξ, τί ἐπηγγείλω διδάσκειν; —τὸ πείθειν ὃν ἂν θέλης·—εἰ μὲν τὸ πείθειν με ἐδίδοξας, ἰδοὺ πείθω σε μηδὲν λαμβάνειν· εἰ δὲ τὸ πείθειν με οὐκ ἐδίδαξας, καὶ οὕτως οὐδέν σοι παρέχω, ἐπειδὴ οὐκ ἐδίδαξάς με τὸ πείθειν; —the similar story of Protagoras and Euathlus about the honorarium to be paid by the latter to the former when he gained his first case; [4]—the fallacy in the dialogue between a crocodile and the father or mother whose child has been seized, called ὁ κροκοδειλίτης or ἄπορος [5]—and the dilemma of Bias: εἰ καλήν, ἕξεις κοινήν· εἰ δὲ αἰσχράν, ἕξεις ποινήν. [6] The ψευδόμενος already mentioned [7] is of the same kind.

The solution of the ἀντιστρέφοντα in these dilemmas depends on the division of the apparently simple conclusion into the two elements which it contains. In the law case of Protagoras and Euathlus (as Bachmann [8] and Bencke [9] have rightly remarked) a different decree must be given in two different conclusions. In the first place, the condition of the bargain was not fulfilled. Euathlus has *until now* won no case, and so is *not yet* obliged to pay the sum. Hence he must *gain* this case. But by this decision the state of the case is altered, and Protagoras must be allowed to bring a second *action*, on the ground

1 *Inst.* v. 10, 69.
2 *De Inv.* iv. 6; cf. *Anon. Prolegom. ad Hermog.* iv. 14.
3 *Anon. Prolegom. ad Hermog.* iv. 14.
4 *Schol. ad Hermog.* p. 180, ed. Walz; *Gell.* v. 10.
5 *Diog. Laert.* vii. 44, 82; *Lucian, Bίων πρᾶσ. 22*: in another form, instead of the crocodile the robber of the daughter of a soothsayer, *Schol. ad Hermog.* pp. 154, 170.
6 *Gell.* v. 11; cf. ix. 16, 5.   7 § 77.
8 *System der Logik*, p. 218.   9 *System der Logik*, p. 140.

of the changed relation, which must be decided in his favour.
It must be granted without hesitation that cases may occur
where the logical distinction cannot actually be realised (as
e.g. in the anecdote of the crocodile, the death of the stolen
child would make any further action needless). For if absurdity once enters into the premises, it must appear in the
conclusion.

Boëthius, like the earlier logicians, reckons disjunctive
judgments and inferences among the hypothetical: fiunt vero
propositiones *hypotheticae* etiam per *disiunctionem* ita: aut hoc
est, aut illud est;—omnis igitur *hypothetica* propositio *vel per
connexionem* (per connexionem vero illum quoque modum, qui
per negationem fit, esse pronuntio), *vel per disiunctionem*.[1]
He puts both of these forms or the whole hypothetical or conditional judgments and inferences in the wider sense as the
complex in opposition to the categorical or predicative as the
simple: praedicativa *simplex* est propositio; conditionalis vero
esse non poterit, nisi ex praedicativis propositionibus *coniunga-
tur*;—ac de *simplicibus* quidem, i.e. de praedicativis syllogismis
duobus libellis explicuimus;—*non simplices* vero syllogismi
sunt, qui hypothetici dicuntur, quos Latino nomine conditio-
nales vocamus ;—necesse est, categoricos syllogismos hypothe-
ticis vim conclusionis ministrare.[2]

Later logicians have made disjunctive judgments and inferences co-ordinate with the hypothetical, because they have
taken the latter term in its narrower sense, but have subsumed
both, with Boëthius, under the notion of the not simple or compound, and so opposed them to the categorical, which are simple
and primitive.

This plan prevails in the *Cartesian* and also in the *Leibnizian* Schools. The frequently mentioned Logique ou l'Art de
Penser [3] divides syllogisms into simple (simples) and compound
(conjonctifs); the former (as in § 120, p. 444) are divided into
incomplexes and complexes, the latter [4] into conditionnels, dis-
jonctifs, and copulatifs. The individual forms essentially

[1] *De Syll. Hypoth.* p. 608.   [2] Ibid. p. 607.
[3] Part ii. ch. ii.   [4] Ch. xii.

agree with the five συλλογισμοί ἀναπόδεικτοι of Chrysippus
(see p. 460).

Wolff says : [1] syllogismus compositus est, cuius vel una, vel
utraque praemissa non est propositio categorica ; he enumerates
here [2] the hypothetical (syllogismus hypotheticus, conditionalis,
connexus) and [3] the disjunctive syllogism (syllogismus disiunc-
tivus).

Leibniz himself subsumes disjunctive inferences under the
hypothetical, after the fashion of the Peripatetics.[4]

Kant [5] first enumerates categorical, hypothetical, and disjunctive syllogisms as *three co-ordinate kinds*, which he refers,
as he does the corresponding judgments, to three supposititious
original and primary notions of the understanding; viz. to the
three categories of Relation—Substantiality, Causality, and
Reciprocity. He abandons the view that the categorical inferences of reason are regular and the others irregular ; for all
three kinds are the products of equally correct and essentially
mutually distinct functions of reason.

This division suffers from the same defects as the corresponding division of judgments (cf. § 68). Kant, however, is correct
when he denies that these *inferences* as such are compound.

§ 124. COMPOUND INFERENCES are combinations of
simple inferences by means of common parts, through
which a final judgment (mediately) is deduced from more
than two given judgments. The individual parts of
the compound inference are either completely or incompletely expressed. In the first case, the *Chain syllogism*
arises (syllogismus concatenatus, catena syllogismorum,
polysyllogismus). This is a series of inferences so
linked to each other that the conclusion of one makes
a premise of the other. That inference in which the

[1] *Log.* § 403. [2] Ibid. § 404. [3] Ibid. § 416.
[4] *Nouv. Ess.* iv. 17, p. 395 in Erdmann's ed. of the Philosophical
Works.
[5] *Log.* § 60 ; *Krit. der r. Vern. Elementarl.* §§ 9, 19.

common proposition is the conclusion is called *Prosyllo-gismus*, and that in which it is the premise, *Episyllo-gismus*. The advance from the prosyllogismus to the episyllogismus (a principiis ad principata) is called *epi-syllogistic*, or *progressive*, or *synthetic*, and the advance from episyllogismus to prosyllogismus (a principiatis ad principia) is called *prosyllogistic*, or *regressive*, or *analytic*.

Thus, e.g. Boëthius[1] concludes *episyllogistically* or *pro-gressively*, for he first forms the syllogism: what furthers (prodest) is good; what exercises or improves, furthers: There-fore what exercises or improves is good,—and continues using the *conclusion* attained as a *premise* (the *major premise*) *of a new syllogism*: misfortune, which happens to the good, serves either (if he is a wise man) to train him, or (if he is a proficient) to improve him. Hence misfortune which befalls the good is good.

In the long mathematical example § 110, the conclusion of 1 is *minor premise* in 3; the conclusion of 3 is *minor premise* in 4, and so on. In this reference the course of demonstration is *progressive*. This chain of inference is *epi-syllogistic* or *progressive*. If there is a medium obstructing the motion of the planets, then the path of the earth cannot be constant nor periodical, but must always become less: If this be the case, then the existence of organisms on the earth cannot have been (nor can remain) eternal. Hence, if there is this medium, organisms must have at one time come into existence, and will wholly pass away. If organisms once existed for the first time on the earth, they must have arisen out of inorganic matter. If this is the case, there has been an original produc-tion (generatio aequivoca). Hence, if this obstructive medium exists, there has been an original production.

Cato argues *prosyllogistically* or *regressively* in Cicero:[2]

[1] *De Consol. Philos.* iv. pr. vii.   [2] *De Fin.* iii. 8, 27.

quod est bonum, omne laudabile est; quod autem laudabile
est, omne honestum est: bonum igitur quod est, honestum est.
This syllogism is supported by a *supplementary proof of a
premise* (the minor: quod est bonum omne laudabile est).
If the *major premise be proved supplementarily*, the inference
is also made *prosyllogistically* or *regressively*. The historical
development of the sciences in its length and breadth should
take this course. For certain general propositions are first discovered (as, e.g. the laws of Kepler) under which the individual
facts are syllogistically subsumed. The highest principles
are discovered later (e.g. the Newtonian law of Gravitation)
from which those general propositions are necessary deductions.
A like course is to be preserved in many cases for didactic
reasons in the exposition of the sciences. In psychology a
similar significance might belong to the fundamental processes of Beneke—the formation of sensations in consequence
of external affections, the formation of traces or unconscious
constructions of memory, of the internal affections, to which
also belongs the calling into consciousness of like thoughts by
the like, and the reconstruction of mental (psychic) powers—
which belongs in Astronomy to Kepler's laws; for from these
processes the individual phenomena of the mental (psychic) life
may be *genetically* explained. The *prosyllogism* which deduces these processes from higher principles has yet to be
sought for. The Herbartian hypotheses, which, even if they
were correct, could not be placed in the same rank with the
principles of Newton, are insufficiently established, and, although enunciated to avoid contradictions, are not free from
internal contradiction. (The monads or the real essences are
not in space, and yet are the substantial elements of what exists
in space; self-maintenance suffices only to maintain what
exists, and yet is sufficient to establish the new, which remains
as a conception after the removal of the existing cause, and
affects in manifold relations other results of self-maintenance.)
Hence they are untenable.

The exposition of the different forms which a combination
of syllogisms admits or excludes, whether they take the form

of *inferences of the First or the other Figures*, appears to be
unnecessary, for the general syllogistic rules enable us to deal
securely with every given case in the enunciation and testing
of chains of reasoning.

§ 125. An ENTHYMEME (ἐνθύμημα, syllogismus decur-
tatus) is a simple inference abbreviated in the expression
by the omission of one of the two premises. The premise which remains unexpressed must be completed in
thought, and thus the enthymeme is logically equivalent
to a fully expressed syllogism. If one or both of the
premises of a simple inference be enlarged by the addition of reasons, the EPICHEIREMA results (ἐπιχείρημα,
aggressio), which is, therefore, an abbreviated compound
inference. The abbreviation, however, has to do only
with the form of the syllogism reduced to a subordinated
proposition which is given as the cause of one of the
premises.

An episyllogistic chain of reasoning whose expression
is simplified by the omission of all the conclusions save
the last, and where those suppressed conclusions are
identical with the major or minor premises of the following syllogisms, is called a *Chain-syllogism* or a
SORITES (σωρίτης, sorites, acervus, syllogismus acer-
vatus). The *Aristotelian Sorites* differs from the *Goclenian* by the arrangement in which the premises follow
each other. The *former* has the form : A is B, B is C,
C is D : ∴ A is D. It advances from the *lower notion to
the higher*. The *minor premises* of all the syllogisms
save the first (e.g. A is C) are not expressed, but are to
be added in thought in the analysis which completes
them. The *Goclenian Sorites*, on the other hand, has
the opposite succession of premises : C is D, B is C, A is

B: ∴ A is D. It advances, so far as the succession of premises is concerned (and if, as in Aristotle's Sorites, the predicate be enunciated before its subject, so far as the succession of notions also is concerned), *from the more* universal to the less universal. The *major premise* of all the syllogisms except the first (e.g. B is D) is to be added in thought.

The scheme may be given for the sake of distinctness:—

Aristotelian Sorites.	Goclenian Sorites.
A is B	C is D
B is C	B is C
C is D	A is B
A is D	A is D

Analysis.	Analysis.
1. A is B (minor premise)	1. C is D (major premise)
B is C (major premise)	B is C (minor premise)
A is C (conclusion)	B is D (conclusion)
2. A is C (minor premise)	2. B is D (major premise)
C is D (major premise)	A is B (minor premise)
A is D (conclusion)	A is D (conclusion)

In the Aristotelian Sorites that conclusion which in the following (or in a great number of members, in each of the following) syllogism becomes the minor premise is not expressed (but is to be added in an analysis which completes the thought). In the Goclenian Sorites that conclusion which in (each of) the following syllogisms becomes the major is omitted. Both forms, the Aristotelian and Goclenian, agree in this, that the conclusion of the first syllogism is the premise (major or minor) of the second. The characteristic (§ 124) of *episyllogistic* procedure lies in this, that one advances from previous to consequent inferences. Hence, both in the Goclenian and in the Aristotelian Sorites the advance is *episyllogistic.* It is a mistake to think the Goclenian *prosyllogistic* or regressive.

The *Enthymeme* must not be considered to be an immediate,
nor the *Epicheirema* a simple influence. The abbreviation of
expression does not change the form of thought.

Examples of Chain-syllogisms may be seen in great numbers in
scientific writings which advance from given hypotheses to final
results. In such writings the form of a chain of thoughts is more
frequently shortly indicated than completely expressed according to the logical schematism. For example, Aristotle[1] concludes
that the exposition of action, the combination of events into the
unity of a complete action or the μῦθος, is the most important
of the elements of Tragedy, from the following premises:
Action is that in which happiness lies; what contains happiness is the end and aim; the end and aim is what is highest:
Therefore action is what is highest. This is true in actual
life. But the unspoken thought must be added: The reproduction of what is actually the highest in the objects reproduced in Tragedy (Action, Character, Thought) is the highest
in Tragedy. Hence it follows that, because action is highest
in real existence, its reproduction or the μῦθος is highest in
Tragedy. In the same sense Aristotle concludes negatively
that the reproduction of character is not highest: Character is a
quality (a ποιόν); Quality is not that in which happiness lies;
that in which happiness does not lie is not the end: What is not
the end is not highest. The unexpressed thought must be added:
The reproduction of what is not actually highest in what is to
be reproduced in Tragedy, is not highest in the work of art.

Aristotle does not, like later logicians, mean by ἐνθύμημα
an abbreviated inference, but an inference of probability. He
says:[2] ἐνθύμημα μὲν οὖν ἐστι συλλογισμὸς ἐξ εἰκότων ἢ ση-
μείων. He classes it[3] among the rhetorical syllogisms. The
Enthymeme, in the Aristotelian sense, when compared with
the scientific or apodictic syllogism, is a mere previous deliberation or consideration producing only subjective conviction
(and so the name signifies, although moderns have strangely
made it refer to the retention of one premise in the mind,

[1] *Poet.* c. vi.   [2] *Anal. Pr.* ii. c. xxvii. p. 70 a, 10.
[3] *Anal. Post.* i. 1, p. 71 a, 10.

ἐν θυμῷ). It is an imperfect form of inference, and therefore has been called by some logicians (according to *Quintil.* Inst. Or. v. 10) 'imperfectus Syllogismus.' The 'imperfection' has been taken to mean imperfection of expression by later logicians.[1]

Boëthius also says in this sense:[2] Enthymema est imperfectus syllogismus, i.e. oratio, in qua non omnibus antea propositionibus constitutis infertur festinata conclusio, ut si quis dicat: homo animal est; substantia igitur est. The ἐπιχείρημα is, in Aristotle, an inference which tests, συλλογισμὸν διαλεκτικόν.[3] It is often useful, in debated questions, to reason by means of a double ἐπιχείρημα, both from the proposition and from its negation, not to be brought sophistically to a standstill by the contradiction, but in order to gain dialectical experience, and, by breaking through the illusion in this way, to come to a sure settlement of the question.[4] There has been some uncertainty amongst the later logicians and rhetoricians, more especially among the Latins, about the meaning of the term. Quintilian[5] ascribes the translation *aggressio* to *Valgius*, and the explanation of the Epicheirema as an 'apodixis imperfecta' to *Caecilius*. This explanation is related to the meaning of Aristotle, but does not exhaust it. According to the later logicians, the Epicheirema agrees with the Enthymeme in this, that the imperfection contained in it lies in the incompleteness of expression, but the Epicheirema is distinguished from the Enthymeme by denoting a certain abbreviation of the compound (or extension of the simple) syllogism.

The term SORITES is not found in *Aristotle*[6] in the sense given above. It came into use later. *Cicero*, for example, uses it,[7] calling it the inference of the Stoics: quod bonum

[1] [This question is fully and clearly discussed by Hamilton, *Lect. on Logic,* i. 388, and *Discus.* p. 154.]

[2] *Op.* ed. Basil. p. 864.   [3] *Top.* viii. 11, p. 162 A, 16.

[4] Ibid. c. xiv. p. 163 A, 36 ff.   [5] *Inst. Orat.* v. 10.

[6] He alludes to the thing itself, *Anal. Pri.* i. c. xxv.

[7] *De Fin.* iv. 18, 50.

sit, id case optabile; quod optabile, id case expetendum; quod
expetendum laudabile;—igitur omne bonum laudabile. The
Goclenian Sorites is not essentially distinct from the so-called
Aristotelian, and corresponds strictly to the Aristotelian Syl-
logism. It gets its name from *Rudolf Goclenius* (1547-1628),
Professor at Marburg, who first explained this form in his
Isagoge in Organum Aristotelis, 1598. In this work he
partially follows Ramus.

[*Hamilton* accepts the justness of these two forms of the
Sorites as a testimony in favour of the scientific accuracy of
his distinction between reasoning in comprehension and reasoning in extension. The Goclenian Sorites, in which the subject
is the containing whole, and the predicate the contained part,
proceeds in the Quantity of *Comprehension*; the Aristotelian
Sorites, in which the predicate is the containing whole, and
the subject the contained part, proceeds in the whole of *Extension.*[1]]

§ 126. An *inference incorrect* in its *formal* relation
(fallacia) is a PARALOGISM if it leads the person reasoning
into error. If there is the intention to deceive, it is
called a SOPHISM. *Formal fallacies* depend partly on a
false comparison of spheres, and partly on the *ambiguity*
of the signification of one and the same notion, more
especially of the middle notion. The Fallacies of the
First kind, which are most worthy of notice, are—

Inferences with a negative minor premise in the
    First Figure,
Inferences with affirmative premises in the Second
    Figure,
Inferences with an universal conclusion in the
    Third Figure; and

[1 Cf. Hamilton's *Lect. on Logic*, i. 380.]

The Fallacia de consequenti ad antecedens in categorical and hypothetical form.

The Fallacies of the *Second kind* are divided into—

(a) *Fallaciae Secundum dictionem*, and (b) *Fallaciae extra dictionem.*

(a) Among the former are reckoned those which proceed from—

Homonymia—i. e. from similarity of name in different things which have no similarity of notion, and where there is, therefore, an ambiguity in the word. The fallacy arises from the reciprocal exchange of the different meanings of the same word.

Prosodia—the fallacy arises from the exchange of words which sound similarly and have the same letters, but are differently accentuated.

Amphiboly—the mistaking syntactical forms which have a double sense. And from

Figura dictionis (σχῆμα τῆς λέξεως)—the mistaking the grammatical form of individual words, especially the interchange of different forms of inflection, of different parts of speech, and of different forms of conception or categories in the Aristotelian sense of the word.

(b) To the *Fallaciis extra dictionem* belong more especially—

Fallacia ex accidente—an interchange of the essential and non-essential.

Fallacia a dicto secundum quid ad dictum simpliciter;

and conversely, *a dicto simpliciter ad dictum secundum quid*—an interchange of the absolute and relative senses of the term considered.

Fallacia secundum plures interrogationes ut unam —neglecting the necessity of dividing a question which, according to its different references, requires several answers.

All fallacies of the second kind contain a more or less hidden *quaternio terminorum*—i.e. four principal terms —or a *Saltus in concludendo*—i.e. a leap or hiatus in arguing.

The doctrine of fallacies has a more didactic and historical than a peculiarly scientific interest. Logic, as the science of thinking and knowing, gives an exposition of the normative laws. Whatever contradicts these laws is fallacious. To enumerate exhaustively all the possible departures from these rules would be a useless waste of work, for error is an ἄπειρον.

It is sufficient to *exemplify* the kinds of fallacies which even practised thinkers often fall into.

When Descartes believed that matter in opposition to mind was without force—entirely passive, a form of thought underlay his belief which, when brought to the form of a simple syllogism, can be represented as a fallacy in the First Figure with a negative minor premise. Mind is active; matter is not mind : ∴ matter is not active. Many defences of negro slavery proceed upon this fallacy. Caucasians have the rights of men ; Negroes are not Caucasians : ∴ They have not the rights of men.

The fallacy resulting from merely affirmative premises in the Second Figure is exemplified in the inference that the Platonic state is essentially identical with the old Hellenic, because both agree in requiring the unconditional submission of the individual to the community. (The inference overlooks the essential difference of the immediate unity in and through a community of disposition, and subordination under a scholastically fostered transcendental wisdom.)

In the Third Figure a universal conclusion would be falsely drawn in the reasoning: All men are inhabitants of the earth; all men are reasonable creatures; all reasonable creatures are inhabitants of the earth.

When from the material truth of certain consequents the validity of the presupposition is inferred, the fallacy de consequente ad antecedens results. It is exemplified in the following. Helmholtz[1] enunciates the proposition: whatever in sense-perception is overcome and converted into its opposite in the intuition-picture by moments which experience has given, undoubtedly cannot be recognised to be sensation (but must be considered as a product of experience and practice). This proposition is equivalent to the proposition from which it proceeds (§ 87) by conversio simplex: whatever in the sense-perception is sensation cannot be overcome (set aside and converted to its opposite) by moments of experience. Now another author[2] gives the following proposition as the equivalent of this. Everything in our sense-perception that is not overcome and converted into its opposite by the moments of experience in the intuition-picture, is sensation. But this proposition is in fact by no means identical with that of Helmholtz. It can only be made equivalent to it by means of the paralogism we are illustrating. The real consequence is only: Something at least which cannot be overcome by the moments of experience is sensation (cf. § 91 or § 85). If we believe, with Helmholtz, that whatever is sensation, cannot be overcome by the moments of experience (sensation being the antecedens, and the impossibility to be overcome the consequens), the assertion is still not equivalent to this, that sensation always is present where this impossibility to be overcome exists. For this same impossibility to be overcome might arise from something else which is not sensation, perhaps from what is à priori, in the Kantian sense of

[1] *Physiol. Optik.* p. 438, Leipzig, 1867.
[2] H. Böhmer, *Die Sinneswahrnehmung*, p. 617, Erlangen, 1868.

the word, or to what had been so firmly established by earlier experience that no later experience can alter it. Cf. § 122. A concealed quaternio terminorum is the most frequent and the most deceptive of fallacies. A fallacy of this kind lies in Plato's inference in the Phaedo: The soul is ἀθάνατος (which according to the connection of the passage is only proved in the sense: according to its essence, so long as it exists, it is never dead): Everything ἀθάνατον (i.e. immortal) is ἀνώλεθρον: Hence the soul is ἀνώλεθρος. So in the inference of Epicurus: Whatever has effects is something ἀληθόν; every perception has effects (psychical): Hence it is something ἀληθές—where the same word now means *actual*, at another time *true*. A quaternio terminorum often lies in the use of such expressions as boni, optimi, &c. which waver between the meanings of: the *aristocracy of talent and character*, and the *aristocracy by birth*, when debating the best form of government. Tertullian's fallacy rests on a quaternio terminorum: It contradicts the conditions of human existence that men should continually live with their heads undermost and their feet uppermost; those at the antipodes must live in this way: hence there are no dwellers at the antipodes. (The first premise is true only for an uppermost and undermost understood from the stand-point of the individuals concerned, and the second true only of an uppermost and undermost understood of the stand-point of the speaker). Calov's inference contains a quaternio terminorum: Changes in the vowels of the Hebrew text of the Bible are inadmissible and criminal because man, liable to error, ought not to touch God's word (where ‘God's word’ means now, really, the transmitted text of the Bible, then, ideally, the Divine Truth). When the Stoics quote as an example of impossibility: ἡ γῆ ἵσταται, using flying in the proper sense of the word, and at the same time exclude by it any motion of the earth, the deceptive form of the expression ἵστασθαι implicitly contains a fallacy of the kind now under consideration. Explicitly stated, it would be as follows: Whatever moves on in open space (without support from beneath) flies; what has no wings (and therefore the earth) does

not fly: Hence what has no wings (and therefore the earth)
does not move on in open space. Logical analysis reveals the
fallacy lurking in the double sense of the expression 'flying,'
and concealed by the enthymemic use of the figurative expression. Cf. § 61: Remarks on Synthetic Definitions; and
§ 137: On Failures in Proof.

Aristotle, in his Περὶ τῶν σοφιστικῶν ἐλέγχων, is led to give
especial attention to the sophisms most discussed in his day.
He defines[1] the σόφισμα to be συλλογισμὸς ἐριστικός, and divides
Sophisms into two chief classes: παρὰ τὴν λέξιν and ἔξω τῆς
λέξεως. In the first class he reckons[2] six kinds: ὁμωνυμία (aequi-
vocatio), ἀμφιβολία (ambiguitas), σύνθεσις (fallacia a sensu diviso
ad sensum compositum), διαίρεσις (fallacia a sensu composito ad
sensum divisum), προσῳδία (accentus), σχῆμα τῆς λέξεως (figura
dictionis). The third and fourth of these, as far as they belong to the fallaciis secundum dictionem, can be classed in
the above-given sense under the notion of Amphiboly. These
two are the mutual exchange of mutual and collective sense,
or of what is true of all individuals, or in every special individual reference, and of what is true only of the sum total of
the individuals.[3]

Aristotle[4] enumerates among the sophisms of the Second
division the following seven kinds: παρὰ τὸ συμβεβηκός (fallacia ratiocinationis ex accidente), τὸ ἁπλῶς ἢ μὴ ἁπλῶς (a dicto
simpliciter ad dictum secundum quid), ἡ τοῦ ἐλέγχου ἄγνοια
(ignoratio elenchi), παρὰ τὸ ἑπόμενον (fallacia ratiocinationis ex
consequente ad antecedens), τὸ ἐν ἀρχῇ λαμβάνειν, αἰτεῖσθαι
(petitio principii), τὸ μὴ αἴτιον ὡς αἴτιον τιθέναι (fallacia de
non causa ut causa), τὸ τὰ πλείω ἐρωτήματα ἓν ποιεῖν (fallacia
plurium interrogationum). These fallacies, however, are partly

---

[1] *Top.* viii. 11.   [2] *De Soph. Elench.* c. iv.

[3] By σχήματα τῆς λέξεως Aristotle means here the grammatical forms
of nouns and verbs, and in *Poet.* c. xix. more especially the forms of
proposition founded upon the various relations of predicate to subject,
which are partly expressed by verbal moods: Imperative, Desiderative,
Threatening, Indicative, Question and Answer.

[4] *Poet.* c. v.

rather fallacies in demonstration (§ 137) and fallacies in single
judgments than properly fallacies of inference. Aristotle, in
his Περὶ σοφιστικῶν ἐλέγχων, gives examples of the fallacies
named by him. Plato's (or a Platonist's) dialogue Euthydemus may also be compared. *Fries* gives ancient and modern
examples, for the most part made up.[1] A detailed and accurate account of fallacies of inference may be found in Mill's
Logic.[2]

Trendelenburg very properly remarks, in reference to the
nebulous, misty character of so many modern speculations, and
to the innumerable fallacies which apparently solve the insoluble
problem of deriving perfection from the imperfect, that a
modern reproduction of Aristotle's work on the solution of
fallacies is a want of the day.[3]

This problem has been attempted by the *Antibarbarus Logicus*
of *Cajus*,[4] but only in a one-sided way, although the author is
somewhat skilful in performing certain police duties within the
province of philosophical thought.

§ 127. INDUCTION (inductio, ἐπαγωγή) is the inference from the individual or special to the universal.

Its form is the following:—

M_1, as well as M_2 and M_3 . . . . is P
M_1, as well as M_2 and M_3 . . . . is S

Every S is P

This inference proceeds from the individual or particular
(M), which ever approaches the universal (S) by successive extension to the universal (S). The inference
of induction in its external form is somewhat like a
conjunctive syllogism of the Third Figure, but is essen-

[1] *System der Logik*, § 109.   [2] 7th ed. ii. 352–401.
[3] *Erläut. zu den Elem. der Arist. Log.* p. 69, 1842.
[4] 1851; 2nd ed. part i., 1853.

tially distinguished from it by its endeavour to reach a universal conclusion.

The expression induction is used in the proper and strictest sense, when inference is made from the *individual*, laid hold of by observation, to the universal. The logical form, however, is the same when inferences are made from smaller groups to the universal which contains them, and this inference also must be recognised as inductive.

The predicate, as well as the subject of the minor premise, may be a plurality in the inductive inference. If the predicate merely is a plurality, the form would be:—

$$\text{M is P}$$
$$\underline{\text{M is } \sigma_1 \text{ as well as } \sigma_2 \text{ and } \sigma_3 \ldots}$$
Everything that is σ_1, as well as σ_2 and σ_3, ... is P.

For example: The earth has inhabitants; the earth is a planet of medium size of a medium distance from the sun, surrounded by an atmosphere whose meteorological phenomena are subject to regular returns: Therefore every planet of the same kind has inhabitants.

This inference advances from the individual or particular (M) to a universal (σ) which approaches (M) by successive limitations. It has not, however, the peculiarly inductive character in so far as the ' everything this is σ_1, as well as σ_2, ... is,' does not yield a truly singular universal notion. The same would be true in the combined form :—

$$\text{M}_1, \text{ as well as M}_2, \ldots \text{ is P.}$$
$$\text{M}_1, \text{ as well as M}_2, \ldots \text{ is both } \sigma_1 \text{ and } \sigma_2 \ldots$$
Everything which is σ_1, as well as σ_2, ... is P.

All these forms may also occur in hypothetical inferences.

The following inference may here serve as an example of induction: The planet Mars moves (as Kepler has proved) in an elliptical orbit round the sun. The planet Jupiter does so also, &c. Hence it is to be concluded that the planets generally move in an elliptical orbit round the sun. Other examples will be contained in the following paragraphs.

Aristotle traces the first methodical use of Induction back to *Socrates* (§ 12). The use of the expression ἐπανάγειν in Xenophon's Memorabilia[1] is worth noticing. It is there said of Socrates, that if anyone contradicted him without alleging his reasons, he always went back to his presuppositions. For example, if the question arose—What citizen is the better, Socrates first sought to find out what was the work of a good citizen in the government of the state, in war, in embassics, and so on:—ἐπὶ τὴν ὑπόθεσιν ἐπανῆγεν ἂν πάντα τὸν λόγον· . . . οὕτω τῶν λόγων ἐπαναγομένων καὶ τοῖς ἀντιλέγουσιν αὐτοῖς φανερὸν ἐγίγνετο τἀληθές. This is going back to the universal not for its own sake, but in order to infer something else from it. In like manner Plato, in the dialogue Phaedo,[3] makes Socrates demand that those in debate go back from a debated proposition to more general and more certain presuppositions. The Socratic 'Induction' in the Aristotelian sense does not lie in this procedure, but in the combination of individual and similar facts whereby a universal proposition arises from the former which becomes certainty. For example, the pilot who understands his business is the most skilful, the physician who understands his business is the most skilful, and thus in all departments he who understands his business is the most skilful.

Plato, like Socrates, makes the comprehension of individuals in the general serve for the formation of notions :[3]—εἰς μίαν τε ἰδέαν συνορῶντα ἄγειν τὰ πολλαχῇ διεσπαρμένα, ἵνα ἕκαστον ὁριζόμενος δῆλον ποιῇ περὶ οὗ ἂν ἀεὶ διδάσκειν ἐθέλῃ. Induction is a mode (εἶδος) of procedure of philosophical thinking which forms the natural presupposition of the opposite method,—deduction from universals to particulars. The method of Abstraction, by which universal notions are formed, and of Induction, by which universal propositions are formed, appear in Plato not yet distinguished from each other.

Aristotle calls Abstraction ἀφαίρεσις,[4] and Induction ἐπαγωγή. He defines Induction thus :[5] ἐπαγωγὴ ἡ ἀπὸ τῶν καθ' ἕκαστον

[1] iv. 6, 13, 14.   [2] P. 101 ε.   [3] Phaedr. 265 p.
[4] Anal. Post. i. 18 and passim.   [5] Top. l. 12.

ἐπὶ τὰ καθόλου ἔφοδος¹ — ἡ δ' ἐπαγωγὴ ἐκ τῶν κατὰ μέρος.

Aristotle makes Induction in the stricter sense co-ordinate with Abstraction, because it leads to the universal judgment or proposition, while Abstraction leads to the universal notion. He often, however, uses ἐπαγωγὴ in a wider sense, which includes Abstraction.⁸ The term ἐπαγωγὴ refers to the successive enumeration of individual members (rationes inferre). Aristotle teaches :⁸—ἀδύνατον δὲ τὰ καθόλου θεωρῆσαι μὴ δι' ἐπαγωγῆς, ἐπεὶ καὶ τὰ ἐξ ἀφαιρέσεων λεγόμενα (i.e. the mathematical especially) ἔσται δι' ἐπαγωγῆς γνώριμα ποιεῖν. He believes, however, that Induction is more a popular than a strictly scientific way of knowledge :⁴ φύσει μὲν οὖν πρότερος καὶ γνωριμώτερος ὁ διὰ τοῦ μέσου συλλογισμός, ἡμῖν δ' ἐναργέστερος ὁ διὰ τῆς ἐπαγωγῆς. On this account Aristotle has not explained the theory of Induction as thoroughly as that of Syllogism. He believes that the only scientific Induction is the perfect (cf. § 128):⁵ δεῖ δὲ νοεῖν τὸ Γ τὸ ἐξ ἁπάντων τῶν καθ' ἕκαστον συγκείμενον· ἡ γὰρ ἐπαγωγὴ διὰ πάντων. He only says, in his logical writings, of the procedure in imperfect induction, that to generalise many experiences of the same kind is admissible only when there is no contrary case :⁶ πρὸς δὲ τὸ καθόλου πειρατέον ἐνστασιν φέρειν· τὸ γὰρ ἄνευ ἐνστάσεως, ἢ οὔσης ἢ δοκούσης, κωλύειν τὸν λόγον δυσχεραίνειν ἐστίν. εἰ οὖν ἐπὶ πολλῶν φαινομένων μὴ δίδωσι τὸ καθόλου μὴ ἔχων ἔνστασιν, φανερὸν ὅτι δυσκολαίνει. The thought that causal connection enables us to generalise is in Aristotle the ruling one in the construction of definite inductions,⁷ but does not attain to a fundamental significance in his logical theory.

Following Aristotle, *Boëthius* defines :⁸ inductio est oratio,

¹ *Anal. Post.* i. 18.
² E.g. in the assertion quoted in § 12, from *Metaph.* xiii. 4, that Socrates was the author of Induction and Definition.
³ *Anal. Post.* i. 18.   ⁴ *Anal. Pri.* ii. 23.
⁵ *Anal. Pri.* ii. 23.   ⁶ *Top.* vii. 8.
⁷ *De Partibus Animalium*, iv. 2, 667 a, 37 ; longevity of animals which have no gall.
⁸ *De Differentiis Topicis*, oper. ed. Basil. 1546, p. 664.

per quam fit a particularibus ad universalia progressio (Syllogism, on the other hand, deduces ab universalibus in particularia). It was reserved for modern times to bring out the full significance of inductive procedure. In the Middle Ages the favourite method of procedure was the deduction of the individual from given principles. In modern times men have sought to find out the principles themselves in a scientific way, and for this purpose required induction. Modern *investigators of nature* use the inductive method along with mathematical induction, and *Bacon of Verulam* outlined the fundamental features of the theory itself. He wished to get at a more methodical procedure than the simple enumeration of individual cases, which may be always contradicted by other cases. Bacon says:[1] Inductio quae procedit per enumerationem simplicem, res puerilis est et precario concludit et periculo exponitur ab instantia contradictoria et plerumque secundum pauciora quam par est et ex iis tantummodo quae praesto sunt pronunciat. At inductio quae ad inventionem et demonstrationem scientiarum et artium erit utilis, naturam separare debet per reiectiones et exclusiones debitas ac deinde post negativas tot quot sufficiunt super affirmativas concludere, quod adhuc factum non est nec tentatum certe nisi tantummodo a Platone, qui ad excutiendas definitiones et ideas hac certe forma inductionis aliquatenus utitur. He seeks to define the correct method of procedure more nearly (although in an insufficient way).

The dogmatic course of development of later philosophy from *Des Cartes* to Leibniz and Wolff did not despise Induction, but did not advance its theory beyond the doctrines of Aristotle. It had more interest in Deduction.

Wolff, however,[2] correctly hints that causal connection enables us to form universal judgments out of individual experiences. He does not give to this procedure the name of imperfect Induction (§ 129), because the reproach of unscientific character still clung to the external apprehension of inductive method, but opposes it to induction as a better procedure.

The empirical tendency for which Locke prepared the way favoured Induction, but, because it turned too much aside from all metaphysical relations, was not able to do much to essentially enrich or deepen the theory of this method.

The latest attempts to carry out what Bacon purposed in his Novum Organum, by aid of the scientific means of our time, and in a way corresponding to the present stand-point of the positive sciences, have mostly proceeded from philosophically-inclined cultivators of natural science. Besides the works (mentioned in § 35) of *Whewell, J. Herschel, J. S. Mill,* and *A. Comte,* we must here notice the treatise of *Apelt,* proceeding upon the philosophical fundamental axioms of Kant and Fries: Die Theorie der Induction, 1854. *Oesterlen* has much that is valuable, more particularly with reference to his special province, in his work, *Medicinische Logik,* 1852. Cf. also *Liebig,* Induction and Deduction (speech delivered in the public session of the Academy of Sciences at Munich on March 28, 1865), who does not sufficiently separate the logical form of Induction from the happy anticipation of scientific results attained by the power of the imagination of the practised investigation familiar with the object. [Cf. also in the same connection *Prof. Tyndall*: On the Scientific Use of the Imagination.]

Upon the *inductive methods of investigation* (in the wider sense of this expression), cf. § 140.

§ 128. PERFECT INDUCTION (Inductio Completa) is that in which the sphere of the subject in the minor premise falls wholly and completely within the sphere of the predicate. This takes place when, by a perfect enumeration of all individuals or particulars, the whole sphere of the universal is exhausted. (By complete enumeration of all M_1, M_n, M_t . . . . the whole sphere of S is exhausted.) Accordingly in this case the

minor premise may be brought by conversion to the
disjunctive form—

Every S is either M_1 or M_2 .... or M_n.

In this way the inference passes over into a conjunctive-
disjunctive syllogism of the First Figure, and is to be
proved, according to the general rules of the syllogism,
from the relation of its spheres. Every S falls within
a sphere, and the whole sphere of all S coincides with a
sphere which itself falls within the sphere of P. Hence
every S is P.

Perfect Induction with an infinite enumeration of
parts is possible in two cases:—

1. When[1] the parts are connected together continuously
in space, so that a survey of all is possible in a finite
(and often in a very short) time. This happens in every
geometrical demonstration when the inference, which
has to do directly with the simple figure it refers to, is
extended and made universally valid for all figures
falling under the like definition.

2. When the parts are not continuously connected,
if it can be syllogistically proved that what is true of a
definite n^{th} part must also be true for the $(n+1)^{th}$ part.
This last method, however, which mostly finds application in Arithmetic, is not purely inductive.

In *Perfect* Induction the sphere of what has the predicate
P, according to the major premise, coincides with what has the
predicate P according to the conclusion. Hence this mode of
inference comes within the general notions of Inference and Induction only in so far as it is seen to be an extreme case, just as
the universal is comprehended under the particular as an extreme

[1] As Beneke remarks, *Log.* ii. 52 ff.

case. So long as the series in the enumeration of the individuals or classes M_1, M_2 .... is not completed, the sphere of S is wider than the sphere of M_1, M_2 .... and the inference results in something more universal. The successive enlargement of the sphere of the subject, or diminution of that of the predicate, leads up to an equality of spheres, never beyond it.

The following are *examples* of Perfect Induction:—
Mercury revolves on its axis; So do Venus, the Earth, Mars, Jupiter, and Saturn. But these are all the old planets: Therefore the whole of the old planets revolve upon their axes.

The angle at the circumference of a circle is half the size of the angle at the centre on the same arc, when the centre of the circle is within the angle at the circumference, when it is in one of its sides, and when it is outside of it. But these three positions are the only ones possible: Therefore the angle at the circumference is always half the size of the angle at the centre on the same arc.

§ 129. Imperfect Induction (inductio incompleta) warrants a particular conclusion only according to syllogistic rules: At least some S is P'; at least something which is both σ_1, σ_2 .... is P'. The conclusion is made universal with more or less probability, and the blank which remains over in the given relations of spheres is legitimately filled up, partly on the universal presupposition of a causal-nexus in the objects of knowledge, partly on the particular presupposition that in the case presented such a causal-nexus exists as connects the subject and predicate of the conclusion. The degree of probability of the inductive inference depends in each case on the admissibility of this last presupposition, and the various inductive operations, the extension of the sphere of observation, the simplification of the observed conditions by successive exhaustion of the unessential, &c., all tend to secure its admissibility.

A fact which establishes an objection against the universal validity of the inference is called an *Instance* (instantia, *ἔντασις*).

The first example in the preceding paragraph (of Perfect Induction) becomes an Imperfect Induction, when either the revolution upon the axis has been observed of some only of the bodies called planets (Mercury, Venus, the Earth, Mars, Jupiter, Saturn), or when, on the other hand, while the given results of observation of all serve as a starting-point, the inference is extended to the whole of the planets (not merely to those called the old planets). The universal conclusion is made probable by the presupposition, that the earth revolves on its axis not because it is the earth, i.e. because it is this definite planet, and Mars not because it is Mars, not because of its proper qualities, but that every one of these planets revolves on its axis, because it is a planet, because of its planetary nature. There is a certain causal-nexus existing between the nature of a planet and (at least the present) revolution upon the axis (which may be founded upon the original nature of the planet). The multitude of observed cases leads us to assert that this relation exists. If it were possible, on the basis of a single observation, to know on *what* causal relation this was dependent, we would not need more cases to establish the inductive connection. If it were possible to know by a single observation whether the earth revolves on its axis or is inhabited, &c. because it is a *planet*, or because it is *this* planet, because of its universal, or because of its individual nature;— whether a stone falls because it is a dense body belonging to the earth, or because it is matter;—whether iron, lead, gold, &c. are heavier than water because they are metals (in which case the metals Sodium and Potassium must be heavier than water, while they are lighter);—whether a medicine heals because of the generic or the specific nature of the medicine used, and of the disease treated, or because of individual and accidental circumstances;—whether the rose which we see has white blossom, has it because it is a rose, &c.;—we would not need to bring in other cases into our induction. We are inclined to come to a decision upon this point after a single, or a few observations, but the primitive inductions thus formed are mostly false. The certain scientific knowledge which recognises whether the judgment forming a ground of the induction contains a predicate which belongs to the subject because of its generic nature, because of its individual nature, or because of accidental circumstances, is not the point from which Induction starts, but its essential aim. Among the many primary inductions, most of which further experience rejects, there are some which are never rejected. These concern the *elementary* relations which have an essential causal character. They form the standard by which all other inductions are to be tested.

The sciences of organic nature have become enlarged by inductively making universal the individual results of observation. The sciences of inorganic nature rest more upon the combination of induction with deductions deduced by the aid of mathematics. The same principles of method find application within the province of mental life. We limit ourselves here to the universal elements of the theory of induction, and refer to the well-known works of Whewell, Mill, Apelt, Oesterlen, and others, for its particular applications in the individual sciences.

The *significance of Induction* as a mean to expand our knowledge rests upon the same reference to a *real conformability to law* (according to the axiom of Sufficient Reason, § 81), on which the possibility of the syllogism as a form of knowledge is founded. It is a mere prejudice which places the one of these forms before the other in scientific value, whether the syllogistic procedure is thought exclusively capable to demonstrate, or whether, on the other side, Induction only is thought able to advance knowledge, and Syllogism to serve merely for the arrangement, explanation, and communication of knowledge already possessed. Propositions which are absolutely highest, and so cannot be syllogistically

deduced, so far as they are neither identical nor analytically
formed judgments, can only be scientifically established by
Induction.

Inductive inference has strict universality when S contains the 'sufficient reason' of P, when P is related to S
as its only possible cause or conditio sine qua non, and, lastly,
when S and P are both necessary consequences of a common
cause, sufficient for P and the only possible cause of S. On the
other hand, Induction leads only to comparative universality,
or to rules which may be limited by exceptions, when S is only
a single co-operative cause or condition of P, or when, on the
other hand, P is not the only possible cause of S, or when S
and P are consequences of a common cause but may also
result singly under different conditions. Lastly, inductive
inference is altogether untenable when no causal-nexus of any
kind can be supposed to exist between S and P.

The correct formation of notions (cf. § 66) is conditioned
by the correct formation of judgments and inferences; and
the latter by the former. The formation of valid *inductions*
especially is very closely related to the formation of *notions*
according to their truly essential attributes. The possibility
of correct inductive generalisations depends upon a good
formation of notions. For a great number of properties and
relations stand in a causal-nexus, on which the validity of
the Induction depends, with the essential attributes of the
object of which (according to § 56) the notion is formed. From
this comes the logical right to refer properties inductively to
the whole species, which have been observed in single individuals of a species, in so far as they are not evidently conditioned by mere individual relations. Contrary cases always
remain possible, however, so long as the kind of causal connection is not clearly known.

The axiom of inductive generalisation which *Newton* enunciates [1] with immediate reference to the physical properties of
bodies:—qualitates corporum, quae intendi et remitti neque-
unt, quaeque corporibus omnibus competunt, in quibus ex-

[1] *Princip. Phil. Nat.* bk. iii.

perimenta instituere licet, pro qualitatibus corporum universorum habendae sunt, may be traced back to the presupposition
of an internal connexion of such properties with the essence of
the bodies.

Since syllogistic procedure is *synthetic*, the inductive,
in so far as it separates the given object into its partly
common, partly special elements, may be called *analytic.*
We cannot agree to the opposition enunciated by Trendelenburg[1] between Induction and the Analytic procedure, according to which the former only sums up the *fact* of the universal
from the individuals, while the latter seeks the universal
cause from the given phenomenon, for the reasons we have
stated (§ 101) when opposing the analogous separation
of syllogism and synthesis. Trendelenburg's so-called 'analytical procedure' must take the inductive form, and scientific induction the 'analytical' element which refers to the
causal-nexus. Hence, every such distinction only corresponds to that of the 'formal' and 'real' *sides* of Induction.

The distinction between *Induction* and *Abstraction* lies in
this, that the former has to do with the universal *proposition*,
and the latter with the universal *notion.* This specific distinction cannot be said to be one of degree only [2]—Induction
leading to universal theorems, and Abstraction to necessary
and fundamental truths. There are not two kinds of universal
conceptions (as *Apelt* asserts),[3] notions and laws; for the law
is not a conception, but is the constant way in which something actually happens, and our consciousness of it is a judgment or combination of conceptions, in which that constancy
is thought to be real. The real nexus of things conformably
to law may be recognised either deductively i.e. syllogistically, or inductively, never à priori in the sense of Kant,
Krause, Fries, and Apelt—not even in Mathematics. Mathematics is certainly not an inductive and empirical science in
the sense that its individual *theorems* must be established by

[1] *Log. Unters.* 2nd ed. ii. 282; 3rd ed. ii. 315.
[2] As Apelt does, *Theorie der Induction*, p. 54 ff., Leipz. 1854.
[3] P. 56.

the method of empirical observation and measurement; they
are syllogistically proved, and their free combination goes far
beyond the forms empirically given : but the certainty of
those mathematical *fundamental propositions* which are synthetical judgments, and especially of the *geometrical axioms*, is
based upon empirical observation and induction. In so far as
this observation and induction do not warrant their absolutely strict and universal validity, what is lacking is supplied
hypothetically (as Dugald Stewart showed) by means of idealising what is given,[1] and these hypothetical elements attain
scientific certainty in the way that all hypotheses do,—by the
agreement of their consequences, of the innumerable individual
theorems which are syllogistically inferred from them, with
each other, and with what is empirically given, which agreement results more and more in every attempt, the more strictly
we construct the figures. When this agreement has been
tested often enough to exclude the possibility of a mistake in
the principles of demonstration, the certainty of the result in
every new deduction is secured before the experience specially
directed to it, or relatively à priori.

The Kantian doctrine of the absolute à priority of the intuition of space would not, even if it were correct, ensure the
necessary truth of the defined individual axioms. That doctrine, however, is only an attempt, which has miscarried, to
explain the mathematical certainty actually existing, and has
its stronghold not in immediate experience, but in the *systematic
concatenation of propositions* attached to this experience. This
systematic concatenation does not *create* the geometrical order,
but reproduces and reconstructs for our consciousness the real
relations which lie essentially in nature itself. Kant hypos-
tatises the formative activity of the mind operating according
to logical laws conditioned by forms of existence into a *product*
called *form*—into the presumptive intuition of space existing à

[1] This does not presuppose ideal pictures ready in human mind
which exist previous to all experience, any more than artistic idealisation presupposes ideal forms existing originally in the mind ; It follows
the hint given by the objects.

priori, and reduces the apodicticity which belongs to the
whole of mathematical thinking in its relation to what is
actually given, to the presumptive distinctive origin of the
mathematical fundamental intuitions, just as is done in other
departments of thought by the doctrine of innate ideas.[1]

Hegel[2] recognises Induction and Analogy to be the bases of
Syllogistic Inference, because the major premise depends upon
those forms. This is true of Induction, and also of Analogy,
in so far as an inference of induction is contained in it (cf. § 131).

Trendelenburg[3] opposes the following question to Hegel's
opinion: Have the necessary primary judgments of Geometry,
which form the basis of a series of inferences, become what they
are from Induction or Analogy? This question, when strictly
defined as we have done it, is decidedly to be answered in the
affirmative. They have been made foundations of mathematical
inference by Induction, aided by Abstraction, Construction,
and Idealisation. Their scientific certainty, however, does not
depend upon Induction alone. It depends more on the fact
that the propositions derived from them syllogistically without exception agree with each other and with experience, for
the smallest mistake lurking in the fundamental axiom would
be increased in these propositions so that it would be sure to be
observed.

Schleiermacher says[4]—'The possibility of the original acts in
the process of Deduction lies in a reference back to the original
acts in the process of Induction:'[5] 'as in the first and second
original moment the process of Deduction must be referred back
generally to the process of Induction.' He is right when he
enunciates the canon in its universality without exception.

Leopold George explains in his Logic the doctrine of science,[6]

[1] Cf. Plat. *De Rep.* vii. 533; Aristot. *Anal. Post.* i. 18; J. Her-
schel, *A Prelim. Disc.* p. 95 ff.; J. S. Mill, *System of Logic,* 7th ed. i.
254 ff.; Beneke, *Log.* i. 73, li. 3, 51, 86, 151 ff.; Drobisch, Pref. to
2nd ed. p. vi. ff.

[2] *Encycl.* § 190. [3] *Log. Unters.* 2nd ed. ii. 342; 3rd ed. ii. 376.
[4] *Dial.* § 279. [5] Ibid. § 238.

[6] *Logik als Wissenschaftslehre,* Berl. 1868, 'dedicated to the manes
of Schleiermacher.'

490 § 130. *The most Notable Errors in Induction.*

and declares that the reference of Induction to the objective
causal-nexus is a circle, since the knowledge of the real nexus is
always based upon incomplete inductions. But this objection
rests upon a confusion of the existence of the causal-nexus and
our knowledge of it. Its existence precedes our inductions,
but our knowledge of it in a universal form results after a multiplicity of special inductions. We generalise at first only
according to mental (psychic) laws of association; our generalisations have logical correctness in so far as they each time
correspond to the objective causal-nexus, and the inductive
methods are really the means of attaining to this correspondence. The highest induction is that by which we recognise
the universal validity of the law of Causality itself.

The question, in how far the inductive knowledge presupposes
mental (geistige) *self-activity* and *forms*, which are brought
from what is within to apprehend what is without, has been sub-
jected to strict investigation by *Beneke.*[1] [This question lies
at the basis of the differences of views held by Whewell and
Mill regarding the nature and aim of scientific methods.
Whewell attributes more to the speculative power of the individual investigator, and seems to consider that the chief part
of scientific method is the construction and testing of hypotheses, and their gradual conversion into scientific conceptions.]

§ 130. The most common FALLACY against the laws
of Induction is that of *false generalisation* (fallacia fictae
universalitatis). This fallacy generally arises either
from the confusion of an Imperfect with a Perfect
Induction, or from the false presupposition of a strict
causal-nexus from subject to predicate of the conclusion
(non causa ut causa, sive post hoc ergo propter hoc).

For example, when the rules for the calculation with powers
are proved in all those relations which subsist along with
positive whole exponents, and these rules without further de-

[1] *Syst. der Logik,* ii. 23 ff.

monstration are taken quite universally, and as valid in powers
with negative fractional and irrational exponents,—this is a
case, so far as the method is concerned, of incorrect generalisation (although as a matter of fact it is not false) or of false
resting upon an *Imperfect* Induction while the Perfect is required and is attainable.

The most numerous and most important examples of false
Inductions which depend upon ignorance of the true causal-
nexus, and the imaginary substitution of a supposititious one,
are afforded by superstition in the inexhaustible multiplicity
of its forms, which, dragged from its thousand hiding-places,
always burrows in new ones. The history of serious investigation, however, makes it evident, in the many errors of
this kind of which it has to report,[1] that man must find scientific truth, the highest point he can reach, as well as moral
sentiment, not ready made like a gift without effort on his part,
but only by long and hard struggle by way of development,
and especially by overcoming his natural propensity to a false
anthropomorphism.

In many cases the *usage of language*, not yet corrected by
science, leads to false inductions. The sphere of the conception, to which the word refers, does not necessarily coincide
with the spheres of those notions, to whose objects the predicate
in question belongs. The variety of connected circumstances
is not easily detected by the superficial glance, and we are apt to
attribute the same predicate to all that we denote by the same
name, until we have learned to subject to logical laws the psychological association of conceptions which the word suggests.[2]

The chapter in *Mill's* Logic on fallacies of generalisation
contains[3] a series of examples of false inductive inferences.

§ 131. The INFERENCE OF ANALOGY (exemplum,
analogia, παράδειγμα, ἀναλογία) is an inference from

[1] Cf. Whewell's important work, *The History of the Inductive
Sciences*, 1839–42.
[2] Cf. Beneke, *System der Logik*, ii. 59 ff.　　[3] 7th ed. ii. 352.

particulars or individuals to a co-ordinate particular or individual. Its Schema is the following:—

$$M \text{ is } P$$
$$\underline{S \text{ is similar to } M}$$
$$S \text{ is } P$$

Or more definitely, since it also gives that in which the similarity consists, the following:—

$$M \text{ is } P$$
$$M \text{ is } A$$
$$\underline{S \text{ is } A}$$
$$S \text{ is } P$$

Sometimes the notion M, sometimes the notion A, sometimes both of the two notions are plural. Hence *three forms* arise, the first of which corresponds to the fundamental form of the Inductive Inference, the second and the third to the secondary forms mentioned above (§ 127). Every inference of Analogy may be resolved into an Inductive Inference of the corresponding form and a Syllogism.

The *First* form of the Inference of Analogy, stated more particularly, is the following:—

$$M_1, \text{ as well as } M_n \text{ and } M_s \ldots \ldots \text{ is } P$$
$$M_1, \text{ as well as } M_n \text{ and } M_s \ldots \ldots \text{ is } A$$
$$\underline{S \text{ is } A}$$
$$S \text{ is } P$$

This is reduced to the Inductive Inference of the first form—

$$M_1, \text{ as well as } M_n \text{ and } M_s \ldots \ldots \text{ is } P$$
$$\underline{M_1, \text{ as well as } M_n \text{ and } M_s \ldots \ldots \text{ is } A}$$
$$A \text{ is } P$$

and to the corresponding syllogism of the First Figure—

$$A \text{ is } P$$
$$S \text{ is } A$$
$$\overline{S \text{ is } P}$$

The *Second* form of the Inference of Analogy is the following:—

$$M \text{ is } P$$
$$M \text{ is } A_1, \text{ as well as } A_n, \text{ and } A_2 \ldots \ldots$$
$$S \text{ is } A_1, \text{ as well as } A_n, \text{ and } A_2 \ldots \ldots$$
$$\overline{S \text{ is } P}$$

This form reduces itself to the inference—

$$M \text{ is } P$$
$$M \text{ is } A_1, \text{ as well as } A_n, \text{ and } A_2 \ldots \ldots$$
$$\overline{\text{Whatever is } A_1, \text{ as well as } A_n, \text{ and } A_2 \ldots \ldots \text{ is } P}$$

and to the corresponding syllogism in the First Figure—

$$\text{Whatever is } A_1, \text{ as well as } A_n, \text{ and } A_2 \ldots \ldots \text{ is } P$$
$$S \text{ is } A_1, \text{ as well as } A_n, \text{ and } A_2 \ldots \ldots$$
$$\overline{S \text{ is } P}$$

The *Third* form of the Inference from Analogy combines the peculiarities of the first two—

$$M_1, \text{ as well as } M_2 \ldots \ldots \text{ is } P$$
$$M_1, \text{ as well as } M_2 \ldots \ldots \text{ is also } A_1 \text{ and } A_2 \ldots \ldots$$
$$\overline{S \text{ is } P}$$

When resolved the two following inferences result:—

$$M_1, \text{ as well as } M_n \ldots \ldots \text{ is } P$$
$$M_1, \text{ as well as } M_2, \ldots \ldots \text{ is also } A_1 \text{ and } A_2 \ldots \ldots$$
$$\overline{\text{Whatever is } A_1 \text{ and } A_2 \ldots \ldots \text{ is } P}$$

and—

> Whatever is both A_1 and A_2 . . . . . is P
> S is both A_1 and A_2 . . . . .
> _____
> S is P

These three forms of the syllogism of Analogy may also occur with *hypothetical* premises.

The following is an *example* of an inference of Analogy of the *first* form:—

Mercury, Venus, the Earth, Mars, Jupiter, and Saturn (the whole of the planets known to the ancients) revolve on their axes from west to east; all these are planets of our system; Uranus also belongs to planets of this system: Hence it probably revolves on its axis from west to east.

The following is an inference of Analogy of the *second* form:—

The Earth supports organic life; the Earth is a planet revolving in an orbit round our sun, turning on its axis, having an atmosphere, the change of seasons, &c.; Mars is a planet revolving in an orbit round our sun, turning on its own axis, having an atmosphere, the change of seasons, &c.: Hence Mars also will probably support organic life.

Of the same form is the inference which Franklin made in November, 1749,[1] and which must be reckoned among inferences of Analogy on the presupposition that the subsumption of the notion of lightning under that of electrical phenomena was not yet made, and the two notions were only thought similar: The electric fluid, as it shows itself in experiments made by us, is attracted by projecting metallic points; this electric fluid and lightning agree in the properties that they give light of the same colour, have a quick motion, are conducted by metals, &c. &c.: Hence it is to be presumed that lightning will also be attracted by projecting metallic points.

The example quoted of an inference of Analogy of the first form passes over into the *third* form, when the community of nature which Uranus has with the old planets is denoted not

[1] Cf. Beneke, *Log.* ii. 119.

only by the general nature of planet, but also by the particular
quality by which all these planets (together with Neptune)
are distinguished from the asteroids, viz. that they are larger
and the only planets which are always at a defined distance from
the sun.

There are not two kinds of Inference by Analogy, the *Per-*
fect and the *Imperfect*, according as the Induction implicitly
contained in it is of the one kind or the other; for if the
Induction is Perfect, the case which is first inferred by Analogy
must be given as a premise. Hence the Inference by Analogy
can only be joined to an Imperfect Induction. All forms of
Analogy are distinguished from induction by the adjoined
syllogism, which concludes from the universal reached by pre-
sumption to the particulars or individuals.

The certainty or probability of the inference by Analogy is
founded on the same moments as that of the Imperfect Induction. It depends on the correctness of the presupposition of a
real nexus conformable to law between A and P. For the
reference to single analogous cases must be true in the *very*
same measure and from the same reasons as the inductive
generalisation. No new uncertainty enters in its syllogistic
subsumption under the universal law for the present held to
be valid, and the reference to the single analogous case is
justified only in so far as a universal conformability to law is
presupposed, according to which the same predicate can also
be added inductively to all those objects which strictly correspond to the same conditions.

The *fallacies* which appear in Analogy, because it is a combination of Induction and Syllogism, are the same as those
which enter into those modes of inference. They depend for
the most part on the false presupposition that the predicate P
belongs to M because of its universal nature A, and therefore
will belong to other A, and to S, while P really belongs to
the specific difference of M which S does not share with it.
So long as a connection conformable to law cannot be presupposed between A and P, the proposition holds good: *illus-*
trations and parables prove nothing.

Examples of false inferences from Analogy lie in the old
belief of the animate nature of the heavenly bodies from the
analogy of men and animals because they were moving beings.
(Cf. § 42.) By a very doubtful analogy the persistence of
mental (psychic) impressions was made parallel with the persistence of a body in a state of rest or motion, according to
the law of inertia.[1] *Mill* gives other examples.[2]

Analogy is related to *Proportion*, but not identical with it.
If we call the P which belongs to M, P', and the P which
belongs to S, P'', the Inference from Analogy may be reduced
to the following formulas:—

$$M : S = P' : P''$$

or

$$M : P' = S : P''$$

In the latter form the A may be reckoned the exponent. But
in most cases this representation is only an illustration, and is
not exactly true. But the cases in which it is exactly true
(as in the so-called 'Rule of Three') do not lead only to the
inference S is P, but also to the nearer determination of P as
P'' (e.g. not merely to the inference that the second quantity
of goods has a value, but also to the calculation of this value);
for the predicate P does not belong to the two subjects M and
S, only in so far as its class-nature A goes, but is also modified
according to the relation of their specific peculiarities (M and
S). An inference of this kind may be called the Inference of
Strict Analogy[3] (as Drobisch does, Log. 3rd ed. § 149).

The first of the examples of the Second form of Analogy,
reduced to the form of *Proportion*, would run: As the Earth
is to Mars, so is the organic life on the earth to the (presupposed) organic life in Mars; or: as the Earth is to its
organisms (exponent: planetary nature), so is Mars to its
organisms (exponent: planetary nature).

Aristotle[4] distinguishes the Inference from Analogy (παράδειγμα) on the one hand from Induction, and on the other from
Syllogism, in this way, that conclusion is made neither from the

[1] Cf. Lotze, *Mikrokosmos*, i. 214.　　[2] *Logic*, 7th ed. ii. 362.
[3] *Analogia Exacta.*　　[4] *Anal. Pri.* ii. 24.

part to the whole, nor from the whole to the part, but from the part to the part. He resolves Inference by Analogy into an inference to the more universal (which is an Inference of *Imperfect Induction*, although Aristotle does not use this term, because he recognises Perfect Induction only ; cf. § 187) and an adjoined syllogism :[1] φανερὸν οὖν ὅτι τὸ παράδειγμά ἐστιν οὔτε ὡς μέρος πρὸς ὅλον, οὔτε ὡς ὅλον πρὸς μέρος, ἀλλ' ὡς μέρος (Δ) πρὸς μέρος (Γ), ὅταν ἄμφω μὲν ᾖ ὑπὸ ταὐτὸ (Β), γνώριμον δὲ θάτερον (Δ, scil. ὅτι τὸ Α αὐτῷ ὑπάρχει). καὶ διαφέρει τῆς ἐπαγωγῆς, ὅτι ἡ μὲν ἐξ ἁπάντων τῶν ἀτόμων τὸ ἄκρον ἐδείκνυεν ὑπάρχειν τῷ μέσῳ καὶ πρὸς τὸ ἄκρον οὐ συνῆπτε τὸν συλλογισμόν, τὸ δὲ καὶ συνάπτει καὶ οὐκ ἐξ ἁπάντων δείκνυσιν.[1] He gives the following example : ἔστω τὸ Α κακὸν, τὸ δὲ Β πρὸς ὁμόρους ἀναιρεῖσθαι πόλεμον, ἐφ' ᾧ δὲ Γ τὸ Ἀθηναίους πρὸς Θηβαίους, τὸ δὲ ἐφ' ᾧ Δ Θηβαίους πρὸς Φωκεῖς. He deduces from the empirically given case that the war made by the Thebans against the Phocians was destructive (Δ is A), by the Imperfect Induction, that, because *that* war was a war against neighbours (Δ is B), every war against neighbours is destructive (B is A). It is then inferred syllogistically that a war of the Athenians against the Thebans (Γ), because this would be a war against neighbours (Γ is B), would be destructive (Γ is A). Hence the three premises are given :—

1. Δ is A,
2. Δ is B,
3. Γ is B.

Aristotle first deduces presumptively from 1 and 2—

4. B is A,

and after this is shown (ὅταν τῷ μέσῳ, sc. τῷ Β, τὸ ἄκρον sc. τὸ Α, ὑπάρχον δειχθῇ διὰ τοῦ ὁμοίου, sc. τοῦ Δ, τῷ τρίτῳ, sc. τῷ Γ), he lastly deduces syllogistically from 4 and 3 the result—

5. Γ is A.

From these two consequences which are contained in the one inference from Analogy, the first is that one on which the final

[1] *Anal. Pri.* ii. 24.
[1] Cf. *Rhet.* i. 2.

K K

decision depends, since the validity of the whole stands and
falls with its validity; the second, or the syllogism, concludes easily and undoubtedly. Aristotle, therefore, bestows
special attention upon the first element of Analogy, and
explains it to be a kind of Induction which is imperfect,
and more rhetorical than scientific, because what is the more
universal is not proved from an exhaustive enumeration
of every individual case, but from one or a few individual
cases. Analogy is related to Induction as the Enthymeme is
to Syllogism:[1] ὡς δ' αὐτὼς καὶ οἱ ῥητορικαὶ συμπείθουσιν· ἡ γὰρ
διὰ παραδειγμάτων, ὅ ἐστιν ἐπαγωγὴ, ἡ δι' ἐνθυμημάτων, ὅπερ
ἐστὶ συλλογισμὸς. Aristotle does not use the term ἀναλογία
with a logical meaning of *Analogy*, but in the sense of mathematical *Proportion*. Theophrastus employs the word in a
logical signification, but in one quite different from what it
now denotes. He calls thoroughly hypothetical inferences
συλλογισμοὺς κατ' ἀναλογίαν.[2] On the other hand, the term:
οἱ κατὰ τὸ ἀνάλογον συλλογισμοί, is used of inferences from
Analogy, and the Schema of mathematical proportion in the
Γαληνοῦ Εἰσαγωγὴ διαλεκτική[3] is applied.[4]

Boëthius,[5] strictly agreeing with Aristotle, teaches : Est
enim *exemplum*, quod per particulare propositum particulare quoddam contendit ostendere hoc modo: oportet a
Tullio consule necari Catilinam, quum a Scipione Gracchus
sit interemptus.—Ex parte pars approbatur.—Exemplum inductionis simile. Quae omnia ex syllogismo vires accipiunt.

The modern development of the *natural sciences* has first
made evident the full scientific value of Analogy as well as of
Induction.[6]

Kant explains[7] Analogy to be the similarity of two quali-

[1] *Anal. Post.* i. 1.   [2] Cf. § 121.   [3] P. 54 sqq.
[4] Cf. Prantl, *Gesch. der Log.* i. 608.
[5] *Op.* p. 864 sqq., ed. Basil. 1546.
[6] Cf. Gruppe, *Wendepunct der Philos. im neunzehnten Jahrhundert,*
p. 34 ff., 1831; and Trendelenburg, *Log. Unt.* ii. 302-309, 2nd ed.,
ii. 378-385.
[7] *Krit. der r. Vern.* p. 222.

tative relations (while mathematical analogy or proportion
proceeds upon the sameness of two relations of size). He allows
that Analogy,[1] like Induction, is in a certain degree useful and
necessary for the purpose of extending the knowledge got by
experience, but ranks these two forms, which he calls 'Inferences of the reflective judgment,' far behind syllogism, which
alone can pretend to the name 'Inference of Reason.' For[2]
'every inference of the reason must give necessity; Induction
and Analogy are therefore not inferences of reason, they are
only logical presumptions or empirical inferences:'[3] 'the universal towards which it (the reflective judgment) advances from
the special is only empirical universality, merely an analogue
of the logical.' Kant does not seek to make any reference in
Logic, or anywhere, to the conformability to law in real existence.[4] But that 'Inference of Reason,' or Syllogism, so highly
exalted above Induction and Analogy, with the purely formal
apprehension, which Kant finds in it, is still less able than
those inferences of the judgment to widen our knowledge. It
only leads in the conclusion to a partial repetition of what wo
already know and have already said in the major premise. It
cannot be a principle of scientific certainty, and Kant himself
makes dependent on it only the 'analytical' forms of thought,
by which all our knowledge already possessed is analysed and
arranged, but no new knowledge attained. Kant will not recognise a source of apodictic certainty in all methods of logical procedure in inference (and in this agrees with the Sceptics, for
the logical theories of those called by him dogmatic philosophers
in the form apprehended by him did not satisfy him). On the
other side, however, Kant could not but recognise (in opposition to the Sceptics) the apodicticity, which he found in the
positive sciences, to be a given fact, and the question how
this apodicticity was possible, to be a problem in the theory of
knowledge. Starting from these two presuppositions, Kant's
own doctrine of knowledge, or the 'Kritik of pure Reason,'

[1] *Log.* § 81.   [2] Ibid. § 81, Remark 2.   [3] Ibid. § 81.
[4] The section in the *Kritik d. r. Vern.* pp. 218–265, upon tho
analogies of experience, has not this tendency.

K K 2

which destroyed so many traditional illusions, could not but
attain to the somewhat mystical character which it indeed
possessed. Kant sought the basis of scientific certainty, which
he could not find in logical laws, outside of them in the supposititious à priori acquired forms of intuition, Categories and Ideas.
He ascribes to the ' I ' of the pure apperception, as an original
act of the spontaneity of every individual, what in truth proceeds from the mental co-operation of individuals and nations,
what is the historical result of the progress of the development of
mankind in the course of centuries, and could only appear in
definite historically-conditioned degrees of culture.[1]

As regards its formal side, Kant teaches[2] that in the inference from Analogy the judgment concludes from many
determinations and properties, in which things of one kind
agree, to the rest of them so far as they belong to a single
principle, or from partial to total similarity; while in Induction the judgment concludes from many to all things of one
kind according to the principle: what belongs to many things
of one genus belongs to the rest of them. Kant accordingly
makes the distinction of Analogy from Induction lie in that
determination which we make the peculiarity of the second
form of Analogy.

Several modern logicians, such as *Bachmann*,[3] [*Hamilton*,[4]
and *Mansel*,[5]] follow his example.

Fries[6] remarks, in opposition to Kant, that the going back
from the universal to the rest of the individuals is the sole
peculiarity of Analogy, and,[7] following Aristotle, reduces
the inference of Analogy to a combination of an Induction with a Syllogism.[8] The chief division of inferences
must be based in any case on the most essential of all differences,—viz. whether conclusion be made from the universal to

[1] Cf. J. G. Fichte, *Werke*, vii. 608. [2] *Log.* § 84.
[3] Ibid. p. 338 ff. [4] [*Lect. on Log.* ii. 166.
[5] *Artis Logicae Rud.* App. pp. 226–228.]
[6] *Syst. der Log.* p. 466. [7] Ibid. p. 436 ff.
[8] [Mansel calls this Analogy, *Example*: cf. *Artis Log. Rudim.*
pp. 95 n, 226.]

the particular, or from the particular to the universal, or (in a combination of those two forms) from the particular to a co-ordinate particular; and the kinds of inference resting on this division have since Aristotle's time taken the names of *Syllogism, Induction,* and *Analogy.* All other distinctions, including that founded on whether the inference is made from one or from several examples of one genus and on the basis of agreement in one or several characteristics, are of comparatively subordinate significance, and are of value only in the further division of those kinds of inference into their species or forms.

Hegel [1] believes that Analogy takes for its abstract scheme the Second Aristotelian Figure (the Third in Hegel's enumeration), just as Induction takes the Third (or the Second according to Hegel). The middle term of the Inference of Analogy is an individual, taken in the essential universality of its genus or essential determinateness. ' The earth has inhabitants; the moon is an earth: Therefore it has inhabitants.'

While Aristotle combines first of all the first two of the three premises Δ is A, Δ is B, Γ is B, in order by an inference from the individual to the general to deduce the proposition: B is A, which then serves, when taken along with the third, for the Major Premise of a Syllogism;—Hegel would combine the second and the third premises: Δ is B, Γ is B (or in the example: the earth is a world, the moon is a world), in order first of all to deduce the proposition: Γ is Δ (the moon is an earth), which then serves, when taken along with the first premise, to be the Minor of a Syllogism. The combination of the premises: Δ is B, Γ is B, only follows the scheme of the Second Aristotelian Figure, in so far as the middle notion B is twice predicate (while it does not follow the law of the syllogistic moods of that Figure, that one premise be negative). The whole process has not the truth which that Aristotelian reduction has. For the subsumption of Γ under Δ is incorrect, and has an apparent validity by the double sense (as Hegel

[1] *Log.* ii. 155 ff., 1834; *Encycl.* § 190.

himself proves [1]) of the notion Δ (*the* earth—*an* earth). The Aristotelian reduction, on the other hand, clearly exhibits with logical accuracy the essence of the inference of Analogy on its certain and on its doubtful side.

§ 132. In so far as the nexus conformable to law between S and P is uncertain in Imperfect Induction or Analogy, the conclusion has only a *problematic* validity. If the reasons for its existence are of more weight than the reasons against, the conclusion has *probability* (probabilitas). If an attempt be made to define more closely the different degrees intermediate between the complete certainty of the conclusion and the certainty of its contradictory opposite, the term *probability* is also used in a wider sense as the common name for the whole of these degrees. The degree of probability in this sense admits in certain cases of *arithmetical* determination, which may have not only probability but also certainty. When different analogies, some of which point to the conclusion and the others to its contradictory opposite, are in general alike applicable, the degree of probability may be represented mathematically as a fraction, whose numerator is formed by the number of cases for, and its denominator by the number of cases compared. The degree of probability of a definite consequence is the relation of the number of cases, which in the same circumstances have led to this result, with the number of cases compared. The latter number must be of a considerable size in empirical statistic (e.g. in determining the liability to death in certain wounds) in order to be able to estimate the degree of probability. It is a fixed quantity if the possible kinds of results (e.g. as in the game of dice) be deduced from the nature of the case, and then lead to the most certain inferences. So far as the different analogies differ in the degree of the possibility of their finding application, a mathematical determination of the degree of probability is generally impossible. In this case a less exact estimation of the degree of probability may be arrived at, which can lay claim to probability only, not to certainty. This kind of estimation of the degree of probability is commonly called the *philosophical* in opposition to the mathematical, but more correctly the *dynamic*, in so far as it depends upon the relative consideration of the internal force of the causes for and against.

The terms *mathematical* and *philosophical* (dynamic) *probability* are not strict enough. It is not the probability but the way of estimating its degree that is mathematical (arithmetical) or dynamic.

The degree $1 = \frac{a}{a}$ denotes, according to the definition given above, complete certainty, for the number of favourable cases is equal to the sum total of all the cases. The degree $0 = \frac{0}{a}$ denotes the certainty of the opposite contradictory, because not one of all the cases is favourable. The degree $\frac{1}{2}$ denotes that the reasons for and against are evenly balanced. The positive fractions from $\frac{1}{2}$ to 1 denote probability in the narrower sense, because the cases for are more numerous than the cases against. Lastly, the positive fractions from $\frac{1}{2}$ to 0 denote improbability in its different degrees. It belongs to Mathematics, not to Logic, to describe more definitely the calculus of probabilities (calculus probabilium).

[Cf. *Mill's* Logic, ii. p. 122 ff.; *De Morgan's* Formal Logic or Calculus of Inference necessary and probable, pp. 170–210; and *Boole's* Laws of Thought, pp. 243 399.]

§ 133. In every Inference formally correct and of strict universal validity *the material truth of the conclusion follows from the material truth of the premises,* but not conversely the latter from the former; and *the material falsehood of at least one of the premises follows from the material falsehood of the conclusion,* but not conversely the latter from the former. A single premise, or all of them, may be false and yet the conclusion true; but it cannot happen that the premises are all true while the conclusion, correctly deduced, is false. Only truth can follow from what is true; but truth as well as falsehood from what is false. The proof for the material truth of the conclusion derived from true premises lies in the logical correctness of the derivation; for the logical laws of the formation of inference, like logical laws in general, are founded on the idea of truth (cf. §§ 3, 75 ff., 101), and a deduction which leads to what is false would prove itself to contradict the logical laws and so to be incorrect, in opposition to the hypothesis. But, if inference from false premises is made conformably to the logical laws, it is not necessary that what follows must be true or must be false. Various relations determine the particular cases.

In *Syllogism* the material truth of the inference correctly deduced from materially true premises is *necessary*; but the material truth of the conclusion can also coexist along with the falsehood of one or both premises. The analogy between inference and calculation should not mislead us to believe that the conclusion can have material truth *only* when several material fallacies balance each other in the premises or hypotheses. The incorrectness of a premise, e.g. of a *major premise* in the syllogistic mood Barbara, may lie in a false generalisation, while the corresponding particular may be true, and the materially true minor premise may seize upon that part to which the predicate of the major actually belongs. For example, all parallelograms may be inscribed in a circle; all rectangles are parallelograms: Therefore all rectangles may be inscribed in a circle. In the same way, the *minor premise* may be false, if it subsumes the S under M instead of under M', and yet the conclusion be true, if P belongs to M as well as to M'. For example, in the enthymeme, ' The sanctity of treaties has no religious reference; and *therefore* is independent of Church doctrines, and of the religious differences of peoples.'[1] Not only that which has no religious reference, but that also which has no *special* religious reference, is independent of the religious differences of peoples.

But this possibility to hit at truth accidentally by a formally correct deduction from what is false is not to be looked at as a proof of the imperfection of the syllogism.[2]

Aristotle taught[3] *ἐξ ἀληθῶν μὲν οὐκ ἔστι ψεῦδος συλλογίσασθαι· ἐκ ψευδῶν δ' ἔστιν ἀληθές, πλὴν οὐ διότι, ἀλλ' ὅτι,* and copiously illustrated the latter relation[4] with reference to single syllogistic figures.

§ 134. HYPOTHESIS is the preliminary admission of an uncertain premise, which states what is held to be a cause, in order to test it by its consequences. Every single consequence which has no material truth, and has been derived with formal correctness, proves the falsehood of the hypothesis. Every consequence which has material truth does not prove the truth of the hypothesis, but vindicates for it a growing probability, which, in cases of corroboration, without exception, approaches to a position where the difference from complete certainty

[1] Klüber, *Völkerrecht,* § 143.
[2] As Vorländer does, *Erkenntnisslehre,* p. 160.
[3] *Anal. Pri.* ii. 2.   [4] c. ii.-iv.

vanishes (like the hyperbola of the Asymptotes). The hypothesis is the more improbable in proportion as it must be propped up by artificial *auxiliary hypotheses* (hypotheses subsidiarine). It gains in probability by *simplicity*, and *harmony* or (partial) *identity* with other probable or certain presuppositions (simplex veri sigillum; causae practer necessitatem non sunt multiplicandae). The content of the hypothesis acquires absolute certainty, so far as it succeeds in recognising the supposed reason to be the only one possible by excluding all others conceivable, or in proving it to be the consequence of a truth already established.

An hypothesis sufficiently confirmed, so far as it lies at the basis of a series of inferences as a common major premise, establishes a *Theory*, i.e. the explanation of phenomena from their universal laws.

The formation of hypotheses is a mean to scientific investigation as justifiable as indispensable. ‘The intelligent man is not he who avoids hypotheses, but he who asserts the most probable, and best knows how to estimate their degree of probability. What is called certainty in a law-case is, at bottom, only a probability of the hypothesis which refuses to admit the possibility of error in the consciousness of the judge.’[1] Hypotheses are necessary in all sciences, if the knowledge of causes is to be reached. Causes as such are not accessible to observation, and, therefore, at first can be thought only under the form of hypotheses, until, with the advance of the sciences, the previously problematic suppositions pass over into knowledge apodictically certain. But to the most ingenious boldness in the invention of hypotheses there must be united the most cautious accuracy in testing them. Scientific hypotheses

[1] A. Lange in the *Zeitschrift für Staatsarzneikunde*, N. S., xi. 1, 138 f., Erlangen, 1858.

are not (as *Apelt* [1] expresses himself) 'assertions which have been floating in the air, and are laid hold of;' they are the results of regular reflection on experiences, and, as premises in tentative deductions, form the necessary preliminaries to adequate knowledge.

In the provinces of the knowledge of nature and of mind, enquiry, which is still incomplete and unconscious of its limits, falls into error when it fancies itself able to distinguish between the absolutely certain and the absurd: it easily changes to Scepticism or Mysticism when this error disappears. A riper enquiry recognises that in all problems where we must proceed upon mere observation, and not with mathematical certainty, the scientific correctness of distinct hypotheses must be the first object of investigation. An essential advance in method in this sense was made in Astronomy, when in the Platonic School, and especially by Heraklides of Pontus, the question to be investigated was not stated in this way,—What positions and motions of the heavenly bodies are to be necessarily accepted on empirical and speculative grounds?—but in this,—What *hypotheses* of regular motions, in themselves possible, can be formed which agree with the facts of observation, so that the phenomena 'may be preserved' (σωθήσεται τὰ φαινόμενα)? Heraklides reckons among these hypotheses that of the motion of the earth. Unfortunately Aristotle misunderstood and destroyed this real advance in method, under the influence of his belief in the capacity of the νοῦς to know principles immediately; for he undertook to decide upon the facts themselves, partly by a rash and erroneous application of speculative and teleological arguments. At the same time, in his logical theory, he does recognise the verification of hypotheses by an appeal to facts, and uses this verification to some extent in his scientific thinking.

The correct construction of hypothesis is a life and death question with Philosophy; for it is the science of the principles which underlie all the sciences, and requires, more than any other, to pass beyond mere experience, and to bring together

[1] *Theorie der Induct.* p. 173.

by comparison very different departments of knowledge. Whoever denies this must abandon philosophy to mere empiricism, or consign it to the old road of immediate à priori intelligence, or to that play of paralogisms,—the so-called ' dialectic method.' Whenever a problem is under consideration, such as the Darwinian Origin of Species, the Wolffian hypothesis of the origin of the Homeric Poems, Schleiermacher's, K. F. Hermann's, Munk's, &c. theory of the arrangement of the Platonic Dialogues, the various theories of the genesis of the Gospels, &c., the most essential condition for carrying on the investigation in a genuinely scientific, and, at the same time, the right and proper way for man, lies in this,—Let all the opposing fundamental opinions be brought under the view of different thoroughly testing hypotheses, and do not let the one opinion (as too often happens if it is the traditional one) be treated from outset as correct, necessary, sound, and rational, and those of opponents considered to be false, arbitrary, unsuitable, or foolish. In scientific investigation every belief which passes beyond the bounds of the scientific probability to be established is necessarily accompanied by illiberality, injustice, and passion, in proportion to the tenacity with which it is maintained; and this tenacity may arise from supposed ethical considerations, as happened to Kant to some extent.

In every comprehensive problem of this kind a great number of single circumstances must necessarily be explained. Now, the student, whatever stand-point he may take, very seldom reaches the unusually favourable position where he is able to found a proof of the certainty, or even of the superior probability, of his view, and of the untenable nature of all opposing opinions upon any one of these circumstances which are to be considered. The conviction of the *certainty* or *superior probability* of an opinion may be scientifically established by a few instances, or even by a single instance, as in the case of Bacon's Experimentum Crucis. In all other instances the possibility only, or the tenableness of an opinion, is the subject of investigation, and the removal of objections which seem to prove that opinion to be untenable. In this investigation it is not only legitimate but advisable to place one's self at the point of view of a given opinion, in order to construct a suitable, complete, and harmonious theory which may embrace all the facts of the case without distortion, by gathering together *admissible* conjectures. Two fallacies are easily fallen into. The one is, that he who argues in one way may perceive a proof for his opinion in the harmony established in this way, although this harmony may entirely differ from the thought itself, since, so long as this opinion is not absolutely confirmed by the arguments in its favour, the possibility of its being contradicted is always open. The other fallacy, which as frequently occurs, is that when an opponent from his stand-point, according to its internal consequences, frames his opinion, and keeps himself free from any confusion between argument for the possibility, and arguments for the necessity of his view, he is, nevertheless, without purely or completely acquiescing in his stand-point, argued against as if the necessity of his opinion were the matter of investigation in every instance. What is uncertain, too, in his statements, which he requires in order to thoroughly carry out his fundamental view of the matter, is made matter of reproach against him. His presuppositions are treated as if they were a mere play of conjecture and evasion, an inadmissible departure from the ground of fact, a creation of hypotheses from hypotheses, reasoning in a circle, or, at least, a capricious acceptance of what is unproved and of what should not be made use of without proof. But the fact of the matter is that he who so speaks has to prove the impossibility of his opponent's statements, not that they are not confirmed by facts, but that they are quite incompatible with facts or with propositions which undeniably follow from the presuppositions of one's opponent, understood as he understands them—because, when *possibility* is denied, it is not enough to show the uncertainty, nor to prove the certainty of other cases, *impossibility* must be demonstrated. In cases of this kind, it is one of the hardest of scientific and ethical problems to give fair play to one's opponent. Our own prejudices are sure to influence us. Yet the effect of the influence of another's stand-point, when it is reached, is of immense value in scientific knowledge. Polemic easily leads to exasperation; it is easy both to abuse it, and to let it alone, because of dislike to the conflicts which it produces; but it is difficult to recognise it, and use it in the right sense as the necessary form which the labour of investigation always takes. Man never attains to a scientific knowledge of the truth without a rightly-conducted battle of scientifically justifiable hypotheses, the one against the other: the scientific guidance of this battle is the *true dialectic method.*

For a long time the emission and the undulation hypotheses have been opposed to each other in optics. They are not to be thought of as fanciful hypotheses which present an incidental conception such as might coincide with the facts, without any warrant that they actually so coincide. Both of them are assertions to be constructed and tested scientifically. One of them must contain the truth, and each of them for some time coincided with all observed facts, although the one appeared better fitted to explain one set, the other another set of facts. At last certain facts were found, in the phenomena of Interference and of Polarisation, which could easily be accounted for on the one hypothesis only, and not on the other. There were four hypotheses on the origin of meteoric stones. The one derived them from earth-volcanoes, the other from atmospheric vapours, the third from volcanoes in the moon, and the fourth gave them a cosmic origin. A stricter comparison of the observed facts with what each hypothesis, developed out into its consequences, led us to expect, showed that none of the first three, but only the fourth, agreed with all the facts of experience. They were, accordingly, seen to be false suppositions, while it was raised to the rank of a scientific theory. Inference from the effect to the only cause possible according to the known laws of nature is no mere hypothesis.

In the same way the circumstance that rays which pass through Comets do not appear to be broken, may be explained either on the hypothesis that Comets are composed of a fine gaseous mass, or on the hypothesis that they are composed of distinct hard bodies. The latter hypothesis, although early proposed, found very little support, until the identity of Comets and Meteoric stones, which cause the appearance of falling stars in the neighbourhood of the earth, favoured this hypothesis (although all the circumstances are not yet explained).

Newton did not merely show that the motions of the heavenly bodies, according to Kepler's three laws, could be explained with mathematical accuracy by the laws of gravitation; he showed that a sufficient explanation could be given *only* on the presupposition of power which acts according to the laws of gravitation, and, consequently, that this cause which sufficed (causa sufficiens) to produce the effects, and which had been already shown to exist as an actual power in Nature (causa vera), in the power of weight upon the earth, was the only one possible. Hence the doctrine of Gravitation, which by itself could only be an hypothesis, became a scientifically established theory ; and in *this* sense Newton very properly refused (in his well-known expression : ' hypotheses non fingo ') to call his doctrine by the term *hypothesis,* which had been used to denote very many earlier fantastic assertions. The inference from the perceivable consequences to the invisible cause was in this case absolutely certain, because this one cause *only* could be proved. The same certainty seldom enters into other departments of investigation, and it can only be reached in the same way. ' Whenever a truly great hypothesis has been established in any of the positive natural sciences, the science is transferred from the province of pure observations to that of philosophical speculation. When the fundamental propositions of mechanics were known, and the integral calculus was discovered, all that could be ascertained from the observed motion of the planets was only the value of the centripetal force for any place which the planet successively occupied. The thought that this value, when found, was to be expressed as proportional to the inverse square of the distance from the sun, and without reference to the path, so that the real path is nevertheless fully ascertained from this statement,—This thought is born of the mind."[1]

Herbart endeavours in his philosophy to get beyond the observed by means of presuppositions which are alone able to solve the contradictions which are contained in what is observed. This hypothetical enlargement of given facts, which proves itself to be necessary, constitutes the essence of his 'method of references.' The apparently simple cause A, which is given, may not be able to establish B; but the question remains, how much A may be enlarged by its accompanying condition A'? The metaphysical application of this method, however, is very uncertain.

Every *philological conjecture* may be considered as an Hypothesis in so far as it finds in the text which it assumes to be the original one the source, not more immediately known to us, of those readings which are to be found in our codices.

Every *historical assertion*, and assertions concerning the truth of reported occurrences, are Hypotheses which must be confirmed in this way, that they alone fully explain the actual shape which the report took, and the further course of the historical occurrence; and that they fully coincide with what was to be expected, as the consequence of nature, of the circumstances and of earlier occurrences. That the 'Koresch' who permitted the Jews to return from their exile and to rebuild the temple was King Cyrus (Kosra), although this has been asserted by Josephus, and is to be accepted on the ground of tradition, must be held to be a mere Hypothesis, so long as reasons worthy of notice are brought against the opinion; for the testimony of Josephus may be explained by the very probable psychological, though unhistorical, identification of a less known person with one better known, and from the interest Josephus had in making the well-known great king appear to be a friend of the Jews. The identification of 'Koresch' with Kuresch, a Babylonian satrap of Artaxerxes Longimanus, of his successor Darius with Darius Nothus, the son of Xerxes and Esther, and, consequently, of Nebuchad-

---

[1] R. Lipschitz in a letter to the Author.

nezzar with Cambyses, is an hypothesis equally justifiable, which, *if* only it explains the facts, is worthy of the rank of an historical truth.

In criminal cases, the two assertions, on the one side of the *guilt*, on the other side of the *innocence* of the person accused, are to be recognised as Hypotheses. The prosecutor and the defendant have to develope each hypothesis into its consequences, and to prove in how far their own hypothesis agrees with the facts obtained by observation and testimony, and how far their opponent's does not. A single case of the *absolute* incompatibility of the opposite hypothesis with any one of the ascertained facts is sufficient to overthrow it, at least, in the form hitherto accepted; but mere uncertainties and difficulties prove nothing. One single circumstance, which admits of one explanation *only*, is more decisive than an hundred others which agree in all points with one's own hypothesis, but are equally well explained on an opposite hypothesis, which has originated from our opponent's side of the question.

The most essential postulate is this—We may not weaken, conceal, or alter any of the consequences of the hypotheses out of deference to the given facts, as little may we darken our vision for the true and simple apprehension of the facts by reference to the consequences of the hypotheses; nor must we reject every explanatory theory, nor every hypothesis preparing a way for a theory, in order to avoid collision with the bare facts. We must first distinctly represent, each by itself, both the consequences of the hypotheses and the facts, and then carefully compare the two. It was in this way that Kepler proceeded when he tested his twenty different forms of path, which he hypothetically took to be the orbit of the planets. He inferred their consequences, by a most laborious mathematical calculation, in order to compare them with the observations of Tycho Brache. The difference of a few minutes determined him to test a new hypothesis in the same way until he found the true orbit: 'sola igitur haec octo minuta viam praeiverunt ad totam astronomiam reformandam.' But mathematical exactness in the development of an hypothesis into its consequences is not attainable in all departments of research, nor is Kepler's perseverance and his single-hearted search after truth a common property of mankind. The motive to the construction of confused notions, and to the use of ambiguous expressions, lies most commonly in the half-perceived divergence between facts and the demands of the system. Science, in this way, is much under the influence of the will; and the truth of knowledge depends upon the purity of conscience. The will has no power *to resist* scientific evidence; but scientific evidence is not obtained without the continuous loyalty of the will.

When natural science, in the whole and in its parts, presents us with the lively and elevating spectacle of a genuinely scientific struggle of different stand-points, the one against the other, we find many cases, especially in the labours of the more eminent men, of a combat between opposed hypotheses-not conducted according to logical laws.

Goethe, although full of the finest natural feeling, and of the most subtle sympathy with organic natural life, was by no means happy in his explanation of the genesis of physical natural phenomena. He very incorrectly expected to see the colours of the rainbow on looking through a prism at a white surface. He saw that the necessary condition of this phenomenon was the presence of a dark boundary line, and he believed that it gave him a proof against the Newtonian doctrine, and in favour of his own explanation of colours, which he said were the children of light and darkness; he did not rest satisfied with the reply that Newton's theory also required the presence of a dark boundary line. The logical analysis of the case would have solved the apparent deception which deceived Goethe. According to logical laws, the Newtonian doctrine could only be contradicted by those facts of experience if an inference of the following kind could be constructed :—If Newton's hypothesis is correct the colour picture must also appear on looking through a prism upon an unbounded field of white; this phenomenon does not occur : Therefore Newton's hypothesis is untenable. But the major premise of this syllogism was never, and could never have been, proved by Goethe, for it is false. The necessity of the dark boundary line follows with strict mathematical accuracy from the Newtonian principle of explanation. The same necessity exists in both hypotheses, although it arises from different causes; hence the fact brought forward will not serve to decide between the two; the ground of decision must be looked for elsewhere.

In the struggle between scientific hypotheses, logical analysis very often renders essential service in settling the true value of single moments. A very instructive example is afforded by the present fluctuating discussion for and against the validity of the *Darwinian development theory*, according to which the higher organisms develope out of those a little lower by successive transformation and improvement acquired in the struggle for existence. This assertion[1] recommends itself, *directly* by its analogy with the embryonal development of the individual, and with the spiritual or mental development of civilised peoples; *indirectly* by the following considerations: We must either suppose that the species of organisms existing on this earth have existed from all eternity, or else that a merely periodic change is eternal, or we must believe in an instantaneous procession of complicated creations from nothing, or, at least, from inorganic materials, or, lastly, we must accept as true a gradual progressive development of the organic from the inorganic, and the higher organisms from the lower. The eternity of existing species[2] and an eternal periodic revolution upon the earth[3] are hardly reconcilable with geological, palæontological, and astronomical facts, for

[1] Made by Charles Darwin in his work, published in 1859, *Upon the Origin of Species in the Animal and Vegetable Kingdoms by Natural Selection.*

[2] Czolbe in his work, *Ueber die Grenzen und den Ursprung der menschlichen Erkenntniss,* Jena and Leipzig, 1865, has lately vindicated this hypothesis in a systematic construction of his mechanico-teleological view of the world. He concedes the extinction of many species and a few small transformations of others.

[3] Volger has adopted this hypothesis.

it presupposes the existence of this earth from all eternity, and it is absolutely untenable if there exists any cause which hinders even in the slightest degree the motion of the planets. The instantaneous creation of complex organisms involves an absolute miracle, transcends the circle of experience, and so is outside of natural investigation. There remains, consequently, for scientific investigation, only the last hypothesis, which is the Darwinian somewhat enlarged. This supposition, however, is itself opposed by the fact, that although lesser transformations may at present be proved from experience, no great transformations such as it presupposes can be pointed out, and that while the succession of organisms in the strata of the earth is undoubtedly kept up, it is by no means without exceptions to its law. But, according to logical laws, if we are only concerned with the *possibility* of the hypothesis, it is an unjustifiable procedure to call these circumstances fundamental objections, and to declare that their explanation is a fundamental condition of the correctness of the hypothesis. For the previous question arises whether a properly constructed hypothesis can include the present condition of organisms which have become stereotyped in hard and fast lines, and which have been formed from organisms more fluctuating, and whose capacity for development only exists now within certain limits, and belongs more to their internal relations, and whether an early, and originally only sporadic, appearance of higher organisms may not be supposed, long before the proportionate final destruction of many lower forms? In this last sense *Virchow* seems to vindicate the *admissibility* of the Darwinian view against the objection of Volger in his speech at the Stettin Association for the investigation of Nature.[1] The *truth* of the Darwinian doctrine has been vindicated by *Häckel*. It is hypothetical, he says, only in its view of the mode of the genesis, and of the number of the original organisms; in other things it is a theory founded on facts, for it explains facts which can be made intelligible in no other way. *Volger*, on

[1] *Bericht über die 38 Versammlung deutscher Naturforscher und Aerzte in September 1863*, p. 71 f., Stettin, 1864.

the other hand, admits the existence of a continuous change
of form,—species pass away and new species are formed from
a common type-species: he will not allow a universal progressive development in the animal world, because higher forms
appear before the lower disappear. 'It is an undoubted fact
that long before those fish-lizards existed, which have been
looked upon as the prophetic forms out of which the pure fish
and the pure lizards were afterwards developed, there were
pure lizard forms belonging to the highest group of lizards.
It is a fact that the Proterosaurus is a dactylopod, and that it
long preceded the first nexipods, Nothosauri, Ichthyosauri, and
Plesiosari. These are facts which are not to be got over. It
is also a fact that real mammals were actually in existence
before those mixed forms, the Ichthyosauri, which should be
the prophetic composite typical forms of vertebrate animals,
and from which, by development combined with analysis,
mammals especially should be produced. The Microlestes of
Plieninger in the Würtemberg is as undoubted a fact as the
Plagiaulax, related to it, and the other mammals of the Port-
land oolite. So long as these facts are not overthrown, a
theory which is founded on the ignorance of these facts cannot be accepted.' But *Virchow's* words aim at vindicating the
admissibility of the theory of development correctly understood. He says, 'We may discover by new observations that
man existed at a time when, according to our conception
hitherto, he did not exist. It may appear that he fought with
the antediluvian bears, while we have hitherto believed that
these bears had vanished long before man came into existence.
It may appear that a lizard existed long before it has been
found to exist up to the present time. But we must remember
that the book of the earth lies open before us in a very few
places only;—Embryology must be our standing-ground,
because there alone we can find any sure knowledge of living
development;—experiences in this department coincide with
universal experience of the mental life;—In the history of
mankind we find solitary great phenomena making their appearance in a period hitherto unenlightened. They remain

long unable to be understood until we see from them that the free development of individual men ever advances and broadens.'

The foundations of the theory of Hypothesis were laid by *Plato* and *Aristotle*. Plato denoted by ὑπόθεσις, in general, a supposition from which something else was deduced; but he used the word in a double sense. In the Phaedo[1] ὑπόθεσις means the presupposition of the more general, which is the cause of the rest, such as participation in the idea which is the cause of qualities. In reference to every presupposition of that kind a double distinction must be made. We must first of all consider what follows from it, and whether it agrees with itself or contradicts itself (—ἕως ἂν τὰ ἀπ᾿ ἐκείνης ὁρμηθέντα σκέψαιο, εἰ σοι ἀλλήλοις ξυμφωνεῖ ἢ διαφωνεῖ), and then, in order to confirm our hypothesis, we must lay down as its reason another, a higher and more general one (ἥτις τῶν ἄνωθεν βελτίστη φαίνοιτο), and go on doing so in this gradually ascending way until we reach something in itself certain (ἱκανόν). Accordingly, Plato will not accept, and rightly, the mere agreement of the consequences of an hypothesis with each other as a sufficient criterion of the *truth* of the hypothesis ;[2] he does not mention the relation of those consequences to the facts of experience ; he seeks demonstration from the more universal, and by that first deduction only reaches a judgment concerning the admissibility of the hypothesis, which can only be proved true by its deduction from a higher principle. He does not, as is now done, prove the truth of the hypothesis by reference to the *truth* of the consequences. The higher principle is a higher idea, and is at the same time a more universal law. In the Republic[3] he uses ὑπόθεσις, on the one hand, to mean what is, because it is the more general, the scientific foundation of the less general ; —fundamental notions, for example, in Arithmetic and Geometry serve as hypotheses from which theorems may be deduced (ψυχὴ ζητεῖν ἀναγκάζεται ἐξ ὑποθέσεων οὐκ ἐπ᾿ ἀρχὴν πορευομένη, ἀλλ᾿ ἐπὶ τελευτήν· —ὑποθέμενοι τό τε περιττὸν καὶ τὸ ἄρτιον καὶ τὰ σχήματα καὶ γωνιῶν τριττὰ εἴδη κ.τ.λι); and, on

---

[1] Pp. 100 A, 101 D, 107 A.   [2] Cf. *Cratyl.* p. 436 c.
[3] vi. 510 sqq.; vii. 533 sqq.

the other hand, in the opposite sense of what serves as the basis for the elevation of a more general—fundamental notions in geometry so far as they serve as spring-boards to elevate to the ideas. He calls this use of the words the truer, and uses, in the same sense of: in itself certain, equivalent to the ἱκανόν of Phaedo, τὸ ἀνυπόθετον, i.c. that which can no longer serve as a basis from which to raise to the more general, because it is itself absolutely the most general (τὸ δ' αὖ ἕτερον τὸ ἐπ' ἀρχὴν ἀνυπόθετον ἐξ ὑποθέσεως ἰοῦσα '—τὰς ὑποθέσεις ποιούμενος οὐκ ἀρχὰς, ἀλλὰ τῷ ὄντι ὑποθέσεις οἷον ἐπιβάσεις τε καὶ ὁρμάς '—ἡ διαλεκτικὴ μέθοδος μόνη ταύτῃ πορεύεται τὰς ὑποθέσεις ἀναιροῦσα ἐπ' αὐτὴν τὴν ἀρχήν). In this last sense the less universal serves as the ground of the knowledge of the more universal, but not as a means of testing the truth of an hypothesis from which it was derived—rather as a foundation, ὑπόθεσις of the Abstraction.[1] In the Dialogue Parmenides[2] it is said that, in order to test an assertion by *antinomies*, not only the Assertion itself, but its opposite must be developed into its consequences (χρὴ δὲ μὴ μόνον εἰ ἔστιν ἕκαστον ὑποτιθέμενον σκοπεῖν τὰ συμβαίνοντα ἐκ τῆς ὑποθέσεως, ἀλλὰ καὶ εἰ μὴ ἔστι τὸ αὐτὸ τοῦτο ὑποτίθεσθαι, εἰ βούλει μᾶλλον γυμνασθῆναι); and, in the (non-Platonic) sentence quoted, this ‘ dialectic ’ procedure is defined to be the training or subjective preliminary conception which conditions scientific knowledge.

Aristotle distinguishes (direct) demonstrative and hypothetical inference (ἡ δεικτικὰς ἢ ἐξ ὑποθέσεως).[3] The apodictic syllogism must conclude from necessary premises, and, therefore, in the first place, from definitions and axioms, i.c. from principles true and immediately certain, which must be a natural prius to what is to be proved, and (as Aristotle and Plato both think) as such must be in itself certain:[4] ἀνάγκη μὴ μόνον προγινώσκειν τὰ πρῶτα ἢ πάντα ἢ ἔνια, ἀλλὰ καὶ μᾶλλον '—μᾶλλον γὰρ ἀνάγκη πιστεύειν ταῖς ἀρχαῖς ἢ πάσαις ἢ τισὶ τοῦ συμπεράσματος). The *Hypothesis*, however, is a pro-

[1] Cf. also *Meno,* p. 86 z ; *Cratyl.* p. 436 c sqq.
[2] Pp. 127 sqq., 131 sqq.   [3] *Anal. Pri.* i. 23.
[4] *Top.* i. 1 ; *Anal. Post.* i. 2.

position in which one of the two members of a contradictory opposite is taken to be true, although its truth is not self-evident as an axiom is: [1] θέσεως δ' ἡ μὲν ὁποτερονοῦν τῶν μορίων τῆς ἀντιφάσεως λαμβάνουσα, οἷον λέγω τὸ εἶναί τι ἢ τὸ μὴ εἶναί τι, ὑπόθεσις. Aristotle calls that hypothetical procedure which was first used in Philosophy by Zeno the Eleatic, and that testing of doubtful propositions which have a certain appearance of truth, by their consequences, dialectical: [2] διαλεκτικὸς δὲ συλλογισμὸς ὁ ἐξ ἐνδόξων συλλογιζόμενος.[3]

In the same sense he calls Zeno the founder of Dialectic.[4] Aristotle attributes to Dialectic not only a didactic value, because it trains to think and is the art of dialogue, but a scientific value, in so far as it is a way to the knowledge, and especially to the critical discovery, of principles:[5] ἔστι δὲ πρὸς τρία· πρὸς γυμνασίαν, πρὸς τὰς ἐντεύξεις, πρὸς τὰς κατὰ φιλοσοφίαν ἐπιστήμας·—ἐξεταστικὴ γὰρ οὖσα πρὸς τὰς ἁπασῶν τῶν μεθόδων ἀρχὰς ὁδὸν ἔχει. Aristotle, however, does not solve the question, whether and in how far the νοῦς recognises principles (ἄμεσα, ἀναπόδεικτα), or whether Induction, Dialectic, and the construction and testing hypotheses in the modern sense are required. Aristotle could not solve it; for on the one side the (Kantian) distinction between judgments formed analytically and judgments formed synthetically is an indispensable preliminary to the solution, and so, on the other side, is the insight into the full meaning of deduction from what is not yet certain for the purpose of clearing the way for the undoubted knowledge of principles—an insight due to the actual course of development of the positive sciences.[6]

In the *middle ages* Hypothesis, for the same reason as Induction,[7] could not be apprehended in a scientific way. Ere logical theory could recognise the full scientific value of hypotheses, positive natural science must first be preceded by the great fact of an earnest battle between scientific hypotheses,

---

[1] *Anal. Post.* i. 2.   [2] *Top.* i. 1.   [3] Cf. *Top.* viii. 11, 14.
[4] Cf. above, § 11.   [5] *Anal. Post.* i. 2.
[6] Cf. Zeller, *Philos. der Gr.* ii. 2; 2nd ed. p. 119.
[7] Cf. § 127.

often prolonged for centuries, and some sure proof of the power
of true and persistent investigation had to be given.

Wolff[1] demanded, in opposition to the judgments of rejection
of earlier logicians : hypothesibus philosophicis in philosophia
locus concedendus, quatenus ad veritatem liquidam inveniendam *viam sternunt*: but gives due warning against the misuse
of hypothesin venditandi pro veritate demonstrata.

Mill remarks :[2] ' Without such assumptions, science could
never have attained its present state : they are necessary steps
in the progress to something more certain; and nearly everything which is now theory was once hypothesis.'

Trendelenburg[3] very properly says that, ' whoever declares
truth to be the present and undoubted possession of the mind
may well fall a prey to sceptical thoughts when he becomes
conscious of this thoroughgoing contest. But the mind has no
inert heritage ; what it has acquired and is master of, it calls
its own possession. This labour is its pride, and is the common
property of the race.' The form of hypothesis is the shape
taken by every notion in the process of construction. Thus
man grows on, regulating his conceptions by their consequences,
and by phenomena. What he knows to be certain is revealed
to him by this correspondence. Science advances in the same
way when it seeks to know, not the mere conception accommodated to the phenomena, but the notion of the cause. Increase is made in that only which lies between the phenomenon
and the notion of the cause, and the synthetic act of the mind
becomes more and more complex and multiform.

§ 135. *Proof* (demonstratio, argumentatio, probatio,
ἀπόδειξις) is the deduction of the material truth of one
judgment from the material truth of other judgments.

Direct Proof (demonstratio directa sive ostensiva,
ἡ δειχτικὴ ἀπόδειξις, or ἡ ἀπόδειξις in the stricter sense,
οἱ δειχτικοὶ συλλογισμοί) deduces the truth of the con-

[1] *Log. Disc. Proel.* § 127.   [2] *Log.* 7th ed. ii. 16.
[3] *Log. Unters.* 2nd ed. ii. 346 f.

clusion from premises, whose truth is presupposed. It is *genetic* (demonstratio genetica) if the ground of proof coincides with the real cause.

INDIRECT or APAGOGIC PROOF (demonstratio indirecta, ἡ εἰς τὰ ἀδύνατον ἄγουσα, or ἀπάγουσα ἀπόδειξις, ἡ εἰς τὸ ἀδύνατον ἀπαγωγή, ὁ διὰ τοῦ ἀδυνάτου συλλογισμός) first shows the material falsehood of a premise, which, the only one uncertain, has been combined with one or several undoubtedly true, from the material falsehood of the conclusion, and then shows the material truth of the contradictory opposite of that premise. By means of a disjunctive major premise, which includes all the possibilities present in the sphere under consideration, indirect proof, by successively excluding all the rest, can raise the one which remains to the rank of certainty. Indirect proof is quite as *powerful in demonstration* as direct proof, i.e. it produces the same strength of conviction of the truth of what is to be proved; but when an affirmative proposition is to be demonstrated, indirect proof must be held to be inferior to the direct, because in indirect proof the ground of knowledge cannot coincide with the real cause as it can do in direct. Indirect proof, however, is quite a justifiable form of knowing the apodictic truth of negative propositions; and the positive knowledge of the truth of principles is not to be reached without it.

The proposition to be proved is called the *Theorem* (theorema).

An *inference* may have formal correctness, it may be an inference and have validity as an inference, although the judgments contained in it are materially false: but a pretended *proof,* whose elements have no material truth, is not a valid proof. The so-called *argumentatio ad hominem* (κατ' ἄνθρωπον), in opposition to the *argumentatio ad rei veritatem* (κατ' ἀλήθειαν), is not a logical form.

The *method of Euclid* in Mathematics is the most perfect specimen of *accuracy* in demonstration. In *this* reference the work of the Alexandrine geometer is unsurpassable. An impartial estimation however will scarcely confirm the judgment of Küstner unconditionally:[1] 'Every text-book of Geometry possesses less of what is of the most value in Geometry, distinctness and certainty, the further it departs from the Elements of Euclid.' It will rather corroborate the judgment of the Cartesians,[2] that it is a mistake on Euclid's part: 'Avoir plus de soin de la certitude que de l'évidence, et de convaincre l'esprit que de l'éclairer;' that he has given too little: ' Des raisons prises de la nature de la chose même pourquoi cela est vrai ;' and ' N'avoir aucun soin du vrai ordre de la nature.' Euclid has sacrificed, in order to obtain this one requisite of strict accuracy (of course the most essential), others which are not incompatible with it.

Tschirnhausen desiderates, next to the greatest possible generalisation, the deduction of every proposition from that doctrine on which it most naturally depends (cf. Chasles, Geschichte der Geometrie, p. 112, Halle, 1839); and Schopenhauer, in the very same sense, requires geometry to base its propositions on existence and not to enunciate ' mousetrap-proofs ' (Mausefallenbeweise).

Proofs should not only be strict, but, where possible, should be *genetic,* i.e. the ground of knowledge should coincide with the real cause. This postulate should and must raise the modern science to a higher rank than Euclid was able to do. A more genetic demonstration is rendered possible by means of analytic geometry and the calculus of infinitesimals. For *analytic geometry* separates the essential and universal relations of quantity which may be represented in formulae, from the accidental forms which they take in single figures. It leads

[1] *Anfangsgr. der Geom.* 4th ed. p. 423; cf. Trendelenburg's *Log. Unters.* 2nd ed. ii. 365; 3rd ed. ii. 399.
[2] *Log. ou l'Art de Penser,* iv. 9.

us, over and beyond the manifold and various considerations, 'accidental views,' and auxiliary inventions happily discovered in individual cases, on which most constructive proofs are based, to the surer and more uniform knowledge of particulars from their common general causes; while the *differential* and *integral calculus* leads us back to the last elements in order to understand the genesis of mathematical notions, and so to comprehend their essence and relations, and thereby to prove the theorems which rest upon them. It is here, therefore, that we can see the greatest simplicity of proof accompanied by the most complete satisfaction to the thinking mind.

Every *indirect* proof is obtained by means of an *Hypothesis.*[1] This hypothesis is not enunciated in the hope that it will perhaps be confirmed by the truth of its logical consequences, but with the express view of overthrowing it by proving the falsehood of one of its consequences, and in this way finding the true assumption by the exclusion of the untenable ones. This procedure serves to establish *principles* in a scientific way, because they, since they are highest and most universal, do not admit of deduction from any higher proposition, and because mere Induction, taken by itself, is not sufficient. The true nature, for example, of infinitely small quantities, or of the differential as a flowing quantity, is shown by means of the following indirect proof. The differential is either of a fixed or of a flowing value. If it is a fixed quantity, it must either be equal to nothing, or in its absolute value greater than nothing. It cannot be nothing, because it has definite relations to other differentials, whereas the relation of nothing to nothing is quite indefinite. (For example, $2 \cdot dx$ can never be made $= dx$, whereas $2 \cdot 0 = 0$. In the same way, the infinitely small circle has its definite relation to its semicircle, the circumference its relation to the radius and its separation from it and from the centre, &c., whereas in the mere point whose extent is $= 0$, all these relations vanish.) But the differential cannot be a fixed quantity different from nothing, because it would not then absolutely disappear in the presence of a finite quantity, and

[1] Cf. § 134.

because in many cases the ascertained result would not be absolutely accurate, whereas its absolute accuracy is from another side apodictically certain (e.g. by means of a proof given in a purely elementary way without the aid of the differential calculus). Hence the differential is not a fixed quantity, but is to be thought of as a flowing one; i.e. that quantity is infinitely little which is determined by going through a series the limit of the value of whose members is zero—that is, a series which has the two following properties:—1. That a member furnished with the same index, and of smaller absolute value, follows every member of the series; and, 2. That whatever fixed number be given, however small this number may be, a member of the series is always to be found whose absolute value is still smaller.

A teleological argument for the existence of God may be given indirectly. In the Kantian disjunction: the world is due either to accident, or to a blind necessity, or to a free cause, it may be laid down and proved that neither the first nor the second assumption corresponds to the given characteristics of the universe, while the third does. The harmonious construction of organisms is only intelligible from the thought ' by which all problems in physics are at bottom solved,' and the finite spirit is only comprehensible from the eternal spirit of God. Still Logic, in so far as it is a doctrine of knowledge, notices this problem only as an example in method. It is not an integral part of its task.[1]

Aristotle explains *Demonstration* (ἀπόδειξις) to be a *species* of the syllogistic procedure, and finds its specific difference in the material *truth* and *necessity* of its premises:[2] ἀπόδειξις μὲν οὖν ἐστιν, ὅταν ἐξ ἀληθῶν καὶ πρώτων ὁ συλλογισμὸς ᾖ, ἢ ἐκ τοιούτων, ἃ διά τινων πρώτων καὶ ἀληθῶν τῆι περὶ αὐτὰ γνώσεως τὴν ἀρχὴν εἴληφεν· διαλεκτικὸς δὲ συλλογισμὸς ὁ ἐξ ἐνδόξων συλλογιζόμενος.[3] ἀνάγκη τὴν ἀποδεικτικὴν ἐπιστήμην ἐξ ἀληθῶν τ' εἶναι καὶ πρώτων καὶ ἀμέσων καὶ γνωριμωτέρων καὶ προτέρων

---

[1] Upon the problem itself and the method of its solution, cf. Trendelenburg, *Log. Unters.* 2nd ed. ii. 406 f., 425 ff.; 3rd ed. ii. 411 f., 461 ff.

[2] *Top.* i. 1.   [3] *Anal. Post.* i. 2.

καὶ αἴτιον τοῦ συμπεράσματος. Aristotle distinguishes *direct* and *apagogic* demonstration:[1] ἀνάγκη δὴ πᾶσαν ἀπόδειξιν καὶ πάντα συλλογισμὸν—δεικνύναι—ἢ δεικτικῶς ἢ ἐξ ὑποθέσεως· τοῦ δ' ἐξ ὑποθέσεως μέρος τὸ διὰ τοῦ ἀδυνάτου.—πάντες γὰρ οἱ διὰ τοῦ ἀδυνάτου περαίνοντες τὸ μὲν ψεῦδος συλλογίζονται, τὸ δ' ἐξ ἀρχῆς ἐξ ὑποθέσεως δεικνύουσιν, ὅταν ἀδύνατόν τι συμβαίνῃ τῆς ἀντιφάσεως τεθείσης. He prefers direct to apagogic demonstration, in so far as direct demonstration infers from what is better known and earlier, or from what is more allied to principles (ἐκ γνωριμωτέρων καὶ προτέρων).[2] The highest principles of demonstration are in themselves indemonstrable, and as immediately certain propositions (ἄμεσα) are known by the νοῦς, they must be better known in themselves, and more self-evident, than what is deduced from them.[3]

Wolff,[4] in order to make the definition of Demonstration conformable with the terminology of the positive sciences, requires from it only the *truth* of all its premises, and admits, besides definitions,[5] axioms, and theorems deduced from them, premises which are based on undoubted facts of *experience.*

Kant[6] explains the dangers of indirect demonstration, and, going too far, would exclude it from pure philosophy.

Trendelenburg[7] has given special attention to the meaning and value of indirect demonstration in the knowledge of principles.

§ 136. REFUTATION (refutatio, ἔλεγχος, ἀνασκευή) is the proof of the incorrectness of an assertion or of a demonstration.

The refutation of an *assertion* is identical with the (direct or indirect) proof of its contradictory opposite.

The refutation of a *demonstration* is accomplished either by weakening the deduction, i.e. by showing that

[1] *Anal. Pri.* i. 23.   [2] *Anal. Post.* i. 23.
[3] Ibid. i. 2 sq.; cf. § 131.   [4] *Log.* § 498.
[5] He follows the example of Melanchthon, *Erotem. Dial. I.* iv. 239.
[6] *Krit. der rein. Vern.* p. 817 ff.
[7] *Log. Unters.* 2nd ed. ii. 396 ff., 425 ff.

what was to be proved does not necessarily follow from the premises, or by proving the material *falsehood* of some premises.

INVESTIGATION (disceptatio) and *scientific disputation* consist in weighing the causes for and against an assertion.

In any thoroughgoing contradiction of an opposed assertion, the refutation of the demonstration must be united with the demonstration of the contradictory opposite. Refutation is most complete when it shows the *cause* of the error, and so destroys the deceptive appearance of correctness.

The knowledge to be produced by a scientific investigation is called the PROBLEM.

The *true apprehension* of the opposite opinion, the capacity to get thoroughly within, and in a measure to sympathise with, the circle of another's thoughts, is an indispensable condition to genuine scientific polemic, but one seldom fulfilled. The power of fulfilling this requisite arises only from a disinterested love of truth. Nothing is commoner in difficult problems than a half and one-sided apprehension of thoughts strange to us, confounding it with a part of our own opinion, and then combating this chimera. The opinion disputed is classed under some abstract category or other, which looks suspicious to common judgment or prejudice; or else an introduction branding it as heretical is prefixed to a garbled statement, in order to prevent the impression which the thought itself even in this form might make, and to confuse the pure sensibility. The contest is transferred to a different province, and, by its construction of suspected consequences, polemic, which ought to serve for the common investigation of truth, is degraded to be an instrument for making attacks on individuals. The experience of all times shows that these perversities are not solely produced by a specially dull and narrow power of thought, and a specially weak and degenerate will. It is a rare power and structure of thought and conscience which can keep itself entirely free from them. It is natural to believe that he himself, or the community to which he belongs, is fully in the right, and that, consequently, his opponents are to be looked on as enemies of the truth, to enquire any more deeply into whose absurd opinions is at least an unnecessary trouble, and is perhaps a violation of truth and loyalty to one's own community. In more favourable cases they may be looked on as we would on sick persons, or on the feeble-minded, or their opinions may be considered to be behind the age, and occupying a stand-point which we have got wholly beyond, towards whom, provided that they are not stiff-necked on their side, a certain degree of humanity, in the shape of a good-hearted forbearance and consideration, is to be shown. To overcome narrowness, and to enter fully within the circle of an opponent's thoughts, and into the motives for his doctrine—which is a very different thing from the languid toleration of indifferentism—presupposes a height of intellectual and ethical character, which is not innate either in individuals or in the race of man, but must be acquired by a long and earnest struggle in development. Yet this is the only path which leads man to truth. His judgment only emancipates who has shown himself to be docile.[1]

When the Problem rests on the opposition of cause and contradictory cause, it bears the character of an *antithesis.* The necessity of solving the contradiction is the greatest spur to scientific research. An example of an unsolved antithesis lies in the relation of the cosmogony to the want of any experience of an original creation.

A theory, to be thoroughly tested, must be tested in a twofold way. On the one hand, the arguments must be tested,—Are they *able* to prove what they are adduced to prove? On the other hand, the doctrine itself, the substance of the proposition constructed upon those arguments, must be tested,—Is

---

[1] Karl Lachmann in the preface to the 2nd ed. of the *Ilias*; cf. Hertz, *Diogr.* p. 179.

it free from all internal contradiction, and is it free from any incompatibility with facts? It is clear that what has been really accurately proved must be free from contradiction, and that what involves a contradiction cannot be accurately proved. Hence a positive result from the first process of testing would render the second superfluous, while a negative result from the second process would render the first superfluous. But we should remember our liability to error, and should so complete our process of testing in both ways, that what remains undeterminate by the result of the one may be determined by the other.

Aristotle defined refutation,[1] ὁ γὰρ ἔλεγχος ἀντιφάσεως συλλογισμός—ἔλεγχος δὲ συλλογισμὸς μετ' ἀντιφάσεως τοῦ συμπεράσματος.[2] He demands that Logic should point out the way in which others have fallen into error,[3] ἀλλὰ καὶ διότι ψεῦδος ἀποδεικτέον, and:[4] οὐ μόνον δεῖ τἀληθὲς λέγειν, ἀλλὰ καὶ τὸ αἴτιον τοῦ ψεύδους κ.τ.λ. Among others *Wolff*, who calls this procedure ' praestantissimum refutandi modum,' follows his example.[5] Wolff, however, prefers a demonstration of the truth to every kind of mere refutation, and does so justly.[6]

Kant[7] urges that, in order to destroy errors, apparent truth, the source of error, should be investigated and explained, and has sought to accomplish this[8] demand by means of his so-called 'dialectic inferences of reason.' He proposes to himself, by means of a thorough-going investigation, to trace the true causes of the delusive errors which arise ' in the fallacies, not of men, but of the pure reason itself.' In this way delusive error, although (like optical deception) it cannot be removed, will no longer lead us astray. The carefulness and thoroughness of this investigation of Kant's, so far as its formal nature goes, commands the admiration and respect of those who must refuse to agree with the material contents of the Kantian doctrine.

[1] *Anal. Pri.* ii. 20.
[2] *De Soph. El.* c. i.
[3] *Top.* viii. 10, 160 a, 37.
[4] *Eth. Nic.* vii. 15.
[5] *Logica.* § 1033.
[6] *Ibid.* § 1035.
[7] *Log. Einl.* vii. a.
[8] *Krit. der rein. Vern.*, transsc. Dial.

§ 137. The FALLACIES which one may fall into lie either in the mode of deducing the conclusion from the premises, or in the premises, or in the conclusion.

Fallacies of the *first kind* comprehend the Paralogisms and Sophisms explained above (§ 126), and fallacies of induction in inductive proof (§ 130).

Fallacies of the *second kind* have to do either with *material truth* of the premises themselves or the *correctness* of their assumption in the case under consideration.

A pretended proof from *false* premises is called *fallacia falsi medii*, when the invalidity consists in combining the middle term with the other notions. In *indirect proof* one of the most common and most prejudicial fallacies arising from incorrectness in the premises results when an *incomplete disjunction* in the *major premise* is erroneously supposed to be complete. An incorrect premise, on which a series of various consequences is based, is called a *fundamental error* (error principalis, or fundamentalis, πρῶτον ψῦδος).

A proposition which may be materially true cannot be *assumed* to be true, and cannot be used as a premise, when it is either identical, in point of fact, with the proposition to be proved, or when its truth may be questioned along with the truth of the proposition to be proved. This is the logical postulate—*assume nothing which is to be proved*. Its neglect is the fallacy of *assuming the point in debate* (τὸ ἐξ ἀρχῆς sive τὸ ἐν ἀρχῇ [scil. προκείμενον] αἰτεῖσθαι, petere id quod demonstrandum in principio propositum est, petitio principii, argumentari ex non concessis tanquam concessis).

Reasoning in a circle (circulus sive orbis in demon-strando) is related to the last fallacy. It proves A by B, then B again by A, or A by B, B by C, C by D . . . . and D or any other element in the demonstration by A.

Fallacies of the *third kind* consist in making a divergence from what is deduced from the premises to what is to be proved, and in the *substitution* of the latter for the former (heterozetesis, ἑτεροζήτησις).

The divergence is either *qualitative* (μετάβασις εἰς ἄλλο γένος) or *quantitative—proving too much* or *proving too little*. When it occurs in a regular refutation, then it may be either the (unconscious) *ignorance* or the (conscious) *change of the point in debate* (ignoratio sive mutatio elenchi, ἡ τοῦ ἐλέγχου ἄγνοια μεταβολή). The confusion of the refutation of a pretended demonstration with the refutation of the fact to be demonstrated is an instance. When *too little* is proved the purpose of the demonstration has not been sufficient; but what is actually proved is not to be absolutely rejected. It has its own value, and may, perhaps, serve as a stepping-stone to a fuller knowledge. When *too much* is proved, if the whole result is correct, no harm is done. What is to be proved is usually able to be obtained by Sub-alternation or Partition from the more comprehensive result. But when the result contains materially false elements, it will show the *characteristics* of some one or other of the various formal or material fallacies in demonstration. In *this* sense the proposition is true: ' Qui nimium probat, nihil probat.'

Subreption (subreptio) is a common name for con-cealed fallacies of any kind, in so far as a sight of the

desired result has led the reasoner astray; but it is more
particularly used of different forms of Heterozetesis.

Truth as well as falsehood may result from *false* premises.[1]
For example, from the systems of the Universe, conceived by
Ptolemy and Tycho de Brahe, the nature and periods of eclipses
of the moon, the duration of the month and of the year, could
be deduced with a certain degree of accuracy. In cases of
this kind the falsehood of the arguments co-exists along with
the truth of the proposition which is not really proved by them.

Indirect proof, when it seeks to establish a positive assertion
by the exclusion of all other conceivable cases, assumes a
strict *disjunction* of the different possible cases. It is often
the hardest part of the task to fulfil this condition with the
strictness required. Indirect proofs are not dangerous in mathematics where a complete representation of the possible cases
may generally be given without difficulty, and with apodictic
certainty; but they are misleading in other departments of
sciences, and especially in sciences such as Philosophy and
Theology, where, after a slight modification of an opinion, the
arguments directed against it, perhaps triumphantly against its
previous form, are no longer appropriate, and the inference for
the truth of the opposite opinion has no logical validity.
The witness borne by the oldest opponents of Socrates to
his guilt rests on an *incomplete disjunction*. Socrates they
believed must either have the sentiments of the old party in
Athens or be a sophist. Now, he had not the first: Therefore he must be the second. The delusion was relatively
necessary because here, as in all similar cases, the higher
stand-point which rises above and combines the two opposed
one-sided views cannot be understood by those who belong to
any of the opposed opinions, since he who understands it is
already raised above them. The apparent proof for the necessity of the χωρισμός of the Idea (cf. above at § 56) depends
on the incomplete disjunction: Ideas existing by themselves
(universalia ante rem)—individuals of sense, overlooking the

ideas inherent in real existence (universalia in re). The apparent proof for the necessity of despotic forms of communities depends on the incomplete disjunction: divine order—human caprice, where the third possibility of rational volition is neglected. A very instructive example is afforded by the lunacy physician, Maximilian Jacobi, whose decision was very famous in its day. When examining the mental condition of a criminal, Reiner Stockhausen, who had been brought to his establishment, he declared that he was not insane, but quite able to account for his own actions because his case did not correspond to any of the six forms into which he himself had classified mental diseases. (He thus overlooked mixed forms.) When brought to the House of Correction the patient soon gave evidence of his insanity.[1]

Kant warns men against *apagogic demonstrations in philosophy,* but the proofs which he himself adduces for the fundamental propositions of his system are apagogical, and suffer from the fallacy of *incomplete disjunction* in the major premises which are stated. Logic, according to Kant, has *nothing* to do with the objects of knowledge. *Therefore* it has to do only with the understanding in itself and in its forms. But a third possibility has been overlooked, that while the objects themselves do not make the object of Logic (and while the task of Logic is not identical with that of Metaphysics, Mathematics, Physics, History, &c.), it is not thinking purely in its relation to itself or its freedom from contradiction, but rather the *relation of thinking to existence,* the agreement of thought with its objects, that is to be explained in Logic. According to Kant experience is *not,* and therefore forms of thought, which belong to us à priori or independently of all experience, are the basis of the apodicticity of our knowledge. Here also a third possibility is overlooked: the ground of apodictic certainty may lie in the order of things—in themselves and the regular manner of sense-affection; we may recognise this order by a thinking

[1] Cf. the tract, *Ueber Reiner Stockhausen,* Elberfeld, 1855, for the one side, p. 119 ff., and for the other, p. 133 ff., where Dr. Richars points out the dangers attending the method of exclusion.

based on experience, whose *action*, which is subject to the sum total of the *logical rules* (regulative *laws*), systematically linking experience together *according to relations lying in experience itself and found there*, does not need to be hypostatised into a series of '*à priori forms*,' which must be added to the given material as a second 'constitutive element.' Just as in the mechanical arts what cannot be done by mere hand labour is accomplished by the hands and machines, which were themselves originally produced by the hands, and not without the hands by magic, so we do not attain to that measure of certainty, which the merely single experience could not give, by means of an à priori magic independent of all experience. We obtain it by thinking, which combines experiences according to logical laws. According to Kant, in the Kritik der praktischen Vernunft, a material ground of determining the will, i.e. one directed to a desired end, is *not* capable of being the principle of morality, *and therefore* the only possible principle of morality is the form of strict universality of law possible without contradiction. Here also the disjunction is complete. A third possibility remains unnoticed, that the principle of ethics is to be sought neither in a mere formless material, nor yet in a form void of all content, but in the *relations* which subsist between various aims, or in *the gradual series of their value*.[1]

An example of a πρῶτον ψεῦδος, from which a series of other errors is derived with a relative necessity, lies in the naïve assumption which is formed from the deception of the senses, and confirmed by the natural vanity of men, that the earth stands still, and is the central body in the centre of the universe, and that the heavens revolve round it in a circle.

The Cartesians made use of a PETITIO PRINCIPII in their polemic against the Newtonian doctrine of gravitation when they looked at the proposition: a body at rest can neither move itself nor any other, as a necessity of thought, founded on the axiom that nothing cannot be a cause of anything, and on

---

[1] Cf. App. D, and the author's article, *Das Aristotelische, Kantische und Herbartische Moral-Princip*, in Fichte's *Zeitschrift*, xxiv. 71 ff., 1854.

the notion of matter, which was fully and exhaustively given in the definition: 'extended substance'—while the chief question in debate was not the validity of this notion of a matter only extended, or of a matter absolutely without power. Kant's attempt to prove his opinion that the First Figure of the Categorical Syllogism is the only regular one[1] is another example of the Petitio Principii. He founds his opinion on the assertion that the law of the First Figure, which enjoins that the Major Premise must be universal and the Minor affirmative, must be the law of all categorical inferences of the reason. But this assertion arises from the definition of the inference of the reason as ' the knowledge of the necessity of a proposition by subsuming what conditions it under a general rule '—a definition which of course applies to the First Figure only and to none of the others. It contains, however, an arbitrary limitation which assumes the very thing Kant has to prove; viz. that there are no simple and regular syllogisms in the other Figures, and that the division of Figures into four is a ' false subtlety.' A Petitio Principii is contained in the objection to the teleological argument :[2] 'since the absolute conformability to plan in nature is *only* the necessity of things, no inference can be made from the conformability to plan in the world to a supernatural cause.' For the ' *only* ' may be called in question. Anton Rée says : ' When an article cannot be fabricated for as little as it costs to bring it from abroad, inclusive of the carriage, it is decidedly better to procure it in the latter way, and rather produce what our land is better able to yield and what we may be able to export.'[3] But the real question is, does such a thing exist? and does it exist in such proportion that the equilibrium between production and consumption is to be produced neither by excessive emigration nor by the hunger-typhus? Rée implicitly assumes as granted, what only a very heedless opponent will grant, and what ought

---

[1] *Von der falschen Spitzfindigkeit, &c.,* and *Logik*, § 56 ff.

[2] Baur, *Kirchengesch. des neunzehnten Jahrh.*, p. 357, Tub. 1862.

[3] *Wanderungen auf dem Gebiete der Ethik*, ii. 147 C, Hamburg, 1857.

to be the chief question to be proved. He commits a Petitio
Principii.

A REASONING IN A CIRCLE happens when we assume,
with Des Cartes, the (objective) reality of what we know with
(subjective) clearness and distinctness, or of what is a (subjective) necessity of our thought; when we found the proof for
the existence of God, or for the validity of the idea of the
Absolute, on this supposition; and when this supposition is
then established by reference to the truthfulness of God, or
by the notion of making absolute harmonious the opposition of
subjectivity and objectivity.

Zeller finds a μετάβασις εἰς ἄλλο γένος[1] when Ast insists on taking the Socratic δαιμόνιον substantially in Plato,
after the analogy of passages in Xenophon; for the inference
of analogy only warrants us in giving the same meaning to
different passages when they occur in the same author. When
the hermeneutical principle of the 'analogy of the faith' is
extended too widely, it becomes the same fallacy.

An IGNORATIO OR MUTATIO ELENCHI occurs when a proof
refuting the hypothesis of innate ideas is opposed by saying
that the ideas have their value, and that the true value of our
thought and action depends upon their theoretical and practical
recognition. It occurs when we oppose the assertion that there
is no synthetic knowledge à priori, or that there is no transcendental freedom in the Kantian sense, by proving or asserting
that science cannot exist without apodictic certainty, nor morality without the determination of the will by ideal motives.
It occurs when it is said that to deny the existence of knowledge à priori (in the Kantian sense) leads to the absurdity of
wishing to prove by the reason (à priori) that there is no reason
(no knowledge à priori). For the question in debate is not the
validity of the ideas, nor the existence of an apodictic certainty,
nor of the faculty of reason, nor of the ethical freedom of the
will. We confuse our opponent's opinion with part of our own
when we substitute our own prejudice that the validity of the
ideas depends upon their special origin, or apodicticity upon

[1] *Philos. der Griechen*, 1st ed. ii. 29.

à priority, and morality upon the unnecessitated removal of the causal nexus, for the *whole* of our opponent's opinion; and having made this confusion, we now argue as if the refusal to admit the false explanation *necessarily* pointed to the denial of the facts themselves (which, however, have been indeed denied by *some* of those who objected to the above-mentioned explanations). Theopomp, the disciple of Isocrates, endeavoured to show that the Platonic explanation of ethical notions was useless, by the argument, that these notions were universally able to be understood without definitions. But Epictetus, the Stoic,[1] objected to this objection, as an ignoratio elenchi, when he insisted (in accordance with the Platonic distinction between science and correct opinion) on the distinction between ἔννοιαι φυσικαὶ καὶ προλήψεις, which we have without philosophy, and the definite conscious knowledge of essences, at which philosophy aims. Another example of mutatio elenchi occurs in the substitution for the refutation of untenable arguments the refutation of the opinion itself, supported by those arguments. For example, a demonstration of the invalidity of supposititious proofs for the existence of a generatio aequivoca sive spontanea (the development of organic forms from dissimilar organic or from inorganic material) is often substituted for the proof of the non-existence of any generatio aequivoca sive spontanea.

The physico-theological argument proves TOO LITTLE. It does not mention the ethical attributes of God. But in so far as it actually shows the certainty of a divine might and knowledge, it is not to be wholly *rejected* (as Kant does) for the sake of the moral argument, but is rather to be complemented by it. Another species of the fallacy of proving too little occurs in Zeno's pretended demonstration that Achilles can never overtake the tortoise, for *whenever* Achilles has reached the place where the tortoise has been, it has made another advance. A mere appeal to the parallelism in the infinite divisibility of space and time does not suffice to solve this very deceptive fallacy; for Zeno could object that, in accordance with this uniformity, the swifter object may reach the slower

[1] *Enchir.* ii. 17.

neither at any time nor at any place. But, in fact, Zeno's argument only proves that, if the two velocities are to each other as 1 : n, the one will not overtake the other within the following series of divisions of time and parts of the way :—

$$1 + \frac{1}{n} + \frac{1}{n^2} + \frac{1}{n^3} + \frac{1}{n^4} + \ldots \text{ in infin.},$$

where the original distance is conceived as a unit of length or as measure of the way, and the time in which the swifter object traverses this unit of length as the unit of time. By omitting the clause : *within this series*, the universal proposition is substituted that the one can never and nowhere overtake the other. The omission would only be correct if it were proved that the sum of that series is infinite, i.e. that, whatever fixed quantity be given, the series developed indefinitely must have a sum which exceeds that quantity. Zeno has not proved this, nor can it be proved; for what is to be proved is false, and its opposite may be shown to be true with mathematical accuracy. The sum of that series, infinitely extended, does not exceed a definite number, viz. $\frac{n}{n-1}$, and only approximates to any fixed difference. Hence it only follows that before a certain finite series of times determined by that quantity has elapsed, and before a corresponding path has been traversed, the quicker object does not attain the greater distance. This is thoroughly true, but is *too little* when compared with what Zeno wished to prove, and believed that he had proved. But the deception arises in this way. Is that quantity of time and that quantity of space, which, so long as we keep within that series, is unattainable, absolutely unattainable?—or must we always keep within the series? Then this is connected with an innumerable number of members, and with the necessity, when these are all individually represented, to attach to every advance, however speedy, a finite and approximately equivalent short time, and also, when the infinite number of divisions of space are *individually represented* in *actual* separation, of representing every one by a finite and, as nearly as possible, proximately equivalent section as small as possible. The series resulting in this way is absolutely unable to be gone over, because its sum (not merely its number of parts) is an infinite quantity. What is true of this latter series is unconsciously transferred, by those who fall into this fallacy, to the first.

Feuerbach's argument against the reality of the idea of God, because it is only an hypostatising of our own existence, is a voucher on behalf of the logical proposition: 'qui nimium probat, nihil probat.' In the logical form used, this argument forms the major premise, which, as such, should be universally true: The multiplication of our own essence in a gradual scale, according to the measure of phenomena, is not a valid form of knowledge, it is only a poetical fiction. But this major premise is untenable, because many other assertions which are evidently false would follow from it (cf. above, § 42). Hence the argument is not convincing, and the decision of the question must be sought on other grounds.

Bonitz[1] refutes an argument of Spengel's by the proof that it would prove *too much*, and therefore that the universal proposition, on which it tacitly rests, is false when he says: 'He who requires the expression ἐξωτερικοὶ λόγοι (in Aristotle) to have the same meaning in every connection, must also give the same meaning to τὰ φυσικά, ἀνατομαί, etc., in every connection—a demand which can evidently not be complied with.'

SUBREPTIONS of all kinds are unavoidable when whole systems are deduced from one or a few principles *only*, while the particular cases which are subsumed under that universal are not reached in any other way (either hypothetically or empirically). The problem of the 'dialectic method,' at least when understood in this sense, is insoluble (cf. above, § 31).

1 In the *Zeitschrift f. öst. Gymn.* p. 227, 1866.

PART SIXTH.

SYSTEM IN ITS RELATION TO THE ORDER OF THE OBJECTIVE TOTALITY OF THINGS.

§ 138. SYSTEM is the orderly combination of mutually related knowledge into one relatively complete whole. *Science* is a whole of knowledge in the form of the system. System is meant to represent in its articulation the articulation of the totality of its (natural or mental) objects, according to the ' *Law of Totality.*' Scientific knowledge finds its perfection in the combination of thoughts, one with the other, into a whole, which in its content and form represents the objective reality.

Scientific propositions and *System* are related to each other as *content* and *form.* But the right form is essential to the content. It is not merely the sum of individual cognitions of scientific significance, nor is their systematic concatenation of merely didactic value. Science, as such, has its true existence only in the systematic form. If (as *Nominalism* assumes) individuals only have real existence, and the sum total of reality is a mere conglomerate of singulars, or if (as the *Critical Philosophy* asserts) all and every arrangement, down to the form of the individual existence itself, is to be looked at as a merely subjective accident imposed by ourselves, then System would have a subjective significance only. But the forms of existence really belong to the reality to be known, and it exists in them.

For the same reason Thought is not (as the *Sensualist Philo-sophers* say) merely a reflex of perception ; it is this mere reflex where perception is the adequate form of knowledge (e.g. in testimony to a deed done the testimony is only a substitute for eye-sight) ; but it is not so in the apprehension of such forms as have corresponding forms of thought (e.g. in a concatenation of mathematical figures which is to become known by demonstra-tion, where the figure only serves to give sensible appearance, or in the knowledge of a causal-nexus, where the perception of suc-cession is itself only a reflex of the thought). In the same way thought is not (as a one-sided *Intellectual Philosophy* assumes) without an empirical basis sufficient for any scientific knowledge whatsoever. The several forms of knowledge are necessarily re-lated to the individual forms of existence, and so is system to the sum total of them all, or to the orderly concatenation of things. Whoever does not know the real articulation of the objects of any science, has not only lost a very useful aid in enabling him to learn it, but has not acquired an essential element of the real knowledge of it itself; and whoever has not got the System does not know this articulation, for the way or form of knowing it is System, and that only.

J. W. Wirth[1] makes the axiom of Totality : ' Strive to bring all your knowledge to the unity of Totality,' co-ordinate with the axioms of Identity and of Sufficient Reason. The logical postulate of the systematic combination of our knowledge may be very suitably brought to the form of a law of thought, but its reference to objective reality should be made more distinctly prominent.

The theory of Division and of Proof is often discussed in Systematic or in Methodology, and this is not inadmis-sible; but it appeared more convenient to treat of the former under the doctrine of the notion, and of the latter under the doctrine of inference. This double possibility arises from the relativity of the notion of *Totality,* and the corresponding relativity of the notion of *System.* It does not alter the logical principle, however.

[1] *Ueber den Real-Idealismus,* in Fichte's *Zeitschrift,* N.S., xli. pt. ii. 196, Halle, 1862.

§ 139. The unity of a system is determined by this, that all the individuals contained in it depend on common principles. A *Principle* is an absolutely or relatively original element on which a series of other elements depends.

A *principle of knowledge* (principium cognoscendi) is the common starting-point of a series of cognitions—viz. the formal and real fundamental intuitions, the fundamental notions and ideas, axioms and postulates.

A *real principle* (principium essendi aut fiendi) is the common basis of a series of real essences or processes.

The principles of knowledge are of two kinds, according as the *individual* or particular, or the *universal*, serves as the starting-point of knowledge. The former do not correspond to the real principles, but form the natural foundations of propaedeutic knowledge; the latter distinctly correspond to real principles and, accordingly, form the foundations of strictly scientific knowledge.

The propaedeutic or method of investigation proceeds *regressively* or ANALYTICALLY to the knowledge of real principles; the purely scientific or constructive method proceeds *progressively* or SYNTHETICALLY from principles to particulars or individuals. But it is by no means always desirable, in an exposition of the sciences, to thoroughly separate the analytic from the synthetic elements. Both are often to be combined with each other in the treatment of individual problems.

Plato enunciated the logical doctrine that all scientific knowledge rests on *principles*, and described more closely the *double* way to and from principles. Philosophy shows itself to have a higher value than the mathematical sciences, because it alone has raised itself to true principles (ἀρχαί), and from these principles descends in pure notions to the less universal, while mathematics deduces its individual theorems from assumptions (ὑποθέσεις) only, which are not the highest axioms.[1]

Aristotle says :[1] εὖ γὰρ καὶ Πλάτων ἠπόρει τοῦτο καὶ ἐζήτει, πότερον ἀπὸ τῶν ἀρχῶν ἡ ἐπὶ τὰς ἀρχάς ἐστιν ἡ ὁδός, ὥσπερ ἐν τῷ σταδίῳ ἀπὸ τῶν ἀθλοθετῶν ἐπὶ τὸ πέρας ἢ ἀνάπαλιν. Like Plato, he ascribes this double problem to our thinking in general: We must ascend from individuals and particulars which lie nearer the senses, and are therefore the earlier and better known for us, to the universals which are the earlier and the better known in themselves, in order from them, as a fundamental basis, to recognise what is particular and individual as their necessary consequences :[1] πρότερα δ' ἐστὶ καὶ γνωριμώτερα διχῶς·—λέγω δὲ πρὸς ἡμᾶς μὲν πρότερα καὶ γνωριμώτερα τὰ ἐγγύτερον τῆς αἰσθήσεως, ἁπλῶς δὲ πρότερα καὶ γνωριμώτερα τὰ πορρώτερον·—ἐκ πρώτων δ' ἐστὶ τὸ ἐξ ἀρχῶν οἰκείων· ταὐτὸ γὰρ λέγω πρῶτον καὶ ἀρχήν.[4] ἁπλῶς μὲν οὖν βέλτιον τὸ διὰ τῶν προτέρων τὰ ὕστερα πειρᾶσθαι γνωρίζειν, ἐπιστημονικώτερον γὰρ τὸ τοιοῦτόν ἐστιν· οὐ μὴν ἀλλὰ πρὸς τοὺς ἀδυνατοῦντας γνωρίζειν διὰ τῶν τοιούτων ἀναγκαῖον ἴσως διὰ τῶν ἐκείνοις γνωρίμων ποιεῖσθαι τὸν λόγον. Aristotle gives as an example, on the one hand, the sensible intuition of body, and the abstractions of surface line and point ; on the other hand, the scientific knowledge of body from the geometrical elements :[3] ἡ γὰρ μάθησις οὕτω γίνεται πᾶσι διὰ τῶν ἧττον γνωρίμων φύσει εἰς τὰ γνώριμα μᾶλλον· καὶ τοῦτο ἔργον ἐστίν, ὥσπερ ἐν ταῖς πράξεσι τὸ ποιῆσαι ἐκ τῶν ἑκάστῳ ἀγαθῶν τὰ ὅλως ἀγαθὰ ἑκάστῳ ἀγαθά, οὕτως ἐκ τῶν αὐτῷ γνωριμωτέρων τὰ τῇ φύσει γνώριμα αὐτῷ γνώριμα. The author of the second book of the Metaphysics[6] explains this Aristotelian thought by the Platonic image,[7] that the eye

---

[1] *De Rep.* vi. 510 sq.; vii. 533; cf. *Phaedr.* p. 265; cf. above, §§ 14, 134.

[1] *Ethic. Nicom.* i. 2.   [1] *Analyt. Post.* i. 2.

[4] *Top.* vi. 4, 141 a, 15.   [3] *Metaph.* vii. 4, § 2 sqq. ed. Schw.

[6] *Met.* ii. (α), 1.   [7] *De Repub.* vii. init.

of our reason dwells originally only in the dim twilight of the sense-world until, trained by exercise, it is able to enter and participate in the bright daylight of the realm of pure thought. But there is an essential difference between the Platonic and the Aristotelian doctrines when the two methods are defined more distinctly. Plato rather requires an ascent to the general notion by means of abstraction, and a descent to the more special notion by means of division; while Aristotle finds this to be a particular instance of the double method of forming inferences—the inductive, which conducts to a knowledge of the universal, and the syllogistic, which, by means of its middle notion, derives the particular from the universal with apodictic certainty. The (Platonic) method of division is only an insignificant part of syllogistic procedure:[1] ὅτι δ᾽ ἡ διὰ τῶν γενῶν διαίρεσις μικρόν τι μόριόν ἐστι τῆς εἰρημένης μεθόδου, ῥᾴδιον ἰδεῖν· ἐστὶ γὰρ ἡ διαίρεσις οἷον ἀσθενὴς συλλογισμός· ὃ μὲν γὰρ δεῖ δεῖξαι, αἰτεῖται, συλλογίζεται δ᾽ ἀεί τι τῶν ἄνωθεν.[2]—οὐδαμοῦ γὰρ ἀνάγκη γίνεται τὸ πρᾶγμα ἐκεῖνο εἶναι τωνδὶ ὄντων. This charge against the Platonic method of division holds good only in so far as this method is synthetic. But division cannot be subordinated as a μικρὸν μόριον under syllogistic procedure; it must take its place beside syllogism as an equally valid form of thought and knowledge of independent value.

Aristotle calls the reduction of given concrete products to their principal elements a solution or analysis, ἀναλύειν,[3] and he was accustomed to cite his logical work itself, because it was a scientific reduction of thinking, and especially of the different modes of inference, under the title of *Analytic.*[4]

Alexander of Aphrodisias[5] says, in harmony with this use of Aristotle: ἀναλυτικὰ δὲ, ὅτι ἡ παντὸς συνθέτου εἰς τὰ ἐξ ὧν ἡ σύνθεσις αὐτοῦ ἀναγωγὴ ἀνάλυσις καλεῖται·—ἡ μὲν γὰρ σύνθεσις ἀπὸ τῶν ἀρχῶν ὁδός ἐστιν ἐπὶ τὰ ἐκ τῶν ἀρχῶν, ἡ δὲ ἀνάλυσις ἐπανοδός ἐστιν ἐπὶ τὰς ἀρχὰς ἀπὸ τοῦ τέλους.

Philoponus[6] directs attention to the use of the terms *analysis*

[1] *Anal. Pri.* i. 31.
[2] *Eth. Nic.* iii. 5; *Anal. Pri.* i. 32.
[3] *Ad Anal. Pri.* f. 4 a.
[4] *Anal. Post.* ii. 5.
[5] Cf. above, pp. 6, 25.
[6] *Ad Anal. Post.* f. 35 a.

and *synthesis* in Geometry. Analysis means finding reasons
for a given theorem; Synthesis is the opposite procedure.[1]

Melanchthon says: ' Geometris usitata nomina sunt et no-
tissima: compositio *Synthesis*, quae à priori procedit; e contra
resolutio seu *Analysis*, quae à posteriori ad principia regre-
ditur.'

The terms *Analysis* and *Synthesis* have been used in Logic
since the time of *Des Cartes*[2] to denote reduction to principles
and derivation from principles.

Newton says (at the conclusion of his Optics) the analytical
must always precede the synthetical in mathematical and
physical investigation. ˛ Methodus analytica est: experimenta
capere, phenomena observare, indeque conclusiones generales
inductione inferre, nec ex adverso ullas objectiones admittere,
nisi quae vel ab experimentis vel ab aliis certis veritatibus de-
sumantur. Hac analysi licebit ex rebus compositis ratioci-
natione colligere simplices, ex motibus vires moventes et in
universum ex effectis causas ex causis particularibus generales,
donec ad generalissimas tandem sit deventum. Synthetica
methodus est: causas investigatas et comprobatas assumere
pro principiis eorumque ope explicare phenomena ex iisdem
orta, istasque explicationes comprobare.

Wolff, following the Cartesian definitions, says:[3] ordo, quo
utimur in tradendis dogmatis, dicitur *methodus*; appellatur
autem methodus *analytica*, qua veritates ita proponuntur, prout
vel inventae fuerunt, vel minimum inveniri potuerunt; methodus e contrario *synthetica* appellatur, qua veritates ita proponuntur, prout una ex altera facilius intelligi et demonstrari
potest; methodus *mixta* est, quae ex utriusque combinatione
resultat. This distinction of the methods is not good as a
definition, because it gives the derivative and not the fundamentally essential characteristics.

[1] *Galen* also speaks of geometrical Analytic, probably in the sense
of Logic expounded according to geometrical methods. He mentions
in his *De Propr. Libr.* xvi. a treatise of his entitled: ὅτι ἡ γεωμετρικὴ
ἀναλυτικὴ ἀμείνων τῆς τῶν Στωϊκῶν ὑπόμνημα ἐν.
[2] Cf. above, § 24.   [3] *Log.* § 885.

545 § 139. *The Principle.   Analysis and Synthesis.*

Kant distinguishes analytic from synthetic *Judgments*,[1] but
prefers to apply to *Method* the terms regressive and progressive
(methodus regrediens a principiatis ad principia, methodus
progrediens a principiis ad principiata).[2]

Hegel[3] assumes that both methods are true in the positive
sciences only because the knowledge conveyed in them relates
only to the 'understanding,' and is only finite knowledge.
The method of philosophical speculation is Dialectic, the form
of the ' Absolute Idea,' of the ' pure reason.' But this Dialectic
is only the supposititious attempt at a synthesis, which does not
yield the results of Analysis.

Schleiermacher requires[4] that the 'process of deduction'
should rest upon a 'process of induction' (and Synthesis upon
Analysis).

Trendelenburg,[5] avoiding both an exclusive empiricism and
the Hegelian theory of ' pure thinking,' sees synthesis to be
the glory of the sciences, but recognises that the condition of
the scientific character of synthesis is its subjection to the
strict discipline of the analytic methods.

Beneke[6] proves how synthesis in all the sciences, mathematics not excepted, is conditioned by previous analysis, and
warns us against betaking ourselves to syntheses à priori,
which, because they are knowledge without foundation, are no
better than caprice and fancy.

The following remark will suffice upon the present *mathematical* use of the expressions *Analysis* and *Synthesis.* Constructive Geometry usually takes the synthetic course of proof,
and leaves the analytic methods to find proofs in solutions of
problems.   However, Geometry, which reckons on the basis of
the systems of co-ordinates, proceeds, by way of preference,
analytically, when it regressively seeks the conditions under
which certain equivalents are satisfied.   It proceeds by means
of algebraical analysis which rests also on this regressive procedure, and is therefore called Analytical Geometry.

[1] Cf. above, § 83.
[2] *Encycl.* § 220 ff.
[3] *Log. Unters.* 2nd ed. ii. 294.
[a] *Logik,* § 117.
[4] *Dial.* § 263.
[5] *Log.* ii. pp. 150–168.

§ 140. The empirical data, from which all scientific investigation in its *regressive* or *analytical* part (or *inductive investigation* in the wider use of the expression) must *start*, are given immediately by external and internal *Perception* (perceptio), and mediately by *Testimony* (testimonium).

Perception when animated by a conscious aim becomes *Observation* (observatio), and when the object admits of the investigation, *Experiment* (experimentum). In experiment we ourselves change the conditions of what happens; we seek to know what conditions are influential and the kind of influence they possess expressly for the sake of the observation, and the answer to the question stated is given by Nature herself.

The *trustworthiness* (fides) of testimony is settled by the general logical rules which govern the inference from the conditioned to the condition, and, more particularly, the construction and verification of hypotheses (§ 134), for this is only a special case of that more general class. The fact to be concluded is the real prius of the testimony. The content of the testimony may have for its ground, either that the event has happened and has been observed exactly in the same way, or that the observation has been influenced by a false apprehension, an untrue recollection, preference of some fancy to strict accuracy, or the confusion of subjective judgment with objective fact. But the witness of an immediate or eyewitness (testis primitivus, proximus, oculatus), who is an immediate witness notoriously or according to the assured concurrence of historical criticism, is

trustworthy, provided that he has been able to apprehend the fact strictly and truly, according to his intellectual and moral condition, and to represent it truly,
and has taken care to do so. The agreement of several
immediate witnesses with each gives to their assertion
a very high probability, if it is proved that they are
independent, that they have not been deceived by the
same deception, nor have been affected and psychologically influenced by the same one-sidedness in apprehension and statement; for a purely accidental agreement in an accidental circumstance has, according to
the laws of the calculation of probability (cf. § 132), a
very high degree of probability in all complicated relations. The trustworthiness of *mediate* witnesses (testes
secundarii, ex aliis testibus pendentes) is determined
partly by their sense and critical capacity, partly and
chiefly by their relation to immediate witnesses. It is
an essential problem, but seldom absolutely soluble, to
discover the genealogy of testimony. The testimony
of later witnesses is suspicious, especially when there is
anything in it to serve a distinct (poetical, national,
philosophical, dogmatic, or practical) tendency, and the
further it stands from the actual occurrences. The
verification of the *subjective* trustworthiness of different
witnesses is reciprocally related to the verification of
the objective probability, which what is attested has in
itself and in connection with undoubted facts. *Criticism* is positive, so far as it has to construct a complete picture of the real previous occurrence, by combining the true elements and excluding the false.

The regressive or analytical investigation seeks to

recognise *real principles* on the basis of admissible
facts. Its knowledge is either given to it in perception
as such, or is innate in the subject in such a way that it
is brought into consciousness by progressive development
—not that it is ascertained by an immediate intuition
of reason, but that it is obtained from the given content
of perception by a *thinking objectively conditioned.* This
thinking fashions the material of perception, not (as an
artist does a block of marble) according to forms, which
are in themselves foreign to it, but (as nature does the
living germ) according to the relations given in itself
and conditioned by the forms of the objective reality.
In reference to this material element, the proposition is
true : ' nihil est in intellectu, quod non fuerit in sensu;'
but the fashioning of the material of (external and internal) perception in thinking is not an operation of less
value, it is the more essential side of the process of
knowledge.

Abstraction leads to the most general *notions* of principle significance. Abstraction, in conjunction with
the idealising activity passing beyond what is given,
fashions what is the higher in science according to scientific laws (as in art according to aesthetic laws), into
the *Idea* (idea in the subjective sense) or into the *regulative* (typical) *notions.*

Judgments which contain scientific *axioms* of value as
principles (axiomata) are framed partly *analytically,*
partly *synthetically.* The former (e.g. the *arithmetical
axioms*) originate by the *resolution* (analysis) of intuitions or notions present before the mind, and have
immediate evidence independent of experience. The

latter (e.g. *axioms of geometry* and the *postulates*, which
are only another form of axioms, and which assert the
possibility of doing what is required) depend partly on
Induction and *Analogy*, partly on *idealisation* and *hypothetical assertion*, accompanied by the verification of
the truth of the hypothesis in its consequences,
which leads to a successive exclusion of the false (by
means of indirect proof) and the confirmation of what
is true. In complicated problems the first attempts at
hypotheses must not include the whole problem. As
many fixed starting points as possible must first be
gained inductively and by means of special hypotheses
and their verification, in order thereby to settle the
principal question. Every principle, if it contains
hypothetical elements, must be verified in its consequences, and hence it is possible to *decide between contradictory elements* in this way, that each shows its true
character in its theoretical and practical consequences.
The axiom: 'contra negantem principia non est dis-
putandum,' is false and inhuman. In a normal development in knowledge, as in life, the lower element is
overcome by the higher, and contradictory principles
equally justifiable find their true place of union in a
common higher principle.

There is no need for a special *'ars inveniendi'* or *'Topic,'*
co-ordinate Logic as the *'ars judicandi,'* such as Christian Wolff
and other logicians, following the view of Leibniz, have desired.
The analytical method which employs the modes of knowledge
explained above in detail, the product of perceptions, intuitions,
notions, judgments, inductions, &c. is the true art of invention,
and so is the synthetic method from its own side. Topic can
only be divorced from Logic when used in the service of Rhe-

torie. *Trendelenburg* says very truly: [1] Disputation or Logic should abolish the chapter De Inventione. When the laws of Logic are once founded on the basis of the individual sciences, they will become much better able to guide one in discovery than could have been the case by means of the previous abstract treatment, whether conducted in the interest of rhetoric or of science.

The true *apprehension of facts*, free from any individual and subjective confusion, is a work of *education.* The teacher, physician, historian and judge, have daily occasion to observe how little men are accustomed to describe the simple facts, and how very much they mix up in the statement (unconsciously and unintentionally) their own opinions and interests. ' It is inconceivably hard, I had almost said impossible, to describe what has been seen or heard wholly and exactly as it has been seen and heard. We often introduce our own feelings without anticipating it, and although we have the strongest and purest love of truth.' [2] ' We see in the descriptions not the things themselves, but only the impressions which they have made upon the soul of our author, and we know that the account of the impression never fully corresponds to the things. It is the business of the historical critic to infer back from the narrative to the first form of the impression, and from this to the actual fact, to remove the additions and changes due to subjective influence, and to restore the objective occurrence.' [3]

The task of the *regressive* (à potiori *inductive*) investigation consists in starting from ascertained individuals, and in explaining everything that follows, where premises are gained sufficient to prove the truth as accurately as possible. The result again serves as a premise for further argumentation, so that, so far as this arrangement goes, all other points of view are noticed only in so far as the final purpose, which consists

[1] *Erläut. zu den Elem. der Arist. Log.* p. viii.
[2] Schiller in Caroline von Wolzogen, *Schiller's Leben*, li. 206, 1830.
[3] *Heinr. von Sybel, Ueber die Gesetze der Historischen Wissens*, p. 12 f.: Bonn, 1864.

in the attainment of the greatest certainty possible, allows free play to each. After that a series of individuals has been thoroughly established in this way, the first thing to be done is to settle what the principles are. When full certainty cannot be attained, the degrees of probability are to be discovered and denoted with as much accuracy as possible.[1] These postulates are equally true for the sciences of Nature and of mental life. *K. O. Müller,* looking upon them as elements of method common to history and the natural sciences, designates them: a quick observation of the events of what is given in experience, the collection of as many individual points as it is possible to find, the enquiry into their regular concatenation according to the laws of probability, and their reference to the given fundamental elements of the universe of nature.

The investigation of *individuals* gains in significance as it can insert itself as a moment in the *sum total of the scientific labour.* Advance in the higher grades of knowledge is not to be made by means of a crude independence, which, trusting to common sense or guided by the idle fancy of personal genius, for the sake of a supposititious 'freedom from prejudice'—which is often only an unscientific persistence in superficial opinions, and full of unripe conceits—despises the study of the investigations of others, or contents itself with half and half apprehension without thorough-going reflection and critical accuracy. Nor is it attained by a compulsory soulless resignation, which, proceeding wholly upon acquired knowledge, and devoted to the safe appropriation and faithful reproduction of treasures produced by creative spirits, leaves unemployed its own power of production. It is attained by reaching an independent insight from the basis of the most accurate acquaintance with the whole development of the science up to this time. In science man, starting from the natural condition of freedom from restraint, must reach true freedom by submission.

The *speculative instinct* aims at the most general principles, and anticipates them in poetical or half-poetical forms before

---

[1] Cf. the remarks on method in my *Platonischen Untersuchungen,* pp. 99, 112, and 268 : Wien, 1861.

strict science is able to recognise them. *Exact investigation* contents itself with the inductive discovery and verification of merely empirical laws, while the first principles cannot be established on the basis of facts with strict accuracy, but is too ready to sacrifice depth to certainty. The *highest problem* is to attain the end, pointed out by speculation, by the methods of exact investigation. Bunsen calls this, more immediately with reference to the Philosophy of History, the ' union of the spirit of the Baconian system with the categories of the German speculative mental Philosophy.' [1]

What may be said upon the history of the doctrines of *Empiricism, Rationalism, Critical Philosophy,* &c., because it must confine itself to the general stand-point of a theory of knowledge, belongs to the whole history of Logic as the doctrine of knowledge. We must therefore here refer to our historical survey.[2]

§ 141. The means which method has at command for the *constructive* or *synthetic* construction of knowledge are: Definition, Division, and Deduction.

Definition ensures the permanence of the result of the process of abstraction, and serves as a foundation for Division and Deduction; and these processes again lead to new definitions.

Division separates the sum total of the scientific material, according to the relations of superordination, subordination, and co-ordination, in the belief that their regular arrangement ensures a true copy of the real relations. They are not reduced to a ready-made scheme, but the schematism, down to its last sub-

---

[1] *Hippol.* i. 276 ; cf. my article *Ueber Idealismus, Realismus und Ideal-Realismus* in Fichte's *Zeitschrift,* vol. xxxiv. 63–82, 1859.
[2] Cf. above, §§ 10–35 ; cf. also expressions in §§ 37 ; 40 ; 44 ; 46 f.; 51 ; 66 f.; 67 ; 73 ; 74 ff.; 89 ; 127 ; 129 ; 131 ; 134 ff.; 138 f.

divisions, is to represent the essence of the content in the form of a natural organisation. The (Kantian) principles of homogeneity, specification, and continuity are to be applied in definition according to the nature of the case, and not as subjective maxims.

Deduction, leading to the results of the processes of Abstraction and Induction, establishes the particular and individual by means of the universal. It authenticates its genetic or teleological necessity in a syllogistic form of thought, by means of a combination of series of reasonings suitable to the case (method of *genetic Explanation*; method of *teleological Speculation*). Deduction can never deduce the reality of the particular and individual without the universal, but it can never deduce it from the universal alone.

According as the definition of notions and division or deduction fills the more prominent place in synthetic knowledge, *Trendelenburg*[1] distinguishes ' *Systems of Arrangement* ' (classifications) and ' *Systems of Development*' (explaining theories). The former take the form of descriptive, the latter of explanatory, natural and mental sciences. But since the arrangement must as much depend on that concatenation of things which is knowable to us, as the possibility of deduction does on the notional arrangement, the end of these elements can never be wholly separated from the other. Each can attain to scientific completion only in and by each other (cf. § 66).

The more *empirical* character of a scientific system is caused by the more frequent use it makes of the regressive or analytical method, in so far as it, keeping to what is given, does not attempt to reach the absolutely highest principles. Its more *speculative* character is caused by the more frequent use it makes of the constructive or synthetic method, in so far as it, starting from first principles, seeks to recognise reality by means of a freely-fashioned product of thought in such a way that in every extension of what is given the path of thought is determined by the aim of knowledge. This opposition is, however, relative only. The so-called empirical sciences, if they wished to deprive themselves of all the thoughts which pass beyond mere experience, would renounce their scientific character. And philosophy, if it would not dissolve into airy fancy, must assume, in order to the regressive knowledge of principles, the whole of the positive sciences. Just as the roof or cupola does not rest immediately on the floor, but the floor bears it by means of the other parts of the building, so philosophy rests on an empirical foundation by means of the positive sciences. The development of one and the other is always reciprocal.[1] In all the sciences without exception speculation requires the empirically given material, and empiricism requires the speculative quickening. Only the relation of these elements to each other is different in different sciences.

Whenever the modifications of the general laws of Logic in their application, according to the difference of the content of different sciences, come into consideration, it becomes a question of PARTICULAR or APPLIED LOGIC (§ 8), and no longer belongs to GENERAL or PURE LOGIC. When we, starting from the facts of self-consciousness in themselves undoubted, have found in the gradual transference of the content and forms of the mental (psychic) world to the outer world, accomplished by means of thinking according to the measure of sense perception, the course of human knowledge, and from the end and aim of knowledge, which is material truth, and which lies in the measure of the attainable agreement of the subjective picture with the objective reality, have conceived the forms of knowledge and the *universal* laws of their structure and combination, we stand at the boundaries of our task.

[1] Cf. the author's article on the *Begriff der Philosophie*, in Fichte's *Zeitschrift*, vol. xlii. 185–199, 1863.

APPENDIX A.

——◆◆◆◇——

ON RECENT LOGICAL SPECULATION IN ENGLAND.

§ 1. THE revival of logical study in England dates from the publication of *Archbishop Whately's* Elements of Logic. Before the appearance of this work, the study of the science had fallen into universal neglect. It was scarcely taught in the universities, and there was hardly a text-book of any value whatever to be put into the hands of the student.[1]

The Elements of Whately was by no means a good text-book. The author wrote without having a very extensive knowledge of his subject, and did nothing to enlarge the science he professed to teach; but he had the great gifts of a clear plain style, good arrangement, and a wonderful power of fresh and interesting illustration. The book, which had no pretensions to scientific accuracy, was nevertheless so successful that probably no text-book on Logic ever went through so many editions. It awakened a real study of Logic, and was the forerunner of a host of logical text-books, which, if they added little to the science they profess to expound, at least showed the national zeal for the study.

§ 2. A more scientific spirit, however, soon showed itself among English logicians, and, when it appeared, took a double direction, due to its twofold origin. Two influences were working in men's minds, that of Kant and that of Hume. The Kantian influence gave us the formal Logic of Hamilton, Mansel, and Thomson; the influence of Hume, the Logic of Mill and Bain.

These two schools, however, do not exhaust the list of scientific English logicians.

Among the formal logicians, the doctrine of a quantified predicate became a leading doctrine, and this prepared the way for the mathematical Logic of Boole. Among the sensationalist logicians the

[1] Cf. Hamilton's *Discussions*, Art. IV. Logic.

doctrine of Induction was most important, and their theories cannot be explained without discussing the relative theories of Dr. Whewell.

We have thus two classes of logicians—Formal and Sensationalist; the former by their doctrine of a quantified predicate inseparably related to the mathematical Logic of Boole, and the latter by their theory of induction closely allied to the inductive Logic of Whewell.

§ 3. The *Formal Logic* of Hamilton, Mansel, and Thomson may be traced to a Kantian influence. These logicians expressly say that they are indebted to Kant for their whole view of the science. They have in many instances borrowed their divisions and terminology from Kant, and they are to be distinguished from other English logicians by strongly asserting the Kantian maxim, that Logic has nothing to do with the objects of knowledge, and, *therefore*, can only be concerned with the forms of thought. They push their theory of Formal Logic much farther than Kant did, however. Kant was not only a logician but a metaphysician, and his logical theories were to a great extent the result of his metaphysical enquiries. The ultimate matter of knowledge, things-in-themselves, was wholly unknown. It was only known in certain relations, when combined with certain forms which were imposed upon it by mind, and by which it was brought into the presence of mind. The invariable and permanent part of knowledge, i.e. that part of it which could form the material of a strict science, was this formal element, and in thinking was the form of thought in its various modifications. There was always some degree of coincidence between Kant's metaphysical and his logical doctrines — a coincidence which indeed expressed itself in the parallelism which he found between the metaphysical and logical categories—and this coincidence kept him from pushing his logical theories to their last consequences. But our English formal logicians were not held back in any such way, and their Logic is a purely formal Logic from beginning to end. They begin by stating the incomplete disjunction—Logic has *nothing* to do with the objects of knowledge (or else it could not be distinguished from metaphysics, &c.); *therefore* it must occupy itself exclusively with the form of thought.[1] The third possibility that Logic treats of, the *relation* of thought to existence, or of the forms of thought in their relation to their objects, does not come into their theory of Logic, though in their practical illustrations of the science it can scarcely be avoided.

The three writers whose names are set at the head of this paragraph, while they must be considered to be thoroughly original and independent thinkers, are yet so far agreed in their views of the science, that,

[1] Cf. p. 533.

in describing the school to which they belong, we may take from each that part which he has most carefully elaborated. Dean Mansel has marked out the sphere and described the work allotted to formal Logic most thoroughly. We must go to Sir W. Hamilton's writings to find how the system is worked out in details. And Archbishop Thomson has given us the only thoroughly elaborated representation of the whole of formal Logic. His Outlines of the Laws of Thought is a text-book for junior students, however, and cannot be taken as a perfect description of Formal Logic in all its parts.

§ 4. According to *Dean Mansel*,[1] Logic is the *science of the formal laws of thought*, or the *science of the laws of thought as thought*. Its province is both *constructive* and *critical*.

Logic as *constructive* takes the three formal laws of thought,[2] and, by applying them to the materials from which notions, judgments, and reasonings are constructed, frames formally these three products of thought. The material must be given ere constructive Logic can act. In forming notions attributes must be given, in forming judgments notions, and in forming reasonings judgments. In the formation of notions all that Logic has to do is to see that the attributes out of which the notion is to be framed are not logically contradictory the one of the other. The material validity is not the question to be considered. 'Centaur' is as correct logically as 'man.' In forming judgments all that Logic is concerned with is to see that the notions put together in the judgment are not self-contradictory. An affirmative judgment is true, formally and logically, whenever the given notions have no attributes which contradict each other; a negative judgment is true, formally and logically, whenever the given notions contain attributes which contradict each other. In forming a syllogism, Logic has only to consider whether the given judgments are free from contradiction, and are put together under such conditions of quantity and quality that the mere act of thought necessarily elicits the conclusion. It has nothing to do with the truth of the premises. 'Purely formal mediate reasoning or syllogism is dependent on the same laws as formal judging, the Law of Identity governing the affirmative categorical syllogism, and the Law of Contradiction the negative; while the subordinate Law of Excluded Middle is called into operation in the immediate inferences of Opposition and Conversion.'[3] This function of

---

[1] Mansel's edition of Aldrich's *Artis Logicae Rudimenta*, pref. lvii-lxxvii, Prolegomena Logica, pp. 181-265.

[2] The laws of Identity, Non-Contradiction and Excluded Middle. The law of Reason and Consequent, commonly given as the fourth law, is excluded by Mansel and Hamilton. Cf. above, p. 231.

[3] *Artis Log. Rud.* p. lxx.

Logic is the same in relation to special classes of these products of thought. For example, in Definition, which is a kind of formation of a notion, all that Logic has to do is to determine the conceivability of the several attributes contained in a given notion by their analysis and separate exposition. If the attributes are compatible the definition is logically valid. On the other hand, Logic as *critical* examines whether notions, judgments, or reasonings are framed in accordance with the laws of thought. It adequately determines the *conceivability* of a notion, the truth or falsehood of an *analytical* judgment, or the validity of a *professedly formal* reasoning. It cannot determine the *real* correctness of the notion, the truth or falsehood of a *synthetical* judgment, or the validity of a reasoning *professedly material.*

Such a view of the nature and province of Logic makes it differ widely from the Logic of Bacon, and indeed from any pre-Kantian Logic whatever; and any attempt to combine under the one name of Logic a Baconian theory of evidence and the description and application of the laws of pure thought cannot but be distasteful to its advocates. Accordingly, Dean Mansel elaborately protests against any such combination. The two disciplines, he contends, are entirely distinct. They differ in the object they treat of, in the nature of the laws they consider, in the conceptions they imply, in the methods they involve, and they use common terms in the most widely different senses.[1]

In short, the distinction between the forms of thought and the objects thought about is pushed to such a length that it becomes forced and unnatural. The vital and important thing in all knowledge, and the real question to be settled in any theory of knowledge, the *relations* of thought to the things thought about, is entirely passed over. And we have an elaborate framework of artificial mechanism instead of the representation of the ways in which the mind works in the attainment of knowledge.

§ 5. It is evident that when Logic becomes only a statement of the fundamental laws of thought with a postulate, and the application of these laws to things thought about, the science becomes much more simple and mechanical than Aristotle, or any other logician who believed Logic to be a theory of knowledge, had ever imagined, and a New Analytic is required to supersede the Old. This New Analytic has never, unfortunately, been worked out to completeness;[2] but we know

---

[1] Cf. *Artis Log. Rud. Prol.* lxxiii.; cf. Hamilton's *Lect. on Logic,* ii. 329 ff.

[2] The completest account given is to be found in *An Essay on the New Analytic of Logical Forms,* &c., by Professor Thomas Spencer Baynes, of St. Andrews. Scattered notices of the *New Analytic* are given in the Appendix to Sir W. Hamilton's *Lectures.*

enough about it to be able to describe it, and also to see how it led, by a strange 'irony of fate,' when we think of the opinions Hamilton held about mathematics and mechanics, to the mathematical Logic of *Prof. Boole* and to the mechanical Logic of Prof. W. Stanley Jevons.

§ 6. According to *Sir W. Hamilton*, the NEW ANALYTIC OF LOGICAL FORMS (1) shows that the distinction between (metaphysical) whole of Comprehension and (logical) whole of Extension runs through all Logic, and gives it another side which has not been recognised; (2) thoroughly enforces the postulate of Logic, and thereby effects numerous simplifications and changes in the science; and (3) constructs a scheme of Symbolical Notation which will display, with mechanical simplicity, propositional and syllogistic forms in all their old and new applications.[1]

§ 7. I. A notion has both *comprehension* and *extension*; it connotes a certain number or whole of attributes, and denotes a certain number or whole of objects. Thus 'man' stands for either the sum total of the attributes which make the *meaning* of the notion, or the sum total of the objects to which the notion may be applied. Unless this double reference be explicitly enounced, the notion is ambiguous. Therefore in propositions and in syllogisms we must make it clear whether we are speaking of the comprehension or of the extension. This is best done by explicitly stating what the ambiguous copula 'is' means. In the sphere of Comprehension *is* means *comprehends in*; man is mortal means: the notion *man comprehends in it* the notion *mortal*. In the sphere of Extension *is* means *is contained under*; man is mortal means: the notion *man is contained under* the notion *mortal*. Now as the two wholes of Extension and Comprehension are always in the inverse ratio of each other, what is smaller in extent is larger in content. When we say 'man comprehends mortal,' the notion *man*, the subject, taken in comprehension, is the greater, and the notion *mortal*, the predicate, is the less; but when we say 'man is contained under mortal,' the notion *mortal*, the predicate, taken in extension, is the greater, and the notion *man*, the subject, is the less. The subject and predicate, which are related to each other as contained part and containing whole in Extension, change places, and become comprehending whole and comprehended part in Comprehension. This reciprocal relation must be noticed, or ambiguity will result. There must therefore be Comprehensive as well as Extensive syllogisms, and the comprehensive syllogism may, in each case, be formed from the extensive by changing the meaning of the copula in the propositions and transposing the premises.

[1] *Lect. on Logic.* p. 250.

This addition of comprehensive judgments and inferences does not recommend itself. The terms 'whole of comprehension' and 'whole of extension,' when applied to notions, are to a certain extent misleading; the words 'connotation' and 'denotation' better express the relations. Denotation is a quantitative relation; it means ability to denote a greater or smaller number of objects; and when we use 'man' denotatively, we can say with correctness 'some men' or 'all men.' 'Man' is then a whole and has parts. But Connotation is a qualitative relation; it means ability to represent certain qualities; and when we use 'man' connotatively we cannot say with correctness 'some man' or 'all man.' 'Man is not a whole that can so be divided. The term 'comprehensive' is still more unfortunate when applied to judgments. It is absurd to say, 'Some men are black-haired,' meaning that some part of the whole of the attributes comprehended under the notion man comprehend the notion black-haired. We may say, the attributes connoted by 'man' are sometimes accompanied by the attributes connoted by the notion 'black-haired,' but this is not a judgment in Comprehension. The truth is that a judgment does not naturally take this double quantity of comprehension and extension. The subject of a judgment is naturally denotative; it denotes an object or objects. While the predicate of a judgment is naturally connotative; it connotes an attribute or attributes (cf. App. B). The same remarks apply to Syllogisms in Comprehension.[1]

§ 8. II. The *postulate* of Logic is—*To state explicitly what is thought implicitly.*[2] The chief result which comes from the rigid enforcement of this postulate, is: that logically we take into account the *quantity* always understood in *thought*, but usually, and for manifest reasons elided in its expression, not only of the *subject*, but also of the *predicate*. On this *quantification of the predicate* the principal changes of the New Analytic are based.[3]

1. The *preindesignate terms* of a proposition, whether subject or predicate, are never to be thought as *indefinite* (or indeterminate) in quantity. *All* or *some* or an equivalent predesignation must be prefixed to each term.[4]

2. A proposition becomes an *equation.* This conception of the nature of a proposition, though given by Hamilton as a result of the application of the quantification of the predicate, is perhaps rather its-

[1] Cf. also Mill, *Exam. of Sir W. Hamilton's Phil.* 3rd ed. p. 488 ff.
[2] This single postulate is elaborated into five rules by Sir Wm. Hamilton; cf. *Lect. on Log.* ii. 252. It is stated variously; cf. Baynes's *New Analytic of Logical Forms,* p. 4.
[3] *Lect. on Log.* ii. 250.
[4] Cf. Baynes's *New Analytic,* p. 5 ff.

cause. For whenever the relation of subject and predicate in a proposition is thought to be, not that of subsistence and inherence or of object and attribute inhering in it, but an equation, we must think the predicate as a quantity which is equal to the subject, and we must think it as quantified, and so exactly correspondent to the subject.

3. Whenever a proposition is conceived to be an equation, and the copula is seen to be equivalent to the sign of equality (=) it is evident that there can no longer be three species of *Conversion*, but only one—that of Simple Conversion (All A=some B, is the same as: some B = all A).[1]

4. Whenever propositions are seen to be equations, inference is greatly simplified. Categorical syllogism is simply the comparison of equal sides of equations, ' it is the product of that act of mediate comparison, by which we recognise that two notions stand to each other in the relation of whole and part, through the recognition that those notions severally stand in the same relation to a third;' and its general laws may very well be gathered into one canon which will guide this comparison. The canon is: ' What worse relation of subject and predicate subsists between either of two terms and a common third term, with which both are related, and one at least positively so—that relation subsists between these two terms themselves.'[2]

5. From this one *canon* all the *species* and *varieties* of *Syllogism* may be evolved.

(1) There are two *kinds* of Syllogism corresponding to the two kinds of logical wholes and parts. These wholes are comprehensive and extensive. Hence there are syllogisms of comprehension and extension. The first clause of the canon—' *What worse relation of subject and predicate subsists between two terms,*' &c., determines these different kinds of syllogism. In the whole of comprehension the predicate is part of the subject, and therefore is worse than the subject. In the whole of extension the subject is part of, and therefore worse than the predicate.[3]

(2) Syllogisms vary in relation to Figure and Mood.

(a) The variation of *Figure* arises from the various positions of the middle term in relation to the extremes, and this is evidently determined by the clause—' *What relation subsists between either of two terms and a common third term.*'

(b) The variation of *Mood* arises from the various quantity and quality of the propositions which make the Syllogism, and this variety is determined by the clause—' *What worse relation of subject and pre-*

[1] Hamilton's *Lect. on Log.* ii. 271 ff.; Baynes' *New Analytic*, p. 31 ff.
[2] Cf. Baynes' *New Analytic*, p. 53 ff.
[3] Ibid. pp. 56, 57.

dicate,' &c. A particular quantity is a *worse* relation than a universal, and a negative quality a *worse* relation than a positive.[1]

6. Logicians have laid down special laws of Syllogism which regulate the inferences in the various Figures. All of them emerge on the neglect to give the predicate explicitly the quantity which implicitly belongs to it, and all of them are rendered useless and most of them false as soon as the quantification of the predicate takes effect. The enunciation of the one supreme canon of Syllogism therefore *abrogates these special laws.*[2]

7. The supreme canon of categorical Syllogism, since it determines all the varieties of Syllogism, will determine the number of syllogistic Figures. A reference to this canon demonstrates the *exclusive possibility of Three Syllogistic Figures,* and *abolishes* the so-called *Fourth Figure.* The clause which determines the variations of Syllogism with respect to Figure is—'What worse relation of subject and predicate subsists between either of two terms and a common third term,' &c., and this clause determines all the variations possible. These are three: for there are only three varieties of relation. The relations are :—

(1) *That in which the common third term is subject of one of the terms,* and the *predicate of the other.* This gives the *First Figure* in Extension and in Comprehension. For example :—

In Extension	In Comprehension
M is contained under P ;	S comprehends M ;
S is contained under M :	M comprehends P :
∴ S is contained under P.	∴ S comprehends P.

(2) *That in which the common third term is predicate of both the other terms.* This gives the *Second Figure,* which admits affirmative as well as negative conclusions. For example :—

Affirmative	Negative
All P is all M ;	All P is all M ;
All S is some M :	No S is any M :
∴ All S is some P.	∴ No S is any P.

(3) *That in which the common third term is subject of both the other terms.* This gives the *Third Figure,* which admits of universal as well as of particular conclusions. For example :—

Universal	Particular
All M is some P ;	All M is all P ;
All M is all S :	Some M is some S :
∴ All S is some P.	∴ Some S is some P.

[1] Baynes' *New Analytic,* p. 74.   [2] Cf. Hamilton's *Le t. on Log.* pp. 285, 345, 350.

The so-called Fourth Figure is a hybrid. Its premises proceed in the whole of Comprehension. For example :—

All P is M ;		All P comprehends M ;
All M is S :	which being inter-	All M comprehends S :
∴ Some S is P ;	preted gives	∴ Some S is contained under P ;

i.e. in the premises the two subjects P and M are greater than the two predicates M and S, while in the conclusion the predicate P is greater than the subject S. This Figure is also useless, for reasoning is scientifically complete without it.[1]

8. Since Syllogism is the result of an act of immediate comparison by which we recognise that two notions stand to each other in the relation of whole and part, through the recognition that these notions severally stand in the same relation to a common third notion, it is not necessary that these notions stand to each other in *the* relation of subject and predicate. And since the syllogistic variation of Figure depends on the varieties of the relations of subject and predicate, Syllogistic Figure is not an *essential variation.* There may be *Unfigured* as well as *Figured Syllogism.*

The UNFIGURED SYLLOGISM is that in which the terms compared do not stand to each other in the reciprocal relation of subject and predicate ;[2] the FIGURED SYLLOGISM, that in which the terms compared have this relation.[3] But if Figure itself be only an accidental variation of Syllogism, one of the Figures, the first, cannot be in itself the only true and valid form of syllogistic inference, and it is absurd to *reduce* the others to that form in order to show their validity. Hence the New Analytic abolishes *Reduction.*

9. But if Reduction be unnecessary, *each Figure* must have an *organic* principle of its own on which it proceeds, and, since all varieties of syllogism are to be evolved from its supreme canon, these canons of the separate Figures are to be evolved from that supreme canon. And since the variation of Figure is determined by the varieties of relation of the extremes with the common third term implicitly given in the supreme canon, the canons of each of the Figures will be formed by explicitly enouncing that particular variety of relation which determines each Figure.

In the *First Figure* the common third term is the subject of the one of the terms and the predicate of the other. Hence the canon of this Figure will be : *What worse relation of determining (predicate), and of deter-*

[1] Cf. Baynes' *New Analytic*, pp. 63-69.
[2] Cf. above, p. 376.
[3] Cf. Baynes' *New Analytic*, p. 153 ; Hamilton's *Lect.* ii. 404.

mined (subject), is held by either of two notions to a third, with which one at least is positively related ; that relation do they immediately (directly) hold to each other, and indirectly (mediately) its converse.

In the *Second Figure*, the common third term is the predicate of both of the other terms. Hence the canon of this Figure will be : *What worse relation of determined (subject) is held by either of two notions to a third, with which one at least is positively related ; that relation do they hold indifferently to each other.*

In the *Third Figure*, the common third term is the subject of both of the other terms. Hence the canon of this Figure will be: *What worse relation of determining (predicate) is held by either of two notions to a third, with which one at least is positively related; that relation do they hold indifferently to each other.*[1]

10. The syllogistic variation of *Mood* was seen to be evolved from the supreme canon of Figured Syllogism. The *true* number of moods is also to be determined by that canon. For the variety of mood depends on the various relations of subject and predicate produced by difference of quantity and quality. Hence the number of moods is to be determined by the number of variations in quantity and quality possible in the premises; and the number of *valid* moods, by the number of those variations in which both premises are not negative, and in which the quantifications of the middle term, whether as subject or predicate, exceed the quantity of the term taken in its whole extent (i.e. where the middle term is distributed). When some others are excluded which have particular conclusions where universal are competent, there remain in all *thirty-six valid Moods*, twelve affirmative and twelve negative. These Moods are all evolved from the supreme canon of Figured Syllogism, and are independent on the variation of the various Figures. Hence they are valid in every Figure. Each one of them may be evolved from the supreme canon without reference to the others, and therefore they are mutually independent. The variation of moods in the different Figures under the Old Analytic was caused by the confusion created by not quantifying the predicate. When that confusion is cleared up the moods are seen to be virtually identical or *relatively equivalent* throughout every variety of schematic difference.

11. In the *Second* and *Third* Figures, where the extremes both hold the same relation to the middle term, there is *not*, as in the first, an *opposition* and *subordination between a term major and a term minor, mutually containing* and *contained, in the counter wholes of Extension and Comprehension.* In the First Figure, since the major term is pre-

[1] Hamilton's *Lect. on Log.* p. 350; cf. *Discussions*, pp. 654, 648.

dicate of the one premise and the minor term subject of the other, in the whole of Extension the major is greater than the middle, and therefore much greater than the minor term; while in the whole of Comprehension the minor is greater than the middle, and therefore much greater than the major term. But in the Second Figure both major and minor terms are subjects in the premises, and in the Third Figure they are both predicates in the premises; and the mutual subordination cannot arise. Consequently, in the *Second* and *Third* Figures *there is no determinate major and minor premise*, and there are *two indifferent conclusions.* For example, we may equally well say—

<table>
<tr><td>Second Figure</td><td></td><td>Third Figure</td><td></td></tr>
<tr><td colspan="2">P M or S M</td><td colspan="2">M P or M S</td></tr>
<tr><td>S M</td><td>P M</td><td>M S</td><td>M P</td></tr>
<tr><td>S P</td><td>P S</td><td>S P</td><td>P S</td></tr>
</table>

Whereas in the *First* Figure the *premises* are *determinate*, and there is a *single direct conclusion.* For example, we must say—

$$\begin{array}{l} M\,P \\ S\,M \\ S\,P; \end{array}$$

and since every proposition is an equation, we may have also the *indirect* conclusion P S.

12. In the First Figure, Comprehension and Extension are in equilibrium, the major and minor terms are reciprocally whole and part, and this Figure is, therefore, common to *Induction* and *Deduction*, indifferently.

In the *Second* Figure, *Extension* is predominant, for the predicate is naturally the greater, and this Figure is, therefore, more appropriate to *Deduction*, which proceeds from the universal to the particular, from what is true of a class to what is true of individuals.

In the *Third* Figure, *Comprehension* is predominant, for the subject is naturally the greater, and this Figure is, therefore, more appropriate to *Induction*, which proceeds from the particular to the universal—from what is true of the individuals which make up a class to what is true of the class itself.

§ 9. III. The scheme of logical notation is meant to show, with mechanical simplicity, all the propositional and syllogistic forms. Sir W. Hamilton[*] intends this scheme to be wholly different in principle and perfection from those which have been previously proposed, but, as Archbishop Thomson says, 'many of the different elements are not new.' This notation 'can represent any relation of the terms, any order of

* *Lect. on Logic.* ii. 251.

the proposition, *any* extent of quantity. The *terms* are represented by *letters*—the extremes by the letters C and Γ, which are each the third letter in its respective alphabet, and the middle term of the syllogism by the letter M—, their *quantity* by the *points*, and the *propositions* by the *lines with the letters.*' ' 'Definite quantity (*all, any*) is indicated by the sign (:); indefinite quantity (*some*), by the sign (, or ,). The *horizontal tapering line* (▬▬—) indicates an *affirmative* relation between the subject and predicate of the proposition. *Negative* is marked by a *perpendicular line* crossing the horizontal (▬╈—). . . . In *Extension*, the *broad end* of the line denotes the *subject*, the *pointed end* the *predicate*. In Comprehension this is reversed; the pointed end indicating the subject, the broad end the predicate. . . . A *line beneath the three terms*

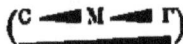

$$(C \text{ ▬◀ } M \text{ ◀▬ } \Gamma)$$

denotes the relation of the *extremes of the conclusion*. . . . In the *Second* and *Third* Figures,—a line is inserted above as well as below the terms of the syllogism, to express the *double conclusion* in those figures. The symbol (⌣—) shows that when the premises are converted, the syllogism remains in the *same mood*; the symbol (✕) shows that the two moods between which it stands are *controvertible into each other* by conversion of their premises.' ²

The mood *Barbara* is thus expressed by Hamilton's notation :—

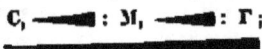

$$C, \text{ ▬◀ } : M, \text{ ◀▬ } : \Gamma ;$$

and the mood Celarent thus :—

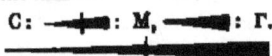

$$C : \text{ ▬╈◀ } : M, \text{ ◀▬ } : \Gamma.$$

This New Analytic is almost entirely based upon the doctrine of the Quantification of the Predicate, and stands or falls with that doctrine. For a criticism of the doctrine, cf. Appendix B, p. 579.

Archbishop Thomson, who does not accept all the results given above, gives the most complete exposition and application of the doctrines in his Outlines of the Laws of Thought.

§ 10. The doctrines contained in this New Analytic of logical forms lead directly to the theories of Boole and Jevons.

A leading characteristic of the Doctrine of the Quantification of the Predicate, and other [recent] theories of a similar kind, is the attempt to assimilate all propositions to the type of mathematical identities, the copula being reduced to a mere sign of identity between the extension of the subject and the quantified Predicate. In *Boole's Laws of Thought*, the analogy thus suggested between the processes of formal Logic and the methods of Arithmetic is worked out into a complete theory of symbolical reasoning developed from fundamental laws, in great part precisely similar to the laws of Operation in Mathematics. That is, the premises of an argument expressing given relations among certain logical elements, Boole undertakes by symbolic methods to eliminate those elements which we desire not to appear in the conclusion, and to determine the whole amount of relation implied by the premises among the elements which we wish to appear, and that in any proposed form. To this end he divides Propositions into Primary Propositions expressing relations between things (Categorical), and Secondary, expressing relations between Propositions (Hypothetical). His method is originally developed with regard to the former class of Propositions, and then is shown to admit of extension to the latter also. A symbolical expression of the reasoning processes, of which language is the instrument, will embrace signs of three kinds. (1) Literal signs, as x, y, &c., representing things as subjects of conception—descriptive signs. [These are really signs of classes, the symbolical method necessarily proceeding in extension.] (2) Signs, as $+$, $-$, $\times$, standing for the mental operations by which conceptions are combined. (3) The sign of identity $=$.

The sign $+$ adds classes. Thus, if x means men and y women, $x+y$ means men and women. Similarly, if z means Asiatics, $x-z$ means men not Asiatics. Again, $z \times z$ means all Asiatics who are men, or all men who are Asiatics. It is thus indifferent whether we write zx or xz, that is, the commutative law holds in logical as in mathematical symbolism. Again, $z(x+y)=zy+zx=zx+zy$; i.e., men and women who are Asiatics, *or* Asiatic men and Asiatic women, *or* Asiatic women and Asiatic men, are all identical conceptions. That is, the *distributive* law of mathematical operation holds here also. Further, the ordinary rule of transposition, by which we may write indifferently $a+b=c$ or $a=c-b$, and the rule by which if $a=b$, $ca=cb$, plainly hold here. There is one limitation only to our right to manipulate logical and mathematical identities by the same rules. From the identity $ca=cb$, which asserts that the a's which are also c's, and the b's which are also c's, are identical, we cannot infer that all a's are b's ($a=b$).

Connected with this peculiarity of logical symbolism is the following remarkable law : xx or x^2 means all x's that are x's, and so is simply =x. This result $x^2 = x$ is, in fact, the keystone of Boole's method when put in the shape $x(1-x)=0$. But to understand the result in this shape we must have a meaning for 1. In arithmetic, 1 satisfies the equation $1 \times y = y$, whatever y is. This will be true in Logic also, if 1 represents a class which contains all y's, whatever y is, that is, if it be the Universe [of logical extension]. This being so, we see at once that $1-x$ means all *not* $-x$'s, and the equation $x(1-x)=0$ means that no x can also be a not $-x$, the law of Contradiction. This very remarkable deduction of the law of Contradiction is almost the only one of Boole's results which can be fully stated without an amount of symbolical apparatus which would be out of place here. But it will be seen that the symbols and methods just described, with the addition of an indefinite v to mark particular terms [e.g. if x means men, vx means some men] suffice to express any proposition as an identity. The symbolically expressed identity may then be manipulated like an equation, save only that we must not divide out a common factor. The equation may take a shape not logically interpretable; but a purely symbolical rule, corresponding to Taylor's theorem in algebra, suffices to reduce any expression, however complex, to a final form, which can at once be read back into ordinary language, and gives exhaustively all the relations logically implied between the elements of the original proposition. If the premises form more than one proposition, the whole system can be reduced to a single final equation, the interpretation of which in like manner exhausts the logical relations implied in the premises. But usually, as in syllogism, it is desired to eliminate one or more middle terms from the conclusion, and here, too, Boole's method is general, providing, by an application of the fundamental principle $x(1-x)=0$, for the elimination of any number of terms from any proposition or system of propositions. Of this general method the laws of syllogism are merely special cases, and cases which, as Boole urges, do not appear to be *fundamental*. On the contrary, he concludes that all reasoning does not consist of elimination, and that syllogism is not the natural type of elimination, and so that the Aristotelian or scholastic logic is not a science but a collection of scientific truths, incomplete and not fundamental.

Proceeding to discuss the Logic of Secondary Propositions, Boole argues thus :—The secondary proposition, ' If X is, Y is,' means that the proposition X is true at the time when Y is true, and so that other secondary propositions may be explained with reference to time. Now, let x, y denote the times during which X, Y are true. Then $x+y$ or $y+x$ will mean the aggregate of these times, xy or yx will be the time during which both X and Y are true. Thus the commutative and

distributive laws hold here also. In short, the laws of operation for
x, y, &c., which now denote parts of *time*, are just the same as the
laws already developed for symbols denoting parts of the universe.
For example, $x(1-x)=0$ has the meaning that the proposition X
cannot be both true and false at the same time, and from this starting
point the whole Logic of Secondary Propositions flows on in the exact
shape taken by the Logic of Primary Propositions. The importance
which ' pure time ' thus acquires in symbolical logic, as in the more
speculative part of modern algebra, is very striking, and Boole remarks
that the theory of Primary propositions might similarly have been
founded on the Conception of space.[1] But that such a use of the
notion of space is not necessary seems to him to be in harmony with
the fact that a geometry of space of more than three dimensions is
analytically possible ; and suggests the observation that there seem to
be grounds for thinking that the manifestation of space to the human
mind, but not that of time, might have been otherwise than it is.
[Boole's work contains also a theory of probability, which need not bo
discussed here, and closes with a striking metaphysical chapter on the
nature of science and the constitution of the intellect.]

§ 11. *Professor W. Stanley Jevons*,[2] like other logicians who base
their systems on the quantification of the predicate, starts with the
doctrine that the proposition is an *equation* of subject and predicate.
He objects to *Dr. Boole's* method, because it ' shrouds the simplest
logical processes in the mysterious operations of a mathematical calculus,'[3] forgetting that it was Dr. Boole's express design to show that
Logic was really a department of mathematics, and its operations ' to be
followed only by highly accomplished mathematical minds.' For this
and other reasons Professor Jevons thinks that the ' true clue to the
analogy of Logic and mathematics has yet to be seized,' and that he
himself has discovered it. He shows that when a proposition is regarded as the equation of two terms, the terms need no longer bo distinguished as subject and predicate, but become convertible, and for the
copula may be substituted the sign of equality ($=$). When the equation is thus taken as the fundamental *form* of inference, and the distinction of subject and predicate abolished, the fundamental *formula* for
reasoning will be : *whatever is true of a thing is true of its like*, and the
fundamental *principle* of reasoning is the SUBSTITUTION OF SIMILARS.

[1] Is there not a confusion here similar to that which led Hamilton (and with
him Boole also) to represent Kant's forms of intuition as forms of thought ?
[2] *The Substitution of Similars the True Principle of Reasoning.* London, 1869.
[3] *Phil. Trans. of the Royal Society of London*, vol. cls. pt. ii, 449.

Deductive power always resides in equality. Difference as such cannot afford any inference. For example, if we have

$$a = b$$
$$\text{we may infer } \begin{array}{c} a \\ c \end{array}, \text{ by substituting } c \text{ for } b; \text{ but if we have}$$

$$a \sim b$$
$$\begin{array}{c} \iota \\ c \end{array}, \text{ where } \sim \text{ is the sign of inequality, there can be no inference.}$$

He shows how the ordinary syllogistic moods may be obtained, simply and directly by means of his fundamental principle, and how all the forms of immediate inference rest upon it; but has not worked out his theory into all its details. The great novelty, however, in Professor Jevons' view of Logic is, that just as Dr. Boole reduced Logic to a mathematical calculus, so he brings it to certain mechanical processes which can be exemplified, or rather performed, by a logical engine. This logical analytical engine is described in the 'Phil. Trans. of the Royal Society of London,' vol. 160, pt. ii. p. 497: *On the Mechanical Performance of Logical Inference.* To such lengths has Formal Logic been developed.

As Professor Jevons' logical theories depend upon the doctrine of the quantification of the predicate, and stand or fall with that doctrine, they do not require to be here discussed. It would not, however, be right to pass from their consideration without noticing that the doctrine of *substitution* of similars, as the true principle in reasoning, which Professor Jevons claims to have discovered and placed in its rightful position, as the fundamental principle of deductive inference, was long before enounced to be so by *Dr. Fr. Ed. Beneke*, was discussed by him (to say nothing of others) in his logical writings, and is so well known and recognised in Germany as *a* logical principle, that most logics devote a paragraph to its discussion.[1]

§ 12. The logical system which has been elaborated by *Mr. J. S. Mill*[2] is very far removed from the systems of Formal Logic mentioned above. Mr. Mill belongs to that school of Philosophy which continental critics are disposed to regard as the typical English. He is the inheritor of the ideas of Hobbes, Locke, and Hume. Logic, and more especially the Syllogistic, has never been a favourite study with these thinkers, and has even been expressly neglected by many of them. Mr. Mill has done this service for his fellow-thinkers; he has taken what they believe to be the dry bones of a dead Scholasticism, and quickened them into life, making them fit for service and labour by inspiring them with the spirit of his sensational philosophy. He has seen the value of a system of Logic to be the iron edge to the wedge of sensationalist metaphysics. Hence it is, that with Mr. Mill, more than with any other logical writer, logical theories are almost entirely dependent on a particular metaphysical solution of problems of knowledge, and logical criticism becomes a defence and attack of metaphysical theories.

Mr. Mill's problem seems to be: Given sensation and a multiplex association as the sole matter and form of knowledge, to construct a theory of evidence which shall fitly appropriate all the old scholastic logical nomenclature, and be for us, with our present opinions, a real Logic. And the task is accomplished with such freshness of insight, that we must admire the ability of the thinker, however much we dissent from the fundamental doctrines on which he builds his theories.

Mr. Mill's logical doctrines cannot be understood nor appreciated apart from the remembrance of the fact, that he believes knowledge to be the joint result of sensation and processes of association. This fact lies at the basis of his logical opinions, and everywhere modifies them. Things are congeries of sensations to which we ascribe a unity, because they are inseparably associated. Judgments are statements of the co-existence of two sets of attributes. Inference is proceeding from one to another set of associated phenomena.

According to Mr. Mill, Logic is the science of the operations of the understanding which are subservient to the estimation of evidence; both the process itself and all other intellectual operations, in so far as they are auxiliary to this. It attempts a correct analysis of the intellectual process called Reasoning or Inference, and of such other mental operations as are intended to facilitate this; then on the foundation of this analysis, it brings together a set of rules for testing the sufficiency of any evidence given to prove any proposition.

Starting from this definition, a theory of Logic falls naturally into three divisions—a theory of *naming*, a theory of *proposition*, and a theory of *inference*.

§ 13. A *Name* is defined to be 'a word or set of words serving the double purpose of a mark to recall to ourselves the likeness of a former thought, and a sign to make it known to others.' Names which stand for individual conceptions, and correspond to the objective individual existences, are not distinguished from names which stand for general conceptions or notions, and correspond in their content to the essence, and in their extent to the genus or species.[1] The categories of Aristotle are considered to be a haphazard classification of Nameable things, and are superseded by one which is considered simpler and better fitted to represent the real nature of the case.[1] The Predicables are also retained but transformed. The objective fact on which this five-fold classification of predicates is made to rest is the *real* existence of kinds. Every class which is a *real* kind, i.e. which is distinguished from every other class by an innumerable number of attributes, may be a genus or a species. Starting from this fact, the five predicables are easily evolved. A *Genus* is a kind which includes other kinds. A *Species* is a kind which does not include other kinds. If it be looked on as a kind with reference to other kinds above it, it is a *Species predicabilis*; if looked on as a kind with reference to individuals below it, it is a *species subjicibilis*. The other three predicables are founded on the connotation of the name of the species. The *Differentia* is that part of the connotation of the specific name, ordinary, special, or technical, which distinguishes the Species from all other species of the Genus to which we are for the time being referring it. The *Property* is an attribute belonging to all individuals of the Species, which, though not ordinarily annoted by the specific name, follows from some attribute so annoted, either by demonstration or causation. An *Accident* is any attribute belonging to the Species, which is neither involved in the name nor follows from any attribute so involved. If it belongs universally to the Species it is *inseparable*; if it does not, it is *separable*.

The great defect in Mr. Mill's theory of names is, that while he distinguishes simply and clearly between the extent and content of notions in his remarks on the denotation and annotation of names, he has not referred these distinctions to their objective realities on which they depend, and to which they conform. The *extent* of the notion depends on the real existence of the species or *kind*. This Mr. Mill acknowledges, but does not apply. The *content* of the notion depends on the real existence of the *essence*. This Mr. Mill denies. He acknowledges no essence but the nominal, which itself depends on the content.

§ 14. In his theory of Predication, Mr. Mill begins by laying down a fundamental principle, the truth of which cannot be too often asserted—propositions are assertions about things, and what is of primary importance to the logician in a proposition is the relation between the two phenomena to which the subject and predicate respectively correspond. He then shows that other theories of predication, and especially the theory of the upholders of Formal Logic, have neglected this fact, and in neglecting it have been led to dwell exclusively on the denotation of the subject and predicate, and to make a proposition the statement of a relation between two classes of objects. A theory of predication must make prominent the *connotation* of the terms used, else it will not express that reference to *fact* which predication involves. In this way Mr. Mill evolves his *attributive theory of predication*—which asserts that the true import of the proposition ' All men are mortal ' is : Whatever has the attributes of man has the attribute of mortality, or : Mortality constantly accompanies the attributes of man. One class of propositions, however, do not assert matters of fact. They only declare the meaning of names. These propositions may be called *verbal,* while others are *real.* A verbal proposition conveys no information to any one who previously understands the full meaning of the term, and when any important consequences seem to follow from such a proposition (as they do in mathematics), these consequences really flow from the *tacit assumption* of the *real existence* of the object so named. The most important class of verbal propositions are Definitions. No Definition is meant to explain and unfold the nature of a thing ; it is simply a proposition declaratory of the meaning of a term. It is always *nominal.* What are called *real* definitions are merely nominal definitions with an implied postulate that the object denoted by the name exists. Mr. Mill's *attributive* theory of the syllogism is based on this theory of Predication and on his explanation of the nature of Demonstrative truth.

When Mr. Mill says that propositions are assertions about things, he does not go deep enough. A proposition is the expression of a relation in thought which corresponds to and mirrors a real relation in things. This real relation is not mere co-existence, it is generally subsistence and inherence. What is represented by the subject is seen to be something which subsists, and what is represented by the predicate is seen to be something which inheres in what subsists. Mr. Mill's fundamental error of refusing to admit the real existence of the essence as he does the real existence of the species prevents him from following out the true theory of predication. The acknowledgment of a real essence would give a unity to the subject which in Mr. Mill's theory it does not possess, and make it something different from the *set of attributes* more or less indefinite, which Mr. Mill makes it to be. This error comes out more especially in the theory of Definition. Definition is not merely the declaration of the meaning of a word—i.e. the statement of the connotation. It is the expression of the Essence. Now Mr. Mill recognises no Essence save the nominal essence, which is merely the approximately correct connotation.

§ 15. *Inference* or reasoning in the most general sense results when a proposition is believed as a conclusion from something else. The so-called immediate Inferences of logicians are not inferences properly speaking, because no new truth is arrived at in the conclusion. Inference only occurs when we proceed from the known to the unknown. Inference in this sense is of three kinds: reasoning from generals to particulars—Ratiocination or Syllogism; reasoning from particulars to generals—Induction; and reasoning from particulars to particulars—a kind not often noted, but the basis of the other two.

Syllogism is usually thought to be the universal type of all reasoning. So far from this being the case, the truth really is that if we take syllogism to be a process of inference at all, we cannot avoid the conclusion that it is a Petitio Principii. If we are to get out of the difficulty, we must distinguish the process of inference from the process of registering the results of inference. The usual theory of the syllogism ascribes to the latter the functions of the former. All true inference is the associative inference from particulars to particulars. We store up the results of such inferences in general propositions, and in this way they become registers of a multitude of past inferences, and short formulæ for making more. The major premiss of a syllogism is such a register and formula. The conclusion is not an inference drawn *from* the formula, but *according* to it. In the syllogism we do not infer, we only decipher our notes. The true logical premiss is the particular facts from which the general premiss was gathered. Hence the dictum of Aristotle does not give a true type nor correct formula for the syllogistic process. Every reasoning may rather be reduced to this form :

Certain individuals have a given attribute ;
An individual or individuals resemble the former in certain other attributes.
∴. They resemble them in the given attribute also.

In this way the legitimacy of every inference is to be decided by the canons of induction ; and general propositions are retained as useful registers and abbreviations in reasoning.

The strongest objections to this theory of the Syllogism may be drawn from the Demonstrative Sciences. They are supposed to have a peculiar certainty of their own, which rests in the force to prove lying in the major premiss. Against such objections Mr. Mill brings his theory of Demonstrative Science, which is based on his theory of Definition. The peculiar certainty and accuracy of Demonstrative (e. g. geometrical) science is fictitious and hypothetical. For every Demonstrative Science depends on Definitions and axioms. Now the axioms of

Geometry are merely generalizations from experience—an experience which constantly recurs, is never broken by contradictory cases nor even by contradictory analogies, and so is very strong. The Definitions, again, do not admit of consequences concerning the nature of things, because they are only declarations of the meanings of words. The consequences deduced follow from the assumption that there is a real thing exactly conformable to the definition. This assumption is only approximately true in Geometry. There are no actual circles exactly correspondent to the definition of a circle, &c. And the conclusions in Geometry are true only in the ratio of the approximate truth of the assumption. The peculiar accuracy in Geometry is therefore *hypothetical*, and any number of sciences might be constructed, having the certainty of Geometry, by combining a set of definitions with a few real axioms.

Mr. Mill's theory of Definition, on which this somewhat strange conclusion regarding the nature of mathematical certainty rests, has been already noticed; but even if his theory of Definition were correct, objections might be taken to the conclusions he founds upon it. Mathematical notions become fruitful and produce mathematical science, not by being verbally defined, but by being actually realised as primitive elements of intuition ;—not as merely subjective elements, but as real elements in *rerum natura*, which the mathematician seeks to apprehend in their primitive *generality* and *simplicity*, and to carry out into their real (not formal) consequences.[1] And no branch of knowledge wherein the notions it contains cannot be apprehended in their primitive generality and simplicity in Intuition, can reach the certainty of Geometry. Wolff's science of Architecture was formed after the plan described by Mr. Mill, but it does not possess mathematical certainty.

§ 16. Mr. Mill's labours in founding a systematic theory of *Induction* cannot be altogether passed over. His primitive type of reasoning is the associative impulse ; and when this has created for itself a basis (the law of Causation) on which it may rest while advancing beyond particulars to generals, and has formed certain rules or canons by which it may so vary its processes as to exclude, more or less thoroughly, the entrance of error (the Inductive Methods), it becomes Induction. Mr. Mill differs from his predecessor in the same department of logical enquiry, Dr. Whewell, in the view he takes of the general character of Induction. He complains that Dr. Whewell does not distinguish between Colligation of facts—i.e. the collection of instances and their union

[1] Cf. two Papers read before the Royal Society of Edinburgh, by Prof. W. R. Smith, 'On Mr. Mill's Theory of Geometrical Reasoning,' and 'Hegel and the Metaphysics of the Fluxional Calculus.'—*Transactions*, vol. xxv.

under a mental conception which binds them together—and Induction proper. The former is mere description. It does not proceed to the unknown. Induction goes beyond the facts either to their *explanation* (i. e. the determination of the conditions under which they now occur), or to their *prediction* (i.e. the determination of the conditions under which similar facts may be expected again to occur). Kepler's theory of the elliptical orbit of the planets was a mere description or Colligation of Facts. Newton's doctrine that the planets are moved by the composition of a centripetal with an original projectile force is an Explanation or Induction.

Dr. Whewell, on the other hand, declares that Mr. Mill, by asserting that the Colligation of Facts is not Induction and that it does not introduce a new element of knowledge, misses one of the most important things in all inductive enquiry—the true meaning and power of the mental conception which binds the facts together. To separate the explanation of facts from their colligation, and to introduce elaborate methods for attaining to this explanation, is to degrade the theory of induction and the philosophy of discovery to a mechanical method, and to neglect too much the peculiar power of the mind to frame scientific ' ideas,' apply modified conceptions of these to the particular instances, and so *explain* the facts. Dr. Whewell would do away with Mr. Mill's inductive methods altogether, and give instead rules for framing suitable conceptions.

                                                      T. M. L.

APPENDIX B.

THE DOCTRINE OF THE QUANTIFICATION OF THE PREDICATE.

The doctrine of the Quantification of the Predicate has held such an important place in all recent English logical speculation, that it deserves to be specially discussed.

The Quantification of the Predicate was discovered and applied with more or less fulness almost simultaneously by Dean Mansel, Archbishop Thomson, and Professor Sir W. Hamilton. But as Sir W. Hamilton has stated, developed, and applied the doctrine in a much fuller and more systematic way than any other, we shall only notice his exposition.[1]

[1] For a statement and discussion of the various partial anticipations of the doctrine of the quantification of the predicate, compare Sir W. Hamilton's *Lect. on Logic*, vol. ii. 298 ff.; and Prof. Thomas S. Baynes' *New Analytic of the Forms of Thought*, p. 81 ff. A word may be added on the claims of two modern writers on Logic, to the discovery of the doctrine, unnoticed in either of these statements. Prof. Beneke, of Berlin (cf. above, p. 219), enounced that *substitution* was the principle of all analytical syllogisms. We advance from the known to the unknown by substituting one notion or one term for another. He saw that this principle implied that what is substituted must be equal or of less extent than that for which it is substituted, and that as predicates are among the terms substituted, their extent must be definitely known. This clearly implied the quantification of the predicate. But Beneke stopped short before enouncing it, and his new analysis of Logic, which really rests on the doctrine, is thus one-sided, confused, and unsystematic. He saw, rightly we believe, that the predicate is really and naturally attributive, not quantitative nor expressive of extent, and would not therefore quantify it in any thorough-going way. He did not see that his doctrine of Substitution involved the quantification of the predicate, and therefore did not abandon the former when he rejected the latter. (Cf. *Syll. Anal. Orig.*, &c., Berol., 1839.)

George Bentham (*A New System of Logic*, &c., Lond., 1827), is said by some to have anticipated Hamilton in enouncing and applying to Logic the doctrine of a quantified predicate. The assertion cannot be justified. He did enounce the fact,

The doctrine of the Quantification of the predicate demands that
the quantity of the predicate be explicitly stated. According to the
common logical rules in force since the days of Aristotle, the predicate
is not regarded as possessing any quantity of its own. When there is
occasion for marking its quantity, as in conversion, a borrowed quantity
dependent on the quality of the proposition is attributed to it. All
affirmative propositions are said to have predicates whose quantity is
particular, e.g. *All men are mortal* when converted becomes *Some
mortal beings are men*, not *all mortal beings are men*. On the other
hand, the quantity of predicates in negative propositions is universal,
e.g. *No merely formal Logic is a true theory of knowledge* when converted becomes *No true theory of knowledge is a merely formal Logic*,
not *Some true theories of knowledge are not a merely formal Logic*.
The doctrine of the quantification of the predicate would make the
quantity of the predicate as self-dependent as that of the subject is,
and would give to the predicate the same quantitative predesignations
which are attached to the subject. The immediate effect of this doctrine is to double the number of the propositional forms. For quantity
is either universal or particular, and each of the four common forms of
propositions takes a double form as its predicate is universal or particular. Thus—

(I.) A. All S are P, becomes
$\begin{cases} \text{All S are all P} & . & \text{AFA.*(1)} \\ \text{All S are some P} & . & \text{AFI.} \quad (2) \end{cases}$

(II.) I. Some S are P, becomes
$\begin{cases} \text{Some S are all P} & . & \text{IFA.* (3)} \\ \text{Some S are some P} & . & \text{IFI.} \quad (4) \end{cases}$

(III.) E. No S are P, becomes
$\begin{cases} \text{Any S are not any P} & . & \text{ENE.} \quad (5) \\ \text{Any S are not some P} & . & \text{ENO.* (6)} \end{cases}$

(IV.) O. Some S are not P, becomes .
$\begin{cases} \text{Some S are not any P} & . & \text{ONE.} \quad (7) \\ \text{Some S are not some P} & . & \text{ONO.* (8)} \end{cases}$

This doctrine of the Quantification of the Predicate is based on the
fundamental postulate of Logic : *State explicitly what is thought im-*

but not with such fulness of meaning and application as was afterwards done.
His chief service lay in this, that he was one of the first to clearly conceive and
assert that a proposition was only an *equation* of the subject and predicate.

* The forms marked with an asterisk are the new ones. F and N are used to
denote affirmative and negative moods, being the first consonants in the verbs
affirmo and nego. Since the subject must be equal to the predicate, vagueness in
the predesignations must be as far as possible removed. *Some* is taken as equivalent to *some* but *not all*, and in negative propositions *all* is discarded for *any*.
All men are not black might mean *some men are black*. It should be noticed that
Archbishop Thomson does not adopt all the new forms, but only the affirmative
ones (1 and 3).

plicity. This postulate has only to be stated to be accepted, and whenever it is accepted, Hamilton thinks, the recognition and acceptance of the quantification of the predicate must follow. This implies, *of course, that the predicate is implicitly thought to be a quantity,* or its explicit quantification would not follow from the postulate of Logic. Unfortunately, the advocates of the doctrine have taken this fundamental conception of the nature of a predicate for granted, and never attempted to prove that the nature of predication presupposes that the natural and true conception of a predicate involves the thought of quantity. All their arguments for their favourite doctrine are founded upon this assumption, and so avoid the real question at issue. Thus Hamilton argues :—

1. It may easily be shown that the predicate is as *extensive* as the subject. We are conscious that the proposition—*All animal is man* or *All animals are men* is absurd, though we make the notion *man* or *men* as wide as possible ; for it does not mend the matter to say—*All animal is all man.* We feel it to be equally absurd, as if we said, *All man is all animal.* Here we are aware that the subject and predicate cannot be made co-extensive. If we are to get rid of the absurdity, we must make the notions co-extensive by restricting the wider. If we say—*Man is animal,* we think, though we do not overtly enounce it, *All man is animal.* And we think—not *all* but *some* animal.

2. Ordinary language quantifies the predicate so often as this determination becomes of the smallest import. This is done directly or indirectly.

   a. We say for example—*Mercury, Venus, &c. are all the planets.* Here the quantification is *direct.*

   b. We say—*Of animals man alone is rational* ; which means *Man-is-all rational animal.* Here the quantification is indirect and *limitative.*

   c. We say—*On earth there is nothing great but man* ; which means *Man-is-all earthly great.* Here the quantification is indirect and *exceptive.*

3. Logicians confess that the predicate is quantified by particularity in affirmative, by universality in negative, propositions. Why the formal quantification should be thus restricted in thought, they furnish us with no valid reason.[1]

Other arguments are added, showing that the quantification of the predicate is not only scientifically correct, but of actual practical value

[1] Hamilton, *Lect. on Log.,* II. 259.

in simplifying and completing a system of Logic. Thus it has been said :

4. The progress of science demands at least the new affirmative forms (Thomson and Mansel).

5. Even the new negative forms are required in logical division (Hamilton).

6. The doctrine removes from Logic many cumbrous constructions and meaningless rules.

These arguments, as has been said, are all repetitions with variations of the original assertion, that the predicate is implicitly thought as quantified, and that this thought should be expressed. Now we do not admit this assumption, and therefore do not feel persuaded by the arguments which it supports. The quantification of the predicate has been urged from the essential nature of the notion as a quantity; but there is a wide difference between a notion taken simply by itself, and a notion taken as the subject or as the predicate of a proposition. A notion considered simply by itself is both quantitative and qualitative. It denotes objects and connotes attributes. A subject notion, however, is naturally quantitative—denoting objects; while a predicate notion is naturally qualitative—connoting attributes. For a proposition in its simple and most natural meaning asserts that *an attribute or quality (the predicate) is or is not possessed by a given object or class of objects (the subject)*. The *inherence* of an attribute in a given *subsisting* object is the natural assertion made by the simple categorical proposition. The relation between subject and predicate is the natural correlative of the real relation which subsists between a substance and its qualities. Hence the predicate does not naturally denote a class of objects. It is not naturally quantitative. We do not naturally think it as quantified. We think of it as expressive of a quality, and of a quality only.[1]

This primary meaning of predication may be elaborated, however, into two secondary meanings. For—

(1). Although the subject is naturally quantitative, denoting an object or part or whole of a class of objects, yet as the object possesses attributes, and objects are arranged in classes, as they do or do not possess certain attributes, the subject notion originally quantitative may be looked on as qualitative. The proposition will then denote the relation of co-existence between two sets of qualities. *The set of qualities* (which are implied by the subject) *are always or sometimes accompanied by the set of qualities* (implied by the predicate). This is Mr. Mill's attributive theory of predication.

[1] Cf. above, § 68, and Braske, *Syllogismorum Analyticorum Origines*, &c., § 4.

(2). Although the predicate is naturally qualitative, connoting a quality or qualities, yet as the presence of a quality or qualities may serve to denote the objects belonging to a particular class, the predicate notion originally qualitative may come to be looked on as quantitative. The proposition will then denote the relation between two classes of objects; and predication may be said to be the *affirmation or negation that one class comes under another class.* This is Sir W. Hamilton's theory of predication, and since it looks on the predicate as a quantity, naturally leads to the quantification of the predicate, and comes to regard every proposition as an equation of subject and predicate.

So far, however, from this being the primary meaning of predication, it is only a secondary and forced interpretation of the fact process, and one which is only applicable in certain cases, viz., when the notion of the predicate can itself become substantive. Whenever the sum total of the objects, to which the quality expressed by the predicate belongs, are not all of the same kind and are not a class, then the predicate cannot be taken substantively, and cannot be quantified. The same limitation belongs to conversion.[1]

T. M. L.

[1] Cf. p. 295.

584

APPENDIX C.

THE DOCTRINE OF ESSENCE.

The paragraph in the text upon our knowledge of the essence (§ 57) involves a certain amount of acquaintance with German modes of thought and expression, and will seem obscure and scarcely intelligible to many English readers. The translator, therefore, thinks it advisable to present, as far as possible, the same thoughts in such a modification of expression and illustration as the necessities of translation forbade in rendering the passage.

(1). The essence is always to be looked upon as a reality existing in *rerum natura.* It is not a merely arbitrary nominal essence, the more or less definite and correct meaning of a term. Now, the very thought of essence implies both *generality* and *simplicity* (on the union of which in the ultimate elements of knowing and being the possibility of science rests), and both these attributes are nowhere so well seen in union as in the Self or Ego, which is related to, and, as it were, mingles with the host of fleeting impressions and phenomena which change and pass (generality), while itself remains stable and self-dependent through all (simplicity). But this Self or Ego is not at first known, nor does it at first exist in us. Like everything else it *grows*, and comes to maturity by growth. At first we have only vague feelings awakened by the relation of our activities and conditions to our present existence and development. What furthers this existence and development is felt with pleasure, what retards it with pain. These pleasures and pains give us vague positive and negative notions of Self. There is one class of feelings which more especially gives us this knowledge—the ethical feelings ; for the one class of actions and conditions which more than any there reveal to us our true independent self existence, is the ethical. When we truly and fully realise that we are set to perform certain duties, cultivate certain virtues, and possess certain rights, we truly and fully realise our own Self—our own essential existence—our own essence.

(2). When once we have attained to the knowledge of our own existence, it is easy by transferring the knowledge, to recognise the essences of other persons. And the knowledge of the essences of others, since it more sharply defines our relations, duties, and rights in connection with theirs, makes our knowledge of our own essence clearer. The knowledge of each acts on the other, strengthening and more sharply defining it.

(3). When once we have reached the knowledge of personal essence, we have only to apply it by analogy to the world of nature, in order to gain a knowledge of the essences of plants and animals. And as our own essence is most clearly realised and defined by the round of duties and rights which encircle us, so their essences must be known and defined by the ends they fulfil, and the functions they are set to perform.

(4). In the same way, the essences of the inorganic objects of nature is determined by the end fulfilled and function performed. It is, however, very difficult to realise them, because we know them almost exclusively through their outward mechanical relations, not by any exhibition of an inward tendency exerted towards the fulfilment of an end.

(5). Artificial objects have only a borrowed independence, and their essence is to be sought for either in their analogy to self-dependent individuals, or in their capability to fulfil the use for which they were intended.

T. M. L.

APPENDIX D.

THE PRINCIPLES OF ETHICS.

TRANSLATED FROM THE GERMAN OF PROFESSOR UEBERWEG.

§ 1. Ethics is the doctrine of the normative laws of human volition and action, which rest on the idea (i.e. on the type-notion) of the *Good*. The place which Ethics occupies in the system of Philosophy is a position after Psychology, on a line with Logic and Æsthetics, and before Pædagogic and the Philosophies of Religion and of History.

§ 2. The psychological basis of Ethics consists in the distinctions of value in the different mental (psychic) functions. These distinctions reveal themselves to us immediately in the feelings, which are connected with them—on the one side in the feelings of pleasure and pain, and on the other in the feelings of approval and shame. The distinction between what aids and what hinders reveals itself in pleasure and pain, and the distinction between higher and lower functions in the feelings of approval and shame. Feelings precede ethical notions and judgments. Their universal existence and importance is based upon the similarity of the human nature and exists in so far as this similarity exists.

§ 3. These distinctions in value are immediately connected with the mental (psychic) functions themselves, and mediately with whatever condition these mental functions. A *Good* is what makes those mental functions possible which are revealed by feelings of pleasure or approval. The sum total of everything Good, belonging to the human race, is the 'Highest Good' in the *collective* sense (*Summum Bonum*). The relative values are connected partly with the connections which exist between the different classes of functions of the individual, or between the actions of the different faculties of the soul (for the actions of the higher faculties are of more value than the actions of the lower), partly with the ties which connect the individual with the surrounding community (since the requirement of a greater number of persons is of more value than the requirement of a lesser number (or of an individual of this number.) The idea (the type-notion) of rational self-regard starts from the first, the idea of the common weal from the second.

§ 4. The whole ethical problem for mankind is gradual approximation to the realisation of the Highest Good. This problem is to be solved by the co-operation of all persons interested. Labour is activity in order to procure any good whatever. The distribution of the sum total of labour among the different members of the community becomes more and more qualitative with the progress of development. Every individual no longer works at the same labour in his own province which others work at in theirs, but each individual endeavours to produce one kind of product, and exchanges with his neighbours for others. The existence of the community is conditioned by a limitation of the share of each member to his labour and the results of his labour. This share is determined partly by the community, by means of the instrument of its collective will, and partly by the individual himself. The sphere of free self-determination which belongs, according to determinations or rules which are universally true, to the individual or to the lesser community within the more comprehensive community, is the *Right* of the individual or of the lesser community. The sum total of these determinations is the 'Right,' in the collective sense of the word, which prevails within the community. To 'Right' corresponds 'Duty,' or the sum total of what every member of the community has to do or to suffer in order to fulfil the final end of the whole. Duty with reference to a sphere of rights to which we do not belong is determined by the will of persons authorised to do so; Duty with reference to our own sphere of rights is determined by our own consciousness. Here arises the distinction between a Duty of Right and a Duty of Conscience. The latter is the 'moral duty' in the stricter sense. The limitation of spheres of Right by each other is determined by means of an order of rights, and this order is maintained by the relation of authority and obedience. He who bears the authority and therefore the power which the authority exercises over the members of the community is its Head. The *State* is the most extensive community under one head which aims at reaching an ethical end by means of the classification of rights. The essential functions of States are: to give laws or the determination of the classification of rights, just decision or the application of this classification of rights to disputable cases, and the choice or direct appointment of individuals by means of the highest choice of the State, and in an analogous way by lesser communities within the sphere of their right.

§ 5. The application of the law to the individual cases follows by means of an inference, whose major premise is the law itself, whose minor is the subsumption of the individual under the subject notion of the law, and whose conclusion is the reference of the predicate notion of the law to the individual. The universality of the major premise of this syllogism may be actually denied by the lawful opinion and action of the members of the State; the subsumption given in the minor premise may be debated between different persons concerned. In both cases the State exercises its lawful function by means of an instrument framed for the purpose by itself—criminal justice and civil justice. The security of the classification of rights, as opposed to the possible contradictory wills of individual persons, is attained by threatening punishment and by means of actual punishment. It is not a correct view of punishment to say that its use is only preventative, and as a warning. The wrong which consists in transgressing upon the arrangement of rights is followed by pain which injures, and is of the same kind as the pain we suffer in our consciousness. This consciousness opposes the motives which incite us to break the laws. In the same way the community opposes punishment to law-breaking, and by not allowing it shows that it is not a participator in the licence. Punishment, limited according to law, is in comparison with direct coercion, the correct measure of personal freedom taking the form of the reaction of ordinance—the State against contradictory individual wills. The highest problem is to avoid, as far as possible, collision by means of the greatest harmony possible between the law of the community and the sentiments of its members.

§ 6. Within his own sphere of rights every person has to co-operate in the gradual realisation of the highest good. In this consists his *moral duty.* The moral law takes the following formula : Act within the limits of your own sphere of duty, so as to solve the great problem of humanity as far as possible. This law demands, above all, that some work be done in each one's vocation, i.e. in the sphere of labour determined by the principle of the division of labour. All other action, however, finds also the criterion of moral value in the demand : each one must strive at all times to make the most valuable or the highest possible contribution to attain the end of mankind, according to the classification of value which is founded upon the essential nature of man. The reason determines how every single end is to be followed out according to its position within the totality of ends (Aristotle postulates this, but not very determinately), according to a mean between its over and under estimation. The egotistic tendency to overestimate our own ends, which tends to disturb our true estimation of their relation to the sum total of the problem of mankind, may be checked by reflecting whether it would be possible or desirable that the maxim of our action should be followed out by all persons, or serve for a principle of universal legislation. But this principle is not to be made of the highest significance in Ethics (as Kant made it). It is rather based upon the Ethical principle of allowing the fullest scope to the realisation of the whole task of mankind. There is a more or less certain approximation of different ends to equivalency in value.

The subordination of individual ends desirable to ourselves under the ethical law is the sum total of ethical duty which falls to us; the subordination of individual ends desirable by others under the ethical law is the sum total of ethical duty which falls to others. This distinction is theoretical only, for practically every kind of duty which concerns ourselves concerns others also.

§ 7. *Virtue* is habit in accordance with the ethical problem, or the ethical aptitude of the will. Habit (as Aristotle has rightly seen) arises from single similar acts of will, and is a permanent tendency of the will. It conditions, again, the subsequent acts of will. It gains its full development when the ethical view becomes the customary one. The ethical view, originally confined to a single instance, passes over into an ethical consciousness which rests on a comparison of feelings by means of thought. The mere performance of deeds commanded by the laws of ethics is Legality; right action accompanied by right feeling, or doing what is good because it is good, is Morality. (Kant has made this distinction, following the Stoical doctrine of *καθῆκον* and *κατόρθωμα*). Development into morality presupposes a struggle between inclination and duty; but the perfection of morality (according to Schiller's doctrine) lies in the harmony of inclination and duty; for (as Aristotle saw) what is best in itself in what is ethically produced appears also to be most desirable, just as what is truly beautiful according to the laws of Æsthetics is the most agreeable. The harmony between inclination and duty is attained in its fullest measure in the exercise of the vocation corresponding to one's individual character.

§ 8. The division of the duties and of their corresponding virtues is founded on the different kinds of purposes contained in the whole problem of mankind, and accordingly on the different kinds of desires and inclinations; but every single duty and virtue stands in a necessary relation to the whole ethical task. The subordination of inclinations, which tend to advance our own interests, to the ethical law recognised by the ethical view is called rational self-regard; and the subordination of inclinations to advance others' interests under the ethical law is called rational love of our neighbour. The following virtues, which have as many classes of corresponding duties, are to be arranged (with Aristotle) by themselves : — Courage, Temperance, Generosity, Honour, Gentleness, Truth, Sociableness, Friendship, and Justice in the narrower sense of the word, which (according to Aristotle) is partly distributive, partly corrective, and this last has partly to do with reward, partly with punishment. ' Distributive Justice ' has to do with the functions of legislation and administration ; ' Corrective Justice ' has reference to reward determined by an already existing order of rights, on which, in disputed cases, the judge must found his decision. Justice in the most comprehensive sense, which (according to Aristotle) is the chief virtue with reference to our fellow-men, may be identified with loyalty to duty. (The virtues called ' dianoetic ' by Aristotle are not virtues in the special sense of the word—i.e. with reference to the adaptability of the *will*).

§ 9. Education is the formation of one capable of being trained to virtue ; Instruction is training to intellectual and technical adaptability. The formation of principles lies in the (Aristotelian) axiom that the individual is to be led from the sensible, which is the earlier for us, to the intellectual, which is the first in itself, so that what is first in itself may come to have the predominance over what is first for us.